ARCHBISHOP ALEMANY LIBRARY
DOMINICAN UNI
SAN RAFAEL, CALIFC

W9-CUG-489

ENCYCLOPEDIA OF THE AGE OF IMPERIALISM, 1800-1914

ENCYCLOPEDIA OF THE AGE OF IMPERIALISM, 1800–1914

Volume 2   L–Z

Edited by **Carl Cavanagh Hodge**

Greenwood Press
Westport, Connecticut • London

Library of Congress Cataloging-in-Publication Data

Encyclopedia of the age of imperialism, 1800–1914 / edited by Carl Cavanagh Hodge.
    p. cm.
    Includes bibliographical references and index.
    ISBN 978–0–313–33404–7 (set : alk. paper)—ISBN 978–0–313–33406–1 (v.1 : alk.
paper)—ISBN 978–0–313–33407–8 (v.2 : alk. paper)   1. History, Modern—19th
century—Chronology—Encyclopedias.   2. Europe—History—1789–1900—Chronology—
Encyclopedias.   3. Europe—History—1871–1918—Chronology—Encyclopedias.
4. Great powers—History—19th century—Chronology—Encyclopedias.   5. Great
powers—History—20th century—Chronology—Encyclopedias.   I. Hodge,
Carl Cavanagh.
    D358.E45 2008
    909.8103—dc22   2007026483

British Library Cataloguing in Publication Data is available.

Copyright © 2008 by Carl Cavanagh Hodge

All rights reserved. No portion of this book may be
reproduced, by any process or technique, without the
express written consent of the publisher.

Library of Congress Catalog Card Number: 2007026483

ISBN-13: 978–0–313–33404–7 (set)
        978–0–313–33406–1 (vol 1)
        978–0–313–33407–8 (vol 2)

First published in 2008

Greenwood Press, 88 Post Road West, Westport, CT 06881
An imprint of Greenwood Publishing Group, Inc.
www.greenwood.com

Printed in the United States of America

The paper used in this book complies with the
Permanent Paper Standard issued by the National
Information Standards Organization (Z39.48–1984).

10 9 8 7 6 5 4 3 2 1

Every reasonable effort has been made to trace the owners of copyright materials in this book,
but in some instances this has proven impossible. The editor and publisher will be glad to
receive information leading to a more complete acknowledgments in subsequent printings of
the book and in the meantime extend their apologies for any omissions.

To Jane, the best of friends, Easter 2007

CONTENTS

LIST OF ENTRIES

LIST OF PRIMARY DOCUMENTS

GUIDE TO RELATED TOPICS

Acts, Conventions, Treaties, and Understandings

Act of Union (1801)
Adams-Onís Treaty (1819)
Adrianople, Treaty of (1829)
Aigun, Treaty of (1858)
Alaska Purchase Treaty (1867)
Amiens, Treaty of (1802)
Anglo-American Treaty (1818)
Anglo-Russian Convention (1907)
Ausgleich (1867)
Australian Colonies Government Act (1850)
Bassein, Treaty of (1802)
Bates Agreement (1899–1904)
Beijing, Conventions of (1860)
Björkö, Treaty of (1905)
Bond of 1844
Boxer Protocol (1901)
British North America Act (1867)
Burlingame Treaty (1868)
Carlsbad Decrees (1819)
Chaumont, Treaty of (1814)
Clayton-Bulwer Treaty (1850)
Concordat of 1801
Corn Laws (1804, 1815)
Cuban Reciprocity Treaty (1902)
Entente Cordiale (1904)
Foraker Amendment (1899)
Franco-Italian Convention (1902)
Franco-Spanish Agreement (1904)
Frankfurt, Treaty of (1871)
French Restoration (1814)

Geneva Convention (1864)
Guadalupe Hidalgo, Treaty of (1848)
Hay-Bunau-Varilla Treaty (1903)
Hay-Herrán Treaty (1903)
Hay-Pauncefote Treaty (1901)
Heligoland-Zanzibar Treaty (1890)
Inkiar Skelessi, Treaty of (1833)
Irish Land Acts (1870–1909)
Kanagawa, Treaty of (1854)
Kittery Peace (1905)
London Straits Convention (1841)
London, Treaty of (1839)
Louisiana Purchase (1803)
Lunéville, Treaty of (1801)
Mediterranean Agreements (1887)
Military Conversations (1906–1914)
Missouri Compromise (1820)
Münchengrätz Convention (1833)
Nanjing, Treaty of (1842)
Navigation Acts
Paris, Declaration of (1856)
Paris, Treaty of (1815)
Paris, Treaty of (1856)
Paris, Treaty of (1898)
Platt Amendment (1901)
Portsmouth, Treaty of (1905)
Pressburg, Treaty of (1805)
Pretoria, Convention of (1881)
Reinsurance Treaty (1887)
Royal Titles Act (1876)
Rush-Bagot Treaty (1817)
Sand River Convention (1852)
San Stefano, Treaty of (1878)

Artists, Intellectuals, Inventors, and Explorers

Asia, the Middle East, the Pacific, and the Polar Regions

Battles

Concepts, Labels, and Slogans

Tirpitz Plan
Treaty Ports
Two-Power Standard
Union
Weltpolitik
White Man's Burden

Conferences and Congresses

Aix-la-Chapelle, Congress of (1818)
Algeciras Conference (1906)
Berlin Conference (1884–1885)
Berlin, Congress of (1878)
Hague Conferences (1899, 1907)
Imperial Conferences
Congress System
Laibach, Congress of (1821)
Troppau, Congress of (1820)
Verona, Congress of (1822)
Vienna, Congress of (1815)

Crises

Agadir Crisis (1911)
Alabama Dispute (1871–1872)
Annexation Crisis (1908–1909)
Armenian Massacres (1894–1896)
Balkan Crises (1875–1878, 1908–1913)
Dogger Bank Incident (1904)
Dreyfus Affair (1894–1906)
Ems Telegram (1870)
Fashoda Incident (1898)
Irish Famine (1845–1850)
July Crisis (1914)
July Monarchy (1830–1848)
July Revolution (1830)
Moroccan Crisis (1905)
October Manifesto (1905)
Oregon Question
Panama Scandal (1892–1893)
Paris Commune (1871)
Perdicaris Affair (1904)
Russian Revolution (1905)
Samoan Crisis
Tampico and Vera Cruz Incidents (1914)
Venezuelan Crisis (1895)

Empires

British Empire
French Empire
German Empire
Habsburg Empire
Japanese Empire
Ottoman Empire

Portuguese Empire (1415–1808)
Russian Empire
Spanish Empire
United States

Europe

Åland Islands
Albania
Alsace-Lorraine
Armenia
Austrian Empire
Austria-Hungary
Bavaria
Belgium
Bohemia
Bosnia-Herzegovina
Bosporus
Bulgaria
Caucasus
Central Powers
Confederation of the Rhine (1806–1813)
Crete
Croatia-Slavonia
Cyprus
Danubian Principalities
Dardanelles
Denmark
Finland
German Confederation
Gibraltar
Greece
Hesse-Cassel
Hesse-Darmstadt
Hungary
Iceland
Ireland
Italy
Kiel
Macedonia
Malta
Montenegro
Moscow
Netherlands, Kingdom of the
Norway
North German Confederation (1867–1871)
Novibazar, Sanjak of
Ossetia
Piedmont-Sardinia, Kingdom of
Prussia
Rumania
Saar
Salonica

Sarajevo
Scandinavia
Schleswig-Holstein
Serbia
Sweden
Trieste
Wales

Institutions

Bashi-Bazouks
Bundesrat
Burschenschaft
Caliph
Caliphate
Chrysanthemum Throne
Commonwealth
Concentration Camps
Conservative Party
Durbar
East India Companies
Frankfurt Parliament (1848–1849)
French Foreign Legion
Great White Fleet
Imperial Federation
Janissaries
Liberal Party
Liberal Unionist Party
Missionaries
Napoleonic Code
Porte, The Sublime
Reich
Reichsbank
Reichstag
Royal Navy
Russian-American Company (RAC)
Suttee
Zollverein

Leaders and Statesmen

Abd-al-Qādir (1808–1883)
Acton, Lord John (1834–1902)
Adams, John (1735–1826)
Adams, John Quincy (1767–1848)
Aehrenthal, Aloys Lexa von (1854–1912)
Andrássy, Gyula, Count (1823–1890)
Asquith, Herbert Henry, Earl of Oxford and
    Asquith (1852–1928)
Balfour, Arthur J. (1848–1930)
Beck-Rzikowsky, Friedrich (1830–1920)
Bentinck, Lord William (1774–1839)
Bethmann-Hollweg, Theobald von (1856–
    1921)

Bismarck, Otto Eduard Leopold von (1815–
    1898)
Bonaparte, Joseph (1768–1844)
Botha, Louis (1862–1919)
Briand, Aristide (1862–1932)
Bülow, Bernhard Heinrich Martin Carl,
    Count von (1849–1929)
Burke, Edmund (1729–1797)
Campbell-Bannerman, Sir Henry (1836–
    1908)
Canning, George (1770–1827)
Caprivi, Count Leo von (1831–1899)
Cardwell, Edward, First Viscount Cardwell,
    (1813–1886)
Castlereagh, Robert Stewart, Viscount
    (1769–1823)
Cavour, Count Camillo Benso di (1810–
    1861)
Chamberlain, Joseph (1836–1914)
Cherniaev, General Mikhail Gregor'evich
    (1828–1898)
Churchill, Lord Randolph (1849–1894)
Churchill, Sir Winston Leonard Spencer
    Churchill (1874–1965)
Clemençeau, Georges (1841–1929)
Cleveland, Grover (1837–1908)
Conrad von Hötzendorf, Franz (1852–1925)
Cromer, Sir Evelyn Baring, First Earl of
    (1841–1917)
Curzon, George Nathaniel, Marquess Cur-
    zon of Kedleston (1859–1925)
Dalhousie, George Ramsay, Ninth Earl of
    Dalhousie (1770–1838)
Dalhousie, James Andrew Broun Ramsay,
    First Marquess of Dalhousie (1812–1860)
Delcassé, Théophile (1852–1923)
Derby, Edward George Geoffrey Smith Stan-
    ley, Fourteenth Earl of (1799–1869)
Derby, Edward Henry Stanley, Fifteenth Earl
    of (1826–1893)
De Valera, Eamon (1882–1975)
Dilke, Sir Charles (1843–1911)
Disraeli, Benjamin, Earl of Beaconsfield
    (1804–1881)
Dost Muhammad Khan (1793–1863)
Elgin, James Bruce, Eighth Earl of (1811–
    1863)
Elgin, Victor Alexander Bruce, Ninth Earl
    of (1849–1917)
Ferry, Jules François Camille (1832–1893)
Fisher, John Arbuthnot, Lord Fisher (1841–
    1920)

Wilson, Woodrow (1856–1924)
Witte, Sergei (1849–1915)
Wolseley, Garnet Wolseley, Field Marshal Viscount (1833–1913)
Wood, Leonard (1860–1927)

Monarchs and Dynasties

Albrecht Friedrich Rudolf, Archduke (1817–1895)
Alexander, King of Yugoslavia (1888–1934)
Alexander I, Tsar of Russia (1777–1825)
Alexander II, Tsar of Russia (1818–1881)
Alexander III, Tsar of Russia
Bonaparte, Louis (1778–1846)
Bonaparte, Louis Napoleon (1808–1873)
Bonaparte, Napoleon (1769–1821)
Bourbon Dynasty (1589–1848)
Bukhara Emirate
Charles, Archduke of Austria (1771–1847)
Charles X, King of France (1757–1836)
Edward VII, King of Great Britain (1841–1910)
Francis Ferdinand, Archduke of Austria (1863–1914)
Francis Joseph, Emperor of Austria (1830–1916)
George III, King of Great Britain (1738–1820)
George IV, King of Great Britain (1762–1830)
George V, King of Great Britain and Emperor of India (1865–1936)
Haakon VII, King of Norway (1872–1957)
Habsburg Dynasty
Hohenzollern Dynasty
Louis XVIII (1755–1824)
Maximilian, Emperor of Mexico (1832–1867)
Mehmet Ali (1769–1848)
Mehmet V, Sultan of Turkey (1844–1918)
Mutsuhito, Emperor of Japan (1852–1912)
Nicholas I, Tsar of Russia (1796–1855)
Nicholas II, Tsar of Russia (1868–1918)
Qing Dynasty (1644–1912)
Victor Emmanuel II (1820–1878)
Victor Emmanuel III (1869–1947)
Victoria, Queen of Great Britain (1819–1901)
Wilhelm I, Kaiser of Germany (1797–1888)
Wilhelm II, Kaiser of Germany (1859–1941)

Movements

Action Française
Anarchism
Anti-Corn Law League
Black Hand
Bolsheviks
Bonapartism
Communism
Decembrists
Freemasonry
Impressionism
Internationalism
Jadidism
Liberal Imperialists
Liberalism
Mensheviks
Mercantilism
Narodna Odbrana
Navalism
Nihilism
Orientalism
Progressivism
Protectionism
Radicalism
Sinn Féin
Slavism
Social Darwinism
Tariff Reform League
Terrorism
Young Ireland
Young Italy (1831)
Young Turks
Wahhabi/Wahhabism
Zionism

Soldiers

Blücher, Gebhard von (1742–1819)
Bonaparte, Napoleon (1769–1821)
Boulanger, General Georges-Ernest (1837–1891)
Campbell, Sir Colin, Baron Clyde (1792–1863)
Clausewitz, Carl von (1780–1831)
Falkenhayn, Erich von (1861–1922)
Foch, Ferdinand (1851–1929)
Gneisenau, August Wilhelm von (1760–1831)
Gordon, Charles George (1833–1885)
Grant, Ulysses S. (1822–1885)
Haig, Douglas (1861–1928)
Hindenburg, Paul von Beneckendorff und von (1847–1934)
Jackson, Andrew (1767–1845)
Jellicoe, John Rushworth (1859–1935)
Mackensen, August von (1849–1945)

MacMahon, Patrice Edmé Maurice (1808–1893)

Moltke, Helmuth von (1800–1891)

Moltke, Helmuth Johannes Ludwig von (1848–1916)

Nelson, Horatio (1758–1805)

Roon, Albrecht von (1803–1879)

Scharnhorst, Gerhard Johann von (1755–1813)

Tirpitz, Alfred von (1849–1930)

Technologies and Inventions

Berlin-Baghdad Railway

Dreadnought

Great Exhibition (1851)

Kaiser-Wilhelm-Kanal

Machine Gun

Oil

Panama Canal

Railways

Steamboats/Steamships

Telegraph

Zoological Gardens

Wars and Conflicts

Achinese War (1873–1907)

Afghan Wars (1838–1842, 1878–1880)

American Civil War (1861–1865)

Andijan Revolt (1898)

Anglo-American War (1812–1815)

Anglo-Burmese Wars (1824–1826, 1852, 1885)

Anglo-Nepal War (1814–1816)

Arrow War (1856–1860)

Ashanti Wars

Australian Frontier Wars (1788–1928)

Austro-Prussian War (1866)

Balkan Wars (1912–1913)

Boer Wars (1880–1881, 1899–1902)

Boxer Insurrection (1900)

Carlist Wars (1833–1840, 1847–1849, 1872–1876)

Crimean War (1853–1856)

Franco-Prussian War (1870–1871)

Indian Wars

Italo-Abyssinian War (1887–1896)

Italo-Turkish War (1911–1912)

Kaffir Wars (1781–1879)

Liberation, War of (1813)

Maji-Maji Rebellion (1905–1907)

Maori Wars (1843–1847, 1863–1870)

Maratha Wars (1775–1782, 1803–1805, 1817–1818)

Matabele Wars (1893–1894, 1896–1897)

Mexican-American War (1846–1848)

Napoleonic Wars (1792–1815)

Opium War (1839–1842)

Peninsular War (1808–1814)

Polish Rebellions

Restoration War (1868–1869)

Russo-Khokandian War (1864–1865)

Russo-Japanese War (1904–1905)

Russo-Swedish War (1808–1809)

Russo-Turkish War (1806–1812)

Russo-Turkish War (1828–1829)

Russo-Turkish War (1877–1878)

Sikh Wars (1845–1846, 1848–1849)

Sino-French War (1883–1885)

Sino-Japanese War (1894–1895)

Sioux Wars (1862, 1876–1877, 1890–1891)

Spanish-American War (1898)

War of the Pacific (1879–1882)

Zulu War (1879)

MAPS

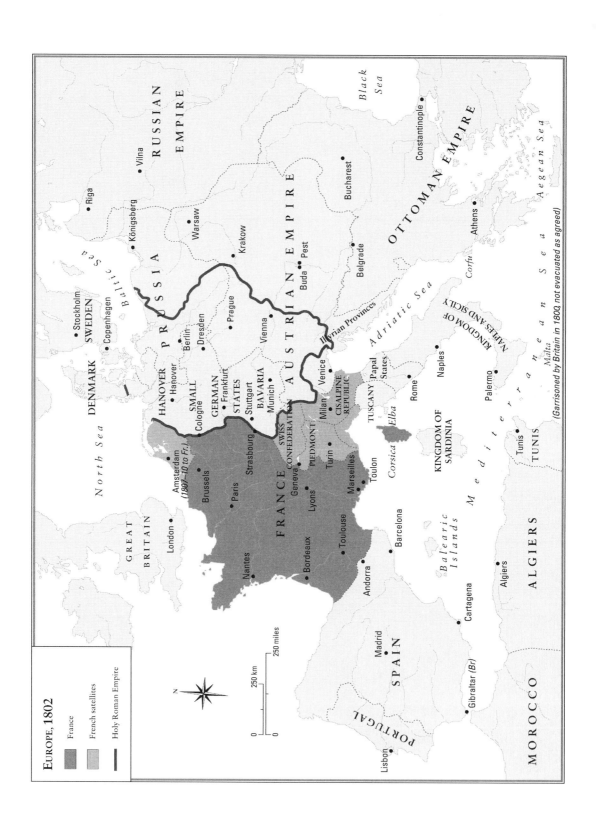

EUROPE, 1802

France

French satellites

Holy Roman Empire

N

250 km
250 miles

RUSSIAN EMPIRE

Black Sea

Aegean Sea

OTTOMAN EMPIRE

Vilna

Riga

Königsberg

Warsaw

Krakow

Bucharest

Constantinople

Athens

Corfu

Adriatic Sea

Buda Pest

Belgrade

Prague

Illyrian Provinces

Venice

AUSTRIAN EMPIRE

Stockholm

SWEDEN

Copenhagen

DENMARK

Baltic Sea

PRUSSIA

Berlin

Dresden

Vienna

HANOVER

Hanover

SMALL
Cologne

GERMAN
Frankfurt

STATES
Stuttgart

BAVARIA
Munich

North Sea

GREAT
BRITAIN

London

Amsterdam
(1807–10 to Fr.)

Brussels

Paris

FRANCE

SWISS
Geneva CONFEDERATION

PIEDMONT

Turin

Milan

CISALPINE
REPUBLIC

TUSCANY Papal
States

Elba

Rome

Naples

KINGDOM OF
NAPLES AND SICILY

Palermo

Corsica

KINGDOM OF SARDINIA

Strasbourg

Lyons

Marseilles

Toulon

Toulouse

Bordeaux

Nantes

Andorra

Barcelona

Balearic
Islands

Mediterranean Sea

Malta
(Garrisoned by Britain in 1800 not evacuated as agreed)

Tunis

TUNIS

ALGIERS

Algiers

SPAIN

Madrid

Gibraltar (Br)

Cartagena

PORTUGAL

Lisbon

MOROCCO

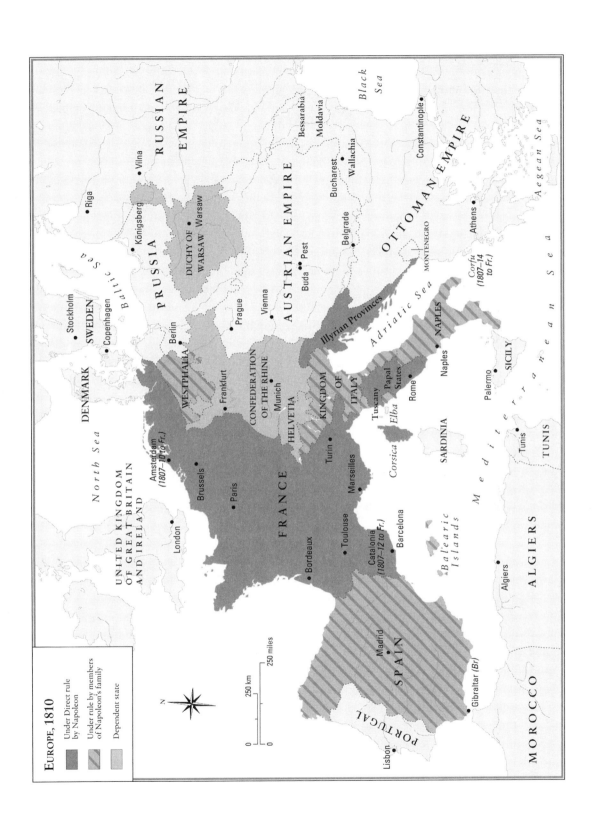

EUROPE, 1810

- Under Direct rule by Napoleon
- Under rule by members of Napoleon's family
- Dependent state

N

250 miles
250 km

RUSSIAN EMPIRE

Riga

Vilna

Königsberg

DUCHY OF WARSAW · Warsaw

PRUSSIA

Berlin

Stockholm
SWEDEN
Copenhagen

DENMARK

Baltic Sea

North Sea

UNITED KINGDOM
OF GREAT BRITAIN
AND IRELAND

London

Amsterdam
(1807–10 to Fr.)

Brussels

WESTPHALIA

Frankfurt

CONFEDERATION
OF THE RHINE

Munich

HELVETIA

Prague

Vienna

AUSTRIAN EMPIRE

Buda · Pest

Belgrade

Bucharest.

Wallachia

Bessarabia

Moldavia

Black Sea

Constantinople

OTTOMAN EMPIRE

MONTENEGRO

Athens

Corfu
(1807–14
to Fr.)

Aegean Sea

FRANCE

Paris

Bordeaux

Toulouse

Marseilles

Turin

KINGDOM
OF
ITALY

Tuscany

Elba

Papal
States

Rome

Illyrian Provinces

Adriatic Sea

NAPLES

Naples

SICILY

Palermo

Corsica

SARDINIA

Mediterranean Sea

Balearic
Islands

Barcelona

Catalonia
(1807–12 to Fr.)

SPAIN

Madrid

PORTUGAL

Lisbon

Gibraltar (Br)

MOROCCO

Algiers

ALGIERS

Tunis

TUNIS

Europe in 1815 After
the Treaty of Vienna

━━━ German Confederation

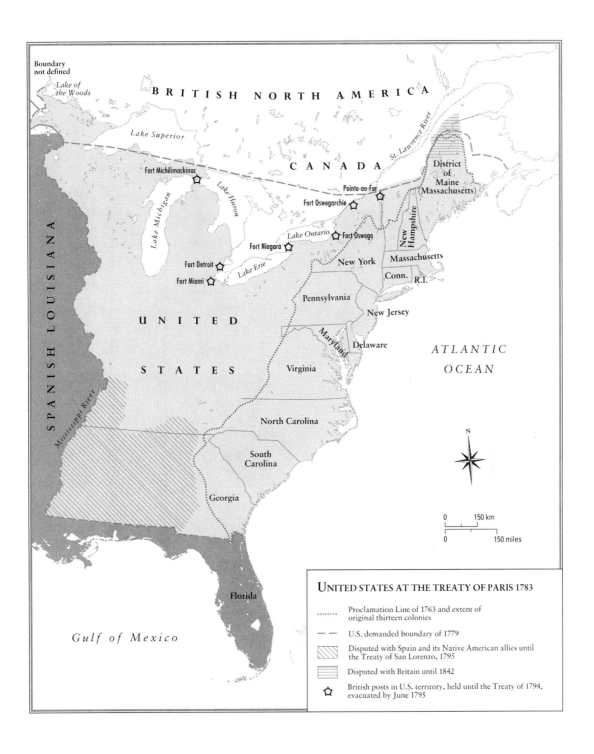

Boundary
not defined

*Lake of
the Woods*

BRITISH NORTH AMERICA

Lake Superior

CANADA

St. Lawrence River

Fort Michilimackinac

Lake Michigan

Lake Huron

Pointe-au-Far

Fort Oswegarchie

Lake Ontario Fort Oswego

Fort Niagara

Lake Erie

Fort Detroit

Fort Miami

District
of
Maine
(Massachusetts)

New
Hampshire

New York

Massachusetts

Conn.

R.I.

SPANISH LOUISIANA

Mississippi River

U N I T E D

S T A T E S

Pennsylvania

New Jersey

Maryland

Delaware

Virginia

*ATLANTIC
OCEAN*

North Carolina

South
Carolina

N

Georgia

Florida

Gulf of Mexico

| 0 | | 150 km |
| 0 | | 150 miles |

UNITED STATES AT THE TREATY OF PARIS 1783

.... Proclamation Line of 1763 and extent of
original thirteen colonies

— — — U.S. demanded boundary of 1779

Disputed with Spain and its Native American allies until
the Treaty of San Lorenzo, 1795

Disputed with Britain until 1842

☆ British posts in U.S. territory, held until the Treaty of 1794,
evacuated by June 1795

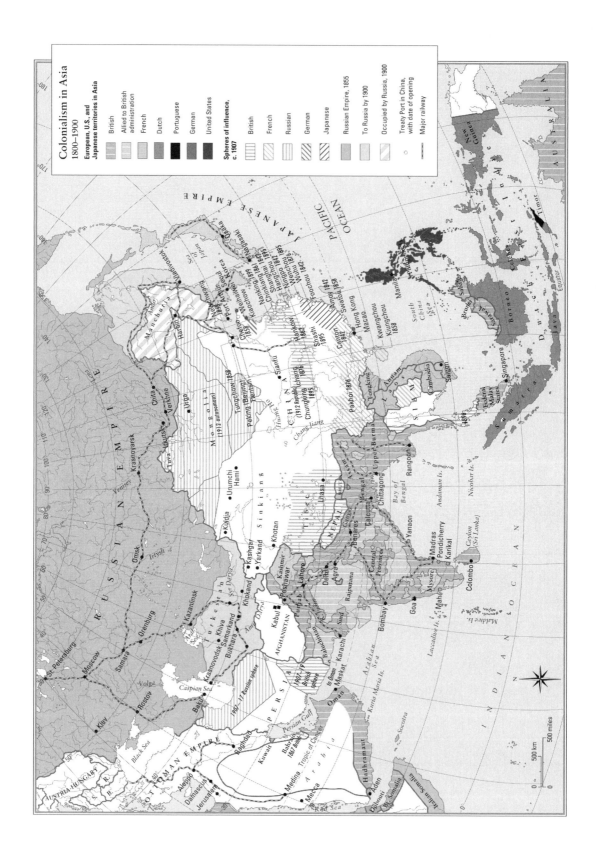

Colonialism in Asia
1800–1900

European, U.S., and Japanese territories in Asia

British
Allied to British administration
French
Dutch
Portuguese
German
United States

Spheres of influence, c. 1907

British
French
Russian
German
Japanese
Russian Empire, 1855
To Russia by 1900
Occupied by Russia, 1900
Treaty Port in China, with date of opening
Major railway

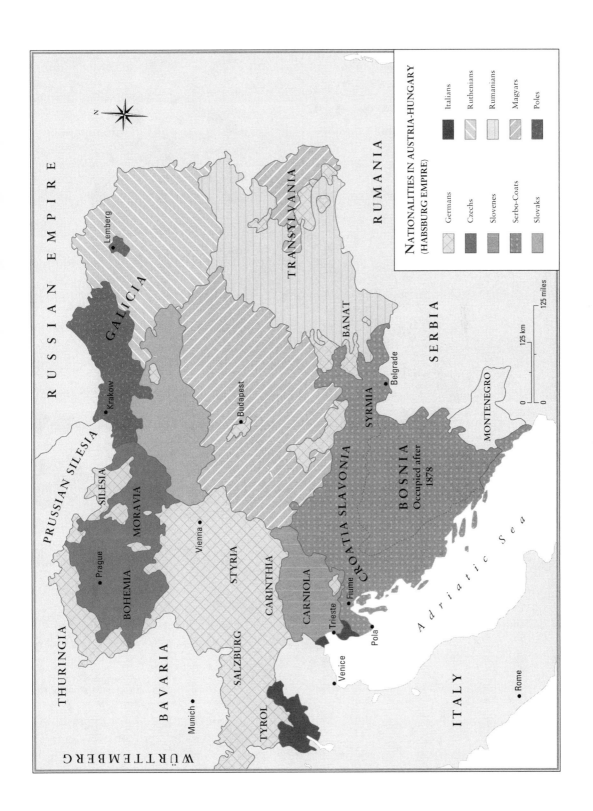

NATIONALITIES IN AUSTRIA-HUNGARY
(HABSBURG EMPIRE)

Germans
Czechs
Slovenes
Serbo-Coats
Slovaks

Italians
Ruthenians
Rumanians
Magyars
Poles

RUSSIAN EMPIRE

PRUSSIAN SILESIA

THURINGIA

WÜRTTEMBERG

BAVARIA

Munich

SALZBURG

TYROL

SILESIA

MORAVIA

BOHEMIA

Prague

Vienna

STYRIA

CARINTHIA

CARNIOLA

Trieste
Fiume
Pola

Venice

ITALY

Rome

Adriatic Sea

GALICIA

Krakow

Lemberg

Budapest

TRANSYLVANIA

BANAT

SYRMIA

CROATIA SLAVONIA

BOSNIA
Occupied after
1878

Belgrade

SERBIA

MONTENEGRO

RUMANIA

N

125 km

125 miles

The Balkans, 1878–1914

Area of Turkey in Europe before Treaty of Berlin, 1878

Area of Turkey in Europe before the Balkan Wars, 1912–1913

Area ceded by Bulgaria to Romania, 1913

Boundaries before the Balkan Wars

Boundaries after the Balkan Wars

Dniester

BESSARABIA

Drava

MOLDAVIA

Prut

Sava

BANAT

ROMANIA

Belgrade

• Bucharest

• Craiova

BOZNIA
Occupied by
Austria, 1878;
annexed, 1908

SERBIA

Black

Sarajevo •

Danube

Sea

HERZEGOVINA

BULGARIA

MONTENEGRO

• Sofia

DALMATIA
(Austria)

• Scutari

Vardar

• Adrianople

Bosphorus

M A C E D O N I A

THRACE

TURKEY
Constantinople •

Albania created
from former
Turkish territory
1913

*Sea of
Marmara*

ITALY

Salonika

ALBANIA

Dardanelles

THESSALY

A e g e a n

TURKEY

to GREECE 1881

S e a

• Smyrna

I o n i a n

Sea

G R E E C E

Ionian Islands

• Athens

N

MOREA

C y c l a d e s

DODECANESE
to Italy, 1912

RHODES

0   100 km

0   100 miles

Cerigo

to Greece, 1913

CRETE

M e d i t e r r a n e a n   S e a

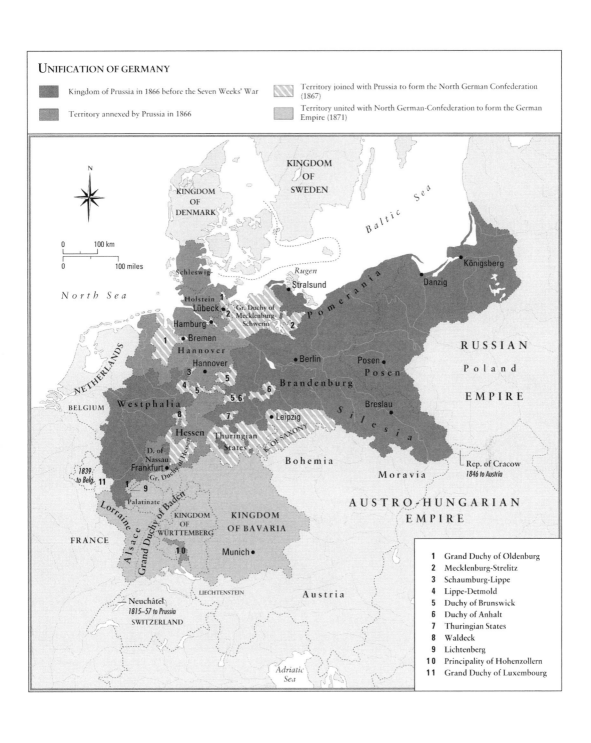

UNIFICATION OF GERMANY

Kingdom of Prussia in 1866 before the Seven Weeks' War

Territory annexed by Prussia in 1866

Territory joined with Prussia to form the North German Confederation (1867)

Territory united with North German-Confederation to form the German Empire (1871)

N

0   100 km

0   100 miles

KINGDOM OF SWEDEN

KINGDOM OF DENMARK

Baltic Sea

Schleswig

Rugen

Stralsund

Königsberg

North Sea

Holstein   **1**

Lübeck   **2**

Hamburg

Gr. Duchy of Mecklenburg-Schwerin

2

Pomerania

Danzig

Bremen

Hannover

Hannover

3

4   5

Berlin

Posen

Posen

RUSSIAN

Poland

EMPIRE

5

5 6

6

Brandenburg

NETHERLANDS

BELGIUM

Westphalia

8

5 6

7

Leipzig

Breslau

Silesia

Hessen

Thuringian States

K. OF SAXONY

Bohemia

Moravia

Rep. of Cracow
1846 to Austria

D. of Nassau

Frankfurt

Gr. Duchy of Hessen

1839 to Belg.   **11**

1   9

Palatinate

AUSTRO-HUNGARIAN EMPIRE

Lorraine

Alsace

Grand Duchy of Baden

KINGDOM OF WÜRTTEMBERG

KINGDOM OF BAVARIA

FRANCE

10

Munich

LIECHTENSTEIN

Austria

Neuchâtel
1815–57 to Prussia
SWITZERLAND

Adriatic Sea

1 Grand Duchy of Oldenburg
2 Mecklenburg-Strelitz
3 Schaumburg-Lippe
4 Lippe-Detmold
5 Duchy of Brunswick
6 Duchy of Anhalt
7 Thuringian States
8 Waldeck
9 Lichtenberg
10 Principality of Hohenzollern
11 Grand Duchy of Luxembourg

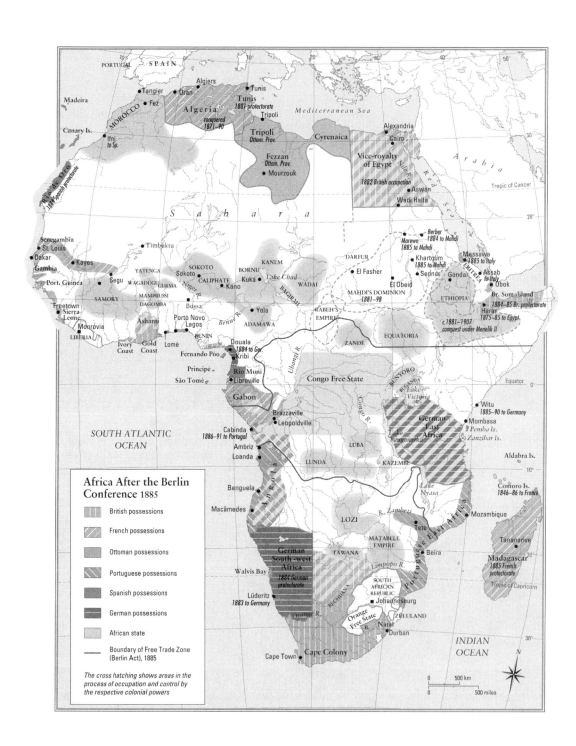

Africa After the Berlin Conference 1885

British possessions

French possessions

Ottoman possessions

Portuguese possessions

Spanish possessions

German possessions

African state

Boundary of Free Trade Zone
(Berlin Act), 1885

*The cross hatching shows areas in the
process of occupation and control by
the respective colonial powers*

PORTUGAL SPAIN

Madeira

Canary Is.

Ifni
to Sp.

MOROCCO

Tangier

Fez

Oran

Algiers

Algeria
conquered
1871–90

Tunis

Tunis
1881 protectorate

Tripoli

Mediterranean Sea

Cyrenaica

Tripoli
Ottm. Prov.

Fezzan
Ottm. Prov.

Mourzouk

Alexandria

Cairo

Vice-royalty
of Egypt

1882 British occupation

Aswan

Wadi Halfa

Arabia

Red Sea

Tropic of Cancer

S a h a r a

Senegambia

St. Louis

Dakar

Gambia

Port. Guinea

Timbuktu

YATENGA

SOKOTO

Sokoto

WAGADUGU

GURMA

MAMPRUSSI

DAGOMBA

BORNU

KANEM

Lake Chad

WADAI

DARFUR

El Fasher

Marewe
1885 to Mahdi

Berber
1884 to Mahdi

Khartoum
1885 to Mahdi

El Obeid

Sednar

Gondar

Massawa
1885 to Italy

Assab
to Italy

Obok

CALIPHATE

Kuka

Kano

BAGIRMI

MAHDI'S DOMINION
1881–98

Mahdi's Dominion

ETHIOPIA

Br. Somaliland
1884–85 Br. protectorate

Harar
1875–85 to Egypt.

Kayes

Segu

SAMORY

Niger R.

Bussa

Benue R.

Yola

ADAMAWA

RABEH'S
EMPIRE

EQUATORIA

c.1881–1907
conquest under Menelik II

Freetown

Sierra Leone

Monrovia

LIBERIA

Ashanti

Ivory
Coast

Gold
Coast

Porto Novo

Lagos

Lomé

BENIN

Douala
1884 to Ger.

Kribi

ZANDE

Fernando Póo

Príncipe

São Tomé

Rio Muni

Libreville

Gabon

Ubangi R.

Congo Free State

BUNYORO

BUGANDA

Lake
Victoria

Equator

Brazzaville

Leopoldville

Witu
1885–90 to Germany

German
East
Africa

Mombasa

Pemba Is.

Zanzibar Is.

Cabinda
1886–91 to Portugal

Ambriz

Loanda

LUNDA

LUBA

Congo R.

KAZEMBI

Lake
Tanganyika

Aldabra Is.

SOUTH ATLANTIC
OCEAN

Benguela

Macâmedes

Angola

LOZI

Lake
Nyasa

R. Zambezi

Comoro Is.
1846–86 to France

Mozambique

Tete

Beira

Portuguese East Africa

Tananarive

Madagascar
1885 French
protectorate

Tropic of Capricorn

German
South-west
Africa

1884 German
protectorate

Walvis Bay

Lüderitz
1883 to Germany

TAWANA

BUCHUANA

MATABELE
EMPIRE

Limpopo R.

SOUTH
AFRICAN
REPUBLIC

Johannesburg

Orange R.

Orange
Free State

ZULULAND

Natal

Durban

Cape Town

Cape Colony

INDIAN
OCEAN

N

0   500 km

0   500 miles

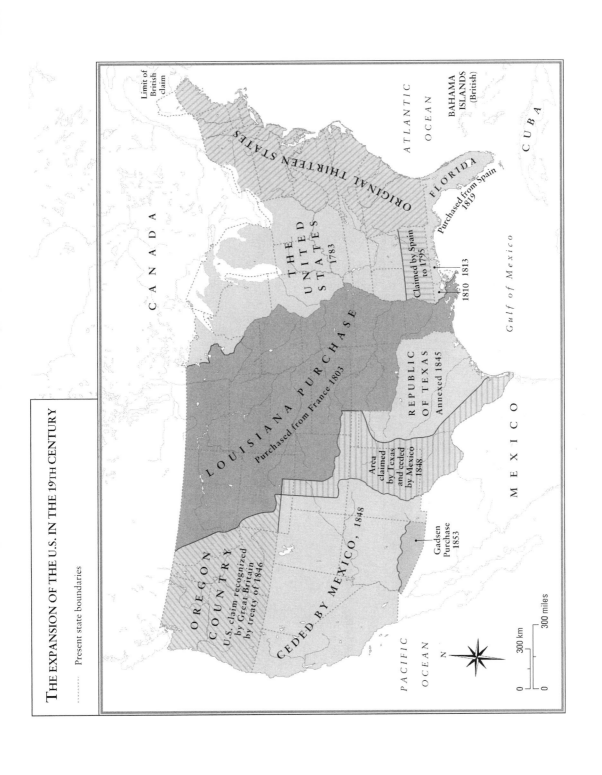

THE EXPANSION OF THE U.S. IN THE 19TH CENTURY

- - - - - Present state boundaries

CANADA

Limit of British claim

ORIGINAL THIRTEEN STATES

THE UNITED STATES 1783

ATLANTIC OCEAN

BAHAMA ISLANDS (British)

CUBA

FLORIDA

Purchased from Spain 1819

Claimed by Spain to 1795

1810 1813

Gulf of Mexico

LOUISIANA PURCHASE

Purchased from France 1803

REPUBLIC OF TEXAS Annexed 1845

OREGON COUNTRY U.S. claim recognized by Great Britain by treaty of 1846

CEDED BY MEXICO, 1848

Area claimed by Texas and ceded by Mexico 1848

Gadsden Purchase 1853

MEXICO

PACIFIC OCEAN

N

300 km

300 miles

0

0

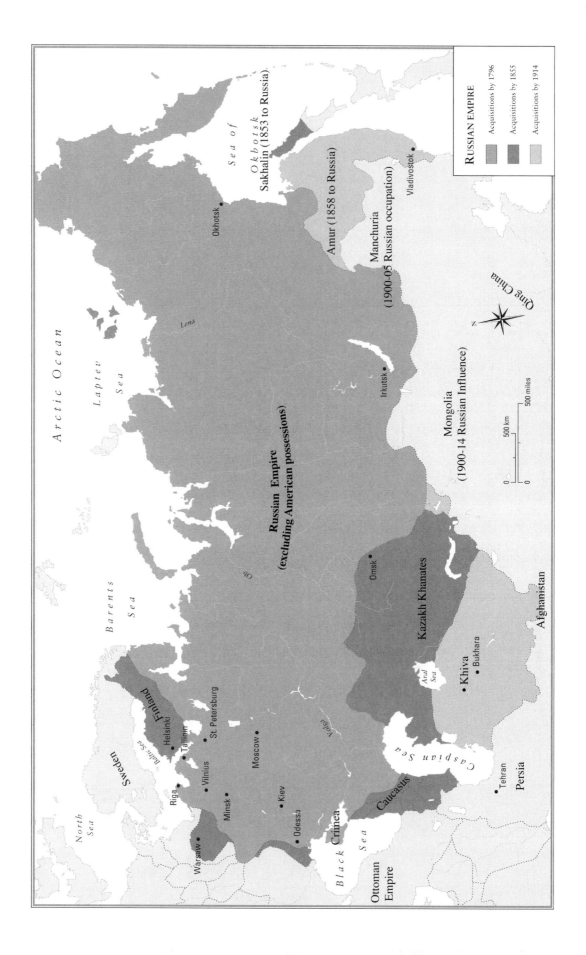

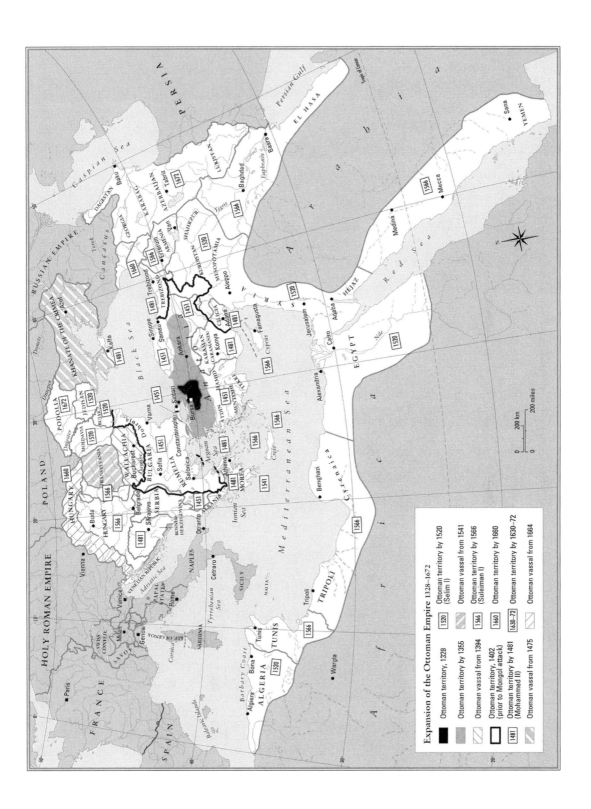

Expansion of the Ottoman Empire 1328–1672

■	Ottoman territory, 1328		▨ 1520	Ottoman territory by 1520 (Selim I)
▨	Ottoman territory by 1355		▨ 1520	Ottoman vassal from 1541
▨	Ottoman vassal from 1394		1566	Ottoman territory by 1566 (Suleiman I)
▢	Ottoman territory, 1402 (prior to Mongol attack)		1660	Ottoman territory by 1660
1481	Ottoman territory by 1481 (Mohammed II)		1630–72	Ottoman territory by 1630–72
▨	Ottoman vassal from 1475		▨	Ottoman vassal from 1664

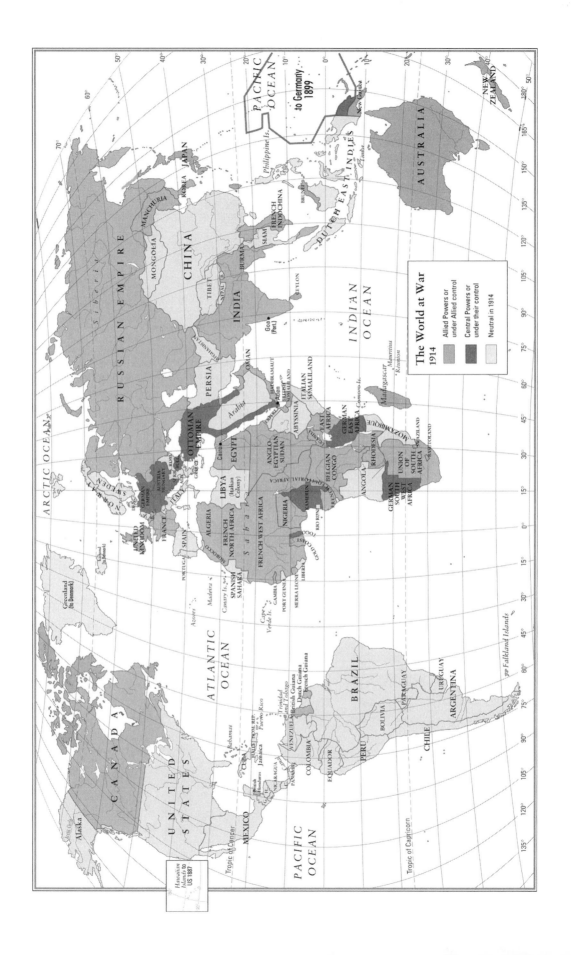

ENCYCLOPEDIA OF THE AGE OF IMPERIALISM, 1800-1914

L

Laibach, Congress of (1821)

The completion of the Congress of **Troppau** and the fourth meeting of the **Congress System,** held from January until May 1821. At the time, a liberal revolution was underway in **Italy,** prompted in part by the apparent success of the Spanish revolution of 1820, and Austria had deployed 80,000 troops to "restore order" in the most disaffected regions. Russian Tsar **Alexander I** was fully under the influence of the Austrian Foreign Minister **Metternich** and, at one point in the congress, advised the French representative that it might be prudent for France to intervene in Spain on the same principle that Austria applied to Italy. The meeting marked another step in British alienation from the Congress system, insofar as Lord **Castlereagh** acknowledged Austria's right to intervene in the particular case of Italy yet rejected any notion of general right of intervention for the Great Powers in the internal affairs of lesser nations as contrary to fundamental British principles and potentially a tyranny in the hands of "less beneficent monarchs." *See also* Austrian Empire.

FURTHER READING: Kissinger, Henry. *A World Restored: Metternich, Castlereagh, and the Problem of Peace 1812–1822.* London: Weidenfeld & Nicolson, 2000.

CARL CAVANAGH HODGE

Lamartine, Alphonse de (1790–1869)

A French poet, author, and politician of the Romantic era, Alphonse de Lamartine was born Mâcon Saône-et-Loire in 1790 to a provincial noble family. During his youth, Lamartine traveled frequently and served briefly in the army. In 1820, he married Maria Birch, an Englishwoman. After his military career ended, Lamartine turned to writing and achieved immediate success with his first major publication, *Méditations poétiques* (1820), a collection of 24 poems, including the famous "Le Lac." He was elected as a member of the *Académie française* in 1829.

Lamartine later strayed from his orthodox Christian upbringing by becoming a pantheist, writing *Jocelyn* (1836) and *La Chute d'un ange* (1838). His romantic idealism influenced his politics. He advocated democratic principles, social justice, and international peace. From 1825 to 1828, he worked for the French Embassy in **Italy** and in 1833 became an elected deputy in the French parliament. Lamartine conducted a lavish tour of the countries in the Orient and wrote an account of his travels, during which he lost his only daughter, under the title *Voyage en Orient*. After the publication of *Voyage en Orient* in 1835, Lamartine focused on prose and wrote several works of history, including his *Histoire des Girondins,* a popular work glorifying the Girondist faction of the French Revolution, and *L'Histoire de la révolution de 1848*. In the wake of the Revolution of 1848 against Louis Philippe, Lamartine headed the provisional government until the establishment of the Second Republic and served as minister of foreign affairs from February 24 to May 11, 1848. Lamartine ran unsuccessfully for the French presidency with Louis Napoleon **Bonaparte,** later Napoleon III, in December 1848.

During the Second Republic, Lamartine was criticized as too moderate. He worked toward the abolition of slavery and the death penalty and supported the national workshop programs advocated by Louis Blanc. With Louis Napoleon's coup d'etat of December 2, 1851 and the end of the Second Republic, Lamartine retired to his writing career hoping to amass enough funds to pay off his enormous debts. Among his later works are *Graziella* (1849) and *Les Confidences* (1852). Lamartine died in obscurity in 1869.

FURTHER READING: Fortescue, William. *Lamartine: A Political Biography.* London: Croom Helm, 1983; Lombard, Charles. *Lamartine.* New York: Twayne, 1973.

ERIC MARTONE

Landshut, Battle of (1809)

Fought northeast of Munich in **Bavaria** on April 21, 1809, the Battle of Landshut was a French victory in the War of the Fifth Coalition over Austrian General Johann Hiller. After his defeat at Abensberg, Hiller withdrew his 35,000 men to Landshut, on the River Isar, pursued by Marshal Jean Lannes. Napoleon had sent Marshal André Masséna to cut them off, but delays allowed Hiller to occupy the town and the bridge. Lannes efforts to dislodge him failed and it took Napoleon's arrival to change things. Napoleon's forces quickly occupied the suburbs and then dispatched troops to capture the bridge. The Austrians put up stiff resistance, but with Masséna threatening his line of retreat, Hiller withdrew toward Neumarkt. Napoleon then sent Marshal Jean Baptiste Bessières after the Austrian with 20,000 men and led the rest of his army toward Eckmühl, determined to crush Archduke **Charles**'s forces. The action at Landshut further split the Austrian army and inflicted heavy losses, including 10,000 men and many guns and supplies. *See also* Bonaparte, Napoleon; Napoleonic Wars.

FURTHER READING: Rothenberg, Gunther Erich. *The Napoleonic Wars.* London: Cassell, 2000.

J. DAVID MARKHAM

Laos

Known as Lan Xang or "land of a million elephants," Laos was founded as a unified state by Prince Fa Ngoum (1353–1373), a Lao, in the year 1353. After the state's disintegration, a long duel between Vietnam and Thailand began over suzerainty of the various kingdoms of Laos. The coming of the French formed an important chapter in the history of the country. The French interest in Laos was subordinate to its interest in Vietnam, and the conquest of Laos was the last stage of French **imperialism** in **Indochina**. There was fierce rivalry among France, Thailand, and Britain for control of the Mekong valley between 1866 and 1893. It was Auguste Pavie, who was responsible for bringing Laos under the French colonial hold. The Franco-Siamese treaty of October 3, 1893, established the French protectorate over Laos. Thailand gave up its claim on the territories of the left bank of the Mekong River. The 1904 Anglo-French treaty spelled out in explicit terms the respective spheres of influence of Britain and France. In exchange for a 25-kilometer neutral zone along the Mekong's west bank, Thailand gave Champassak and Sayaboury provinces to the French in 1904 and 1907, respectively. France had thus completed the conquest of Indochina over a period of 50 years ending in 1907. In the same year, the Indochinese Union was created out of four protectorates, Annam, Tonkin, Laos, and Cambodia.

French colonial policy was formulated from Hanoi and Laos functioned as a colony of Vietnam. A system of "cross racial administration" was applied, pitting various ethnic groups against each other. Education and health sectors were neglected. Taxation system was oppressive. The response of the Lao to French administrative measures was not passive. In the beginning of twentieth century, resistance movements led by individuals and tribes developed, and the rebellion of a district chief of Savannakhet, Phocodout, in 1901, took two years suppress. Resistance by the Alec and Loven tribes of Bolovens plateau was provoked by French attempts to collect taxes and regulate commerce. In 1908, Va Nam Phoum led a revolt in Phong Saly and Nam Tha provinces. As they were isolated, the insurrections were unsuccessful; however, they generated a tradition that later helped in fostering Lao nationalism. *See also* French Empire.

FURTHER READING: Mishra, Patit Paban. *A Contemporary History of Laos.* New Delhi: National Book Organization, 1999; Stuart-Fox, Martin. *A History of Laos.* Cambridge: Cambridge University Press, 1997; Toye, Hugh. *Laos: Buffer State or Battleground.* London: Oxford University Press, 1968.

PATIT PABAN MISHRA

Lapse Doctrine

A device used by the British East India Company, starting in the 1830s, for bringing the princely states of **India** under its control. The doctrine maintained that the company had the right to any states whose ruler died without a direct male heir to uphold succession. Such rulers had hitherto been succeeded by adopted sons, but the lapse doctrine forbade the practice except in special cases. During his service as governor-general, Lord **Dalhousie** used the doctrine to annex Jhansi, Nagpur, Punjab, Sambalpur, and Satara, thereby causing considerable anxiety, among even the most cooperative of Indian rulers, that no dynastic succession was secure. Among the other causes, the **Indian Mutiny** of 1857 was a product of lapse doctrine's predatory attack on tradition, so that after the defeat of the rebellion the policy was formally renounced. *See also* East India Companies.

FURTHER READING: James, Lawrence. *Raj: The Making and Unmaking of British India.* New York: St. Martin's, 1997.

CARL CAVANAGH HODGE

Laswari, Battle of (1803)

A sharp and bloody engagement of the Second **Maratha War.** In late September 1803, a Maratha chief named Abaji took command of the 9,000 westernized Maratha infantry and 4,000 to 5,000 cavalry in northern **India.** After the fall of Agra, Abaji retreated toward Jaipur. In October, General Gerald Lake, commander of British troops in northern India, advanced toward him with 10,500 soldiers. On November 1, Lake caught up with the Maratha force at the village of Laswari. The left of the Maratha line was posted in the village while a rivulet with steep banks covered the right. The Marathas deployed 74 guns in their center. Because of the grass and dust blown by the arrival of British cavalry, Lake was unable to realize the strong position of the Maratha line. He launched his first and second cavalry brigades on the Maratha left while the Third Cavalry Brigade attacked the Maratha right. The cavalry charges were driven back by Maratha infantry and artillery.

At noon, Lake's infantry arrived, and he threw it against the Maratha right. The infantry was organized in a column formation of two lines. Lake himself led the first line consisting of the Seventy-Sixth Regiment and two sepoy battalions. One cavalry brigade threatened the Maratha left. The Maratha artillery was able to stop the infantry line, while the cavalry launched an attack against the Lake's infantry. But Lake's two reserve cavalry brigades countered, and, in close quarter combat, the light Maratha cavalry had no chance against the disciplined dragoons mounted on bigger horses. Although Lake's force suffered 838 casualties, Laswari finally set the seal on the disintegration of Maratha power in north India. *See also* British Empire.

FURTHER READING: Wolpert, Stanley. *A New History of India.* New York: Oxford University Press, 2005.

KAUSHIK ROY

Laurier, Sir Wilfrid (1841–1919)

Prime minister of **Canada** from 1896 to 1911, Wilfrid Laurier was born in rural Quebec, the son of a farmer. After a classical education, he studied law at McGill University. Laurier established himself as a lawyer and newspaper proprietor in the small town of Arthabaska, Quebec. Elected to the Dominion Parliament in the Liberal sweep of 1874, Laurier held his seat even when Sir John A. Macdonald's Tories came back into power in 1878. Laurier spoke in favor of the Metis rebel Louis Riel, executed for treason in 1885, but reacted with studied ambiguity to other English-French and parallel denominational issues dividing Canadians. Laurier became leader of the Liberal Party in 1887, and after Macdonald's death in 1891 and the Conservatives' inability to produce a compelling successor, he won power in 1896.

As a Liberal, Laurier was a free trader and hence opposed to Macdonald's protectionist national policy. But in obeisance to imperial feeling as well as the antitariff views of his supporters, Laurier, in 1897, lowered tariffs on the goods of nonprotectionist countries, which effectively meant Britain. In the imperial climate of the diamond jubilee of that year, Laurier was seen as a pioneer of Imperial Preference, a strange fate for a free trader who opposed schemes for imperial consolidation or centralization. During the Boer War, Laurier's government agreed, in response to English-Canadian opinion, to recruit and equip a relatively small number of volunteers for service in South Africa, a policy that alienated some of his more nationalist Quebec supporters. In the face of the Edwardian naval race, Laurier declined to contribute to the Royal Navy, but did found, in 1910, the Royal Canadian Navy for coastal defense, immortalized by its imperialist opponents as the "tin pot navy."

In response to an American initiative, Laurier negotiated a treaty of trade reciprocity with the **United States.** He fought the election of 1911 on the issue, losing to Sir Robert Borden, who saw **free trade** with the United States as a threat to imperial cohesion. During World War I, Laurier supported the war effort but opposed the conscription policies of Borden's government, losing the election of 1917 decisively. Laurier is remembered as a Canadian nationalist who attempted to reconcile Canada's French and English populations. *See also* Boer Wars; Dominion; Imperial Preference.

FURTHER READING: Skelton, O. D. *The Life and Letters of Sir Wilfrid Laurier.* 2 vols. Toronto: S. B. Gundy, 1921.

MARK F. PROUDMAN

Lausanne, Treaty of (1912)

See Italo-Turkish War (1911–1912)

Leipzig, Battle of (1813)

Also known as the "Battle of the Nations," Leipzig was the largest engagement of the War of the Sixth Coalition. Fought from October 16 to 19, 1813, between 185,000 French with 600 guns under Napoleon, and 220,000—rising to 300,000—Allies (Russians, Prussians, Austrians, and Swedes) with 1,400 guns, Leipzig was the decisive engagement of the campaign in Germany and forced Napoleon to abandon his hold over Central Europe.

Failing to capture the Prussian capital, Berlin, Napoleon retired to Leipzig, in Saxony, where he established defensive positions against three converging Allied armies advancing in an arc around the northern, eastern, and southern approaches to the city. On October 16, Russian forces under Barclay de Tolly attacked the southern portion of Leipzig, but were thrown back by a French counterattack. The Prussian commander, General Gerhard von **Blücher,** opened a simultaneous assault against the position held by Marshal Marmont, but notwithstanding their numerical superiority, the Prussians failed to oust the French before darkness brought the fighting to a close. Reinforcements arrived for both sides during the night, raising the forces to 150,000 French—27,000 having fallen on the first day—and 300,000 Allied troops, 35,000 having become casualties. October 17 saw only sporadic fighting, as Napoleon narrowed his front and consolidated his hold within the city itself.

The next day the Allies attacked several sectors at once. Although the French withstood the onslaught, conceding little ground to their opponents, Napoleon was acutely aware that he had to preserve a line of retreat, as he could not long sustain his position against mounting numbers. During the night he therefore began withdrawing his army over the single remaining bridge spanning the river Elster. When the bridge was prematurely blown, however, Prince Poniatowski's corps of 20,000 French and Poles was stranded in the city, together with 15,000 wounded left behind in the city's hospitals. The battle cost the French at least 70,000 killed, wounded, and taken prisoner, including many generals and 150 guns. The Allies lost heavily themselves: approximately 54,000 killed and wounded, but such losses—unlike those suffered by the French—could be replaced. Victory on this scale cleared the way for the Allied advance on Paris in 1814. *See also* Bonaparte, Napoleon; Liberation, War of; Napoleonic Wars.

FURTHER READING: Chandler, David G. *The Campaigns of Napoleon*. London: Weidenfeld & Nicolson, 1995; Hofschröer, Peter. *Leipzig 1813*. London: Osprey, 1993; Nafziger, George. *Napoleon at Leipzig—The Battle of the Nations 1813*. Chicago: Emperor's Press, 1996; Petre, F. Loraine. *Napoleon's Last Campaign in Germany, 1813*. London: Greenhill Books, 1992; Smith, Digby. *1813 Leipzig: Napoleon and the Battle of the Nations*. London: Greenhill Books, 2001.

GREGORY FREMONT-BARNES

Lenin, Vladimir Il'ich (1870–1924)

Revolutionary and **Bolshevik** leader who orchestrated the Russian Revolution of 1917, which led to the establishment of a communist regime in Russia and its territories. Vladimir Ulyanov—Lenin was a pen name he adopted in 1901—was born in Simbirsk, Russia, to an average, respectable family; his father was a school teacher and administrator. As a child, Lenin was a good student whose childhood was uneventful until, when he was 17, his older brother was hanged for a failed attempt on the tsar's life. That same year, Lenin participated in a student demonstration and was expelled from Kazan University where he was studying law; his brother's revolutionary activity, of course, had not helped his case. The young Vladimir was permanently affected by these events and the social isolation that followed.

He was eventually readmitted to the university and finished his law degree, but while there, he became involved in a Marxist group and began to read the works of the father of Russian Marxism, Georgi Plekhanov. In the spirit of Karl Marx, Lenin believed liberal reforms were only a temporary fix, not the solution, to the working class's problems. In 1895, Lenin and several other Marxists founded the League of Struggle for the Emancipation of the Working Class. By the end of the year, however, the members of the League were arrested. Lenin spent 14 months in jail and then he was sentenced to three years' exile in Siberia.

In 1900, Lenin was released from exile, returned to Russia, and founded a revolutionary newspaper, *Iskra* (*Spark*). In 1902, he published *What Is to Be Done?* in which he argued that a successful Marxist organization should be led by a small group of dedicated and professional revolutionaries, who would be more effective and harder for the authorities to catch. Lenin believed that the working class, on its own, would not develop political consciousness, but only "trade-union consciousness." Thus they needed help from revolutionary intellectuals who would guide them until, over time, the leaders would come from the working class itself.

It was also in 1902 that part of the *Iskra* board moved to London, and there Lenin met Lev Davidovich Bronstein, who became known as Leon **Trotsky.** In 1903, the Russian Marxists gathered for a second time where they were split by disagreements over questions of organization and policy. It was during these disagreements that the names Bolshevik and **Menshevik** emerged. In 1905, the Bolsheviks held their own congress in London. Meanwhile, to fund Bolshevik efforts, Lenin and other Bolsheviks resorted to robbing banks; among those involved in this activity was Joseph Djugashvili, Stalin. In 1911, in Paris, Lenin met Inessa Armand, with whom he began a romantic relationship. In 1912, Lenin and some of his staunchest supporters founded a newspaper in St. Petersburg called *Pravda,* or "truth."

When war broke out in 1914, Lenin was arrested; he was soon released and fled to neutral Switzerland. The outbreak of World War I shattered any immediate hope of a unified international workers' organization; Social Democrats all over Europe supported their countries' war effort. Faced with this new challenge, Lenin reformulated his interpretation of Marxism to explain the current war. The result was his book, *Imperialism, the Highest Stage of Capitalism,* written in 1915–1916, which argued that capitalism directly leads to **imperialism:** as capitalist nations strive to find markets for their products, they will ultimately come into competition with one another, which will lead to war—an idea from *The Communist Manifesto.* But Lenin also believed that as capitalism entered its highest stage, so did the proletariat. So Lenin's book was not only an explanation for World War I but also a prediction of revolution. When the first Russian Revolution broke out in February 1917, Lenin was in exile in Switzerland. Writing from Switzerland, Lenin made it clear that he opposed the newly created Provisional Government and hoped to topple it; he also expressed his intent and desire to take Russia out of the war. Consequently, France and Italy, both allies of Russia, would not allow Lenin passage to Russia.

The German government, however, was more than happy to help Lenin get home, on the condition that he travel in a sealed train car so that he could not foment revolution along the way. So Lenin, Krupskaya, and 32 other Bolsheviks arrived on April 3, 1917 in St. Petersburg (now called Petrograd to eliminate the German root of the city's previous name). Lenin immediately set out to get the other Bolsheviks to adopt his stance against the war and to take control of the Petrograd Soviet.

During the summer of 1917, Lenin struggled to convince the Bolsheviks to accept his interpretation. Meanwhile, Bolshevik party membership grew rapidly and the position of the Provisional Government weakened. During this time, Trotsky returned to Russia and joined the Bolsheviks. By the fall of 1917, Alexander **Kerensky** and his Provisional Government were severely weakened and discredited, and the only thing between Lenin and revolution was the hesitancy of his fellow Bolsheviks. From Finland, Lenin continued to call for a seizure of power, and in early October he went to Petrograd and tried to convince the other leading Bolsheviks of his plan. Until late in the evening of October 24, the majority of the Central Committee of the Bolshevik Party did not imagine that the overthrow of the Provisional Government would take place before the opening of the All-Russian Congress of Soviets the next day. Lenin, however, was persistent and persuasive. On October 25, 1917, the Bolsheviks executed a small military coup that passed unnoticed by most residents in Petrograd. In the following months, Lenin and the Bolsheviks worked to consolidate power and eliminate opposition, but by the summer of 1918, a civil war had erupted between the Bolsheviks, or Reds, and anti-Bolshevik forces, or Whites. The civil war raged for three years. By 1922, Lenin was chairman of the council of people's commissars and the uncontested leader of both the Communist Party and the Soviet government. *See also* Hobson, John Atkinson; Imperialism; Russian Empire.

FURTHER READING: Lenin, V. I. *Imperialism, the Highest Stage of Capitalism.* New York: International Publishers, 1993, c1939; Lenin, V. I. *What Is to Be Done? Burning Questions of Our Movement.* Peking: Foreign Languages Press, 1973; Pipes, Richard, ed. *The Unknown Lenin: From the Secret Archives.* With the assistance of David Brandenberger; basic translation of Russian documents by Catherine A. Fitzpatrick. New Haven, CT: Yale University Press, 1996; Service, Robert. *Lenin: A Biography.* Cambridge, MA: Harvard University Press, 2000; Theen, Rolf H. W. *Lenin: Genesis and Development of a Revolutionary.* Princeton, NJ: Princeton University Press, 1973; Williams, Beryl. *Lenin.* Harlow, England: New York: Longman, 2000.

LEE A. FARROW

Leopold II, King of Belgium

See Belgium

Lesseps, Ferdinand de (1805–1894)

A French engineer and entrepreneur, born to a family of career diplomats, Lesseps was fascinated both by the culture of **Egypt** and by the patterns of commercial trade between East and West. It was after his retirement from the diplomatic service that Lesseps, encouraged by the accession to the viceroyalty of Egypt of Said Pasha in 1854, revived the Napoleonic idea of a canal connecting Mediterranean and Red Seas across the Isthmus of Suez. Despite the initial skepticism of British investors and the open hostility of the British government, Lesseps secured sufficient financial backing from France to begin digging in 1857. The **Suez Canal** opened in 1869.

Fired by extraordinary self-confidence and influenced by the social ideas of the Saint-Simonians, Lesseps turned from his Suez triumph to the more ambitious and difficult project of a canal across the Isthmus of **Panama** in 1875. Riding the Suez reputation of *Le Grand Français* bestowed on him by Léon **Gambetta,** Lesseps appealed to small investors to raise capital but grossly underestimated the cost of the Panama project. Work began in 1881, but, when little progress was made over the following eight years, falling stock values and corruption precipitated the **Panama Scandal.** Lesseps and his son Charles were found guilty of mismanagement and sentenced to a lengthy imprisonment. Charles alone served one year. After his death at 89, Lesseps's reputation was rehabilitated with an array of posthumous national honors. *See also* French Empire.

FURTHER READING: Beatty, Charles. *Lesseps of Suez: The Man and His Times.* New York: Harper Brothers, 1956; Karabell, Zachary. *Parting the Desert: The Creation of the Suez Canal.* New York: Random House, 2003.

CARL CAVANAGH HODGE

Lewis and Clark Expedition (1804–1806)

The first overland expedition of discovery across the **United States** to the Pacific Ocean and back, mandated by President Thomas **Jefferson** as the Corps of Discovery, following the **Louisiana Purchase.** Serving as the private secretary of President Jefferson, Meriwether Lewis (1774–1809) was selected by Jefferson in 1803 to lead the expedition. Accompanying Lewis was Second Lieutenant William Clark (1770–1838) of the United States Army, a veteran of many Indian wars. They were instructed to forge business relations with tribes they encountered in the West. The president also asked them to record the plants, animals, minerals, and geography they encountered and in particular to determine whether there existed a transcontinental water route for westward expansion. Jefferson was concerned about establishing an American presence in the West, as British and Canadian trappers had made inroads there.

Lewis and Clark, accompanied by approximately 50 men, spent the winter of 1803 in the St. Louis area. In the spring of 1804, they sailed up the Missouri River. In the winter they made it to what is now the Dakotas, and they camped among the Mandan Indian tribe. Early in 1805, they set out to cross the West. They were accompanied by Sacajawea, a Shoshone Indian woman who guided them across the Rockies. In November 1805, the party finally reached the Pacific Ocean. In July 1806, the expedition split into two groups, Lewis and his team turning back through Blackfoot territory while Clark returned through Crow territory. They eventually rejoined in present-day North Dakota where the Yellowstone River flows into the Missouri and arrived in St. Louis in September. Their explorations resulted in establishing relations with many Western tribes; discovering passages through the Rockies; and providing important botanical, zoological, and geological information about much of the West. The expedition was instrumental in opening the trans-Mississippi region to white settlement. In 1807, Jefferson appointed Lewis governor of the Louisiana Territory. Clark became the first governor of the Missouri Territory in 1813. *See also* Manifest Destiny.

FURTHER READING: Ambrose, Stephen E. *Undaunted Courage: Meriwether Lewis, Thomas Jefferson, and the Opening of the American West.* New York: Simon & Schuster, 1996; Dillon, Richard H. *Meriwether Lewis: A Biography.* Santa Cruz, CA: Western Tanager Press, 1988; Raum, Elizabeth. *Meriwether Lewis.* Chicago: Heinemann Library, 2004.

GENE C. GERARD

Lewis, Meriwether

See Lewis and Clark Expedition

Liaoyang, Battle of (1904)

A major battle in the **Russo-Japanese War,** fought between August 24 and September 4, 1904. In early August 1904, after defeats at Motien Pass and Dashiqiao, Russian forces in **Manchuria** under General Alexei Kuropatkin fell back on the city of Liaoyang with Japanese forces in pursuit. The battle began on August 25, with the Russians attempting to turn the flanks of the Japanese army.

On August 26, the Japanese counterattacked, seizing Kosarei Peak and Hung-sha Pass southeast of Liaoyang and forcing the Russians to abandon their outer defensive perimeter. On August 31, the Japanese First Army crossed the Tai-tzu River northeast of Liaoyang. Fearing encirclement, Kuropatkin ordered Russian forces to abandon Liaoyang on September 4 and regroup near Mukden. Japan won the battle, but its forces suffered heavier casualties, 23,600 out of 125,000 troops deployed while the Russians suffered 17,900 casualties out of a force of 158,000. *See also* Japanese Empire; Russian Empire.

FURTHER READING: Connaughton, Richard M. *Rising Sun and Tumbling Bear: Russia's War with Japan.* New York: Cassell, 2004; Warner, Denis Ashton, and Peggy Warner. *The Tide at Sunrise: A History of the Russo-Japanese War, 1904–1905.* London: Frank Cass, 2001.

ADRIAN U-JIN ANG

Liberal Imperialists

A faction within Britain's **Liberal Party** in the late nineteenth and early twentieth centuries, the Liberal Imperialists were notable for their lack of enthusiasm for Irish **Home Rule,** for their defense of **free trade** within the **British Empire,** and for their support for moderate social reform. The Liberal Imperialists included some of the most talented figures in the Liberal Party, such as Lord **Rosebery,** H. H. **Asquith,** Sir Edward **Grey,** and R. B. **Haldane,** and as many as a third of the Liberal members of the House of Commons. The Liberal Imperialists were clever men looking for a new program for their party and for power within that party. They made their bid for influence at a time when the Liberal Party, always an uneasy coalition, appeared to be floundering. Yet the Liberal Imperialists failed and never came close to success. One contemporary sneered that they were politically inept "babes in intrigue." In part the Liberal Imperialists failed because they were regarded as disloyal and not true Liberals and in part because their most important leader, Lord Rosebery, was self-destructive as a party politician. He had charm, eloquence, and intellect, but he lacked the personal ambition that might have motivated him to compromise. Unlike Rosebery, other Liberal Imperialists chose to advance their careers at the expense of their ideology. It is easy to date the end of Liberal Imperialism. In December 1905, leading Liberal Imperialists joined a ministry headed by a mainstream Liberal, Sir Henry **Campbell-Bannerman.**

It is less easy to date the beginnings of Liberal Imperialism. Some historians see its origins in the 1880s or with the general election of 1892. Others date it as late as the Boer War (1899–1902). It is also difficult to identify Liberal Imperialism's general theme. A revival of Lord Palmerston's mid-century Liberal nationalism? Social imperialism, combining domestic reform with an emphasis on empire? A cross-party movement for national efficiency? Promoting the financial interests of the City of London? Placing less stress on program, some historians emphasize the intraparty struggle for power. The leading historian of the Liberal Imperialists focuses on the period 1888–1905 and identifies them as "a post-Gladstonian elite." The Liberal Imperialists sought to reconstruct their party on lines different from that of its old leader W. E. **Gladstone.** Among other things, this meant freeing the Liberal Party from an electorally disastrous program that gave priority to Irish Home Rule and that included miscellaneous demands of "faddist" single-cause lobbies such as prohibition by local option. The Liberal Imperialists regarded themselves as representatives of the national interest and not of mere sectional interests. They despised the Newcastle Programme of 1891, assembled by the National Liberal Federation, as a miscellaneous collection of concessions to narrow factions.

It is not easy to generalize about the Liberal Imperialists. Although they created two organizations—the Liberal Imperialist League in 1900 and the Liberal League 1902—essentially they were a group of individuals who did not always agree with one another. More important, the focus that gave them a sort of unity changed over the years. At first, it had little to do with imperialism, and it never bothered much with **India,** the most important part of the empire. Perhaps the Liberal Imperialists can be understood as Liberals who wanted the Liberal Party to be a moderate and patriotic party that supported practical domestic reforms and kept foreign affairs and the conduct of wars out of partisan politics. The philosopher T. H. Green probably influenced their ideas. Many intellectuals outside Parliament hoped that the Liberal Imperialists might advance their agendas, as for example, Benjamin Kidd, H. J. Mackinder, and even the Fabian socialists Sidney and Beatrice Webb.

Vague slogans often substituted for detailed policies. For instance, Liberal Imperialists called for a clean slate in devising a party program. This rhetorical strategy sidestepped the practical political problem of how to deal with old commitments such as Irish Home Rule. Liberal Imperialists called for what they described as sane imperialism. This middle way between aggressive expansion and Little Englander dislike of empire did not provide clear guidance. It merely implied that realists should avoid making decisions based on ideology. The Liberal Imperialist desire for reforms that promoted national efficiency similarly lacked clarity. Bitter disputes over education and temperance, for instance, made compromise difficult. In many ways the Liberal Imperialists had much in common with Joseph **Chamberlain,** the Radical turned Liberal Unionist, at least until he advocated protective tariffs. Of course, Rosebery lacked Chamberlain's ruthlessness.

In the late 1880s, many of the politicians later identified as Liberal Imperialists developed the friendships that would provide the personal basis for Liberal Imperialism. In 1892, when Gladstone formed his last government, several of the future Liberal Imperialists obtained office. At one time they had admired John Morley, an old-fashioned Gladstonian, but increasingly they considered Lord Rosebery, the foreign secretary, as their leader. He briefly served as prime minister in 1894–1895. A year later he resigned as party leader and, although only 49, claimed that he had retired from public life. In practice, he intermittently quarreled with his immediate successor as party leader, Sir W. V. Harcourt, and then with his replacement, Sir Henry Campbell-Bannerman. The relatively young Liberal Imperialist group regarded Harcourt and Campbell-Bannerman as elderly mediocrities and longed for Rosebery's return. In the late 1890s, imperialism became a distinguishing feature of this factional revolt. How were Liberals to react to the Conservative government's decision to send an army into the Sudan and the subsequent Fashoda crisis that threatened war with France? How were Liberals to respond to the war in South Africa with the Boer republics? As self-proclaimed patriots, the Liberal Imperialists almost always backed the government. In 1901, Campbell-Bannerman denounced British concentration camps in South Africa, where many women and children had died of disease, as "methods of barbarism." Although Campbell-Bannerman had not attacked the war as a whole, the Liberal Imperialists reacted as if he had allied himself with the so-called pro-Boers, such as David Lloyd George, who opposed the war itself as wrong. The Liberal Imperialists wanted Campbell-Bannerman out as leader.

In 1903, when Joseph Chamberlain called for tariff reform, he helped heal the Liberal divisions at least partially. Free trade was a principle on which all Liberals could unite. At the end of 1905, most prominent Liberal Imperialists such as Asquith accepted office under Campbell-Bannerman, despite their previous criticisms of him. Rosebery was isolated and politically irrelevant. As a coherent faction, the Liberal Imperialists no longer existed. *See also* Boer Wars; Ireland.

FURTHER READING: Matthew, H.C.G. *The Liberal Imperialists: The Ideas and Politics of a Post-Gladstonian Elite.* London: Oxford University Press, 1973; Searle, G. R. *A New England? Peace and War, 1886–1918.* Oxford: Clarendon Press, 2004.

DAVID M. FAHEY

Liberalism

Liberalism was the hegemonic ideology of the Anglo-Saxon powers during the nineteenth century. Although not uncontested, it was the ideology that was able to establish the terms in which other contemporary ideologies—from John Calhoun's pseudo-feudalism and Benjamin **Disraeli**'s romantic Toryism to the socialisms of Marxists and also of the Fabians—had to define themselves. The term *liberalism* was used most obviously to name the ideology of the **Liberal Party,** although that party did not exist until the middle of the century. On the European continent, liberalism was generally understood to be the philosophy of constitutional government, although by such a standard, everyone in the nineteenth-century Anglo-Saxon world was a liberal.

The term *liberal*, borrowed from the Spanish, originally had a connotation of enlightenment, and entered political language with the liberal Tories of the 1820s. The term *liberal conservative* was often applied to the free trading followers of Sir Robert **Peel,** who formed the core of the mid-Victorian Liberal Party. Although it is impossible to define liberalism with reference to some dogmatic premise to which all liberals must assent, a number of core characteristics can be identified. Perhaps the most obvious is constitutionalism and a related concern for liberty. The autonomy of the individual has always been valued by liberals, as the central place of that value in John Stuart **Mill**'s *On Liberty* made clear. Liberalism is also a rationalist ideology: it believes that reason can understand and improve the world, and consequently liberals often characterized themselves as the party of enlightenment as against the obscurantism imputed to their opponents. In common with their Whig predecessors, liberalism sees history as an essentially progressive process; the Whig view of constitutional development was thus congenial to liberals. Liberalism was usually an anticoercive ideology, generally, although not always, opposed to the use of force in politics, although this did not prohibit force where reason was believed to have failed, and few liberals became full-fledged pacifists.

Liberalism emphasized freedom of contract and the importance of voluntary cooperation and was normally hostile to assertive state action. As such, free market economics has often been thought—most notably by marxists—the centerpiece of liberalism, the ostensible ideology of the bourgeoisie. **Free trade** was certainly the centerpiece of British liberalism. Nevertheless, free trade commanded only minority support in the **United States,** neither of whose major parties thought to call itself liberal, and free trade never attained the hegemonic status it had in Britain in the settlement colonies. Three prominent strains of liberal thought can be identified: (1) the Lockean, or contractual, which emphasized the importance of free, uncoercive individual choice, and which led to doctrines of right or liberties; (2) the Benthamite, or utilitarian, strand of liberalism, associated with Jeremy **Bentham**'s influential successors the philosophical radicals, which emphasized the importance of rational human happiness and presented powerful arguments against preexisting social orders, but for which liberty was only an instrumental good; and (3) an eminent tradition of political economy that went back to Adam **Smith** and David Ricardo, and that emphasized the importance of individual choice in (usually) free markets, informed liberalism. There were latent contradictions between the first two strands of liberalism, although neither thought itself incompatible with classical political economy. The relation of liberalism to imperialism was ambiguous. On the one hand, liberalism presented powerful arguments for colonial self-government. On the other, some liberals contested the suitability for self-government of what they saw as irrational or inferior peoples or cultures. Most ideological liberals were anti-imperialists, and anti-imperialism was strongest on the radical, which is to say radically liberal, wing of the Liberal Party. There was a strong tradition of liberal anticolonialism, going back to Adam Smith and Jeremy Bentham. It was nevertheless possible to argue on liberal grounds that the expansion of the liberal and free trading British empire was preferable to that of other, illiberal and protectionist empires, and there was a powerful group of liberal imperialists around the turn of the century, including once and future prime ministers such as Lord **Rosebery** and H. H. **Asquith.** *See also* Anti-Corn Law League; Cobden, Richard; Liberal Imperialists.

FURTHER READING: Berlin, Isaiah. *Four Essays on Liberty.* London: Oxford University Press, 1969; Hirschmann, Albert O. *The Passions and the Interests: Political Arguments for Capitalism before Its Triumph.* Princeton, NJ: Princeton University Press, 1977; Howard, Michael. *War and the Liberal Conscience.* London: Temple Smith, 1978; Mill, John Stuart. *On Liberty.* Edited by David Spitz. New York: W. W. Norton, 1975; Read, Donald. *Cobden and Bright: A Victorian Political Partnership.* London: Edward Arnold, 1967; Smith, Adam. *An Inquiry into the Nature and Causes of the Wealth of Nations.* 2 vols. Edited by W. B. Todd. Indianapolis: Liberty Press, 1976.

MARK F. PROUDMAN

Liberal Party

In British politics, the Liberal Party was the nineteenth-century successor to the Whigs of the Stuart and Hanoverian eras. In their own minds, the Liberals were the party of reform, liberty, and progress. Although in socialist dogma they were the party of the bourgeoisie, they usually attracted the support of those, from religious nonconformists to workers, who felt themselves excluded from power. From the middle of the nineteenth century to its breakup after World War I, the Liberal Party was one of two British parties—the other being the Tories, alternately called the **Conservative Party** or Unionists—that had a serious chance of winning office.

Before the 1870s, political parties did not have much in the way of formal organization: the term *party* applied to groups of MPs (i.e., members of Parliament) who tended to vote together, and contemporaries could speak intelligibly of the radical party or the protectionist party. The term *liberal* as the designation of a political inclination first came into wide use to describe the Liberal Tories of the 1820s. In the years following the split of the Tory Party over the **Corn Laws** in 1846, it became common to refer to the diverse and fissiparous assemblage of radicals, Peelites—followers of Sir Robert **Peel,** including most notably William **Gladstone**—and Whigs that supported **free trade** and other ostensibly enlightened policies as "the great Liberal Party." The Liberals kept the Tories from more than brief periods of minority government in the generation before Benjamin **Disraeli**'s great victory of 1874. It was after one such interlude—Lord **Derby**'s government of 1858–1859—that Lord Palmerston became prime minister after the famous Willis's rooms meeting in which radicals, Whigs, and former Peelites agreed to act together. The term *Whig,* being anathema to radicals, Palmerston's government and its successors were normally called Liberal.

A formal Liberal electoral organization, the National Liberal Federation (NLF), was founded in 1877, employing the machinery of Joseph **Chamberlain**'s National Education Federation. The NLF played a role in Gladstone's convincing victory at the polls in 1880, as did the strident opposition of many among the party's nonconformist base to Disraeli's imperial and eastern policies. In 1886, however, the Liberal Party split over the issue of Irish **Home Rule.** Many Liberals followed Chamberlain's lead into alliance with Lord **Salisbury**'s Tories, and thence into the Conservative Party itself. The Liberals were largely excluded from power, with the exception of the years 1892–1895, until 1906. During this period, the Liberal Party was paralyzed by divisions between its radical and liberal imperialist wings. The Liberal governments of H. H. **Asquith** put through a number of reformist measures, including old-age pensions, the Parliament Act of 1911 restricting the power of the Lords, and the Third Irish Home Rule bill, never put into effect. Asquith fell from power in 1916, and the former radical David **Lloyd George** took office at the head of a Tory-dominated coalition. The party divided into Asquith and Lloyd George wings just as many among its more progressive followers were defecting to the rising Labour Party. Lloyd George, the last Liberal prime minister, fell from power in 1922.

It is of course difficult to say with any precision what a political party stands for, but if there was one fixed point of Liberal faith, it was free trade. The attitude of **liberalism** to the empire was more ambiguous: although imperialism has more often been associated with conservatism, some of the most bellicose and successful of British statesmen, from Palmerston to Lloyd George, were in fact Liberals. *See also* Liberal Imperialists.

FURTHER READING: Searle, G. R. *The Liberal Party: Triumph and Disintegration.* London: Palgrave, 2001; Vincent, John. *The Formation of the British Liberal Party.* London: Constable, 1966.

MARK F. PROUDMAN

Liberal Unionist Party

Liberal Unionists was the name given to those who left the Gladstonian **Liberal Party** in opposition to William **Gladstone**'s defeated Irish **Home Rule** bill of 1886.

The Unionists were initially a faction, and by no means an entirely conservative faction, of the Liberal Party, including well-known radicals like Joseph Chamberlain and John Bright. The Unionist split of the Liberal Party ended definitively the long period of Victorian Liberal predominance and ushered in almost two decades of largely Tory rule.

The so-called **Unionist** party was formed by a coalition of the **Liberal Unionists** with the Conservative Party or Tories under Lord **Salisbury** in the aftermath of the split of the Liberal Party in 1886. Although in the 1880s, the term *Unionist* designated a Liberal Unionist, in the 1890s it came to be used to describe any supporter of Salisbury's Conservative governments. By the Edwardian era, when Irish Home Rule was once more put forward by the Liberals, the distinction between Conservatives and formerly Liberal Unionists had largely disappeared, and the term *Unionist* became a synonym for Conservative. The Conservative Party officially renamed itself the Conservative and Unionist Party in 1912. The term *Unionist* fell from favor after Irish independence but was only formally dropped in 1970. *See also* Ireland.

FURTHER READING: Lubenow, W. C. *Parliamentary Politics and the Home Rule Crisis*. Oxford: Clarendon Press, 1988.

MARK F. PROUDMAN

Liberation, War of (1813)

The latter half of the War of the Sixth Coalition, following Napoleon's disastrous campaign of 1812 in Russia. The latent nationalism that had blossomed since Prussia's humiliation in 1806 finally exploded, bringing King Frederick William III into alliance with Tsar **Alexander I** of Russia. The theater of operations shifted to Germany, where Napoleon rapidly cobbled together a new army of raw recruits, reservists, and the remnants of his *Grande Armée*. The Russians and Prussians confronted the French in Saxony, one of the principal states of the French-allied Confederation of the Rhine which continued to maintain its links with Napoleon. After driving back a Russian attack at Lützen on May 2, Napoleon went in pursuit of the Allies, defeating them at Bautzen on May 20. By a two-month armistice agreed to at Plaswitz on June 4, both sides sought to recover their strength in anticipation of further fighting in the autumn. The Allies strengthened their alliance by the treaties of Reichenbach on June 14–15, binding Britain, which would offer substantial subsidies to her allies, with Russia and Prussia in exchange for the mutual promise of no separate peace with France.

Napoleon met Emperor Francis of Austria on June 26 but refused Habsburg mediation, after which Austria joined the Allies and declared war on France on August 11. In his last major victory, Napoleon defeated the Allies at the Saxon capital of **Dresden** on August 27, but his corps commanders, operating independently thereafter lost a succession of minor, although collectively significant, actions at Grossbeeren, Kulm, and Dennewitz. As a result of these setbacks, Napoleon was obliged to withdraw and concentrate most of his troops around **Leipzig,** where the largest battle of the Napoleonic Wars—involving over half a million combatants and fought over several days in mid-October—left the French decisively defeated and obliged to retreat to the Rhine. All of Napoleon's German allies abandoned him and French control in central Europe collapsed as the Allies marched west. A Bavarian force failed to halt Napoleon at Hanau October 30, and the French reached Mainz on November 5. By the end of the year the Allies were poised along the Rhine for the invasion of France. *See also* Bonaparte, Napoleon.

FURTHER READING: Fremont-Barnes, Gregory. *The Napoleonic Wars, vol. 4: The Fall of the French Empire, 1813–1815.* Oxford: Osprey, 2001; Lawford, James. *Napoleon's Last Campaigns, 1813–15.* New York: Crown Publishers, 1977; Petre, F. Loraine. *Napoleon's Last Campaign in Germany, 1813.* London: Greenhill Books, 1992.

GREGORY FREMONT-BARNES

Liberia

A West African state founded in 1821 by freed American slaves, sponsored by the American Colonization Society and funded in part by the U.S. Congress. President James **Monroe,** who favored a gradual elimination of slavery, had developed the idea as early as 1801 in correspondence with President Thomas **Jefferson** after the Gabriel slave rebellion in Virginia, where Monroe then served as governor. In 1819, Monroe secured an appropriation of $100,000 from Congress to resettle recaptured and illegally traded slaves in Africa.

Monroe referred to Liberia as "a little America, destined to shine in the heart of darkest Africa," but the settlers encountered resistance from the local inhabitants who resented both the presence of the newcomers and the suspension of the local slave trade. With assistance from the U.S. Navy, the settlers nonetheless established themselves at Cape Messurado in 1822 and eventually established a capital at Christopolis, which they renamed Monrovia in 1824. After retiring from presidential duties, Monroe served as the first president of the American Colonization Society. The society governed Liberia until 1847, when it declared itself an independent republic modeled after the United States. The settlers ruled over the native population as a hereditary aristocracy, denying them the vote and other rights of citizenship.

FURTHER READING: Liebnow, J. Gus. *Liberia: The Evolution of Privilege.* Ithaca, NY: Cornell University Press, 1969.

CARL CAVANAGH HODGE

Libya

The North African Ottoman provinces of Tripoli and Cyrenaica together composed Libya, which became of predatory interest to **Italy** after the French occupation of Tunisia to the west in 1881 and the British occupation of **Egypt** to the east in 1882. As the economic potential of a territory that was mostly desert was limited and the opportunities for emigration there modest, Italian ambitions in Libya were in large part the product of nationalist zeal and the accurate perception that Ottoman hold on the provinces was too weak to withstand a determined challenge.

With the Moroccan Crisis of 1911, Italy's opportunity came to strike while avoiding the open objections of Britain or France. It therefore announced that its obligation to protect the Italian community in Tripoli required military intervention, and Libya became the centerpiece of the **Italo-Turkish War.** Although Italy formally acquired Libya from the Porte by the terms of the Treaty of Lausanne in 1912—the name Libya had fallen into disuse and was revived by the Italians—Arab *guerrilla* resistance at one point required as many as 100,000 troops to suppress. *See also* Africa, Scramble for; Ottoman Empire.

FURTHER READING: Beehler, W. H. *The History of the Italian-Turkish War.* Annapolis: Advertiser-Republican, 1913; Wesseling, H. L. *The European Colonial Empires, 1815–1919.* London: Pearson Education, 2004.

CARL CAVANAGH HODGE

Ligny, Battle of (1815)

Part of Napoleon's **Waterloo** campaign during the Hundred Days that witnessed his return from exile and final defeat. Returning from exile at Elba, Napoleon realized that there was no hope of a negotiated settlement with the Allied coalition. The emperor decided to strike first and marched to the French border at Charleroi, hoping to defeat the combined British-Prussian army. Crossing into **Belgium,** Napoleon sent Marshal Michel Ney to deal with the Duke of Wellington at the crossroads of **Quatre Bras,** as Marshal Emmanuel de Grouchy marched toward Field Marshal Gebhard von **Blücher** at Ligny. Napoleon brought forward the Imperial Guard behind Grouchy when he realized an opportunity to defeat the Prussians existed. Napoleon attacked Blücher on the afternoon of June 16. When the Prussians appeared near breaking, Napoleon launched the guard forward in the early evening hours, and the Prussians finally gave way. Blücher himself tried to check the rout and was, for a period of time, lost to his army.

General Augustus **Gneisenau** reorganized the Prussian Army for a retreat north toward Wavre, rather than toward the east. This decision eventually proved fatal to Napoleon. Although Napoleon dispatched Grouchy to prevent the Prussians from rallying to the Duke of **Wellington,** Grouchy instead lost contact with Blücher's forces. When Blücher resumed command, he moved quickly to support Wellington on the afternoon of June 18, during the climactic Battle of Waterloo. *See also* Bonaparte, Napoleon; Napoleonic Wars.

FURTHER READING: Hofschröer, Peter. *The Waterloo Campaign.* Mechanicsville, PA: Stackpole Books, 1998.

THOMAS D. VEVE

Limited Liability

The status of limited liability gives a business a legal personality separate from that of its shareholders and limits the liability of shareholders for the debts incurred by the business, normally to the amount of their investment. The development of limited liability laws facilitated the growth of joint stock companies owned in the main by nonactive shareholders: a shareholder knew that his potential losses in the event of business failure were limited to the amount of his investments and had legal protection against being pursued at law for debts incurred by a company whose daily operations he knew little about. By removing a powerful disincentive to investment, limited liability laws mobilized large amounts of capital, including the savings of small investors.

Although limited liability companies had long been known before the passage of limited liability laws, the status had required a special charter, granted by the crown or a legislature, similar to those granting monopolies or other privileges to entities such as the British East India Company. In Britain a Limited Liability Act of 1856 made the status generally available; in the **United States** corporate law was generally a state matter, and limited liability laws were often resisted until the late nineteenth century. Limited liability principles became part of the Prussian Commercial Code in 1861 and then spread quickly to other German states; France passed similar laws in 1863 and 1867. Because such laws stimulated investment by the growing European middle class, they put an enormous pool of capital at the disposal of overseas investment and thus contributed to intensified imperial competition in the second half of the nineteenth century. *See also* East India Companies.

FURTHER READING: Ferguson, Niall. *The Cash Nexus: Money and Power in the Modern World, 1700–2000.* New York: Basic Books, 2002; Freedman, C. E. *Joint Stock Enterprise in France, 1807–1867: From Privileged Company to Modern Corporation.* Chapel Hill: University of North Carolina Press, 1979; Hunt, B. C. *The Development of the Business Corporation in England, 1880–1867.* Cambridge, MA: Harvard University Press, 1936.

MARK F. PROUDMAN

Lincoln, Abraham (1809–1865)

Sixteenth President of the **United States** and commander-in-chief of the Union during the **American Civil War** (1861–1865). Lincoln's nomination by the Republican Party for the presidency and subsequent election was itself prominent among the reasons for the secession of Southern states and the outbreak of civil war, insofar as his policy of opposition to the spread of **slavery** to new states was well known. Lincoln also publicly identified the survival of slavery to be the singular source of the national crisis and linked his opposition to its expansion to an implied willingness to use force to preserve an indissoluble constitutional union.

After the creation of the Confederate States of America on February 4, 1861, and the capture of the federal Fort Sumter in April of the same year, Lincoln took an active interest in the prosecution of the Union war effort. He was ill-suited to the issuance of strategic orders to Union commanders in the field, but until Lincoln discovered the fighting qualities of Ulysses S. **Grant,** few successive Union commanders were well-suited to the aggressive prosecution of the war. Lincoln's blockade of the southern ports gave the Civil War an international dimension—quite apart from the anticipated predations of European powers in the Americas in the event of the disintegration of the Union. It led to a confrontation with Britain in the **Trent Affair,** a diplomatic crisis adroitly defused by Lincoln's Secretary of State William Seward.

Yet as the war progressed, Lincoln's understanding of its military imperatives became evermore sophisticated, and his appreciation of the importance of the political dimension to the strategic balance was brilliant. Lincoln followed the Union victory at **Antietam** with the Emancipation Proclamation of January 1,

1863, in which he proclaimed the freedom of slaves solely in the secessionist states and thereby kept the loyalty of four slave states that had remained in the Union. The war thereafter became a crusade for liberty, in which Lincoln forced the United States to live up to the ideals of its constitution and preserved its unity in its hour of maximum peril, just as the growing industrial and military might of the Union laid the foundation for the emergence of a Great Power. *See also* *Alabama* Dispute.

FURTHER READING: Donald, David. *Lincoln.* New York: Simon and Schuster, 1995; McPherson, James. *Battle Cry of Freedom.* New York: Oxford University Press, 1988; Oates, Stephen B. *With Malice toward None.* New York: Harper Perennial, 1977.

CARL CAVANAGH HODGE

Lissa, Battle of (1866)

A naval engagement of the **Austro-Prussian War.** On July 16, the Italian fleet of 34 warships, including 12 ironclads, was ordered to attack the island of Lissa to prepare for troop landings. The Austrian fleet of 27 warships, including seven ironclads, arrived at Lissa on the morning of July 20. Admiral Wilhelm Tegetthoff formed his fleet into three V-shaped wedges; the charge of the Austrian warships through the Italian line turned the battle into a frantic melee, with ships chasing after one another, all obscured by the smoke from cannon and engines. There was more confusion on the Italian side as the Italian commander, Carlo di Persano, changed flagships at the last moment. His subordinates, unaware of the transfer, kept looking to the wrong ship for signals. Neither side's guns were effective, but the Austrians rammed several Italian warships. The Italian fleet retreated in chaos after one ironclad sank and a second caught fire and exploded, leaving the Austrians in control of the Adriatic. As a result **Italy**'s plan to open up a front on Austria's Dalmatian coast had to be abandoned. *See also* Habsburg Empire.

FURTHER READING: Sondhaus, Lawrence. *The Habsburg Empire and the Sea.* West Lafayette, IN: Purdue University Press, 1989; Wawro, Geoffrey. *The Austro-Prissian War: Austria's War with Prussia and Italy in 1866.* New York: Cambridge University Press, 1996.

DAVID H. OLIVIER

List, Friedrich (1789–1846)

A German economist of formative impact, Friedrich List established himself as an expert for administrative matters in Württemberg, but was forced into exile to the **United States.** Having returned to Saxony in 1832, he advocated the extension of the **railway** system in Germany and developed a theory of protection that stressed national welfare, including tariff protection for the transition to an industrial economy. The establishment of the *Zollverein* in 1834, a customs union between the majorities of the German states, was due largely to his enthusiasm.

List maintained that a nation's prosperity depended on its productive forces, including scientific discoveries, advances in technology and transport, educational facilities, an efficient administration, and some kind of self-government. Germany, List argued, needed for economic progress an extended territory from the North Sea to the Mediterranean and an expansion of commerce. The German national spirit after unification was receptive to List's writing. His ideas became the economic foundation of unified Germany.

FURTHER READING: Henderson, William Otto. *Friedrich List. Economist and Visionary, 1789–1846.* London: Franc Cass, 1983.

MARTIN MOLL

Liverpool, Charles Banks Jenkinson, Second Earl of (1770–1828)

Lord Liverpool was prime minister of Great Britain from 1812 until 1827. Remembered as a stern and unbending Tory—"the arch-mediocrity" in Benjamin **Disraeli**'s inaccurate epithet—and often associated with the Peterloo massacre and the Six Acts of 1819, he also skillfully managed the closing years of the **Napoleonic Wars,** the rapid rapprochement with France in their aftermath, and the economic liberalization of the 1820s. Descended from minor gentry who had become prosperous East India merchants—"nabobs" in the parlance of the day—Jenkinson was educated at Charterhouse and Christ Church, Oxford.

Jenkinson entered Parliament for a pocket-borough on leaving Oxford and rapidly rose in prominence, serving on the Board of Control for **India.** He also visited Europe to observe the armies and served actively in the militia. In 1796, his father was created earl of Liverpool, from which time Jenkinson was known by the courtesy title of Hawkesbury. Under that name he became foreign secretary in the government of Henry Addington, in which post he was responsible for the negotiations leading to the peace of **Amiens,** an achievement that did his future prospects little good.

He served as home secretary in William **Pitt**'s last administration and also under the duke of Portland from 1807–1809. When Portland's ministry was replaced by that of Perceval in 1809, Liverpool, as he had then become, became secretary for war. As secretary for war, he steadfastly supported the duke of Wellington's initially unpopular peninsular campaign. Liverpool became prime minister after the assassination of Perceval in 1812. As premier, he revoked the orders-in-council, which had provoked war with the **United States,** but his move came too late to prevent war. In the European diplomacy of 1814 and 1815, his chief concern was to secure the independence of weaker nations while avoiding a Carthaginian peace with France. Social unrest following the peace, however, provoked repressive legislation, which further damaged the government's popularity.

Intellectually convinced of the arguments for **free trade,** it had nevertheless been Liverpool's government, which initially brought in the **Corn Laws.** In the growing prosperity of the 1820s, his government, with William **Huskisson** at the Board of Trade, began to simplify and lower tariffs, especially on primary products. Liverpool suffered a stroke and retired in 1827 and died the next year. Liverpool was distinguished more by industry and commonsense than by ostentation, a fact that perhaps explains why he—who after all served as prime minister for a period equaled only by Pitt and Walpole—has suffered in reputation by comparison with more flamboyant contemporaries like George **Canning,** Pitt, and Lord **Castlereagh.** In securing a lasting European peace in 1815, his government established the conditions for Britain's prosperity and imperial expansion later in the century. *See also* Conservative Party; Peninsular War.

FURTHER READING: Gash, Norman. *Lord Liverpool.* London: Weidenfeld and Nicolson, 1984.

MARK F. PROUDMAN

Livingstone, David (1813–1873)

Scottish explorer, **missionary,** and philanthropist, David Livingstone was born in Blantyre Works, Lanarkshire. Of humble origins, he was nonetheless able to save sufficient money to attend medical school in Glasgow and win a degree in 1840. In 1841, the London Missionary Society assigned Livingstone to Bechuanaland, although he had sought instead to be sent to China, where he set to work converting the indigenous population to Christianity, treating disease and combating the local slave trade.

In 1852, Livingstone organized an expedition across the Kalahari Desert to Lake Ngami and in 1851 explored the Zambezi River. In 1852, he began the explorations of Central Africa that ultimately won him a national and international reputation—the capstone of which was the discovery and naming of Victoria Falls—as a great geographer. Livingstone was appointed British consul for eastern Africa, a position through which he continued his explorations, discovering Lake Nyasa in 1859, and became an ever more determined enemy of slavery and slave trading.

In 1865, he became British consul to Central Africa and embarked on his last, greatest, and fatal expedition, the central goal of which was to understand the watershed of Central Africa and to locate the sources of the Congo and Nile Rivers. The Nile, he thought, could be the artery for bringing Christian civilization from the Mediterranean to the heart of the continent. He disappeared for many years until he was at last found at Ujiji on Lake Tanganyika by the American explorer Henry **Stanley.** Livingstone carried on his explorations against the gathering predation of disease until he succumbed in April 1873, having opened vast new territory to British influence—not least of all by force of his personal humanity. *See also* Africa, Scramble for; British Empire.

FURTHER READING: Huxley, Elspeth. *Livingstone and the African Journeys.* New York: Saturday Review Press, 1974.

CARL CAVANAGH HODGE

Lloyd George, David (1863–1945)

David Lloyd George was British prime minister during World War I, a progenitor of the welfare state, and both a critic and practitioner of **imperialism.** Lloyd George came from a lower middle class family of schoolteachers, farmers, and tradesmen. He was raised in Caernarvonshire, Wales, and began his career as a radical and Welsh nationalist, but ended it as the effective leader of the Tory party.

Lloyd George was first elected to Parliament for a north Wales constituency in 1890. He defended the rights of religious nonconformists and pushed for the disestablishment of the Anglican Church in Wales, both emotive issues among Welshmen and Liberals at the time. Lloyd George went so far as to attempt to lead a movement for Welsh Home Rule in the mid-1890s, a stance far outside the mainstream of **Liberal Party** politics. He first became prominent on the national scene as a determined opponent of the South African War, expressing the view—common on the left at the time—that the war had been caused by capitalist interests seeking to annex the Rand gold fields; at one point, Lloyd George was forced to flee for his life from a jingo mob. The fiery young radical was brought into the cabinet as president of the Board of Trade under Sir Henry **Campbell-Bannerman** in 1905.

When H. H. **Asquith** succeeded Campbell-Bannerman in 1908, Lloyd George became chancellor of the exchequer. In that role he introduced old-age pensions, paid for by the so-called people's budget of 1909, which introduced a land tax, taxes on drink, and a more steeply progressive income tax. The Lords—"five hundred men chosen at random from amongst the unemployed," as Lloyd George referred to them—rejected his budget, provoking the election of January 1910, in which the Liberals secured a narrow majority. After a second general election in December 1910, with a very similar result, the Liberals were able to pass not merely Lloyd George's budget but also the 1911 Parliament Act, which limited the power of the Lords to that of delay alone.

Lloyd George was a close friend in these years of Winston **Churchill,** first lord of the admiralty, which to some extent reduced his radical opposition to naval spending. His Mansion House speech of 1911 warned the Germans against aggression, and it was taken all the more seriously because it came from an erstwhile radical. With the coming of war in 1914, Lloyd George as chancellor played an important role in paying for it and in negotiating more flexible work rules with the unions in war-related industries. In May 1915, the cabinet was reconstructed, with some Tories coming into office, and Lloyd George assumed the immensely important post of minister of munitions. After Kitchener's death, Lloyd George became in July 1916 secretary for war. Amidst growing disenchantment with Asquith, particularly among the Tories, Lloyd George became prime minister in December 1916—the radical and anti-imperialist had become a war leader with Tory support.

As prime minister, Lloyd George was a consistent opponent of the war of attrition on the western front, constantly seeking ways to win victory in other theaters. His wartime leadership was marked by a dogged determination to persevere against all odds, and also by nearly continuous struggles over strategy with his generals. Lloyd George's dependence on the support of Tory Members of Parliament deepened the divisions in the Liberal Party occasioned by his 1916 split with Asquith. The victory of 1918 brought Lloyd George—"the man who won the war," as he was popularly known—to the height of his prestige. He won the postwar 1918 election by a huge majority, with the backing of a coalition of Tories and his own so-called coalition Liberal backers. Although Lloyd George talked of building "a land fit for heroes," the immediate focus of his government was the 1919 peace talks. Lloyd George negotiated the Treaty of Versailles, but he considered its punitive attitude to Germany a mistake, a view that led to him to support appeasement in the 1930s.

Without a political party of his own—he was an outsider to the **Conservative Party** and had occasioned a bitter split in the Liberal Party—Lloyd George's support rapidly withered in the postwar years. He resigned in the face of a 1922 scandal in which certain of his aides were discovered to have been essentially selling honors and peerages. Although there was periodic talk of his reentering government, and he continued to advocate far-reaching social reforms, his political career was over. *See also* Boer Wars.

FURTHER READING: Grigg, John. *Lloyd George.* 3 vols. London: Methuen, 1973–1985; Morgan, Kenneth O. *Lloyd George.* London: Weidenfeld and Nicolson, 1974.

MARK F. PROUDMAN

Lobengula Khumalo (1833–1894)

The last king of the Matabele in present-day Zimbabwe, Lobengula Khumalo held the throne from 1870 until his death. In 1893, Lobengula came into conflict with the British South Africa Company both over mining rights and over his attempts to reestablish Matabele authority over the Mashona people who were increasingly employed by Europeans. Although he had agreed to mining concessions with Cecil **Rhodes** in 1888, Lobengula had underestimated the scope of Rhodes's commercial ambitions and attempted to limit the company's encroachments into Mashonaland. In the resulting **Matabele War** of 1893, he was defeated and fled his capital of Bulawayo after torching the city. He died of smallpox in 1894. The British took over Matabeleland and named it Rhodesia. *See also* British South Africa Company.

FURTHER READING: Cloete, Stuart. *Against These Three.* Boston: Houghton Mifflin, 1945.

CARL CAVANAGH HODGE

London Convention

See Anglo-American Treaty

London Straits Convention (1841)

An international agreement signed by Austria, France, Great Britain, the **Ottoman Empire,** Prussia, and Russia, which reaffirmed the principle that the Ottoman Straits—the **Bosporus** and **Dardanelles**—were to be closed to all warships of foreign powers when the Ottoman Empire was at peace. Anglo-Russian agreement over the straits, which had been a matter of contention since the signing of the Treaty of **Inkiar Skelessi** in 1833, was brought about due to mutual concerns over the resumption of hostilities between the Ottomans and their Egyptian vassal in 1839. The resolution of outstanding differences was largely due to Anglo-Russian diplomatic cooperation and Anglo-Ottoman military cooperation, which prevented the Ottoman Empire from suffering yet another near collapse at the hands of their Egyptian vassal, **Mehmet Ali.** On British insistence, the Russians did not negotiate a renewal of the Treaty of Inkiar Skelessi. Instead, both powers—joined by the Austrians, Prussians, and Turks—signed the London Convention for the Pacification of the Levant on July 15, 1840, and the London Straits Convention on July 13, 1841. The former prefigured the ultimate settlement to this phase of the problems in the Near East by offering Mehmet Ali hereditary title as governor of Egypt, providing he abandon his Syrian holdings, return the Ottoman fleet—which had defected to Alexandria in the summer of 1838—and continue to acknowledge the suzerainty of and pay tribute to the Ottoman Sultan. The London Straits Convention grew out of a desire on the part of the British and Russian governments to come to satisfactory arrangement between themselves—with the cooperation of the Porte and other great powers—as to the status of the Straits.

The convention was an outgrowth of the desire by the Great Powers to restore a semblance of balance to Near Eastern relations in the wake of a series of crises that had threatened the very existence of the Ottoman Empire. The regulations regarding the straits laid down in it essentially remained in force during the remainder of the life of the Ottoman Empire, and its terms remained in force until the end of World War I. The Treaty of **Paris** (1856), which ended the **Crimean War,** reaffirmed the Convention while also neutralizing the Black Sea. *See also* British Empire; Eastern Question.

FURTHER READING: Anderson, M. S. *The Eastern Question 1774–1923.* London: Macmillan, 1966; Hale, William. *Turkish Foreign Policy 1774–2000.* London: Frank Cass, 2000; Hurewitz, J. C., ed. *The Diplomacy of the Near and Middle East, A Documentary Record: 1535–1914.* Vol. 1. Princeton, NJ: D. Van Nostrand and Co., 1956; Jelavich, Barbara. *A Century of Russian Foreign Policy 1814–1914.* Philadelphia: J. B. Lippincott, 1964; Karsh, Efraim, and Inari Karsh. *Empires of the Sand: The Struggle for Mastery in the Middle East 1789–1923.* Cambridge, MA: Harvard University Press, 1999.

ROBERT DAVIS

London, Treaty of (1839)

The final settlement of the dispute over Belgian independence from the Netherlands after the Belgian revolt against Dutch rule had established an independent monarchy in 1830. The Netherlands acknowledged Belgian sovereignty, and the River Scheldt was declared open to the commerce of both **Belgium** and the Netherlands. The treaty was a diplomatic triumph for the British foreign secretary, Lord **Palmerston,** who considered the independence of the smaller constitutional states of Europe a vital national interest of Great Britain. It was also a triumph for international cooperation insofar as Austria, Britain, France Prussia, and Russia collectively guaranteed the independence and perpetual neutrality of Belgium. *See also* July Crisis; Schlieffen Plan.

FURTHER READING: Hayes, Carlton J. H. *A Political and Social History of Europe.* New York: Macmillam, 1926; Schroeder, Paul W. *The Transformation of European Politics, 1763–1848.* Oxford: Clarendon, 1996.

CARL CAVANAGH HODGE

Louis XVIII (1755–1824)

Installed by the Congress of **Vienna** after the defeat of Napoleon **Bonaparte,** Louis, Comte de Provence, became king of France as Louis XVIII. He was born at Versailles on November 17, 1755, to dauphin Louis, son of Louis XV, and Maria Josepha of Saxony. In June 1791, he had fled France and become the leader of the *émigrés,* seeking help of European monarchs in the royal conspiracy against the French Revolution. He assumed the title of regent of France in 1792 after Louis XVI was guillotined and Louis XVII died in prison, and he styled himself as Louis XVIII with a manifesto of restoration of monarchy, aristocracy, and the Church.

As king, he would have liked to rule with absolute power, but he knew well that return to the prerevolutionary *ancien régime* was impossible. Nationalism and democratic ideas had taken roots. The Royal Charter of 1814 retained religious toleration, equality before law, the Bank of France, and the Napoleonic Code. Although Royal prerogative was asserted, monarchy was to be constitutional. When Napoleon entered Paris in March 1815, Louis XVIII had to flee for the duration of the Hundred Days. After the Battle of **Waterloo,** he again returned to France "in the baggage of the allies" to rule France from July 1815. The ultras, more Royalist than the king, controlled the Chamber of Deputies after the elections. The ultras pursued a program of repressive measures against political opponents and settled many scores with old enemies from the Revolutionary days. Alarmed at the "White Terror," Louis XVIII dissolved the Chamber in September, and liberals got an upper hand. The moderate ministries undertook the task of reconstruction in an admirable way.

The ultras were seething with anger at the policy of moderation and got their chance after the heir apparent Duke of Berri, nephew of Louis XVIII, was assassinated. The events of neighboring Spain in 1820 had generated antirevolutionary fear in France, so the ultras secured control of the Chamber of Deputies in November 1820 and instituted a reactionary program. The ministry of Comte de Villèle was a victory of aristocracy over bourgeoisie and *ancien régime* over the Revolutionary era. It sent troops to quell the Spanish revolutionaries, muzzle the press, create a ministry of Church affairs, and public instruction. In the elections of February–March 1824, the ultras returned with a thumping majority and the liberal opposition was in a minority. In foreign policy Louis deferred to the judgment and diplomatic skills of Talleyrand who set France in a course of rehabilitation as a legitimate Great Power. He died on September 16, 1824, at Paris and **Charles X** continued the reactionary tendency. *See also* Bonapartism; Congress System; Talleyrand, Charles-Maurice de.

FURTHER READING: Lever, E. *Louis XVIII.* Paris: Fayard, 1988; Macaulay, Thomas B. *Napoleon and the Restoration of the Bourbons.* New York: Columbia University Press, New Edition, 1977; Mansel, Philip. *Louis XVIII.* New York: Sutton Publishing, 1999.

PATIT PABAN MISHRA

Louisiana Purchase (1803)

The 1803 purchase by the **United States** from France of the land west of the Mississippi River, consisting primarily of the Mississippi and Missouri River basins. The purchase makes up most of what is known as the Great Plains today.

Until the end of the French and Indian War in 1763, the entire Mississippi River basin, along with the Great Lakes region, was controlled by France. With the defeat of France in that war, its North American empire was dismembered, with Great Britain taking the land east of the Mississippi, except for the port of New Orleans, and Spain receiving New Orleans and the land to the west. The United States gained control of the British share in 1783 with their victory in the American Revolution, and Napoleon **Bonaparte** forced Spain to return its share to France in 1800.

President Thomas **Jefferson** approached Napoleon in 1803 in an effort to purchase New Orleans. Napoleon countered with an offer to sell the entire region. Napoleon had reclaimed Louisiana as part of a plan to restart France's colonial empire, but the slave revolt in the Caribbean French colony of **Haiti** and the British control of the seas convinced Napoleon that the concept was more trouble than it was worth. Despite misgivings at the constitutionality of the purchase, Jefferson jumped at the offer. For $15 million the United States had bought a vast land that was largely unexplored by Europeans.

For his money, Jefferson got the multicultural seaport of New Orleans, an outlet for American produce being floated down the Mississippi, and a rogues' gallery of sophisticated Creole elites, shady traders, and outright pirates. He also got St. Louis, a nominally French town near the confluence of the Missouri and Mississippi Rivers that by 1803 was largely American. Finally, he got a vast land with perhaps hundreds of Native American tribes, many of whom had never even seen a white person. None of these people, European or Native American, had been consulted concerning the transfer. The borders of the purchase were only vaguely defined but were eventually resolved. The **Adams-Onís** Treaty between Spain and the United States in 1819 established the southern border as roughly that of current-day Texas, Louisiana, and Oklahoma, extending into the Rocky Mountains. The Anglo-American Convention of 1819 established the border between British North America and the United States at the 49th parallel.

Relations with the actual inhabitants of the Great Plains were not as easily resolved. American immigration into the region continually displaced the Native Americans, resulting in three generations of conflict and Native American dislocation. The major effect of the Louisiana Purchase was to ensure that the United States was transformed from a series of states along the Atlantic Seaboard to a continental power with room for extensive population growth, at the expense of the Native Americans whose land was transferred by the purchase. *See also* Indian Wars; Lewis, Meriwether; Manifest Destiny.

FURTHER READING: Ambrose, Stephen. *Undaunted Courage: Meriwether Lewis Thomas Jefferson and the Opening of the American West*. New York: Simon & Schuster, 1996; Fleming, Thomas. *The Louisiana Purchase*. Hoboken: J. Wiley, 2003; Tucker, Robert W., and David C. Hendrickson. *Empire of Liberty: The Statecraft of Thomas Jefferson*. New York: Oxford University Press, 1990.

JOESPH ADAMCZYK

Lucknow Residency, Siege of (1857)

A central drama of the **Indian Mutiny.** When the **sepoy** regiments in Lucknow, on the Gumti River 270 miles east of Delhi, mutinied, the British residents and soldiers took shelter within the Lucknow Residency. In the residency, there were 855 British soldiers and 153 male civilians. In addition, there were 500 women and children. About 712 Indian soldiers remained loyal. On June 30, 1857, 10,000 rebels—sepoys and townsmen—laid siege to the residency. The residency was an imposing building. It was in three stories with a lofty colonnaded verandah. The outer part was barricaded with chests and boxes. A spiral staircase led to the roof from which one could gain an elevated view of the city and the adjoining countryside. A line of parapet and a ditch shielded the residency compound. Guns and mortars protected the parapet. The British officers feared that the rebels might receive reinforcement from Kanpur. So a battery was constructed to enfilade the road from Kanpur.

During the siege mutineer sharpshooters, who took positions along the mosques and houses surrounding the residency, caused most of the losses to the garrison. Before the outbreak of the mutiny, Henry Lawrence, the British chief commissioner, was repeatedly requested by the engineers to demolish all these buildings, but had always replied to "spare the holy places, and private property too as far as possible." Despite their numerical superiority, the failure of the rebels to take residency reflected their inadequacy in waging siege warfare by scientific methods. First, rebel bombardment by the heavy guns failed to destroy the British batteries within the residency. Second, both the defenders of the residency and the rebels resorted to mining and counter-mining to blow each other's positions; however, the British always had the upper hand by virtue of their training in engineering operations. The siege was relieved when Sir Colin **Campbell**'s force reached Lucknow in November 17, 1857, but the residency was not retaken until March 1858. *See also* British Empire; India.

FURTHER READING: David, Saul. *The Indian Mutiny, 1857*. London, Viking, 2002; Farwell, Byron. *Queen Victoria's Little Wars*. New York: W. W. Norton, 1972.

KAUSHIK ROY

Lüderitz, Frans Adolf Eduard (1834–1886)

Merchant adventurer and cofounder of Germany's first colony in Southwest Africa, Frans Lüderitz was the son of a prosperous tobacco dealer from Bremen. Lüderitz inherited a fortune and took to traveling. Together with Heinrich Vogelsang, also in throes of boredom of inherited wealth, in 1883 he purchased a parcel of land from the Khoikhoi in modern-day Namibia for the equivalent of £100. It was later extended and named, absurdly, Lüderitzland. In 1884, Berlin announced, even more absurdly, that Lüderitzland was a protectorate of the Reich. This action is widely considered the birth of the German colonial empire. *See also* Africa, Scramble for; German Empire; Herrero Revolt.

FURTHER READING: Henderson, W. O. *The German Colonial Empire 1884–1919*. London: Frank Cass, 1993; Pakenham, Thomas. *The Scramble for Africa*. New York: Random House, 1991; Smith, Woodruff D. *The German Colonial Empire*. Chapel Hill: University of North Carolina Press, 1978.

CARL CAVANAGH HODGE

Lugard, Frederick Dealtry, Baron Lugard of Abinger (1858–1945)

British soldier, diplomat, and colonial administrator best known for his articulation of the British policy of **indirect rule**. Born in **India** to missionary parents, Lugard was educated in England and later returned to the subcontinent in 1878 as a young army officer. Over the next decade he served in campaigns in **Afghanistan, Sudan,** and **Burma** before leaving the army in 1887 to volunteer his services to British chartered companies working to open the interior of East Africa to European trade. After leading an expedition to suppress the **slave trade** around Lake Nyasa, in 1889 he assumed command of the Imperial British East African Company's (IBEAC) garrison in **Uganda** and quickly intervened in a local civil war in an effort to increase British influence in the region. Upon hearing that the IBEAC wanted to abandon portions of the East African interior rather than administer so large and volatile a territory, Lugard returned to England in 1892 and spent the next two years successfully lobbying the British government to declare a protectorate over Uganda.

Lugard returned to Africa in 1894 where he worked for the Royal Niger Company, racing against French expeditions to sign treaties of protection with chiefs on the middle portion of the Niger River. Over the next decade, first as commander of the newly created West African Frontier Force (1897–1899) and then as high commissioner for Northern Nigeria (1900–1906), Lugard used a combination of diplomacy and force to expand British holdings in West Africa.

While on home leave in Britain he was knighted for his service in 1901, and in 1902 he married Flora Shaw, former colonial editor for the *Times* of London. Because his wife's health could not tolerate the Nigerian climate, in 1907 Lugard left Africa and took up a new post as Governor of **Hong Kong.** In 1912, he was appointed Governor of **Nigeria** and charged with the task of uniting its two halves into a single colony. Building on lessons learned during his earlier service in northern Nigeria, he became committed to the doctrine of indirect rule, whereby colonial administrators relied heavily on traditional indigenous political authorities to implement official policy. As this doctrine, which Lugard articulated in his 1922 book entitled *The Dual Mandate in British Tropical Africa,* had the benefit of being both cheaper and less likely to arouse opposition to the colonial presence, it was soon adopted throughout British Africa. Lugard returned to Britain after World War I and became one of its leading colonial authorities through his prolific writings and his work on the League of Nations Permanent Mandates Commission. He was raised to the peerage in 1928 in recognition for his many years of service to the British Empire. *See also* Africa, Scramble for; British East Africa, British Empire.

FURTHER READING: Cavendish, Richard. "The Fall of Kano." *History Today* 53 (2003): 52; Crowder, Michael. "Lugard and Colonial Nigeria: Towards and Identity?" *History Today* 36 (1986): 23–29; Mellor, Bernard. *Lugard in Hong Kong: Empires, Education and a Governor at Work, 1907–1912.* Hong Kong: Hong Kong University Press, 1992; Perham, Dame Margery Freda. *Lugard.* 2 vols. London: Collins, 1955–1960; Thomson, Arthur. *Lugard in Africa.* London: R. Hale, 1959.

KENNETH J. OROSZ

Lunéville, Treaty of (1801)

A peace treaty signed on February 9, 1801, between the French Republic and the Holy Roman Empire, under its Austrian Habsburg emperor, Francis II, which concluded Franco-Austrian hostilities in the War of the Second Coalition (1799–1801). It essentially confirmed the previous terms of the Treaty of Campo Formio of April 1797, which had ended the War of the First Coalition (1792–1797). Again, Belgium, the left bank of the Rhine, Lombardy, Milan, Modena, and some small territories were ceded by the Habsburg monarch to France. However, in an exchange that benefited the Habsburg monarchy by consolidating its boundaries, they were again given Venetia and its Dalmatian possessions as far south as Cattaro, which the French had originally seized in April 1797. Tuscany passed to the Spanish Duke of Parma, and its Habsburg former grand duke was to be indemnified in Germany.

The treaty reestablished the international Congress of Rastadt, suspended in April 1799, where the European ambassadors would implement the treaties. Its main task would now be the reorganization of Germany's states, which secularized the many ecclesiastical lands and significantly reduced the number of larger surviving states. French satellite republics were reestablished in Batavia, (Holland), Helvetia (Switzerland), Cisalpine (northern Italy), and Liguria (Genoa), although France agreed to evacuate her forces from all of them. The war between France and Great Britain would continue for another year until the Treaty of **Amiens** of March 1802. France's failure to honor her pledge to evacuate the satellite republics would lead to renewed war with Great Britain in 1803 and eventually the War of the Third Coalition of 1805. *See also* Napoleonic Wars.

FURTHER READING: Rodger, A. B. *The War of the Second Coalition, 1798–1801.* Oxford: Clarendon, 1964; Shroeder, Paul W. *The Transformation of European Politics, 1763–1848.* Oxford: Clarendon, 1994.

DAVID HOLLINS

Luxemburg, Rosa (1871–1919)

A German revolutionary leader and socialist theorist, Rosa Luxemburg was born in Russian Poland, into a Jewish middle class family. She became involved in revolutionary politics when she was still at school. In 1889, state repression forced her into exile in Switzerland. Luxemburg entered the University of Zurich, where she earned a doctorate in political sciences. When she moved to Germany in 1898, she had already established herself as a marxist speaker and thinker. In 1899, Luxemburg published "Reform or Revolution." She opposed Eduard Bernstein who had rejected Karl **Marx**'s theories of class struggle and concluded that revolution was unnecessary. Bernstein's theory of gradual reform of capitalism was utopian, Luxemburg argued.

Luxemburg became a leader of the Social Democratic Party's (SPD) left wing, taught at party school in Berlin, and developed ideas about general strike as a political weapon. In 1912, she published "The Accumulation of Capital," in which she tried to prove that capitalism would inevitably collapse, and she interpreted **imperialism** as a conflict between capitalist nations for places to dump their excess industrial production and thus forestall crises. After differences with the SPD, Luxemburg and Karl Liebknecht founded the radical Spartacus League in 1916. During World War I, Luxemburg spent long times in prison for her opposition to the German war effort. She welcomed the October Revolution in Russia as a precursor of world revolution; however, Luxemburg participated reluctantly in the Spartacist uprising in Berlin against the new SPD government. Luxemburg and Liebknecht were arrested. While being transported to prison, the couple was murdered on the night of January 15 to 16, 1919 by *Freikorps* soldiers.

Next to Liebknecht, Luxemburg was the most important representative of the left-wing socialist, antimilitarist, and internationalist positions in the SPD before 1918. Luxemburg combined political commitment, scientific analysis, and the quest for empowerment as a woman. She was an advocate of mass action, spontaneity, and workers' democracy. A passionate critic of capitalism as well as dictatorial tendencies within Bolshevism, Luxemburg argued that there could be no real socialism without democracy. For Luxemburg, Marxism was not a theoretical system, but a method of examining economic and social changes. *See also* Bolsheviks; German Empire; Militarism.

FURTHER READING: Abraham, Richard. *Rosa Luxemburg: A Life for the International.* Oxford, New York: Berg, 1989; Ettinger, Elzbieta. *Rosa Luxemburg: A Life.* Boston: Beacon Press, 1986.

MARTIN MOLL

M

Macaulay, Thomas Babington, First Baron (1800–1859)

An English historian, political commentator, cabinet minister, and imperial administrator, Thomas Babington Macaulay was raised by evangelical Christians, but became a secular Whig, although, as a man of his time, he was never a democrat. A brilliant speaker, writer, and controversialist, he made his reputation early writing on literature—his primary interest—and politics for the leading Whig intellectual journal, the *Edinburgh Review*. Macaulay first entered Parliament in 1830, and established himself as a powerful speaker on the side of reform.

In 1834, Macaulay went to **India** as a senior legal official. While there, Macaulay wrote his famous Minute on Indian Education, which proclaimed with the self-confidence of the age that half a shelf of European learning was worth more than all the fabled wisdom of the East and argued that Indian students should be trained in English rather than Arabic or Sanskrit. Although it had little immediate effect on Indian life, the creation of an Anglophone intelligentsia in India eventually had momentous consequences.

Returning to England in 1839, Macaulay served briefly as secretary of war in the last years of Melbourne's government and began work on his famous *History of England*. The first two volumes were published in 1848 and were widely understood—Macaulay made the case elsewhere in so many words—to argue that the Whig revolution of 1688 and reform bill of 1832 had enabled England to avoid the revolutions that swept Europe in 1848. Further volumes of his history came out in the 1850s, commanding record-breaking royalties; but his health failed, and he died in 1859, still a relatively young man, having brought his story no further than the death of William III. Macaulay's works have been criticized on many grounds, but they remain vivid reading even today. From an imperial point of view, Macaulay expressed the confidence of a nation at the height of its power and convinced of the unique value of its heritage.

FURTHER READING: Clive, John. *Macaulay: The Shaping of the Historian.* New York: Knopf, 1973; Lord Macaulay. *The Works of Lord Macaulay: Complete.* Edited by Lady H. Trevelyan.

London: Longmans, Green, 1875; Trevelyan, G. O. *The Life and Letters of Lord Macaulay.* London: Longmans, Green, 1876.

MARK F. PROUDMAN

Macdonald, Sir John A. (1815–1891)

The first prime minister of the **Dominion** of **Canada,** John Macdonald had established himself in a law practice at Kingston, Ontario by the age of 21. As a young man, he served in the militia on the loyal side against the rebels of 1837, and in the subsequent Fenian raids. First elected to the assembly of the province of Canada in 1844, as a Tory he opposed **responsible government** and the extension of the franchise. But when a Reform government passed the Rebellion Losses Bill of 1848, effectively introducing responsible government and provoking riots among Montreal Tories, Macdonald remained among the moderate conservatives who resisted calls for annexation to the United States. Within a short space of years, he was a leader of the so-called Liberal Conservatives, holding office as attorney general almost constantly from 1854 to 1867.

Macdonald initially opposed proposals to create a federal union of the British colonies in North America. The victory of the north in the **American Civil War** and a subsequent spate of Fenian raids, however, moved him toward support for a British North American federation. Macdonald became the first prime minster of the Dominion of Canada, holding office from the creation of the Dominion in 1867 to 1873, when he was forced to resign because of allegations that he had accepted favors from the leader of a railway syndicate. During his first term as prime minister, the Dominion purchased the **Hudson's Bay Company**'s lands in western Canada, part of which became the province of Manitoba. Although Macdonald supported French and Catholic rights in Manitoba, his government also put down the Métis Red River rebellion of 1870. Elected again in 1878, "the old chieftain" died in office in 1891.

During this final decade in office, Macdonald saw the completion of the **Canadian Pacific Railway,** the incorporation of **British Columbia** into the Confederation, and the suppression of the Northwest rebellion of 1885. He implemented a "national policy" of tariffs aimed at supporting domestic industry, thus cementing Tory support in the industrializing central provinces. Macdonald was a keen supporter of Canada's ties to the British Empire and an admirer of his contemporary, the British Prime Minister Benjamin Disraeli. Although his opponents accused him of sheer opportunism, he played a central role in creating the self-governing Dominion of Canada. *See also* British North America Act; Canada; Dominion.

FURTHER READING: Creighton, Donald. *John A. Macdonald.* 2 vols. Toronto: MacMillan, 1955.

MARK F. PROUDMAN

Macedonia

A geographical region in the Balkans under Ottoman rule until the twentieth century. The creation of Greek, Serbian, and Bulgarian national identities in the nineteenth century resulted in Macedonia becoming a focus of the national ambitions of all three governments. Macedonia became part of Bulgaria in the Treaty of **San Stefano** in March 1878 but returned to Ottoman control by the Congress of **Berlin** the following July. In the 1890s, the governments sponsored rival armed groups who fought the Muslims and one another. The conflict was not simply over territory but over peoples whom the governments and peoples of **Greece,** Bulgaria, and **Serbia** considered were their brothers and sisters.

All three sides used propaganda, education, and violence to achieve their ends. The Greek cause linked nationality to the allegiance of the Orthodox of Macedonia to the Patriarchate of Constantinople and the Greek rite. Education was the focus of propaganda. The Greek cause suffered outside of the Aegean regions, because the people of the interior were mostly Slav. Nevertheless, the propaganda effort and the violence adopted in the 1890s managed to win the Greek cause some support in central Macedonia. The Greek government became more involved after the death of Pavlos Melas, a Greek army officer, in 1904.

Bulgaria sponsored the largest organization fighting for the autonomy of Macedonia, the Internal Macedonian Revolutionary Organization (IMRO). The organization was founded in 1893 by a group of Bulgarian revolutionaries led by Hristo Tatarchev and Dame Gruev under the name Bulgarian Macedonian-Adrianople Revolutionary Committee. In 1902, it became the Secret Macedonian-Adrianople Revolutionary Organization and in 1906 the Internal Macedonian-Adrianople Revolutionary Organization. It disbanded itself during the Bulgarian occupation of Macedonia (1915–1918), but was revived in 1920 and took the name IMRO. At first the Committee wanted to unite all those—Bulgarians, Greeks, Vlachs, and Turks— dissatisfied with Ottoman rule in Macedonia and the Adrianople Vilayet and obtain political autonomy for the two regions. When the Ottomans discovered a depot of ammunition near the Bulgarian border in 1897, however, repressions against committee activists led to its transformation into a militant organization, which engaged in attacks against Ottoman officials and punitive actions against suspected traitors. The launch of pro-Serb and pro-Greek *guerrilla* organizations into Macedonia further militarized and nationalized IMRO and the people of Macedonia. The Bulgarian cause dominated in central and northern Macedonia and was also strong in southern Macedonia.

A Croatian historian, Spiridon Gopcevic—also known as Leo Brenner—made the greatest contribution to Serbian propaganda. In 1889, he published his ethnographic study "Macedonia and Old Serbia," which argued that there were 2 million Serbs in Macedonia and only 200,000 Greeks and 50,000 Bulgarians. Other such "scholars" published similar works. Such views were transferred into practice in the educational system drastically from 1878. The Society of Saint Sava in Belgrade gave scholarships to talented Orthodox Macedonians, turning them into staunch supporters of the Serbian cause. Nevertheless, the Serbian cause in Macedonia was less successful than the Bulgarian and Greek, with success restricted to the northern and western districts of Tetovo, Skopje, Gostivar, Debar, Kicevo, and Kumanovo.

In 1912, the governments of Greece, Bulgaria, and Serbia put their differences aside to join forces against Ottoman rule. Despite support in Bulgaria, as well as in Macedonia, for the establishment of an autonomous Macedonian province under a Christian governor, Sofia agreed to the partition of Macedonia, but without fixing its borders the conflict became a battle of armies. The Greek army beat the Bulgarians to Salonica, while Belgrade and Sofia disputed the division of Macedonia.

In June 1913, Bulgaria's Tsar Ferdinand, without consulting the government and without any declaration of war, ordered Bulgarian troops to attack the Greek and Serbian troops in Macedonia. The intervention of the Romanian and Ottoman armies tilted the scales against Bulgaria. Vardar Macedonia was incorporated into Serbia and Greece secured Aegean Macedonia. The region was the primary battleground of the Second Balkan War. During the Greek advance at the end of June, the army set fire to the Bulgarian quarter of the town of Kukush and more than 150 Bulgarian villages around Kukush and Serres, driving 50,000 refugees into Bulgaria. In retaliation the Bulgarian army burned the Greek quarter of Serres. *See also* Balkan Wars; Eastern Question; Ottoman Empire.

FURTHER READING: Anderson, M. S. *The Eastern Question 1774–1923.* London: Macmillan, 1966; Gerolymatos, André. *The Balkan Wars: Conquest, Revolution, and Retribution from the Ottoman Era to the Twentieth Century and Beyond.* New York: Basic Books, 2002; Hammond, N.G.L. *A History of Macedonia.* Oxford: Clarendon Press, 1972.

ANDREKOS VARNAVA

Machine Gun

A generic term for an automatic weapon capable of firing small-arms ammunition continuously and rapidly. The first cyclic firing weapon constructed was probably James Puckle's Defence gun from 1718. The Gatling gun, constructed by Richard Jordan Gatling in 1861, was the first to see action, notably in the **American Civil War** at the Battle of **Antietam** in 1862. It fired 300 rounds per minute. British troops used Gatling guns against the **Ashanti** in 1874 and the **Zulu** in 1879. Another early type was the Gardner Gun, adopted by the British Army in 1879. These were not true machine guns, however, as their feeding mechanism had to be operated manually, but most European armies acquired them. Early cyclic firing weapons were regarded as artillery, being large, bulky, and wheel mounted. Consequently, they were deployed as such, in clusters far behind the front firing lines. This rendered them almost useless, a lesson learned particularly by the French in the **Franco-Prussian War.**

Sir Hiram Maxim, an American settling in Britain in 1881, constructed the first true machine gun. The Maxim gun was presented to the British Army in 1884. It had a recoil driven feeding mechanism and water-cooled barrel, could fire six hundred .45-caliber rounds per minute, and was effective against area targets at a range up to 2,000 meters. It proved indispensable in Britain's colonial wars in the late nineteenth century. It first saw action in 1885 in the Red River Rebellion in Canada and was especially devastating against the human wave assaults in the **Matabele War** of 1893 in South Africa. By 1900, the colonial troops of all the Great Powers were equipped with machine guns.

The **Russo-Japanese War** was the first to witness battles between large forces equipped entirely with breech-loading and rapid-fire weapons. By World War I, most machine guns were based on the Maxim concept, like the German Machingewehr 08, although shorter, lighter, and mounted on a tripod or bipod. One notable exception was the unreliable French Saint-Etienne M1907. On the eve of the war, however, the French developed the excellent Hotchkiss Modèle 1914, with a gas-driven loading mechanism.

FURTHER READING: Headrick, Daniel R. *The Tools of Empire: Technology and European Imperialism in the Nineteenth Century*. New York: Oxford University Press, 1981; Keegan, John. *The Face of Battle*. London: Jonathan Cape, 1976.

FRODE LINDGJERDET

Mackensen, August von (1849–1945)

A Prussian field marshal, August von Mackensen was born on December 6, 1849, in Saxony. Mackensen joined the *Leibhusaren Regiment* in 1869 and fought in the **Franco-Prussian War** of 1870–1871. He was appointed to the Prussian general staff in 1880. In 1891, he became Alfred von **Schlieffen**'s adjutant and in 1901, he was named Kaiser **Wilhelm II**'s personal adjutant and General *á la Suite*. During World War I, Mackensen served on the Eastern Front as corps commander in the Eighth Army and played a major role in the German victory at the Battle of Tannenberg. Commanding the Ninth Army, he subsequently served in the Polish campaign and received the *Pour le Mérite* in November 1914.

In May 1915, commanding the Eleventh Army, he won a victory at Gorlice-Tarnow that led to his promotion to field marshal. He subsequently commanded the campaign against **Serbia** and led the Danube Army in Romania, where he spent the rest of the war in charge of the occupation army. After the war, Mackensen, who was now a war hero, was used by the National Socialists for propaganda purposes. Mackensen opposed aspects of the National Socialist regime, but supported the German war effort in World War II. He died at aged 95, on November 8, 1945.

FURTHER READING: Schwarzmüller, Theo. *Zwischen Kaiser und 'Führer': Generalfeldmarschall August von Mackensen. Eine politische Biographie*. Paderborn: Schöningh, 1995; Showalter, Dennis. *Tannenberg. Clash of Empires*. Washington, DC: Brassey's, 2004.

ANNIKA MOMBAUER

Mackinder, Sir Halford (1861–1947)

A geographer, theorist of Britain's world role, and a prominent supporter of British imperialism. A polymath, Mackinder studied both modern history and the sciences at Oxford before becoming active in the University extension movement, which attempted to make university-level education more widely available. Interest in geography was considerably heightened in the late nineteenth century by the expansion of the British Empire. After delivering an influential lecture to the Royal Geographical Society, Mackinder was appointed to the first position in geography at Oxford, and went on to play an important role in establishing geography as an academic discipline there and elsewhere.

Originally a **Liberal Imperialist** in politics, Mackinder was converted to the cause of imperial preference, and became a Conservative, sitting as Tory Member of Parliament for a Glasgow constituency from 1910 to 1922. Mackinder's most influential work was *Britain and the British Seas* of 1902, which surveyed British history in the light of the country's maritime position. *Britain and the British Seas* concluded that

Britain, as the center of the global capitalist system and the world's major creditor nation, would have to remain a strong naval and military power.

In making the argument that British capitalism required an empire, Mackinder anticipated by a couple of months the more famous but parallel argument of J. A. **Hobson** that capitalism caused imperialism; the differences between the two men were as much moral as analytical, both holding that capital export was central to imperialism. Mackinder was also known for arguing that the power that dominated the "world island" of Eurasia would dominate the world, an intellectual articulation of the old rationale for Britain's traditional balance-of-power policy of opposing potential European hegemons. *See also* Balance of Power; Strategy.

FURTHER READING: Blouet, Brian W. *Halford Mackinder: A Biography.* College Station: Texas A&M University Press, 1987; Mackinder, H. J. *Britain and the British Seas.* London: William Heinemann, 1902.

MARK F. PROUDMAN

MacMahon, Patrice Edmé Maurice (1808–1893)

A marshal of France and president of the French Republic (1873–1879), Patrice MacMahon descended from an Irish soldier who had settled in France in the seventeenth century. MacMahon entered the army during the reign of **Charles X** and first distinguished himself during the conquest of **Algeria.** During the **Crimean War,** he led the French assault on Malakoff in September 1855. During the Austro-Piedmontese War, MacMahon's actions at in the Battle of Magenta were in large part responsible for a Franco-Piedmontese victory and earned him the rank of Marshal along with the title of Duke of Magenta.

As governor of Algeria between 1864 and 1870, he fought in a number of colonial campaigns before returning to France to command the First Corps during the **Franco-Prussian War.** He was defeated as Weissenburg and Fröschwiller and then finally captured at Sedan. After repatriation, MacMahon commanded the troops that suppressed the Commune of Paris with the loss of some 800 troops against an estimated 20,000 Communards. He was elected the second president of the **Third Republic** in May 1873, thereby disappointing the royalists, who hoped he would restore the monarchy. *See also* Thiers, Adolphe.

FURTHER READING: Brogan, Denis. *The Development of Modern France, 1870–1939.* London: Hamish Hamilton, 1940.

CARL CAVANAGH HODGE

Madagascar

A large island in the Indian Ocean off the east coast of Africa that in the early nineteenth century was of interest to Britain. Governed at the time by the Hova Empire, whose rulers sought to modernize their army and open the island to new technology, the Hova King Radama I was in 1828 offered arms, ammunition, and training by British troops, who had established a beachhead in the coastal town of Tamatave, in exchange for the abolition of slavery and rights for Christian

missionaries. His successor on the Hova throne, Queen Ranavalona I then expelled all missionaries. During the 1860s, missionaries were permitted to return, and by the end of the decade the queen and many Hova leaders were of the Protestant faith.

French interest in Madagascar dated to 1840 but became more active in the 1880s, when France demanded the right to declare a protectorate over Madagascar, was refused by Queen Ranavalona II, and prosecuted a war against the Hova until a treaty yielded partial control in 1885. French imperial ambition on the island then entered a new phase in 1890, when Britain and Germany gave France a free hand in return for recognition of their own protectorates in East Africa. Yet Hova resistance continued, and in 1894 the French parliament voted to fund a large expedition. In fact, two separate expeditionary forces were sent and in September 1895 reached the capital, Tananarive. Initially, Ranavalona was permitted to keep her throne, and the French commander, General Joseph Gallieni, became governor-general. As rebellions persisted, however, Ranavalona was removed by force and sent into exile in Algeria. *See also* Africa, Scramble for; French Empire; Heligoland-Zanzibar Treaty.

FURTHER READING: Brown, Mervyn. *A History of Madagascar.* Princeton, NJ: Markus Wiener, 2000; Ellis, William. *History of Madagascar.* London: Fisher, Son, & Co., 1838; Wesseling, H. L. *The European Colonial Empires, 1815–1919.* London: Longman, 2004.

CARL CAVANAGH HODGE

Madison, James (1751–1836)

American founding father, statesman, and fourth President of the **United States,** James Madison was born March 16, 1751, the first of the 10 children of Eleanor Conway and James Madison, Sr., a major landowner in Orange County, Virginia. Madison was a dedicated student and natural scholar. He graduated from the College of New Jersey, now Princeton University, in 1771, where he studied government, history, law, ethics, and Hebrew and founded the American Whig Society. After returning to Virginia, Madison played a prominent role in the state's politics from 1775 to 1780.

With the arrival of the American Revolution, Madison was chosen as a delegate to the Virginia Convention of 1776 and subsequently was the youngest delegate to the Continental Congress. His keen awareness of the flaws of the 1781 Articles of Confederation made Madison a major intellectual influence at the Federal Convention at Philadelphia in 1787 and—through the *Federalist* papers, coauthored with Alexander **Hamilton** and John Jay—as prominent a figure as any of the founding generation in articulating the spirit of the Constitution of the United States. Madison then served under Jefferson as secretary of state from 1801 to 1809, was involved in the **Louisiana Purchase,** and grappled with the dilemma of American neutrality during the **Napoleonic Wars,** wrongly assuming Britain's blockade of Europe to be the greater threat to American shipping rights.

Succeeding Thomas **Jefferson** in the presidency in 1809, Madison demonstrated that intellect is no passport to executive acumen by transforming the neutral rights issue into an unnecessary and imprudent conflict, the **Anglo-American War** of 1812, with the British Empire. The American invasion of **Canada** went very badly; American troops managed to burn the parliament of Upper Canada, but British troops returned the favor by invading the United States and torching the White the next year. Further calamities were avoided when the war ended with the Treaty of Ghent. "Mr. Madison's War," as his critics named the conflict, profited the United States nothing save the emergence of Andrew **Jackson** as a national hero in the Battle of New Orleans after the peace had already been signed.

FURTHER READING: Banning, Lance. *The Sacred Fire of Liberty: James Madison and the Founding of the Federal Republic.* Ithaca, NY: Cornell University Press, 1995; Horsman, Reginald. *The Causes of the War of 1812.* Philadelphia: University of Pennsylvania Press, 1962; Stagg, J.C.A. *Mr. Madison's War: Politics, Diplomacy and Warfare in the Early American Republic, 1783–1830.* Princeton, NJ: Princeton University Press, 1983.

CARL CAVANAGH HODGE

Madras

A port city, present-day Chennai on **India**'s southeast coast, Madras was founded by Francis Day, an English **East India Company** representative, in 1639. The East India Company had been granted a charter by Queen Elizabeth in December 1600 for a monopoly on all English trade east of the Cape of Good Hope. Company merchants sought to create trading outposts allowing direct access to highly valued Indian textile sources. Day's land grant from the Nayak of Poonamallee, the local ruler of the Vijayanagar Empire, fulfilled that objective. By the eighteenth century, Madras became the most important city in South India. In the next two centuries Madras, along with Bombay and Calcutta, came to represent one of three legs of the powerful British Empire in India. The city served as the capital of the Madras Presidency, comprising most of South India.

The port was captured by a French force in 1746, but the British regained control in 1749 through the Treaty of Aix-la-Chapelle and subsequently fortified the base to withstand further attacks from the French and Hyder Ali, the Sultan of Mysore. By the late eighteenth century the British had conquered most of the region around Tamil Nadu and the modern-day states of Andhra Pradesh and Karnataka to establish the Madras Presidency. Under British rule the city grew into a major urban center and naval base. With the advent of railways in India, Madras was connected to the other towns such as Bombay and Calcutta, facilitating communication and trade with the hinterland. In 1857, a university was founded in Madras; thereafter, its commercial and intellectual importance made the city a center of Indian nationalism. In 1909, an artificial harbor capable of servicing ocean-going ships was completed at Madras. It was the only Indian city to be attacked by the Central Powers during World War I, by the German light cruiser S.M.S. Emden. *See also* British Empire; India.

FURTHER READING: Krishnaswami, Nayudu W. S. *Old Madras.* Madras: Solden, 1965; Krishnaswamy, S. *The Role of Madras Legislature in the Freedom Struggle, 1861–1947.* New Delhi: Indian Council of Historical Research, 1989; Mukherjee, Nilmani, *The Ryotwari System in Madras, 1792–1827.* Calcutta: Firma K. C. Mukhopadhay, 1962; Ramaswami, N. S. *The Founding of Madras.* Madras: Orient Longman,1977.

JITENDRA UTTAM

Mafeking, Siege of (1899–1900)

The most famous of three sieges fought during the Boer War of 1899–1902, in which Transvaal General Piet Cronjé surrounded Mafeking on October 13, 1899, trapping a small British and Cape colonial force consisting of 1,500 whites and 5,000 black Africans under Colonel Robert Baden-Powell. The garrison constructed forts, thereby convincing the Boers not to storm the defenses; but on October 24, Cronjé began to bombard the town with a large-caliber artillery piece. The siege became a boring affair, with shelling on both sides, and with Baden-Powell forced to institute strict rationing to stave off starvation inside the overcrowded town. Sorties and minor Boer attacks punctuated the siege, but neither side made any substantial progress. Two British relief columns, one approaching from the south and the other from the north, met on May 15, 1900, broke through the Boer lines the next day and relieved Mafeking that evening. Baden-Powell's defense became popularized as one of the great epics of the Victorian period. *See also* Boer Wars.

FURTHER READING: Flower-Smith, Malcolm, and Yorke, Edmund, eds. *Mafeking: The Story of a Siege*. New York: Covos-Day Books, 2000; Gardner, Brian. *Mafeking: A Victorian Legend*. London: Cassell, 1966.

GREGORY FREMONT-BARNES

Magenta, Battle of (1859)

A critical engagement of the Austro-Piedmontese War. In 1858, France and Piedmont-Sardinia formed an alliance against Austria. Sardinian war preparations provoked the Habsburg monarchy to give an ultimatum to Piedmont-Sardinia and finally to wage war. Austrian forces failed to take the offensive and were pushed back near Palestro at the end of May 1859. In the first of two major battles, 54,000 French-Sardinian troops under the French Emperor Napoleon III defeated 58,000 Austrian troops under General Count Ferenc Gyulai on June 4, 1859. The battle took place near the town of Magenta, west of Milan and east of the Ticino River in northern **Italy** and resulted in heavy losses on both sides. In the aftermath of their victory, the Franco-Sardinian forces were able to take control of Lombardy, but it was the Battle of **Solferino** on June 24, 1859, that decided the war. *See also* Habsburg Empire; MacMahon, Marshal Patrice.

FURTHER READING: Berkeley, G. F.-H. *Italy in the Making*. Cambridge: University Press, 1932; Hearder, Harry. *Italy in the Age of the Risorgimento, 1790–1870*. New York: Longman, 1983.

GUENTHER KRONENBITTER

Maghreb

Derived from *al-Maghrib,* the western half of North Africa, the Maghreb now includes the five countries north of the Sahara desert—Tunisia, Algeria, Morocco, Libya, and Mauritania, as well as the western Sahara. The Maghreb was the bastion of Berber civilization before Arab influences began to spread through the region.

The Maghreb is also pervaded by black African culture, as well as European colonial influences.

Although the entire Maghreb was colonized, the impact of French colonial rule varied. Although Mauritania did not experience any major changes brought about by colonialism, French colonial rule over Algeria was the most extensive. The French were unable to subdue anti-French movements in the vast land of Mauritania. In Algeria, however, the French managed to decimate the anticolonial religious and nationalist movements by the late 1840s. In contrast to limited French colonial involvement in Mauritania, Tunisia, and Morocco, many French citizens, known as *pied-noirs* lived in Algeria, relegating the native Algerians to an inferior status, and Algeria was integrated as part of metropolitan France.

In 1881, the French established a protectorate in Tunisia to deflect other European ambitions in North Africa, especially Italian designs on Libya. Traditional ruling structures and institutions were therefore preserved in Tunisia. Morocco's location at Africa's gate to the Mediterranean and status as a target of French ambitions after 1904 made it the flashpoint of two **Moroccan Crises.** In 1912, Morocco was partitioned between Spain and France, although the latter gained control over most of the country in terms of territory and resources. *See also* Africa, Scramble for; French Empire.

FURTHER READING: Abun-Nasr, Jamil M. *A History of the Maghrib.* Cambridge: Cambridge University Press, 1971.

NURFADZILAH YAHAYA

Mahan, Alfred Thayer (1840–1914)

A U.S. naval officer known for his histories of British naval power. He attended Columbia and the U.S. Naval Academy before being commissioned into the U.S. Navy at the beginning of the **American Civil War.** He was president of the U.S. Naval War College from 1886 to 1889, where he wrote *The Influence of Sea Power upon History* (1890) and the *Influence of Sea Power upon the French Revolution and Empire* (1892). Mahan retired from active service in 1896, and was subsequently promoted vice-admiral.

His books argued that a blue water fleet such as Horatio Nelson's could command the seas, thus giving control of global commerce to the primary naval power. He also argued, however, that possession of a naval fleet required a significant national merchant fleet, and he was quite pessimistic as to the prospects of his own country ever building such a merchant fleet. His books were widely read in Britain and Germany yet failed to stimulate any large-scale American shipbuilding, although they had some influence on Theodore **Roosevelt,** Winston **Churchill,** and Kaiser **Wilhelm II.** Mahan's materialist approach to history saw commerce as a central component of power and was widely shared at the time, as was his view that a successful power must almost necessarily possess an overseas empire. He also advocated American expansion in the Pacific. *See also* Navalism; Strategy; Trafalgar, Battle of; United States.

FURTHER READING: Beale, Howard K. *Theodore Roosevelt and the Rise of America to World Power.* Baltimore: The Johns Hopkins University Press, 1984; Keegan, John. *The Price of Admiralty.*

London: Hutchinson, 1988; Mahan, A. T. *The Influence of Sea Power upon History, 1660–1783.* London: Sampson, Low, Marston, 1890; Seager, Robert. *Alfred Thayer Mahan: The Man and His Letters.* Annapolis, MD: Naval Institute Press, 1977.

MARK F. PROUDMAN

Mahdi

In Islamic eschatology, the Mahdi was the divinely guided leader who would fill the world with justice. In popular Islam, the idea of the Mahdi is often associated with messianic expectations. In Sudanese history, the Mahdi is most commonly a reference to Muhammad Ahmad al-Mahdi (1848–1885). He was a major religious leader and the founder of the Mahdist movement in the **Sudan.** He was born in the Dongola area and received a relatively thorough religious education. He became a strong critic of what he believed was the prevailing immorality of the social and political leaders of his day. His own zeal and the general expectations combined to create the conviction that he was the anticipated Mahdi. His support grew rapidly and government attempts to stop the movement militarily failed. By January 1885, the Mahdi's forces had taken Khartoum and most of the northern Sudan was under his control. He tried to create an organization modeled on the early Islamic community. Muhammad Ahmad died in **Omdurman** not long after the conquest of Khartoum. The descendants of the Mahdi have played an important role in twentieth-century Sudanese history. *See also* Gordon, Charles George.

FURTHER READING: Collins, Robert O. *The Southern Sudan, 1883–1898: A Struggle for Control.* New Haven, CT: Yale University Press, 1964; Holt, P. M. *The Mahdist State in The Sudan, 1881–1898: A Study of Its Origins, Developments and Overthrow.* Oxford: Clarendon Press, 1970.

MOSHE TERDMAN

Mahmud I (1696–1754)

Mahmud I was the 24th Ottoman Sultan (1730–1754). A revolt of the **Janissaries** put him on the throne of the **Ottoman Empire.** After restoring order to the empire in Istanbul in 1730, Mahmud I suppressed the Janissary rebellion in 1731 and waged war against Persia between 1731 and 1746. The Ottomans managed to retain control of Baghdad but lost Armenia, Azerbaijan, and Georgia to the Persians. He led successful wars against Russia in 1736 and Austria in 1737, concluded by the treaty of Belgrade in 1739, which restored North Serbia and Belgrade to the Ottoman Empire. He was a patron of the arts and also carried out reform of the army.

FURTHER READING: Fleet, Kate, ed. *The Ottoman Empire in the Eighteenth Century.* Roma: Instituto per l'Oriente, 1999; Quataert, Donald. *The Ottoman Empire, 1700–1922.* New York: Cambridge University Press, 2000.

MOSHE TERDMAN

Mahmud II (1785–1839)

The 30th Sultan of the **Ottoman Empire,** Mahmud II ruled during a period of rapid decline (1808–1839). During his reign, the empire lost Bessarabia in the

Russo-Turkish War of 1806–1812; **Serbia** in the Greek War of Independence, 1821–1829; and control of Syria and Palestine to the armies of Mehemet Ali of **Egypt** in the 1830s. Mahmud was nevertheless among the more successful sovereigns of the Ottoman Empire insofar as he attempted—and in part succeeded—in imposing overdue modernizing reforms to Ottoman governance. He abolished the court of confiscations and stripped rebellious provincial pashas of their power. In 1826, he destroyed the **Janissaries** and reasserted the absolute power of the sultan; he also reformed finances and ended some of the more arbitrary practices of the Ottoman justice system by edict. In 1839, Mahmud also initiated the *tanzimat,* a period of sustained modernization, but neither he nor his successors reversed the trend of imperial decline, and the empire became increasingly dependent on British and then German support to resist further territorial losses. *See also* Crimean War; Russian Empire.

FURTHER READING: Goodwin, James. *Lords of the Horizons.* London: Chatto & Windus, 1998; Quataert, Donald. *The Ottoman Empire, 1700–1922.* New York: Cambridge University Press, 2000; Shaw, S. J. *History of the Ottoman Empire and Modern Turkey.* Cambridge: Cambridge University Press, 1976.

CARL CAVANAGH HODGE

Maji-Maji Rebellion (1905–1907)

A revolt in **German East Africa** that was brutally suppressed by the colonial authorities. Together with the equally brutal German response to the **Herero Revolt** in South West Africa, the suppression of the Maji-Maji Rebellion helped trigger the **Dernburg Reforms,** which significantly altered German colonial policies. The underlying cause of the Maji Maji revolt was African resentment over colonial tax policies, the introduction of forced labor, and the steady weakening of traditional elites. From the start of their colonial presence in East Africa, the Germans faced a chronic labor shortage caused by low wages and competition from better paying British commercial ventures across the border in Kenya and Uganda.

The arrival of white settlers after the turn of the century quickly exacerbated the situation, when the settlers demanded access to African labor in order to develop their own self-sustaining farms and plantations. In an effort to resolve the labor issue, the Germans began using forced labor for road and railroad construction, introduced a head tax in 1898, and implemented quotas for the mandatory production of cash crops like cotton in 1902. While three measures were deeply unpopular, their impact was compounded by the steady weakening of traditional elites who were not only charged with enforcing German policies, but were also in the process of losing control over the local retail trade to a growing Indian immigrant population first introduced to the region in the 1890s as part of the British railroad construction boom in neighboring Kenya and Uganda.

The German colonial administration's refusal to relax labor and tax policies in the wake of a 1903–1904 drought proved to be the final straw and caused long simmering animosities in German East Africa to erupt into outright rebellion in August 1905. The Maji Maji revolt, which began with the destruction of cotton fields in the Rufiji River Valley as a symbolic gesture of defiance, took its name from the rebels' belief that anointing themselves with a potion of water—*maji* in Swahili—castor oil, and millet would provide protection by magically turning German bullets into water. As the rebellion spread, it quickly evolved into a campaign of violence against German officials, settlers, and missionaries. Germany responded by sending in reinforcements armed with machine guns who combined military action with a scorched earth policy to stamp out the last vestiges of the revolt and punish those responsible. African casualties from the fighting and the resultant famine are estimated at 250,000. *See also* German Empire.

FURTHER READING: Capeci, Dominic J. Jr., and Jack C. Knight. "Reactions to Colonialism: The North American Ghost Dance and East African Maji-Maji Rebellions." *Historian* 2 (1990): 584–602; Falola, Toyin, ed. *Sources and Methods in African History: Spoken, Written, Unearthed.* Rochester, NY: University of Rochester Press, 2003, pp. 295–311; Iliffe, John. *Tanganyika under German Rule, 1905–1912.* Cambridge: Cambridge University Press, 1969; Monson, Jamie. "Relocating Maji Maji: The Politics of Alliance and Authority in the Southern Highlands of Tanzania 1870–1918." *Journal of African History* 39 (1998): 95–121; Redmond, Patrick. "Maji Maji in Ungoni: A Reappraisal of Existing Historiography." *International Journal of African Historical Studies* 8 (1975): 407–424.

KENNETH J. OROSZ

Malta

An island in the central Mediterranean Sea, south of Sicily and east of Tunisia, Malta was ruled by the Knights of St. John of Jerusalem, a chivalric and monastic order that went back to the Crusades, until conquered by the French under Napoleon Bonaparte in 1798. It was then occupied by the British, who in 1800 ejected the French. By the Treaty of **Amiens** in 1802, Britain agreed to withdraw but then refused to do so in the face of other French violations of the temporary peace.

In 1815, Britain remained in Malta, using its excellent fortified harbor at Valetta as a major base for the **Royal Navy.** Malta's strategic value to the British Empire was enhanced by the fleet build during the Crimean War, 1854–1856, and by the opening of the Suez Canal in 1869. Malta's Grand Harbor was vital to the British war effort after 1914, and the island remained a British possession until the mid-twentieth century. *See also* Mahan, Alfred Thayer; Navalism; Strategy.

FURTHER READING: Blouet, Brian W. *The Story of Malta.* New York: F. A. Praeger, 1967; Lee, Hilda I. *Malta 1813–1914: A Study in Constitutional and Strategic Development.* Valletta: Progress Press, 1973; Rodger, N.A.M. *The Command of the Ocean: A Naval History of Britain, 1649–1815.* New York: W. W. Norton, 2004.

MARK F. PROUDMAN

Malthus, Thomas Robert (1766–1834)

An Anglican clergyman, prominent political economist, and author of the doctrine that constricted food supplies must determine economic life. He had an unconventional education, for a clergyman, at a dissenting academy, and then at Cambridge. From 1805, Malthus taught at the **East India Company**'s college at Haileybury. Malthus first published his *Essay on the Principle of Population* in 1798, although he subsequently revised it extensively. The central argument of the essay was that while population, independent of other variables, would grow geometrically, food supply could only grow arithmetically. Population therefore tended, extraneous factors to one side, to outgrow food supply. Using the moral ideas of his time, however, Malthus saw various restraints on population growth, including misery, vice, and moral restraint. This grim arithmetic led to economics being baptized "the dismal science."

The idea that a growing population competed for limited resources inspired Charles **Darwin** with his idea of the survival of the fittest. Often remembered almost exclusively as "Population Malthus," Malthus was nonetheless credited by Keynes with having stressed the importance of effective demand, as against the emphasis on supply, and assumption that supply would create demand, characteristic of other classical political economists. In domestic policy, and particularly from the point of view of poor relief—a controversial topic at the time—Malthus's doctrines on population tended to reinforce the notion that the poverty and suffering of a large proportion of the population was a part of the natural order of things, while being at the same time avoidable through moral prudence. From an imperial point of view, Malthus served to establish in the popular mind the idea that the food supplies available on a small and crowded island were inherently limited. This implied that the **Corn Laws,** as restrictions on imports, exacerbated an already parlous situation. It implied secondly that substantial emigration was both necessary and beneficial to the country and to the emigrant. The desirability of settlement colonies became in the nineteenth century an idea accepted across the political spectrum. *See also* Cobden, Richard; Free Trade.

FURTHER READING: Peterson, William. *Malthus.* Cambridge, MA: Harvard University Press, 1979; Smith, Kenneth. *The Malthusian Controversy.* London: Routledge & Paul, 1951; Winch, Donald. *Malthus.* New York: Oxford University Press, 1987.

MARK F. PROUDMAN

Manchu Dynasty

See Qing Dynasty

Manchuria

A largely artificial geographical term corresponding roughly to the northeastern Chinese provinces of Liaoning, Jilin, and Heilongjiang, as well as portions of Inner Mongolia. The Chinese refer to the region simply as *dongbei*, "the northeast." Historically, the region of Manchuria was the home of various nomadic ethnic tribes of Mongol or Tungus origin that frequently posed a threat to more established Chinese dynasties to the south. In 1644, the newly centralized state of the Manchu, a Tungus tribe descending from the Jurchen, overthrew the Chinese Ming dynasty in 1644 to establish the **Qing** dynasty, which ruled China to 1912. Under the Qing, until the late nineteenth century the Manchu homelands—hence Manchuria—were off limits to those of non-Manchu ethnicity, as the Qing emperors sought to preserve and promote the region as sacred to Manchu identity even as the Manchu imposed their rule over China.

With heightened imperial rivalries in Northeast Asia from the nineteenth century, the region became a bone of contention between a declining Qing state, Meiji Japan, and late imperial Russia. With the decline of Chinese power, Japan and Russia simultaneously developed a keen interest in Manchuria for its abundant natural resources. The Japanese check of Russian interests in Korea in the course of the early and mid-1890s further spurred Russian interest in Manchuria. With the laying of the Russian Trans-Siberian Railway, begun in 1887, that state began to seek out an ideal warm water port as the railway's terminus. One such candidate was the naturally protected harbor of **Port Arthur** at the tip of China's Liaodong Peninsula in southern Liaoning province. On the strength of its decisive victory in the First **Sino-Japanese War,** 1894–1895, fought partly in Manchuria, Japan seized the Liaodong Peninsula as part of its peace settlement with China but was forced to retrocede it with the 1895 Triple Intervention of Russia, France, and Germany. Japan's diplomatic reversal was followed soon thereafter in 1898 by a Russian forced lease from China of railway rights through eastern Manchuria. To administer its newly leased territories along the railway line, Russia developed both Port Arthur and the nearby city of Dalny, present-day Dalian. In 1900, Russian troops, along with those of six other Western powers and Japan, helped suppress the largely antiforeign **Boxer Insurrection.**

Following the Boxer's defeat, Russian troops proceeded to seize large portions of northeastern Manchuria, including the entire Liaodong Peninsula, heightening Russian-Japanese tensions. Such imperial rivalries came to a head in the **Russo-Japanese War** of 1904–1905, which witnessed the defeat of Russia and the reestablishment of Japanese control over the Liaodong Peninsula in the form of a lease with China for the so-called Guandong Territory, a term referring roughly to northeast China. Japan soon thereafter established the Guandong governor-general and Guandong Army with the duty of administering and protecting the Japanese-leased territories there.

Through the early twentieth century, Japanese interest in Manchuria continued apace with the development of the South Manchurian Railway Company, the influx of large numbers of Japanese migrants and officials, and the development regional industry. Also of increasing influence was the Guandong Army headquartered at Port Arthur. The army became a political tool of more radical elements in the Japanese government and military. In 1931 elements of the Guandong Army staged the Manchurian Incident, leading to the establishment of the puppet state of Manchukuo, headed by the last Qing emperor, the full seizure of Liaodong, and the outbreak of the Second Sino-Japanese War in 1931. *See also* Japanese Empire; Russian Empire.

FURTHER READING: Lensen, George Alexander. *Balance of Intrigue: International Rivalry in Korea and Manchuria, 1884–1899.* Tallahassee: University Presses of Florida, 1982; Stephan, John J. *The Russian Far East: A History.* Stanford, CA: Stanford University Press, 1994.

DANIEL C. KANE

Manifest Destiny

A slogan of American territorial expansion that was coined in the 1840s. Justificatory rhetoric throughout the continental expansion of the **United States** was clothed in various garbs, of which Manifest Destiny is the best known, and to invoke a diversity of principles such as natural law or geographical predestination all tailored to meet the same end—an extraordinary ideological cocktail concocted to assist an exceptional, and evident future sanctioned by providence. Its most illustrious forerunner was probably John Quincy Adams whose "hemispheric" dreams left no room for the European nations on the North American continent. The phrase "manifest destiny," was presumably coined by the lawyer, editor, journalist, and diplomat John L. O'Sullivan who twice used his felicitous formulation, first in his *United States Magazine and Democratic Review* about the annexation of Texas and next in the *New York Morning News* about the acquisition of Oregon. The phrase owes its lexical status to the assertion that the American claim to the latter was the "best and strongest," because "that claim is by the right of our manifest destiny to overspread and to possess the whole of the continent which Providence has given us for the development of the great experiment of liberty and federated self-government entrusted to us."

Its author unmistakably captured the mood of the times, the expansionist fever of the 1840s, yet very few historians mention the fact that O'Sullivan's Manifest Destiny, as applied to territorial expansion, was nonviolent, that the man was a cultural nationalist who hoped for the creation of a genuinely American literature, and that he was the discoverer and publisher of several talented writers of his day. Manifest Destiny—a multifaceted and elusive doctrine that looms much larger than O'Sullivan's 1845 editorial views—ought from the start to be relativized and divested partly of its Americanness. Every great nation—England, France, Spain, Holland, for example—has at some time in its history claimed to have a special destiny and has justified that claim in racial and/or religious, if not mystical, terms. And expansionistic nationalism—usually territorial conquest—has generally been the corollary of a regional or world destiny.

The English colonists of the seventeenth and eighteenth centuries were true to their fatherland's "Anglo-Saxon" destiny. Had not England long felt predestined to take over and develop the New World, viewing herself as the only nation capable of such a colossal undertaking? It can be argued that nineteenth-century Americans elaborated a self-serving, expansionist doctrine, which, despite its native trappings, was in no small degree rooted in the European past and culture in that it echoed specifically Britain's own cult of the Anglo-Saxons' superiority, destiny, and mission and more generally the Western world's belief in its role as the vehicle of progress in Africa, Asia, and the Americas.

The United States is the only nation to have consistently sought to shape the world in its own image. As a matter of fact, American nationalism from the start *was* unique and, paradoxically, laid claims to universality: alone among the nations of the earth, the United States was "the embodiment of an idea"; the English tradition of liberty; and the war for independence was fought to uphold "the birthright of mankind." "It has been our fate as a nation," Richard Hofstadter once observed, "not to have ideologies but to be one." The young republic had none of the usual attributes of nationhood: a historically defined territory, a common religion, and distinctive cultural or spiritual features. Initially, its unifying element was the cult of freedom, realized through representative government. Empire building by way of westward expansion came next, uniting the American people through the frontier experience and strengthening their budding nationalism. Vastness of territory would soon come to be regarded as a blessing, contrary to Montesquieu's view that smallness was the surest guarantee of virtue and health for a republic.

The significance of Manifest Destiny divides historians. Daniel J. Boorstin for one contends that the new nation's destiny was more "uncertain" than "manifest" at first and that the Founding Fathers gave little thought to the potential conquest of the continent. Many historians of continental expansion have scrutinized, and generally criticized, the motives behind territorial aggrandizement, be they economic, political, or cultural. Most have challenged the validity and relevance of the Manifest Destiny ideal. But all recognize the impact of this legitimizing myth of empire on popular beliefs about U.S. history, if not on foreign policymaking. It should be noted that the component parts of that myth underlie the nationalist-imperialist ideologies of other nations—witness "the **White Man's Burden,**" "Nordic supremacy," "*la* **mission civilisatrice,**" "*sacro egoismo,*" and the like.

The reactivation of Manifest Destiny apropos of the acquisition in the late nineteenth century of noncontiguous territories certainly underscores the similarity and continuum between continental and overseas expansion, although some American scholars are reluctant to admit the identical character of the two movements. Lexical disagreements may conceal ideological ones; "expansionism" fares better than "imperialism." The use of the latter term still generates unease and controversy among historians and therefore requires some caution on the part of their readers. Nevertheless, dictionary definitions do reflect a form of historical consensus; with time many radical historians, thanks to the quality of their research, have influenced the more orthodox scholars and even achieved respectability, as in the case of William Appleman Williams, the New Left revisionist and founder of the "Wisconsin School." In the 1970s, many of his scholarly contributions were regarded as so many ideological tracts. Today even the most conservative historians acknowledge the importance of his work and pay lip service if not tribute to his views. His best-known book, *The Tragedy of American Diplomacy,* has become a classic.

There still is room for disagreement in the analysis of causes and effects, of motivations and accomplishments. Manifest Destiny, in particular, whether viewed as a driving force, a rhetorical device, an ideal, an *a posteriori* justification of conquest, or the quintessential expression of American nationalism, permits a host of interpretations or nuances. For Ronald Reagan in his 1964 speech, "A Time for Choosing," America was "a beacon of hope to the rest of the world" and "the dream of America" was "the last best hope of man on earth." Whether the United States is or not "the last best hope of man on earth" is open to question, but the problem is that it thinks it is. If its continued self-righteous perception of itself as democracy incarnate distinguishes it from other democracies, its self-serving justificatory rhetoric does not, for all nations with liberal traditions evince great disingenuousness when it comes to the least palatable manifestations of their self-interest and great ingenuity in concealing them under the guise of piety or altruism. *See also* California; Indian Wars; Jefferson, Thomas; Louisiana Purchase; Monroe Doctrine; Mexican-American War; Spanish-American War.

FURTHER READING: Boorstin, Daniel J. *The Americans.* 3 vols. New York: Random-Vintage, 1973; Graebner, Norman A. *Empire on the Pacific: A Study in American Continental Expansion.* New York: Ronal Press Co., 1955; Hietala, Thomas R. *Manifest Design: Anxious Aggrandizement in Late Jacksonian America.* Ithaca, NY: Cornell University Press, 1985; Horsman, Reginald.

Race and Manifest Destiny: The Origins of American Racial Anglo-Saxonism. Cambridge, MA: Harvard University Press, 1981; Kohn, Hans. *American Nationalism: An Interpretative Essay.* New York: Macmillan, 1957; Merk, Frederick. *Manifest Destiny and Mission in American History: A Reinterpretation.* New York: Knopf, 1963; Osgood, Robert E. *Ideals and Self-Interest in America's Foreign Relations.* Chicago: University of Chicago Press, 1953; Stephanson, Anders. *Manifest Destiny: American Expansionism and the Empire of Right.* New York: Hill and Wang, 1995; Weinberg, Albert K. *Manifest Destiny: A Study of Nationalist Expansionism in American History.* New York: AMS Press, [1935] 1979.

SERGE RICARD

Manila Bay, Battle of (1898)

The first battle of the **Spanish-American War,** whereby the **United States** defeated Spain, acquired colonies in the Caribbean and the Pacific, and joined the ranks of the Great Powers. On April 25, 1898, the United States declared war on Spain. Three days later, Commodore George Dewey steamed from Mirs Bay, located just up the China coast from neutral British Hong Kong, toward the Spanish colonial possession of the Philippines.

Backed by Assistant Secretary of the Navy Theodore **Roosevelt,** Dewey had become commander of the U.S. Asiatic Squadron in November 1897. With the cruiser *Olympia* as his flagship, Dewey commanded a squadron of five cruisers and three gunboats. Dewey's squadron arrived in Manila Bay on the evening of April 30. Early the next morning, Dewey commenced operations against the Spanish fleet at the Cavite naval station under the command of Admiral Patricio Montojo y Pasarón. Before the day ended, Montojo's entire fleet was destroyed. Dewey's victory was accomplished with only eight American servicemen wounded. The Spanish forces reported 167 killed and 214 wounded.

Dewey's squadron then silenced Cavite's shore batteries and established a naval blockade. After Major General Wesley Merritt arrived with ground troops, the United States took control of the capital city of Manila on August 13, marking the end of Spanish colonial rule in the Philippines. Filipino nationalists proclaimed independence and established a republic under Asia's first democratic constitution, but Spain ceded the Philippines to the United States in the Treaty of Paris that ended the Spanish-American War in December 1898. Subsequently, the United States suppressed the Filipino independence movement headed by Emilio Aguinaldo, who waged an insurrection against the U.S. occupying forces until his capture in April 1901.

News of his victory at Manila Bay made Dewey a national hero in the United States, and he was promoted to admiral of the navy, a position created especially for him by the U.S. Congress. Dewey returned home to become president of the newly created General Board of the Navy Department, in which capacity he was instrumental in helping now President Theodore Roosevelt display American power through the world tour of the U.S. Navy's **Great White Fleet** from 1907–1909. The Philippines was granted independence from the United States on July 4, 1946. *See also* Cuba; Monroe Doctrine; McKinley, William; Navalism.

FURTHER READING: Balfour, Sebastian. *The End of the Spanish Empire, 1898–1923.* New York: Oxford University Press, 1997; Hattendorf, John B. "The Battle of Manila Bay." In Jack Sweetman, ed. *Great American Naval Battles.* Annapolis, MD: Naval Institute Press, 1998, pp. 175–197; Lehman, John. *On Seas of Glory: Heroic Men, Great Ships, and Epic Battles of the American Navy.* New York: Free Press, 2001; Symonds, Craig L. *Decision at Sea: Five Naval Battles That Shaped American History.* New York: Oxford University Press, 2005.

DAVID M. CARLETTA

Maori Wars (1843–1847, 1863–1870)

Two conflicts between the forces of the **British Empire** and the Maori people in New Zealand, in both cases arising from disputes over territory. The first was triggered by the violation of the 1840 Treaty of Waitangi, according to which the Maori agreed to sell goods solely to British merchants in return for protection and the guarantee that they could retain their land. When the New Zealand Company attempted to survey land to which it had no claim, a meeting between company officials and the Maori ended in the Wairau Massacre where more than 20 Europeans perished. Thereafter the Maori chief, Hone Heke, launched a series of raids against settler towns, and not until Sir George Grey took control of British forces were the Maori defeated.

The peace thereby established fractured in 1859, however, when individual Maoris again sold land that by tribal tradition was held in common. The Second Maori War, also known as the Taranaki Wars, was a more serious affair—even though it was punctuated by a truce—because the Maori fought with greater determination and often used *guerrilla* tactics. Still by 1872, the Maori had lost half their population and most of their land.

FURTHER READING: Gibson, Tom. *The Maori Wars: The British Army in New Zealand.* London: L. Cooper, 1974; Sinclair, Keith. *The Origins of the Maori Wars.* Wellington: New Zealand University Press, 1957.

CARL CAVANAGH HODGE

Maratha Wars (1775–1782, 1803–1805, 1817–1818)

Three wars of the late eighteenth and early nineteenth centuries occasioned by the encroachment of the East India Company against the territory and authority of the Maratha Confederacy of south-central **India.** In the first the company involved itself in a succession crisis of the Maratha leadership, yet was defeated at the Battle of Telegaon in January 1779 and forced to sign a treaty relinquishing all territory and revenue it had taken from the Maratha since 1775. The company renewed its campaign in 1780 with a larger force and managed a series of victories that resulted in the Treaty of Salbai in 1782.

Renewed conflict within the confederacy 20 years later again tempted British intervention, initially in the form of the Treaty of **Bassein** in which the company agreed to support the Peshwa Baji Rao II against his rival Jaswant Rao Holkar by stationing company troops on his domain in return for revenue-yielding authority within the territory. Three Maratha clans, however, promptly raised forces to eject the British, so on August 7, 1803, the company declared war and deployed two armies—one under General Gerard Lake, the other under Major-General Arthur Wellesley, later the Duke of **Wellington**—and inflicted a series of defeats on the Maratha, the most important at **Assaye** and **Laswari.** Ultimately the Maratha forces were chased into the Punjab, and the Treaty of Sarji Anjangaon, dictated at bayonet-point, ceded additional territory between the Jumma and Ganges Rivers to the company.

In the Third Maratha War the company was prompted by raids by freelance Pindari horsemen into company territory—horsemen the Marathas were by treaty obliged to restrain, yet often indulged or encouraged—as reason enough to eliminate what remained of Maratha power. It fielded an army of more than 20,000 men to mop up the Pindaris before bringing the Maratha to battle for a final defeat at Mahidpur in December 1817. The war dragged on into April 1818, but at the end of it, the company was in possession of all of Baji Rao's territory. *See also* East India Companies.

FURTHER READING: James, Lawrence. *Raj: The Making and Unmaking of British India.* New York: St. Martin's 1997; Keay, John. *The Honourable Company.* London: Harper Collins, 1991; Kincaid, C. A., and Rao Bahadur D. B. Parasnis. *History of the Maratha Peoples.* 3 vols. New York: Oxford University Press, 1925.

CARL CAVANAGH HODGE

Marengo, Battle of (1800)

The decisive last-minute *victoire politique* of French First Consul Napoleon **Bonaparte** over the Austrian army under General der Kavallerie Michael Melas, which secured Napoleon's grip on political power in Paris in the aftermath of the Brumaire coup of 1799. Despite having assembled his Army of the Reserve, nominally under the command of General Louis André Berthier, in western Switzerland in early 1800, Bonaparte was wrong-footed by the surprise Austrian advance toward the key city port of Genoa, held by French troops under General André Masséna, in mid-April. He was forced to make a hasty march over the St. Bernard Pass to cross the Alps into Italy in mid-May and, aided by a local double-agent, reached Milan on June 2. After Bonaparte's advance-guard under Lieutenant General Jean Lannes defeated Feldmarschalleutnant Ott at Montebello on June 9, the 29,000 French marched to engage the 31,000 strong Austrian army near Alessandria. Meanwhile, Genoa had surrendered to the Austrians on June 4, although Masséna was allowed to rejoin the campaign and joined General Suchet in a march north from the coast. French troops were also marching from Turin, adding to Melas' fear of being encircled.

Partially deceived by the same agent acting for the Austrians, Bonaparte dispatched large forces to the north and south during June 13, as he believed the Austrians would try to break out north, while troops from Genoa would advance from the south. The French advance-guard, now under Lieutenant General Claude-Victor Perrin, seized Marengo village that evening. However, 8 A.M. on June 14 brought Melas' surprise advance against the main French army under General Berthier, as the Austrians sought to fight their way out directly eastward. Initially, the two Austrian assaults across the Fontanone stream near Marengo village were repelled and Lannes reinforced Perrin's right wing. At 11 A.M., Bonaparte realized the true situation and recalled the detachments, while moving his reserve forward. On the Austrian left wing, Ott had taken Castel Ceriolo and then, on his own initiative, sent his small advance-guard to tackle Lannes' flank. Melas took his chance and tried to push cavalry across the Fontanone on his right wing, but it was routed by French cavalry under General François Kellerman. Nevertheless, a third assault on Marengo village succeeded after bitter fighting, and by 2:30 P.M. the Austrians had broken the French position. The French were driven back east into the main vine belt just as Bonaparte reached the battlefield. In a desperate move to halt Ott's column coming from the north, Bonaparte committed his consular guard, but they were surprised and destroyed by Oberst Frimont's cavalry. Knowing that French troops under General Charles Louis Desaix were approaching, Bonaparte organized a steady withdrawal eastward from about 4:15 P.M. toward San Giuliano, followed by an Austrian column led by Chief of Staff, Feldmarschalleutnant Zach. Desaix's arrival around 5:30 P.M. stabilized the French position as his infantry delayed the Austrian pursuit. Just north of Cascina Grossa, the pursuing Austrian troops met a mix of musketry and artillery fire, which covered a surprise flank attack by Kellerman's cavalry. The French cavalry threw the Austrian column into disordered flight, and a wave of French troops then shattered the center of Melas' army. Exhausted after fighting all day, many Austrian infantry surrendered or fled back over the Bormida River, while in the north Ott failed to intervene. Both sides had sustained about 2,100 casualties, with another 2,500 Austrians captured. The next day, the Armistice of Alessandria obliged the Austrians to evacuate northwestern Italy. Had Bonaparte failed at Marengo, his authority back in France might well have been overthrown by Jacobins or royalists. *See also* Habsburg Empire; Napoleonic Wars.

FURTHER READING: Arnold, J. *Marengo and Hohenlinden.* Lexington, VA: Napoleon Books, 1999; Furse, G. *Marengo and Hohenlinden.* London, 1903; Hollins, D. *Marengo.* Oxford: Osprey Military Publishing, 2000; Rose, J. Holland. *The Revolutionary and Napoleonic Era, 1789–1815.* London: Cambridge University Press, 1935.

DAVID HOLLINS

Marconi, Guglielmo

See Telegraph

Marmont, Auguste Frédéric Louis Viesse de (1774–1852)

A marshal of the **French Empire** under Napoleon **Bonaparte,** Auguste Marmont was trained as an artillerist and served as Napoleon's aide-de-camp during his Italian campaign, 1796–1797, and expedition to Egypt, 1798–99. He helped Napoleon seize power in the coup of Brumaire in 1799 and in the following year distinguished himself in command of the artillery at the Battle of **Marengo.** He served for five years as governor of Dalmatia, where he proved himself both effective and popular with the people. He replaced Marshal Masséna in command of an army in Spain in 1811, but was decisively defeated and severely wounded at the Battle of Salamanca the next year. He was transferred for service in Germany, where he fought the Allies as they pushed Napoleon's forces back into France itself in 1814. Defeated at Laon, Marmont concluded a secret convention with the Allies and surrendered his corps, making continued French resistance impossible—a betrayal for which neither Napoleon nor the French people ever forgave him.

FURTHER READING: Chandler, David, ed. *Napoleon's Marshals.* London: Weidenfeld & Nicolson, 2000; Delderfield, R. F. *Napoleon's Marshals.* New York: Cooper Square Publishers, 2002; Macdonell, A. G. *Napoleon and His Marshals.* New York: Prion Books, 1996.

GREGORY FREMONT-BARNES

Marx, Karl (1818–1883)

German philosopher and political activist whose theories on the development of capitalism and vision of a future socialist society were a compelling influence on both the democratic and nondemocratic socialist movements of the late nineteenth and early twentieth centuries. Born in Trier, Germany, to a Jewish family that had converted to Christianity, Marx studied in Bonn and Berlin between 1835 and 1841 and was powerfully influenced by the theories of Georg **Hegel** on the historical dialectic, as well as by French utopian thought and the economic theory of Adam **Smith** and David **Ricardo.**

Marx moved to France and then to **Belgium** and fell in with exiled German socialists for whom he drafted his most celebrated pamphlet, *The Communist Manifesto,* in collaboration with Friedrich **Engels.** He participated in the revolutionary disturbances of 1848 and was forced by their failure and charges of treason leveled against him to flee to London, where he remained for the rest of his life developing his interpretations of political class conflict and the economic laws of capitalist society. These culminated in his most important work, *Das Kapital,* the first volume of which was published in 1867. British politics mystified Marx, above all the nonrevolutionary civility of British trade unions, but he nonetheless took part in the establishment of the International Workingmen's Association, better known as The International, in 1864.

Marx and his family lived in poverty in London. This condition was mitigated in part by the financial support of his collaborator, Engels, and by correspondence work for newspapers. Marx was, in fact, at his best in analyses of current events thrown against his grasp of broad historical change, above all in his interpretation of the transition from feudalism to capitalism and the function the state as the political agent of the most productive social and economic forces. In developing his ideas about future revolutionary trends, however, Marx extrapolated too aggressively from contemporary trends; in some instances misinterpreted their meaning altogether; and frequently succumbed to the very utopianism he professed to despise. Marx's ideas were most influential among German and Russian socialists, but because he died before European socialist movements had matured, his most important disciples, ranging from Karl **Kautsky** in Germany to V. I. **Lenin** in Russia, differed fundamentally on how to realize Marx's vaguely articulated vision of a future socialist society—with disastrous consequences.

Marx was uncompromising in his condemnation of the impact of industrial capitalism on the wage laborers of Europe. He held that European dominion over non-European peoples was motivated by the same fundamental material greed that had built "satanic mills" from Manchester to Lille and Essen, but he also argued that European capitalism could play a progressive role in European overseas colonies by destroying the social bases of "Oriental despotism" founded on social caste and sustained by slavery. This argument lost out entirely among the socialists of pre-World War I for whom capitalism and **imperialism** were joined at the hip—and in all places, in all times, necessarily wicked in intention and consequence. *See also* Internationalism.

FURTHER READING: Hook, Sidney. *Marxism and Beyond.* Totowa, NJ: Rowman and Littlefield, 1983; McLelland, David. *Karl Marx: A Biography.* New York: Palgrave-Macmillan, 2006; Padover, Saul. *Karl Marx: An Intimate Biography.* New York: McGraw-Hill, 1978.

CARL CAVANAGH HODGE

Masaryk, Tómaš (1850–1937)

A Czech philosopher and statesman, Tómaš Masaryk was born on March 7, 1850, in Moravia. He was the son of a Slovak carter who lived with his family in a predominately Catholic city of Hodonín in the Hungarian part of the **Habsburg Empire.** Between 1872 and 1876, Masaryk studied philosophy at the universities of Brno and Vienna and in 1882 became professor of philosophy at the University of Prague. One year later he founded *Athenaeum,* a journal devoted to Czech science and culture. During the 1890s, Masaryk wrote several books on Czech history and nationality, such as *The Meaning of Czech History* in 1895, and *Jan Hus* along with *Karel Havlicek* in 1896.

For Masaryk, the Czech national revival in the nineteenth century was the continuation of the Czech reformation, and he considered Czech humanism as the basis for a modern Czech democracy. But Masaryk's opinion on the significance of Czech reformation for Czech modernization was criticized by respected Czech scholars like Josef Kaizl (1854–1901), who thought that the Czech question was a national, not a religious problem. Nevertheless, Masaryk stimulated Czech national discourse from a moralist-philosophical point of view. As a member of the Young Czech Party, Masaryk became a member of the Reichsrat, the Austrian parliament, from 1891 to 1893, and then from 1907 to 1914 as delegate of the Realist Party, but rejected a Czech separation from the Habsburg Empire. His opinion changed with the outbreak of World War I when he had to flee Austria to avoid arrest. In exile in Geneva and then in London, he became a strong advocate of Czech independence in union with the Slovaks. In 1917, Masaryk went to Russia to organize Slavic resistance to the Habsburg Empire, one year later he visited U.S. President Woodrow Wilson to convince him of an independent Czechoslovak state. After World War I, Masaryk became the first president of the Czechoslovak Republic.

FURTHER READING: Beld, A. van den. *Humanity: The Political and Social Philosophy of Thomas G. Masaryk.* The Hague: Mouton, 1976; Novák, Josef, ed. *On Masaryk: Texts in English and German.* Amsterdam: Rodopi, 1988; Soubigou, Alain. *Thomas Masaryk.* Paris: Fayard, 2002.

EVA-MARIA STOLBERG

Matabele Wars (1893–1894, 1896–1897)

Two short conflicts between indigenous African and British forces, initially caused by the migration of the Matabele people into Southern Rhodesia just as the **British South Africa Company** became an important presence there. Originally a branch of the **Zulu,** the Matabele people under Moselekatse refused to pay tribute to **Shaka** and were forced by punitive Zulu attacks against them to flee to the Orange Free State and Transvaal where they made raids on the Bantu, but in 1836, they suffered defeat at the hands of the Boers. Moselekatse then took the Matabele north of the Limpopo River and made raids against the local Mashona.

In 1893, the British South Africa Company insisted that these raids be stopped and sent an expedition against the Matabele when the raids persisted. A force of 1,200 volunteers led by Leander Starr **Jameson** and armed with Maxim guns inflicted terrifying defeats on the Matabele at Shangani River and Imbembese. By February 1894, most of the Matabele had surrendered. In March 1896, the Matabele revolted and inflicted heavy losses on isolated settlers and their families.

Regular British troops were sent to put down the rising, which spread to include the Mashona. The Matabele finally laid down their arms in October 1897 in response to British military pressure and a conciliatory diplomatic approach by Cecil **Rhodes** who promised attention to the Matabele grievances. A much harsher line was adopted with the Mashona, and several of their religious leaders were executed. *See also* Africa, Scramble for; Boer Wars; British Empire.

FURTHER READING: Glass, Stafford. *The Matabele War.* Harlow: Longmans, 1968; Laing, D. Tyrie. *The Matabele Rebellion, 1896.* London: Dean & Son, 1897; Mason, Philip. *The Birth of a Dilemma: The Conquest and Settlement of Rhodesia.* Westport, CT: Greenwood, 1982; Ranger, Terence. *Revolt in Southern Rhodesia, 1896–97.* London: Heinemann, 1967.

CARL CAVANAGH HODGE

Matiners' War

See Carlist Wars

Mauritius

An island of only 650 square miles directly east of **Madagascar** in the Indian Ocean. Although it had been settled for less than 400 years, Mauritius was visited by the Arabs before the tenth century, the Malays in the 1400s, and the Portuguese in 1510. It was occupied in 1598 by the Dutch, who named it after Prince Maurice of Nassau. The Dutch left in 1710, and in 1715 the French took possession, renaming it Ile de France. The French built a harbor in the island called Port Louis, which became the capital of Mauritius and an important center for trade, privateering, and naval expeditions against British vessels on their way to and from India. Mauritius was captured by the British in 1810, during the **Napoleonic Wars,** and was formally ceded to Britain in 1814. To offset the labor problem arising from the abolition of slavery in the **British Empire,** the French planters of the sugarcane were allowed to import indentured laborers from India, whose descendants constitute nowadays the majority of the population. Mauritius achieved independence on March 12, 1968.

FURTHER READING: Simmons, Smith Adele. *Modern Mauritius: The Politics of Decolonization.* Bloomington: Indiana University Press, 1982; Wright, Carol. *Mauritius Newton Abbot.* Devon: David & Charles Limited, 1974.

MOSHE TERDMAN

Maxim Gun

See Machine Gun

Maximilian, Emperor of Mexico (1832–1867)

The archduke of Austria and emperor of **Mexico,** Ferdinand Maximilian of Austria was born in Vienna in July 1832. The younger brother of Emperor Francis Joseph I, he became commander of the Austrian navy in 1854 and governor-general of the Lombardo-Venetian kingdom in 1857. In the war of 1859, the Habsburgs lost Lombardy to Piedmont-Sardinia, and Maximilian lost his post. Persuaded by the French Emperor Napoleon III (see **Bonaparte, Louis Napoleon**) and Mexican conservatives who were scheming to topple President Benito Juárez, Maximilian accepted the offer of the Mexican throne in 1863.

After his arrival in Mexico, Maximilian had to face massive armed resistance. In this civil war Maximilian depended on the financial and military support of Napoleon III. When the **United States** threatened to intervene in 1865, Napoleon III disengaged and left Maximilian with little chance of success. Nevertheless, Maximilian refused to flee the country and was arrested by Juaréz' forces. He was executed by republican troops near Querétaro in June 1867. *See also* Habsburg Empire.

FURTHER READING: Bérenger, Jean. *A History of the Habsburg Empire, 1780–1918.* London: Longman, 1997; Bridge, Francis R. *The Habsburg Monarchy Among the Great Powers, 1815–1918.* New York: St. Martin's, 1990; Kann, Robert A. *The Multinational Empire: Nationalism and National Reform in the Habsburg Monarchy, 1848–1918.* 2 vols. New York: Octagon Books, 1964; Taylor, A.J.P. *The Habsburg Monarchy, 1809–1918.* Chicago: University of Chicago Press, 1976

GUENTHER KRONENBITTER

Mazzini, Giuseppe (1805–1872)

An Italian patriot, philosopher, and champion of republican government, Giuseppe Mazzini was born the son of a doctor in the port city of Genoa and enlisted in the Carbonari in the 1820s. His revolutionary activities resulted in arrest in Sardinia in 1830, but the next year he fled to Marseilles where he founded the **Young Italy** movement with the mission of uniting the states and kingdoms of the Italian peninsula into a republic. Mazzini held that national unification could be accomplished only by popular insurrection, a romantic political reflex typical of liberal movements of the time. His open advocacy of this approach, however, got him banned not only from Italy but also from France.

Mazzini was equally attracted to ornate conspiratorial projects. From refuge in Switzerland he concocted a plot to use Polish exiles in Switzerland and France to launch an invasion of Savoy, the ancestral home of Piedmont-Sardinia's ruling family, on the calculation that the action would touch off popular risings in **Italy,** France, Germany, and Switzerland itself—leading to the creation of a republican and neutral Confederation of the Alps. The easy defeat of the raid by Piedmontese forces badly damaged Mazzini's status a republican leader. In exile in Marseilles and London, he nurtured the idea of a republican brotherhood of nations and founded a Young Europe movement.

The revolutionary year of 1848 found Mazzini back in Milan, now coordinating his efforts with Giuseppe **Garibaldi**; in 1849 he headed the governing triumvirate of the Roman Republic. When it fell, Mazzini's influence waned as Garibaldi's waxed. The nationalist movement gravitated toward unification under the House of Savoy, as Garibaldi and Count **Cavour** assumed its leadership. Mazzini rejected national unification under a crown and continued to agitate for a republic. By 1868, when he settled in Lugano, Switzerland, only 15 miles from the Italian border, Mazzini was no longer a political force in his homeland.

FURTHER READING: Griffith, Gwilym Oswald. *Mazzini: Prophet of Modern Europe*. New York: H. Fertig, 1970; Mack Smith, Denis. *Mazzini*. New Haven, CT: Yale University Press, 1994; Schroeder, Paul W. *The Transformation of European Politics, 1763–1848*. Oxford: Clarendon, 1994.

CARL CAVANAGH HODGE

McKinley, William (1843–1901)

The 25th president of the **United States,** William McKinley led the country in war against the Spanish Empire in 1898 and laid the foundations for an overseas empire and a strong international presence of the United States. A civil war hero from Ohio who served in the U.S. Congress from 1877 to 1882 and again from 1885 to 1891 and as governor of Ohio from 1892 to 1896, McKinley had little interest in foreign policy and no international experience before he assumed the presidency in 1896.

Confronted with the Cuban struggle for independence, McKinley refused to recognize the Cuban revolutionaries and urged Spanish reforms of colonial rule with limited local sovereignty. The president opposed annexation schemes for Cuba, as he interpreted the inclusion of a multiracial society into the United States as detrimental for the American body politic. Once confronted with the deterioration of Spanish control over the island, public outrage over the brutal Spanish policy of forced Cuban resettlements, and the sinking of the *U.S.S. Maine* in Havana harbor, however, McKinley asked Congress for a declaration of war.

McKinley interpreted American victory in the **Spanish-American War** of 1898 as a unique opportunity to strengthen the U.S. informal empire in the Caribbean with control over Cuba and understood the new colonial empire, which among other possessions encompassed the Philippines and Hawaii, as stepping-stones to the Asia market. He staunchly supported the acquisition of colonies in a powerful national debate between expansionists and anti-imperialists over the merits of empire and gained reelection in 1900. For McKinley, the colonial empire strategically and commercially complemented American hegemony in the Caribbean and safeguarded his administration's claim to access to markets on the Asian mainland under the **Open Door** diplomacy of 1899 and 1900. In 1900, during the **Boxer Insurrection,** McKinley dispatched 2,500 soldiers to participate in a multinational expedition to protect foreign legations against Chinese rebels. McKinley was assassinated on a visit to the Pan-American Exposition in Buffalo, New York, in September 1901. *See also* Monroe Doctrine, Panama Canal; Roosevelt, Theodore.

FURTHER READING: Dobson, John. *Reticent Expansionism: The Foreign Policy of William McKinley*. Pittsburgh: Duquesne University Press, 1988; Gould, Lewis L. *The Presidency of William McKinley*. Lawrence: University of Kansas Press, 1982; Musicant, Ivan. *Empire by Default*. New York: Henry Holt, 1998.

FRANK SCHUMACHER

Mediterranean Agreements (1887)

Initially, the Mediterranean Agreements were a series of bilateral agreements signed between Britain and **Italy** on February 12, 1887, and between Britain and Austro-Hungary on the following March 24. These initial exchanges received further clarification in a trilateral exchange of notes, ratified on December 12, 1887, known as the Second Mediterranean Agreement. The agreements pledged the participants to the maintenance of the status quo in the Eastern Mediterranean and adjacent seas. In effect, this also meant that should the status of Bulgaria, the **Ottoman Empire,** the Balkans, **Egypt,** or Tripoli be altered by outside powers or internal unrest, these three powers would work in coordination together.

Although considerably short of a formal alliance, the agreements marked a decade long period in which Britain associated its interests in European diplomacy closely with the powers of the **Triple Alliance,** composed of Germany, Austro-Hungary, and Italy. Several factors led to this alignment. On the part of the British, friction with Russia over the delineation of the Afghan frontier—the Penjdeh crisis of 1885—and especially divergent positions regarding Bulgaria pushed London to look for diplomatic partners to check the Russians. Continued friction with France over the nature of the British occupation of Egypt since 1882 precluded such an agreement between those two powers and led the British to turn instead toward Berlin and Vienna. A domestic crisis in France resulting in the Boulanger episode worried France's neighbors, particularly Germany and Italy, about possible adventurism in French foreign policy.

The Italians had been pursuing an alliance or alignment with Britain since the early 1880s, in part to win British support against French expansion in North Africa. In particular, the Italians felt they had been cheated when France stole a march on them in Tunisia in 1881. In both the case of Italy and Austro-Hungary, Otto von **Bismarck** encouraged an approach to the British, hoping to force Britain to serve as the lead check on Russia's Balkan designs, while allowing him to maintain his support for the *Dreikaiserbund.* At the same time, the association of Britain with Italy and Austro-Hungary also helped Bismarck successfully negotiate the extension of the Triple Alliance, especially with Italy, which was signed on February 20, 1887. The Mediterranean Agreements in many ways marked the high point of Anglo-German relations before the tension-prone reign of Kaiser **Wilhelm II.** *See also* Africa, Scramble for; Eastern Question; Great Game.

FURTHER READING: Bridge, F. R. *From Sadowa to Sarajeva: the Foreign Policy of Austria-Hungary 1860–1914.* London: Routledge & Kegan Paul, 1972; Kennedy, Paul. *The Rise of the Anglo-German Antagonism 1860–1914.* London: George Allen & Unwin, 1982; Langer, William L. *European Alliance and Alignments 1871–1890.* New York: Alfred A. Knopf, 1962; Lowe, C. J. *The Reluctant Imperialists: British Foreign Policy 1878–1902.* New York: Macmillan, 1967; Lowe, C. J. *Salisbury and the Mediterranean: 1886–1896.* London: Routledge and Kegan Paul, 1965.

ROBERT DAVIS

Mehmet Ali (1769–1848)

Also known as Muhammad Ali, Mehmet Ali was Ottoman *pasha,* or governor, of **Egypt.** Originally from Albania, Mehmet Ali, a driven and ambitious man, made himself into the most powerful subject of the Ottoman Sultans in the early nineteenth century and on several occasions threatened to replace his nominal overlords with his own imperial pretensions. In the wake of Napoleon **Bonaparte**'s Egyptian campaigns, the province was restored to nominal Ottoman control. The chaotic situation in Egypt and the many difficulties faced by Ottoman authorities in Constantinople, however, provided an ideal opportunity for Mehmet Ali's own designs.

By 1811, he had displaced the Ottoman governor and brutally suppressed the Mamlukes, former slave soldiers and the traditional power brokers of Egypt for hundreds of years. His modernization programs, although creating considerable tension in Egypt itself, focused on strengthening the Egyptian economy and building a modern army on European lines, often trained by French officers looking for work in the aftermath of the Napoleonic Wars. His success was considerable enough to cause concern in Constantinople. Sultan Mahmud II, Mehmet Ali's nominal suzerain, ordered the Egyptian army to Arabia to suppress the **Wahhabi** movement, which threatened Ottoman control of the Hijaz. Success against the Wahhabis emboldened Mehmet Ali, who soon dispatched one son at the head of an army of conquest into the **Sudan,** another to aid his suzerain in the suppression of the Greek revolt, all the while toying with plans for the conquest of North Africa. When he reaped what he deemed insufficient reward for his assistance against the Greeks, Mehmet Ali turned against Mahmud and sent his son Ibrahim at the head of an Egyptian army to invade the neighboring Ottoman province of **Syria.** This led to a major crisis in the Near East in 1832–1833 in which it seemed that the **Ottoman Empire** was on the verge of collapse, perhaps to be replaced by an Egyptian Empire in its stead.

Only the unlikely intervention of Russia on the side of the Ottomans checked Mehmet Ali's ambitions. Six years later Mahmud II again tried to deal with his overly ambitious vassal by reconquering Syria, only to suffer major reverses yet again. This time the Ottomans had to rely on British assistance to drive Ibrahim out of Syria. In the end, Mehmet Ali never succeeded in establishing a fully independent Egyptian state, but from 1841 on, he secured hereditary title as Ottoman governor of Egypt. His family was to rule Egypt, although as Ottoman subjects until World War I, until the end of the monarchy in 1952. *See also* Inkiar Skelessi, Treaty of; Russian Empire.

FURTHER READING: Dodwell,Henry. *The Founder of Modern Egypt: A Study of Muhammed Ali.* Cambridge: Cambridge University Press, 1931; Fahmi, Khaled. *All the Pasha's Men: Mehmed Ali, His Army, and the Making of Modern Egypt.* Cambridge: Cambridge University Press, 1997; Karsh, Efraim, and Inari Karsh. *Empires of the Sand: The Struggle for Mastery in the Middle East 1789–1923.* Cambridge, MA: Harvard University Press, 1999; al-Sayyid Marsot, Afaf Lutfi. *Egypt in the Reign of Muhammad Ali.* Cambridge: Cambridge University Press, 1984.

ROBERT DAVIS

Mehmet V, Sultan of Turkey (1844–1918)

Born in Constantinople, Mehmet V succeeded to the throne of the **Ottoman Empire** when the **Young Turks** deposed his brother, Abdul Hamid II, in 1909. His father was one of the most progressive sultans of the empire, and Mehmet was raised as a reformer and with an excellent knowledge of Arabic, Persian, and Islam. During his reign the Ottoman Empire lost **Tripoli** and the Dodecanese Islands to **Italy** and most of its remaining Balkan possessions between 1911 and 1913. Mehmet lost his remaining power to the Revolution of the Committee of Union and Progress in January 1913, and from that time, Enver and Talat Pashas controlled the government and Mehmet became a symbolic sovereign without authority. Germany gained increasing influence over Turkish affairs, resuming the construction of the **Berlin-to-Baghdad Railway** in 1911. Mehmet sided with the Central Powers in

World War I. He died shortly before the Ottoman surrender and was succeeded by his brother, Muhammad VI.

FURTHER READING: Ahmad, Feroz. *The Making of Modern Turkey.* London: Routledge, 1993; McCarthy, Justin. *The Ottoman Peoples and the End of Empire.* London: Arnold, 2001; Yapp, M. E. *The Making of the Modern Near East 1792–1923.* London: Longman Group UK Limited, 1987.

ANDREKOS VARNAVA

Meiji Restoration (1868–1912)

A palace coup of 1868, which overthrew the Tokugawa Shogunate and "restored" power to the Japanese emperor, followed by the rapid socioeconomic and political changes that occurred during the reign of the Meiji emperor from 1868 to 1912. In 1868, a coup led by disgruntled nobles toppled the enfeebled Tokugawa Shogunate that had ruled Japan since the feudal era, shifted power to the emperor, and moved the imperial court from Kyoto to Tokyo. The political revolution of 1868 vested *de jure* sovereignty in the emperor, but *de facto* power was wielded by the *genro,* an oligarchy of nobles and former samurai. The new Meiji government governed a militarily weak and economically backward nation threatened by Western encroachment, and under the banner of *fukoku Kyohei*—a rich nation, and a strong military—embarked on a series of reforms that radically transformed and modernized Japanese society.

The Meiji government abolished feudalism, made large investments in modern infrastructure and industries, and introduced a national education system. The government dispatched Japanese students overseas to study the latest aspects of Western science and technology, and foreign experts were hired to teach in Japan. Military modernization was a key goal of the Meiji government, and a conscript national army based on the Prussian model and a modern navy based on the British Royal Navy were established. In 1877, the government used the army, trained in modern European infantry tactics and equipped with the latest weaponry, to quell the Satsuma Rebellion and destroy the last vestige of Samurai resistance to the Meiji reforms. The Meiji Constitution, based on the Prussian constitution, was drafted by Hirobumi Itō and adopted in 1889. Elections for the first diet were held in 1890, but suffrage was limited to the wealthiest 1 percent of the population. In the later Meiji period, Japan triumphed in the **Sino-Japanese War** and **Russo-Japanese War,** negotiated an alliance with Britain, and abolished the unequal treaties with the Western powers. By the end of the Meiji period, Japan was counted among the ranks of the Great Powers. *See also* Anglo-Japanese Alliance; Chrysanthemum Throne; Japanese Empire.

FURTHER READING: Beasley, William G. *The Meiji Restoration.* Stanford, CA: Stanford University Press, 1972; Jansen, Marius, ed. *The Emergence of Meiji Japan.* New York: Cambridge University Press, 1995; Jansen, Marius. *The Making of Modern Japan.* Cambridge, MA: Belknap Press of Harvard University Press, 2002.

ADRIAN U-JIN ANG

Melville, Henry Dundas, First Viscount (1742–1811)

Henry Dundas, Viscount Melville, was a major architect of British naval and **India** policy. Dundas was the Scottish lieutenant of his close friend William **Pitt** the

Younger, and as first lord of the admiralty in Pitt's last administration has been credited with creating the fleet that won the Battle of **Trafalgar.** Dundas initially made his name as a legal reformer in Scotland and a supporter of Lord North in London. He was one of the earliest to back Pitt as an alternative to the unworkable 1783 coalition of North and Charles James **Fox.** The American war of 1775–1783 had convinced Dundas that Britain should aim at an empire of trade rather than settlement, it being his view that colonies of emigrants would inevitably seek independence. He applied these insights in Pitt's 1784 India bill, which discouraged Britons from settling permanently in India and also strengthened the control of the ministry over the East India Company; Dundas duly became the first president of the board of control on that office's creation in 1793.

On the creation of the office of secretary of state for war and colonies in 1794, Dundas took that post. He was throughout the 1790s a staunch advocate of a naval, imperial, and economic war against the French, as opposed to campaigns on the European continent. He left office on Pitt's resignation in 1801, but returned, again under Pitt, as first lord of the admiralty in 1804. There he energetically organized the building of ships of the line. The closing stages of his career were marred by a corruption scandal, which resulted in his having the dubious distinction of being the last British minister to have been impeached by the House of Commons, although he was acquitted in the House of Lords. *See also* East India Companies; Royal Navy.

FURTHER READING: Ehrman, John. *The Younger Pitt.* 3 vols. Stanford, CA: Stanford University Press, 1996; Fry, Michael. *The Dundas Despotism.* Edinburgh: John Donald Publishers 1972; Marshall, P. J. *Problems of Empire: Britain and India, 1757–1813.* London: Allen and Unwin, 1968; Rodger, N.A.M. *The Command of the Ocean.* New York: W. W. Norton, 2004.

MARK F. PROUDMAN

Menelik II, Emperor of Ethiopia (1844–1913)

The Ethiopian emperor who secured Ethiopian independence in the midst of the scramble for **Africa** by defeating Italian colonial aspirations at the Battle of **Adowa.** Menelik began his political career in 1865 by ousting a usurper and reclaiming his birthright as king of Shewa, one of the many semi-independent kingdoms in central **Ethiopia.** Over the next 15 years he concentrated on consolidating his position while simultaneously strengthening his claim to the imperial throne by negotiating with European powers, many of whom sold him modern weaponry for use in annexing neighboring kingdoms and safeguarding important trade routes.

Upon the death of Johann IV in 1889, Menelik declared himself emperor and signed the Treaty of Wachali recognizing Italian claims to **Eritrea.** Menelik met **Italy**'s subsequent claims that the treaty also established an Italian protectorate over Ethiopia with vigorous denials and, in 1896, a crushing military defeat at Adowa that guaranteed Ethiopia's continued independence. He spent the remainder of his reign working to suppress the slave trade and modernize Ethiopia via the construction of railroads, telephone lines, and the creation of a new capital at Addis Ababa. In 1909, Menelik was forced to relinquish the throne to his grandson Lij Yasu after a series of paralytic strokes left him incapacitated. *See also* Abyssinia; Somaliland.

FURTHER READING: Darkway, R.H.K. *Shewa, Menelik, and the Ethiopian Empire.* London: Heinemann, 1975; Henze, Paul B. *Layers of Time: A History of Ethiopia.* New York: Palgrave, 2000; Marcus, Harold G. *The Life and Times of Menelik II: Ethiopia, 1844–1913.* Oxford: Oxford University Press, 1975.

KENNETH J. OROSZ

Mensheviks

A faction of Russian Social Democrats that emerged during the Social Democrats' 1903 London conference, the result of bitter clashes over questions of organization and policy. The leader of the Menshevik faction was Julius Martov, who favored a broad conception of the party, open to all who accepted Karl **Marx**'s principles. In opposition, Vladimir **Lenin** stressed that the revolutionary party should be a secret, disciplined, hierarchical organization. During this conference the infamous names **Bolshevik** (from the Russian, *bol'she,* meaning larger) and Menshevik (from *men'she,* or smaller) emerged. These two factions never reconciled their views and thereafter developed sharply different organizations, programs, and expectations for a future revolution. In 1917, the Mensheviks opposed Lenin's plan to violently overthrow the Provisional Government; later, many joined the counter-revolutionary Whites in the Civil War of 1918–1921. After 1921, many Mensheviks were arrested and exiled, and under Stalin many were imprisoned and executed. *See also* Russian Empire.

FURTHER READING: Ascher, Abraham, ed. *Mensheviks in the Russian Revolution.* Ithaca, NY: Cornell University Press, 1976; Basil, John. *The Mensheviks in the Revolution of 1917.* Columbus, OH: Slavica Publishers, 1984; Haimson, Leopold, ed. *The Mensheviks: From the Revolution of 1917 to the Second World War.* Chicago: University of Chicago Press, 1974.

LEE A. FARROW

Mercantilism

A set of principles and assumptions prevalent during in the development of European capitalism between 1500 and 1800, according to which national governments regarded competition for access to and distribution of wealth as a prime responsibility of the state. The supporters of mercantilist policy were generally less concerned with articulating a systematic economic theory than with enhancing national power and prosperity, a project they customarily assumed to be in large part predatory and therefore requiring a concentration of military and financial power. Because mercantilists also commonly held that the available wealth and trade available globally was fixed, they favored the acquisition of overseas colonies as a vital interest of the state in the pursuit of raw materials for domestic industry, precious metals, inexpensive labor, and markets. This zero-sum competition for wealth logically favored the development of large merchant marine fleets, professional armies and navies along with the construction of docks, warehouses, and repair facilities both at home and at strategic locations in overseas territorial possessions.

Mercantilist policy also sought to achieve a positive balance of trade through high tariffs on the import of manufactured goods and the export of raw materials, combined with low tariffs on the import of raw materials along with an aggressive promotion of the export of finished goods. Raw materials were to be made readily and cheaply available to domestic industry, and foreign manufactures were to be kept out. Domestic industry, in other words, was to have monopolistic access to the home market while being given every advantage in exporting to foreign markets. A related phenomenon was the development of gold and silver mines in overseas colonies and the national hoarding of precious metal supplies. In the case of the Spanish Empire, monopolistic control of trade with colonies was so fanatically applied that it suffocated commerce and ultimately put Spain at a disadvantage against less restrictive competitors such as England and the Netherlands.

The argument that in fact mercantilist practice was inherently counterproductive to wealth accumulation—and antithetical in many cases to wealth creation—became the central thesis of Adam **Smith**'s *Wealth of Nations*. With the nineteenth-century embrace of the **free trade** principle, despite the slower application of free trade practice, mercantilism acquired a pejorative association with absolutist regimes in an increasingly liberal age. The return of protectionism in the late nineteenth century, however, occasioned a revival of the mercantilist spirit and the popularity of economists such as Friedrich **List** in the newly created **German Empire.** At the same time intensified imperial competition among the European powers for territory in Africa in the last quarter of the century had an unmistakable mercantilist flavor. *See also* East India Companies; Navalism.

FURTHER READING: Clough, Shepard, and Charles Cole. *Economic History of Europe*. Boston: Heath, 1952; Heckscher, Eli F. *Mercantilism*. Translated by Mendel Shapiro London: Allen & Unwin, 1955; Horrocks, John Wesley. *A Short History of Mercantilism*. London: Methuen & Co., 1925; Thomas, Parakunnel Joseph. *Mercantilism and East India Trade*. New York: A. M. Kelly, 1965.

CARL CAVANAGH HODGE

Metternich, Prince Klemens Wenzel Nepomuk Lothar, Fürst von (1773–1859)

One of the greatest statesmen of the nineteenth century, Prince Metternich was born in the Rhineland but entered the Austrian diplomatic service and served at The Hague, Dresden, Berlin from 1803 to 1806, and Paris from 1806 to 1809, where he became well acquainted with Napoleon **Bonaparte.** He was instrumental in persuading Emperor Francis I to open hostilities with France in 1809, notwithstanding Austria's defeat in the Austerlitz campaign only four years earlier. After the defeat of Archduke Charles at Wagram in July, Metternich replaced Count Stadion at the Foreign Ministry on October 8 and negotiated the Treaty of **Schönbrunn,** by which Austria ceded substantial territory to France and her allies. Between 1809 and 1813, a period in which Austria acted as a nominal ally of France, Metternich helped arrange the marriage between Napoleon and the emperor's daughter, Marie Louise. Metternich maintained amicable relations with France while the Habsburg Empire built up its forces and finances, expanding the army beyond the limits set by Schönbrunn. He also arranged for Austria to supply a contingent of troops for Napoleon's invasion of Russia in 1812, although by secretly informing

Tsar Alexander that Austrian participation constituting nothing more than lip service to the French, Metternich understood the advantage of keeping Austria's options open.

When Napoleon's fortunes waned as a consequence of the retreat from Moscow, Metternich withdrew Count Schwarzenberg's forces from the alliance in February 1813 and sought a general negotiated peace. After an interview with Napoleon in Dresden on June 26, at which time Metternich secured an armistice between the two sides, he became convinced that Austria should throw in her lot with the Allies. Austria formerly entered the war in August in alliance with Russia and Prussia, although unlike the latter, he did not appeal to the nationalist instincts of his people for fear of sparking off separatist movements within the multiethnic **Habsburg Empire.**

Never on good terms with **Alexander I,** Metternich enjoyed good relations with the British foreign secretary, Lord **Castlereagh,** with whom he regularly conferred from January 1814. As the Allied armies crossed the Rhine and France appeared destined to be vanquished, Metternich sought to establish a postwar settlement in which France—with or without Napoleon in power—might serve as a counterweight to the growing power of Russia, as well as to Austria's traditional rival, Prussia. In conjunction with Castlereagh, Metternich is regarded as the architect of the settlement reached in 1815 at the Congress of **Vienna,** where his adept diplomacy averted war between Russia and Prussia through compromise over the fates of Poland and Saxony. He secured territorial gains for Austria, particularly in northern Italy, and extended Habsburg influence into the new German Federation. He also brought Austria into the Holy Alliance with Russia and Prussia. Metternich's principal long-term policy, influenced by his anticonstitutional, reactionary position, was to maintain the status quo of the restored monarchies through the cooperation of the Great Powers, particularly in combating resurgent revolutionary movements. Ironically, he was forced from office on March 13, 1848, by the revolution that broke out in Vienna in that year. *See also* Balance of Power; Congress System; Holy Alliance; Liberation, War of.

FURTHER READING: Kissinger, Henry. *A World Restored: Metternich, Castlereagh and the Problems of Peace, 1812–1822.* London: Weidenfeld & Nicolson, 1957; Milne, Andrew. *Metternich.* Totowa, NJ: Rowman and Littlefield, 1975; Palmer, Alan. *Metternich.* New York: Harper & Row, 1972; Schwarz, Henry Frederick. *Metternich, the "Coachman of Europe": Statesman or Evil Genius?* Boston: Heath, 1962.

GREGORY FREMONT-BARNES

Mexican-American War (1846–1848)

A war in which **Mexico** ceded the present-day area from **Texas** to **California** to the **United States,** establishing the boundary between the two nations at the Rio Grande River and extending the United States "from sea to shining sea." Conflict over Texas and the American President James Polk's expansionist politics precipitated hostilities on April 25, 1846. When both nations signed the Treaty of **Guadalupe Hidalgo** on February 2, 1848, the United States fulfilled its self-proclaimed **Manifest Destiny** to expand westward.

Polk won the presidency on an expansionist platform in 1845, leading to the annexation of then independent Texas. As Texas became the 15th slave state, an infuriated Mexican government broke diplomatic relations with the United States; Mexico never recognized its former territory's independence. In response, Polk incurred further ire by sending an envoy to Mexico City with an offer to settle Texas's disputed lower boundary at the Rio Grande and purchase Mexico's territories to the west. When the government refused to negotiate, Polk ordered General Zachary Taylor to advance his troops through the disputed area to the Rio Grande.

Mexican cavalry, considering this an act of aggression, attacked an American patrol on April 25. Congress declared war on May 13, 1846. Polk argued that Mexico had shed "American blood on American soil." Taylor proceeded to push southwest into Mexico along the Rio Grande to defeat troops at Palo Alto, Resaca de la Palma, and Monterrey and in February 1847, at Buena Vista against Mexican hero General Antonio Lopez de Santa Anna. A second force under General Stephen W. Kearney seized New Mexico and occupied California by January 1847. Finally, General Winfield Scott led an army from the coast to Mexico City, where he defeated Santa Anna in September 1847. Mexico ceded more than 500,000 square miles to the United States for $15 million and $3.25 million in American claims against the government. The United States became a continental power with vast natural resources and access to newly discovered gold in California.

Territorial expansion had its costs. Approximately 13,000 Americans and 50,000 Mexicans died during the war, most from disease rather than bullets or bayonets. The conflict lasted much longer than expected, costing the United States close to $75 million. The war bitterly divided Americans along sectional lines; discredited many of the moderate voices who had previously held sway; contributed mightily to the breakdown of the two-party system; and helped bring about the **American Civil War,** which claimed in excess of 600,000 lives.

FURTHER READING: Bergeron, Paul H. *The Presidency of James K. Polk.* Lawrence: University of Kansas Press, 1987; Pletcher, David M. *The Diplomacy of Annexation: Texas, Oregon and the Mexican War.* Columbia: University of Missouri Press, 1973; Weinberg, Albert I. *Manifest Destiny: A Study of Nationalist Expansionism in American History.* Baltimore: The Johns Hopkins University Press, 1935.

JOHN FAITHFUL HAMER

Mexico

Mexico was a constitutional monarchy immediately after securing independence from Spain in 1821, a federal republic after 1824, and a country without durable peace until after 1867. Home to the Olmec and Mayan civilizations until the ninth century, present-day Mexico was largely conquered by the Aztec Empire in the fourteenth century. The next wave of conquest, from Spain, had destroyed Aztec power by the mid-1520s, but full Spanish control was not accomplished until 1600. Spanish rule in Mexico was oppressive and occasioned many rebellions, but all were easily defeated until Spain itself became the object of Napoleonic conquest in the **Peninsular War.** A series of revolts—starting with the peasant and Indian rising led by Hidalgo y Costilla, 1810–1811, and succeeded by that of Jose Maria Morelos y Pavón, 1811–1815—prompted limited reforms from Spain; but the critical breakthrough to independence came from a rival of Morelos, Augustín de Iturbide, who, in 1822, proposed a Mexican monarchy separate from the Spanish throne. Iturbide and the throne were then replaced in 1824 by the proclamation of a republic with Guadalupe Victoria as its first president.

After General Antonio López de Santa Anna championed the defeat of Spanish forces attempting to reconquer Mexico in 1825, he was able to translate popular appeal into the capture of the presidency in 1833. He also revoked the federal constitution and in 1836 faced a rebellion in **Texas,** which led to that territory's independence from Mexico and his loss of the presidency after Santa Anna's army lost the Battle of San Jacinto River on April 21. Santa Anna returned to the presidency again in 1841 and 1846, on the latter occasion seizing control of the army and leading it and his country to a humiliating defeat in the **Mexican-American War.** Even then Santa Anna was able to return to power in 1853 before the liberal revolution of 1855 finally rid Mexico of him for good. Unable to fade away entirely, Santa Anna was involved in the ensuing civil war and the French intervention that led to the farcical empire of **Maximilian** in 1863.

With the restoration of the republic in 1867, Mexico embarked on a period of comparative peace and economic progress, most notably under the *de facto* dictatorship of Porfirio Díaz between 1876 and 1911. The period following Díaz's ouster took Mexico into a new phase of revolution combined with punitive expeditions by the **United States** into its territory in retaliation for incidents along the border. *See also* California; Manifest Destiny.

FURTHER READING: Bazant, Jan. *A Concise History of Mexico, from Hidalgo to Cárdenas, 1805–1940.* New York: Cambridge University Press, 1977; Callcott, Wilfrid Hardy. *Santa Anna: The Story of an Enigma Who Was Once Mexico.* Hamden, CT: Archon, 1964; Cheetham, Nicolas. *History of Mexico.* New York: Crowell, 1971.

CARL CAVANAGH HODGE

Michelet, Jules (1798–1874)

One of France's foremost nineteenth-century historians, Jules Michelet was born in Paris less than a decade after the French Revolution. Michelet worked from a young age in his father's print shop; however, in 1817, he passed the *baccalauréat* with high honors. He then held a variety of teaching positions until 1822, when he was appointed specifically to teach history—only recently added to the curriculum, and still viewed with suspicion by the government—at the Collège Sainte-Barbe. In 1827, Michelet was invited to teach philosophy and history at the École Normale and later became keeper of the national historical archives from 1831 to 1852 and held a Chair at the Collège de France from 1838 to 1851.

Michelet came to believe that the study of world history revealed a progressive movement from enslavement to liberty and that France had a crucial role to play in the next phase of world history—the unification of humanity. Hence, he sought to acquaint himself with every possible detail of France's past. In doing so, he produced a vast body of historical work. His massive *History of France* was published in 17 volumes between 1833 and 1869. His *History of the French Revolution*—1847–1853, seven volumes—and *History of the Nineteenth Century*—1872–1874, three volumes—were also written on a grand scale and in a florid, literary style.

Michelet eventually came to see the French Revolution as the moment when nations, and France in particular, attained the final stage of self-consciousness. His glowing patriotism and intense sense of what it meant to be French, combined with a strong current of enlightenment universalism, meant that he came to view France as "the brilliant culmination of universal history." As he recalled in retrospect, "I arrived both through logic and through history at the same conclusion: that my glorious motherland is henceforth the pilot of the vessel of humanity." He believed that these views were justifiable because France had built its identity on the principles of liberty, equality, and fraternity. The popularity of Michelet's work waned sharply after his death, but it was extremely well received during his lifetime and inspired in many significant public figures both patriotism and a belief in the unique mission of France to disseminate the values of the revolution abroad. *See also Mission Civilisatrice.*

FURTHER READING: Kippur, S. A. *Jules Michelet, a Study of Mind and Sensibility.* New York: State University of New York Press, 1981.

PAUL LAWRENCE

Mickiewicz, Adam Bernard (1798–1855)

Renowned Polish nationalist poet, born to a *szlachta* (noble) family in the Lithuanian province of the **Russian Empire.** During his studies at the University of Vilnius in the 1820s, Mickiewicz became involved in a secret circle that agitated for Polish-Lithuanian freedom from tsarist rule. In 1823, Mickiewicz was arrested for his political engagement and was banished to Central Russia. Tsarist supervision was loose, however, and in 1825 Mickiewicz visited the Crimea, which inspired a collection of sonnets, the so-called Crimean Sonnets. Three years later he published the narrative poem "Konrad Wallenrod," which glorified the fights of the Lithuanians against the Teutonic Knights in the Middle Ages. The poem was an indirect attack on any foreign rule over **Poland**-Lithuania and therefore also of Russian rule. It escaped the Russian censors who allowed the publication. There was much pathos in Mickiewicz's poems, especially in "Pan Tadeusz," which described his homeland, Lithuania, on the eve of Napoleon's intervention into Russia in 1812.

During the 1830s, Mickiewicz traveled to Germany, **Italy,** and France. In 1840, he was honored to be appointed to the newly founded chair of Slavonic languages and literature in the College de France in Paris. Mickiewicz's thinking was deeply influenced by the mystical philosopher Andrzej Towianski. Religious mysticism and patriotic feeling characterized lyrics that had an influential impact on the Polish national movement in the nineteenth century. During the **Crimean War** of 1853, the poet went to Constantinople to form a Polish regiment fighting against the Russians. Two years later, Mickiewicz suddenly died of cholera.

FURTHER READING: Debska, Anita. *Country of the Mind: An Introduction to the Poetry of Adam Mickiewicz.* Warsaw: Burchard Edition, 2000.

EVA-MARIA STOLBERG

Militarism

Militarism is an excessive influence of military over civil institutions in the political realm, customarily combined with the popularization of military virtues in the social sphere. The term became a common pejorative in Europe during the late nineteenth century, usually in criticism of the increasing attention given to military demands and considerations among the priorities of national governments. In the last quarter of the century in particular, critics could point to the sheer ubiquity of the military in the maintenance, by large and small states alike, of heavier armaments and greater land and sea forces than ever before. The public acceptance of such forces as essential to national defense—partly in light of the scale of European conflict during the **Napoleonic Wars** at the beginning of the nineteenth century, partly due to a perceived need to protect overseas commerce and colonies at its end—afforded the military class enormous social prestige in the high summer of nationalist patriotism in the decades leading to World War I.

Viewed from this perspective, the father of nineteenth-century militarism was Bonaparte, both in his conception of war as a clash of whole peoples rather than professional armies and equally through Napoleonic France's intoxication with the martial spirit. Among the nations most traumatized by Napoleonic conquest, **Prussia** produced not only Clausewitz but also a *Junker* military class at the head of an army that under Otto von **Bismarck** united the German states by force. It is no exaggeration to say that, between the victory of 1871 that created a **German Empire** and the war of 1914, which destroyed it, the army was for many Germans the quintessence of national virtues. It was a society, the novelist Theodore Fontane noted, in which it was hardly possible to turn a corner without bumping into a uniform. Indeed, the militarization of society so ubiquitous in Germany was also evident in the other European powers. Monarchs and their families appeared in public, whenever possible in military dress and wherever possible to review columns of troops. An awed public meanwhile embraced military values of discipline, self-sacrifice, and physical courage—along with the acceptance of the inevitability of major armed conflict as a test of personal and national character. *See also* Jingoism; Navalism; Social Darwinism; War Studies.

FURTHER READING: Berghahn, Volker R. *Militarism: The History of an International Debate, 1861–1979.* Leamington Spa: Berg, 1981; Craig, Gordon. *The Politics of the Prussian Army, 1640–1945.* New York: Oxford University Press, 1955; Howard, Michael. *War in European Society.* New York: Oxford University Press, 1976; Vagts, Alfred. *A History of Militarism.* New York: Meridian, 1959.

CARL CAVANAGH HODGE

Military Conversations (1906–1914)

Anglo-French military staff discussions of 1905 to 1914, subsequent to the Entente Cordiale of 1904. They were originally authorized by the faltering Tory government of A. J. **Balfour,** but received their most significant impetus from Edward **Grey,** foreign secretary in the new Liberal government of 1905. Grey, a Liberal Imperialist with a comparatively realist view of international relations, kept the conversations secret from his more radical cabinet colleagues. The conversations discussed the deployment of a relatively small—by continental standards—British expeditionary force of about half a dozen divisions to operate against potential German invaders in cooperation with the French Army.

Conversations continued over a number of years, but assumed renewed seriousness after the 1911 **Agadir** crisis. The conversations were conducted under the explicit conditions that no British commitment was implied; nevertheless they acclimatized the British command structure, including both the military and senior ministers, to thinking of themselves as French allies. The military conversations were a significant part of the increasing division of the major powers into two hostile blocs in the years before 1914. *See also* Entente Cordiale; July Crisis.

FURTHER READING: Herrmann, David G. *The Arming of Europe and the Making of the First World War.* Princeton, NJ: Princeton University Press, 1996; Keegan, John. *The First World War.* London: Hutchinson, 1998.

MARK F. PROUDMAN

Mill, John Stuart (1806–1873)

The preeminent intellectual of Victorian Britain and the central philosopher of nineteenth-century **liberalism.** Brought up according to the educational theories of his father James Mill, a follower of Jeremy **Bentham,** and also a prominent philosopher, historian of British India, and political theorist, Mill famously mastered Greek at three and was functioning as his father's editorial assistant by early adolescence. Mill had a famous mental breakdown, recounted in his *Autobiography,* occasioned by Macaulay's *Essay on Government* of 1829, which led him to question the more dogmatic aspects of his father's worldview. Mill's friendships ran across political boundaries and included at one point Carlyle and many other key figures. His political journalism in the 1830s was radical in the sense of being rationalist and opposed to aristocratic privilege. In imperial affairs, he was a fierce opponent of slavery and supported Canadian self-government. Mill's *Principles of Political Economy* of 1848 became the standard text of classical political economy, although, in contrast to the dogmatically anti-interventionist beliefs of most mid-Victorian liberals, it allowed a surprisingly wide scope for governmental intervention in the economy.

Mill's economic views moved leftwards throughout his career. The posthumously published "Chapters on Socialism" reflected an increasing self-identification as a socialist, although that term indicated more of a disposition to see society whole than a commitment to a specific program. One area in which he early supported government economic intervention was in the encouragement of state-assisted emigration to settler colonies. In 1851, he married Harriet Taylor, widow of a Unitarian businessman. Before their marriage, gossip of an illicit affair between Mill and Taylor led Mill increasingly to isolate himself from society. In 1859, he published what is possibly his most famous work, the small book *On Liberty,* advancing the radically libertarian principle that society may interfere with a person's liberty only to prevent harm to others, but then retreating from its more extreme implications by showing the scope of human connections. Mill's primary work of political philosophy was the *Representative Government* of 1861; it was an argument for active citizenship and made the case for a franchise that was at once wide and based on active involvement in the community. Mill was briefly member of Parliament for Westminster from 1866 to 1868, but practical politics did not suit him, and he was not reelected in part because of his high-minded refusal to campaign or to incur election expenses.

During his time in Parliament, he supported the passage of the second reform bill, although his attempt to extend the franchise to women was greeted with laughter; it was a position he later defended in *The Subjection of Women* of 1869. Mill led the **Jamaica** committee that protested the violent reaction of Governor Eyre to native disturbances; humanitarian causes were a consistent feature of his career and advocacy; however, Mill's relationship to imperialism was ambiguous. As chief examiner in the East India Company, in succession to his father, he defended the company's activities, and he resented its abolition following the **Indian mutiny.** He could be authoritarian in his attitudes, declaring in the *Liberty*, that peoples not capable of self-government needed, "an Akbar or a Charlemagne, if they are so fortunate as to find one." And yet, on specific issues, at least outside India, he almost invariably supported colonial self-government, emancipation, and opposed military intervention, the 1867 **Abyssinian** expedition being a rare exception to the latter. His primary importance, from the point of view of empire, must remain his anticoercive and rationalist liberalism. *See also* East India Companies.

FURTHER READING: Mill, John Stuart. *Collected Works.* Edited by J. M. Robson et al. 33 vols. Toronto: University of Toronto Press, 1963–1991; Ryan, Alan. *The Philosophy of John Stuart Mill.* London: Macmillan, 1970.

MARK F. PROUDMAN

Milner, Alfred, Viscount Milner (1854–1925)

Governor of the **Cape Colony** and high commissioner for other British South African colonies during the **Boer War** of 1899–1902, and subsequently secretary of war during the closing months of World War I. Milner was educated at Balliol College, Oxford, where he fell under the influence of the social reformer Arnold Toynbee. Milner began his political career as a liberal and always had an interest in social reform and a conviction of the power of intelligent leaders to act for good. He served as private secretary to the Liberal Unionist G. J. Goschen while the latter was Chancellor of the Exchequer in the government of Lord Salisbury. In 1889, he went to **Egypt** to work in a financial capacity under Lord Cromer; this marked the beginning of his career as an imperial proconsul.

Appointed high commissioner in South Africa in 1897, he negotiated with the Transvaal President Paul Kruger over the contentious issue of the rights of British subjects—most of them miners and entrepreneurs—in the Afrikaner republics. Milner's high-handed manner played a role in the failure of the Bloemfontein negotiations of 1899, and the subsequent Afrikaner ultimatum, which led to war. After the conquest of the Transvaal and the Orange River colony, Milner attempted to organize the political system of the united South Africa created by the war so as to give a predominant role to British and Anglophone settlers, under the guidance of his own Oxbridge-educated elite, sometimes referred in sarcastic allusion to Plato as "guardians." In this he failed, and by the time of his 1906 recall it was clear that South Africa's political future would be dominated by the Afrikaners. Opposition to Irish Home Rule led Milner into cooperation with the Tories, and it was with their support that he was brought into David **Lloyd George**'s cabinet in 1916. He had much to do with appointment of Marshal Foch as allied generalissimo in the crisis caused by the German offensive of the spring of 1918, and was subsequently appointed to the War Office. After the war, he served briefly as colonial secretary and died in 1925. Milner is remembered, not inaccurately, as the prototype of an overly imperious pro-consul. *See also* Chamberlain, Joseph.

FURTHER READING: Gollin, A. M. *Proconsul in Politics: A Study of Lord Milner in Opposition and Power.* London: MacMillan, 1963; Milner, Alfred. *Constructive Imperialism.* London: National Review, 1908; Packenham, Thomas. *The Boer War.* New York: Random House, 1979.

MARK F. PROUDMAN

Miranda, Francisco de (1750–1816)

A Venezuelan revolutionary known as "the Precursor" of Spanish-American independence who took part in three great political events: The American Revolution, the French Revolution, and the South American wars of emancipation from Spanish rule. Miranda was born in Caracas on March 28, 1750. His father, an immigrant from the Canary Islands, was a successful businessman. The colonial Miranda encountered prejudice from higher-status Iberian-born elites, who under the Spanish Bourbons enjoyed political and social privileges in Spain's overseas empire. After attending university, Miranda sailed to Spain to purchase a commission in the Spanish Army, with whom he served in North Africa. In 1780, after a treaty with France brought Spain into the American Revolution, Miranda sailed to Cuba in a Spanish expedition that cooperated with the French in attacking English colonies in the West Indies. Accused of misuse of funds in 1783, he fled to the United States, where he met many of the leaders of the American Revolution, including George **Washington.**

Encouraged by the American Revolution, Miranda advocated Spanish-American independence. In 1785, he returned to Europe and under the relentless surveillance of Spanish agents traveled widely in an attempt to solicit funds. Many European leaders and aristocrats became Miranda's patrons, including the Empress Catherine the Great, whom Miranda visited in Russia in February 1787. In France in 1792, Miranda joined the French Revolution and in September became a lieutenant general in the French Army, fighting with Charles-François Dumouriez's forces, known as the Army of the North, which battled Prussians and Austrians near the Belgian border. Consequently, Miranda's name was inscribed in the Arc de Triomphe in Paris. Maximilien Robespierre and the radical Jacobins distrusted Miranda, whose alignment with the revolution's moderate republican Girondist faction led to his imprisonment during Robespierre's Reign of Terror. Disillusioned with the French Revolution, Miranda left France in January 1798 for Britain, where for years he unsuccessfully urged Prime Ministers William **Pitt** and Henry Addington to fund an invasion for Spanish-American liberation.

Returning to the United States in 1805, Miranda privately raised a volunteer force of approximately 180 men to attack Venezuela. In February 1806, Miranda's mercenary soldiers left New York on board the *Leander.* For more than a month Miranda and his men took shelter in **Haiti,** which in January 1804 had become the world's first independent black republic. While there, Miranda chartered two additional U.S. schooners. Prepared for the arrival of the three vessels near Puerto Cabello in April 1806, Spanish colonial military leaders defeated Miranda and forced him to flee to the island of Aruba. On his second attempt in August 1806, Miranda captured the town of Coro, but the townspeople failed to join his uprising against the Spanish crown. Defeated again, Miranda sailed to London.

In 1808, Napoleon **Bonaparte** installed his elder brother Joseph Bonaparte on the Spanish throne after obtaining the abdication of Charles IV and his son Ferdinand VII. With French forces occupying Spain, a junta was created in Venezuela that claimed to rule on behalf of the deposed monarch, Ferdinand VII. Two years later, Miranda returned to Venezuela, which formally declared independence from Spain on July 5, 1811. Spanish loyalist forces under General Juan Domingo Monteverde, however, were too strong for Miranda and his supporters. In July 1812, Miranda signed an armistice with Monteverde and prepared to leave Venezuela. Seized by Spanish loyalists, Miranda was shipped back to Spain. He died in the prison of La Carraca in Cádiz on July 14, 1816. Venezuela won independence in federation with Colombia and Ecuador in 1821, breaking away to form a separate country in 1830. *See also* Bourbon Dynasty; Spanish Empire.

FURTHER READING: Harvey, Robert. *Liberators: Latin America's Struggle for Independence, 1810–1830.* Woodstock: Overlook Press, 2000; Nicholson, Irene. *The Liberators: A Study of Independence Movements in Spanish America.* New York: Praeger, 1969; Polanco Alcántara, Tomás. *Francisco de Miranda: Ulises, Don Juan o Don Quijote?* Caracas: Editorial Ex Libris, 1997; Racine, Karen. *Francisco de Miranda: A Transatlantic Life in the Age of Revolution.* Wilmington: Scholarly Resources, 2003.

DAVID M. CARLETTA

Missionaries

Missionaries played a major, albeit complicated and unofficial, role in the new **imperialism** of the nineteenth century. Until the 1820s, missionary activity was largely confined to existing colonial holdings in the New World, coastal regions of China, and portions of South East Asia. In Asia, obstacles to further expansion included prohibitions by the British and Dutch East India Companies on missionary activity in their holdings, lest it alienate potential trade partners and interfere with commerce. As for **Africa,** missionaries were discouraged from moving beyond existing mission fields in Portuguese Angola and Mozambique by a combination of physical danger from disease, African resistance, and opposition from practitioners of the transatlantic **slave trade** who worried about the effects that evangelical efforts would have on their operations.

The onset of the Industrial Revolution and the success of the abolitionist movement changed all that. Europe's Industrial Revolution not only estranged workers from religion, it also created a host of social problems including alcoholism, declining standards of living, and growing crime rates. Churches responded to these threats by developing temperance movements, schools, hospitals, orphanages, and urban missions to return the poor to God. As these European-based mission societies took shape, their members began talking about the need to expand their efforts and evangelize among so-called heathen populations elsewhere in the world. These calls gained additional impetus from the abolitionist movement, which highlighted the horrors of slavery and the transatlantic slave trade. When the East India Company's charter was amended in 1813 to allow missionary activity in **India,** the floodgates opened and missionaries rushed out to both Asia and Africa. By the early nineteenth century, Protestant missions from the United States and various European nations were active in Africa, Asia, and the Pacific. Catholics, on the other hand, were still reeling from the effects of the French Revolution and the dissolution of the Jesuit order and therefore preferred to concentrate the bulk of their efforts until the 1870s on winning people back to the faith in Europe. Thereafter interdenominational rivalries ensured that Catholic missionaries flocked to new mission fields around the world in an effort to make up for lost time.

Once in place, missionaries like David **Livingstone** helped promote interest in potential colonial areas through their work as explorers. Others helped pioneer ethnography and anthropology by studying and writing up their observations of indigenous cultures and societies. In the process, these early scholars made European business concerns aware of the commercial possibilities of colonial possessions. Missionaries soon joined business leaders in creating powerful colonial lobbying groups that pressured European parliaments to take on new colonies, arguing that only European rule could provide the necessary political stability that would enable both evangelical and commercial activities to flourish. For example, missionaries, merchants, and land speculators successfully joined forces and induced the British government to assume formal control over **New Zealand** in 1840. As French participation in the Second Opium War and their invasion of **Indochina** illustrates, the need to protect missionaries from indigenous peoples could also lead to additional colonial expansion. Once the late nineteenth century scrambles for territory began, missionaries not only cheered on Europe's acquisitions in the belief they would facilitate evangelical work by providing political stability, some also actively facilitated colonial expansion by serving as translators during negotiations with interior peoples. The most notorious and controversial example concerns efforts by Cecil **Rhodes**'s British South Africa Company to secure mineral rights from Lobengula, king of the Ndbele in what is now Zimbabwe. Although Charles Helm, a member of the London Missionary Society, attested to having fully translated and explained the details of the negotiations leading up to the October 1888 Rudd Concession, Lobengula's subsequent repudiation of the agreement on the grounds that it was inaccurate gave rise to allegations that Helm deliberately mistranslated the document to facilitate a British takeover of Lobengula's lands.

Regardless of their location, missionaries played an active role in shaping and carrying out the New Imperialism's so-called "civilizing mission." Christian missions used the pulpit, schools, and hospitals to spread their religious message and teach the indigenous peoples about Western civilization and cultural norms. For example, missions argued against polygamy, polytheism, initiation rites, and secret societies, while simultaneously extolling the virtues of literacy, science, Christian morality, and Western notions of child rearing. Missionary societies also paid their own way by creating trading companies, workshops, and school gardens that were designed to generate working capital and teach Western notions of discipline and a European work ethic. Although Protestant missionaries were more likely than their Catholic counterparts to make regular use of local languages in churches and schools, all missions played a role in aiding the spread of European languages through colonized areas by offering at least some foreign language classes in their schools.

In addition to aiding the importation of European languages to colonized areas, missionaries also helped spread European gender norms as part of the civilizing mission. As products of their times, the governing boards of most missionary societies found it difficult to overcome Victorian notions about the frailty of women, their suitability for work outside the home, and the dangers of exposing them to unsupervised attention from natives and male missionaries alike. Nevertheless, most mission societies concluded that some female missionaries were a necessity if they were to successfully reach native women whose own societies and cultures often placed them out of reach of male missionaries. This was especially important given the prevailing wisdom that converting native women ensured future generations of converts as mothers passed on their beliefs to their children. As a result, missions recruited men and married couples most heavily, but they also turned to single women when necessary to reach as many potential converts as possible. Regardless of their marital status, female missionaries serving in colonies found themselves in an ambiguous position. Although they were often given more freedom to travel and work outside the home than if they had stayed in the metropole, female missionaries also faced strict limits on acceptable behavior, were expected to be obedient to heavily patriarchal mission hierarchies, and were usually confined to tasks like nursing, teaching school, and running Bible study classes.

Western women were not the only ones affected by mission work. Efforts to reach out to native women often upset the balance of indigenous societies in many different and often conflicting ways. Missionaries often held up polygamy, payment of bride price, and women's involvement in agricultural labor as examples of native backwardness. Consequently missions worked hard to abolish all three. Unfortunately, the campaign against polygamy often forced converts to abandon all but their first wives. Similarly, the combination of missionary emphasis on the notion that a woman's primary role was to be a wife and mother plus ongoing campaigns against the custom of men paying a bride price when marrying, a concept seen in the West as a form of slavery, and the fight to end the use of women as agricultural laborers undermined the value of women in many native societies, as their participation in remunerative work raising crops was no longer being acknowledged. Missions also found that their efforts to provide native women with an education, both academic and practical, often aroused protest from traditionalists in native society who openly complained that educated women upset the natural social order by becoming independent and less obedient to their husbands and fathers.

Missionary relations with European merchants, settlers, and government officials were ambivalent. In some areas, such as German **Cameroon,** Catholic missionaries were not only welcomed by merchants and government authorities, they were given active support in the form of land grants, transportation, cheap supplies, and advice. In French and Belgian colonies, however, Catholics fared less well. **Leopold II** banned them entirely from the Congo, a prohibition that lasted until 1908. The eruption of turn-of-the-century anticlerical sentiment in France led to a steady decline in relations between Catholic missionaries and colonial officials throughout the French Empire. Personality clashes and fierce interdenominational rivalries also played an intermittent role in souring official views of missionaries as the different societies engaged in a war of rhetoric, accusations and counter accusations against one another in the struggle to win the hearts and minds of indigenous peoples.

As if that were not enough, missionaries often created new problems that tarnished their reputations in the eyes of settlers, traders, and administrators alike. Not only were missionaries tainted by the whiff of having "gone native" as a product of their living in close proximity to colonized peoples, the expansion of their mission fields and their many reform campaigns sometimes provoked violent uprisings from native peoples that not only had to be put down with force but also adversely affected commerce. The **Indian Mutiny,** for example, was triggered in part by allegations that the British were actively seeking to convert Indian soldiers to Christianity. Toward the end of the nineteenth century, missionaries anxious to regain the trust of native peoples and expand the pace of their conversion efforts began championing native rights and argued against the sale of alcohol, the use of forced labor, and the expropriation of native lands. These activities often led to charges of unpatriotic behavior and earned the missionary community the enmity of the white colonial population.

Native reactions to missionaries were similarly ambivalent. Missionaries were successful in gaining real converts among colonized peoples, but many chose to take advantage of mission schools and hospitals simply in an effort to better their own circumstances and were quite astute at exploiting interdenominational rivalries to get what they wanted. In Cameroon, for example, pupils of mission schools frequently threatened to defect to rival denominations unless their demands for more academic subjects in mission school curricula were met. By the second generation of contact with missionaries, colonized peoples often chafed under restrictions placed on them by white missionaries. Disputes over leadership roles within local churches led some African congregations to split and develop into the so-called Ethiopian churches of West and South Africa. In other areas, indigenous peoples fused elements of Christianity with traditional culture and religious practices to create their own distinct religious movements. Examples include China's **Taiping Rebellion** and the proliferation of African Independent Churches.

Although missionaries continued to play an active role in colonial life through the twentieth century, their activities were seriously curtailed by the onset of the two World Wars. The export of hostilities to colonies combined with chronic shortages of manpower, supplies, and funds forced missions throughout the European colonial empires to curtail their activities. The post-1945 rise of colonial nationalism and the granting of independence to former colonies in the 1960s further complicated missionary work, as former colonies sought to shake off symbols of colonial domination. *See also* Belgian Congo; British Empire; French Empire; German Empire; *Kulturkampf; Mission Civilisatrice;* Opium Wars.

FURTHER READING: Beidelman, T. O. *Colonial Evangelism.* Bloomington: Indiana University Press, 1982; Bickers, Robert, and Rosemary Seton, eds. *Missionary Encounters: Sources and Issues.* Richmond, Surrey: Curzon, 1996; Christensen, Torben, and William R. Hutchinson, eds. *Missionary Ideologies in the Imperialist Era 1880–1920.* Copenhagen: Aros, 1982; Etherington, Norman. *Missions and Empire.* Oxford: Oxford University Press, 2005; Hastings, Adrian. *The Church in Africa: 1450–1950.* Oxford: Clarendon Press, 1994; Holtrop, Pieter, and Hugh McLeod, eds. *Missions and Missionaries.* Rochester: Boydell Press, 2000; Porter, A. N. *Religion versus Empire? British Protestant Missionaries and Overseas Expansion, 1700–1914.* Manchester: Manchester University Press, 2004; Sundkler, Bengt, and Christopher Steed. *A History of the Church in Africa.* Cambridge: Cambridge University Press, 2000.

KENNETH J. OROSZ

Mission Civilisatrice

A slogan, expressed in the coin of doctrine, of French colonialism of the late nineteenth century, initially championed by Jules **Ferry**. Its central idea was that France had a unique mission to civilize the world, which could both elevate the nation's moral character after the humiliating defeat of the **Franco-Prussian War** and enlighten non-European peoples to the superiority of French culture. Coincidentally, the *mission civilisatrice* could assimilate colonial populations and ease colonial rule while enhancing French influence abroad at a time of increased imperial competition from other European powers—advantageous collateral benefits of a high-minded policy. Behind the slogan was the notion that the colonial policy of the Third Republic ought to be qualitatively different from that of the Second Empire by appealing to the ideals of 1789. Cultural enlightenment in the colonies was to have the effect of making overseas subjects citizens of a global civilization for which secular and democratic France was the model and capital. As a colonial policy the *mission civilisatrice* had two critical shortcomings. Its ideals too often stood in grotesque contrast to the brutal reality in many of France's colonies, while forcing colonial peoples to become French usually cultivated resentment rather than a sense of elevation. *See also* White Man's Burden.

FURTHER READING: Burrows, Mathew. "Mission Civilisatrice: French Cultural Policy in the Middle East." *The Historical Journal* 29, 1 (1986): 109–135; Conklin, Alice L. *Mission to Civilize: The Republican Idea of Empire in France and West Africa, 1895–1930*. Stanford, CA: Stanford University Press, 1997.

CARL CAVANAGH HODGE

Missouri Compromise (1820)

The legislative outcome of a bitter dispute between the House and the Senate of the United States Congress over the status of new states admitted to the Union. The quarrel was a collision of two realities of early American nationhood: slavery and rapid territorial expansion. The creation of new states from the enormous territory of the **Louisiana Purchase** upset a tentative balance that had been applied hitherto in which free states and slave states were admitted alternately to the Union. Under Spanish and then French rule slavery had been legal in even the northern regions of the Louisiana Territory.

Although the Compromise of 1820 admitted Missouri as a slave state and Maine as a free state simultaneously, it also made slavery illegal in any territory north of 36°30' latitude. The constitutionality of the Missouri Compromise was struck down in 1857 by the U.S. Supreme Court over the status of a slave who had fled Missouri to live in a free state. The decision infuriated abolitionists and hastened the day when the United States would have to become, in Abraham Lincoln's words, "all one thing, or all the other." *See also* American Civil War; Manifest Destiny; Mexican-American War.

FURTHER READING: Stephanson, Anders. *Manifest Destiny: American Expansionism and the Empire of Right*. New York: Hill and Wang, 1995; Weeks, William E. *Building the Continental Empire: American Expansionism from the Revolution to the Civil War*. Chicago: Ivan R. Dee, 1997.

CARL CAVANAGH HODGE

Mobilization Crisis

See July Crisis

Moldavia

See Danubian Principalities

Moltke, Helmuth von (1800–1891)

Helmuth von Moltke was a Prussian strategist and military modernizer. On graduation from the Military Academy of Denmark, Moltke entered the Danish service, but in 1822, he joined the Prussian army. He was seconded to Turkey as a military adviser between 1835 and 1839. In 1857 he became chief of the Prussian General Staff. Moltke advocated a system in which officers would be able to coordinate their units almost instinctively, without the need for specific orders. His idea was decentralization of command structure to achieve greater concentration of forces on the battlefield. This would allow movement in separated columns, leading to coordination for a decisive strike. By exploiting **railway** transportation and **telegraph** communication, Moltke hoped to bring greater numbers of troops to bear at crucial junctures.

Moltke attempted to implement such a system in the **Schleswig-Holstein War** of 1864, but his directives were ignored. The **Austro-Prussian War** in 1866, however, was different. Moltke was permitted both to plan and direct the action. The Prussian army entered Austria in three columns. They converged on the enemy at **Königgrätz** on July 3, thereby securing victory. When a war with France became imminent in 1870, no one argued with Moltke's plan for the campaign. Moltke correctly estimated that the French would concentrate their forces in two areas and that the Prussians should drive one great wedge between these concentrations, destroying first one and then the other before they could join together. The first French army was engaged in two great battles. The second French army was encircled at **Sedan** and had to surrender. Victory in the **Franco-Prussian War** was thus his greatest professional triumph. Taken together, Moltke's victories paved the way to the establishment of a unified **German Empire.** Wilhelm I made him a count, promoted him to field marshal, and made him the first chief of the German general staff. Moltke resigned in 1888, having grown deeply distressed over the influence of the belligerent clique that surrounded **Wilhelm II.** In 1890, Moltke warned that when a war broke out, its result would be incalculable.

As the architect of the modern German general staff, Moltke was a preeminent military innovator. For him, military **strategy** had to be understood as a system of options. He gave his subordinates liberty in making decisions, because he believed that no battle plan could survive contact with the enemy and that his military successes were due to the elasticity of his strategy. *See also* Bismarck, Otto von; German Empire; Wilhelm I.

FURTHER READING: Bucholz, Arden. *Moltke, Schlieffen, and Prussian War Planning.* New York: St. Martin's, 1991; Citino, Robert M. *The German Way of War.* Lawrence: University of Kansas Press, 2005; Morris, William O. *Moltke: A Biographical and Critical Study.* New York: Haskell House, 1971.

MARTIN MOLL

Moltke, Helmuth Johannes Ludwig von (1848–1916)

Known as "The Younger," Helmuth von Moltke was a Prussian general, chief of the German general staff from 1906 to 1914, and nephew of the victorious General Field Marshal Helmuth von **Moltke** of the German Wars of Unification. Moltke participated in the Franco-Prussian war of 1870-1871 and enjoyed a military career that benefited from his uncle's support, serving as his personal adjutant until 1891, as well as from the favor of Kaiser **Wilhelm II.** He became the monarch's personal adjutant in 1891. By 1904, he had advanced to general quartermaster in the general staff, taking over as its chief from Alfred von Schlieffen in January 1906. He was the kaiser's preferred candidate, although there was concern from within the military about his suitability for this important position.

From 1906, Moltke was responsible for German war planning and the preparation of the German army for the event of war. His time in office was characterized by his frequent demands for preventive war and by his fear of Russia, a country he felt would in the near future become invincible. Like his predecessor, he had to prepare Germany for a war on two fronts, and he adjusted the so-called **Schlieffen Plan** to changing circumstances. By 1914, Germany had but one plan for the eventuality of a European war. The German army was to concentrate its efforts in the West and violate the neutrality of Luxembourg and **Belgium.**

When war broke out in August 1914, Moltke soon lost confidence. The ill-fated Battle of the Marne destroyed his war plan and led to his dismissal in favor of Erich von **Falkenhayn.** Moltke never accepted his fate and attempted intrigues against his successor to regain his influential position. Instead, he was relegated to being the deputy chief of staff in Berlin, responsible for administrative matters only.

After his death in June 1916, Moltke became a perfect scapegoat, first for the lost Battle of the Marne and, after 1918, for the lost war. Countless critics blamed him for adulterating Schlieffen's deployment plan and for not being skilled enough to lead Germany to victory. His belief in anthroposophy, shared by his wife Eliza, led to further bad press and called into question not just his wartime leadership but also his suitability for leading the general staff. This view was only partially revised from the 1930s onward, although in recent years his military skills have received more favorable estimations, but his role in the outbreak of the war now receives rather more criticism.

FURTHER READING: Citino, Robert M. *The German Way of War.* Lawrence: University of Kansas Press, 2005; Moltke, Eliza von, ed. *Helmuth von Moltke. Erinnerungen, Briefe, Dokumente, 1877–1916.* Stuttgart: Der Kommende Tag, 1922; Mombauer, Annika. *Helmuth von Moltke and the Origins of the First World War.* New York: Cambridge University Press, 2001.

ANNIKA MOMBAUER

Monroe Doctrine (1823)

A sphere-of-influence statement enunciated by and named for James **Monroe,** the fifth President of the **United States,** in his annual message of 1823. The statement was occasioned by encroachments by Russia in the northwest of North America and alarm over a possible intervention by the Quadruple Alliance—Russia, Prussia, Austria, Britain—to assist Spain in regaining her former Latin American possessions. It stated that "the American continents, by the free and independent condition which they have assumed and maintain, are henceforth not to be considered as subjects for future colonization by any European powers," and further cautioned that "we should consider any attempt on their part to extend their system to any portion of this hemisphere as dangerous to our peace and safety." Additionally, it pledged American non-interference in the "still unsettled" affairs of Europe.

In point of fact, the actual authorship of the pronouncement against European colonization and interference in the New World belongs to Secretary of State John Quincy **Adams.** James Monroe's warning did not worry the Old World unduly at the time. The continental powers had no concrete plans in November and December 1823 for reconquering the lost Spanish colonies, and British disapproval of use of force against the newly independent Latin American republics was actually more effective in cold-showering any serious thought of a European intervention.

The Monroe Doctrine was laid to rest for two decades until President James K. Polk reactivated it as a defensive measure in 1848 by proclaiming American opposition not only to colonization and reconquest by Europe, but also to any cession of territory in the Western Hemisphere to a European power. This new interpretation reflected both expansionist momentum and American uneasiness over the fate of the Western territories, which coincided with renewed European encroachments—real or imagined—in the Yucatán and the Caribbean. The doctrine had evolved into the geopolitical expression of two of the myths that most influenced U.S. foreign policy: exceptionalism and mission. It was shortly to become a national principle. Napoleon III's Mexican ambitions and **Maximilian**'s short-lived reign from 1864 to 1867, like Spain's reoccupation of Santo Domingo in 1861–1864, caused the United States to reassert the Monroe Doctrine vigorously during the Civil War years. The 1860s and 1870s saw its consolidation into diplomatic dogma first with William Seward's repeated protests against France's designs in Mexico and Spain's scheming in the Caribbean, and next with Ulysses S. Grant's and Hamilton Fish's insistence on the no-transfer principle. In later years the ever-increasing interest in an isthmian canal would lead to the gradual substitution of the Monroe Doctrine for international law in the Western Hemisphere. By 1895, the doctrine had become the affirmation of American preeminence in the New World—the outcome of the **Venezuelan Crisis** being evidence that Great Britain, despite the irritation of the Foreign Office, tacitly approved of that supremacy.

Exceptionalism and messianism finally triumphed with the proclamation and application of the **Roosevelt Corollary** to the Monroe Doctrine, which explicitly turned the Caribbean into the United States' "backyard." As a matter of fact, in his annual message of December 1904, Theodore Roosevelt enunciated not simply a corollary to the Monroe Doctrine but a wholly new diplomatic tenet: the United States was to act as policeman of the Western Hemisphere; it was to put to use the right of interference it continued to deny the European powers. Of course, U.S. interventionism had been at work in Latin America long before the 1904 pronouncement that was to legitimate it. But the great North American republic for the first time, as the 26th president was well aware, was now strong enough to monopolize interference in the New World; not only did it possess industrial and agricultural might, but it had acceded to world power status in 1898 at the close of the splendidly profitable **Spanish-American War.** This new condition called for a new diplomacy, especially in that part of the globe where the United States was pre-destined by geography to play a leading role. Monroe's doctrine had the weakness that nowhere was American preeminence clearly stated. A "corollary" was needed to remedy that omission and give the hitherto defensive dictum a markedly assertive coloration.

The catalysts for this were no other than Germany's aggressiveness in the Venezuela affair of 1902–1903 and the projected isthmian canal, which by 1904 had become a reality thanks to the controversial acquisition of the Canal Zone, for Roosevelt had "taken" **Panama** the year before. It was out of the question to tolerate more European interventions in the Caribbean; the protection of the approaches of the future waterway, the defense, in other words, of the Panamanian lifeline, demanded that the latter be turned into an American lake. Despite its toning down in 1923 and 1928 and notwithstanding its official repudiation at the 1933 and 1936 pan-American conferences, the Roosevelt Corollary to the Monroe Doctrine remained in force unofficially and continued to guide hemispheric policy in both World Wars and during the Cold War. *See also* Manifest Destiny; Russian Empire; Spanish Empire.

FURTHER READING: Collin, Richard H. *Theodore Roosevelt's Caribbean: The Panama Canal, the Monroe Doctrine, and the Latin American Context.* Baton Rouge: Louisiana State University Press, 1990; LaFeber, Walter. *The New Empire: An Interpretation of American Expansion, 1860–1898. 1963.* Ithaca, NY: Cornell University Press Paperbacks, 1987; Merk, Frederick. *The Monroe Doctrine and American Expansionism.* New York: Knopf, 1966; Perkins, Dexter. *A History of the Monroe Doctrine.* Boston: Little, Brown, 1963; Ricard, Serge. "Monroe Revisited: The Roosevelt Doctrine, 1901–1909." In Marc Chénetier and Rob Kroes, eds. *Impressions of a Guilded Age: The American Fin de Siècle.* Amsterdam: Amerika Instituut, Universiteit van Amsterdam, 1983; Smith, Gaddis. *Last Years of the Monroe Doctrine.* New York: Hill and Wang, 1994.

SERGE RICARD

Monroe, James (1758–1831)

The American statesman James Monroe was U.S. secretary of state (1811–1817), secretary of war (1814–1815), and fifth president of the **United States** (1817–1825). In his early years as a politician, Monroe joined the anti-Federalists in the Virginia Convention. He then moved on to become a United States senator in 1790. From 1794 to 1796, he served as minister to France. As envoy extraordinaire under the direction of President Thomas **Jefferson,** he helped to negotiate the **Louisiana Purchase.** Monroe was elected president of the United States in 1816 and was reelected in 1820. His presidency is labeled as "The Era of Good Feeling," mostly because partisan politics were comparatively placid.

As president, Monroe initiated negotiations with Britain leading to the **Rush-Bagot Treaty** of 1817, which demilitarized the Great Lakes and laid the groundwork for peaceful relations between the United States and British North America. In the **Anglo-American Treaty** of 1818, he then furthered the cause of pacific relations with the British Empire in the West by establishing agreement on joint claims to the Oregon Territory. Lastly Monroe rounded out the project of formal territorial consolidation by settling with Spain the control of East Florida and delineating the border between Mexico and the Louisiana Purchase in a diplomatic situation highly advantageous to the United States, which produced the **Adams-Onis Treaty** of 1819.

Meanwhile, decree from Tsar Nicholas I in 1821 established territorial claims for Russian North America that overlapped with American and British claims along the Pacific Coast. Monroe successfully contested these claims and secured the Russo-American Convention of 1824 in which the Tsar agreed to pursue no Russian settlement south of 54°40′ north latitude and recognized joint Anglo-American control of Oregon. To these continental territorial settlements Monroe added in the resettlement of freed slaves in West Africa in what became **Liberia,** governed by the American Colonization Society until 1847.

During his presidency Monroe therefore earned a reputation as a conservative man and as a president who preferred the path of compromise. But he was also an avid expansionist, and the message he delivered to Congress on December 2, 1823, which became well known as the **Monroe Doctrine,** was among the most ambitious assertions of territorial interest in modern history. In it Monroe proclaimed that Americans should be free from future European colonization or interference in American affairs; he also stated that the United States would remain neutral in Europe's wars. Any attempt by a European power to extend its territory into the Western Hemisphere would be seen as a threat to the United States. The doctrine guided policies of the United States for decades, remaining influential to this day. On retirement Monroe returned to his home in Virginia, where he died on July 4, 1831. *See also* British Empire; Madison, James; Manifest Destiny; Russian Empire; Spanish Empire.

FURTHER READING: Ammon, Harry. *James Monroe: The Quest for National Identity.* Charlottesville: University Press of Virginia, 1990; Cunninghan, Noble E. *The Presidency of James Monroe.* Lawrence: University of Kansas Press, 1996; O'Shei, Tim, and Joe Marren. *James Monroe.* Berkley Heights: Enslow Publishers, 2002.

ARTHUR HOLST

Montenegro

The Latinized name for Crna Gora, a small mountainous region of the Balkans intermittently under Ottoman occupation. Because of its difficult terrain and the fighting quality of its people, Montenegro was able to establish *de facto* independence when all its neighbors were Ottoman subjects. This was officially recognized by the Porte in 1799, but clashes with the Turks continued. In 1852, an Ottoman army invaded Montenegro but withdrew in the face an Austrian threat of intervention. When Montenegro supported a Slav uprising in Herzegovina in 1860, the Turks moved against it yet again and were again forced to accept Montenegro's autonomy and boundaries.

In 1878, the Treaty of **Berlin** established its complete independence, although Austria-Hungary was given a naval protectorate on Montenegro's Adriatic coast. In 1912, Montenegro was the first state to declare hostilities against the Porte in the **Balkan Wars,** and it emerged from the Balkan conflicts almost double in size. In August 1914, it sided with Entente Powers but spent much of the war under Austro-Hungarian occupation. *See also* Ottoman Empire.

FURTHER READING: Hall, Richard C. *The Balkan Wars, 1912–1913: Prelude to the First World War.* London: Routledge, 2000; Schurman, Jacob Gould. *The Balkan Wars, 1912–1913.* New

York: Cosimo Classics, 2005; Stevenson, Francis Seymour. *A History of Montenegro*. New York: Arno, 1971.

CARL CAVANAGH HODGE

Monterrey, Battle of (1846)

An early battle of the **Mexican-American War, 1846–1848.** As part of a three-pronged offensive to seize northern **Mexico,** Major General Zachary Taylor's Army of Occupation advanced on Monterrey in summer 1846. Natural and constructed obstacles rendered this provincial capital virtually impregnable. Fortified heights and the winding Rio Santa Catarina protected the city to the south and west, while a network of redoubts guarded its eastern flank. To the north, a massive fortress, the citadel, commanded the approaches to the city. The Mexican commander, General Pedro de Ampudia, had 7,500 regular troops, plentiful artillery, and weeks to prepare for the expected American attack.

Without proper siege guns and considerably outnumbered, Taylor boldly divided his army of 6,000 effectives on September 20 and executed a double envelopment of the city. One division struck from the west, while the bulk of his force attacked from the east. Taylor's audacious strategy and his troops' perseverance despite heavy losses completely unnerved Ampudia, and the Mexican commander missed the opportunity to defeat in detail Taylor's divided army. Facing heavy canon and musket fire from the strongly entrenched defenders, the Americans in two days of hard fighting battered their way into the city proper. With streets barricaded, stone houses loop-holed, and rooftops garrisoned, further advance required clearing the defenders street by street and house by house. Nevertheless, the two wings of Taylor's army gradually closed on the city's central plaza.

On September 24, Ampudia asked for terms. Taylor granted an eight-week armistice and allowed Mexican forces to withdraw from the city unmolested. Infuriated, President James K. Polk immediately repudiated the truce and lost all confidence in Taylor. His situation, however, had been critical and a final assault would have decimated his exhausted and battered army. Capturing the fortress-city by any means was nonetheless an impressive feat, and Monterrey served as a major American base for the remainder of the war. *See also* Manifest Destiny; Texas.

FURTHER READING: Bauer, K. Jack. *The Mexican War, 1846–1848*. Lincoln: University of Nebraska Press, 1992; Eisenhower, John S. D. *So Far from God: The U.S. War with Mexico, 1846–1848*. New York: Random House, 1989; McCaffrey, James M. *Army of Manifest Destiny: The American Soldier in the Mexican War, 1846–1848*. New York: New York University Press, 1992; Smith, Justin H. *The War with Mexico*. 2 vols. Gloucester, Mass: Peter Smith, 1963.

DAVID R. SNYDER

Moreno, Mariano (1778–1811)

One of the leading republican leaders in the early years of **Argentina**'s struggle for independence. Moreno was an active figure in local politics in Buenos Aires during the first decade of the nineteenth century. Trained in theology and law, in 1810 he produced a key pamphlet, *Representación de los hacendados y labradores,* which asserted the logic and the benefits of free trade and challenged colonial commercial restrictions. Its publication made him one of the leading liberal intellectuals in Buenos Aires. He helped introduce a broader range of anti-imperialist ideas by translating French revolutionary tracts into Spanish. When the city council declared independence in 1810, he served in the first revolutionary government formed in 1810. Moreno's belief in a centralized government and his preference for a single country rather than a collection of provinces in place of the defunct colony alienated many of his peers. Sent on a diplomatic mission to Europe, he died at sea. *See also* Spanish Empire.

FURTHER READING: Bagú, Sergio. *Mariano Moreno*. Buenos Aires: EUDEBA, 1966.

DANIEL K. LEWIS

Moroccan Crisis (1905)

One of a string of international incidents that threatened to embroil Europe in war before 1914. In April 1904, France and Britain resolved some of their longstanding differences over Morocco and Egypt. When France attempted to enforce a reform program in Morocco in early 1905 and to extend its influence in the region, Germany decided to challenge France and provoked an international crisis. Arguably, Germany was less concerned for its economic interests in the region than for its international prestige. Resentful at not having been consulted by France and Britain over Morocco and worried about the recently concluded **Entente Cordiale,** Germany wanted to demonstrate that it was a power that could not simply be bypassed on important colonial matters. Friedrich von Holstein, a senior figure in the German Foreign Office, felt that Germany could not allow its "toes to be trodden on silently." The German Chancellor, Bernhard von **Bülow,** persuaded a reluctant Kaiser **Wilhelm II** to land in the port of Tangiers on March 31 to stake Germany's claim and to ensure the Sultan of Germany's support.

In addition Germany sought to undermine the Entente and to intimidate the French. During the ensuing diplomatic crisis, Germany insisted on the dismissal of the anti-German French Foreign Minister Théophile **Delcassé** and even threatened France with war. In 1904–1905, the Russians were losing their war against Japan, and in January 1905, revolution further weakened Russia, so that France could not rely on Russian support during the crisis. Germany's bullying had the opposite effect, however, and led to a strengthening of the Entente. At the international conference at **Algeciras** in 1906, convened at the insistence of the German government, Germany was diplomatically isolated and unable to achieve its aim of limiting the extension of French interests in Morocco.

During and after the crisis, Germany began to feel the full effects of its own expansionist foreign policy. British involvement in a future war was now more likely and as a result, Italy, allied to Germany and Austria since 1882, would be a less reliable ally, for it would be unable to defend its long coastlines from Britain and might therefore opt to stay neutral in a future war. France also looked on Germany as a likely future enemy. Far from splitting its potential enemies, Germany had only managed to strengthen their resolve to oppose Germany if necessary. *See also* German Empire; *Weltpolitik*.

FURTHER READING: Anderson, Eugene N. *The First Moroccan Crisis, 1904–1906.* Hamden, CT: Archon, 1966; Joll, James, and Martel, Gordon. *The Origins of the First World War.* London: Longman, 2006; Rich, Norman. *Friedrich von Holstein. Policy and Diplomacy in the era of Bismarck and Wilhelm II.* 2 vols. Cambridge: Cambridge University Press, 1964..

ANNIKA MOMBAUER

Morocco

One of the Barbary States of Northwest Africa, effectively independent since the Middle Ages but poor and territorially ill defined. Morocco supported the *jihad* of **Adb el-Qadr** against French dominion in Algeria, for which it suffered brutal retaliation in 1845. Morocco's next clash with a European power came in 1859 in the form of invasion by Spain. Spain was not only geographically proximate to Morocco but also had been intermittently involved there going back to the fifteenth century. The invasion of 1859, however, was in response to Moroccan raids against outposts in northern Africa. A Spanish force captured the town of Tetuán in February 1860, and Morocco was forced to pay an indemnity and to cede more territory to Spain around the towns of Ceuta and Melilla.

A second war followed in 1892. From 1863 onward, Morocco was of increasing interest to France. In 1904, an Anglo-French agreement gave France a free hand in Morocco in exchange for French acceptance of British supremacy in Egypt. Later the same year a secret agreement between France and Spain divided the country into spheres of influence. Thereafter, Morocco became the object of the **Moroccan Crisis** of 1905 and the **Agadir Crisis** of 1911, which brought Britain and France closer together and prefigured World War I. *See also* Africa, Scramble for; Algeciras Conference; French Empire.

FURTHER READING: Porch, Douglas. *The Conquest of Morocco.* New York: Knopf, 1982; Terrasse, Henri. *History of Morocco.* Translated by Hilary Tee. Casablanca: Éditions Atlantides, 1952.

CARL CAVANAGH HODGE

Morse, Samuel F. B. (1791–1872)

The inventor of the **telegraph,** Samuel Morse was born to a prominent New England family. In 1805, Morse entered Yale University and subsequently studied art in London. In 1815, he returned to Boston and opened an art studio. For the next 14 years he painted portraits but was never financially successful. In the 1830s, Morse began to consider how electricity could be used to send messages over a wire. In 1832, he invented a device that could send messages by opening and closing an electric circuit and another that could receive the messages and record them on paper as dots and dashes—the code that later bore his name. Morse continued to make improvements in his devices for the next few years, thanks to the financial support of Alfred Vail, a wealthy young man he had previously tutored in art. Morse filed a patent for an "electric telegraph" in 1837, but was unable to generate enough financial backing to market his communication system.

The **United States** Congress finally allocated some money in 1843 to build the first telegraph line between Washington, D.C., and Baltimore, Maryland. On May 24,

1844, Morse transmitted the first telegraph message to Alfred Vail in Baltimore. Morse petitioned Congress for a grant of $100,000 to design a telegraph system for the nation, but was turned down. Morse turned to Vail. With other business partners the two generated funding that enabled them to connect much of the nation by a telegraph line. In 1858, Morse founded the Magnetic Telegraph Company, after having finally achieved considerable financial success. By the time Morse died in 1872, a telegraph line connected the United States and Europe.

FURTHER READING: Silverman, Kenneth. *Lightning Man: The Accursed Life of Samuel F. B. Morse.* Philadelphia: Da Capo Press, 2004.

GENE C. GERARD

Moscow

The capital and core of Russia. The name of Moscow first appears in Russian chronicles under the year 1147, now considered the birth date of the city, although the region was settled by various Slavic tribes probably in the tenth and eleventh centuries. During this early period in Russian history, from about 1054 to 1240, when the Kievan state became fragmented into individual principalities, Moscow seems to have been little more than a border town of the much larger principality of Vladimir. In 1547, Ivan IV, better known as The Terrible, was the first ruler to be crowned tsar and thereafter to use this title regularly and officially both in governing his land and in conducting foreign relations. In doing so, he made it clear that Moscow was no longer just one of many principalities; Russia had entered a new historical phase called Muscovite Russia. Ivan continued to expand the reach of Moscow, conquering Kazan and Astrakhan and building the famous St. Basil's cathedral in celebration of those victories.

From this point forward, Moscow would be the capital and center of the developing Russian Empire, remaining so until Peter the Great built his new capital at St. Petersburg in 1703. In 1812, after the bloody Battle of **Borodino,** Moscow was occupied briefly by Napoleon **Bonaparte**'s troops. Although Napoleon ultimately retreated, the city suffered much destruction by both Russians and the retreating French troops. Fortunately, the spectacular churches of the Kremlin and its surrounding area, many dating back to the sixteenth century, survived. After the **Bolshevik** Revolution of 1917, Moscow became the capital once more and served as the seat of the government during the Soviet regime and the center of the country's transformation. *See also* Napoleonic Wars; Russian Empire.

FURTHER READING: Crummey, Robert O. *The Formation of Muscovy, 1304–1613.* London and New York: Longman, 1987; Palmer, Alan. *Napoleon in Russia.* London: Andre Deutsch, 1967; Presniakov, A. E. *The Formation of the Great Russian State.* Chicago: University of Chicago Press, 1970.

LEE A. FARROW

Moscow, Retreat from (1812)

Napoleon **Bonaparte**'s retreat from the Russian capital after his disastrous invasion of that nation. After the significant military defeats at **Austerlitz** and Friedland in 1805 and 1807 respectively Russia was forced to sign the Treaty of **Tilsit** and maintain peaceful relations with France from 1807 to 1812. During this period, Russia was part of Napoleon's **Continental System,** a reluctant collaboration of subjugated or conquered European nations who, through various trade embargos, were supposed to help Napoleon bring England to its knees. Russia's participation in this system, however, was only a product of Napoleon's military power, not common interests, for Russia had a long trading relationship with England. Moreover, Tsar **Alexander I** was suspicious of Napoleon's ambitions in Eastern Europe and the Mediterranean. When it became apparent that Alexander would no longer cooperate, Napoleon decided to invade Russia. He amassed an army of 600,000 men, 200,000 animals, and 20,000 vehicles and entered Russia in late June 1812. The Russians retreated eastward avoiding battle and drawing the French further into Russia and destroying everything as they went. Finally in September, the Russians took their stand at **Borodino,** under the leadership of Field Marshal Mikhail Kutuzov. Although the French won, they lost 40,000 men and failed to destroy the Russian army. Napoleon's forces then proceeded to Moscow, arriving on September 14, 1812.

Napoleon had expected to be greeted by a delegation of nobles; instead, he found the city abandoned and in flames. Napoleon took up headquarters in Moscow and waited for Alexander to admit defeat. When Alexander refused, Napoleon was faced with the grim prospect of staying in Moscow through the bitter Russian winter. He decided to retreat and on October 19, 1812, 95,000 troops left Moscow. Napoleon ordered them to destroy many of Moscow's great monuments, like St. Basil's Cathedral. During their retreat, French forces experienced cold, hunger, and attacks by Russian peasants and cossacks. Moreover, Russian troops prevented the French from taking a new road as they moved west, forcing them to leave by the same road they had entered, through land that was stripped and devastated. In the end, only about 30,000 of Napoleon's troops made it to the Russian border. Napoleon, traveling in disguise, reached Paris on December 18. The campaign had been a failure and was the beginning of the end of Napoleon's unbeatable war machine. Adolph Northern's painting, *Napoleon's Retreat from Moscow,* commemorates the Russian disaster. *See also* Napoleonic Wars; Russian Empire.

FURTHER READING: Caulaincourt, Armand Augustin Louis. *With Napoleon in Russia: The Memoirs of General de Caulaincourt, Duke of Vincence. From the original memoirs as edited by Jean Hanoteau.* Edited by George Libaire. New York: W. Morrow and Company, 1935; McConnell, Allen. *Tsar Alexander I.* New York: Crowell, 1970; Riehn, Richard K. *Napoleon's Russian Campaign.* New York: McGraw-Hill, 1990; Walter, Jakob. *The Diary of a Napoleonic Foot Soldier.* Edited and with an Introduction by Marc Raeff. New York: Doubleday, 1991.

LEE A. FARROW

Mudki, Battle of (1845)

The opening battle of the First **Sikh War** in the small village of Mudki in northwestern **India.** With war winds blowing, the Sikh army, the **Khalsa,** led by Lal Singh and Tej Singh, crossed the Sutlej River into British territory on December 11. The Sikhs did not go on the offensive immediately. Seven days after crossing the Sutlej, on December 18, the Sikh army advanced against British forces at Mudki, where Lieutenant General Sir Hugh Gough, commander-in-chief in India, had about 10,000 troops assembled.

At about 4:00 P.M., the Sikhs opened fire and an artillery duel ensued. Then, after the Sikh cavalry was repulsed, the British infantry, 12 battalions in all, went on the attack and pushed back the Sikh army. The battle continued into the night and confusion reigned. Death by friendly fire was not uncommon. The British had 870 casualties, 215 killed and 655 wounded; the Sikhs lost an estimated 300 killed. Although not a decisive win, the British considered Mudki a victory. *See also* British Empire.

FURTHER READING: Bruce, George. *Six Battles for India: The Anglo-Sikh Wars, 1845–6, 1848– 9.* London: Arthur Barker, 1969; Cook, Hugh. *The Sikh Wars: The British Army in the Punjab, 1845–1849.* London: Leo Cooper, 1975; Crawford, E. R. "The Sikh Wars, 1845–9." In Brian Bond, ed. *Victorian Military Campaigns.* New York: Frederick A. Praeger Publishers, 1967; Farwell, Byron, *Queen Victoria's Little Wars.* New York: W. W. Norton & Co., 1972.

DAVID TURPIE

Mukden, Battle of (1905)

The Battle of Mukden was the last major land battle of the **Russo-Japanese War** and the largest in history to that point. After the fall of Port Arthur, the Japanese began augmenting their forces in Manchuria for an assault on Russian positions in Mukden, which began on February 20, when the Japanese Fifth Army attacked the Russian left flank. On February 27, the Japanese launched a general attack on the right flank and despite heavy losses threatened to roll up the Russian flanks and encircle Mukden. General Kuropatkin ordered the evacuation of the city on March 10. The retreating Russian armies disintegrated, but the exhausted Japanese failed to destroy them. Mukden cost the Russians about 90,000 casualties out of 350,000 troops, and Japanese casualties were about 75,000 of 300,000. Russian defeats at Mukden and Tsushima prompted the tsar to accept an offer of mediation to end the war from President Theodore **Roosevelt** of the **United States.** *See also* Kittery Peace; Portsmouth, Treaty of; Tsushima, Battle of.

FURTHER READING: Connaughton, Richard. *Rising Sun and Tumbling Bear: Russia's War with Japan.* London: Weidenfeld and Nicolson, 2003; Ethus, Raymond A. *Theodore Roosevelt and Japan.* Seattle: University of Washington Press, 1974; Warner, Dennis, and Peggy Warner. *The Tide at Sunrise.* London: Angus and Robertson, 1975; White, John Albert, *The Diplomacy of the Russo-Japanese War.* Princeton, NJ: Princeton University Press, 1964.

ADRIAN U-JIN ANG

Münchengrätz Convention (1833)

A set of agreements reached by Count **Metternich** and Tsar **Nicholas I** in a meeting at the village Mnichovo Hradiště, then Münchengrätz, in the present-day Czech Republic. They agreed that the **Russian Empire** and **Habsburg Empire** would cooperate in sustaining the **Ottoman Empire** against collapse but to act in concert if such a collapse became imminent. They also agreed to guarantee their respective possessions in Poland and pledged mutual assistance in the event of a Polish rebellion. At the time, Austria's problems in Central Europe required Russian cooperation, but Metternich wanted simultaneously to restrain Russian territorial opportunism over Ottoman decline. He therefore sought a Russian commitment to the maintenance of the diplomatic status quo generally and linked it to a shared fear of liberal revolt. A month later a third agreement was added when Prussia, too, declared a willingness to assist the Habsburg and Russian monarchies in defeating a liberal revolt. *See also* Congress System; Eastern Question; Holy Alliance.

FURTHER READING: Schroeder, Paul. W. *The Transformation of European Politics, 1763–1848.* Oxford: Clarendon, 1994.

CARL CAVANAGH HODGE

Mutsuhito, Emperor of Japan (1852–1912)

The emperor who presided over the transformation of Japan from a feudal realm into a modern nation and empire. Known posthumously as the Meiji Emperor, Mutsuhito assumed the crown in 1867 and became the preeminent symbol of the dramatic changes and extraordinary accomplishments still associated with the era of "enlightened rule" of the **Meiji Restoration:** national unity, modernization, industrialization, military victory over China and Russia, and empire in Southern Manchuria, Korea, and Taiwan.

Although an imposing figure of stocky build, bushy brow, and calculated reticence, the Meiji Emperor, unlike European monarchs in the Age of Absolutism or even the German kaiser on which the modern Japanese imperial institution was modeled, wielded primarily symbolic power. Emperors had theoretically reigned in Japan from 660 B.C., but from the twelfth through early nineteenth centuries, the most powerful warriors, *samurai,* in the land had actually ruled. Mutsuhito and his courtiers were living in obscurity in Kyoto, the traditional capital of the imperial family, when suddenly plucked to serve as the central symbol of a modern nation.

The "restoration" of authority to the emperor was a convenient pretext for the dramatic overthrow of the warrior family that had ruled Japan for more than 250 years, the **Tokugawa.** A boy of only 15 in 1867, Mutsuhito was useful not only in conferring political legitimacy on the young samurai usurpers of power but ultimately in fashioning an entirely new national polity. The founders of modern Japan painstakingly transformed the imperial institution into the central symbol of a modern nation and empire. All political, diplomatic, social, and economic reforms were promulgated in the emperor's name. The Meiji constitution of 1889 described the emperor as "sacred and inviolable" and placed all executive, legislative, and judicial powers in his hands.

Although the samurai founders of modern Japan actually ruled in their capacity as imperial "advisers," Mutsuhito became the official face of Imperial Japan. First introduced to his subjects in a series of six Grand Circuits between 1872 and 1885, Mutsuhito's symbolic presence grew enormously during the **Sino-Japanese** and **Russo-Japanese** Wars. He was described as enduring the privations of a soldier at war and portrayed as the heroic and caring commander-in-chief in woodblock prints, war songs, and magic lantern shows. Mutsuhito's death in July 1912 spurred deep and widespread mourning and ushered in a period of wrenching national uncertainty. *See also* Chrysanthemum Throne; Japanese Empire.

FURTHER READING: Beasley, W. G. *The Meiji Restoration.* Stanford, CA: Stanford University Press, 1972; Fujitani, Takashi. *Splendid Monarchy, Power and Pageantry in Modern Japan.* Berkeley: University of California Press, 1996; Keene, Donald. *Emperor of Japan: Meiji and His World, 1852–1912.* New York: Columbia University Press, 2002.

FREDERICK R. DICKINSON

N

Nanjing, Treaty of (1842)

The first of the so-called unequal treaties concluded between China and the Great Powers. Signed August 29, and followed by supplementary treaties in July and October 1843, it concluded the First **Opium War.** The treaties provided for Guangzhou, Xiamen, Fuzhou, Ningbo, and Shanghai to be opened to conduct trade as "treaty ports." They exempted British nationals from Chinese law and permitted the raising of foreign settlements in these ports, which were also subject to **extraterritoriality**.

The Nanjing Treaty abolished the system of *gonghang* in which 13 Chinese firms monopolized trade with Western countries and permitted British merchants free trade in China. The treaty included a most-favored-nation clause, which extended to the British any privileges negotiated from the Chinese by other countries. Further, the treaty violated China's territorial integrity with the outright cession of Hong Kong to Britain. *See also* Boxer Insurrection; Extraterritoriality.

FURTHER READING: Beeching, Jack. *The Opium Wars.* London: Hutchinson, 1975; Waley, Arthur. *The Opium War through Chinese Eyes.* Stanford, CA: Stanford University Press, 1968.

ADRIAN-U-JIN ANG

Nansen, Fridtjof (1861–1930)

A Norwegian scientist, diplomat, and explorer, Fridtjof Nansen crossed Greenland on skis in 1889; sailed across the Arctic Ocean in 1893–1896, and wrote many dissertations on these and other of his voyages. His energetic diplomatic effort secured support from the European Great Powers for Norwegian independence from Sweden in 1905, and he served as ambassador to London (1906–1908). He was also a deputy to the League of Nations, where he coordinated international aid efforts in the Ukraine during the Russian civil war (1919–1921), led the repatriation of Greek and Turkish deportees after World War I, and coordinated the aid distribution to the Armenians in 1925. In 1922, he received the Nobel Peace Price for his efforts.

FURTHER READING: Stenersen, Øivind Libæk, and Stenersen, Ivar. *A History of Norway: From the Ice Age to the Age of Petroleum.* Lysaker: Dinamo Forlag, 2003.

FRODE LINDGJERDET

Napoleon I

See Bonaparte, Napoleon

Napoleon III

See Bonaparte, Louis Napoleon

Napoleonic Code

Established by Napoleon **Bonaparte** in 1804, the Napoleonic Code became the foundation of the French legal system. The adoption of the French Civil Code (*Code civil des Français*), popularly called the *Code Napoléon,* realized a goal of the French Revolution. Formulated in 84 sessions of the Council of State, many of which were presided over by Napoleon himself, the code ended the chaotic and complicated legal system that had developed in France since Roman times and with it much of the freedom of judges to rule creatively in cases. The code was composed of 2,281 articles covering civil rights and duties, marriage, divorce, the mutual obligations of parents and children, and the division of property among children of a family. Later, other articles were added dealing with civil procedure, commerce, criminal justice, and penal standards. Judges became part of a tribunal system and applied the code in an administrative manner. The new system was hailed as a great achievement at the time, because it curtailed judicial power and elevated legislative power as representative of the people. The legal system was greatly simplified and made intelligible to the average person. The code's simplified and "rational" character was also favored by advocates of rule by reason.

Napoleon favored a uniform system of law for his empire, so the code was imposed on much of the territory he conquered, especially **Italy,** southern and central Germany, and the Duchy of Warsaw. It was also exported to French colonies, former French colonies, and to the former Spanish colonies in South America. Its administration made judges judicial bureaucrats and placed the weight of the law on the side of the State. Authoritarian governments found it useful for exercising a tighter control over the people than was the case in the Anglo-Saxon Common Law system. In North America, the code was adopted in Louisiana in 1821 and in Québec in 1866. *See also* French Empire.

FURTHER READING: Martin, Xavier. *Human Nature and the French Revolution: From the Enlightenment to the Napoleonic Code.* New York: Berghahn Books, 2001; Rose, J. Holland. *The Revolutionary and Napoleonic Era, 1789–1815.* Cambridge: Cambridge University Press, 1935; Young, Brian J. *The Politics of Codification: The Lower Canadian Civil Code of 1866.* Montreal: McGill-Queen's University Press, 1994.

ANDREW J. WASKEY

Napoleonic Wars (1792–1815)

A period of more or less continuous conflict between France and shifting coalitions of the other Great Powers of Europe, finally ending with Napoleon's defeat at **Waterloo** and the inauguration of the Congress system of European diplomacy. The War of the First Coalition properly belongs to the French Revolutionary period, the ascent of Napoleon **Bonaparte** to the position of first consul in November 1799 marking the beginning of the Napoleonic era. There were six anti-French coalitions in all, a seventh only if the Anglo-Prussian combination that fought Napoleon at **Ligny, Quatre Bras,** and **Waterloo** between June 15 and 18, 1815, is included. The First Coalition (1792–1797) opposed Revolutionary France with Austria and Prussia, later joined by Britain, the Netherlands, Spain, Naples, the Papal States, and Piedmont-Sardinia. The Second Coalition (1798–1801) confronted Napoleonic France and Spain with Austria, Britain, Naples, Portugal, Russia, and Turkey. The Third Coalition (1805–1806) allied Britain with Austria and Russia, and the Fourth Coalition (1806–1807) added Prussia. The Fifth Coalition (1809) corresponded with Napoleon's creation of the **Continental System** and the prosecution of the **Peninsular War.** It combined Austria and Britain with Portugal. The Sixth Coalition, also known as the Grand Alliance, was orchestrated by Lord **Castlereagh** in 1812–1813 and brought Britain into alliance with Austria, Prussia, Sweden, Russia, and the smaller German states of Bavaria, Saxony, and Württemberg. It ended with Napoleon's abdication in April 1814. The Congress of **Vienna**'s labors to establish a post-Napoleonic Europe were already underway when Napoleon escaped from exile to begin the campaign of the Hundred Days that Waterloo ended. After more than 20 years of rolling conflict, European diplomacy looked to recover its equilibrium, a task made newly complicated by revolutionary and Napoleonic upheaval.

This was particularly true in light of nature and consequences of the wars just concluded. The Napoleonic revolution in warfare began on August 23, 1793, with a decree of the revolutionary government that until such time as French territory had been cleared of foreign armies, all Frenchmen would be on permanent requisition for military service. With the reorganization of French army and the establishment of planned national war economy by Lazare Carnot, the French republic looked to defend itself by prosecuting war on an unprecedented scale. During the period of the Terror at home—roughly November 1793 to July 1794—this vastly larger army was additionally used to reflect the spirit of the regime by fighting with patriotic zeal and annihilating ferocity. France's new tool of war might nevertheless not have saved it from humiliating defeat at the hand of the professional armies of the European powers arrayed against the revolution, had it not come into the hands of an aggressive military innovator.

Napoleon Bonaparte was without peer or precedent in the use of combined arms—infantry, cavalry, and artillery deployed flexibly, both in combination and in sequence, as demanded by circumstance—to strike an opposing army with sudden and overwhelming force at its weakest point. He first demonstrated this at the head of the Army of Italy against a succession of Austrian and Piedmontese generals at Millesimo, Mondovi, and Lodi in 1796–1797. Napoleon demonstrated both strategic vision and a dangerous degree of recklessness with his early and ill-conceived expedition to Egypt in 1798. A British fleet commanded by Horatia **Nelson** destroyed the French fleet in **Aboukir Bay** and stranded Napoleon's army in Egypt. At that time, all of Napoleon's major victories were yet to come, but the episode at Aboukir Bay testified to a British determination to check Napoleonic ambition with repeated and spectacular setbacks.

The storied triumph at **Marengo** in Italy during the war against the Second Coalition was in fact a near disaster, but Napoleon was saved by the action of General Louis Desaix. This was in part a product of Napoleon's leadership, insofar as he promoted soldiers on the basis of demonstrated merit, encouraged them to take initiative, and often entrusted his ablest generals with enormous responsibilities. With this ability to recognize talent and harness it, Napoleon combined a comprehensive reorganization of France's army, especially between 1801 and 1805, along the lines that became the norm for European armies for the next century and a half. The army was divided into army corps, each of which contained two or three divisions of infantry and cavalry of about 8,000 men supported by mobile field artillery. Each division had two brigades, each brigade two regiments, and each regiment two battalions.

When campaigning, Napoleon typically dispersed his corps for the purpose of masking his intentions. He would bring them together again to converge on any enemy army at a place and time of his choice. This required an intuitive understanding of maps, distance, and terrain in order to coordinate the movement of hundreds of thousands of troops from several directions to confront an enemy at the point of convergence with an assault of stunning intensity. The most basic ingredient of the enterprise, impatience, was supplied by Bonaparte himself. He infused his generals with the imperative for speed. His infantry undertook long and fast marches, often under appalling conditions, for the reward of crushing victory and plunder that Napoleon repeatedly delivered in engagements large and small. This formula smashed a combined Austrian and Russian army at **Austerlitz** in 1805 and demolished a Prussian-Saxon force at Jena-Auerstädt in 1806. After a rebuke by the one Russian army at **Eylau** in February 1807, the Grand Armée destroyed another at Friedland the following June. This compelled from Tsar Alexander I the Treaty of **Tilsit**. Victory over the Fourth Coalition found Napoleon at the apex of his success, a situation flawed only by the destruction of the combined French and Spanish fleets off **Trafalgar** by Nelson in October 21, 1805. This freed Britain and the implacably anti-Napoleonic government of William **Pitt** from the fear of invasion and enabled it to continue its support for continental coalitions against France.

The war of the Fifth Coalition in 1809, which included the **Peninsular War** in Spain, began the slow process of Napoleon's defeat. The Sixth Coalition, occasioned by his disastrous invasion of Russian in June 1812 and subsequent retreat of Moscow, completed it at the Battle of **Leipzig** in October 1813. Bogged down in Spain by British regulars and Spanish *guerrillas* even as he threw an army of 600,000 against Russia, Napoleon's forces were overextended, undersupplied, and more than ever frequently confronted by enemy armies that had mastered his art of war. At Leipzig, otherwise known as the Battle of the Nations, three allied armies totaling 335,000 men converged on 190,000 French. After Wellington's victory at **Vitoria** in Spain in June 1813, France itself was under invasion from the north and south. The Hundred Days that led to Waterloo represented the last hurrah of Napoleonic pluck and little more. After 1809, Bonaparte's destruction was ever more probable because Britain and Russia—one the world's greatest sea power, the other a great land power—could not be subdued. The other powers he had also repeatedly humiliated ultimately added their weight to the overwhelming coalition against him. Finally, the most humiliated among them, Prussia, had been driven by Napoleonic arms to initiate the social and military reforms and, at the direction of Carl von **Clausewitz,** make its own contribution to the Age of Total War. *See also* French Empire; British Empire; Pax Brittanica.

FURTHER READING: Bell, David A. *The First Total War.* Boston: Houghton Mifflin, 2007; Blanning, T.C.W. *The French Revolutionary Wars, 1987–1802.* London: Arnold, 1996; Esdaile, Charles. *The Wars of Napoleon.* New York: Longman, 1995; Gat, Azar. *War in Human Civilization.* New York: Oxford University Press, 2006; Howard, Michael. *War in European History.* New York: Oxford University Press, 1976; Johnson, Paul. *Napoleon.* New York: Viking, 2002; Rothenberg, Gunther E. *The Napoleonic Wars.* London: Cassell, 1999.

CARL CAVANAGH HODGE

Narodna Odbrana

Narodna Odbrana, the People's Defense, was a Serbian nationalist organization founded in 1908 in reaction to the Austro-Hungarian annexation of the former Ottoman provinces of Bosnia and Herzegovina. Initially intended to defend ethnic Serbians newly subjected to Austro-Hungarian rule by training and equipping volunteers for armed struggle, it was ordered by the Serb government to reduce tensions with Vienna and to limit itself to cultural activities. It was thereupon immediately replaced by a more militant and secret organization, the **Black Hand.** Narodna Odbrana was indirectly implicated in the assassination of Austro-Hungariam heir Archduke Franz Ferdinand in June 1914, insofar as Black Hand agents operating in Sarajevo eluded detection by Austrian intelligence by using Narodna Odbrana as a cover for their activities. Narodna Odbrana therefore was cited explicitly in the Austrian ultimatum to **Serbia** of July 23, 1914 as an organization to be immediately dissolved. *See also* Habsburg Empire; July Crisis; Ottoman Empire.

FURTHER READING: Albertini, Luigi. *The Origins of the War of 1914.* 3 vols. Translated by Isabella M. Massey. New York: Oxford University Press, 1952.

CARL CAVANAGH HODGE

Navalism

A strategic vogue of the late nineteenth century based mostly on the writings of Alfred Thayer **Mahan,** which held that the possession of an oceanic navy to be an indispensable attribute of a **Great Power.** Mahan, a naval officer and lecturer at the U.S. Naval War College, published *The Influence of Sea Power on History, 1660–1783* in 1890 and followed it two years later with *The Influence of Sea Power on the French Revolution and Empire.* In each he attempted to demonstrate that in the age of commercial capitalism, the sea power of England had provided that country both with security and a commanding control of global ocean lanes sufficient to make it the de facto dominant power of Europe. Owing to the time and place of the release of these books—the United States in the 1890s—Mahan's broader interpretation of the importance of sea power in shaping history, although compelling enough in its own right, was well received by a political leadership predisposed to embrace it implications. Both Theodore **Roosevelt** and Henry Cabot

Lodge used Mahan to further the cause of a strong American navy at a time when the rapid commercial expansion of the United States might be threatened by European colonialism.

But Mahan's books were also instantly popular in Britain and were promptly translated into Japanese and several European languages. Mahan's following in the upper reaches of several governments was almost cultish, especially in Germany where Wilhelm II found in it an intellectual vindication of **Weltpolitik;** the Kaiser rhapsodized that a battleship represented "a consummate expression of human purpose and national character." When British naval muscle forced France to back down in the confrontation over **Fashoda** in 1898, Wilhelm mused that the poor French had forgotten to read their Mahan. In fact, they had not. From the 1880s, both France and Russia were devoting significant resources to the development of fast cruisers—both for commerce-raiding and hit-and-run tactics against stronger navies—as an alternative to constructing battle-fleets. It was initially the naval policies of France and Russia that in 1889 led to the adoption of the **two-power standard** and the passage of the British Naval Defence Act. In Germany, the **risk fleet theory** of Admiral von **Tirpitz**'s then sought to challenge this standard for British naval supremacy with the construction of a fleet large enough only to challenge the Royal Navy specifically in the home waters of the North Sea. Calculations of this sort ultimately drove First Sea Lord Sir John Fisher to change the naval arms race qualitatively with the introduction of the **Dreadnought** in 1906.

The **Russo-Japanese War** meanwhile intensified Great Power interest in naval power as possibly the decisive factor in future major conflict. After the brilliant Japanese triumph in the straits of **Tsushima,** debate raged over specific lessons to be learned from the engagement—the role played by large-caliber long-range guns as opposed to short-range, small-caliber yet rapid-firing guns—but not over its general lesson. The Japanese naval triumph was apparently even more vital to the outcome of the war than Trafalgar had been to the **Napoleonic Wars** a century earlier. Whereas Napoleon **Bonaparte** had lasted for 10 more years after **Trafalgar,** Russia sought peace terms within three months of Tsushima. *See also* Fisher, Sir John; Strategy.

FURTHER READING: Keegan, John. *The Price of Admiralty.* London: Hutchinsion, 1988; Lambert, Nicholas A. *Sir John Fisher's Naval Revolution.* Columbia: University of South Carolina Press, 1999; Langer, William L. *The Diplomacy of Imperialism, 1890–1902.* New York: Alfred A. Knopf, 1968; Massie, Robert K. *Castles of Steel: Britain, Germany and the Winning of the Great War at Sea.* New York: Random House, 2003; Spector, Ronald. *At War at Sea: Sailors and Naval Combat in the Twentieth Century.* New York: Viking Penguin, 2001.

CARL CAVANAGH HODGE

Navarino, Battle of (1827)

The last major naval action under sail, Navarino was fought on October 20, 1827, during the Greek War of Independence (1821–1832) between an Egyptian-Turkish fleet at anchor in the Greek harbor of Navarino and a combined British, French, and Russian fleet. The governments of Britain, France, and Russia, in sympathy with the

Greek struggle against Ottoman oppression, demanded that Egypt and Turkey withdraw their troops from **Greece.** Both countries refused and brought reinforcements to Navarino, where a Turko-Egyptian squadron had anchored. A combined British, French, and Russian naval force entered the harbor and anchored amongst the opposing ships.

The ensuing battle was little more than a slugging match of artillery, with no maneuver. The Turko-Egyptian fleet, heavily outgunned, was annihilated, with three-quarters of its vessels sunk or set on fire by their own crews to prevent capture. The Allies lost about 700; their opponents' losses, although not known, are thought to have been very large. *See also* Ottoman Empire.

FURTHER READING: Woodhouse, Christopher. *The Battle of Navarino.* London: Hodder and Stoughton, 1965.

GREGORY FREMONT-BARNES

Navigation Acts

A series of mercantilist provisions designed to protect English shipping, as well as to secure huge profits at the cost of colonies. English customs practices aimed at the Dutch in 1651 had banned foreign vessels from shipping goods from non-European ports to English ports. They also forbade vessels from third-party countries to ship goods through European ports to England. The 1707 Navigation Acts imposed duties and restricted trade with all British colonies. A favorable balance of trade was maintained for the colonial power by exporting more finished goods to the colonies and importing raw materials. Heavy duties were imposed on export of molasses and sugar from the French West Indies to the 13 American colonies by the Molasses Act of 1733. These restrictions were a factor in both the Anglo-Dutch Wars and the American Revolution.

By the beginning of nineteenth century, mercantilism had fallen into disfavor, and the British government began to move toward a policy of *laissez faire*. The British merchant marine was supreme, and the Navigations Acts could be dispensed with. Moreover, British trade was hampered by retaliatory duties imposed by the Netherlands, Prussia, and Portugal. With the Treaty of Ghent in December 1814, Britain and the United Stares settled their commercial disputes and abolished mutual restrictions on trade. As president of the Board of Trade, William Huskisson promoted **free trade** principles in the Reciprocity of Duties Bill of June 1823. The bill did away with certain restrictions imposed on foreign ships bringing goods to British ports and made no distinctions between British vessels and those of foreign countries agreeing to trade reciprocity. Duties on imported items like raw foreign wool, imported raw, and manufactured silk were lowered.

The Navigation Acts were finally repealed in 1849, as Britain's domination of world shipping permitted the removal of a monopoly of trade with the colonies. In the self-governing colonies, tariffs could even be imposed on goods from Britain. The long-term effect was beneficial, as British shipping increased by 45 percent within two decades. With improved shipping technology and industrial supremacy, Britain witnessed no serious rival to British domination of world trade and shipping in the nineteenth century. *See also* British Empire; Mercantilism.

FURTHER READING: Dickerson, Oliver M. *The Navigation Acts and the American Revolution.* New York: Octagon Books, 1978; Harper, Lawrence A. *The English Navigation Laws: A Seventeenth-Century Experiment in Social Engineering.* New York: Columbia University Press, 1939; Trevelyan, G. M. *History of England.* 2nd ed. London: Longmans, 1966.

PATIT PABAN MISHRA

Nelson, Horatio (1758–1805)

A British admiral victorious in the greatest naval actions of the **Napoleonic Wars** and among the most celebrated military leaders of the period. Small in stature and less than physically robust as a boy, Nelson was nonetheless from an early age self-confident to the point of conceit. He demonstrated a recurrent capacity to make and take chances. At the age of 12, he asked to be taken to sea by his uncle, Captain Maurice Suckling, on a Royal Naval expedition to the Falkland Islands during a crisis with Spain. In 1777, Nelson was commissioned a lieutenant and two years later promoted to captain. He served in the American Revolution, but after 1787 had no command until 1793, when Britain went to war with Revolutionary France.

Under the command and tutelage of Admiral John Jervis, commander of the **Royal Navy** Mediterranean fleet, Nelson established a reputation for exceptional daring and imaginative tactics. These won him a promotion to rear admiral and a knighthood after his performance in the Battle of Cape St. Vincent in 1797. By that year he had also lost an eye and an arm in action. The next year Nelson was ordered to blockade the French fleet in the Mediterranean but failed to interdict the crossing of Napoleon **Bonaparte**'s army to **Egypt.** This he quickly redeemed by pouncing on the French fleet at anchor in **Aboukir Bay** at the mouth of the Nile River, sinking or capturing 11 battleships and two frigates and stranding Napoleon's army in Egypt. Nelson's spectacular victory heartened potential British allies on the continent and was a factor in the formation of the Second Coalition against France. Nelson's warrior renown back in England now shielded his professional and personal life against charges of insubordination in action and ruinous scandal for his affair with Emma Hamilton, the wife of the British ambassador in Naples.

In 1800, Nelson was transferred to the Baltic and placed under the command of Admiral Sir Hyde Parker. In the Battle of Copenhagen, Nelson pressed the attack against the Danish fleet in direct violation of Parker's orders to disengage in the thick of the action. Emerging again with a lopsided victory, for his dashing disobedience he was made a viscount and commander of the Baltic fleet. After the brief peace of the Treaty of Amiens, Nelson was recalled to the Mediterranean and ordered to prevent the combined French and Spanish fleets from escorting an invasion force against England. In the effort he shadowed the French fleet under Admiral Pierre Villeneuve across the Atlantic to the West Indies and back before it was finally able to rendezvous with the Spanish fleet at Cadiz. Under pressure from Napoleon the combined fleets finally sailed and were brought to battle by Nelson off Cape **Trafalgar** on October 21, 1805. In all, 17 French and Spanish ships were sunk or captured, and the threat of a French invasion of England lifted. Trafalgar thus had strategic consequences for the remainder of the Napoleonic Wars, as a secure England could now support and subsidize allies on the continent. The cost of the triumph, however, was the death of Nelson himself. Felled by a sniper, he did not live to see the end of the battle. His body was returned to London in a brandy cask and interred at St. Paul's cathedral. Beyond his enormous contribution to Britain's struggle against Napoleon, Nelson's tactical brilliance and will-to-combat set a standard for generations of Royal Navy captains and bequeathed a mythic status both to that navy and the British Empire for almost a century. *See also* British Empire.

FURTHER READING: Rodger, N.A.M. *The Command of the Ocean: A Naval History of Britain, 1649–1815.* New York: W. W. Norton, 2004; Southey, Robert. *Life of Nelson.* London: HarperCollins, 2004; Sugden, John. *Nelson, A Dream of Glory.* London: Pimlico, 2005; Vincent, Edgar. *Nelson: Love and Fame.* New Haven, CT: Yale University Press, 2003.

CARL CAVANAGH HODGE

Nepal

A kingdom centered on the Katmandu Valley north of **India** in the Himilayas. Nepal was ruled by a number of caste and ethnic groups such as the Brahman, Chetri, Newar, Sherpa, and Tharu, and divided into as many as 50 principalities before it was united under Prithvinarayan Shah in 1743 who became Raja of Gurkha and established the Shah dynasty, 1743–1955. The Gurkhas expanded to Garhwal in the west and Sikkim in the east, bringing them into conflict with the East India Company. The southern boundary of Nepal with India, the Terai, the submontane belt, also led to a border dispute. In 1792, Nepal and the company signed a commercial treaty, but it was abrogated by a faction that came to power in 1794. Between 1795 and 1796, the British made economic and diplomatic overtures to Kathmandu but were ignored before they finally signed a 13-article treaty on October 26, 1801. Nepali hostility to the treaty, however, caused Lord Wellesley (1760–1842), governor-general from 1798–1805, to unilaterally terminate it.

Between 1813 and 1823, however, Francis Rawdon Hastings, first marquis of Hastings (1754–1826), served as governor-general of India and commander-in-chief of the Indian Army. He was determined to continue the expansion of the East India Company's territorial holdings in South Asia and initiated wars against the Pindaris, the Marathas, and Nepal. Hastings gave an ultimatum to Nepal in March 1814, ordering Kathmandu to recognize British authority over the border districts of Sheoraj and Butwal or face invasion. The British invaded but then withdrew in May as the malaria season approached. The Nepalese reoccupied the territory as the British prepared for full-scale war at the end of the rainy season. In September 16,000 troops marched into Nepal, but Nepali resistance delayed British victory until they had captured Kathmandu and forced the Treaty of Sugauli of 1815. It deprived Nepal of Garhwal, Sirmur, and Kumaon in the west, and Sikkim and Morung in the east and a slice of territory to the south, in all about one-third of its territory. It also forced a British resident on Kathmandu. From the war the British learned the difficulty of defeating the Gurkhas and accordingly accepted Nepal as a buffer state with China.

The **Indian Mutiny** of 1857 dramatically changed the relationship with Nepal as Jang Bahadur, the first of the hereditary Rana Dynasty of prime ministers (1846–1877), sent some 6,000 soldiers to aid the British. As a result, Britain restored the Terai lands to Nepal and established an entente with Nepal, allowing it to retain its internal autonomy and its isolationist policies, although it was treated as a protectorate. In the treaty of December 21, 1923, the British recognized Nepal's independence.

FURTHER READING: Shaha, Rishikesh, *Modern Nepal: A Political History 1769–1955.* 2 vols. New Delhi: Manohar, 1990.

ROGER D. LONG

Nesselrode, Count Karl Robert (1780–1862)

A long-serving Russian diplomat and head of the Russian delegation at the Congress of **Vienna,** Count Nesselrode was thereafter a leading statesman of the **Holy Alliance.** Born in Lisbon, where his father served as Russian ambassador, Nesselrode had a background and education that was nonetheless German, qualities considered attractive in the Russian foreign service of the nineteenth century. Frustrated in his attempt at a navy career by chronic seasickness, he joined the army and then the diplomatic service under Tsar Alexander I and quickly proved a cool and reliable professional and assisted in the negotiations leading to the Treaty of **Tilsit.**

After his role as an architect of the Holy Alliance, Nesselrode was a major influence in one capacity or another—between 1845 and 1856 he served as chancellor—for the next 40 years. Nesselrode was instinctively cautious and believed that Russian diplomacy ought to be also. He therefore opposed many of the ambitions of the Pan-Slavic movement in the Balkans, rejected imperial expansion in Asia, and favored conciliation rather confrontation with the **Ottoman Empire,** a policy that led to the Treaty of **Inkiar Skelessi** in 1833. Nesselrode also opposed the policy of **Nicholas I** in the Crimea but was unsuccessful in preventing the **Crimean War.** In 1856, it was on Nesselrode's counsel that **Alexander II** accepted the terms of peace. *See also* Russian Empire.

FURTHER READING: Goldfrank, David M. *The Origins of the Crimean War.* London: Longman, 1994; Ingle, Harold N. *Nesselrode and the Russian Rapprochement with Britain, 1836–1844.* Berkeley: University of California Press, 1976; Royle, Trevor. *Crimea: The Great Crimean War, 1854–1856.* London: Palgrave, 2000.

CARL CAVANAGH HODGE

Netherlands, Kingdom of the

Established in 1814 through a union of Holland, Belgium, and Luxemburg, the Kingdom of Netherlands was the successor state of the United Netherlands or Dutch Republic (1581–1795). During the seventeenth century, the Dutch Republic dominated world trade and built a large overseas empire. It came into conflict with an emerging rival, England, in the Anglo-Dutch Wars of 1652–1654 and 1665–1667, but thereafter was directly menaced by France under Louis XIV. In 1795, the republic was conquered by Revolutionary France and was annexed outright by Napoleonic France in 1810. The Congress of **Vienna** then reestablished Dutch independence in 1814 in the wake of Napoleon's overthrow. The kingdom nonetheless had ethnic and religious tensions that were aggravated by the economic division of the country between an agrarian Holland and industrial Belgium. **Belgium** seceded in 1830, and its independence was recognized in 1839 both by the Netherlands and by the Great Powers in the Treaty of London. The Duchy of Luxemburg then became independent in 1890.

During the nineteenth century, therefore, Netherlands was a colonial power in decline. As a result of the **Napoleonic Wars,** it lost overseas territories to Britain and never wholly recovered them. Its commercial health was in large part dependent on the resources of the Dutch East Indies, the exploitation of which were partly the cause of revolts in **Java** starting in the 1820s and lasting until the 1890s.

FURTHER READING: Israel, Jonathan. *The Dutch Republic.* Oxford: Clarendon, 1995; Schama, Simon. *Patriots and Liberators: Revolution in the Netherlands, 1780–1813.* New York: Alfred A. Knopf, 1977.

CARL CAVANAGH HODGE

New Brunswick

A nineteenth-century British settlement colony south of the Gulf of the St. Lawrence, north of the Bay of Fundy, and west of **Nova Scotia.** It was originally inhabited by native tribes and by French Acadian settlers. Many of the latter were expelled in the eighteenth century in response to their doubtful loyalty to the British Empire. As a consequence of the American War of Independence, an influx of loyalist Americans swelled the population, and led to the 1784 severance of New Brunswick from Nova Scotia. They gave the colony a pro-British and often Tory character. New Brunswick was particularly important as a source of masts for the **Royal Navy.** The exact line of demarcation of the boundary with the United States became a controversial issue in the 1830s, as rival parties of lumbermen clashed in contested territories, and troops were called out on both sides.

The boundary question was settled by the **Webster-Ashburton Treaty** of 1842, and New Brunswick ceased to be a cause of international concern. Like all British North American colonies, relations between the imperially appointed governor, his officials, and a popularly elected assembly were contentious in the early nineteenth century, with issues such as lands and revenues at the center of disputes. New Brunswick was among the last North American colonies in which the principle of **responsible government** became active, waiting until 1854. In 1867, New Brunswick entered the Dominion of **Canada** as one of the initial four provinces, along with Nova Scotia, Quebec, and Ontario. *See also* British North America Act.

FURTHER READING: MacNutt, W. S. *New Brunswick: A History, 1784–1867.* Toronto: Macmillan, 1963.

MARK F. PROUDMAN

Newfoundland

An island off the east coast of **Canada,** first visited by Vikings, and in the modern era by John Cabot in 1497. Its fertile fishing grounds, especially on the grand banks, have long been known and exploited by fishermen from various Western European nations.

The island was annexed to Great Britain by Sir Humphrey Gilbert in 1583, but its exact dimensions remained unknown until its shores were mapped by James Cook in the 1760s.Newfoundland enjoyed prosperity during the Napoleonic Wars, in large part as a result of sales of fish to the army in the **Peninsula War.** Newfoundland was ruled by Admirals until 1825; an assembly was granted in 1832. **Responsible government** was effectively granted in 1855. Although entry into the Canadian confederation was discussed, a tentative agreement to that effect was repudiated by the island's electorate in 1868. Charles F. Bennett, a leading opponent of confederation, became prime minister of the colony in 1869. Confederation was rejected because it was felt that the interests, particularly in regard to the fishery, of Newfoundland conflicted with those of the mainland Maritime provinces. Newfoundland's politics in the late nineteenth century were dominated by fisheries disputes with France and the United States, and it was often felt that the imperial government represented the island's interests without enthusiasm. In World War I, however, Newfoundlanders fought with distinction, the Royal Newfoundland Regiment being almost wiped out on the Somme, and many fishermen serving in the **Royal Navy.**

FURTHER READING: Rowe, Frederick W. *A History of Newfoundland and Labrador.* New York: McGraw-Hill, 1980.

MARK F. PROUDMAN

New Guinea

A large island off the northern coast of **Australia,** likened to hell by the French explorer Louis de Bougainville because of the cannibalism common among its native Negrito, Melanesian, and Papuan peoples. From the time it was first "claimed" by a European power—Spain in 1545—New Guinea was the object negligent imperialism. No power sought New Guinea as a commercial prize in its own right, but British, Dutch, German, and even Australian commercial interests sought at least to exclude each other. In 1884, however, Germany annexed the northeast of the island and named it, appropriately, Kaiser Wilhelmsland. This prodded Britain to declare a protectorate in the southeast later the same year. The two powers agreed on a boundary dividing the island in half in 1885, but Germany surrendered its territory to Australia with the outbreak of World War I.

FURTHER READING: Griffin, James. *Papua New Guinea: A Political History.* Richmond: Heinemann Educational, 1979.

CARL CAVANAGH HODGE

New Zealand

A Pacific island **Dominion** of the British Commonwealth since 1907. The islands were first settled by the Maori, an Eastern Polynesian people thought to have arrived between 800 and 1300. New Zealand's first European visitor, Abel Janszoon Tasman, came in 1642 in the service of the Dutch **East India Company** and named the islands after Zeeland, his home in the southernmost province of the Netherlands. James Cook charted the islands in 1769–1770. American and British whalers frequented the islands in the 1790s; the first Protestant **missionaries** arrived in 1814. The first British settlers came to New Zealand during the 1820s, but a determined effort in colonization began on the north island in the 1840s under the leadership of Edward Wakefield, a Quaker philanthropist and advocate of what he called "scientific" colonial settlement who also accompanied Lord Durham to Canada as an advisor in 1838. Wakefield believed that overseas colonies should yield a social benefit to Britain through the emigration of surplus population, not by forced removal or transportation but rather through the sale at attractive prices of "waste lands" in the colonies. In 1837, he established the New Zealand Association, a political lobby to persuade the British government to sell land in New Zealand to English settlers. In 1840, a delegation of Maori chiefs signed the Treaty of Waitangi with the New Zealand Company in which they surrendered their sovereignty to the British crown while retaining their property rights.

In the 1840s and 1850s, New Zealand was on course for a federal system, the New Zealand Constitution Act of 1852, establishing provincial legislatures for six settlement areas and a national legislature with overarching fiscal authority. Conflicting interpretations of property rights became the source of bitter conflict between the Maori and the increasing numbers of settlers pouring into the country in response to the offer of land, the final acquisition of which violated the terms negotiated at Waitangi. The **Maori Wars** of the 1840s and 1860s ultimately left the Maori devastated but were followed by rapid economic development from the 1870s onward, especially in the expansion of pastureland for the production of meat and dairy products. In 1875, however, New Zealand abolished the provincial legislatures and established a unitary political system. In the 1890s, it also rejected federation with **Australia**. *See also* Canada; Responsible Government.

FURTHER READING: Belich, James. *Making Peoples: A History of the New Zealanders from the Polynesian Settlement to the End of the Nineteenth Century.* Honolulu: University of Hawai'i Press, 2001; Sinclair, Keith. *The Origins of the Maori Wars.* Wellington: New Zealand University Press, 1957.

CARL CAVANAGH HODGE

Ney, Michel (1769–1815)

A famous Napoleonic marshal and Napoleon **Bonaparte**'s most loyal subordinate. Ney reached the rank of brigadier general in 1796 and commanded a division three years later. He distinguished himself in the Low Countries, on the Rhine, and in Switzerland during the Revolutionary Wars. Napoleon appointed him a marshal in 1804. During the campaign of 1805, Ney performed brilliantly at Elchingen against the Austrians, and later at **Eylau** and **Friedland** against the Russians in 1807. He was not very successful in the **Peninsular War,** where his relations with Marshal Masséna were poor.

He commanded III Corps during the invasion of Russia and distinguished himself during the retreat from Moscow. Leading the rearguard, Ney performed heroically and is believed to have been the last Frenchman to cross the border into Poland, having led the last remnants of the *Grande Armée* to safety. He fought in almost every battle thereafter in Germany and France, and joined Napoleon during the Hundred Days, but failed to achieve victory at **Waterloo** in his capacity as *de facto* battlefield commander, as the emperor remained well behind the front line. He was court-martialed and shot for treason by the restored Bourbons. *See also* Napoleonic Wars.

FURTHER READING: Atteridge, A. H. *Marshal Ney: The Bravest of the Brave.* Uxfield: Naval and Military Press, 2001; Chandler, David, ed. *Napoleon's Marshals.* London: Weidenfeld & Nicolson, 2000; Delderfield, R. F. *Napoleon's Marshals.* New York: Cooper Square Publishers, 2002; Horricks, R. *Marshal Ney: The Romance and the Real.* London: Archway, 1988; Macdonell, A. G. *Napoleon and His Marshals.* New York: Prion Books, 1996.

GREGORY FREMONT-BARNES

Nicholas I, Tsar of Russia (1796–1855)

Tsar of Russia from 1825 to 1855. Unlike his elder brothers, whose education was largely overseen by their liberal grandmother, Catherine the Great, Nicholas's education was guided by his mother and militaristic father, Paul I, who admired all things Prussian. It was the way in which his reign began, however, with the **Decembrist** uprising, that pushed him further along the path of conservatism. In December 1825, with the announcement of **Alexander I**'s death, a group of intellectuals, long disgruntled by the slow progress of liberalism in Russia, staged an attempted coup. After a lengthy standoff, Nicholas used troops to disperse the would-be revolutionaries, and began a reign dominated by conservative and reactionary policies.

Nicholas inherited a country with many problems: industrial backwardness, an outdated socioeconomic order based on serfdom; an enormous, corrupt, and ineffective bureaucracy; and an impoverished nobility. Nicholas, however, believed in the soundness of the current social and political order and was unwilling to share his power. He chose instead to rule through an extreme form of absolute monarchy, combined with an emphasis on orthodoxy and nationality, set forth in 1833 in a doctrine called "Official Nationality." Domestically, Nicholas surrounded himself with military men and avoided the use of consultative bodies, preferring to govern through ad hoc committees and personal institutions. His conservatism made it difficult to implement any real reforms, particularly regarding the crucial issue of serfdom, which remained virtually untouched during his reign. Nicholas did succeed, however, in producing a new law code, the first since 1649, and also enacted some minimal reforms to improve the conditions of state peasants, but any hope of further reform ceased with the outbreak of revolutions across Europe in 1848.

Frightened by these revolutions, Nicholas became reactionary. He forbade Russians from traveling abroad; further restricted university admissions, autonomy, and academic freedom; and increased censorship. In foreign affairs, Nicholas also displayed conservatism, putting down an uprising in Poland in 1830, and imposing a policy of "Russification." His relationship with the **Ottoman Empire** was less consistent; he supported the Ottoman sultan in his struggles with internal challenges from the Egyptians but challenged the Turks on the question of which church, the Greek Orthodox or Roman Catholic, should have guardianship over the Holy Places in Jerusalem, Bethlehem, and Nazareth. This conflict led to the **Crimean War** (1853–1856), during which Nicholas died in 1855. *See also* Russian Empire.

FURTHER READING: Kagan, Frederick W. *The Military Reforms of Nicholas I: The Origins of the Modern Russian Army.* New York: St. Martin's Press, 1999; Lincoln, W. Bruce, *Nicholas I.*

Dekalb: Northern Illinois Press, 1989; Pintner, Walter McKenzie. *Russian Economic Policy under Nicholas I.* Ithaca, NY: Cornell University Press, 1967.

LEE A. FARROW

Nicholas II, Tsar of Russia (1868–1918)

The last tsar of Russia, Nicholas II and his family were murdered by the **Bolsheviks** after the Russian Revolution of 1917. Born on May 6, 1868, Nicholas was the eldest son of Alexander III. He officially became heir to the throne in March 1881 when his grandfather was assassinated by a revolutionary's bomb. As a boy and young man, Nicholas is often described as sensitive, emotional, soft-spoken, and meek. He grew up in a large family, with two sisters and two brothers. They spent most of their time in the suburbs of St. Petersburg at the royal residence called Gatchina, where Alexander III isolated himself and his family after his father's assassination. Alexander's strong mistrust of liberal reforms came to dominate his political and personal life, as well as the education of his children. In 1884, Nicholas met his future wife, Alexandra, the granddaughter of the English Queen Victoria, at the wedding of Alexandra's older sister, Ella, to Nicholas's uncle, Sergei—Nicholas was 16; Alexandra was 12. Five years later Alexandra appeared at the Russian court again, this time as a prospective bride for Nicholas, at his insistence. Although his parents disapproved, Nicholas and Alexandra became engaged in 1894. Only six months later, when Alexander III died in October, it became urgent for the new tsar to wed his fiancée. The ceremony took place on November 14, 1894.

It is generally accepted that Nicholas never wanted to be tsar. Although he met his duties throughout his reign, he always felt that it was taking time away from his family and from the time that he liked to spend outdoors. To make matters worse, his reign got off to a bad start. When he ascended the throne, the Russian people had great hopes that his reign would be different. These hopes led naive local councils to submit proposals and requests for all sorts of reforms that included a modest consultative role in the government. In January 1895, Nicholas and Alexandra presented themselves to the public for the first time and in the speech that followed, Nicholas called the suggestions of these councils "senseless dreams." Many viewed the meeting as a bad omen. Nicholas's inability to differentiate between the ideas of moderate reformers and the dangers of extremists pushed many liberals to the left. Nicholas's reputation was further damaged by another event the next year when, during the celebration following the Tsar's formal coronation on May 26, 1896, crowds at Khodynka Field stampeded, resulting in 1,300 deaths. Despite the tragic events of the day, that evening Nicholas and Alexandra attended a ball thrown by the French ambassador in their honor. Although they visited the injured in the days after the tragedy, the public remembered only one thing—that the royal couple had attended a ball on the night after so many lives had been lost. Henceforth, that tragic day became known as "Bloody Saturday" and the tsar became known as "Bloody Nicholas." Under Nicholas, the Russian government continued to severely curtail civil rights, censor the press, and tightly monitor education. In addition, religious persecution grew; Jews encountered restrictions and there were more pogroms. The policy of Russification continued, especially against the Finns who were subjected to Russian laws and military service. In other realms, Nicholas was less resistant to change. He pursued an active policy of industrialization, led by his father's, and now his, minister of finance, Sergei **Witte.** In addition to railroad construction, Witte expanded iron, steel, textile, and oil production. In response to this industrial growth, Russia's two major cities, Moscow and St. Petersburg, grew as peasants moved to the city to find factory work, creating a large, but poor, working class.

These were not the only problems that Nicholas had to face in the early years of his reign. There were also international tensions, in particular between Russia and Japan. In the wake of the **Meiji Restoration,** Japan began to industrialize and to pursue a more aggressive foreign policy. Tensions had been growing between Russia and Japan for a decade, beginning with the construction of the **Trans-Siberian Railroad** and conflicting interests in **Manchuria.** On February 8, 1904, Japan executed a sneak attack on the Russian fleet at Port Arthur on the Liaotung Peninsula. The subsequent **Russo-Japanese War** was a humiliating defeat for Russia. After the annihilation of a Russian fleet in late May 1905, Russia agreed to an armistice and signed a peace treaty in August 1905 at Portsmouth, New Hampshire. The peace treaty came none too soon, for as fighting ceased, Russia was already in the grip of what came to be known as the Revolution of 1905. In January 1905, a strike broke out in St. Petersburg that culminated in a protest march to the Winter Palace. Nicholas tried to respond to the crisis—he established a commission of inquiry to look into the January disaster and met with a group of factory representatives to assure them of his concern—but his changes were minimal and failed to address the underlying problems. When strikes continued, Nicholas issued a manifesto in March, declaring his intention to create a consultative assembly; in addition, he proclaimed religious toleration and repealed some legislation against ethnic minorities. Even in this manifesto, however, Nicholas emphasized his authority and condemned all those who challenged that authority. In the summer of 1905, there were more strikes, peasant uprisings, and occasional rebellions in the armed forces, the most famous being the mutiny on the battleship *Potemkin* in the Black Sea.

Meanwhile, the promised assembly, or duma, was rigged in such a way that it would be ineffectual. In October 1905, the population erupted in protest once again, culminating in an enormous general strike that lasted from October 20 to 30. Nicholas was forced to grant concessions, outlined in the October Manifesto. This document guaranteed a variety of civil liberties, such as freedom of speech, religion, and association. In addition, it promised a Duma with true legislative functions. It resulted in little substantive change, but the October Manifesto nonetheless split the opposition, temporarily satisfying many liberals and moderates. The new political order, however, still faced many challenges. The tsar was reluctant to concede any legal authority to the Duma and repeatedly tried to limit its activities. On the other hand, Duma representatives and nonrepresentatives alike continued to call for reform.

The domestic situation was only aggravated by the outbreak of World War I in 1914. Russian forces performed well initially but quickly began to suffer major losses at the hands of the Germans. In 1915, Nicholas made a fateful decision to lead Russian forces at the front himself, leaving the country in the hands of his German-born wife and her spiritual advisor, the peasant monk, Grigorii Rasputin.

Nicholas was at the front when demonstrations erupted in Petrograd (St. Petersburg) in February 1917. Railroad strikes prevented him from making it back to the capital and, faced with the hopelessness of his situation, Nicholas abdicated the throne, both for himself and his son, the young heir to the throne, Alexei. Nicholas and his family were then moved to one of their palaces outside of Petrograd and kept under guard. In the spring of 1918, they were moved to Ekaterinburg, in the Ural Mountains, where they were all murdered under order of the Bolsheviks in July, bringing to an end the Romanov Dynasty that had ruled Russia since 1613. Their bodies were destroyed and then dumped and lay in an undisclosed location for decades. After the collapse of communism, their remains were located and given an official burial in St. Petersburg; Nicholas, his wife, and children were also canonized as saints in the Russian Orthodox Church. *See also* July Crisis; Russian Empire.

FURTHER READING: Fuhrmann, Joseph T. *The Complete Wartime Correspondence of Tsar Nicholas II and the Empress Alexandra: April 1914–March 1917.* Westport, CT: Greenwood Press, 1999; Lieven, D.C.B. *Nicholas II: Twilight of the Empire.* New York: St. Martin's Press, 1994; Lincoln, W. Bruce. *In War's Dark Shadow: The Russians before the Great War.* Oxford: Oxford University Press, 1983; Radzinsky, Edvard. *The Last Tsar: The Life and Death of Nicholas II.* New York: Doubleday, 1992; Verner, Andrew. *The Crisis of Autocracy: Nicholas II and the 1905 Revolution.* Princeton, NJ: Princeton University Press, 1990.

LEE A. FARROW

Nietzsche, Friedrich (1844–1900)

A German philologist and philosopher of the nineteenth century, among the most misunderstood and disputed minds of his and our time. In the words of historian Golo Mann, "his work was a catastrophe which presaged and predicted Europe's general catastrophe." His major contributions, *Thus Spake Zarathustra, Beyond Good and Evil, The Will to Power,* and *Ecce Homo* were little appreciated while he lived. This resulted in a professional and intellectual isolation that made some of Nietzsche's later writing shrill and polemical in nature.

Some of his more controversial ideas—for example that of the *Übermensch* or superman, a free intellect unrestrained in thought and action by conventional morality and contemptuous of weakness, sentiment, and compassion—were influenced by his idolatry of Napoleon **Bonaparte** and were appropriated by the Nazis in the 1930s to lend an intellectual sheen to Adolf Hitler's "will to power." In the Second Reich of Otto von **Bismarck** and **Wilhelm II,** however, Nietzsche's elegantly articulate cultural criticism was merciless in its condemnation of German nationalism, popular anti-Semitism, and what he called the "proletarianization of civilization." He broke with Richard Wagner, a friend and influence, over Wagner's anti-Semitism and the "horned Siegfried" heroes of his operas. In many ways a product of the Germany he professed to loathe, Nietzsche lacked any capacity for moderation even in his sanest moments. He was instinctively drawn to incendiary assertions. But in his vision of a future world of wars and revolution he was prophetic. *See also* Nihilism.

FURTHER READING: Kaufmann, Walter. *Nietzsche: Philosopher, Psychologist, Antichrist.* Princeton, NJ: Princeton University Press, 1968; Mann, Golo. *The History of Germany since 1789.* Translated by Marion Jackson. London: Chatto & Windus, 1968; Stern, Fritz. *The Politics of Cultural Despair: A Study in the Rise of the Germanic Ideology.* Berkeley: University of California Press, 1974.

CARL CAVANAGH HODGE

Nigeria

A territory in West Africa that became a formal British colony in 1906. British colonization of Nigeria was a gradual process, which involved a combination of local British economic activity and metropolitan impulses stimulated by strategic concerns during the "Scramble for Africa." British control in Nigeria was exercised through a system of **indirect rule,** usually associated with the first governor-general, Frederick **Lugard.** Nigeria is a large territory—distinguished by social, economic, and cultural differences between the coast and the interior—and it therefore proceeded to independence as a federation to accommodate these differences.

During the early nineteenth century British missionaries were active on the Yoruba coast, but the major British presence in the region that would later become Nigeria was the Royal Niger Company. The company expanded its operations through a combination of trade in palm oil, alliances with local chiefs, and military conquest. By the 1890s, the company had established a trade monopoly and tried to push down the price paid to Africans for their palm oil, which stimulated a native rebellion in 1894. Although the company was strong enough to suppress the rebellion it caught the attention of the British government. The government was concerned about the activities of the company because it was operating in an area in which British and French imperial ambitions clashed. To minimize the risk that the company might drag Britain into a war with France, the government extended its formal control by purchasing the company's rights as the administering power. Company officials continued to act as the agents of the government, expanding British influence in the disputed areas, and in 1897 they were authorized to use force against French patrols. Meanwhile the British government negotiated with the French to demarcate their respective spheres of influence in the region, upon which they agreed in the Anglo-French Convention of June 14, 1898.

Frederick Lugard, who had served as the Royal Niger Company's military leader, was instrumental in the development of British rule in Nigeria over the next 25 years. He first served as high commissioner of the Northern Nigerian Protectorate from 1900 to 1906, during which time he imposed British overlordship on the Muslim emirs of that region. After serving as governor of Hong Kong, Lugard returned to Nigeria as governor-general in 1912, and by the outbreak of World War I he had successfully united the administration of North and South Nigeria. Lugard has often been credited with establishing the principles of indirect rule, by which the British governed at minimal expense through the extant authority of African tribal leaders. In fact the British had used such techniques for a long time in **India.**

Lugard's rule brought a number of positive developments in Nigeria, not the least of which was the gradual abolition of slavery. However, Lugard and several other British colonial administrators who served under him and went on to become governors in other African colonies tended to resist the development of an educated indigenous elite, which caused friction and resentment. In Nigeria and other West African colonies, the culture of the prosperous southern coastal regions was very different from the northern interior. Africans along the coast had been exposed to contact with Europeans for a much longer period. They had become Christian, were relatively wealthy and literate, and had therefore developed expectations that they would play a greater role in British administration. In the longer term, the distinction between the partially westernized African elite in the south and the majority of the African tribal population in the north had significant implications for independence. The British fully recognized this fact and during the 1950s, Nigeria was ushered along a path to independence as a federal state, which it achieved in 1960 under the leadership of Abubakar Tafawa Balewa. *See also* Africa, Scramble for; British Empire.

FURTHER READING: Flint, John E. "Frederick Lugard: The Making of an Autocrat, 1858–1943." In L. H. Gann and P. Duigan, eds. *African Proconsuls: European Governors in Africa.* New York: Free Press, 1978; Hargreaves, John D. *West Africa Partitioned.* 2 vols. Madison: University of Wisconsin Press, 1985; Lugard, Sir Frederick. *The Dual Mandate in British Tropical Africa.* London: W. Blackwood & Sons, 1922; Perham, Margery. *Lugard.* 2 vols. Hamden: Archon, 1968.

CARL PETER WATTS

Nihilism

A philosophical doctrine most prodigiously articulated by German philosophers Friedrich **Nietzsche** (1844–1900) first and foremost and then Martin Heidegger (1889–1976). Nihilists were also followers and sympathizers of the Nihilist movement, a cultural and political movement that emerged in 1860s Russia. Etymologically "nihilism" comes from the Latin *nihil,* meaning "nothing." The earliest documented mention is that of the French *nihiliste,* in a 1787 French dictionary that references the use of the term in 1761 in a context where it meant "heretic." The term was used by the German philosopher Friedrich Heinrich Jacobi (1743–1819) in his critique of Immanuel Kant's concept of speculative reason, instead of which Jacobi favored faith and revelation as instruments of understanding.

The fundamental position of nihilism is that the world and human existence in particular have no meaning, which renders superfluous the notions of purpose, truth, or value. This Nietzsche applied to Christianity, which, according to him, had removed meaning from earthly existence and transferred it to a hypothetical afterlife. He saw the materiality of lived experience as the only means of recuperating meaning and nihilism as the ethical reaction to the realization that "God is dead." Heidegger's claim was that lived experience, "being in the world" as such, is no longer possible because all that is left, all that humans have left to operate with, is the illusion of value and the sense of life has been reduced to its exchange and appreciation.

In literature nihilism was made popular by the Russian novelist Ivan Turgenev (1818–1883) who used the term in *Fathers and Sons,* published in 1882 to characterize the attitude of the contemporary intelligentsia in Russian society. These intellectuals protested the social stagnation base of tsarist Russia and demanded reforms. Their social activism peaked in the 1870s with the creation of several secret organizations like the Circle of Tchaikovsky, Land and Liberty, and the People's Revenge. From Land and Liberty emerged *Narodnaia Volia,* People's Will, the first organized revolutionary party in Russia, from which the name of the movement, Narodik, and the philosophy of Narodism were derived. Eventually they did embrace **terrorism** as a revolutionary resource. Early in 1881, a group of young nihilists organized a plot to assassinate Tsar **Alexander II** who had already known several attempts on his life. The plot was carried out on March 13, near the Winter Palace in St. Petersburg, when he was attacked with hand grenades and killed by Ignacy Hryniewiecki (1856–1881), a Polish mathematics student from Lithuania. The Poles, living in various areas occupied by Russia since the fourth Partition of Poland in 1795, were at the being subjected to Russification. Hryniewiecki was wounded and died in the attack. Following this incident nihilism was classified as a destructive ideology and associated with terrorism in a manner similar to anarchism. *See also* Anarchism; Narodna Odbrana.

FURTHER READING: Cunningham, Conor. *Genealogy of Nihilism: Philosophies of Nothing and the Difference of Theology.* London: Routledge, 2002; Wilshire, Bruce. *Fashionable Nihilism: A Critique of Analytic Philosophy.* Albany: State University of New York Press, 2002.

GEORGIA TRES

Nile, Battle of the

See Aboukir Bay, Battle of

North German Confederation (1867–1871)

The North German Confederation (*Norddeutscher Bund*) was a transitional stage in the unification of the German states after the Prussian victory in the **Austro-Prussian War** of 1866. It involved the union of **Prussia** with 21 other German states north of the Main River. Otto von **Bismarck** drafted its constitution, which made **Wilhelm I,** King of Prussia, the Confederation's president and himself its chancellor. A *Bundesrat* or Federal Council of 43 seats—17 of which were Prussia's—shared legislative authority with an elected lower house, the Reichstag; but the chancellor was generally unaccountable to the legislature, retained control over the military budget, and provided the link between the crown and people. The *Zollverein* extended a degree of unity with the states of southern Germany until Prussia's victory over France in 1871 brought Baden, Bavaria, and Württemberg into political union with the Confederation to form the **German Empire** under Wilhelm I. *See also* German Empire.

FURTHER READING: Clark, Christopher. *Iron Kingdom: The Rise and Fall of Prussia, 1600–1947.* Cambridge: Belknap, 2006; Mann, Golo. *The History of Germany since 1789.* Translated by Marion Jackson. London: Chatto & Windus, 1968.

CARL CAVANAGH HODGE

Norway

A Danish domain dragged into the **Napoleonic Wars** in 1799. A seafaring nation highly dependent on grain import, Norway suffered badly under blockade from the **Royal Navy,** and only the recent introduction of the potato saved Norwegians from famine. The Treaty of Kiel transferred the rule of Norway to victorious Sweden. But in the short interregnum in 1814, a Norwegian constitution and parliament were established. The parliament controlled the legislative powers and the judiciary, and the king the executive.

The ruling class of civil servants made up only a tiny faction of the population, less than 3 percent in 1815. Males over 25 years old enjoyed suffrage, provided they had a certain income or sufficient landed property. Full universal suffrage for men and women was introduced in 1913. Although the majority of the population were yeomen, the first half of the nineteenth century saw a growing population in general and a rising number of *husmenn*, peasants renting land, paying either a fee or in labor, servants and laborers, numbering 173,000 in 1801 and 261,000 in 1850. Also, ever more marginal lands were cultivated. The situation for these groups was mixed, however, and many were able to combine farming with fishing and forestry, and agriculture saw a wave of modernization around the mid 1840s and 1850s, called *det store hamskiftet*, the great transformation or more literally "the great shedding." Many emigrated to the **United States** from the 1860s, and only from Ireland did a larger proportion of the population emigrate to North America.

A radical social rising around 1850, the Thranites, was quashed, but at the same time the yeomen asserted themselves as a political force along side the civil servants. Their agenda was lower taxes and small government, as well as a greater degree of local self-rule. A major breakthrough in the latter came with an 1837 law, dividing Norway into municipalities. The ideals of the 1814 constitution, as well as the civil servant class were liberal. Servitude was banned and certain civil rights guaranteed.

From the 1840s, there was a significant improvement of internal communications. The first railroad opened in 1854, but only from the 1870s did railroad building really gather pace. By 1853, steamers covered almost the entire coast. From 1850 to 1880, Norway's merchant fleet grew from the eighth to the third largest in the world, stimulated by Great Britain's repeal of their **Navigation Acts** in 1849, a general liberalization of world trade and the availability of skilled sailors at low wages. From the 1880s, Norwegian high seas shipping also shifted to steam. The nineteenth-century Norwegian economy followed a boom and bust pattern, but long-term growth was ensured by the steady reduction of government regulations, stimulating growth of industry and crafts both in the cities and rural areas. Norway's old industries—shipbuilding, mining, and forestry—still thrived; but from the 1870s new, export-oriented industries of wood-processing, food canning, and electrolysis emerged, based on innovation and abundance of hydroelectric power. The most famous single industry, perhaps, was Norsk Hydro's production of artificial fertilizer. Many new industries were financed by overseas capital, and legislation was introduced to ensure national ownership of natural resources toward the end of the period. Domestic finance also saw the introduction of cooperative banking, especially in rural areas. Cooperative solutions were also chosen in many areas relating to agriculture, that is in dairy processing.

Norway, too, was swept by the nationalist sentiments throughout Europe after 1848. The medieval greatness of the Vikings and folklore came into fashion, but a more long-lasting effect manifested itself in a prolonged struggle for national independence. Until the 1840s, the civil servant class had kept Swedish overtures for more integration at bay. From then on, the king was put on the defensive. Following an impeachment of the government in 1884, parliamentarism asserted itself, and the first political parties were established: Venstre, the Left, and Høyre, the Right, in 1884. The Norwegian Labor Party soon followed in 1887. The late nineteenth century also brought a surge of organizations in every aspect of public life besides pure politics, from religious societies, culture, in labor and trade, sports, and leisure activities.

In addition to the more fundamental cleavage produced by the desire of national independence, Norway also had a different alignment regarding foreign trade. Sweden was oriented toward continental Europe and chiefly Germany, but Norway's greatest trading partner was Great Britain, and, as a seafaring nation, good relations with the British as the rulers of the seas was paramount to Norwegian national interest. The dispute leading to the final abolition of the union with Sweden in 1905 came after Norway demanded separate foreign legations. On the basis of referenda Norway chose independence, but maintained the monarchy and handed the throne to the Danish Prince Carl, who became King Haakon VII. Following independence, Norway pursued expansion in form of explorations and land claims in polar areas and stayed neutral in World War I. *See also* Scandinavia.

FURTHER READING: Barton, H. Arnold. *Sweden and Visions of Norway Politics and Culture, 1814–1905.* Carbondale: Southern Illinois University Press, 2003; Moses, Jonathon Wayne. *Norwegian Catch-Up: Development and Globalization before World War I.* Aldershot: Ashgate Publishing 2005; Stenersen, Øivind Libæk, and Ivar Stenersen. *A History of Norway: From the Ice Age to the Age of Petroleum.* Lysaker: Dinamo Forlag, 2003.

FRODE LINDGJERDET

Nova Scotia

A British colony on the northeast coast of North America, and from 1867 a province of the Dominion of **Canada.** In the eighteenth century, Nova Scotia included what later became **New Brunswick** and Prince Edward Island. It was the only British colony on the coast of North America to remain loyal during the War of American Independence and thereafter saw a large influx of loyalist refugees, almost tripling its population. The port of Halifax, first settled in 1749, became a major British naval base, and was particularly important during the Anglo-American War of 1812. Although Lord **Durham**'s report of 1839 concerned the Canadas, and not Nova Scotia, it was quickly picked up by Nova Scotian reformers, who successfully demanded responsible government for themselves.

In February 1848, Nova Scotia became the first British colony in which the principle was put into effect. Although Nova Scotia participated in the negotiations among the British North American colonies leading to the formation of the Dominion of Canada under the **British North America Act** of 1867, a majority of members hostile to confederation was elected in the first federal election. An effort to persuade the British Parliament to repeal Nova Scotia's entry into the confederation failed, and the province became reconciled to its membership in the Dominion. Its economy in the nineteenth and well into the twentieth century centered on fish, lumber, coal, and shipping. *See also* Responsible Government.

FURTHER READING: Pryke, Kenneth G. *Nova Scotia and Confederation, 1864–1874.* Toronto: University of Toronto Press, 1979.

MARK F. PROUDMAN

Novipazar, Sanjak of

A corridor of territory wedged between **Montenegro** and **Serbia.** At the Congress of **Berlin** in 1878, **Austria-Hungary** was authorized to keep troops in the Ottoman district (*Sanjak*) of Novipazar on a permanent basis. The territory along the Lim River was judged to be of strategic value because it connected **Bosnia-Herzegovina,** occupied and administered by the **Habsburg Empire** since 1878, to Ottoman Macedonia. The Sanjak of Novipazar also formed a buffer between the kingdoms of Serbia and Montenegro. It was reasoned that an Austro-Hungarian military presence there would safeguard the Habsburg's monarchy's economic and political interests on the Balkan Peninsula. In 1908, Austria-Hungary's foreign minister Aloys Lexa von **Aehrenthal,** decided to surrender the right to station troops in the Sanjak of Novipazar to mollify Ottoman and international reactions to the unilateral annexation of Bosnia-Herzegovina. After the defeat of the **Ottoman Empire** in the First Balkan War of 1912, the Sandjak of Novipazar was annexed by Serbia and Montenegro. *See also* Balkan Wars.

FURTHER READING: Jelavich, Barbara. *History of the Balkans.* New York: Cambridge University Press, 1983; Pavlowitch, Stevan K. *A History of the Balkans, 1804–1945.* New York: Addison-Wesley Longman, 1999; Taylor, A.J.P. *The Struggle for Mastery in Europe, 1848–1918.* Oxford: Clarendon, 1954.

GUENTHER KRONENBITTER

O

October Manifesto (1905)

The response of **Nicholas II** to Revolution of 1905 in Russia. By 1900, Russia faced serious problems: a changing social structure, a growing revolutionary movement, and political stagnation. Coupled with the disastrous **Russo-Japanese War** of 1904–1905, these factors led to social unrest and revolution. Nicholas attempted to placate the public with this document that guaranteed civil liberties: freedom of religion, speech, assembly, and association and freedom from arbitrary arrest and imprisonment. It also created a Duma with the power to approve all proposed laws and promised further reform in the future. In principle, it created a constitutional monarchy; in reality, Nicholas had no intention of sharing power. Once order was restored it became clear that very little had been accomplished by the revolution. For the tsar, however, the manifesto split the opposition, satisfying liberals and moderates and temporarily stripping the revolutionary movement of much of its strength. *See also* Bolsheviks; Lenin, Vladimir Illyich.

FURTHER READING: Figes, Orlando. *A People's Tragedy: The Russian Revolution, 1891–1924.* New York: Penguin, 1996; Freeze, Gregory L. *From Supplication to Revolution: A Documentary Social History of Imperial Russia.* Oxford: Oxford University Press, 1988; Pipes, Richard. *The Russian Revolution.* New York: Vintage, 1990; Shanin, Teodor. *Russia, 1905–07: Revolution as a Moment of Truth.* New Haven, CT: Yale University Press, 1986.

LEE A. FARROW

Oil

The vernacular for petroleum, a naturally occurring liquid composed of hydrocarbons, the industrial use of which increased dramatically during the nineteenth century. Much of the exploration and industrial development of uses for oil was done by American oil companies. Oil usage was low at the beginning of the period. Small quantities were gathered from natural oil seeps to be used as pitch to seal boats, as axle grease or for medicinal purpose. In the 1840s, Canadian Abraham Gesner invented kerosene, and the first modern oil well was sunk in 1848 by the Russian engineer F. N. Semyonov near Baku on the Caspian Sea. It soon replaced whale oil as the fuel for lighting in homes and offices. By 1900, gasoline for internal combustion engines and heavy oil to power ships—especial naval vessels, since the age of sail depended on massive quantities of coal for fuel—had caused the demand for oil to increase dramatically. Together with the importance of oil to industrial development generally, the invention of the Parson's turbine engine increased the range of ships, for commerce and naval warfare, and made oil a strategic commodity.

The growing demand for oil was supplied by the cable-tool method of oil well drilling. In 1859, Captain Edwin L. Drake drilled the first oil well in western Pennsylvania. The rotary drill method was used in 1901 at Spindletop, Texas, to bring in the first gusher. Discoveries were made in California, Canada, the Dutch East Indies, Iran, Mexico, Peru, Romania, and Venezuela and elsewhere by increasingly powerful oil companies, the greatest of which was John D. Rockefeller's Standard Oil Trust. The Anglo-Persain Oil Company, founded in 1909, was the first company to exploit the oil potential of the Middle East. *See also* Globalization.

FURTHER READING: Giddens, Paul Henry. *The Early Petroleum Industry.* Philadelphia: Porcupine Press, 1974.

ANDREW J. WASKEY

Omdurman, Battle of (1898)

A critical engagement resulting in the reestablishment of Anglo-Egyptian control over the Upper Nile Valley. Fought on September 2, 1898, during the British campaign against the Dervishes of the Sudan, Omdurman brought Lord **Kitchener** to prominence. Kitchener's army of 26,000 men, half British and half Egyptian, came under attack in its fortified encampment near Omdurman by 40,000 Dervishes commanded by the **Mahdi,** who, despite fanatical perseverance, failed to make headway against the concentrated **machine guns** and modern repeating rifles of their opponents. Having repulsed the tribesmen, Kitchener then marched toward Omdurman where the Dervishes, on rallying, attacked again, including a force concealed in a ravine, which although driven off by a lancer charge, inflicted heavy casualties on the horsemen. Modern technology proved too much even for the bravery of the Dervishes, who fled leaving 20,000 casualties on the field while inflicting only 500 on the Anglo-Egyptians. *See also* Africa, Scramble for; British Empire; Egypt; Fashoda Crisis.

FURTHER READING: Featherstone, Donald, *Omdurman 1898: Kitchener's Victory in the Sudan.* Oxford: Osprey Publishing, 1994; Pollock, John. *Kitchener: The Road to Omdurman.* London: Constable, 1999; Ziegler, Philip, *Omdurman.* London: Leo Cooper, 2003.

GREGORY FREMONT-BARNES

Open Door

A **free trade** principle promoted by the **United States** following Japan's victory in the **Sino-Japanese War** and motivated by a concern to contain the establishment of exclusive spheres of influence by the Great Powers in **China.** In September 1899, Secretary of State John Hay directed a series of circular diplomatic notes toward Britain, France, Germany, Italy, Japan, and Russia. The first note called on the powers to regard China as an open international market yet to pledge noninterference with commerce within existing spheres of influence. It also sought the retention of tariff duties collected by the Chinese government on goods at all treaty ports and the application of the duty without discrimination as to the country of origin. Lastly, it called for all nations to be treated equally in terms of harbor fees and railway duties.

Most of the other powers announced their willingness to make a declaration of agreement—the British government noted its "pleasure," the Russian its "happiness"—but compliance was another matter. Above all, the Open Door Notes testified to an increased American engagement in international affairs generally, along with a special interest, following the acquisition of the Philippines in the **Spanish-American War,** in the affairs of the Western Pacific. At the time the United States had no capacity to enforce Open Door principles, and the other powers, save Italy, had no intention of being bound by them. American interest in the region nonetheless asserted itself again five years later with Theodore **Roosevelt**'s mediation of a peace in the **Russo-Japanese War.** *See also* Boxer Insurrection.

FURTHER READING: Brands, H. W. *Bound to Empire: The United States and the Philippines.* New York: Oxford University Press, 1992; May, Ernest. *Imperial Democracy: The Emergence of America as a Great Power.* Chicago: Imprint, 1991.

CARL CAVANAGH HODGE

Opium War (1839–1842)

A conflict that opened China physically to political, economic, and social influences from the outside world and heralded the period of unequal treaties in which the Great Powers carved out spheres of influence to exploit the country's markets and resources. By the late eighteenth century, Britain had established trading ties with China in the belief that it was a natural market for British manufactured wares. While Britain imported tea, silk, spices, and porcelain, a largely self-sufficient China demonstrated little interest in purchasing Western goods, which resulted in a deteriorating trade deficit for the British. British merchants found a product for which a Chinese demand existed, opium, and started a highly profitable but illicit trade.

By the early 1800s, the large-scale trade in opium from British **India** had reversed the trade deficit and created widespread misery as millions of Chinese became addicted to the drug. In 1839, in an attempt to deal with social and economic dislocations caused the opium trade, the emperor issued 39 articles that imposed severe penalties, including death, for smoking and smuggling opium. A special commissioner, Lin Zexu, was dispatched to Guangzhou (Canton) to ensure that the regulations were enforced. Lin arrested thousands of addicts and demanded that foreign merchants surrender their inventory of opium. The British chief superintendent of trade in Canton, Captain Charles Elliot, was forced to turn over 20,283 chests of opium to Lin, who proceeded to destroy them publicly. Elliot, however, refused to hand over British sailors accused of killing a Chinese national, insisting on the right of extraterritoriality. The situation escalated when Lin ordered Canton completely closed to foreign trade. The British dispatched a naval force to China and hostilities commenced in November 1839. Chinese military forces were no match for the British and were forced to sue for peace. The Treaty of **Nanjing** of August 29, 1842, and the supplementary treaties of July and October 1843 concluded the First Opium War, and were the first of the so-called unequal treaties. Between them, the treaties provided that the ports of Guangzhou, Xiamen, Fuzhou, Ningbo, and Shanghai be open to British trade and residence, as well as the cession of Hong Kong in perpetuity to Britain. A Second Opium War, the **Arrow War,** erupted in 1856. *See also* Qing Dynasty.

FURTHER READING: Beeching, Jack. *The Opium Wars.* London: Hutchinson, 1975; Tan, Chung. *China and the Brave New World: A Study of the Origins of the Opium War, 1840–42.* Durham, NC: Carolina Academic Press, 1978; Waley, Arthur. *The Opium War through Chinese Eyes.* Stanford, CA: Stanford University Press, 1968.

ADRIAN U-JIN ANG

Orange Free State

A Boer republic of South Africa established when Boer settlers migrated north from the Cape Colony during the Great Trek to escape British rule. Britain annexed the territory in 1848 but in 1854 returned it to the Boers in the Bloemfontein Convention, at which time it acquired its name. From the 1860s to the 1890s, the Orange Free State prospered because of the discovery of diamonds and gold in the Transvaal to the north. Railroads were built from the Cape Colony across its territory even as demand for its agricultural products increased.

The Free State established a customs union with the Cape Colony, but it was not from this economic connection that its political autonomy was imperiled. Rather, it formed an alliance with the Transvaal following the **Jameson Raid** in 1895 and was thus drawn directly into the Second **Boer War** in 1899. After the war, the Orange Free State was again joined to the British Empire as the Orange River Colony. The colony was given responsible government in 1907 and in 1910 became a province of the Union of South Africa as the Orange Free State.

FURTHER READING: Pakenham, Thomas. *The Boer War.* New York: Random House, 1979; Were, Gideon. *A History of South Africa.* New York: Africana Publishing Company, 1974.

CARL CAVANAGH HODGE

Oregon Question

A territorial dispute involving the lands west of the Rocky Mountains to the Pacific Ocean and between latitudes 42° and 54°40', encompassing approximately a half-million square miles. Until the early nineteenth century, the United States, Great Britain, Spain, and Russia each asserted colonial rights to the territory, based on either discovery, exploration, or settlement. Spain conceded its title to Oregon to the United States in 1819 with the **Adams-Onís Treaty,** and in treaties with the United States and Britain in 1824 and 1825 respectively Russia renounced its rights. Although the Oregon territory was on the periphery of the British and American empires, both powers valued it for its economic and strategic potential. Britain sought to divide the territory on the basis of settlement, extending the U.S.-Canadian border along latitude 49° to the Columbia River, then following the river to the Pacific Ocean. The United States refused, biding its time until in a stronger position to assert its claims. Instead of a final settlement, for more than 20 years after the 1818 Convention, the United States and Britain established a joint occupation of Oregon that was open to equal settlement.

Awareness of Oregon intensified in the United States as a consequence of the 1842 Wilkes expedition, as thousands of migrants pioneered across the Oregon Trail. The popularity of Manifest Destiny, abundant fertile lands, a deep water port, and a burgeoning commercial interest in the Orient made Oregon high priority for many Americans. Publicly, President James K. Polk insisted that all of Oregon was U.S. territory, echoing jingoist demands of "54°40' or Fight!," but privately he promoted compromise at 49°. The British desired to retain the disputed territory between 49° and the Columbia River, but were unwilling to go to war for it. British Foreign Secretary Lord Aberdeen, realizing that American migration would not abate and that American war cries were intensifying, that Britain was unable to defend Oregon, and that the fur trade was stagnant, conceded the disputed territory. The Buchanan-Pakenham Treaty of 1846—also known as the Oregon Treaty and the Treaty of Washington— established the American-Canadian border at 49°, extending through the Strait of Juan de Fuca. The final settlement resolved a longstanding Anglo-American colonial dispute, guaranteed the United States greater access to the Pacific Ocean and Oriental markets, and paved the way for American redevelopment of Oregon. The steady influx of Euro-American culture in subsequent decades undermined traditional indigenous tribal societies, resulting in their eventual displacement or annihilation. *See also* Canada; Jingoism; Lewis and Clark Expedition; Manifest Destiny.

FURTHER READING: Merk, Frederick. *The Oregon Question: Essays in Anglo-American Diplomacy and Politics.* Cambridge, MA: Harvard University Press, 1967.

JONATHAN GANTT

Orientalism

A term fraught with political and cultural baggage referring vaguely to the East and long used to refer to collectively, if imprecisely, to the diverse societies east and south of Europe. The term *Orientalism* was originally used to name the expertise of specialists in Semitic and Indo-European languages and societies. Sir William "Oriental" Jones was the archetypal Orientalist; an official of the **East India Company,** he noted the similarities between Sanskrit and classical Greek, and hypothesized the now widely accepted common origins of the languages of India and those of Europe. In British India, the term *Orientalist* referred to those such as Jones who did not think that the cultures they studied should be ranked below that of the West. By contrast, anglicizers such as Thomas Babington **Macaulay** held that Oriental learning was obsolete and that Indians should be trained in the language and culture of the superior Western society.

Outside **India,** the term *Orientalist* was in general applied to students of Islamic and Asian languages and societies, and normally implied great and recondite learning. In the arts, Orientalism referred to the use of the Orient as a setting or character, symbolizing a diverse range of attributes from splendor to squalor, majesty to decadence. This was true in 1819 for Goethe's *West-östlicher Diwan*, a collection poems inspired by the Persian poet Hafiz, as well as for Richard Strauss's *Salome*, an opera first performed in Dresden in 1905. In 1978, Edward Said published his study—some would say his polemic—*Orientalism*, which argued that Orientalists had constructed a hostile caricature of the Orient designed to justify imperial conquest. Though Said's work has been subjected to destructive criticism on many grounds, under his influence the term *Orientalism* has become almost impossible to use in its earlier sense; for many, especially in leftist and so-called postcolonial circles, it signifies the imposition of hostile categories on oppressed peoples rather than erudition. *See also* Kipling, Rudyard; Imperialism.

FURTHER READING: Irwin, Robert. *For Lust of Knowing: The Orientalists and Their Enemies.* London: Allen Lane, 2006; Lewis, Bernard. "The Question of Orientalism." *The New York Review of Books,* June 24, 1982; Said, Edward. *Orientalism.* New York: Norton, 1978.

MARK F. PROUDMAN

Ossetia

A region in the Caucasus and lying between Russia to the north and Georgia to the south. Ossetia consists of two parts, North Ossetia and South Ossetia, both of which were absorbed into the **Russian Empire.** Under Catherine II (1762–1796), Russia first advanced into the Caucasus region and established a military presence at the town of Vladikavkaz in North Ossetia, and in the eighteenth century Russia absorbed North Ossetia. Between 1801 and 1806, Russia annexed South Ossetia with its main town of Tskhinvali as part of the process of acquiring all of the Kingdom of Georgia. The Ossetians speak an Iranian language, Ossetic, unrelated to either Russian or Georgian. Ossetians are mostly Orthodox Christian in the south and Sunni Muslim in the north. Because of its long association with Georgia, South Ossetia had a strong imprint of Georgian culture.

FURTHER READING: Geyer, Dietrich. *Russian Imperialism: The Interaction of Domestic and Foreign Policy, 1860–1914.* New York: Berg, 1987; Rywkin, Michael. *Russian Colonial Expansion to 1917.* London: Mansell, 1988; Seton-Watson, Hugh. *The Russian Empire, 1801–1917.* Oxford: Clarendon Press, 1967.

JONATHAN GRANT

O'Sullivan, John Louis (1813–1895)

The probable coiner of the expression **Manifest Destiny.** A lawyer, journalist, editor, and diplomat and onetime U.S. minister to Portugal, O'Sullivan used this immortal phrase in 1845, first in his *United States Magazine and Democratic Review*—a leading Democratic and nationalist organ—about the annexation of Texas and next in the *New York Morning News* about the acquisition of Oregon. O'Sullivan, who was arrested twice on account of his **filibuster** activity, was among other things a cultural nationalist who endeavored to promote a genuinely American literature.

The discoverer and publisher of Nathaniel Hawthorne, a lifelong friend, and Walt Whitman, he also published such authors as William Cullen Bryant, Henry David Thoreau, Ralph Waldo Emerson, Edgar Allan Poe, George Bancroft, and John Greenleaf Whittier. *See also* California; Jingoism; Mexican War; Oregon Question.

FURTHER READING: Haynes, Sam W., and Morris, Christopher, eds. *Manifest Destiny and Empire: American Antebellum Expansionism.* No. 31: The Walter Prescott Webb Memorial Lectures. College Station: Texas A&M University Press, 1997; Pratt, Julius W. "The Origin of 'Manifest Destiny.'" *American Historical Review* 32 (1927): 795–798.

SERGE RICARD

Ottoman Empire

The Ottoman Empire originated as one of more than a dozen small Anatolian principalities that came into existence in the wake of the Mongol invasions of the thirteenth century. These Turkish principalities were Islamic warrior states whose ongoing military confrontations with Christian Byzantium were inspired by religious motives, as well as by a desire for material gain. The tradition of *ghaza*, warfare against non-Muslims for the purpose of extending the domains of Islam, was a driving force among the Muslim frontier warriors (*ghazis*), and the *ghazi* spirit played a decisive role in shaping the Ottoman Empire.

Much about the early history of the Ottoman state remains obscure, but its beginnings are usually traced to the achievements of a Turkish chieftain named Osman, the ruler of one of the smaller *ghazi* principalities. During the early 1300s, Osman's *ghazi* warriors achieved a series of military successes against the Byzantine forces. These victories enhanced Osman's reputation and attracted other chieftains and tribesmen to his realm. The growing military power at Osman's disposal enabled him and his son Orhon to expand their domains in northwestern Anatolia. In 1326, Orhon captured the city of Bursa from the Byzantines and made it the capital of his state. As Orhon's *ghazi* principality made the transition from a frontier society to an established state, his subjects came to be known by his family name, Osmanlis, or Ottomans. The sense of belonging to a single dynastic house created sentiments of solidarity and loyalty that gradually transcended tribal affiliations.

Ottoman Expansion

By the middle of the fourteenth century, the Ottomans had expanded to the shores of the Sea of Marmara, which forms part of the water connection between the Black Sea to the north and the Aegean Sea to the south. Over the course of the next two centuries, all of southeastern Europe came under direct Ottoman control. The Ottomans not only added new European territories to the domains of Islam, but they also extended their rule to the Arab lands where Islam had originated. The transformation of the Ottoman state into a world power began with the conquest of the city of Constantinople. On May 29, 1453, following a long siege, the forces of Sultan Mehmet II, the Conqueror, entered the Byzantine capital and brought an end to Constantinople's role as the symbolic center of eastern Christendom. Henceforth known as Istanbul, the city became the seat of the Ottoman government and was restored to its former splendor by Mehmet II's program of reconstruction and repopulation.

The occupation of Istanbul provided the Ottomans with an unparalleled strategic base from which to dominate the Black Sea and the Eastern Mediterranean. Mehmet the Conqueror constructed shipyards in Istanbul; gathered skilled carpenters, merchants, and sailors from the coastal regions under his rule; and forged an Ottoman navy that eventually drove Venice from the Eastern Mediterranean and established the Ottomans as the supreme maritime power from the Adriatic to the Black Sea. The creation of a fleet also enabled the Ottomans to conquer and occupy such strategic Mediterranean islands as Rhodes (1522), Cyprus (1570), and Crete (1664).

The creation of a successful navy was accompanied by improvements in the Ottoman land army that made it the most formidable military force of the sixteenth and seventeenth centuries. At the heart of the Ottoman military superiority was the development and extensive use of gunpowder weapons. The Ottomans adapted artillery technology to serve their special needs, most notably by developing light field guns that could be transported on wagons to distant battlefields. These guns were used against the feudal armies of Europe, whose infantrymen still fought mainly with pikes. These technological advantages enabled the Ottoman armed forces to defeat the armies of both Europe and the Middle East.

The Ottomans sent their army regularly to the east to repel the advances of the Safavid Empire of **Iran.** When Sultan Selim I led the Ottoman army on an eastern campaign in 1516, his objective appeared to be the occupation of the Safavid imperial capital at Tabriz. However, he decided instead to neutralize the threat posed by the Mamluk Empire, which was centered in Egypt but which also controlled Syria and certain territories in southern Anatolia. The Ottoman army drove the Mamluks out of Syria, and, in early 1517, Selim marched his forces across the Sinai Peninsula and captured Cairo. This victory resulted in the Ottoman acquisition of most of the classical heartlands of Arab Islam and brought about the integration of the Arab and Ottoman Islamic traditions.

The Ottoman conquest of the Arab lands established the sultans as the supreme rulers within the universal Islamic community. They were recognized as the protectors of the holy cities of Mecca and Medina and therefore assumed the important duty of ensuring the security of the annual pilgrimage. To fulfill this responsibility, and also to contain the expansive Portuguese seaborne commercial empire, Selim ordered the creation of a Red Sea fleet. Although the Ottomans proved unable to compete with the Portuguese in the Indian Ocean, their domination of **Egypt** allowed them to establish hegemony in the Red Sea and to incorporate Yemen, on the Arabian Peninsula, into their empire. In addition, Selim's occupation of Egypt enhanced the Islamic standing of the Ottoman sultans by enabling them to gain access to the title of **caliph.** After the Ottoman conquest of Egypt, the reigning caliph was taken to Istanbul and allegedly transferred the title to Selim and his successors in the Ottoman dynasty.

Although Sultan Suleyman the Magnificent (1520–1566), the most powerful of the Ottoman rulers, achieved important military victories at sea and on the eastern front, he was primarily a *ghazi*-inspired sultan who concentrated on pushing the Ottoman frontier deeper into Europe. In 1520, Suleyman led the Ottoman forces in the capture of Belgrade, which became the primary staging ground for subsequent Ottoman campaigns. During the rest of the 1520s, Budapest and most of Hungary were brought under Ottoman control. Then, in 1529, Suleyman laid siege to Vienna, the **Habsburg** imperial capital and the gateway to central Europe. Although the outskirts of Vienna were destroyed and the city walls were breached in several places, the defenders held out until the threat of winter forced the Ottomans to begin their long withdrawal to Istanbul.

In the years to come, Suleyman's European campaigns consolidated Ottoman rule in Hungary and Serbia, but the sultan was unable to mount another siege of Vienna. Central Europe was beyond the limits of Ottoman territorial expansion; the area that did lie within those limits was so extensive—stretching from the Danube to Yemen, from Albania to the northern shores of the Black Sea, and from **Algeria** to Baghdad—that the Ottoman Empire was, at Suleyman's death in 1566, the major European, Mediterranean, and Middle Eastern power. It was not only the leading Islamic state of the sixteenth century, it was a world empire of vast influence and territorial expanse.

Ottoman Rule

At the pinnacle of the Ottoman hierarchy was the sultan-caliph, an absolute monarch whose right to rule was derived from his membership in the house of Osman. As the Ottoman state changed from a *ghazi* principality to a world empire, the sultans instituted an imperial council, or *divan*, to deal with the increasingly complex affairs of government. The *divan* was presided over by the grand vizier, the most powerful official in the government hierarchy whose court was referred to as the *Bab-i Ali*, or Sublime **Porte,** most usually in the context of Ottoman diplomacy. He was the absolute deputy of the sultan and acquired the right to exercise executive authority in the sultan's name. During the reigns of weak sultans, the *grand viziers* sometimes assumed extensive powers and made decisions without consulting the monarch.

The three major groupings within the Ottoman ruling elite were the military, the civil service, and the religious establishment. The two main branches of the Ottoman armed forces came from quite different sources. The provincial cavalrymen, or *sipahis*, were freeborn Muslims who fulfilled an administrative as well as a military function. In an attempt to maintain a large army without making huge cash payments, the sultans awarded *sipahis* the rights to the income from agricultural land, known as *timars*. Each *sipahi* was assigned a specific *timar* from which he was allowed to collect the taxes that served as his salary. In return, the *sipahi* was expected to maintain order in his *timar,* to report for military service when called on by the sultan, and, depending on the size of his income, to bring with him a certain number of armed and mounted retainers.

Although *sipahis* and their retainers made up the bulk of the Ottoman armies, the most efficient imperial military unit was the professional standing infantry corps known as the **Janissaries.** In the fourteenth century, the Ottomans institutionalized a method for procuring slaves from among their European Christian subjects. Known as the *devshirme,* a collecting system, it consisted of a levy every few years on adolescent male Christian children from the European provinces of the empire. The children were removed from their families and taken to Istanbul, where they were converted to Islam, tested and screened, and then trained for service in the empire. Most of them were eventually enrolled in the ranks of the Janissary corps, which, at its peak in the fifteenth and sixteenth centuries, was the outstanding military unit in Europe.

As a centralized imperial state, the Ottoman Empire was characterized by an immense and elaborate bureaucracy. The Ottomans drew on the administrative traditions of the Byzantines, the Iranians, and the Arabs to create a highly differentiated civil service. Most of the middle-level Ottoman civil servants were freeborn Muslims who received on-the-job training as apprentices in one of the several ministries. Along with the bureaucratic and military elite, the *ulama* formed the third pillar of the Ottoman ruling class. The Ottomans endeavored to establish *shari'ah* norms of justice by organizing the *qadis,* judges, into an official hierarchy and arranging for their appointments in the various administrative subdivisions of the empire. Over the course of time, an official known as the *shaykh al-Islam* emerged as the chief religious dignitary of the empire. He oversaw the appointment of *qadis* and *madrasah* teachers in the far-flung Ottoman territories and acquired status as the official whose legal opinion the sultans sought when they contemplated the introduction of certain administrative and fiscal measures.

The European Challenge

The once prevalent idea that the Ottoman Empire entered into a period of decline after the reign of Suleyman is no longer accepted. It is perhaps preferable to view the Ottoman experience from the seventeenth to the twentieth centuries as a period of transformation during which the Ottomans struggled to find a new imperial synthesis in a changing international environment. External factors, most prominent among them the penetration of European merchant capital into the empire, caused a wrenching dislocation of the Ottoman economy. Beginning in the late sixteenth century, Ottoman raw materials, normally channeled into internal consumption and industry, were increasingly exchanged for European manufactured products. This trade benefited Ottoman merchants but led to a decline in state revenues and a shortage of raw materials for domestic consumption. As the costs of scarce materials rose, the empire suffered from inflation, and the state was unable to procure sufficient revenues to meet its expenses. Without these revenues, the institutions that supported the Ottoman system, especially the armed forces, were undermined.

The penetration of European manufactured goods into the empire and the eventual domination of Ottoman commerce by Europeans, and their protégés were facilitated by a series of commercial treaties, known as the Capitulations, which the Ottoman sultans signed with the Christian states of Europe. The first Capitulation agreement was negotiated with France in 1536. It allowed French merchants to trade freely in Ottoman ports, to be exempt from Ottoman taxes, and to import and export goods at low tariff rates. In addition, the treaty granted extraterritorial privileges to French merchants by permitting them to come under the legal jurisdiction of the French consul in Istanbul, thus making them subject to French law. The first treaty was the model for subsequent agreements signed with other European states.

The Capitulations were negotiated at a time of Ottoman military domination and were intended to encourage commercial exchange. When the military balance between Europe and the Ottomans tilted in favor of Europe, however, European merchants, backed by the power of their states, were able to exploit the Capitulations to the disadvantage of the Ottomans. The treaties not only had a devastating effect on the Ottoman economy, but they also had long-term political implications.

By granting the various consuls jurisdiction over their nationals within the Ottoman Empire, the Capitulations accorded the consuls extraordinary powers that they abused with increasing frequency in the course of the nineteenth century.

External economic factors combined with a range of domestic problems, such as incompetent sultans, succession struggles, and political discord within the court, weakened the effectiveness of the central government. The shortage of revenue and the rise of inflation had a devastating effect on the large numbers of state employees on fixed salaries and created an atmosphere that fostered bribery and other forms of corruption. And finally, the government's inability to make regular payments to the Janissaries or to fund the acquisition of new military equipment meant that the Ottoman armed forces lost the absolute dominance that they had earlier possessed.

This loss of dominance was manifested on the battlefield. In 1683, the Ottomans mounted a second siege of Vienna, but they were defeated outside the city walls. In the 1690s, the Ottomans engaged in simultaneous wars with **Austria** and **Russia** and were defeated on both fronts. The Treaty of Karlowitz, signed with Austria in 1699, ceded most of Hungary to the Hapsburgs and marked the first major surrender of European territory by the Ottomans. The next year, the sultan signed a treaty with Peter the Great acknowledging the Russian conquest of the northern shores of the Black Sea. From this point on, the Ottomans were on the defensive.

During the eighteenth century, the Ottoman forces defeated the Austrian army in two wars as well as the Russian army in two wars. These victories may have led the Ottoman ruling elite to conclude that the armed forces of the state were as relatively powerful as ever. That this was not true was demonstrated in the Ottoman-Russian war launched by the Ottomans in 1768. In the course of this war, the Russian Baltic fleet entered the Mediterranean and destroyed an Ottoman fleet off the coast of Anatolia. The land war was equally devastating for the Ottomans, as the Russian forces drove them out of Romania and the Crimea on the Black Sea. The settlement that ended the war, the Treaty of Küchük Kaynarja (1774), was one of the most humiliating agreements ever signed by the Ottomans. In addition to ceding territory, the sultan granted Russia the right to construct a Greek Orthodox church in Istanbul and to make representations to the Ottoman government on behalf of the Greek Orthodox community. These provisions laid the foundation for Russia's claim to be the protector of the entire Greek Orthodox *millet*, the Ottoman term for a self-governing religious community, within the Ottoman Empire.

Decline, Reform, Decline

Thus beginning in the early eighteenth century, the Western powers achieved and maintained military, political, and economic superiority over the Middle East. In the nineteenth century, Russia's drive towards the sea, leadership of the Orthodox Christians, and promotion of **pan-Slavism** combined at times to produce an aggressive Middle East policy. Russian troops went into the **Balkans** during the 1806–1812 conflict with the Ottomans, the Greek struggle for independence in the 1820s, the Rumanian uprising of 1848, the **Crimean War** of 1853–1856, and the **Russo-Turkish War** of 1877–1878.

The **Eastern Question** centered on whether Russia would gobble up the Ottoman Empire's European possessions, especially the straits, or be prevented from doing so by the other Great Powers. In the nineteenth century, many feared that if Russia ruled the Balkans and controlled the straits, all Europe would be at the mercy of the tsars. The **Habsburg Empire** bordered directly on Ottoman-held lands in southeastern Europe. It conquered Hungary in 1699 and naturally hoped to move down the Danube River toward the Black Sea. The Habsburgs also wanted to control lands south of the Danube, especially **Bosnia** and **Serbia.** The interests of the Habsburg emperors seem to have been mainly economic, but they also saw themselves as carrying an old crusading tradition against the Muslim Ottomans. As various Balkan states wrested their independence from the Ottoman Empire, the Habsburgs would often step forward as their patron, protector, and trading partner.

The **British Empire,** suspicious of Russia's aims during the nineteenth century, tended to back Austria in the Balkans. This suspicion also led to a general British policy aimed at preserving the Ottoman Empire against all outside attempts to divide or control its territory. The overriding reason for this policy was that Britain wanted to ensure a safe route to **India** for its navy and merchant ships. From about 1820, the beginning of steamship travel and better overland communication made it faster and safer to transship goods and people across Egypt or Mesopotamia, both of which were Ottoman lands. In a further attempt to secure its shipping routes to India, Britain also took Aden in 1839 and Cyprus in 1878, occupied Egypt in 1882, and made treaties with most of the Arab rulers along the Gulf from Oman to Kuwait.

The best friend of the Ottomans was usually France. Its strategic location, with major ports on both the Atlantic and the Mediterranean, made France a frequent contender for the mastery of Europe. Up to the nineteenth century, its greatest rival in the Mediterranean was the Habsburg Empire, which tended to bring France into alliance with the Ottomans. France claimed to have the oldest capitulatory treaty, and its merchants and investors were almost always foremost among Europeans doing business with the Ottomans. Religion, too, furthered the French connection. When Russia claimed to protect Orthodox Christians under Ottoman rule, France advanced similar claims on behalf of Catholics.

To stop the annexation of its territories, the Ottoman government attempted internal reform, which should be divided into three phases. In the first, such reformers as the Korpulu viziers of the late seventeenth century tried to restore the administrative and military system to what it had been when the empire was at its height in the sixteenth. When this failed, some of eighteenth-century sultans and viziers tried a selective westernizing policy, primarily in the army, but this second phase did not check Russia's advance into the Balkans or **Napoleon**'s occupation of Egypt. In the third phase of Ottoman reform, mainly in the nineteenth century, the government tried to westernize many parts of the empire in an effort to halt the secession or annexation of its territories.

Sultan Selim III (1789–1807) was aware of the European designs on his country, as well as its internal problems, with some provinces in open revolt and a serious shortfall in tax revenues. He planned a full-scale housecleaning, a *nizam-i-jedid,* that would reform the whole Ottoman government. But with the military threat so imminent, Selim concentrated on creating the westernized elite army to which the name *nizam* is usually applied. The training of the *nizam* soldiers had to be carried out secretly. The Janissaries feared that an effective fighting force, trained by European instructors and using modern weapons, would expose them as useless parasites of the state. They also were not about to let their privileges be jeopardized by military reform, however necessary. As a result, they revolted, slaughtered the new troops, and locked up Selim. While **Mahmud II** held power, from 1808 to1839, the whole empire fell into disorder. Several of the Balkan provinces had become independent in all but name under local warlords. A nationalist uprising of the Serbs threatened to affect other subject peoples. Local landowners in parts of Anatolia were taking the government into their own hands, and the garrisons in such Arab cities as Aleppo and Mosul were held by dissident mamluk or Janissary factions. Russia was at war with the empire and had invaded its Danubian principalities. Although the Sultan wanted to reform and strengthen the Ottoman Empire, he also realized that westernizing reforms had to include all aspects of Ottoman government and society, not just the military; reformed institutions would work only if those they replaced were wiped out, and any reform program must be preceded by careful planning and mobilization of support.

At first, Mahmud kept a low profile, quietly cultivating groups that favored centralization of Ottoman power, and slowly built up a loyal and well-trained palace guard to be used eventually against the Janissaries and their supporters. In 1826, he ordered a general attack on the Janissaries. This time the sultan had a strong army, the *ulama*, the students, and most of the people on his side. As a result, the **Janissaries** were massacred, their supporting groups abolished, and their properties seized for redistribution among Mahmud's backers. This action cleared the way for a large-scale reform program. Highest priority went to developing a new military organization to replace the Janissaries, for the Greeks, backed by the Great Powers, were now rebelling against Ottoman rule. Mahmud gathered soldiers from all parts of the old military system into his new army, which was issued European uniforms and weapons and put in the charge of Western instructors. Ottoman youths had als to be trained in technical fields closely tied to the military; existing schools of military and naval engineering were therefore expanded, a new medical college founded, and new institutions later set up to teach military sciences.

The general aim of the reforms was to concentrate power in the hands of the sultan and his cabinet. The ministries of the government were organized more tightly to eliminate overlapping jurisdictions and superfluous posts. In addition, Mahmud abolished the system of military land grants that had sustained the *sipahis* since the beginning of the empire. He also had to overcome opposition from most local and provincial officials, the feudal *sipahis,* the traditional government scribes, and the *ulama.* Often he failed. Too many members of the Ottoman ruling class had a vested interest in the status-quo. Worse still, westernization did not save the army from losing wars. By 1829, the Greeks had won their independence, their success due mainly to intervention by Russia, which in the Russo-Turkish War of 1828–1829 gained significant new territories east of the Black Sea. The advances of Ibrahim Pasha al Wali's Egyptian armies into **Syria** were yet another blow to Ottoman prestige, especially when Mahmud's new army failed to dislodge them. Outside help would be needed if the empire was to survive. The first choice should have been France, but that country was backing **Mehmet Ali** and Ibrahim, so Mahmud turned instead to Russia. In the Treaty of **Inkiar Skelessi,** Russia agreed in 1833 to defend the territorial integrity of the Ottoman Empire.

Britain, however, believed that the treaty gave Russian warships the right to use the straits, from which Western navies were excluded, so London campaigned against the threat of Russian domination in Istanbul. In a commercial treaty signed in 1838, the Porte increased Britain's capitulatory privileges and limited to 9 percent its import tariffs on British manufactures. This relatively low rate stimulated British exports to the Ottoman market, thus wiping out many Ottoman merchants and artisans who could not compete against British mechanized production. But another result of the 1838 treaty was to increase Britain's economic interest in the Ottoman Empire and hence its desire to keep the empire alive.

Mahmud II died while Mehmet Ali's army was invading Anatolia, whereupon the sultan's navy defected to Alexandria. Mahmud's successor was Abdulmejid (1839–1861), who reigned during the reform era of the *Tanzimat*. The guiding man of the early *Tanzimat* was Mahmud's foreign minister, Mustafa Reshid, who happened to be in London seeking British aid against **Mehmet Ali** at the time Abdulmejid took over. On the advice of both the British and Reshid, the new sultan issued a proclamation called the Noble Rescript of the Rose Chamber, which authorized the creation of new institutions guaranteeing his subjects' fundamental rights, assessing and levying taxes fairly, and conscripting and training soldiers. Mustafa Reshid had an entourage of young and able officials who believed that liberal reforms would save the Ottoman Empire. Almost all aspects of Ottoman public life were restructured. This restructuring meant creating a system of state schools to produce government clerks; reorganizing the provinces so that each governor would have specified duties and an advisory council; extending the network of roads, canals, and rail lines; and developing a modern financial system with a central bank, treasury bonds, and a decimal currency.

The *Tanzimat* was not a total success. The subject nationalities expected too much from the 1839 rescript and were disappointed by the actual reforms. Balkan Christians did not want centralization of power; they wanted autonomy. Some now sought outright independence. The Rumanians rebelled in 1848, and it took a Russian invasion to quell their revolt. Without firm British backing, the Ottoman reform movement would have collapsed altogether. Britain's insistence on upholding Ottoman territorial integrity was on a collision course with Russia's attempt to increase its influence in the Balkans; the result was the Crimean War of 1853–1856. The Ottoman Empire, aided by British and French troops, defeated Russia and regained some territory.

The price for Western support was a new official proclamation, Sultan Abdulmejid's Imperial Rescript of 1856. All Ottoman subjects, whether Muslim or not, were now to enjoy the same rights and status under the law. Many Ottoman Muslims objected to giving Jews and Christians the same rights and status as themselves, an act contrary to the basic principles of the *Shari'ah*. The *Tanzimat* reforms, however, continued in such areas as land ownership, codification of the laws, and reorganization of the *millets*. Nationalism in the modern sense first appeared among such Christian subjects as the Greeks and the Serbs, who were closer to Western or Russian cultural influences. As nationalist movements proliferated in the Balkans, the Ottoman rulers grew even more worried about how to hold the empire together. Westernizing reforms were their first answer, but these raised more hopes than they could meet and did not create a new basis of loyalty. The reformers began pushing the idea of Ottomanism, loyalty to the Ottoman Empire, as a framework within which racial, linguistic, and religious groups could develop autonomously but harmoniously. To this the New Ottomans of the 1870s added the idea of an Ottoman constitution that would set up an assembly representing all peoples of the empire. The constitution was drawn up in 1876, with several nationalist rebellions going on in the Balkans, war raging with Serbia and Montenegro, and Russia threatening to send in troops. The New Ottomans seized power in a coup and put on the throne Abdulhamid II (1876–1909), who promised to uphold the new constitution. The ensuing Russo-Turkish War put the empire in such peril that almost no one could have governed under the constitution. Abdulhamid soon suspended it and dissolved parliament. For 30 years, he ruled as a dictator, appointing and dismissing his own ministers, holding his creditors at bay, keeping the Great Powers sufficiently at odds with one another so that they would not carve up the Ottoman Empire, and suppressing all dissident movements within his realm.

Many Ottomans, especially if they had been educated in Western schools, thought that the only way to save the empire was to restore the 1876 constitution, even if it meant overthrowing Abdulhamid. Many opposition groups were formed, but they tend to get lumped together as the **Young Turks.** The key society was a secret order founded at the military medical college in 1889 by four cadets, all Muslim but of several nationalities. It came to be known as the Committee of Union and Progress (CUP). Over time, many groups within Ottoman society accepted the CUP program that the empire must be strengthened militarily and morally, all religious and ethnic groups must be put on an equal footing, the constitution must be restored, and Sultan Abdulhamid must be shorn of power. In July 1908, the CUP inspired a military coup that forced Abdulhamid to restore the Ottoman constitution and elections were held for a new parliament. The coup did not ward off disintegration, however, as Austria annexed Bosnia, Bulgaria declared its independence, and Crete rebelled, all in late 1908. Hopes for rapid economic development were dashed when a French loan deal fell through in 1910. The next year, **Italy** attacked the Ottoman Empire in an attempt to seize Libya; Italian success was assured when Bulgaria and Serbia joined forces in 1912 and attacked the empire in the Balkans. In a few months, the Ottomans lost almost all their European lands. Even **Albania** rebelled in 1910 and later won Great Power recognition as an independent state. These losses were the beginning of the end of the Ottoman Empire, which was dissolved in the aftermath of World War I. *See also* Balkan Wars; Disraeli, Benjamin; Greece; London Straits Convention; San Stefano, Treaty of.

FURTHER READING: Ahmad, Feroz. *The Making of Modern Turkey.* London: Routledge, 1993; Cleveland, William L. *A History of the Modern Middle East.* Boulder, CO: Westview Press, 1994; Fisher, Sydney Nettleton, and William Ochsenwald. *The Middle East: A History.* New York: McGraw-Hill Publishing Company, 1990; Goldschmidt, Arthur, Jr. *A Concise History of the Middle East.* Boulder, CO: Westview Press, 1983; Karsh, Efraim, and Inari Karsh. *Empires of the Sand: The Struggle for Mastery in the Middle East 1789–1923.* Cambridge, MA: Harvard University Press, 2001; Mansfield, Peter. *A History of the Middle East.* New York: Viking Penguin, 1991; McCarthy, Justin. *The Ottoman Peoples and the End of Empire.* London: Arnold, a member of the Hodder Headline Group, 2001; Perry, Glenn E. *The Middle East: Fourteen Islamic Centuries.* Upper Saddle River, NJ: Prentice-Hall Inc., 1997; Yapp, M. E. *The Making of the Modern Near East 1792–1923.* London: Longman Group UK Limited, 1987.

MOSHE TERDMAN

Oyama, Iwao (1842–1916)

A Japanese soldier and hero of the Meiji period, Oyama was born into a samurai family and served in the Boshin War of 1868–1969, which overthrew the Tokugawa

Shōgunate, and also in the Satsuma Rebellion of 1877. In the interim he attended the École Spéciale Militaire de Saint-Cyr in France and witnessed France's defeat in the Franco-Prussian War; he also studied foreign languages in Geneva and achieved fluency in Russian. After promotion to major general, Oyama was a key figure in the establishment of the Imperial Japanese Army that routed the Satsuma rebels. He commanded the Second Army in the **Sino-Japanese War** and captured Port Arthur and the fortress of Weihaiwei. Oyama was promoted to the rank of field marshal and, as chief of general staff in 1904, appealed successfully to the emperor for permission to go to war against Russia. As commander of the Manchurian army in the **Russo-Japanese War,** Oyama inflicted defeats on the Russian army at Liaoyang, Shaho, and **Mukden.**

Oyama was elevated to the rank of *koshaku,* roughly the equivalent of a duke, and subsequently served as war minister and as lord keeper of the Privy Seal. He was awarded the Order of the Golden Kite and the Order of the Chrysanthemum. In 1906, he was also given the newly established Order of Merit of the British Commonwealth by King George VII. The town of Oyama in British Columbia is named after him. *See also* Japanese Empire; Meiji Restoration; Russian Empire.

FURTHER READING: Beasley, W. G. *Japanese Imperialism, 1894–1945.* New York: Oxford University Press, 1987; Matsusaka, Yoshihisa Tak. *The Making of Japanese Manchuria, 1904–1932.* Cambridge, MA: Harvard University Asia Center, 2001; Myers, Ramon H., and Mark R. Peattie, eds. *The Japanese Colonial Empire, 1895–1945.* Princeton, NJ: Princeton University Press, 1984.

CARL CAVANAGH HODGE

P

Palmerston, Henry John Temple, Lord (1784–1865)

The Liberal prime minister of Great Britain from 1855 to 1865, with a hiatus in 1858–1859, and often foreign secretary in the preceding decades. Although he did not set out to expand the **British Empire,** Palmerston was the last Liberal prime minister able to position the **Liberal Party** as the voice of an assertive British nationalism. Palmerston first entered politics as a supporter of William **Pitt** the Younger; he was first elected to the House of Commons in 1807 after several unsuccessful attempts. He attained office at an unusually young age as secretary for war under Spencer Perceval in 1809. Palmerston sympathized with the growing movement for reform in the 1820s, and eventually resigned from the duke of Wellington's cabinet in 1828 over its refusal to contemplate even small measures of electoral redistribution.

He became foreign secretary in Lord Grey's Whig government of 1830, and held that post when the Whigs or Liberals were in power over most of the following 25 years. Palmerston was a cautious reformer in domestic matters, and his foreign policy generally supported liberal causes where it could. In European affairs, he supported Italian, Hungarian, and Polish nationalism, but not to the extent of seriously offending major powers. In imperial affairs, he waged war against China in 1839–1842 and again from 1857–1860, opening Chinese ports to British commerce in the **Opium Wars.** He sought to put down the slave trade, threatening Portugal and Brazil, and expanding British power around the coasts of Africa as he did so. In the famous Don Pacifico affair of 1850, he used the Royal Navy to collect minor debts owed a British citizen by the Greek government, famously proclaiming that the Englishman, like the Roman of old, could say, "*civis Romanus sum.*" Unusually, Palmerston served as home secretary in Lord Aberdeen's government of 1852–1855, thus avoiding blame for the blunders that led to the **Crimean War.** When Aberdeen fell because of his handling of the war, Palmerston became prime minister on the back of popular feeling that the war needed more vigorous prosecution.

As prime minister, Palmerston was generally friendly toward Louis Napoleon **Bonaparte**'s France, so much so that he fell from power in 1858 over the Conspiracy to Murder bill, put forward in response to an assassination attempt against Napoleon that had been plotted in Britain, a bill perceived to be craven in its attitude to the French. The minority Tories being unable to govern, Palmerston came back into power in 1859, and remained prime minister until his death in 1865. He preserved a friendly neutrality toward France and Sardinia during their 1859 war with Austria, kept Britain out of the American Civil War, and admitted that support for Denmark in the 1864 war over Schleswig-Holstein was beyond Britain's power. Critics on both left and right observed that Palmerston was more cautious in dealing with Americans and Prussians than with Greeks and Chinese, and accused him of hypocrisy; defenders credited his pragmatism. Although personally an aristocratic Whig and a man about town, Palmerston was effective as a democratic politician, using his forthright British nationalism to attract support from all classes—an appeal later taken over by Benjamin **Disraeli.** Palmerston is perhaps best understood as a nationalist: he believed that Britain was a great power that should use its power abroad for good and in its own interests, two purposes that did not in his mind often conflict. *See also* Liberalism; Pax Brittanica.

FURTHER READING: Bell, H.C.F. *Lord Palmerston.* 2 vols. London: Longmans, Green, 1936; Chamberlain, Muriel. *British Foreign Policy in the Age of Palmerston.* London: Longman, 1980; Steele, E. D. *Palmerston and Liberalism.* Cambridge: Cambridge University Press, 1991.

MARK F. PROUDMAN

Panama

A province of Colombia until 1903. Colombia's rejection of the **Hay-Herrán Treaty** on August 12, 1903, greatly disappointed the province of Panama and sparked off its secession. The conspirators, prodded and manipulated by a Frenchman, Philippe Bunau-Varilla, a frustrated stockholder of the New Panama Canal Company who had been chief engineer of the initial organization, all lived on the Isthmus and were all connected, one way or another, to the isthmian railroad company: Senator José Augustín Arango, Doctor Manuel Amador Guerrero, Senator José Domingo de Obaldía, governor of the province, as well as lesser figures. They formed a junta headed by Arango in late May, began to establish contacts in Washington in September, and eventually received unofficial assurances by early October.

On November 3, 1903, the Panamanian secessionists launched their revolution with the blessing of the **United States,** and the next day proclaimed the independence of the Isthmus—recognized by Washington on November 6. Arango headed the provisional government, which appointed Bunau-Varilla minister plenipotentiary to Washington. Signed on November 18, the **Hay-Bunau-Varilla Treaty** was less advantageous than the abortive Hay-Herrán accord and virtually made Panama an American **protectorate.** Obaldía would ultimately succeed the discredited Bunau-Varilla as Panamanian minister to Washington, then Amador as president of the Isthmian republic. *See also* Monroe Doctrine; Roosevelt Corollary.

FURTHER READING: Bunau-Varilla, Philippe. *Panama: The Creation, Destruction, and Resurrection.* New York: McBride, Nast and Co., 1914; McCullough, David. *The Path between the Seas: The Creation of the Panama Canal, 1870–1914.* New York: Simon and Schuster, 1977.

SERGE RICARD

Panama Canal

An interoceanic waterway across the Panamanian isthmus initially envisaged by Spanish conquerors in the sixteenth century. Between the sixteenth and the twentieth centuries there was an isthmian road that suddenly became vitally important in 1848 with the California Gold Rush, as unloading and reloading were less time-consuming than rounding Cape Horn. After 1855, an American railroad had linked **Panama** and Colón. After completing the Suez Canal, Ferdinand de **Lesseps** obtained in 1880 the right to build a canal alongside that railroad, where the isthmus was only 50 kilometers wide. Lesseps gave up in 1889 as a consequence of tremendous, unforeseen financial and material difficulties, an episode known in France as the **Panama Scandal,** which rocked the Third Republic.

At the turn of the century American interest in the canal, for reasons of security, prestige, and trade, was increased by the acquisition of **Hawaii** and the **Philippines;** and it actually underlay the annexation of Puerto Rico and the supervision of Cuba at the close of the war with Spain. The only problem was the Clayton-Bulwer Treaty of 1850, which provided that the **United States** and Great Britain would exercise joint control over the projected canal. The British at first attempted to use its abrogation to increase their bargaining power in the Alaskan boundary controversy, but they quickly gave in when they realized that the U.S. Congress was ready to pass a bill that would nullify it and empower the McKinley administration to build a Nicaraguan canal under exclusive American control. A new accord was negotiated on February 5, 1900, the **Hay-Pauncefote Treaty,** which stipulated that the United States could build and own an isthmian canal but could not fortify it. The nonfortification clause, which conformed to the past policy of neutralization, was loudly opposed by the jingoes, who predicted seizure of the future canal by enemies of the United States; it was also denounced by the Democrats—appropriately, for 1900 was an election year. Lastly, it infuriated such Anglophobes as the Irish- and German-Americans.

Although the British were shocked by American pretensions, they eventually yielded when it became clear that the United States intended to go ahead and build the isthmian waterway. Britain was in any event busy fighting the Boers in South Africa and could do without further problems in the Caribbean. In fact, Britain acknowledged American supremacy in the Caribbean and was to reduce her fleet there in light of the fact that the United States could prove a powerful ally that would maintain the status quo in the Western Hemisphere against her great rival, Germany. The Second Hay-Pauncefote Treaty, concluded on November 18, 1901, stripped London of any right to control the canal.

To this point the choice of the most suitable route—through Nicaragua or across Panama—had been pending. On November 16, 1901, two days before the Second Hay-Pauncefote treaty was signed, the Walker Commission, appointed in 1899 by President William **McKinley** and headed by Rear Admiral John G. Walker, recommended the Nicaraguan route. The directors of the New Panama Canal Company—successor to the former de Lesseps organization—who had been asking the huge sum of $109 million for their holdings, suddenly dropped their price to $40 million when faced with the prospect of a Nicaraguan canal. This substantial saving possibly convinced President Theodore **Roosevelt** and the Walker Commission that the Panama site was best, or at least made them overcome their hesitations, for engineering opinion was divided. The Canal Commission reversed its recommendation on January 18, 1902, but at about the same time, the House of Representatives clearly indicated its preference for the Nicaraguan route by a vote of 308 to 2.

Such indecision might have resulted in further postponements but for a timely volcanic eruption on the island of Martinique, which raised fears about a similar risk in Nicaragua, and the astute and efficient lobbying of the New Panama Canal Company, represented by William N. Cromwell, a New York attorney, and Philippe Bunau-Varilla, a Frenchman who had been chief engineer of the first company and now was a large stockholder in the new one. On June 28, 1902, the Spooner Act was passed: the Nicaraguan bill was amended so as to provide for a Panama Canal. The president was now to secure from Colombia a right of way across the Isthmus of Panama, "within reasonable time and upon reasonable terms," or to turn to Nicaragua if this proved impossible. Early in 1903, Secretary of State John Hay practically wrested from Bogota's chargé in Washington, Tomás Herrán, an agreement that seriously compromised Colombian sovereignty and aroused popular indignation and political opposition in Colombia: the Hay-Herrán Treaty stipulated that the New Panama Canal Company would receive $40 million and Colombia $10 million as well as a $250,000 annuity, and granted the United States perpetual control of a zone six miles wide across the isthmus. The treaty was signed on January 22, 1903, and ratified unamended by the U.S. Senate on March 17. Its unanimous rejection by the Colombian senate five months later, on August 12, surprised and incensed Roosevelt. He had set his heart on the Panama route—which engineering opinion then rightly regarded as the best option—and was not going to have his plans thwarted by the "Bogotá lot of jack rabbits," who should not "be allowed permanently to bar one of the future highways of civilization," despite the existence of an alternative in Nicaragua.

The likelihood of a revolution in Panama quickly became public knowledge in Washington. Panama had a long history of uprisings against the central government. The 1903 secession was caused both by Panamanian disappointment at losing the commercial advantages the construction of the canal was expected to bring and by isthmian nationalism. The conspirators soon received indirect assurances that the White House would do nothing to jeopardize their plans. Later events would show how the Bunau-Varilla had anticipated the U.S. government's reaction and its new reading of the Bidlack-Mallarino Treaty of 1846 by which the United States had obtained a right of transit for its nationals, but not of construction. Juridically, American intervention was justified by its Article Thirty-Five, and the resort to force on or about the Isthmus was a half-century-old tradition, always in support of the central government. This time, Washington would choose inaction and even help the rebellion by stopping Colombian reinforcements.

A prodigious acceleration of history took place in late October 1903, for which the annals of diplomacy offered few precedents, if any at all. On October 31, the Colombian senate adjourned without having reconsidered its position on the canal question, thus destroying all hopes of a quick settlement. On November 3, the Panamanian secessionists successfully launched their "bloodless" insurrection thanks to Washington's active, preferential neutrality. The independence of the province was officially proclaimed the next day and recognition of the new republic of Panama granted by the United States on November 6. Bunau-Varilla was appointed minister plenipotentiary to Washington with full negotiating powers. Two weeks after the revolution the isthmian waterway issue was settled. On November 18, the two countries signed the Hay-Bunau-Varilla Treaty, which virtually made Panama an American **protectorate**. In exchange for the sum of $10 million and a $250,000 annuity in gold coins, it granted to the United States "in perpetuity the use, occupation and control" of a zone of land across the isthmus 10 miles wide, and it authorized Washington to fortify the canal and to guarantee and maintain the independence of the new republic. The New Panama Canal Company received its $40 million, Colombia nothing. Theodore Roosevelt, who waxed lyrical to defend the right of the province to break with a corrupt and inept government, would forever claim, not altogether unconvincingly, that the end justified the means, which he did not find particularly objectionable, as his government was morally right in "taking Panama" inasmuch as it had allegedly received a "mandate from civilization." He never concealed his conviction that it was better to polemicize about his action for half a century than to do so about the project.

The Panama Canal—a lock canal—was inaugurated on August 3, 1914. The payment of $25 million to Colombia in 1920, after Roosevelt's death, was in many ways an admission of guilt and a belated effort to atone for past wrongdoing. *See also* Monroe Doctrine; Roosevelt Corollary.

FURTHER READING: Collin, Richard H. *Theodore Roosevelt's Caribbean: The Panama Canal, the Monroe Doctrine, and the Latin American Context.* Baton Rouge: Louisiana State University Press, 1990; LaFeber, Walter. *The Panama Canal: The Crisis in Historical Perspective.* New York: Oxford University Press, 1978; Mack, Gerstle. *The Land Divided: A History of the Panama Canal and Other Isthmian Canal Projects.* New York: Octagon Books, 1974; Marks, Frederick W., III. *Velvet on Iron: The Diplomacy of Theodore Roosevelt.* Lincoln: University of Nebraska Press, 1979; McCullough, David. *The Path between the Seas: The Creation of the Panama Canal, 1870–1914.* New York: Simon, 1977.

SERGE RICARD

Panama Scandal (1892–1893)

An investment scandal in which the misplaced hopes and lost fortunes of small stakeholders in the Panama Canal project of Ferdinand de **Lesseps** became a political earthquake in French politics. As the architect of the Suez Canal, Lesseps enjoyed a national reputation as possibly the greatest Frenchman of his time—a reputation he used to entice small investors to back the construction of a canal across Panama, partly with unrealistic initial estimates of its ultimate cost, partly through misunderstanding of its enormous engineering difficulties, and partly through concealment of colossal financial mismanagement. Financial authority over the Panama Canal Company was exercised by Baron Jacques de Reinach, a German Jew, Italian Baron, and naturalized French citizen who symbolized the new world of cosmopolitan finance in late nineteenth-century Europe.

In the critical stage, when the canal was behind schedule and massively over budget, the government permitted the company to float a lottery-loan for 750 million francs, which, upon failure, put the company into liquidation. The resulting inquiry and trial savaged the reputation of the Radical Party in parliament, especially George **Clemençeau,** and contributed to a virulent wave of anti-Semitism across the country. Edouard Drumont's 1,200 page book, *La France Juive,* sold tens of thousands of copies with its explanation of how France and its honest peasantry—in reality the victims of a garden variety failure in finance capitalism—had been conquered and pillaged by Jews. *See also* Dreyfus Affair.

FURTHER READING: Brogan, Denis. *The Development of Modern France, 1870–1939.* London: Hamish Hamilton, 1940.

CARL CAVANAGH HODGE

Pandu Nadi, Battle of (1857)

A secondary although important engagement of the **Indian Mutiny.** To prevent General Henry Havelock's relieving force from reaching Kanpur, the rebels fortified the masonry bridge over the river at Pandu Nadi. The rebels dug trenches on both sides of the river, which were filled with their infantry. In addition, they deployed two 24-pounder guns to sweep the approach to the river. The river itself was a raging torrent. Havelock had no pontoon equipment; neither were country boats readily available. On July 15, he sent forward an artillery battery and launched a decoy attack with his cavalry toward the center of the rebel position. The Madras Fusiliers equipped with rifles attacked both the flanks of the rebel line. Shrapnel from the guns and firing from the Enfield rifles forced the rebels to withdraw. In their hurry, the sepoys failed to blast the bridge, so that Havelock secured the bridge and the road to Kanpur at the cost of 22 casualties. *See also* British Empire; India.

FURTHER READING: David, Saul. Th*e Indian Mutiny, 1857.* London, Viking, 2002; Watson, Bruce. *The Great Indian Mutiny.* New York: Praeger, 1991.

KAUSHIK ROY

Pan-Slavism

A nineteenth-century cultural and intellectual movement that postulated that the cultural and linguistic affinities of the Slavic peoples could serve as the basis for a political association of all Slavs. Pan-Slavism began among Slavic intellectuals living within the **Habsburg Empire** who did not seek independence from Vienna but desired that the Slavic peoples under Habsburg rule receive equality with the Germans and Hungarians. Eventually the movement spread to Russia where it transformed into a political movement to induce the tsarist government to fight for the liberation of Orthodox Christian Slavs from the **Ottoman Empire.**

The Russian interest started in the 1850s as Russia lost its right to protect the Orthodox Christians in the Ottoman Empire as a result of its defeat in the **Crimean War.** Deprived of its unique role in Eastern Europe based on common religion, the Russian interest changed into one based on ethnolinguistic affiliation. As part of their cultural program, Russian Pan-Slavs established Slavic benevolent societies to bring foreign students from the Austrian and Ottoman Empires to Moscow for education in the hope of instilling bonds of friendship with their Slavic brothers. They anticipated that this common culture would inevitably lead to political unity among all Slavs under the leadership of Russia, given that Russia was the only independent Slavic country in the world.

The leading figure in the Russian Pan-Slav movement was Nikolai Yakovlevich Danilevsky (1822–1885), who advocated a political union of all Slavs under Russian auspices with a capital in Constantinople. Such a political vision would have required the dismemberment of the Ottoman and Habsburg Empires and therefore it was generally rejected by the tsarist government. Nevertheless, the mission to liberate Slavic peoples from the Turkish yoke was taken up by some Russian intellectuals who redefined their own struggle against tsarist autocracy as an external struggle against Ottoman tyranny. The idea that Russia could act as an emancipator for the Balkans rather than the policeman of Europe appealed to leftists. Meanwhile conservative Russian Pan-Slav thinkers supported the fight against Turkey to free the little Slavic brothers so that they could at last naturally gravitate around big brother Russia. When Bulgarians, Serbs, and Montenegrins rose up against the Turks in 1875–1876, Pan-Slavist public opinion in Russia clamored for tsarist military intervention. The Russian government was reluctant to act, but Russian volunteers streamed into the Balkans to join the cause of Slavic liberation. Ultimately, the tsarist government did go to war against the Ottomans in 1877, and the Russian victory led to independence for **Serbia** and Montenegro and autonomy for Bulgaria. *See also* Balkan Wars; Eastern Question; July Crisis; Russian Empire.

FURTHER READING: Jelavich, Barbara. *Russia's Balkan Entanglements, 1806–1914.* New York: Cambridge University Press, 1991; Kohn, Hans. *Pan-Slavism: Its History and Ideology.* New York: Vintage Books, 1960; Ragsdale, Hugh. *Imperial Russian Foreign Policy.* Cambridge: Cambridge University Press, 1993; Seton-Watson, Hugh. *The Russian Empire, 1801–1917.* Oxford: Clarendon Press, 1967.

JONATHAN GRANT

Paraguay

Effectively an independent state in South America as of 1811. Spanish explorers established a settlement in Asunción, on the eastern bank of the Paraguay River, in 1537. Its isolation and conflicts with Native Americans, Portuguese raiders, and Jesuits led its citizens toward a tradition of autonomy. In 1776, it became part of the newly organized Viceroyalty of the Río de la Plata. The change created resentment and conflict that would further alienate the territory from Spain.

Paraguayan militia forces played an important role in the successful effort to defeat a British military invasion of the Río de la Plata in 1806 and 1807. The two surprise victories against British forces encouraged independence sentiments at the end of the region's colonial era. Napoleon **Bonaparte**'s invasion of Spain in 1807 set in motion a series of events that led the town council of Asunción to declare its independence from Spain and from the rebel movement in Argentina in 1811. The revolutionary junta pursued policies that isolated Paraguay and promoted its military capabilities. By 1814, José Gaspar Rodríguez de Francia emerged as dictator. He enforced strict border controls that maintained the country's independence. He also strictly regulated trade, which limited the influence of European and North American merchants who hoped to capitalize on the collapse of Spanish authority as the independence struggle developed.

Francia's death in 1840 left the country in the control of dictators who modernized the military and promoted limited, state-controlled development of the economy.

During this period, the government allowed limited contacts with European companies that helped the country develop its economic infrastructure. Francisco Solano López, who inherited dictatorial powers from his father, Carlos Antonio López, set Paraguay on a disastrous course in 1864 through attempts to expand Paraguay's borders at the expense of the Argentine Confederation and the Brazilian Empire. The ensuing War of the **Triple Alliance,** which pit Paraguay against the combined forces of **Argentina, Brazil,** and Uruguay, led to the utter destruction of Paraguay. It ceded disputed territories to its neighbors, lost as much as two-thirds of its population, and experienced political and economic instability as a result of its defeat for the following seven decades. *See also* Spanish Empire.

FURTHER READING: Whigham, Thomas. *The Paraguayan War.* Vol. 1 Lincoln: University of Nebraska Press, 2002; Whigham, Thomas. *The Politics of River Trade: Tradition and Development in the Upper Plata, 1780–1870.* Albuquerque: University of New Mexico Press, 1991; Williams, John Hoyt. *The Rise and Fall of the Paraguayan Republic, 1800–1870.* Austin: University of Texas Press, 1979.

DANIEL K. LEWIS

Paris Commune (1871)

A socialist government that ruled Paris for two months from March 28 to May 26, 1871, following the **Franco-Prussian War,** and named itself the Commune in evocation of the Jacobin Assembly of 1793. The capital city of France had refused to accept the terms of peace with Prussia, which had been negotiated by Adolphe **Thiers,** the head of the new national government. The Paris National Guard, a creature of the Commune, prepared to resist the entry of the German army and began to station cannons at various parts of the city, disrupting commercial life in Paris. This forced Thiers to step in, causing a more general uprising in Paris. The Paris National Guard refused to back down and the government was forced to retreat to Versailles. There was a strong left-wing sentiment in Paris as shown by municipal elections, which led to the installation of the Paris Commune at Hôtel de Ville on March 20.

A civil war erupted between the Commune and the Versailles government. Starting on May 21, the Commune was violently suppressed by the national government in brutal street fighting. The casualty rate was very high, as more than 20,000 members of the Commune died. Many public buildings such as the Hôtel de Ville were destroyed by fire. The Commune's memory became a power symbol to the insurrectional tradition of the French left but also bequeathed a legacy of class hatred to the country.

FURTHER READING: Brogan, Denis. *The Development of Modern France, 1870–1939.* London: Hamish Hamilton, 1940; Edwards, Stewart. *The Paris Commune, 1871.* Chicago: Quadrangle, 1971; Shafer, David A. *The Paris Commune.* New York: Palgrave Macmillam, 2005.

NURFADZILAH YAHAYA

Paris, Declaration of (1856)

Along with the **Treaty of Paris of 1856,** the Declaration of Paris was part of the diplomatic settlement of the **Crimean War.** The Declaration, however, dealt specifically with the rules of naval warfare. It abolished privateering and established the principle that neutral flags protected enemy goods, except for the contraband of war. It also stipulated that neutral goods other than war contraband would not be liable to capture under the enemy's flag and that naval blockades had to be maintained by sufficient and present force in order to be binding. All maritime states of any importance accepted the declaration, with the exceptions of Spain and the **United States;** Spain finally acceded in 1907; the United States agreed to the Hague Convention principles in the same year. *See also* Ottoman Empire.

FURTHER READING: Piggott, Francis Taylor. *The Declaration of Paris, 1856: A Study.* London: University of London Press, 1919.

CARL CAVANAGH HODGE

Paris, Treaty of (1815)

Occasionally referred to as the Second Peace of Paris, the terms imposed on France after the Hundred Days and Waterloo. After Napoleon **Bonaparte** abdicated for the second time, his opponents—Britain, Austria, Russia, and Prussia—signed a peace treaty on November 20, a harsher treaty than the treaty of 1814, whose terms were still binding.

The treaty of 1814, signed after Napoleon's first abdication, was considered too lenient, something that was attributed to the superb diplomatic skill of French statesman Charles Maurice de **Talleyrand.** According to the treaty of 1815, France was to cede territories such as Saar and Savoy. The boundaries of France were reduced to those of 1790. In addition, the French were also ordered to pay 700 million francs in indemnities, a portion of it to build additional fortresses in **Belgium** and Germany. A corps of Allied troops, not exceeding 150,000 men, to be paid for by France, was to occupy some parts of France for five years as a precaution and temporary guarantee to neighboring countries, and the four powers confirmed their alliance against France for the next 20 years. *See also* Congress System.

FURTHER READING: Schroeder, Paul W. *The Transformation of European Politics, 1773–1848.* Oxford: Clarendon, 1994.

NURFADZILAH YAHAYA

Paris, Treaty of (1856)

Signed at the Congress of Paris, on March 30, 1856, the treaty ending the **Crimean War** between Russia and the **Ottoman Empire,** whose allies—France, Britain, and Sardinia-Piedmont—were also party to the treaty. The principalities of Moldavia and Walachia were granted the right to hold national assemblies and have independent constitutions, and the former gained the southern part of Bessarabia from Russia; however, the Ottomans regained nominal suzerainty over both principalities. A referendum was to decide whether residents of the two principalities favored unification. The Black Sea was made neutral; warships and military fortifications were forbidden there. On the land perimeter surrounding the Black Sea, the stationing of military weapons was also banned. The Danube River remained open to all ships regardless of national origin. *See also* Paris, Declaration of.

FURTHER READING: Baumgart, Winfried. *The Peace of Paris, 1856.* Translated by Ann Pottinger Saab. Santa Barbara: ABC-Clio, 1981.

NURFADZILAH YAHAYA

Paris, Treaty of (1898)

The Treaty ending the **Spanish American War** and transferring control of **Cuba,** Guam, **Puerto Rico,** and the **Philippines** from Spain to the **United States.** The acquisitions of these territories gave the United States a global presence and thrust the country further into the imperial rivalries in the Far East and Latin America. Major issues at the peace conference, which lasted from October 1, 1898, to December 10, 1898, dealt with responsibility for the Cuban debt, valued at $400 million, and the status of the Philippines. The Cuban debt represented the expense of Spanish administration of Cuba, the cost of suppressing previous Cuban revolts, and the price of several other Spanish ventures in the Western Hemisphere. Although Spain wanted the United States to assume responsibility for the debt, American representatives refused to accept the responsibility or to force it on any future Cuban government. In compensation and to lessen the loss of the Philippines, the United States agreed to pay Spain $20 million.

Acquisition of the Philippines proved controversial, especially in the U.S. Senate, and led to the formation of the American Anti-Imperialist League, which campaigned extensively for the defeat of the Treaty of Paris. The treaty seemed doomed to failure until William Jennings Bryan, the Democratic candidate for president in 1900, urged his supporters to vote for ratification. Bryan supported the treaty because he wanted the upcoming presidential election to focus on domestic issues and because passage of the treaty would allow the issue of American imperialism and the Philippine question to be separated from the peace negotiations. The move stunned the anti-imperialists and gave the treaty the boost it needed in the Senate. The Senate approved the Treaty of Paris 57 to 27 and President McKinley signed the treaty on February 6, 1899. *See also* Monroe Doctrine; Roosevelt Corollary.

FURTHER READING: Brands, H. W. *Bound to Empire: The United States and the Philippines.* New York: Oxford University Press, 1992; Healy, David. *The United States in Cuba, 1898–1902: Generals, Politicians, and the Search for Policy.* Madison: University of Wisconsin Press, 1963.

JAMES PRUITT

Parnell, Charles Stewart (1846–1891)

An Irish nationalist politician, Charles Stewart Parnell, although raised Protestant, nonetheless came to the fore of a deeply Catholic movement and mastered both parliamentary and extra-parliamentary tactics in pursuit of the cause of **Home**

Rule. During the Irish Land War of 1879–1882, Parnell resorted to boycott tactics to wring concessions from the Liberal government of William **Gladstone.** He entered parliament in 1875 and in 1880 was elected chairman of the Irish parliamentary party.

In the election of 1885, Parnell and the Nationalist Party captured 85 seats at Westminster and as a consequence controlled the balance of parliamentary power between the Liberals and the Conservatives. When Gladstone returned to office in 1886, he tabled the first Home Rule Bill but was defeated when 93 Liberals voted against it. The defeat triggered a new election that same year, and a Conservative majority was returned. Parnell's fortunes thereupon went into steep decline, in part because of wholly fallacious charges leveled against him by his political enemies but also as a consequence of a wholly genuine affair with the wife of a friend that led to divorce court and ended in his removal as leader of the Irish party. *See also* Conservative Party; Ireland; Liberal Party.

FURTHER READING: Hurst, Michael. *Parnell and Irish Nationalism.* London: Routledge & Kegan Paul, 1968; Lyons, F.S.L. *Charles Stewart Parnell.* Dundalk: Dublin Historical Association, 1963.

CARL CAVANAGH HODGE

Pašić, Nikola (1845–1926)

Nikola Pašić was a Serbian politician, who, from 1903 until 1918, served as **Serbia**'s prime minister. His years before 1914 were marked by continuing dissent with the military, who demanded a Greater Serbia. With the assassination of the Austro-Hungarian heir to the throne on June 28, 1914, Pašic found himself implicated in the murder. Pašić, however, succeeded in placing responsibility for World War I with Austria-Hungary. A German-Austrian offensive in the autumn of 1915 swept the Serbians into exile. Pašić opposed a union of Serbs, Croats, and Slovenes that took place in December 1918. He found himself out of power but served as the Serbian representative at the Paris Peace Conference. Pašić returned as premier in 1921, and again for two years before his death.

FURTHER READING: Albertini, Luigi. *The Origins of the War of 1914.* 3 vols. Translated by Isabella M. Massey. New York: Oxford University Press, 1952; Radan, Peter, and Aleksandar Pavković, eds. *The Serbs and Their Leaders in the Twentieth Century.* Aldershot-Brookfield-Singapore-Sydney: Ashgate, 1997.

MARTIN MOLL

Pax Britannica

Pax Britannica, the concept of a "British Peace" facilitated by the creation of the **British Empire,** was consciously modeled on the Pax Romana of the ancient Mediterranean world. The Pax Britannica was, paradoxically, upheld by almost continuous warfare on the peripheries of Britain's colonial empire yet accompanied by relative lack of Great Power conflict in Europe, 1815–1853, by virtue of the **Congress System.** The era overlapped with the reign of Queen Victoria (1837–1901), especially its first half, a period of remarkable British prosperity and imperial confidence. It was made possible by several factors: first, the establishment of industrial and commercial primacy; second, the possession of the largest empire in history, consisting of both formal colonies and extensive spheres of influence; third, the maintenance of British naval high seas supremacy; and fourth, a capacity for the projection of military power, provided mainly by the Indian Army. It is important to recognize that the Pax Britannica was also a cultural edifice underpinned by a number of ephemeral advantages, which eroded toward the end of the nineteenth century. The actual and potential challenges of emerging European and non-European powers produced an anxious ruling elite in Britain and its colonies by the turn of the twentieth century.

The British had a sense of imperial mission to bestow the benefits of their civilization upon native peoples of its overseas possessions. There was a particular desire to civilize the "Dark Continent." British missionaries began work in West Africa as early as 1804, and were not easily deterred by tropical disease or the hostility of indigenous peoples—a determination that made many of them martyrs to their cause. Missionaries sought not only to Christianize indigenous peoples but also to civilize them, by teaching them English and changing their mode of dress, standards of hygiene, and housing. British missionaries were also active in **India** yet had consciously refrained from interfering with Indian customs during the eighteenth century. There was therefore widespread discontent when missionaries prevailed on the British authorities to legislate against traditional Indian practices such as *sati*. The imposition of British norms of law and order was a prevalent feature of the Pax Britannica but was not always acceptable to colonial societies, as the **Indian Mutiny** of 1857 demonstrated.

The Pax Britannica was partly a result of the industrial revolution, which took off first in Britain from the middle of the eighteenth century and was firmly established by the time that Queen Victoria ascended the throne in 1837. By the middle of the nineteenth century, Britain produced about half the world's commercial cotton cloth, while heavy industrial output was even more impressive, accounting for around two-thirds of the world's coal production, half its iron, and almost three-quarters of its steel. Britain was also the world's leading investor, banker, insurer, and shipper. The returns on overseas investments increased from £10.5 million per annum in 1847 to £80 million in 1887, by which time Britain had more than £1000 million invested abroad. Britain was the primary world carrier, and consolidated this lead in the mid-nineteenth century with the switch from sail to steamships, which was another advantage conferred by early industrialization. The progressive adoption of a **free trade** policy in the1840s and 1850s underpinned British economic dominance because, as the world's leading manufacturer, Britain could produce and sell commodities more cheaply than its competitors. If foreign governments attempted to exclude British merchants from markets, the Royal Navy opened them up at gunpoint. By 1890 Britain had more registered shipping tonnage than the rest of the world's carriers combined. The City of London was the center of most international financial transactions, including private and public loans, currency exchange, insurance, and the sale and purchase of commodities.

The possession of colonies was an obvious sign of the Pax Britannica. At the end of the **Napoleonic Wars,** Britain was unquestionably the most dynamic of the European imperial powers. Throughout the nineteenth century Britain continued to add new territories to its empire and by the early twentieth century, it covered one-quarter of the earth's land surface and encompassed roughly the same proportion of the world's population. The formal empire is often divided for analytical purposes into three elements: the areas of white settlement, the Crown colonies, and India. The white territories of **Canada, Australia, New Zealand,** and later, South Africa, acquired self-government and became known as the Dominions. In 1815, the total white population of the empire was just 550,000; but by 1911, this had risen to almost 19 million, and trade with the Dominions was worth £175 million annually. The Crown colonies, such as Trinidad, Ceylon, and Hong Kong, were governed directly from London and are therefore sometimes described as the dependent empire. The value of trade with many Crown colonies diminished dramatically over the course of the nineteenth century: for example, in 1815, the West Indies provided 17.6 percent of Britain's trade, worth £15.4 million per annum, but a century later the figures were just 0.47 percent and £6.6 million. India was administered by a combination of Crown officials and representatives of local British interests in an arrangement known as "double government." In economic terms, India was by far the most valuable individual part of the formal empire. By 1911, the Indian population was more than 300 million, which provided Britain with a huge market, and the value of annual trade was £120 million. India was also strategically significant, and Britain acquired many colonies during the nineteenth century simply to protect communication routes to India.

Yet the formal Empire was only one component of British imperialism in the nineteenth century. As the historians John Gallagher and Ronald Robinson argued, equating the size and character of the empire solely with those areas over which Britain exercised formal jurisdiction is like judging the extent of an iceberg according to the part that shows itself above the waterline. It is notable that almost 70 percent of British emigrants between 1812 and 1914, more than 60 percent of British exports between 1800 and 1900, and more than 80 percent of British capital investment overseas from 1815 to 1880 went to British spheres of influence as South East Asia, Central and South America, and Africa. Britain's informal presence in Africa developed into formal rule in the last quarter of the nineteenth century as a result of competition from other colonial powers, particularly France.

The **Royal Navy** discharged a number of vital functions that underpinned the Pax Britannica. It kept the British Isles free from the threat of invasion, protected and extended Britain's overseas commerce, and projected military force overseas from garrisons in Britain and India. The Royal Navy was powerful partly because of its sheer size. By the mid-nineteenth century it consisted of around 240 ships, crewed by 40,000 sailors. The Naval Defence Act of 1889 established the **two-power standard,** by which the Royal Navy was supposed to be maintained at a strength that was equivalent to the next two biggest navies combined. Another factor that contributed to Britain's naval power was its technical development. When France began launching armored warships in 1858, the British responded by constructing ironclads like HMS *Warrior,* with superior speed and firepower. Finally, a global network of strategic bases and coaling stations extended the reach of the Royal Navy to deal with many actual or potential threats to British interests. When China attempted to restrict trade with British merchants, it suffered crushing naval defeats in the **Opium War** of 1840–1842 and the Arrow War of 1856–1860. As a result of the Treaty of **Nanjing,** China ceded Hong Kong to Britain and opened five ports to trade, with a resident consul in each, although full diplomatic recognition was withheld until the Treaty of Tientsin in June 1858. Yet the Royal Navy could also be used for humanitarian purposes. By 1847, for example, 32 warships of the West African squadron were engaged in the suppression of the slave trade.

Traditionally, Britain did not field large armies, but its control of the Indian Army provided a significant military reserve of around 180,000 troops, which accounted for more than 60 percent of total manpower in British garrisons overseas in the 1880s. The Conservative Prime Minister Lord Salisbury once remarked that India was "an English barrack in the Oriental Seas from which we may draw any number of troops without paying for them." Indeed, the Indian Army served in more than a dozen imperial campaigns in Africa and Asia during the second half of the nineteenth century. The Indian Army was therefore a significant element of the Pax Britannica, for without it the cost of maintaining imperial control would have been much higher. Lord Curzon, viceroy of India, went so far as to proclaim in 1901 that "as long as we rule in India we are the greatest power in the world. If we lose it we shall drop straight away to a third rate power."

It is tempting to identify the Pax Britannica as shorthand for British global dominance during the nineteenth century, but contemporaries perceived it differently, as a cultural edifice rather than a political relationship. The extent of British power during the nineteenth century can also be easily overstated, for it was always limited to those areas in which the Royal Navy could operate. Further, the economic and strategic platforms on which Britain's international lead rested after 1815 were temporary. During the last quarter of the nineteenth century competition from other European powers—France, Germany, Italy, and Russia—and non-European powers—the United States and Japan—challenged Britain's commercial, naval, and imperial preeminence, which caused considerable anxiety about the future of the empire. Yet despite this anxiety the empire continued to grow, and when it did finally vanish during the two decades after World War II, its legacy included widespread use of the English language, belief in Protestant religion, economic globalization, modern precepts of law and order, and representative democracy. In these respects traces of the Pax Britannica are still very much in evidence today. *See also* Balance of Power; Navalism; *Weltpolitik*.

FURTHER READING: Chamberlain, Muriel. *'Pax Britannica'? British Foreign Policy, 1789–1914.* London: Longman 1988; Eldridge, C. C. *England's Mission: The Imperial Idea in the Age of Gladstone and Disraeli, 1868–1880.* Chapel Hill: University of North Carolina Press, 1974; Gallagher, John, and Robinson, Ronald. "The Imperialism of Free Trade." *Economic History Review* 6/1 (1953): 1–15; Hyam, Ronald. *Britain's Imperial Century, 1815–1914.* New York: Palgrave, 2002; Kennedy, Paul M. *The Rise and Fall of British Naval Mastery.* London: A. Lane, 1976; Morris, Jan. Pax Britannica: *The Climax of an Empire.* London: Faber, 1968; Perris, Henry Shaw. *Pax Britannica: A Study of the History of British Pacification.* London: Sidgwick & Jackson, 1913; Porter, Andrew, ed. *The Oxford History of the British Empire. Volume III: The Nineteenth Century.* Oxford: Oxford University Press, 1999.

CARL PETER WATTS

Peel, Sir Robert (1788–1850)

A reforming British prime minister, notable above all for his repeal of the **Corn Laws.** Peel was born to a wealthy Lancashire cotton manufacturer, chalked up an impressive academic record at Harrow and Christchurch, studied law at Lincoln's

Inn, and was elected a Tory member of Parliament for Cashel at the age of 21. Peel had the gift of oratory and a lucid understanding of the substance of a policy issue. With these qualities he combined an unrepentant ability to change his mind. From 1812 to 1818, he served as chief secretary in **Ireland,** where he was a consistent opponent of Catholic interests and opposed Catholic Emancipation. As Home Secretary in 1822 and again from 1828 to 1830, he reformed prisons and founded the Metropolitan Police, its constables ever after known as "Bobbies."

In 1829, he reversed positions on Catholic Emancipation and steered the Catholic Emancipation Act through Parliament. Briefly prime minister (1834–1835), Peel resigned and used his *Tamworth Manifesto* to declare support for reforms undertaken by the Whig ministries of Lord Grey and Lord Melbourne and to reconstitute the Tories as the **Conservative Party.** Elected as the head of a majority Conservative government in 1841, Peel passed the Factory Act of 1844 and the Bank Charter Act of 1844 and was prompted by the Irish potato famine, in a combination of conviction and opportunism, to repeal the protectionist Corn Laws. This break in favor of **free trade** cost Peel his government, as a majority of his party opposed it and it passed with Radical and Whig votes. Conservative rebels against Peel's policy, led by Benjamin **Disraeli,** brought down the government in June 1846.

FURTHER READING: Crosby, Travis L. *Sir Robert Peel's Administration.* Hamden, CT: Archon, 1976; Evans, E. J. *Sir Robert Peel: Statesmanship, Power and Party.* New York: Routledge, 2006; Jenkins, T. A. *Sir Robert Peel.* New York: St. Martin's, 1999.

CARL CAVANAGH HODGE

Peninsular War (1808–1814)

Known in Spain as the War of Independence, a Napoleonic War fought on the Iberian Peninsula and in southern France between British, Spanish, and Portuguese forces on the one hand and those of France on the other. Napoleon **Bonaparte,** frustrated with the Portuguese refusal to submit to his anti-British **Continental System,** invaded Portugal in 1807 with the acquiescence of Spain. Equally frustrated with the inefficiency of Spanish cooperation with his war effort, he then used his troops to evict the Bourbons from the Spanish throne, putting in their place his brother Joseph in July 1808. This provoked a popular Spanish uprising, bloodily repressed by the French. Britain, looking for an opportunity to carry the war to Napoleon, sent an expeditionary force to Portugal, a traditional ally.

British forces under Sir Arthur Wellesley defeated the French at Vimeiro, forcing them to leave Portugal under a controversial armistice, the convention of Cintra. Simultaneously, a British army under Sir John Moore advanced into Spain, but was obliged to retreat on the port of **Corunna,** Moore being killed in January 1809. In April, Wellesley returned to Portugal, leading an army east along the River Tagus into central Spain. After holding their own in hard-fought defensive battle at Talavera on July 27–28, 1809, the British were obliged to withdraw for lack of supplies. But Napoleonic forces had not hitherto been driven from many battlefields, and Wellesley was raised to the peerage as Viscount **Wellington,** notwithstanding Whig predictions of disaster. Supported by the government in London, and in particular by the then Secretary at War, Lord Liverpool, Wellington remained on the strategic defensive in 1810, fighting effective defensive battles against the advancing French under Marshal Masséna, and eventually retreating into prepared positions outside Lisbon, the famous lines of Torres Vedras.

The French withdrew from Portugal for lack of supplies in the spring of 1811, a year characterized by bloody sieges of fortresses on the Portuguese-Spanish border. Two major fortresses, Cuidad Rodrigo and Badajoz, fell in the early months of 1812. As French forces were drawn down for the coming invasion of Russia, Wellington advanced into Spain, defeating the French at Salamanca on July 22 and going onto Madrid, before being forced to retreat once more on his bases on the Portuguese border. In 1813, Wellington advanced into Spain by a northern route, depending for support on the Spanish Biscay ports. Wellington inflicted a major defeat on the French at Vittoria on June 21, 1813, and, after sharp engagements in the Pyrenees, advanced into southern France. The abdication of Napoleon and the treaty of Fontainbleau concluded European hostilities. The French forces had attempted to live off the countryside, as was their practice elsewhere in Europe, thereby incurring the hostility of the Spanish, whereas Wellington made a practice of paying for requisitions and preventing looting by ferocious discipline and a system of military police. Wellington's much smaller forces were able to use the aid of the Spanish guerillas to keep the French forces dispersed, and for valuable intelligence. The Peninsular war created the term *guerrilla* originally to name popular resistance to foreign occupation, now transferred to any small-unit, unconventional forces. The Peninsular War also saw the collapse of the Spanish Latin-American Empire. In some ways, it established the pattern of future guerrilla wars: guerrillas can wear down large conventional forces, but generally cannot prevail without secure base areas of conventional forces on their own side. *See also* Napoleonic Wars; Spanish Empire.

FURTHER READING: Esdaile, Charles. *The Peninsular War: A New History.* London: Allen Lane, 2002; Gates, David. *The Spanish Ulcer.* New York: Norton, 1986; Glover, Michael. *The Peninsular War, 1807–1814, A Concise Military History.* Hamden, CT: Archon, 1976.

MARK F. PROUDMAN

Perdicaris Affair (1904)

A diplomatic incident arising after a supposed **United States** citizen, Ion Perdicaris, was kidnapped along with his English stepson by a Moroccan revolutionary, Mulai Ahmed er Raisuli. President Theodore **Roosevelt** responded by threatening to "send in the Marines." The eventual outcome saw Perdicaris returned and Roosevelt's domestic and international status enhanced.

At the time Morocco was nominally under the rule of Sultan Mulia Abdul-Aziz, with Tangier having a number of well-to-do neighborhoods, although outside of the capital the hinterland was lawless and ruled by revolutionaries. On May 18, 1904, Raisuli stormed the Tangier home of millionaire Perdicaris and took him hostage, demanding a ransom and to be made governor of two districts surrounding Tangier. Tension rose as stories likening Raisuli to a Barbary pirate circulated in the international press. Through quiet diplomatic channels Roosevelt enlisted support from Europe's leading powers in exerting pressure on the Moroccan Sultan to pay off Raisuli, but to much greater public fanfare he dispatched seven ships of the **Great**

White Fleet to the African coast. While the Fleet headed east on June 21, news arrived in Washington that the Sultan would concede to Raisuli's demands. Thus it was at the behest of Roosevelt that the Sultan struck a deal with Raisuli and the navy never landed the Marines.

The incident was important for Roosevelt in domestic politics. Although delivered by Secretary of State John Hay to the Moroccans in the form of a diplomatic note, the Wild-West style call of "Perdicaris alive or Raisuli dead!" became synonymous with Roosevelt as it became public at the 1904 Republican convention. The subsequent release of Perdicaris ensured Roosevelt was the overwhelming favorite for the 1904 election. A fuller version of the Perdicaris affair emerged later. At the time of the incident Perdicaris was no longer an American citizen having renounced his citizenship to avoid his family assets being seized during the **American Civil War.** Furthermore, almost 40 years later Roosevelt's knowledge of this prior to his rallying cry came to light. The potential political ramifications of this for Roosevelt's standing in terms of international embarrassment, as well as a reelection campaign were well understood by Hay at the time, who saw that it was "a bad business," which would require the Administration to "keep it excessively confidential."

That they did at the time served to enhance Roosevelt's international position at a point where he sought to forward U.S. foreign policy by speaking softly and carrying a big stick following his role in the creation of the **Panama Canal** Zone and anticipating his role as peacemaker in the **Russo-Japanese War** and mediator at the 1905 **Algeciras Conference,** which stabilized Morocco position as North Africa's last independent nation. *See also* Jingoism.

FURTHER READING: Burton, David H. *Theodore Roosevelt: Confident Imperialist.* Philadelphia: University of Pennsylvania Press, 1968; Marks, Frederick W. *Velvet on Iron: The Diplomacy of Theodore Roosevelt.* Lincoln: University of Nebraska Press, 1979; Morris, Edmund. *Theodore Rex.* New York: Random House, 2001.

J. SIMON ROFE

Persia

A conventional European designation for Iran, in general use in the West until 1935, although the Iranians themselves had long called their country Iran. Persia is still widely used as an alternate for Iran. From its founding in the sixth century B.C. until its conquest by Alexander the Great in the fourth century B.C., Persia was the dominant power of the ancient world. After an interlude of Greek rule lasting a century or so, Persian power revived under two native dynasties: the Arsacid, or Parthian, and the Sassanian, or neo-Persian. Persia held at bay the empires of Rome and Byzantium for more than seven centuries before finally succumbing to the rising power of Islam in the middle of the seventh century A.D.

The Islamic conquest was aided by the material and social bankruptcy of the Sassanids; the native populations had little to lose by cooperating with the conquering power. Moreover, the Muslims offered relative religious tolerance and fair treatment to populations that accepted Islamic rule without resistance. It was not until around 650, however, that resistance in Iran was quelled. Conversion to Islam, which offered certain advantages, was fairly rapid among the urban population but slower among the peasantry. The majority of Iranians did not become Muslim until the ninth century. One important legacy of the Arab conquest was Shia Islam. It was not until the sixteenth century, under the Safavids, that a majority of Iranians became Shias. Shia Islam became the state religion.

After the death of Malik Shah in 1092, Iran once again reverted to petty dynasties. During this time, Genghis Khan brought together a number of Mongol tribes and led them on a devastating sweep through China; and in 1219, he turned his forces west and quickly devastated Bukhara, Samarkand, Balkh, Merv, and Neyshabur. Before his death in 1227, he had reached western Azarbaijan, pillaging and burning cities along the way. The Mongol invasion was disastrous to the Iranians. Destruction of qanat irrigation systems destroyed the pattern of relatively continuous settlement, producing numerous isolated oasis cities in a land where they had previously been rare. A large number of people, particularly males, were killed; between 1220 and 1258, the population of Iran dropped drastically. The Safavids (1501–1722), who came to power in 1501, were leaders of a militant Sufi order. The rise of the Safavids marks the reemergence in Iran of a powerful central authority within geographical boundaries attained by former Iranian empires. The Safavids declared Shia Islam the state religion and used proselytizing and force to convert the large majority of Muslims in Iran to the Shia sect. The Safavid Empire received a blow that was to prove fatal in 1524, when the Ottoman Sultan Selim I defeated the Safavid forces at Chaldiran and occupied the Safavid capital, Tabriz.

In 1794, Agha Mohammad Qajar established the rule of the Qajar dynasty that lasted until 1925. The Qajars revived the concept of the shah as the shadow of God on earth and exercised absolute powers over the servants of the state. Early in the nineteenth century, however, the Qajars began to face pressure from two great imperial powers, Russia and Britain. Britain's interest in Iran arose out of the need to protect trade routes to India, whereas Russia's came from a desire to expand into Iranian territory from the north. In two disastrous wars with Russia, which ended with the Treaty of Gulistan in 1812 and the Treaty of Turkmanchay in 1828, Iran lost all its territories in the Caucasus north of the Aras River. Then, in the second half of the century, Russia forced the Qajars to give up all claims to territories in Central Asia. Meanwhile, Britain twice landed troops in Iran to prevent the Qajars from reasserting a claim to Herat. Under the Treaty of Paris in 1857, Iran surrendered to Britain all claims to Herat and territories in present-day **Afghanistan.**

The two great powers also came to dominate Iran's trade and interfered in Iran's internal affairs. They enjoyed overwhelming military and technological superiority and could take advantage of Iran's internal problems. Iranian central authority was weak; revenues were generally inadequate to maintain the court, bureaucracy, and army; the ruling classes were divided and corrupt; and the people suffered exploitation by their rulers and governors. During World War I, Britain and Russian, now allied against the Central Powers, occupied the country and used it as a base of operations against the Ottoman Turks. *See also* British Empire; Great Game; Ottoman Empire; Russian Empire.

FURTHER READING: Ansari, Ali. *Iran.* New York: Routledge, 2004; Arberry, A. J. *The Legacy of Persia.* Oxford: Clarendon, 1953; Daniel, Elton L. *The History of Iran.* New York: Greenwood, 2000; Ghirshman R. *Iran from the Earliest Times to the Islamic Conquest.*

Harmondsworth: Penguin, 1954; Olmstead, A. T. *History of the Persian Empire.* Chicago: University of Chicago Press, 1948; Payne, Robert. *The Splendor of Persia.* New York: Knopf, 1957; Shuster, M. W. *The Strangling of Persia.* Washington, D.C., 1987. Reprint of 1912 edition.

JITENDRA UTTAM

Peters, Carl (1856–1918)

Explorer, adventurer, and colonial enthusiast behind the colonization of **German East Africa.** Convinced that Germany's economic survival depended on the acquisition of colonies, in March 1884 Peters helped found the *Gesellschaft für Deutsche Kolonisation* (Society for German Colonization), a colonial lobby that was absorbed three years later by the *Deutsche Kolonialgesellschaft* (German Colonial Society). Not content with Germany's recent colonial acquisitions in South West Africa, **Togo,** and **Cameroon,** Peters carved out a German sphere of influence in East Africa in late 1884 by signing treaties with interior tribes. Although initially unsanctioned by the German government, in February 1885 Otto von **Bismarck** made Peters's protectorate official and granted him and the newly created German East Africa Company a charter to administer the new colony. Over the next several years he took part in expeditions to explore the interior and extend the German protectorate deeper inland.

After the creation of an official German colonial administration in East Africa, Peters served from 1891 to 1897 as Imperial High Commissioner in Kilimanjaro before being relieved of his position amidst allegations of misuse of power and mistreating Africans. Thereafter, he spent 1899–1901 exploring the Zambezi river basin in search of commercial possibilities before being rewarded in 1905 with official rehabilitation by the German government. He returned to Germany full time in 1909 and spent the remainder of his life writing his memoirs and several books on international politics. *See also* Africa, Scramble for; Berlin, Conference of; German Empire; Uganda; Zanzibar.

FURTHER READING: Henderson, W. O. *The German Colonial Empire 1884–1919.* London: Franck Cass, 1993; Perras, Arne. *Carl Peters and German Imperialism 1856–1918: A Political Biography.* Oxford: Clarendon, 2004; Reuss, Martin. "The Disgrace and Fall of Carl Peters: Morality, Politics and Staatsräson in the Time of Wilhelm II." *Central European History* 14 (1981): 110–141.

KENNETH J. OROSZ

Philippines

A group of islands in the Western Pacific, colonized by Spain by way of **Mexico** between 1565 and 1571 and ceded to the **United States** at the end of the **Spanish-American War.** Practically none of the imperialists of 1898 had imagined the annexation of the Philippines as a colony, either before or during the conflict. Commodore George Dewey's victory at **Manila Bay,** on May 1, 1898, was to open new expansionist vistas in the Pacific. After the Spanish rout in **Cuba** three months later, Washington hesitated between several solutions: a return of the islands to Spain, independence, or partial or complete control under conditions to be defined.

The dispatch of an expeditionary corps, early in the summer of 1898, that was larger than the one sent to Cuba was in itself an avowal of intentions, a war measure that very much suggested a preemptive bid. If annexing the archipelago was not quite on the cards yet, relinquishing it was already unthinkable. Similarly, it was out of the question to recognize, let alone tolerate, the native nationalist sentiment and to cooperate or compromise with the Filipino patriots. At no time would the latter be regarded as valid negotiators. On September 16, President William **McKinley** decided in favor of the acquisition of the main island, Luzon; on October 28, he demanded from Madrid the cession of the whole archipelago. Even before the peace treaty of December 10 was ratified, at a time when juridically the Philippines were still Spanish, the president, by an executive order of December 21, 1898, proclaimed U.S. sovereignty over all of the islands.

From June 1898 to January 1899, the Filipino patriots repeatedly gave proof of their political maturity, which the American authorities took pains to ignore. The independence of the archipelago was proclaimed on June 12, 1898, and a provisional revolutionary government set up on June 23. An elected constituent assembly undertook to draft a constitution that was approved in mid-January 1899 and promulgated on January 21. Two days later the Philippine Republic was officially inaugurated with Emilio Aguinaldo as president. When it eventually dawned on the Filipinos that they had driven out their Spanish overlords only to fall under the American yoke, they rebelled again.

On February 4, 1899, the United States embarked on its first colonial war. It matters little whether American or Filipino troops were responsible for the outbreak of hostilities two days before the Senate's ratification of the Treaty of **Paris.** In a sense the Upper Chamber's approval was a foregone conclusion, for, in Richard E. Welch's terse formulation, it "was faced not with a decision to acquire the islands but with a decision of whether or not to repeal their annexation." The Philippine-American War lasted over three years. The percentage of casualties for the U.S. Army was one of the highest in American history. Aguinaldo was captured by ruse on March 23, 1901. On April 1, he took the oath of allegiance and on April 19, he called upon his countrymen to accept American rule. The military governorship was ended on July 4, 1901.

In many respects the acquisition of the Philippines became a bone of contention in American politics at the turn of the nineteenth century, simply because the Republican Party obstinately tried to turn into a colony a territory located thousands of miles from Washington. In fact, the imperialist rationale, although not its mode of implementation, received unanimous support at a time when the United States was moving on to a new stage in its irresistible growth. The great debate of 1898–1900 between imperialists and anti-imperialists witnessed a confrontation between two categories of expansionists—extremists and moderates. Theodore **Roosevelt** achieved an acceptable, hence workable and durable, synthesis when he drew closer to the latter following his accession to the presidency. The Philippine Government Act of July 1, 1902, created an elective assembly and provided measures for the betterment of social and economic conditions on the islands. Roosevelt next proclaimed a general amnesty, which was enough to still public criticism almost completely; and on July 4, 1902, declared the insurrection to be officially over, although sporadic fighting continued for a few more years. *See also* Hawaii; Panama Canal; Japanese Empire; Open Door.

FURTHER READING: Alfonso, Oscar M. *Theodore Roosevelt and the Philippines, 1897–1909.* Quezon City: University of the Philippines Press, 1970; Linn, Brian M. *The U.S. Army and Counterinsurgency in the Philippine War, 1899–1902.* Chapel Hill: University of North Carolina Press, 1989; Miller, Stuart C. *"Benevolent Assimilation": The American Conquest of the Philippines, 1899–1903.* New Haven, CT: Yale University Press, 1982; Rystad, Göran. *Ambiguous Imperialism: American Foreign Policy and Domestic Politics at the Turn of the Century.* Lund, Sweden: Esselte Studium, 1975; Welch, Richard E., Jr. *Response to Imperialism: The United States and the Philippine-American War, 1899–1902.* Chapel Hill: University of North Carolina Press, 1987.

SERGE RICARD

Piedmont-Sardinia, Kingdom of

A territory of northwestern **Italy** united under the House of Savoy by the Treaty of Aix-la-Chapelle in 1748. The kingdom was conquered by Napoleon **Bonaparte** in 1796 but recovered its independence at the Congress of **Vienna** in 1814. Liberals in the kingdom began to agitate for constitutional government in the 1820s, yet made the critical breakthrough only under King Charles Albert in the landmark year of 1848. Piedmont was thereafter active in the Risorgimento to unite Italy but was thwarted at the battles of Custozza and Novara in the effort to prize Lombardy from Austrian rule. Under **Victor Emmanuel III** and Count **Cavour,** the effort was rejoined by way of an alliance with France against Austria in 1859. It was successful in joining Piedmont to the Kingdom of Italy in 1861, although Savoy and Nice were ceded to France in compensation for alliance services rendered. *See also* Napoleonic Wars.

FURTHER READING: Di Scala, Spencer M. *Italy: From Revolution to Republic, 1700 to the Present.* Boulder, CO: Westview Press, 1998; Hearder, Harry. *Italy in the Age of the Risorgimento, 1790–1870.* New York: Longman, 1983.

CARL CAVANAGH HODGE

Piłsudski, Jozef (1867–1935)

Polish nationalist, soldier, and political leader, Jozef Piłsudski was born into a Polish *szlachta* (lower nobility) family that had been actively involved in the 1863 **Polish Rebellion.** His education took place during the height of the Russification efforts. His teachers' "system was to crush as much as possible the independence and personal dignity of their pupils," he later said of his schooling. In 1887, he was arrested by the Russian police and exiled to Siberia for five years on a charge, almost certainly false, of participating in an assassination attempt on the tsar. He was again arrested in 1900, but escaped after feigning mental illness and went into exile in Austria. In 1905, during the **Russo-Japanese War,** he went to Japan where he unsuccessfully tried to convince the Japanese to raise an anti-Russian army from the Polish conscripts it had captured.

Back in Austrian Poland after the war, he founded a military organization called *Bojawa,* or "Fighting Organization." Piłsudski rejected traditional terrorist activities, such as assassination of imperial officials, which he felt were not only ineffective but led to reprisals against civilians. Instead, his organization confined itself to rescuing Polish nationals condemned to death and to robbing banks and mail trains. By

1910, Piłsudski had also organized a "Riflemen's Association," which was tolerated by the Austrians as training for reservists. When World War I broke out, this force became the Polish Legion and fought as part of the Austrian army. In the last years of the war, Piłsudski was arrested by the Germans; in the chaos of the last days of the war, he was released and sent to Warsaw, the Polish capital. There he was named commander-in-chief of the newly forming nation. From that point, he essentially led Poland, although usually unofficially, without a formal position, until his death in 1935. *See also* Napoleonic Wars; Russian Empire.

FURTHER READING: Jedrzejewicz, Wacław. *Piłsudski, A Life for Poland.* New York: Hippocrene Books, 1882; Pilsudska, Alexandra. *Piłsudski: A Biography.* New York: Dodd, Mead, 1941.

JOSEPH ADAMCZYK

Pitt, William (1759–1806)

Prime minister of the United Kingdom from 1783 to 1801, and again from 1804 to 1806, Pitt was the fourth child of William Pitt, later first earl of Chatham, who had distinguished himself as prime minister during the Seven Years' War (1756–1763). The younger Pitt studied at Cambridge before first practicing law and then entering Parliament at the age of 21 in January 1781. His maiden speech demonstrated Pitt's mastery of the language and his skill as a debater—talents he would go on to use in opposing the government's policy of war against the United States, and in advocating economic reforms to reduce government spending and reduce the king's powers of patronage. He also advocated parliamentary reform by denouncing the system of rotten boroughs and calling for a redistribution of constituencies inequitably represented in the House of Commons.

When Lord Shelburne became prime minister in July 1782, Pitt was made chancellor of the exchequer, and thereafter became a staunch political opponent of the prominent Whig politician, Charles James **Fox.** In December 1783, Pitt himself became prime minister, so enabling him to institute a number of successful policies for reducing the massive national debt, specifically the introduction of his Sinking Fund and a range of innovative taxation schemes. When he failed to achieve Parliamentary reform in 1785, however, he thereafter ceased to pursue that object. As a war leader in the 1790s, Pitt lacked the strategic vision necessary to effectively oppose revolutionary France. Nevertheless, he was instrumental, together with his foreign secretary, Lord Grenville, in consolidating the First Coalition (1792–1797), although he confined his material contribution to the war effort to naval activity and small-scale military operations on the Continent. During the Second Coalition (1798–1801), he again dissipated British resources, although his provision of substantial financial payments to Austria, Russia, and various other continental allies played an important role in maintaining resistance against Revolutionary France.

Pitt resigned from office in 1801 over differences with **George III** on the issue of Catholic Emancipation, a measure that the king refused to support on the grounds that it would violate his coronation oath. Pitt initially supported Henry Addington, his successor in office, as well as the Peace of Amiens with France, but when war resumed in May 1803, he gradually came to oppose government policy and returned to office for his second ministry a year later. Pitt was instrumental in raising the Third

Coalition—Britain, Russia, Austria, and Sweden—against France, personally conceiving, in January 1805, detailed plans for the reconstruction of postwar Europe. With the decisive triumph of the French at **Austerlitz** in December and the refusal of Prussia to join the Allies, however, Pitt's fragile health finally gave out, and he died from a combination of overwork and the cumulative effect of years of heavy drinking. *See also* Napoleonic Wars.

FURTHER READING: Duffy, Michael. *The Younger Pitt.* New York: Longman, 2000; Ehrman, John. *The Younger Pitt: The Consuming Struggle.* London: Constable, 1996; Ehrman, John. *The Younger Pitt. The Reluctant Transition.* London: Constable, 1986; Ehrman, John. *The Younger Pitt: The Years of Acclaim.* New York: Dutton, 1969; Hague, William. *William Pitt the Younger.* London: HarperCollins, 2004.

GREGORY FREMONT-BARNES

Platt Amendment (1901)

Passed by the U.S. Congress without serious opposition, the Platt Amendment defined the postoccupation political relationship between the **United States** and the new Cuban Republic. The legislation placed limitations on Cuban sovereignty by barring the new Cuban government from entering into any agreement with a foreign power that infringed on the independence of **Cuba** or granted the right to colonies or military bases in Cuba. It also prohibited the government from accumulating a debt larger than the ordinary revenues of the island could pay. Article Three, the clause most objectionable to the Cubans, granted the United States the right to "intervene for the preservation of Cuban independence, the maintenance of a government adequate for the protection of life, property, and individual liberty, and for discharging the obligations . . . imposed by the Treaty of **Paris** on the United States. . . ." The Platt Amendment obligated the Cuban Republic to ratify the actions of the U.S. military government, to continue the sanitation measures introduced during the occupation, and to sell or lease to the United States land for coaling or naval stations.

The United States called for the Cubans to embody the same terms in a formal treaty with the United States and to incorporate them into the Cuban Constitution. Initially the Cuban Constitutional Convention and the Cuban populace rejected and denounced the Platt Amendment. Yet pressure from the United States and the recognition that the occupation would not end without acceptance of the Platt Amendment eventually forced the Cubans to accept the measure. Despite assurances to the contrary, the Platt Amendment became a pretext for American meddling in internal Cuban affairs. It laid the foundation for future American Caribbean policy and the **Roosevelt Corollary** to the **Monroe Doctrine.** The United States abrogated the Platt Amendment in 1934 as part of the good neighbor policy. *See also* Cuban Reciprocity Treaty; Protectorate.

FURTHER READING: Healy, David. *The United States in Cuba, 1898–1902: Generals, Politicians, and the Search for Policy.* Madison: University of Wisconsin Press, 1963; Marks, Frederick W. *Velvet on Iron: The Diplomacy of Theodore Roosevelt.* Lincoln: University of Nebraska Press, 1979.

JAMES PRUITT

Pobedonostsev, Konstantin Petrovich (1827–1907)

An influential statesman in Russian imperial politics under Tsar Alexander III (1881–1894) and Tsar **Nicholas II** (1894–1917). After his studies at the School of Law in St Petersburg, Pobedonostsev began his career as an official in a department of the Russian Senate in Moscow. Between 1860 and 1865, Pobedonostsev became professor of civil law at the Moscow State University and was instructed by Tsar **Alexander II** (1885–1881), a promoter of reforms and modernization, to teach his sons law and administration management. Pobedonostsev also took part in the reform of the Russian judicial system in order to make the Russian autocracy more effective, but he never doubted the superiority of Russian autocracy over Western democracy.

As Pobedonostsev was an uncompromising conservative, he had a decisive impact on the Tsar's son and successor, Alexander III. After the assassination of Alexander II, Alexander III installed a repressive and authoritarian regime that was deeply influenced by Pobedonostsev's ideology. As chief procurator of the Holy Synod beginning in 1880, Pobedonostsev's ultraconservatism resulted from his orthodox belief. Pobedonostsev thought that human nature was sinful without a strong religious education. Consequently, he rejected Western ideals of freedom for the **Russian Empire;** independence and democracy as demanded by young Russian intellectuals Pobedonostsev considered as an "outburst of juvenile nihilism." Pobedonostsev spoke respectfully of England, but he thought that individual freedom and democracy would fit the English character but not the Russian. Pobedonostsev also denied any education for the Russian worker and peasant classes because they had to learn to live by the work of their hands. Any intellectual education would harm their productive force. As the head of the Russian Orthodox Church until the revolution of 1905, Pobedonostsev had an immense influence on domestic policy, especially on religion, education, and censorship. Although in domestic politics he propagated a most repressive policy toward nonorthodox religions—especially toward Jews—and non-Russian ethnic minorities, he was familiar with European and American literature and philosophy.

FURTHER READING: Byrnes, Robert. *Pobedonostsev: His Life and Thought.* Bloomington: Indiana University Press, 1968; Pobedonostsev, Konstantin P. *Reflections of a Russian Statesman.* London: G. Richards, 1898; Thaden, Edward. *Conservative Nationalism in Nineteenth Century Russia.* Seattle: University of Washington Press, 1964.

EVA-MARIA STOLBERG

Poland

See Polish Rebellions

Polar Imperialism

The polar regions were and are an object of imperial ambition. The Arctic held riches in form of oil, baleen, and ivory from sea mammals, and exploitation of these resources started here in the seventeenth century. Fisheries, prestige, adventurism, and, toward the end of the nineteenth century, prospects of rich mineral resources also inspired entrepreneurs and states to venture to the extreme north of the globe.

Sea mammals had become scarce in the Arctic by then, and attention was increasingly directed toward the Antarctica. The precondition for lasting expansion by Europeans into these areas came with the age of discoveries and its development of seaworthy vessels capable of navigating icy polar waters, and the organizational skill associated with modern society.

When the first Europeans arrived, Spitzbergen, the Arctic ice shelf, and Antarctica with its surrounding islands were void of peoples; and hunter-gatherer societies only thinly populated Northern Canada, Greenland, and Arctic Russia. Rich fisheries, petroleum deposits, and the absence of subjugated peoples who could or are willing to assert forceful claims of sovereignty has prolonged the age of imperialism in polar areas into the twenty-first century, and it even extends to the oceans and the continental shelves below. Major contested areas are the Antarctica proper (contested by several powers), the Falkland Islands (between Britain and **Argentina**), and the Barents Sea (between Russia and **Norway**). In support of these claims on land and sea, past explorers and practices play an important role.

FURTHER READING: Peterson, M. J. *Managing the Frozen South: The Creation and Evolution of the Antarctic Treaty System.* Berkeley: University of California Press, 1988; Sufford, Francis. *I May Be Some Time: Ice and the English Imagination.* New York: St. Martin's, 1997.

FRODE LINDGJERDET

Polish Rebellions

A succession of nationalist risings aimed at reestablishing a unified Polish state. In the seventeenth and eighteenth centuries, Poland was a terrain of contention between Prussia and the **Russian Empire.** While the eighteenth century was the era of the partitions, Polish dreams of independence awakened in the Napoleonic period. Polish volunteers joined Napoleon **Bonaparte**'s army in the hope that the French emperor's wars with Prussia, Austria, and Russia would realize an independent Polish state. Napoleon pursued his own policy in Central and Eastern Europe. In 1807, he established the Duchy of Warsaw on territory that formerly belonged to Prussia and that had been part of old Poland, but the duchy was a French puppet regime with a limited self-government. When in 1809 Józef Poniatowski, nephew of Stanislaw II August, demanded some territories back that had been annexed by Austria in the second partition, the Russians invaded the duchy in 1813. Two years later with the defeat of Napoleon at Waterloo, all Polish dreams of national independence through French expansion vanished.

The Congress of **Vienna** sealed the dissolution of the Duchy of Warsaw and left most of the terms of the last Polish partition valid. After 1815, Poles became discontented with a political order in Europe that restored a rigid conservative rule as an expression of the growing influence of the Holy Alliance of Austria, Prussia, and Russia, the powers responsible for the statelessness of the Polish nation. Polish nationalism exploded in a series of armed rebellions in the nineteenth century. After the Congress of Vienna, nearly three-quarters of Polish territory belonged to the Russian Empire. At first, Tsar **Alexander I** established a Kingdom of Poland, granted a liberal constitution, a national army, and limited cultural autonomy of Poles within the Russian Empire, but these concessions did not satisfy the Polish dream of independence. From the 1820s onward, the Russian regime became more repressive, and many Polish secret societies were established to drive out the Russians. In November 1830, the Polish army rebelled in Warsaw. The rebels hoped for aid from France, but it failed to come. The rebels' reluctance to abolish serfdom, moreover, gambled away all sympathies of the Polish peasantry. One year later, the Russian army crushed the revolt and 6,000 rebels fled into French exile. The tsarist government abolished the Polish constitution and the army.

Nevertheless, Polish nationalist activities were organized by exiles in Paris. One of the prominent leaders, Adam Czartoryski, tried to win international support in order to gain independence from the Russian Empire. But Czartoryski's vision was not undisputed among Polish intellectuals in Paris. He sought to establish a Polish monarchy based on a conservative ideology that denied any political participation of peasants and workers. The radicals wanted an independent Polish republic and the abolition of serfdom. When in 1846 the peasantry of Austrian Poland rebelled against the gentry, the oppression by the Habsburg regime was so harsh that it undermined the social basis of the Polish nationalists, as they split into rival factions and lacked the financial sources to participate actively in the European revolutions of 1848 and 1849. The Polish uprising on the Russian-occupied territory in January 1863 also failed because the intellectual leaders of the national movement did not succeed in mobilizing the peasantry. In August 1864, the Russian army crushed the rebellion. The former Kingdom of Poland was abolished, and the territory came under the dictatorship of Governor-general Mikhail Murav'ev. By then the leaders of the Polish national movement realized that Polish independence was a long process, and they preferred peaceful means by education and economic development.

In the second half of the nineteenth century, the time for a Polish independence was not ripe, as the **German Empire,** established in 1871, and the Russian Empire sought, respectively, to Germanize or Russify their Polish minorities. Only Austria-Hungary guaranteed Poles a cultural autonomy in return for loyalty. Galicia received a semi-autonomous parliament, the Galician *sejm.* The universities of Kraków and Lwów became centers of Polish cultural and scientific renaissance that attracted many Polish students from Germany and Russia, but not before the collapse of the German, Russian, and **Habsburg Empires** in World War I could Poland become an independent republic. *See also* Napoleonic Wars; Pan-Slavism.

FURTHER READING: Kutolowski, John F. *The West and Poland: Essays on Governmental and Public Responses to the Polish National Movement, 1861–1881.* New York: Columbia University Press, 2000; Porter, Brian A. *When Nationalism Began to Hate. Imagining Modern Politics in Nineteenth Century Poland.* New York: Oxford University Press, 2000.

EVA-MARIA STOLBERG

Political Economy

A field of interdisciplinary study drawing on economics, law, and political science to understand the mechanism by which political structures, institutions, and the policies influence market behavior. Within the discipline of political science, the term refers to modern liberal, realist, Marxian, and constructivist theories concerning the relationship between economic and political power among states. This is also of concern to students of economic history and institutional economics.

Economists, however, often associate the term with game theory. Furthermore, international political economy is a branch of economics that is concerned with international trade and finance, and state policies that affect international trade, such as monetary and fiscal policies. Others, especially anthropologists, sociologists, and geographers, use the term *political economy* to refer to neo-Marxian approaches to development and underdevelopment set forth by theoreticians such as Andre Gunder Frank and Immanuel Wallerstein.

To study the economies of states, the discipline of political economy was developed in the eighteenth century. In 1805, Thomas **Malthus** became first professor of political economy at the East India Company College at Haileybury in Hertfordshire. In an apparent contradistinction to the theory of the physiocrats, which viewed land as the source of all wealth, political economists such as John Locke, Adam **Smith,** and Karl **Marx** proposed the labor theory of value. According to this theory, labor is the real source of value. Political economists also attracted attention to the accelerating development of technology, whose role in economic and social relationships grew ever more important. Until the late nineteenth century, however, the term *economics* generally superseded the term *political economy*.

By the second half of the nineteenth century, *laissez-faire* theorists started to argue that the state should not regulate the market, that politics and markets operated according to different principles, and that political economy should be replaced by two separate disciplines, political science and economics. Around 1870, neoclassical economists such as Alfred Marshall began using the term *economics*. Institutions that taught politics and economics jointly, such as Oxford University, did not adopt this terminological preference and appointed the mathematical economist Francis Edgeworth to the Drummond Chair of Political Economy in 1891. Political economy remained in use for the study of economies seen through the lens of government action, even though many economists also study the effects of government. Political economy primarily refers to "systems" of economy, either Wallerstein's "world system" or emergent systems, and the free market is often an important subject of discussion. *See also* Corn Laws; Free Trade; Imperialism.

FURTHER READING: Best, Michael H., and William E. Connolly. *The Politicized Economy.* Lexington, MA: DC. Heath, 1982; Kindleberger, Charles P. *Historical Economics: Art or Science?* New York: Harvester/Wheatsheaf, 1990; Lindblom, Charles A. *Politics and Markets: The World's Political-Economic Systems.* New York: Basic Books, 1977; Phelps, Edmund S. *Political Economy: An Introductory Text.* New York: W. W. Norton, 1985; Staniland, Martin, *What Is Political Economy? A Study of Social Theory and Underdevelopment.* New Haven, CT: Yale University Press, 1985.

JITENDRA UTTAM

Port Arthur

Port Arthur is the former name of the port city of Lüshun at the tip of China's Liaodong Peninsula in Liaoning Province, approximately 30 kilometers south of the city of Dalian. Port Arthur takes its name from Royal Navy Lieutenant William C. Arthur, who briefly occupied the harbor in 1858. Port Arthur's natural harbor and strategic position, commanding the northern Yellow and Bohai Seas, resulted in its fortification in the 1880s by Qing China and its choice as headquarters for the developing Beiyang Fleet. The port played a major role in the **Sino-Japanese War** of 1894 when it was captured by Japanese troops after a short siege. On the strength of its peace settlement with China in 1895, Japan briefly occupied the city along with the Liaodong Peninsula yet was forced to withdraw in response to the Triple Intervention of Russia, France, and Germany.

In 1898, Russia occupied Port Arthur as part of its lease of railroad rights in Manchuria. It soon extended a spur of the Trans-Siberian Railway to the port, increasing the location's strategic and commercial value. During the **Russo-Japanese War** of 1904–1905, the port was again occupied by Japan after a prolonged siege and, with the defeat of Russia, became the headquarters of the Japanese Guandong (Kwantung) Leased Territories, taking on a major role in Japan's occupation and development of **Manchuria.** *See also* Japanese Empire; Russian Empire; Port Arthur, Siege of; Trans-Siberian Railroad.

FURTHER READING: Matsusaka, Yoshihisa Tak. *The Making of Japanese Manchuria, 1904–1932.* Cambridge, MA: Harvard University Asia Center, 2001; Stephen, John J. *The Russian Far East.* Stanford, CA: Stanford University Press, 1994.

DANIEL C. KANE

Port Arthur, Siege of (1904–1905)

A costly but important Japanese victory in the **Russo-Japanese War.** Indecisive Russian command failed to halt the landing of Japan's Second Army on the Liaotung Peninsula from May 5–19, 1904. General Oku Yasukata skillfully directed the Japanese advance and defeated the Russians guarding the narrow isthmus at Nanshan on May 25, which isolated Port Arthur. After the battle, Oku led his army north to engage the main Russian army, while the Third Army commanded by General Nogi Maresuke, who had captured Port Arthur 10 years earlier in the Sino-Japanese war, landed at Dalny, east of Port Arthur, and advanced on **Port Arthur.**

Russian commanders made little effort to interfere with Nogi, and reinforcements by the end of July had built his force to 80,000 soldiers and 474 artillery pieces. The Japanese began probing Russian defenses in July and launched their first assault on August 7. This and successive assaults suffered heavy casualties, forcing Nogi to proceed cautiously and build extensive siege works. The key Russian position on 203 Meter Hill did not fall until December 5, but afterwards Japanese artillery on that hill shelled the city regularly. Russian General Anatolii M. Stessel surrendered the city and its garrison of 32,000 soldiers and sailors on January 2, 1905, despite ample stocks of food and munitions. Russia suffered 31,000 casualties during the siege, and Japan suffered 59,000 casualties. *See also* Tsushima, Battle of.

FURTHER READING: Jukes, Geoffrey. *The Russo-Japanese War, 1904–5.* Oxford: Osprey, 2002; Warner, Denis, and Warner, Peggy. *The Tide at Sunrise: A History of the Russo-Japanese War, 1904–1905.* London: Frank Cass, 2002.

STEPHEN K. STEIN

Porte, The Sublime

"The Sublime Porte" or simply "the Porte" was the name given to the Ottoman government at Constantinople. The name derives from the French translation of the Turkish *Bâbiâli* ("High or Lofty Gate," or "Gate of the Eminent"), which was the official name of the gate that gave access to the Sultan's palace in Constantinople, where justice was formerly administered and later where the Grand Vizier resided with the offices of the main departments of state. The French phrase has been adopted, because at one time French was the language of European diplomacy. The court of Constantinople was also known as the Seraglio. The name was no longer used when Mustafa Kemal Atatürk founded the Turkish Republic. *See also* Ottoman Empire.

FURTHER READING: Alderson, D. *The Structure of the Ottoman Dynasty.* Oxford: Clarendon, 1956; Inalcik, H. *The Ottoman Empire: The Classical Age, 1300–1600.* London: Weidenfeld and Nicholson, 1973.

ANDERKOS VARNAVA

Portsmouth, Treaty of (1905)

The diplomatic settlement of the **Russo-Japanese War.** The war broke out with Japan's surprise attack on Port Arthur on February 8, 1904, but it was caused by Russia's hegemonic ambitions in Manchuria. The conflict was a severe blow to the Open Door diplomacy of the **United States** and a serious threat to the integrity of China. After the battle of Mukden, decided in favor of Japan between February 23 and March 10, 1905, President Theodore **Roosevelt** was indirectly approached as a possible mediator. He was aware of two major stumbling blocks: Tokyo's demands for a war indemnity and for the surrender of Sakhalin Island, which St. Petersburg adamantly resisted.

The peace talks began at Portsmouth, New Hampshire on August 9, 1905, and Roosevelt monitored them from a distance for two weeks, tirelessly stepping in to break every deadlock. Eventually, the Japanese were willing to restore the northern half of Sakhalin to Russia while Russia seemed ready to conclude peace if any reference to what might be interpreted as a war indemnity was abandoned. The accord agreed to on August 23 finalized terms that surprised the American president. They were less favorable to Tokyo than those he had earlier wrung from St. Petersburg. Unknown to him, the Russian envoy had in fact cleverly guessed and used to his country's advantage Japan's eagerness to reach a settlement. Signed on September 5, 1905, the Treaty of Portsmouth was a compromise agreement that froze the new power equilibrium that had resulted from the battle of Mukden six months earlier. The Japanese, who had dropped their demand for financial compensation, received the southern half of Sakhalin, the Guangdong concession, which comprised Port Arthur, and the Russian rights to the south-Manchurian railroad—although the region remained open to international trade and investments. The Russians kept the northern half of Sakhalin, as well as their control over the Kharbin-Changchun railroad in northern Manchuria, and recognized Japanese predominance in **Korea,** with the blessing of the United States given that American policy included acceptance of a Japanese

Korea. In all, Russia did not lose as much as her defeat ought to have entailed; she retained a foothold in China and remained an Asian power that could still counteract Japanese influence—a welcome preservation of the balance of power in the Far East. Theodore Roosevelt's single-handed peacemaking feat at Portsmouth was crowned by the 1906 Nobel Peace Prize. *See also* Japanese Empire.

FURTHER READING: Esthus, Raymond A. *Double Eagle and Rising Sun: The Russians and Japanese at Portsmouth in 1905.* Durham, NC: Duke University Press, 1988; Neu, Charles E. *An Uncertain Friendship: Theodore Roosevelt and Japan, 1906–1909.* Cambridge, MA: Harvard University Press, 1967; Trani, Eugene P. *The Treaty of Portsmouth: An Adventure in American Diplomacy.* Lexington: University of Kentucky Press, 1969.

SERGE RICARD

Portuguese Empire (1415–1808)

In the nineteenth century, the empire of Portugal was already in advanced decay. From the fifteenth century, Portugal had been a leading maritime power, advantaged by its location to play a precocious role in the European exploration and exploitation of Africa, India, and South America. Portugal also established the Atlantic **slave trade**, linking the longstanding slave trade within the African continent with the demand for labor in South America in particular. By the seventeenth century, **Brazil,** formally a Portuguese possession since 1500, was absorbing more than 40 percent of all slaves shipped to the Western Hemisphere. In addition Portuguese traders played a dominant role in the early spice trade linking Cape Verde with Mozambique, **India,** China, and Japan.

Portugal's vulnerabilities in maintaining a far-flung colonial empire were twofold. The country's comparatively small population hampered its capacity to settle the interior of many of the territories to which it laid claim. Plain bad luck played a role here, when in 1755 the Lisbon earthquake of 1755 killed more than 100,000 of a city population of 275,000. Moreover, Portugal itself was vulnerable to constant threat from other continental powers and was as often the object of the rivalries of England, France, and Spain as it was master of its own destiny. Napoleon **Bonaparte**'s invasion and occupation of Portugal in 1807 marked the beginning of the **Peninsular War** and the end of the empire that had begun with the Portuguese conquest of Ceuta across the Strait of Gibraltor in 1415. In 1808, the Portuguese court was transferred to Brazil, and in 1815 the colony was made the United Kingdom of Portugal, Brazil, and Algarves. The court did not return to Portugal until 1821 by which time the self-confidence of the Brazilians had built an unstoppable appetite for independence, which they secured under Dom Pedro I in 1822. The loss of Brazil to Portugal marked a decline as symbolic as Britain's loss of India in 1947.

In the nineteenth century Portugal therefore concentrated on consolidating and expanding its holdings in Africa—Cape Verde, São Tomé and Principe, Guinea-Bissau, Portuguese West Africa (Angola), and Portuguese East Africa (Mozambique)—but at a time of intensifying competition among the other European power on that continent. The attempt to link Portuguese Angola and Mozambique across the continent east-to-west was blocked in 1890 by Britain's project to link Egypt with South Africa north-to-south. Portugal's last major imperial gambit, therefore, was to participate as a loser in the great Scramble for **Africa.** *See also* Netherlands; Habsburg Empire; Slavery; Spanish Empire.

FURTHER READING: Birmingham, David. *Portugal and Africa*. New York: St. Martin's, 1999; Boxer, C. R. *The Portuguese Seaborne Empire*. London: Hutchinson, 1969; Russell-Wood, A.J.R. *The Portuguese Empire, 1415–1808*. Baltimore: The John Hopkins University Press, 1998.

CARL CAVANAGH HODGE

Pozzolo, Battle of (1800)

The last victory for Republican France over the Austrian army, fought on December 25–26, 1800, in northeastern Italy. In late November, Feldzeugmeister Graf Bellegarde concentrated his 50,000 Austrian troops to cross the Mincio river, but news of defeat at **Hohenlinden** on December 3 made him hesitate, while French commander, General Brune went on the offensive with 70,000 men. Lieutenant General Dupont's troops crossed the Mincio on December 25 at Pozzolo and constructed a bridge. Reinforced by Lieutenant General Suchet, he beat off an Austrian counterattack and by midday, had secured Pozzolo village. An hour later, Bellegarde attacked the village, while more troops moved along the riverbank to attack the bridge. Feldmarschalleutnant Kaim seized Pozzolo and drove the French back to the bridge, but French artillery on the opposite bank prevented the Austrians from taking the bridge. Dupont reassembled his division and led a renewed assault, which recaptured Pozzolo, while Suchet sent another division over a second bridge. Pozzolo changed hands three times in bitter fighting. A French general assault took the village for a fifth time, but Austrian cavalry and dusk prevented any further advance.

The next morning, Suchet crossed another bridge at Monzambano in thick fog, heading for the Monte Bianco hills, where half of Bellegarde's troops were positioned. Suchet assaulted the hills and drove the Austrians back on Salionze, while Lieutenant General Delmas attacked Valeggio village, which would change hands three times. The French reinforced their positions around Pozzolo, while an Austrian counterattack on Monte Bianco failed. During the night, Bellegarde decided not to renew the action, but retreated across the Adige River. *See also* Habsburg Empire; Napoleonic Wars.

FURTHER READING: Blanning, T.C.W. *The French Revolutionary Wars, 1787–1802*. London: Arnold, 1996; Fremont-Barnes, Gregory. *The French Revolutionary Wars*. Oxford: Osprey, 2001.

DAVID HOLLINS

Pressburg, Treaty of (1805)

A peace treaty signed on December 26, 1805, in the capital of Hungary, now Bratislava in Slovakia, which ended hostilities between Austria and France in the Third Coalition war after Napoleon **Bonaparte**'s decisive victory at **Austerlitz** on December 2. The key southern German states and the Batavian Republic (Holland) also signed. Austria recognized Napoleon as king of **Italy** and ceded the western part of Venetia to the kingdom; however, Napoleon failed to keep his promise to separate the Italian monarchy from the French crown. The electors of Bavaria and

Württemburg were made kings. Austria was forced to hand over her most western territories, the Tyrol and Vorarlberg to Bavaria; the remaining *Vorlände,* enclaves in southwestern Germany, were given to Baden and Württemburg. In return, Austria was given the lands of the Elector of Salzburg, who in their place received the formerly Bavarian Principality of Würzburg.

The abandonment of the titles of elector by these rulers and the termination of the Holy Roman Emperor's right to call on military contingents from southern Germany was a clear signal that the thousand-year-old Holy Roman Empire was at an end. Napoleon established the **Confederation of the Rhine** on July 18, 1806, and Habsburg Emperor Francis II confirmed the Empire's dissolution two weeks later. Napoleon's domination of Central Europe was expressed in a clause, under which France guaranteed Austria's territorial integrity. Austria agreed to pay an indemnity of 40 million French francs. The Franco-Russian war would continue for another 18 months. *See also* Habsburg Empire; Napoleonic Wars.

FURTHER READING: Castle, I. *Austerlitz: Napoleon and the Eagles of Europe.* London: Pen & Sword, 2005; Schroeder, Paul W. *The Transformation of European Politics, 1763–1848.* Oxford: Clarendon Press, 1994.

DAVID HOLLINS

Pretoria, Convention of (1881)

Signed on August 3, 1881, the Convention of Pretoria laid down the principal terms of the peace agreement that concluded the First Boer War of 1880–1881 between Britain and the Afrikaner insurgents of the recently annexed Transvaal. A final major British defeat at Majuba Hill helped the Transvaal cause and ensured recognition of the independent Afrikaner republic. The price was accepting the British Crown's suzerainty, that is, handing over control of foreign relations and policy toward the indigenous African population. It was also specified that the republic may not expand westward. Because this agreement was considered unsatisfactory, a delegation led by Transvaal president Paul **Kruger** renegotiated the terms, the resulting document being the London Convention of 1884.

Despite important concessions, including the granting of treaty making powers with the Orange River Free State, as well as western territorial gains by the now renamed Afrikaner state, the South African Republic, the crucial objective of full sovereignty was not formally ceded, even though the phrase "the suzerainty of Her Majesty" was now deleted from the text. Ultimately the mounting tensions resulting from continued British interference led to the Second Boer War of 1899–1902. *See also* Boer Wars; British Empire; Orange Free State; Sand River Convention.

FURTHER READING: Falwell, Byron. *The Great Anglo-Boer War.* New York: Harper & Row, 1976; Pakenham, Thomas. *The Boer War.* New York: Avon Books, 1979; Smith, Iain R. *The Origins of the South African War, 1899–1902.* New York: Longman, 1996.

GÁBOR BERCZELI

Primo de Rivera y Orbañeja, Miguel (1870–1930)

A Spanish general and dictator who fought devotedly to prevent first the final fall of the **Spanish Empire** and then the fall of the Spanish monarchy. He was unsuccessful in both cases. Primo de Rivera was born in Jerez, **Spain,** on January 8, 1870, into a prominent military family. He joined the army in 1884 and advanced in rank through his participation in the Spanish colonial wars in Morocco, **Cuba,** and the **Philippines** in the 1890s. He became general in 1912. In 1915 he was appointed governor of Cádiz; in 1919 he became captain general of Valencia and Madrid, and then Catalonia, in 1922. In 1921, after the death of his uncle, Primo de Rivera became Marqués de Estella. From Barcelona he organized, with the approval of King Alfonso XIII and large support that included the Catalan high bourgeoisie, the trade unions, and the *latifundistas,* a military coup d'état that took place on September 13, 1923, ending the *turno* system under which the leading political parties took turns in power.

He had married Casilda Sáenz de Heredia in 1902. She died in 1908 after bearing him six children. The first born, José Antonio, would become the founder of the *Falange Española,* Francisco Franco's eventual political base. His sister Pilar ran the women's section of the Falange and is known to have said that, "there is nothing more detestable than an intellectual woman." José Antonio and his brother Fernando were taken prisoners and executed in the first year of the Spanish Civil War.

FURTHER READING: Ratcliff, Dillwyn F. *Prelude to Franco: Political Aspects of the Dictatorship of General Miguel Primo de Rivera.* New York: Las Americas, 1957.

GEORGIA TRES

Progressivism

An American political and social movement of the late nineteenth century that influenced the spirit of territorial expansionism policy in the two decades before 1914. The most dramatic example of the emergence of the **United States** as an imperial power was the **Spanish-American War** in which it eliminated Spanish influence in the Western Hemisphere and also gained possession of the **Philippines,** Guam, Puerto Rico, and Samoa.

By the late 1890s, the American economy was producing more than it could consume, leading to a search for new markets abroad. At the same time, the economic success enjoyed by the country came at the expense of the industrial working class. The project of domestic reform championed by the Populist and Progressive movements—prodding the administrations of William McKinley and Theodore **Roosevelt** to take steps to improve the condition of the working class and to end monopolies and trust corporations—was also felt in its most ebullient moments in the increasingly popular notion that the United States had both moral obligations and a responsibility to humanity more generally. In the case of the war with Spain over **Cuba,** the older traditions of **Manifest Destiny** and the **Monroe Doctrine** were married in the mind of Progressives to a crusading moralism that clamored for the United Sates to rescue Cubans from the oppression of Spanish rule. Roosevelt referred to it as "militant decency" and observed that America's chief usefulness to humanity "rest(s) on our combining power with high purpose." This relationship between American imperialism and progressivism continued into the presidential terms of William Howard **Taft** and Woodrow **Wilson** and stalled with the onslaught of World War I, after which it was rearticulated as liberal internationalism.

FURTHER READING: Freidel, Frank. *The Splendid Little War.* New York: Dell, 1958; McDougall, Walter. *Promised Land, Crusader State.* Boston: Houghton Mifflin, 1997; McGerr, Michael. *A Fierce Discontent: The Rise and Fall of the Progressive Movement in America, 1870–1920.* New York: Free Press.

CARL CAVANAGH HODGE

Protectionism

A set of economic policies promoting favored domestic industries by using high tariffs and regulations designed to discourage imports. Historical variants of protectionism have included **mercantilism,** a trade policy aimed at maximizing currency reserves by running large trade surpluses, and import substitution, a trade policy in which targeted imports are replaced by local manufactures to stimulate local production. Mercantilist policies of Britain created a major burden on the colonies; thus protectionism became a significant cause of the revolution in America. Having achieved independence, however, many Americans advocated protectionist policies similar to those that they had earlier condemned.

Alexander **Hamilton** laid the theoretical basis for economic protectionism and modern economic nationalism. He set forth a dynamic theory of comparative advantage based on an import-substitution industrialization strategy of economic development, which supports the superiority of manufacturing sector over agriculture. In his work, *National System of Political Economy,* German economist Friedrich **List** argued that: (1) the **free trade** theories of classical British economists were the economic policy of the strong; (2) there was no "natural" or immutable international division of labor based on the law of comparative advantage; (3) the division of labor was merely a historical situation resulting from prior uses of economic and political power. List and other German economic nationalists advocated political unification, development of railroads to unify the economy physically, and erection of high tariff barriers to foster economic unification, protect the development of German industry, and create a powerful German state.

The **Netherlands** was among the first countries to take trade as a route to prosperity and developed into the commercial center of Europe as a consequence. Shipping and shipbuilding grew, giving Amsterdam control of the Baltic grain trade and making it a naval center and entrepôt for heavy goods. By the seventeenth century, the Dutch were the richest people on earth. By the late 1600s taxes and tariffs nevertheless began to creep upward, which had the twofold effect of diminishing trade while increasing wages, as workers demanded more money to compensate them for the increased cost of living. Skilled workers and commerce gradually moved to new locations, such as Hamburg, where taxes and tariffs were lower. By the end of the 1700s, the Netherlands even abandoned its traditional neutrality and suffered major defeats in war with England.

As the Dutch were removing medieval restrictions on trade in the sixteenth century, England was beginning to open its market as well. In the early part of the century, usury laws were no longer enforced, restrictions on the export of unfinished cloth were relaxed, and certain differential duties were abolished. Enforcement of remaining trade restrictions was also generally reduced. Unfortunately, this initial era of free trade was short-lived. The end of the seventeenth century saw another revival of protectionism. In the decades after the 1776 publication of Adam **Smith**'s *The Wealth of Nations,* **free trade** wholly won the intellectual battle. The remnants of mercantilism were extensive, however, as were restrictions on domestic trade dating back to the Middle Ages. The free-trade campaign began in 1820 and concluded with the repeal of the Corn Laws in 1846 and of the Navigation Acts in 1849. The Anglo-French Commercial Treaty of 1860 cemented the principle of freedom to trade. From then until World War I, Great Britain practiced a largely free-trade policy.

The U.S. Congress adopted the first tariff in 1789 with its principal purpose being to raise revenue. Rates went from 5 to 15 percent, with an average of about 8 percent. In 1816, however, Congress adopted an explicitly protectionist tariff, with a 25 percent rate on most textiles and rates as high as 30 percent on various manufactured goods; however, the first wave of protectionism peaked in 1828. In the late nineteenth century, Republicans called for tariffs to protect American manufacturing. Benjamin Harrison's defeat of Democrat free trader Grover Cleveland led to passage of the McKinley tariff in 1890. Protectionist tariffs remained the bedrock of economic policy of the Republican Party for the next 20 years. The Underwood tariff of 1913, passed early in the administration of President Woodrow **Wilson,** liberalized trade somewhat; but as soon as the Republicans returned to power after World War I, they raised tariffs again.

During the **Tokugawa** period, from the seventeenth through the nineteenth centuries, the era of shogun rule, Japan was almost totally isolated from the outside world. Although they had some limited contact with the Dutch and Portuguese, the Japanese were forbidden to travel abroad or even build oceangoing ships. Thus, Japanese feudalism lasted hundreds of years after its collapse in Europe, and industrialization there was nascent long after the industrial revolution that swept Western Europe. Trade played an important role in Japanese economic development after the **Meiji Restoration.** Although foreigners initially dominated trade, the Japanese quickly learned how to compete; they imported foreign technology and techniques and rapidly incorporated them into Japanese industry. By the late 1800s, Japan almost practiced a policy of free trade because treaties with foreign powers generally prohibited any restraint on trade and because the government was not heavily involved in the economy.

Germany has often been cited as a model of protectionism. However, an examination of German history, as well as a deeper reading of List, does not confirm the efficacy of protectionism as a path to prosperity. Although List favored protection against imports from outside Germany, he was adamant about abolishing all trade barriers, including tolls, within Germany itself. Eventually, List's view prevailed with the establishment of the German customs union, the *Zollverein,* in 1833. By 1854, virtually every German state had joined the union. List favored protection primarily for political reasons—to further the cause of German unification. Insofar as he had an economic rationale for restricting imports, it was based on the now-discredited infant industry argument. But protection, in List's view, was only temporary.

Until 1879, Germany's tariffs were comparatively low. In that year, however, Germany adopted a protective tariff policy for the first time. Although protectionism was promoted by the usual special interests, such as the iron and steel industry, it was held in check by the large agricultural sector that sought open world markets and increased agricultural productivity. What tipped the political balance toward protection was the central government's need for revenue. World War I brought a complete breakdown in trade between Germany and its European enemies.

FURTHER READING: Barbour, Violet. *Capitalism in Amsterdam in the Seventeenth Century.* Baltimore: Johns Hopkins University Press, 1950; Henderson, W. O. *The Zollverein.* Chicago: Quadrangle, 1959; Hilton, Boyd. *Corn, Cash, Commerce: The Economics of the Tory Governments, 1815–1830.* New York: Oxford University Press, 1977; List, Friedrich. *The National System of Political Economy.* New York: A. M. Kelly, 1966; O'Rourke, Kevin H., and Jeffrey G. Williamson. *Globalization and History.* Cambridge, MA: MIT Press, 1999; Pierenkemper, Toni, and Richard Tilly. *The German Economy during the Nineteenth Century.* New York: Berghahn Books, 2004; Wallich, Henry C. *Mainsprings of the German Revival.* New Haven, CT: Yale University Press, 1955.

JITENDRA UTTAM

Protectorate

A protectorate was a poorly defined institution or form of governance, suggesting in generic terms a form of international guardianship by a Great Power over a weak state or a territory. The declaration of overseas protectorates by imperial powers in the late nineteenth century was a response to the fact that the acquisition of new colonial territories—itself in part a product of colonial competition among the Great Powers—proceeded at a pace faster than the establishment of colonial administration. A ruler who placed his territory under the protection of a Great Power retained his sovereignty over domestic affairs yet surrendered his authority over foreign affairs to the Great Power in return for its military protection. Depending on the importance of a protectorate, however, it was not unusual for the degree of administrative intrusion into its domestic affairs to increase to the extent that life for the population was hardly distinguishable from that in a full colony.

In colonial projects as in war, protectorates were often deemed appropriate in the case of territorial and tribal entities thought to be too politically immature or vulnerable to be covered by international law. The device could be applied to a smaller European entity, as in the case of British protection of the Ionian Islands in 1809 during the **Napoleonic Wars,** or extended to large overseas territory, such as France's declaration of a protectorate over Morocco in 1912. In each case the stronger power sought for strategic expedience to establish a military presence in the protected territory without assuming the full burden of colonial rule. During the Scramble for **Africa** this meant that, for example, that British Somaliland on the Horn of Africa became a British protectorate in 1884, while neighboring French Somaliland was given the same status in 1884–1885. With the new French protectorate poised at the narrows between the Red Sea and the Gulf of Aden, Britain made the island of Socotra, at the mouth of the Gulf of Aden, a protectorate in 1886 and added a protectorate in Hadramaut on the north shore of the Gulf in 1888. *See also* Imperialism; Indirect Rule.

FURTHER READING: Pakenham, Thomas. *The Scramble for Africa*. New York: Random House, 1991; Wesseling, H. L. *The European Colonial Empires, 1815–1919*. London: Pearson Education, 2004; Wilson, Henry S. *The Imperial Experience in Subsaharan Africa*. Minneapolis: University of Minnesota Press, 1977.

CARL CAVANAGH HODGE

Prussia

Officially Brandenburg-Prussia since the unification of the Duchy of Prussia with the Margraviate of Brandenburg under the Hohenzollern Dynasty in 1618, named the Kingdom of Prussia after 1701, a north German state transformed during the last half of the eighteenth century into a Great Power under the enlightened absolutism of Frederick II, better known as "the Great." A resource-poor and strategically vulnerable state was made into a force to be reckoned with through the introduction of a civil code, a professional bureaucracy, economic centralization, fiscal prudence, education reform, and the development of a highly professional standing army. Frederick II then tested Prussian arms in the Silesian Wars from 1740 to 1763 and managed to add Habsburg lands to Prussia's territory. Under King Frederick Wilhelm II, Prussia acquired additional territory through the partition of Poland.

The French Revolution and **Napoleonic Wars** were for Prussia as traumatic as for any of the other continental powers but were also critically formative. Preoccupied with its rivalry Austria and even yet more apprehensive over the long-term threat posed by the **Russian Empire,** Prussia failed to appreciate either the full political implications of revolutionary France or martial strength of its Napoleonic successor. A policy of prevarication and neutrality was not set aside until the Fourth Coalition, which Prussia joined in October 1806 only to see its armies and those of its new Austrian ally soundly thrashed at Saalfeld, **Jena,** and Auerstädt. The humiliation of defeat and Napoleonic occupation—in which, after all, Napoleon **Bonaparte** viewed Prussia as a way-station on the road to greater glory in Russia—prompted sweeping reforms under Frederick Wilhelm III. Prussian forces formed a major portion of the allied armies at **Leipzig** in 1813 and were decisive in Napoleon's final defeat at **Waterloo** in 1815. Prussia then realized significant territorial gains at the Congress of Vienna and then propelled itself into a new era of bureaucratic reform under **Stein** and Hardenberg; military reform under **Scharnhorst, Gneisenau,** von **Roon,** and Maunteuffel; land reform under von Schön and von Schroetter; and education reform under von Humboldt. Prussia adamantly and successfully resisted the European liberal movement of the 1840s and 1850s to become, after 1860, a modernizing absolutist state presiding over rapid and thorough industrialization. Under Otto von **Bismarck,** who became chief minister in 1862, Prussia also became the principal agent for the economic and political unification of the German states, through the extension of the **Zollverein** on the one hand and successful wars against Denmark in 1864, Austria in 1866, and France in 1871 on the other. The proclamation of the *Deutsches Reich* or **German Empire** at Versailles in January 1871, with Wilhelm I of Prussia as German Emperor, represented the capstone of the unification project and marked the dawn of a new era in German and European history. *See also* Austro-Prussian War; Clausewitz, Carl von;

Confederation of the Rhine; North German Confederation; Franco-Prussian War; Junker; *Realpolitik*.

FURTHER READING: Carsten, F. *The Origins of Prussia*. Oxford: Clarendon, 1954; Clark, Christopher. *Iron Kingdom: The Rise and Downfall of Prussia, 1600–1947*. Cambridge, MA: Belknap Press, 2006; Craig, Gordon A. *Germany, 1866–1945*. New York: Oxford University Press, 1978; Schroeder, Paul W. *The Transformation of European Politics, 1763–1848*. Oxford: Clarendon, 1994.

CARL CAVANAGH HODGE

Przheval'skii, Nikolai Mikhailovich (1839–1888)

A Russian zoologist and explorer, Nikolai Mikhailovich Przheval'skii was born in Smolensk and was educated both there and at the Academy of the General Staff in St. Petersburg. Przheval'skii served in Poland and taught geography at Irkutsk before his explorations. He was committed to exploration of Inner Asia and aided Russian attempts to gain important scientific knowledge about the region. He carried out four major geographic expeditions to the Ussuri River basin, Tibet, Mongolia, the Tian-shan Mountains, Lake Issyk-kul, and other areas of Inner Asia during the 1870s and 1880s. He discovered the horse named *Equus przewalskii* during his travels to the former Dzungan region and was the first westerner to locate wild Bactrian camels in Inner Asia. Przheval'skii likely saw himself as fulfilling the role of a David Livingstone or Henry Morton Stanley for the **Russian Empire** by exploring the "heart" of Inner Asia.

He received the financial and logistical support of the Russian Geographical Society for his journeys and regarded himself as an agent of scientific progress. Przheval'skii was celebrated by the Russian public as a great explorer; after his death from typhus in 1888, monuments were erected commemorating his exploits. One was located at Issyk-kul, the place of his death, and another was placed in St. Petersburg. In 1893, Alexander III decreed that the Kirghiz city of Karakol be renamed Przhevalsk. Przheval'skii kept detailed accounts of his journeys and later published his findings in *Mongolia, the Tangut Country* (1875) and *From Kulja, Across the Tian-Shan to Lob-Nor* (1879). His first book was translated into English, French, and German.

Przheval'skii's three-year journey to Tibet from late 1870 to 1873 was the event that made him a public figure. Przheval'skii dreamed of finding the Dalai Lama at Lhasa, but his hopes were not realized. His travel companion and successor as Inner-Asian explorer, Petr Kozlov, and another of his closest friends, Panteley Teleshov, were introduced to the Dalai Lama in 1905. Throughout his career, Przheval'skii emphasized the importance of Inner Asia to Russia's **Great Game** competition with Great Britain. He hoped to establish some degree of Russian imperial control over Tibet and Mongolia. Upon his return from his expeditions to Inner Asia, he brought back 16,000 specimens of approximately 1,700 species of plant life. *See also* Russian Empire.

FURTHER READING: Przheval'skii, Nikolai Mikhailovich. *From Kulga, Across the Tian-Shan to Lob-Nor*. Translated by E. Delmar Morgan. London: Sampson Low, Marston, Seale, & Rivington, 1879; Przheval'skii, Nikolai Mikhailovich. *Mongolia, the Tangut Country, and the Solitudes of Northern Tibet*. London: S. Low, Marston, Searle, & Rivington, 1876; Rayfield, Donald. *The Dream of Lhasa: The Life of Nikolai Przhevalsky (1839–88) Explorer of Central Asia*. Athens: Ohio University Press, 1976.

SCOTT C. BAILEY

Puerto Rico

Officially the Commonwealth of Puerto Rico, an eastern Caribbean island, named originally Boriquen by the indigenous Taíno Indians, and self-governing entity associated with the **United States.** Between 1509 and 1898, the island was under Spanish colonial rule. After 1815, Puerto Rico experienced opposition to Spanish rule and was granted **Home Rule** in November 1897.

After victory in the **Spanish-American War** of 1898, the United States acquired Puerto Rico in the Treaty of **Paris** on December 10, 1898. With a population of less than a million and little bilateral commerce, this most distant island of the Greater Antilles, more than a thousand miles east of Miami, was of particular strategic value to the United States, as it guarded the Mona Passage, a key shipping lane to Central America and the envisioned interoceanic canal. It thus complemented **Cuba** in Washington's notions of an "American Mediterranean," and served a function similar to that of Malta for the **British Empire.**

The American colonial government placed great emphasis on social engineering and educational reforms. As part of a campaign to "Americanize" the island's Hispanic institutions, Washington created a school system that mirrored that in the United States. English became the official language in all schools, as American teachers and missionaries flooded the island between 1905 and 1915. In addition, the United States executed a substantial program of infrastructure improvements, sanitation measures, public inoculations, and educational reforms.

Initially welcomed as liberators, many Puerto Ricans quickly rejected the new colonial rulers as they granted the locals inferior political rights to those experienced under the Spanish crown. The first interim military government lasted until April 1900, when the U.S. Congress passed the **Foraker Amendment,** which set the legal framework for the civil government of Puerto Rico until 1917. This first Organic Act of Puerto Rico made the dollar legal currency, set up colonial administration with a governor appointed by the president, made the U.S. Supreme Court arbiter of the Puerto Rican legal system, and denied the locals citizenship. At the same time, the act established a system of taxes and tariffs on Puerto Ricans despite their lack of representation. The island was considered an unincorporated territory belonging to, but not part of, the United States with no prospect of eventual statehood. Much of the debate over its colonial status was highly charged with racial and cultural discrimination towards the island's Hispanic population. The Jones Act of 1916 confirmed the territorial doctrine but granted Puerto Ricans U.S. citizenship. *See also* Monroe Doctrine; Panama Canal.

FURTHER READING: Burnett, Christina Duffy, and Burke Marshall, eds. *Foreign in a Domestic Sense. Puerto Rico, American Expansion, and the Constitution.* Durham, NC: Duke University Press, 2001; Caban, Pedro A. *Constructing a Colonial People: Puerto Rico and the United States, 1898–1932.* Boulder, CO: Westview, 2000.

FRANK SCHUMACHER

Pultusk, Battle of (1806)

After the French army's overwhelming success at Jena-Auerstadt, Napoleon **Bonaparte** sought to deliver a crushing blow to the Prussian and Russian armies. On December 26, Marshal Lannes' Fifth Corps soon faced Russian General Bennigsen's army near Pultusk, on the Narew River, 30 miles north of Warsaw. A division of Lannes' Fifth Corps, led by General Claparede, attempted to gain the town but was eventually repulsed, not the least because of the horrid winter weather. Another French division arrived and the French pushed forward. Benningsen's right withdrew to stronger positions and neither side was able to gain advantage. The Russians abandoned their positions under cover of darkness, but the French were unable to pursue. The battle was essentially a draw, although the French held the field. Napoleon put his army into winter quarters, but in less than two month's time, they would fight again at the Battle of **Eylau.** *See also* Napoleonic Wars.

FURTHER READING: Rothenburg, Guenther. *The Napoleonic Wars.* London: Cassell, 1999.

J. DAVID MARKHAM

Punjab

The historic homeland of the Sikhs in northwestern **India,** bordering on **Afghanistan** to its west. Its eastern portion was annexed to British India as a **protectorate** in 1846 as result of the First **Sikh War.** The western Punjab was added in 1849 after the second and more bitter Sikh War. Under Dalhousie the entire Punjab now came under direct administration, as British India extended as far west as the banks of the Indus River. An Anglo-Indian force, the Punjab Irregular Force, was established and quickly acquired a reputation as an effective unit. The Punjab was conspicuously loyal during the Indian Mutiny of 1857 and, as a region, became such an important source of military recruits for the Rāj that, by 1914, it accounted for 60 percent of the Indian Army. *See also* Khalsa.

FURTHER READING: James, Lawrence. *Rāj: The Making and Unmaking of British India.* New York: St. Martin's, 1997.

CARL CAVANAGH HODGE

Qasim-uli

See Kasimov, Kenesary

Qing Dynasty (1644–1912)

Also known as the Ch'ing or Manchu dynasty, the Qing Dynasty comprised a succession of emperors from **Manchuria** who ruled **China** from 1644 until 1912. The foreign Qing gained acceptance by adopting Chinese language, culture, and institutions and by ensuring a period of peace and prosperity lasting until the late eighteenth century. The nineteenth-century Qing rulers failed to deal with population pressure, institutional decline, corruption, and the economic and social consequences of opium imports from British **India.** They were slow to recognize the threat posed by the Western powers and thwarted attempts at administrative, military, and economic reform. While maintaining themselves in power despite the **Taiping** and **Boxer Insurrections** they were increasingly discredited by repeated military defeat and the concessions to foreign powers. Qing rulers flirted with radical reformism (Kuang-hsü in 1898), with anti-Western resistance in alliance with the Boxers (Tz'u-hsi in 1900),and with cautious modernization, but gradually lost support and had to abdicate after the 1911 revolution. *See also* Open Door; Opium Wars.

FURTHER READING: Gernet, Jacques. *A History of Chinese Civilization.* New York: Cambridge University Press, 1982; Hsieh, P. C. *The Government of China, 1644–1911.* Translated by J. R. Foster. Baltimore: The Johns Hopkins University Press, 1925; Hsü, Immanuel C. *The Rise of Modern China.* New York: Oxford University Press, 2000.

NIELS P. PETERSSON

Quadruple Alliance (1815)

An agreement concluded between Britain, Austria, Russia, and **Prussia** on November 20, 1815, the same day as the second Treaty of **Paris,** by which the signatories pledged not only to uphold the peace with royalist France, but to prevent the return of Napoleon **Bonaparte.** The four powers also pledged to hold regular congresses, headed by sovereigns or chief ministers, whose purpose was to preserve continental stability and to discuss matters of common interest. The alliance inaugurated the **Congress System** by which peace in Europe was preserved for the subsequent 40 years. As a result of the Congress of **Aix-la-Chapelle** in 1818, France was invited back into the fold of Great Powers as an equal guardian of European stability, thereby rendering the Quadruple Alliance in effect a Quintuple Alliance. *See also* Balance of Power; Vienna, Congress of.

FURTHER READING: Kissinger, Henry. *A World Restored: Metternich, Castlereagh, and the Problem of Peace 1812–1822.* London: Weidenfeld & Nicolson, 1957; Lowe, John. *The Concert of Europe: International Relations, 1814–70.* London: Hodder & Stoughton, 1991.

GREGORY FREMONT-BARNES

Quatre Bras, Battle of (1815)

The first engagement of Napoeon **Bonaparte's Waterloo** Campaign, fought on June 16, 1815, between the left wing of Napoleon's army under Marshal Michel **Ney** with 24,000 men, and an Anglo-Allied force of fluctuating strength under the Duke of **Wellington.** When Napoleon crossed the Belgian border the previous day, he ordered Ney to seize the crossroads and village of Quatre Bras, while Napoleon himself proceeded with the bulk of his army to engage the Prussians under Marshal Gebhard von **Blücher** at nearby **Ligny.** Ney took most of the village, but with the gradual arrival of British reinforcements in the early afternoon, Wellington was able to counterattack with 32,000 men and force back Ney. Meanwhile, the Comte d'Erlon's corps of 20,000 French troops, through mistaken orders, had been marching and countermarching during the afternoon, failing to reinforce either Ney or Napoleon. The French lost more than 4,000 at Quatre Bras to the Allies' 5,400.

FURTHER READING: Hofschröer, Peter. *Waterloo 1815: Quatre Bras and Ligny.* London: Leo Cooper, 2005; Robinson, Mike. *The Battle of Quatre Bras.* Staplehurst, Kent, UK: Spellmount Publishing, 2005.

GREGORY FREMONT-BARNES

Québec

Known as Lower Canada before 1867, Québec was a British colony that became a province of the Dominion of **Canada** under the **British North America Act.** Conquered by the British in the Seven Years' War of 1757–1763, and then given an extensive western hinterland by the Quebec Act of 1774, it was severed from Upper Canada—the future Ontario—by William **Pitt** the Younger's Constitutional Act of 1791, which was an attempt to extend the British constitution to Quebec. It created an assembly elected under a property franchise and an appointive legislative council. The British-appointed governor ruled through an executive council of his choosing.

This led rapidly to tensions and, as in other British North American colonies, control over colonial revenues was disputed between the British-appointed governor and the popularly elected assembly. Quebec's politics were further complicated by divisions between the French-speaking majority and the English-speaking minority. The *parti patriote* in Quebec claimed that revenues should fall entirely under popular control, which would have placed effective control of the government in the hands of the French majority. More radical members of the *patriotes* moved toward republicanism and led a brief rebellion in 1837, coincident with the rebellion of William Lyon Mackenzie in Upper Canada. Both were easily put down by British troops. The rebellions of 1837 led to the report of Lord **Durham,** and thence to the unification of the Canadas into one colony with the object of assimilating the French population into the larger English Canadian majority. The united province of Canada was granted **responsible government** in 1848, to the anger of much of Quebec's British population, who rioted against the large role given to French Canadians in the newly autonomous government. The united Canadas were divided into the separate provinces of Ontario and Quebec within the new Dominion of **Canada** in 1867, thus re-creating a political unit with a French-speaking majority. *See also* British Empire.

FURTHER READING: Ouellet, Fernand. *Lower Canada, 1791–1840.* Toronto: McClelland and Stewart, 1980; Wade, Mason. *The French Canadians, 1760–1945.* London: Macmillan, 1955.

MARK F. PROUDMAN

Quintuple Alliance (1818)

See Quadruple Alliance

R

RAC

See Russian-American Company

Race

A category in physical anthropology to define groups of people of common origin characterized by a series of common morphological traits. In the political anthropology and social thought of the Age of **Imperialism,** a means of categorization applied unscientifically to mark social, cultural, political, economic, psychological, and other sorts of inequality among groups of people. In both cases the concept is deeply connected with notions of culture, population, ethnicity, and language. Morphological differences among peoples was noted in ancient natural philosophy, major representatives of which believed that external peculiarities of human beings reflected character, intelligence, cultural, and mental abilities of their bearers. This assumption was broadly illustrated in the contacts of the Ancient Greeks and Romans with the barbarian world.

At the Era of Great Discoveries, the tradition had a woeful influence on the treatment of the aboriginal inhabitants of newly opened territories of northern and southern America, southern Africa and the eastern part of Asia. Equally, the maintenance of the **slave trade** gave birth to a series of attempts to allege and explain the superiority of Europeans over their colonial subjects, just as in the **United States** racist and racialist thinking became an integral part of the gathering political struggle between slave owners and abolitionists. It should be noted, nevertheless, that racial discrimination was never unique to the representatives of European civilization. Racially determined social differentiation was common in precolonial Africa, Asia, and **India.** In Africa it helped to sustain slave-based empires.

In nineteenth-century Europe, the ideas of Carl Linnaeus, Charles Darwin, and Thomas Huxley brought a new wave of attention to the race concept in scientific and social thought. Two main trends developed: racial classification and explanation of specific differences. During the second half of the century, the latter trend itself split into two tendencies, one was connected with examination of different factors influenced on the formation of peculiar morphological traits; the other concentrated on the propagation of a revised version of racial theories. All of the latter were based on a common concern with tracing the cultural differences and social and political inequality among peoples to the determining factor of race. Particularly noteworthy is Joseph-Arthur Gobineau, who formulated ideas about deterministic role of racial differences in the history of humankind. Based on his thesis about innate inequality of mental characteristics and the capacity to create, comprehend and maintain cultural heritage, Gobineau believed in the primacy of a so-called Aryan race over other races and connected with Aryans all ancient civilizations, resorting to numerous falsifications in the effort. Gobineau's ideas were later integrated into the racial mythology of Nazi Germany. Another direction was connected specifically with the treatment of the black population of sub-Saharan Africa. This thesis, for the first time strictly formulated by J. Gent at the mid-1860s, created grounds for further studies in this field of representatives of **Social Darwinism**, who used racism as a crucial argument in favor of the primeval character of social inequality and social struggle. Mixed with the material greed accompanying European, American, and Japanese expansion, it fuelled the zeal with which imperial slogans such as **Manifest Destiny, White Man's Burden,** and *mission civilisatrice* were propagated and in its most virulent form—as in King Leopold's Congo—had genocidal implications. *See also* Afghan Wars; Herero Revolt; Pan-Slavism; Sino-Japanese War; Zulu War.

FURTHER READING: Banton, Michael. *Racial Theories.* Cambridge: Cambridge University Press, 1987; Benedict, Ruth. *Race and Racism.* London: Routledge & Kegan Paul, 1983; Bowler, Peter J. *Biology and Social Thought. 1800–1914.* Berkeley: Office for History of Science and Technology, University of California, 1993; Shanklin, Eugenia. *Anthropology and Race.* Belmont: Wadsworth, 1994.

OLENA V. SMYNTYNA

Radetzky, Josef (1766–1858)

An Austrian military leader, Josef Count Radetzky of Radetz was born November 1766 in Trebnice, Bohemia. His military career started in 1784, when he joined the Austrian army. As an officer he gained experience in the wars against the **Ottoman Empire** and Revolutionary France. In the **Napoleonic Wars,** he held commanding positions in several campaigns. At the Battle of **Leipzig** in 1813, he was chief of staff of the allied commander Prince Karl Philip Schwarzenberg. Unsuccessful in his efforts to reform the Austrian army, he nevertheless became one of the most influential military leaders in Austrian history. As commander-in-chief of the Austrian army in Northern Italy since 1831, Radetzky improved the fighting capabilities of his troops. In the revolution of 1848–1849, Radetzky defeated the Italian forces challenging Habsburg control over northern Italy decisively at Custoza 1848 and Novara 1849. From 1850 to 1857, he served as governor of Lombardy-Venetia. He died January 1858 in Milan. *See also* Habsburg Empire.

FURTHER READING: Regele, Oskar. *Feldmarschall Radetzky.* Vienna: Herold Verlag, 1957.

GUENTHER KRONENBITTER

Radicalism

A nineteenth-century term referring to an ideology of radical individualism. In English, the term *radical* was often a contraction of *philosophic radical*, the name given to the followers of Jeremy **Bentham,** and most radicals in the first half of the century looked to his doctrines for inspiration. As the term's Latin etymology implies, radicals went, or believed they went, to the roots of a question. The Benthamite practice of reasoning from the root premise that social policy should aim at the maximization of social happiness, or utility, provided a powerful weapon against traditional mores and usages, and especially against prescriptive royal, aristocratic, and ecclesiastical privileges. While not necessarily egalitarians or democrats, radicals were normally individualists who supported meritocracy.

Although the word *radical* was often used in the twentieth century as a synonym for *extreme,* nineteenth-century radicals in the latter half of the century found themselves outflanked on the left by various kinds of socialists, and in some countries anarchists. Radicals were for most of the century on the extreme left of the British parliamentary political spectrum. In France, the radicals looked back to the revolution and were defined by their antimonarchism, a position that ceased to be particularly radical in the later sense of the term following the advent of the Third Republic in the 1870s. Radicals were generally anti-aristocratic and—especially but not solely in Catholic countries—anticlerical. Radicals in Britain were antimilitary, the services being associated with the aristocracy, but in theory, if not always in practice, they were less opposed to the navy, which was seen as a more meritocratic and also a more defensive institution.

Whereas in Britain many radicals were almost if not absolutely pacifist, French radicalism looked back to the *levée en masse* of 1792 and indulged few such tendencies. Radicals supported private property, and British radicals were almost by definition free traders, although the petit-bourgeois supporters of French radicalism were not. Radicals were often anti-authoritarian and antigovernment—government being seen as an aristocratic tool—and in favor of individual liberties. Their veneration of individual autonomy led some radicals to an opposition to socialism as earnest as their earlier hatred of aristocracy, while others from a radical tradition—including figures as divergent as H. M. Hyndman, founder of the first specifically British Marxist party, the Social Democratic Federation, and Joseph **Chamberlain**—were led by their radical egalitarianism to the view that meaningful personal equality required that free market individualism would have to be supplemented or supplanted by a more positive kind of state action. Radicals were an important, and arguably the leading, component of the coalition that made up the Victorian **Liberal Party.** By 1914, much of the original radical program had been achieved, and arguments from social utility and human happiness often went in socialist rather than radically individualist directions; by this time the term was losing much of its original meaning, yet retained an antimilitarist valence. In imperial affairs, the philosophic radicals began by following Bentham in their opposition to commercial colonies and their support for self-government in settlement colonies, Lord "Radical Jack" **Durham** in **Canada** being a prime example of the latter. Later in the century, radical individualism, support for Free Trade, and an inherited distaste for the aristocratic military led most self-described radicals to follow the likes of John Morley in opposing imperialism, and they formed the backbone of the anti-imperialist wing of the Liberal Party. *See also* Boer Wars; Free Trade; Clemençeau, Georges; Liberalism.

FURTHER READING: Burgess, Glenn, and Matthew Festenstein, eds. *English Radicalism, 1550–1850.* New York: Cambridge University Press, 2007; Fraser, Peter. *Joseph Chamberlain: Radicalism and Empire, 1868–1914.* South Brunswick: A. S. Barnes, 1967; Maccoby, S. *English Radicalism.* 6 vols. London: George Allen and Unwin, 1961.

MARK F. PROUDMAN

Raffles, Sir Thomas Stamford (1781–1826)

As a scholar, colonial administrator, and founder of **Singapore,** Sir Thomas Stamford Raffles played an important role in creating the **British Empire** in the **Far East.** While serving with the East India Company in Penang, Raffles came to the attention of Lord Minto, governor-general of **India,** owing to his expertise in local history, language and culture, and was asked to participate in an expedition to take **Java** from the Dutch in 1811. Raffles later served as lieutenant governor of Java from 1811–1816, where he concentrated on reforming local administration, taxes, and land tenure.

In 1817, he was knighted and returned to Asia as lieutenant governor of Bencoolen, a small port in western Sumatra. The following year he convinced his superiors to authorize a new British settlement at the southeastern end of the Malacca Straits to ensure British access to vital trade routes. Raffles landed in Singapore in 1819, signed treaties with local rulers placing them under British protection, and over the next several years was instrumental in turning it into a major British port. Two years before his death, Raffles retired from colonial service and returned to England where he helped found the London Zoo and continued his career as an Asian scholar.

FURTHER READING: Alatas, Syed Hussein. *Thomas Stamford Raffles, 1781–1826: Schemer or Reformer?* Singapore: Angus and Robinson, 1971; Collis, Maurice. *Raffles.* London: Century, 1988; Stewart, R.M.J. "Raffles of Singapore: The Man and the Legacy." *Asian Affairs* 13 (1982): 16–27.

KENNETH J. OROSZ

Railways

Along with steamships, the **telegraph,** advances in military hardware, and improvements in tropical medicine, railways were critical vehicles for the advancement of European empires, both formal and informal. From their initial development in Great Britain and the **United States** in the early part of the nineteenth century, railways became the key element of modern industrial infrastructure. They served to tie new areas of the world into the developing global marketplace of the nineteenth century, represented the power of the European imperial state, and often times became the focus of or intensified rivalries of the European powers themselves for influence or control of the non-European world.

As early as 1830, a British parliamentary committee had authorized an expedition under the command of Colonel Francis Chesney to explore the possibility of establishing a combined railway-steamer route from Ottoman Syria through the Euphrates Valley for the purposes of improving communication with India. As events proved, this expedition was ahead of its time; however, the notion of railway development through the ancient routes of the Fertile Crescent remained alive. In 1888, Sultan Abdulhamid II of the **Ottoman Empire** began granting concessions to a German-backed consortium for a rail line that would link Constantinople to the Persian Gulf. Capital shortfalls and international tensions, particularly with the British and French who both viewed German railway construction in the Ottoman Empire with suspicion, long delayed this project, which became known as the **Berlin-Baghdad** line. On the eve of World War I, significant stretches of the line in what are modern-day Syria and Iraq were not completed, and it was only after the war, when the Ottoman Empire had ceased to exist and Germany's imperial pretensions were at a nadir, that the line was completed.

In colonies of white settlement, support for railways was often highly desired because it helped get the crops of colonial subjects to market quicker. British financial support was often critical in the development of these lines. In the case of **Canada,** financial support for the **Canadian Pacific** Railway was used as a lever to encourage Canadian federation as a means of binding what were otherwise ethnically diverse provinces together. The Canadian Pacific line helped cement the union between **Quebec** and Ontario on the one hand and the prairie provinces and **British Columbia** on the other. This example is one of the most clear-cut cases of economics rationale and strategic imperative—the British government encouraged the federation of Canada in no small part so that the territories would not be swallowed up by the United States—combining together in the construction of an imperial rail line.

The expansion of Russian military railways into Central Asia in the 1880s was essential to the conquest of the khanates of Bukhara, Khiva, Samarkand, and Merv. British concern over Russian expansion into Central Asia, particularly regarding the security of India, helped spur the **Great Game,** a struggle for influence that would eventually stretch from Istanbul to Tibet. The British responded in part to this threat from Russian railway imperialism by extending their own strategic rail system up into the Northwest frontier, including a line to Quetta in modern Pakistan. The ambitious project for a **Trans-Siberian** Railway, begun under the direction of the Russian Minister of Finance Sergei Witte in 1891, also served to tie Russia's semi-colonial holdings in Siberia and the Far East closer to Russia.

Railway development came late to the **Qing** empire, where conservative bureaucrats and members of the Manchu dynasty long resisted the intrusiveness of the railroad and feared—perhaps rightfully so—the degree of influence it would give European powers in their empire. After **China**'s defeat by the Japanese in the **Sino-Japanese War,** the Russians took advantage of Chinese weakness to secure a concession for the extension of their own Trans-Siberian across Chinese **Manchuria.** This line, known as the **Chinese Eastern** Railway, considerably shortened Russian access to Vladivostok, their warm-water port on the Pacific. After the "Scramble for Concessions" in China in 1898, a spur line was added to **Port Arthur.** The Chinese Eastern Railway was an important focus of the imperial rivalries of Russia and Japan in East Asia. Only after the Qing court belatedly and disastrously threw its lot in with the **Boxer Insurrection** in 1900 did it turn its attention to granting lucrative railway concessions to foreign consortiums. This was seen as a method of securing funds to help pay off the large indemnity that China was forced to pay after the

Boxer Insurrection. European railway development in China and belated Qing attempts to assert centralized control over them, however, were responsible for a huge groundswell of Chinese indignation at these foreign intrusions. Resistance, often focused on the provincial level, lead to widespread "railway recovery" movements. These played an important role in the rebellions of 1911 that toppled the Qing government.

In **Africa,** too, European **imperialism** was often abetted by railway development. In many cases the gunboat and quinine were more fundamental to successful European penetration of the continental interior, but railways, too, played their role. Rival Anglo-French visions for empire in Africa—often more the product of imperial adventurers on the spot than home governments themselves—resulted in the race to **Fashoda** in 1898. The French were looking to build an empire in North Africa that would be bound by a trans-continental railway stretching from west to east. The British moved to Fashoda to block French access to the headwaters of the Nile, but subimperialists like Cecil Rhodes dreamed of a British-controlled line stretching from the Cape to Cairo. Although Rhodes's vision remain unrealized, more modest lines such as the Kenya-Uganda Railroad opened East Africa to commerce and began the process of white settlement in the temperate highlands of Kenya.

Railway development was also critical to the opening up of the Americas. British capital was heavily involved in financing railway development in the United States and Latin America. The invention of refrigerator cars allowed the Argentinian Pampas to become a key supplier of beef for the British world, and helped tie that country into the global economy. Although railway imperialism, the extension of European influence, and sometimes control through the construction of railway lines certainly did exist, it is a complicated and amorphous enough subject that it deserves to be studied specifically case by case. Often railways could serve as means of resistance for indigenous people as they did for the assertion of European control. Considerable work remains to be done studying the complex dynamic of dominance and resistance and the role played by elements of technology, especially railways, in this process. *See also* American Civil War; Franco-Prussian War.

FURTHER READING: Adas, Michael. *Machines as the Measures of Men: Science, Technology, and Ideologies of Western Dominance.* Ithaca, NY: Cornell University Press, 1989; Davis, Clarence B., and Kenneth E. Wilburn, Jr., eds. *Railway Imperialism.* Westport, CT: Greenwood Press, 1991; Huenemann, Ralph. *The Dragon and the Iron Horse: The Economics of Railroads in China, 1876–1937.* Cambridge, MA: Harvard University Press, 1984; Karkar, Yaqub. *Railway Development in the Ottoman Empire.* New York: Vantage Press, 1972; Kerr, Ian J. *Building the Railways of the Raj, 1850–1900.* Delhi: Oxford University Press, 1995; Marks, Steven G. *Road to Power: The Trans-Siberian Railroad and the Colonization of Asian Russia 1850–1917.* Ithaca, NY: Cornell University Press, 1991; McMurray, Jonathan S. *Distant Ties: Germany, the Ottoman Empire, and the Construction of the Baghdad Railway.* Westport, CT: Praeger, 2001; Showalter, Denis. *Railroads and Rifles: Soldiers, Technology, and the Unification of Germany.* Hamden, CT: Archon Books, 1975.

ROBERT DAVIS

Raison d'État

For "reasons of state," a doctrine intimately related to *Realpolitik* and concerned fundamentally with the centrality, security, and vitality of the state. It is associated above all with Armand Jean du Plessis, Cardinal de Richelieu (1585–1642), first minister of France from 1624 to 1642, whose statecraft cast aside the medieval tradition of universal moral values as the animating principle of French policy and asserted instead that the well-being of the state overrides ordinary considerations of morality, personal and political loyalty, and restraint. The doctrine held further that the protection of the vital interests of the state in the conduct of foreign policy—an especially perilous realm—must necessarily be supreme over the interests of civil society and that the normal restrictions of legality, too, must give way to necessity whenever the state's interests are deemed to be imperiled.

The European nineteenth century, baptized in war by a French state incomparably more powerful than that of Richelieu, then shaken by liberal and nationalist revolutions, and finally subject to intensified and militarized Great Power competition within Europe and around the world, became a playground for *raison d'état*. Where "national" or "imperial" interests were thought to be at stake, the most baleful excesses were routinely excused. In comparatively liberal political systems such as Britain and France, the ruthless conduct of imperial policy was intermittently subject to criticism and censure, especially when, as in the case of the Second Boer War, its excesses became widely known. In **Prussia** and the **German Empire** forged by Otto von **Bismarck,** however, *raison d'état* was deeply embedded in the governmental culture and increasingly rested on the unexamined assumption that state power supplied its own legitimacy. *See also* Boer Wars.

FURTHER READING: Auchincloss, Louis. *Richelieu.* New York: Viking, 1972; Church, William Farr. *Richelieu and the Reason of State.* Princeton, NJ: Princeton University Press, 1972.

CARL CAVANAGH HODGE

Rāj

The Hindi word for "rule," and a commonly used reference to the British colonial regime on **India.** The East India Company was founded on December 30, 1600, and company representatives arrived at Surat in 1608, Madras in 1639, Bombay in 1668, and Calcutta in 1690. After 1763, it became the paramount power in India. The Regulating Act of 1774 extended the control of the British government over the East India Company's possessions in India, which the India Act of 1784 extended when it created a Board of Control. Lord Cornwallis, through his 1793 Code of Forty-Eight Regulations and his Permanent *Zamindari* Settlement, introduced the concept of alienable private property into Bengal and created a new class of landlords who embraced Western education and became partners of the British. In Madras a settlement directly with the cultivators, the *Ryotwari* Settlement, was introduced. English common law was introduced and the Rāj was backed up with overwhelming military force. The company founded an "East India College" at Haileybury in 1809 to train administrators to administer this system. From Madras and Bengal the British control extended their presence through the Mysore Wars (1767–1799), the **Maratha** Wars (1775–1819), the **Sikh Wars** (1845–1849), and, from 1826, the **Anglo-Burmese Wars.**

The Charter Acts of 1793, 1813, 1833, and 1853 extended but modified company rule and it discontinued all commercial operations in 1833. It ruled India on behalf of the British government through the governor-general. After company rule was wound up after the **Indian Mutiny** of 1857, the Government of India Act of 1858 created a secretary of state for India who assumed direct responsibility through a viceroy who was also the governor-general. The viceroy was assisted by an executive council of which the commander-in-chief was a member. A "collector" headed each of the 235 districts of India, and departments such as accounts, archaeological survey, customs, education, forests, geological survey, jails, meteorological survey, mint, opium, pilot service, post office and telegraph, police, public works, registration, salt, and survey extended the Rāj to every almost every area of Indian life. The Crown of British rule, Queen Victoria, was in 1877 proclaimed Empress of India.

In 1861, the government passed the first of a number of Indian Councils Acts. Madras and Bombay received legislative assemblies and new councils were created for Bengal in 1862, the North-West Frontier Province in 1886, and Burma and the Punjab in 1897. The Government of India Act of 1909 enlarged the Indian Legislative Council and the provincial assemblies and a nonofficial majority and separate electorates were established. This was the basis of the Government of India Acts of 1919 and 1935. By 1914, the British had created a veritable Rāj that had incorporated India into the global capitalist system, brought modern educational institutions, the British system of representative government, British legal principles, and the English language. *See also* East India Companies.

FURTHER READING: James, Lawrence. *Rāj: The Making and Unmaking of British India.* London: Little, Brown, 1997; Judd, Denis. *The Lion and the Tiger: The Rise and Fall of the British Rāj, 1600–1947.* New York: Oxford University Press, 2004.

ROGER D. LONG

Ranke, Leopold von (1795–1886)

One of the most significant figures in the development of the historical profession during the nineteenth century. Born in Wiehe (Saxony) into an old Lutheran family, Ranke studied in Leipzig and initially taught at a grammar school in Frankfurt an der Oder. It was here that he wrote his *History of the Latin and Teutonic Nations, 1494–1514,* published in 1824. This piece is chiefly significant for Ranke's expressed intention henceforth to reveal history *Wie es eigentlich gewesen,* "as it actually was." Appointed to a chair at the University of Berlin in 1825, where he remained until 1871, Ranke aimed to turn history into an exact science, via the methodical evaluation and use of primary sources, and via the strict avoidance of value judgments. And yet, although history, for Ranke, had replaced philosophy as the "science" that offered insights into the human condition, he retained a belief in a divine plan for humanity. For him, existing political states, insofar as they were results of historical growth, were "moral energies" or "thoughts of God." For Ranke, aiming to reveal history as it actually was primarily meant revealing the evolution of the existing order of things as God had willed it.

Thus Ranke's influential methodology did not imply objectivity in the contemporary sense. While not all professional historians, particularly later in the century, agreed with Ranke's belief that what had developed historically was sanctioned by God's will, many certainly shared his focus on the state as a quasi-mythical category. As Otto von **Bismarck** used **Prussia** to transform Germany into a nation-state, historians emerged among the most vocal advocates of the project. This is perhaps unsurprising considering the close links between the German state and the historical profession. Ranke himself was appointed royal historian by Friedrich Wilhelm IV in 1841, and ennobled by **Wilhelm I** in 1865. The quantity of his work is as impressive as the quality, and the German edition of his complete works numbered 54 volumes. Such was his influence that, toward the end of his life, the American Historical Association, formed in 1884, chose Ranke as its first honorary member and pronounced him "the father of historical science."

FURTHER READING: Donovan, S. M., and K. Passmore, eds. *Writing National Histories. Western Europe since 1800.* London: Routledge, 1999; Iggers, G. *Historiography in the Twentieth Century.* London: University Press of New England, 1997; Krieger, Leonard. *Ranke: The Meaning of History.* Chicago: University of Chicago Press, 1977.

PAUL LAWRENCE

Realpolitik

The German word for political realism, generally referring to the advancement of the national interest unrestrained by ethical or ideological concerns, more specifically a foreign policy based on pragmatic concrete goals rather than theory or ideals, the latter being *Idealpolitik*. Otto von **Bismarck** is often credited with having coined the term, following Count **Metternich**'s tradition in **balance-of-power** diplomacy, but it was first used by the historian August Ludwig von Rochau who, in 1853, published *The Principles of Realpolitik, Applied to the Political Conditions of Germany.*

The ancient Greek historian Thucydides, who wrote the *History of the Peloponnesian War,* is often cited as an intellectual forbearer of *Realpolitik*. One of the most articulate proponents of the doctrine was Niccolò Machiavelli (1469–1527), best known for *The Prince,* and Rochau's work was in substance a neo-Machiavellian doctrine of the natural law of power. The tradition of *Realpolitik* was further refined and transmitted by Richelieu's *raison d'état.* Bismarck's foreign policy adhered to *Realpolitik* in its clear-headed consciousness of **Prussia**'s, then Germany's, "conditions" with as much attention given to its limitations and inherent vulnerabilities as to its considerable capabilities. Under **Wilhelm II,** *Realpolitik* was abandoned in favor of a *Weltpolitik* disdainful of Bismarck's caution. It paved the way for an intense European arms race, increasing tensions between alliances, and World War I. *See also* Bülow, Bernhard von; German Empire.

FURTHER READING: Jensen, Kenneth M., and Elizabeth P. Faulkner. *Morality and Foreign Policy: Realpolitik Revisited.* Washington, DC: United States Institute of Peace, 1992; Schild, Georg. *Between Ideology and Realpolitik: Woodrow Wilson and the Russian Revolution, 1917–1921.* Westport, CT: Greenwood Press, 1995; Wayman, Frank W. *Reconstructing Realpolitik.* Ann Arbor: University of Michigan Press, 1994.

JITENDRA UTTAM

Régiment Étranger

See French Foreign Legion

Reich

A term casually used to refer to an empire of the German peoples. It is most accurately applied to the Second Reich, officially the *Deutsches Reich* but also called the *Deutsches Kaiserreich,* proclaimed on the German victory in the **Franco-Prussian War** in 1871 and enduring until 1918. Its predecessor, the *Heiliges Römisches Reich der deutschen Nation* or Holy Roman Empire, was referred to by German nationalists as the First Reich, and the term *Drittes Reich* or Third Reich was adopted by Nazi propagandists to evoke a sense of imperial continuity. In fact, Germany's official name, *Deutsches Reich,* remained unchanged since 1871 through the Weimar Republic and into the Nazi Era. Between 1933 and the Nazi defeat, however, it was referred to as the *Großdeutsches Reich* or Greater **German Empire.**

FURTHER READING: Mann, Golo. *The History of Germany since 1789.* Translated by Marion Jackson. London: Chatto & Windus, 1968.

CARL CAVANAGH HODGE

Reichsbank

A federal reserve bank for the **German Empire,** established by the bank law of March 14, 1875. The legal successor of the Prussian central bank, the *Reichsbank* was officially under the aegis of a board of directors nominated by the German emperor. As the members of the board were appointed for life, the bank's policy was relatively independent from political intervention.

The bank's tasks were to regulate monetary circulation in the **Reich,** as well as to circulate paper money. Contrary to the provisions of the Bank of England and those of the Banque de France, the *Reichbank's* statutes laid down that only one-third of the circulating money had to be covered by foreign currency and gold. It is important to note that the *Reichsbank* never was an instrument to manage the economy through conscious monetary policy. During the years of depression, the bank did nothing to stabilize the economy; quite the contrary, its procyclical policy aggravated the existing instability. As the *Reichsbank* was a privately owned corporation, its main activity was making money. The influence of financiers and businessmen ensured that state intervention continued to be kept at a minimum. Of all national institutions, the shift in power from the old agrarian elite to the new forces of trade and industry became most apparent in the *Reichsbank.*

FURTHER READING: Henning, Friedrich-Wilhelm. *Handbuch der Wirtschafts- und Sozialgeschichte Deutschlands.* Paderborn: Schöningh, 1991; Lütge, Friedrich. *Deutsche Sozial- und Wirtschaftsgeschichte.* Berlin: Springer, 1960; Seeger, Manfred. *Die Politik der Reichsbank von 1976–1914 im Lichte der Spielregeln der Goldwährung.* Berlin: Duncker & Humblot, 1968; Stern, Fritz. *Gold and Iron: Bismarck, Bleichröder and the Building of the German Empire.* New York: Random House, 1977.

ULRICH SCHNAKENBERG

Reichstag

Established by the constitution of April 16, 1871, the **Reichstag** was the popularly elected lower house of the legislature of the **German Empire.** Although the chancellor and the state secretaries were not responsible to the national assembly and the institution was thus seriously flawed from its inception, its deputies wielded nevertheless considerable power when it came to the elaboration of the budget.

Modeled with a few minor adaptations on the constitution of the German Confederation from July 1, 1867, and on the former *Zollparlament,* the parliament of the members of the **Zollverein,** the Reichstag disposed of the essential power of the purse. As the time where government could reign by decree was definitely over, the executive's dependence on the legislature and the resulting bargaining power of the Reichstag should not be underestimated. Moreover, the monarch had the right to convoke and prorogue Parliament, but no right to veto its decisions.

On the other hand, both contemporary commentators and historians have stressed the Reichstag's weakness compared to the mighty position of the British House of Commons and the French *Assemblé Nationale.* The assembly's functions were indeed subject to substantial restraints. Its budgetary powers were constricted when it came to military spending, the lion's share of the Reich's expenditure. Searching for a compromise between the demands of the representatives of the people and the postulations of the army, it was finally agreed that parliament would decide only every seven years on laws concerning the costs of the military. Although the Reichstag was in a position to veto any bill, it needed to secure the approval of the federal *Bundesrat* to actually make a law. Also, its controlling powers were gravely hampered by the actuality that the Reichstag did not dispose of a vote of confidence. The most formidable threat to the chamber's independence, however, was a dissolution mechanism laid down in the constitution stipulating that a resolution of the *Bundesrat* sanctioned by the Emperor sufficed to dissolve the Reichstag.

In stark contrast to most other European states, the constitution of 1871 introduced universal manhood suffrage including a secret ballot. Elections were held according to the electoral law of 1871, which provided for a majority system in single member constituencies. In spite of accelerating migration to the cities, however, the constituencies were never adapted to population shifts. As a consequence, in 1912 the smallest constituency consisted of 50,000 inhabitants, and the biggest constituency counted more than a million heads. This amounted to a gross discrimination of the left-leaning conurbations to the advantage of the more conservative rural areas. The antiparliamentarian roadblocks of the 1871 constitution ensured that no member of the Reichstag ever became part of the government. Although the chancellor depended on the support of the chamber's majority to pass legislation, a stable and reliable coalition of parties that supported the government seldom existed. Otto von **Bismarck** was disdainful of parliamentarianism, and bitter confrontations between government and Reichstag factions occurred frequently, especially with the Social Democrats and the Catholic Center Party.

With the extension of the modern state and a general centralizing tendency, the influence of the Reichstag nevertheless grew. Increasingly, the government began to form previews on important legislative proposals with the major party leaders before introducing the bill in the *Bundesrat.* Although the Reichstag visibly gained in importance, the kaiser and successive chancellors continued to prevent its members from deciding on pivotal matters, most notably in military affairs and foreign policy.

FURTHER READING: Brandt, Hartwig. *Der lange Weg in die demokratische Moderne.* Darmstadt: Wissenschaftliche Buchgesellschaft, 1998; Cullen, Michael S. *The Reichstag: German Parliament between Monarchy and Federalism.* Berlin: Bebra, 1999; Schnabel, Franz. *Deutsche Geschichte im 19. Jahrhundert.* München: Deutscher Taschenbuch Verlag, 1987; Stürmer, Michael. *Das ruhelose Reich. Deutschland 1866–1918.* Berlin: Siedler, 1983; Willoweit, Dietmar. *Deutsche Verfassungsgeschichte.* Munich: Beck, 2004.

ULRICH SCHNAKENBERG

Reinsurance Treaty (1887)

A hastily formulated secret treaty between Germany and Russia. By 1886, it was obvious the Russians would no longer agree to renew their participation in the Three Emperors' Alliance, set to expire in 1887. To compensate for this, Otto von **Bismarck** masterminded a series of agreements in 1887 designed to keep Russia and France in check. One of those agreements was the Reinsurance Treaty, negotiated secretly with Russia and effective for three years from June 18, 1887. It stated that one country would remain neutral if the other became involved in a war. The only exceptions were if Germany started a war with France, or if Russia started a war with Austria-Hungary. In early 1890, the new German Chancellor Leo von **Caprivi,** on the advice of the Foreign Office, refused to renew a treaty which appeared to run counter to Germany's obligations to Austria-Hungary and the **Triple Alliance.** This left Russia free to pursue other options, specifically an alliance with France. *See also Dreikaiserbund;* German Empire; Habsburg Empire; Russian Empire; Triple Entente.

FURTHER READING: Kennedy, Paul. *The Rise and Fall of the Great Powers.* London: Unwin Hyman, 1988; Langer, William L. *European Alliance and Alignments 1871–1890.* New York: Alfred A. Knopf, 1962; Taylor, A.J.P. *The Struggle for Mastery in Europe, 1848–1914.* Oxford: Clarendon, 1954.

DAVID H. OLIVIER

Responsible Government

The mid-nineteenth-century extension of self-government to British colonies possessing representative legislatures. The British North American colonies had been granted representative government—that is to say elected assemblies—at various stages in the eighteenth century. In the 1830s and 1840s, British North American colonists adopted a variety of stratagems to win responsible government. The rebellions that engulfed Lower **Canada** and Upper Canada in 1837 and 1838 were in part driven by this agenda. Moderate reformers who rejected rebellion, like Robert Baldwin in Upper Canada, Louis-Hippolyte LaFontaine in Lower Canada, and Joseph Howe in Nova Scotia, pressed the point with British policymakers in measured and reasoned tones, insisting that their agenda was not to sever the colonies from the mother country, but merely to achieve the British system of cabinet government.

In the wake of the 1837 rebellions, the first earl of **Durham** was sent as governor-in-chief of British North America, commissioned to investigate the causes of colonial discontent. While Durham remained in Canada only a few months, his *Report on the Affairs of British North America* (1839), or Durham Report, offered a proposed solution to Canada's unrest. He advocated a union of the colonies of Upper and Lower Canada, and recommended responsible government, something traditionally considered incompatible with colonial status. Durham looked to the model of the British system and argued that implementing the system in Canada would require no new colonial theory and would entail only extending the principles of the British constitution and accepting the logical consequences of representative government. The governor should appoint an executive council with support from a majority of the assembly. The matters over which Britain should retain control were comparatively few, Durham argued: the constitution, foreign relations and trade, and public lands.

Britain's Colonial Office, however, was as yet unprepared to concede self-government to the colony. Lord John Russell, secretary of state for the colonies, insisted that the British constitution could not be copied in a colonial possession. Complications would arise if the governor received conflicting advice from his colonial administration and the imperial cabinet. Britain's ultimate willingness to change this policy and surrender the right of self-government has been attributed to a number of factors. Although Britain's own constitutional system was held up as a model by colonial reformers, conventions limiting the sovereign's power of independent action were still in a fluid state before the 1830s. The hardening of constitutional conventions in Britain was thus a necessary antecedent to any attempt to introduce party government in the colonies.

The key factor that has been cited in Britain's policy shift is the move to **free trade.** It is not surprising that a reconsideration of colonial policy would be tied to the mid-nineteenth-century dismantling of centuries of mercantilist doctrine, as that doctrine had provided the rationale for the acquisition of colonies in the first place. The Whig administration of Lord John Russell assumed power in Britain in 1846, with the Third Earl **Grey** in the Colonial Office. The **Corn Laws,** a system of tariffs on wheat, had just been repealed under the previous administration of Robert **Peel,** and Canadian wheat merchants who had prospered under a system of protection in the British market were hard hit by the change. A loss of imperial protection on timber followed.

The loosening of the economic ties of empire was accompanied by a loosening of political ties. Soon after assuming the Colonial Office portfolio, Grey encapsulated his views on responsible government in a famous dispatch to Sir John Harvey, lieutenant-governor of **Nova Scotia.** This 1846 dispatch instructed Harvey to follow the constitutional analogies of the mother country. His executive council should remain in power only as long as they enjoyed the confidence of the assembly. The governor still possessed reserve powers, but these should be used sparingly and discreetly. Grey warned Harvey that the government of the British North American provinces should not be carried on in opposition to the wishes of the inhabitants. Nova Scotia thus became the first self-governing colony in the British Empire. In January 1848, following an election in which the previous Conservative administration was defeated, Harvey called on Nova Scotia's Reform Party to form a government. Nova Scotia reformer Joseph Howe liked to boast that while Canada had experienced a rebellion in its quest for political change, Nova Scotia won responsible government before any other colony in the empire, without "a blow struck or a pane of glass broken." The eighth earl of Elgin, who arrived in Canada as governor in chief in 1847, then recognized the principle of responsible government in that colony. The results of the spring 1848 election made it clear that Canada's Reform Party held more seats in the legislature, and Elgin accordingly called on Louis-Hippolyte LaFontaine and Robert Baldwin, the leading reformers in the French and English sections of the colony, to form a government.

The shift toward responsible government should not be confused with an adoption of wholesale democracy, nor was it the opening wedge of republicanism in British North America. Both Elgin and Grey were committed to preserving a constitution in which the monarchy, aristocracy, and popular will would be held in balance. Elgin rejected any constitutional model that proposed to eliminate the sovereign; the check of the crown was essential. Borrowing de Tocqueville's phrase, Elgin asserted that a "tyranny of the majority" was "not the more tolerable because it is capricious & wielded by a Tyrant with many heads." By the 1850s, the principle of responsible government was nonetheless conceded in the Australian colonies as well. An 1852 Colonial Office dispatch set out this objective for New South Wales, Tasmania, Victoria, and South **Australia,** although the implementation was slightly delayed by controversies over an elected upper house. The imperial government approved the extension of responsible government to **New Zealand** in 1854 and afterward to other colonies. In 1931, the Statute of Westminster formally extended to these self-governing dominions complete autonomy over foreign affairs. *See also* British North America Act.

FURTHER READING: Buckner, Phillip A. *The Transition to Responsible Government: British Policy in British North America, 1815–1850.* Westport, CT: Greenwood Press, 1985; Craig, Gerald M., ed. *Lord Durham's Report.* Toronto: McClelland & Stewart, 1963; Ward, John Manning. *Colonial Self-Government. The British Experience, 1759–1856.* Toronto: University of Toronto Press, 1976.

BARBARA J. MESSAMORE

Restoration War (1868–1869)

Known in Japan as the Boshin War, this civil war was sparked by the proclamation of a "restoration" of imperial rule in January 1868, commonly referred to as the **Meiji Restoration.** The defeat by June 1869 of all forces loyal to the Tokugawa regime paved the way for the emergence of modern Japan. The arrival of Commodore Matthew **Perry** and a squadron of American ships in Uraga Bay in July 1853 seriously threatened the authority of the Tokugawa family, whose head, the supreme warlord (shōgun), had ruled Japan for more than two and half centuries. Following their submission to American demands for open trade, the Tokugawa confronted opposition from two powerful traditional enemies: the Satsuma and Choshu fiefdoms.

The failure of the shōgun's second punitive expedition against Choshu in 1866 inspired a coup in January 1868. Satsuma and Choshu samurai conspired with allies in the imperial court to strip the shōgun of his title and "restore" authority to the emperor. Although the imperial family technically reigned, it had not actually ruled Japan since the advent of warrior rule in the twelfth century.

The restoration decree marked the beginning of a four-phase war between followers of the shōgun and their rivals, now called "imperial forces." In the first phase, 4,500 troops from the Satsuma, Choshu, and Tosa domains defeated 15,500 troops loyal to the shōgun in the battle of Toba-Fushimi, south of Kyoto. The shogun approved a peaceful surrender of his capital, Edo (present-day Tokyo) in May 1868. It took until July 1868, however, to suppress disgruntled loyalists in

Edo in the second phase of the war. The third phase took place in the summer and autumn of 1868 and pitted imperial forces against a confederation of northern fiefdoms under the Aizu domain. Finally, in June 1869, the final holdout—naval commander Enomoto Takeaki—was vanquished after having led the bulk of the Tokugawa fleet northward and establishing a separate regime in the northern-most island of Hokkaido.

Although the great powers remained officially neutral during the restoration war, they retained an eye for commercial and political opportunities. Scottish merchant Thomas B. Glover supplied the Choshu domain with half a million rifles; the French government approved the sale of sixteen 12-inch grooved cannon to the shōgun. By January 1867, French officers had begun training the shōgun's army in Western military technique and "the manners of French civilization." *See also* Japanese Empire.

FURTHER READING: Beasley, W. G. *The Meiji Restoration*. Stanford, CA: Stanford University Press, 1972; Totman, Conrad. *The Collapse of the Tokugawa Bakufu, 1862–1868*. Honolulu: University of Hawaii Press, 1980.

FREDERICK R. DICKINSON

Retreat from Moscow (1812)

See Moscow, Retreat from

Rhodes, Cecil (1853–1902)

A British and South African politician, businessman, and imperial visionary, Cecil Rhodes was the founder of his eponymous colony, Rhodesia, and a major figure in South African and imperial politics in the last decades of the nineteenth century. Rhodes was the son of an Anglican clergyman. He went to Natal at the age of 17 to farm cotton with his elder brother, in part because it was thought that the South African climate would help his always-dubious health. Rhodes and his brother soon decamped to the newly discovered diamond fields near the town of Kimberley, where Rhodes did moderately well as a diamond miner, acquiring a large number of friends among prominent miners, and by 1873 having enough money to take himself off to Oriel College, Oxford.

On his return from Oxford, Rhodes and his partners formed the company that became De Beers to purchase mining claims in the Kimberley area. By operating on a larger scale than individual claim holders, and also by providing pumping services to others, Rhodes' company prospered. In the early 1880s, De Beers solidified its control over the diamond fields, forcing out small independent producers. From the 1880 annexation of the diamond-producing region to the Cape Colony, Rhodes represented the area in the Cape legislature, although not without accusations of corrupt electoral practices. Rhodes had absorbed imperialist ideas from his earliest days—his first will of 1872 went so far as to leave all his property to the colonial secretary—and he never wavered in his faith that the Anglo-Saxon peoples should rule the world in the interests of progress. His involvement in South African politics, his mining interests, and his imperial ideology combined to convince Rhodes that Britain needed to expand in Africa. As so often in imperial history, it was the local "man on the spot" who was determined to push the frontiers of empire forward, often against the will of the government in London and even its local officials. In 1886, gold was discovered on the Rand, in the Transvaal. Rhodes largely missed out on the Rand gold rush, but the discovery convinced him that Britain must expand to the north, both to control the growing power of the Transvaal and to preempt annexations by other European powers.

In 1889, Rhodes obtained from Lord Salisbury's government a charter for the **British South Africa Company,** on the basis of a dubious concession from the Matabele king Lobengula, aided by a certain amount of hype about the mineral potential of central Africa and a number of well-connected British aristocrats and other prominent figures on the company board. In 1890, the famous pioneer column of 200 settlers and about 500 British South Africa Company police marched north into the interior, where they founded the settlement of Fort Salisbury, later the capital of Rhodesia. Also in 1890, Rhodes himself became premier of the **Cape Colony,** putting him in the anomalous position of being both the senior South African politician and the owner of two of the largest commercial operations in the subcontinent, De Beers and the British South Africa Company. Rhodes won the premiership with the backing of an almost equally anomalous coalition of Anglophone liberals and the Afrikaner Bond. As Premier, he put through at the behest of the latter laws limiting the black franchise and native land rights. Simultaneously, the company fought and won a brief but successful war with the Matabele in 1893, securing its control over Rhodesia and eliminating the kingdom of Lobengula. The scandal arising from the **Jameson Raid** of 1895, in which company forces invaded the Transvaal, brought Rhodes's contradictory position as statesman and capitalist, and at once exponent of British and Afrikaner interests, to a head. He was forced to resign the cape premiership, and shortly thereafter a Second **Matabele War** of 1896—this time requiring the intervention of imperial troops—led to his temporary resignation as director of the British South Africa Company.

The company's combination of political connections and stock market manipulation at home with wars of conquest abroad—proceedings compared by Rhodes's admirers to the conquests of the East India Company—did much to bring capitalist and economically motivated imperialism into disrepute in the minds of many Britons, especially on the left. At the outbreak of the Second Boer War in 1899, Rhodes was in the diamond-mining town of Kimberley, whose defense he helped organize during the Boer siege. His health declining and his attention diverted by personal troubles, he took little further part in the course of the war. He died in 1902, leaving a large bequest to fund the Rhodes scholarships and other imperial causes. *See also* Boer Wars; British Empire.

FURTHER READING: Galbraith, J. S. *Crown and Charter: The Early Years of the British South Africa Company.* Berkeley: University of California Press, 1974; Newbury, Colin. *The Diamond Ring: Business, Politics and Precious Stones in South Africa, 1867–1947.* Oxford: Clarendon, 1989; Rotberg, Robert I. *The Founder: Cecil Rhodes and the Pursuit of Power.* New York: Oxford University Press, 1988.

MARK F. PROUDMAN

Ricardo, David (1772–1823)

A prominent and methodologically innovative political economist. Of a Jewish family and trained as a stockbroker, he broke with Judaism and his family, while becoming a successful broker and early amassing a fortune. Drawn to political economy by reading Adam **Smith,** and a friend of James Mill and Thomas **Malthus,** he wrote extensively on the inflation of paper money subsequent to the wartime suspension of convertibility into bullion. He then took up the newly introduced **Corn Laws,** arguing that the interests of landlords were opposed to those of every other class. In 1817, Ricardo published his chief work, the *Principles of Political Economy and Taxation.* He became a member of Parliament in 1819, spoke for the reduction of tariffs, the paying down of the national debt, and the moderate reform of parliament; he was highly respected in the House of Commons for his knowledge of economic questions.

While he evinced great respect for Smith, Ricardo disagreed with him on a number of points, most of all his theory of value. Ricardo's *Principles* were notable above all for their use of mathematical techniques in the attempt to deduce from original premises the rate of profit; in this it is accurate to see Karl **Marx** as a Ricardian. Ricardo claimed to show that the rate of profit tended to fall with a necessity he compared to gravitation, but for the significant caveat that technical progress could overcome this downward force. The immediate political consequences of Ricardo's doctrines were to demonstrate that agricultural rents—which is to say, aristocratic incomes—increased with the price of food: "a rent is paid because corn is high." The idea that high food prices went straight into aristocratic rents was a powerful force behind the abolition of the Corn Laws and the establishment of **free trade.** Although Ricardo's closely argued study of the question was not as widely read or cited as the work of Smith, it provided intellectual ammunition to the advocates of free trade. Like Smith, Ricardo was opposed to exclusive colonial systems. Also like Smith, his primary impact on imperial policy was indirect, through the establishment of classical political economy, with its free trade implications, as the hegemonic authority on its subject. *See also* Cobden, Richard; Corn Laws.

FURTHER READING: Peach, Terry. *Interpreting Ricardo.* Cambridge: Cambridge University Press, 1993; Sraffa, Piero, and M. H. Dobb. *The Works and Correspondence of David Ricardo.* 11 vols. Cambridge: Cambridge University Press, 1973.

MARK F. PROUDMAN

Riel Rebellions (1869–1870, 1885)

Two revolts, led by the brilliant, charismatic, and delusional Louis Riel, of the Métis—a mixed French-Indian people of the Red River Valley in present-day Manitoba—against the encroachment of the Dominion of **Canada** on their territory. The first rebellion, better known as the Red River Rebellion, was a by-product of the creation by the British North America Act of the Canadian confederation and its westward expansion into territory also coveted by the **United States.** The Canadian government purchased the enormous territory of Rupert's Land, of which the Red River Settlement was on a tiny portion, from the **Hudson's Bay Company** in 1869 and appointed a governor who immediately set about surveying land occupied by Métis and not yet officially transferred to Canada. Riel set up a provisional government, arrested leaders of the local pro-Canada movement, and negotiated a settlement making the Red River settlement part of the new Canadian province of Manitoba. An expeditionary force of British regulars and Canadian militia led by Colonel Garnet Wolseley was sent on a 1,000-mile march, initially to occupy the new territory but later to arrest Riel after it was learned that he tried and executed one of the pro-Canada leaders. When the force arrived Riel had fled to the United States.

The second rebellion came about after Riel's return to Canada and the attempt to replicate the Red River Settlement and its government at village of Batoche. This time the Canadian government of John A. Macdonald was in a position to launch an immediate military response and to supply it by way of the newly constructed railway. The rebellion was crushed and Riel tried and convicted for treason. Despite pleas for clemency in Canada and from the United States and Britain, he was hanged in November 1885. *See also* Canadian Pacific Railway.

FURTHER READING: Stanley, George. *Louis Riel.* Toronto: Ryerson Press, 1963.

CARL CAVANAGH HODGE

Risorgimento

See Italy

Risk Fleet Theory

A naval strategic theory formulated by German Admiral Alfred von **Tirpitz.** Whereas the **Tirpitz Plan** was developed to challenge British naval dominance of the high seas with a formidable German battle fleet, the risk fleet theory articulated in a memorandum in 1900 observed that the German fleet need not be strong as the **Royal Navy,** because the latter would in the case of war not be in a position—given the burden of the defense of a worldwide empire—to concentrate its entire fleet against Germany for a battle in the home waters of the North Sea. A German fleet, the theory posited, need therefore be powerful enough only to inflict serious damage on the Royal Navy and thus compromise the latter's capacity to meet and defeat other enemies. Britain would not risk a major battle with the German High Seas Fleet because the potential damage to Britain's strategic position, even in victory, would be too great.

The theory specifically and Germany's naval buildup generally were crafted to nullify Britain's **two-power standard** for naval supremacy. In this it succeeded, yet it also backfired to Germany's disadvantage. Britain's response to the German challenge was a radical recalibration of the naval arms race by way of the development of the *Dreadnought,* which abandoned quantitative advantage in numbers of ship for qualitative superiority in firepower. Moreover, Tirpitz was in error about the risks Britain was willing to take to destroy the German fleet. In the spring of 1916, the Royal Navy did in fact hazard an all-out contest with the High Seas Fleet off Jutland. It sustained but also inflicted heavy losses—and retained dominance of the North Sea for the remainder of the war. *See also* Tirpitz Plan.

FURTHER READING: Keegan, John. *The Price of Admiralty.* New York: Viking, 1989; Scheer, R. *Germany's High Sea Fleet in the World War.* New York: P. Smith, 1934. Steel, Nigel, and Peter Hart. *Jutland 1916: Death in the Gray Wastes.* London: Cassell, 2003.

CARL CAVANAGH HODGE

Roberts, Frederick Sleigh, Earl Roberts of Kandahar and Pretoria (1832–1914)

A talented and popular British general, Roberts made his name fighting in **India, Afghanistan,** and **South Africa,** becoming commander-in-chief of the British Army in 1900. Roberts was commissioned into the **East India Company**'s army in 1851, and won the Victoria Cross during the **Indian Mutiny.** He was an artillery officer who served much of his career in the quartermaster's department, and subsequent to the abolition of native artillery units after the mutiny was absorbed into the British army. He served with Napier's expedition to **Abyssinia** in 1868.

Roberts was then appointed to command on the **Punjab** frontier in 1878, as tensions with Afghanistan rose. After the initial British occupation of Kabul, a temporary peace lasted until the British resident at Kabul and his aides were murdered. Roberts led an avenging force into the city, and controversially executed those held responsible for the murders. An uprising near Kandahar led Roberts to lead a picked force to defeat the Afghans and occupy that city, winning him public renown. He subsequently rose to command the Indian Army, where his chief preoccupation was the perceived danger of a Russian advance through Afghanistan. Roberts was elevated to the peerage in 1892, and left the Indian command in 1893. Following Britain's initial defeats in the Boer War, Roberts was appointed to command there in December 1899, the same month in which his son was killed in the action that won him, like his father, a Victoria Cross. Roberts led a successful advance across South Africa, occupying Pretoria on June 5, 1900, but failing to destroy the Boer forces entirely or to capture their leaders—another two years of guerilla warfare lay ahead.

Roberts returned to Britain to succeed Lord Wolseley as commander-in-chief of the British Army. In retirement, he led the National Service League, which campaigned for the introduction of peacetime conscription to counter the German threat. A firm Unionist, he advised the Ulster Volunteer Force and supported the refusal of many officers to serve against Ulster during the Curragh "mutiny" of 1914. He died in November 1914 while visiting troops in France. *See also* Boer Wars; British Empire.

FURTHER READING: Childers, Erkine. *War and the Arme Blanche.* London: E. Arnold, 1910; Hannah, W. H. *Kipling's General: The Life of Field-Marshal Earl Roberts of Kanahar.* London: Lee Cooper, 1972; Roberts, Frederick Sleigh. *Forty-One Years in India.* New York: Longman, Green & Co., 1898.

MARK F. PROUDMAN

Roon, Albrecht von (1803–1879)

Prussian war minister from 1859 to 1873, Albrecht von Roon joined the Prussian army in 1816. In 1835, he entered the general staff. Recognizing the army's inefficiency, he occupied himself with schemes for reform. In 1859, Roon became war minister. His proposals to create an armed nation by a universal three years' service met with strong opposition. It was not until after heavy fighting against a hostile parliament that Roon succeeded. It required the **Austro-Prussian War** of 1866 to convert opposition into support. Roon's system produced convincing results in the **Franco-Prussian War** in 1870–1871. After that, Roon's ideas were copied throughout Europe. Roon was created a count and a field marshal, and in 1871, he succeeded Otto von **Bismarck** as Prussian prime minister for one year. *See also* Moltke, Helmut von; Gneisenau, August Wilhelm von; Prussia; Scharnhorst, Gerhard von.

FURTHER READING: Citino, Robert M. *The German Way of War: From the Thirty Years War to the Third Reich.* Lawrence: University Press of Kansas, 2005; Wawro, Geoffrey. *The Franco-Prussian War: The German Conquest of France in 1870–1871.* New York: Cambridge University Press, 2003.

MARTIN MOLL

Roosevelt Corollary

President Theodore **Roosevelt**'s codicil to the 1823 **Monroe Doctrine,** which ordained that the Western Hemisphere was the domain of the **United States** and that it would police the area to the exclusion of other powers. The corollary built on the Monroe Doctrine's original premise that the Western Hemisphere should not be within Europe's sphere of influence but has variously been described as skewing, reinterpreting, and perverting its original intent. It was formally espoused in his annual message to Congress on December 6, 1904. Roosevelt stated that adherence to the Monroe Doctrine "may force the United States, however reluctantly, in flagrant cases of such wrong doing or impotence, to the exercise of an international police power."

Roosevelt's Corollary bore the hallmarks of his sense of mission and keen historical interest in the role of the United States in the Western hemisphere. As such it was a manifestation of a wider conception of United States security attributed to the thinking of Alfred Thayer **Mahan,** which placed an emphasis on security beyond the immediate shores of the nation. After the **Royal Navy**'s withdrawal from the region, the president shared Mahan's view of an implicit agreement with Great Britain based on shared values and an Atlanticist outlook.

Following the conclusion of the Spanish-American war of 1898, which had seen the United States post its intent to use military force in the area, Roosevelt was motivated by a desire to protect the **Panama Canal.** This became a rationale itself for preventing a European presence in the approaches to the canal that stretched throughout the Caribbean and to the Hawaiian islands in the Pacific. Roosevelt was also concerned that the internal weaknesses of the Latin American Republics, particularly in the field of economics following European pressure to collect debts in the 1902–1903 Venezuelan affair and in 1903 in the Dominican Republic, could provide a rationale to the Europeans to insist on intervention. This reinforced in Roosevelt's mind the importance of legitimating America's capacity to intervene across the region.

For Roosevelt this was not new. In May 1904, Secretary of State Elihu Root had read a letter from the president to the Cuba Society of New York stating "Brutal wrongdoing, or an impotence which results in a general loosening of the ties of a civilized society, may finally require intervention by some civilized nation, and in the Western Hemisphere the United States cannot ignore this duty." In these words it is possible to both Roosevelt's zeal and a benevolent quality to his corollary, despite it having imperial overtones at the same time. This latter quality did not go unnoticed in Latin America and gave rise to considerable anti-American feeling when the United States subsequently intervened militarily. For good or ill, therefore, the Roosevelt Corollary marked United States assuming an unchallenged position of preeminence in the Western Hemisphere. *See also* Navalism.

FURTHER READING: Marks, Frederick W. *Velvet on Iron: The Diplomacy of Theodore Roosevelt.* Lincoln: University of Nebraska Press, 1979; Morris, Edmund. *Theodore Rex.* New York: Random House, 2001; Ricard, Serge. "The Roosevelt Corollary." *Presidential Studies Quarterly* 36/1 (2006).

J. SIMON ROFE

Roosevelt, Theodore (1858–1919)

Theodore Roosevelt served as the 26th President of the **United States** from 1901–1909 and was a major architect of American expansionist foreign policy. Roosevelt was born in New York City on October 27, 1858, the scion of an old aristocratic family of Dutch origin. He graduated from Harvard College in 1880 and embraced a political career in 1881 as a Republican reformer. He served as assemblyman from the 21st district of New York City in the New York State Assembly from 1881 to 1884, as U.S. Civil Service commissioner in Washington between 1889 and 1895, and as president of the New York City Board of Police Commissioners from 1895 to 1897. He was appointed assistant secretary of the Navy by President William **McKinley** in 1897, and he resigned a year later to take part in the **Spanish-American War** as lieutenant-colonel of the First United States Volunteer Cavalry regiment, known as the "Rough Riders." He returned to civilian life a war hero after his heroic charge up San Juan Hill and was twice elected governor of New York, much to the displeasure of the local Republican boss. To neutralize him, the Republican National Convention nominated him as President McKinley's running mate—the winning ticket—in the 1900 election. On September 6, 1901, McKinley was shot at the Buffalo Pan-American Exposition and died eight days later. On September 14, 1901, Roosevelt took the oath of office as President of the United States, the youngest ever to assume the office.

A convergence of factors made Theodore Roosevelt the most popular statesman of his generation and the first news-generating president: his close relationship with newspapermen; his colorful and endearing personality; his unbounded energy; his virile postures as a soldier, hunter, and westerner; his consummate showmanship; his eclectic tastes; his frequent eccentricities; and the many controversies that he initiated, to say nothing of his adorable but turbulent children. The White House made ideal news material and easy copy at all times, and a welcome antidote to journalistic routine.

Theodore Roosevelt's dedication to **progressivism** is best illustrated by his 1902 legislative record, criticized by both the Republican Old Guard's "stand pat reactionaries" and the "lunatic fringe" radicals. His administration's unexpected enforcement of the Sherman Anti-Trust Act against the Northern Securities Company; imaginative handling of the Pennsylvania anthracite coal strike; appointment to the Supreme Court of Oliver Wendell Holmes, one of the greatest jurists of the twentieth century; and the Newlands Reclamation Act, which inaugurated a national conservation policy—stepped up between 1902 and 1909, often in defiance of Congress—testify to an enduring progressive legacy.

Several other measures may be regarded as part of the Roosevelt's Square Deal program, although he coined the phrase during the 1904 campaign. In 1903, a Department of Commerce was created, with a Bureau of Corporations to assist the President in watching corporate dealings. The same year the Elkins Anti-Rebate Act forbade the railroads from granting rebates to large companies. It was reinforced by the 1906 Hepburn Act, which empowered the Interstate Commerce Commission to set rates and to examine the railroads' bookkeeping, and which prohibited the carrying of commodities unrelated to the companies' usual operations. More important still, inasmuch as they achieved a major precedent, the Pure Food and Drug Act and the Meat Inspection Act of 1906 made the national government the overseer of the consumer's health and safety.

A longtime apologist of Anglo-Saxon expansionism, the new president was in no way perplexed by the colonial gains of 1898; on the contrary, he welcomed them as the inevitable corollary of greatness. In his eyes the colonial venture of the turn of the century marked a mutation from Monroeism to internationalism, from hemispheric responsibilities to global commitments. Roosevelt was better prepared to deal with foreign policy than most of his predecessors, being blessed with three formidable assets: a cosmopolitan upbringing, an impressive knowledge of world history, and an international network of friends and acquaintances in American and foreign diplomatic circles. Yet Roosevelt's realism, inventiveness, and professionalism in the handling of European-American or Japanese-American relations are only part of the story, for he was to evince less restraint and less acumen in dealing with "inferior" races or peoples, in China, the **Philippines,** or the Caribbean. Witness his brutal reaction to the Chinese boycott of American goods in 1905, his ranting diatribes against Emilio Aguinaldo and his followers during the 1899–1902 Philippine-American War, and his spiteful dismissal of Colombian objections to the **Hay-Herrán Treaty** in 1903. Setting Theodore Roosevelt in context tends to mitigate these shortcomings and to highlight the innovative character of his diplomacy; it also evidences his momentous encounter with his times. The historian and theoretician of expansion would turn out to be a fitting chief executive for the newly born imperial republic of the turn of the century. In fact, the Americans of 1900 who endorsed the acquisition of an empire adopted the Rooseveltian thesis of historic continuity as expounded in his *Winning of the West,* conquest and settlement were rooted in the Anglo-Saxon past.

A tradition-inspired innovator, Roosevelt showed his firm grasp of international politics in a new age, such as the need for Anglo-American cooperation and solidarity. With national greatness and national security foremost in his mind, he continued to advocate and promote preparedness, strengthened U.S. supremacy in the Western Hemisphere by adding his "corollary" to the **Monroe Doctrine** in 1904, and cautiously discarded isolation in an attempt to effect the world balance of power in a manner conducive to peace and therefore beneficial to the United States, given the global framework of its security. The 26th President's geopolitical clear-sightedness was too novel, however, to win easy acceptance and support from his contemporaries; the old isolationist reflex had to be reckoned with whenever foreign policy ventured too far from American shores.

Unsurprisingly, the main diplomatic episodes that Roosevelt personally handled—the Venezuelan and Moroccan crises, the **Russo-Japanese War**—directly concerned the two powers that he always considered as potential enemies, Germany and Japan. During the **Venezuelan Crisis** of 1902–1903, he discreetly but vigorously forced Berlin to pay heed to the Monroe Doctrine. His so-called ultimatum was a reminder that he most probably communicated verbally to the German envoy in February 1903. Roosevelt was also instrumental in the controversial acquisition of the **Panama Canal** Zone, after Colombia's rejection's of the Hay-Herrán Treaty; the Canal Zone was secured thanks to a timely revolution on the Isthmus, which Washington government passively encouraged, and a new treaty signed between the newly independent Republic of Panama and the United States on November 18, 1903. Unknown to most of his contemporaries, he secretly acted as mediator in the **Moroccan Crisis** of 1904–1906, which opposed Germany to France, and endeavored both to appease the German emperor and to safeguard French interests, notably during the 1906 **Algeciras Conference.** His greatest diplomatic triumph was his ending of the 1904–1905 Russo-Japanese War by way of the mediation at the Portsmouth Peace Conference and the signing of the Treaty of **Portsmouth** on September 5, 1905. His masterful peacemaking won Roosevelt the Nobel Peace Prize in 1906. He later tried to defuse the Japanese-American crisis triggered by the exclusion of Oriental pupils from San Francisco's schools. The tension between Washington and Tokyo partly justified his decision to send the Great White Fleet on a world cruise on December 16, 1907, the most powerful motive being the chief executive's wish to publicize the need for building up the navy. The return of the fleet on February 22, 1909, shortly before he left office, was a crowning achievement for the outgoing president. His friend William Howard **Taft** succeeded him on March 4, 1909.

As ex-president, Roosevelt continued to make the headlines and to be active in politics. On leaving the White House, he spent a year hunting big game in Africa then toured Europe for three months before going back home. The Ballinger-Pinchot controversy in 1909–1910 led to his estrangement from Taft, of whom he became increasingly critical. Despite his 1904 statement to the contrary, he announced his decision to run again for president. He was denied the nomination by the Republican Party, broke with it, and founded the Progressive Party. The three-cornered fight of 1912 ensured the election of the Democratic candidate, Woodrow **Wilson.** From 1915 until his death, the former president waged his ultimate political battle, first on behalf of preparedness and intervention, then, after American entry into the Great War, against Wilson's projected peace settlement. It was on the whole a lonely, quixotic crusade that eventually gathered momentum and culminated posthumously, in a sense, with the U.S. Senate's rejection of the Versailles Treaty, following a battle in which the Big Stick diplomatist's "alter ego," Henry Cabot Lodge, played a leading part. Theodore Roosevelt died in his sleep in Oyster Bay, New York, on January 6, 1919. *See also* Mahan, Alfred Thayer; Navalism; Roosevelt Corollary.

FURTHER READING: Beale, Howard K. *Theodore Roosevelt and the Rise of America to World Power.* Baltimore: The Johns Hopkins University Press, 1984; Brands, H. W. *T. R.: The Last Romantic.* New York: Basic Books, 1997; Dalton, Kathleen. *Theodore Roosevelt: A Strenuous Life.* New York: Knopf, 2002; Gould, Lewis L. *The Presidency of Theodore Roosevelt.* Lawrence: University of Kansas Press, 1991; Harbaugh, William H. *Power and Responsibility: The Life and Times of Theodore Roosevelt.* Newtown, CT: American Political Biography Press, 1997; Marks, Frederick W., III. *Velvet on Iron: The Diplomacy of Theodore Roosevelt.* Lincoln: University of Nebraska Press, 1979; Morris, Edmund. *Theodore Rex.* New York: Random House, 2001; Ricard, Serge.

Théodore Roosevelt: principes et pratique d'une politique étrangère. Aix-en-Provence: Publications de l'Université de Provence, 1991; Tilchin, William N. *Theodore Roosevelt and the British Empire: A Study in Presidential Statecraft.* New York: St. Martin's Press, 1997.

SERGE RICARD

Root, Elihu (1845–1937)

An American lawyer and statesman who played a prominent role in the development of a legal and administrative framework for the colonial empire of the **United States.** During his term as secretary of war (1899–1904), Root laid the foundations of an American approach to colonial governance in **Puerto Rico** and the **Philippines** and to informal empire in **Cuba.**

Based on a close reading of British imperial experience, Root's approach combined benevolent paternalism with military enforcement of colonial control. He supported extensive social engineering measures and limited political reforms in the colonies but defended the brutal suppression of indigenous resistance to American rule and questioned the abilities of the colonized for self-government on cultural and racial grounds. He designed a legal framework that allocated the overseas possessions a status of unincorporated territories with no constitutional rights for the colonial subjects. In the case of Cuba, Root supported reforms for Cuban independence but simultaneously devised important legal mechanisms, such as the **Platt Amendment** of 1901, which facilitated continued American control over Cuban affairs through intervention rights and a Cuban-U.S. lease agreement for a naval base at Guantánamo Bay.

Between 1905 and 1909, Root served as secretary of state and reformed the consular service, improved relations with Latin America, negotiated mutual recognition of U.S. and Japanese colonial possessions, as in the Root-Takahira Agreement of 1908, and supported a legal framework for the arbitration of international disputes. Root served in the U.S. Senate from 1909 to 1915 and received the Nobel Peace Price for his efforts at international arbitration in 1912. *See also* Monroe Doctrine; Japanese Empire.

FURTHER READING: Jessup, Philip C. *Elihu Root.* New York: Dodd, Mead, 1938; Leopold, Richard W. *Elihu Root and the Conservative Tradition.* Boston: Little, Brown, 1954; Zimmermann, Warren. *First Great Triumph. How Five Americans Made Their Country a World Power.* New York: Farrar, Straus and Giroux, 2002.

FRANK SCHUMACHER

Rorke's Drift, Battle of (1879)

A minor but celebrated engagement of the **Zulu War** that followed quickly on the Zulu victory at **Isandhlwana** in January 1879. At a mission station by a ford of the Buffalo River 25 miles southeast of Dundee in South Africa, a British force of 139 men, 35 of whom were ill, defended a small hospital compound against repeated attacks by a 4,000-man Zulu impi for 12 hours until the Zulu force abandoned the assault. The British force was commanded by two officers hitherto notable for no distinguished service, Lieutenant John Rouse Merriot Chard of the Royal Engineers and Lieutenant Gonville Bromhead of B Company of the 24th Regiment.

In response to repeated Zulu charges, the defenders fired a total of 20,000 rounds of ammunition and inflicted heavy losses on the enemy. At its height, the battle degenerated into savage hand-to-hand combat, and the mission hospital was set afire. The defenders counted 17 dead and 10 wounded after the fighting subsided. Zulu losses have been estimated as low as 400 and as high as 1,000. In all, 11 Victoria Crosses were awarded for the defense of Rorke's Drift, the highest ever given for a single engagement. In 1880, Alphonse de Neuville completed a superb painting, *The Defence of Rorke's Drift 1879*, which today hangs in the Art Gallery of New South Wales.

FURTHER READING: Farwell, Byron. *Queen Victoria's Little Wars.* New York: W. W. Norton, 1972; Knight, Ian. *The National Army Museum Book of the Zulu War.* London: Sidgwick & Jackson, 2003.

CARL CAVANAGH HODGE

Rosas, Juan Manuel de (1793–1877)

Military commander who helped the Federalists defeat the *Unitario* government of Buenos Aires and then helped develop the power and wealth of the city and province of Buenos Aires in **Argentina.** Rosas gained title to land as a result of his skill as a rancher. He helped organize a militia cavalry that campaigned against Native American raiders on the Argentine *pampa.* Increasingly opposed to the efforts of the government to unify all of Argentina's provinces into a single country, he turned his military and political skills against Buenos Aires. He became governor of the province in 1829. The legislature granted him absolute power, and he remained in charge until 1852. To protect and promote the interests of landowners and exporters, Rosas used his military power to regulate the flow of trade on the Río de la Plata. His attempts to force merchants to trade only with Buenos Aires led to wars with **Brazil,** Great Britain, and France, as well as conflicts with other provincial governments. *See also* ABC Powers.

FURTHER READING: Lynch, John. *Argentine Dictator: Juan Manuel de Rosas 1829–1852.* Oxford: Clarendon, 1981.

DANIEL K. LEWIS

Rosebery, Archibald Philip Primrose, Earl of Rosebery (1847–1929)

In 1894–1895, Rosebery was briefly prime minister of Great Britain, during which time Britain declared a protectorate over **Uganda.** Rosebery served with distinction as foreign secretary during William **Gladstone**'s brief administration of 1886, negotiating a peaceful resolution to a crisis in Bulgaria. On the fall of Gladstone's government over the issue of Irish **Home Rule,** Rosebery was one of few Liberal peers to remain with the Gladstonians. Rosebery became foreign secretary once again in Gladstone's fourth government of 1892–1894, and succeeded the latter on his resignation. Gladstone's resignation was provoked by his opposition to increased naval spending, and Rosebery's brief government remained divided on questions related to military spending and imperial expansion, with many of the **Liberal Party**'s core supporters opposed to both.

Rosebery was a Liberal Imperialist, and as such something of a mentor to younger Liberal Imperialists such as H. H. **Asquith** and Edward **Grey.** Although a cautious diplomat, Rosebery is remembered for defending imperial expansion, particularly in Africa, as "pegging out claims for posterity," a remark that reflected the widely held contemporary view that colonies were a necessary source of long-term wealth and power. His government fell on a vote pertaining to army preparedness, and in the subsequent election, the Tories and Unionists led by Lord **Salisbury** were able to accuse the Liberals of being insufficiently supportive of Britain's imperial position. Rosebery did not again hold office, and for the rest of his life was a somewhat quixotic figure pining for an unlikely kind of nonparty government. *See also* Liberal Imperialism.

FURTHER READING: James, Robert Rhodes. *Lord Rosebery.* London: Weidenfeld and Nicolson, 1964.

MARK F. PROUDMAN

Royal Navy

The British navy, the Royal Navy, was the world's dominant naval force throughout the nineteenth century. The Royal Navy emerged from the wars of the French Revolution and Empire with a reputation for invincibility established by its successive victories over the Danish, Dutch, Spanish, and—most of all—the French navies. Its primacy was established by the great victory of **Trafalgar** in 1805, although commerce-raiding and blockades continued until the end of the Napoleonic wars. Although the Anglo-American War of 1812 produced a number of embarrassing defeats in frigate actions, the Royal Navy successfully reasserted itself. In the long peace that followed the French wars, the Royal Navy provided protection to Britain's increasingly far-flung trade routes, its power thereby being an immediate and necessary precondition of the growth of British and indeed Western global economic supremacy.

The Royal Navy was also active in the campaigns against slavery and the slave trade, and against piracy. As naval ships were often the only British forces in distant regions, such as the coasts of Africa and **China,** sailors and marines frequently operated ashore in furtherance of British interests. They played a major role in victories over the Chinese in the so-called **Opium Wars** of 1839–1842, 1857, and 1859–1860, and in operations against slavers and against hostile tribes in Africa. Whereas British power was maintained by small naval forces—often single ships—in more remote areas not dominated by another western power, in home and Mediterranean waters Britain maintained significant fleets of major warships. Warships changed radically throughout the nineteenth century. The introduction of steam engines, at first as auxiliary power, radically changed ship design, as did the advent of iron cladding followed by iron construction. Disputes between advocates of paddlewheels, which were vulnerable and interfered with armament, and screw propellers were resolved in favor of the latter. The fleets used in the **Crimean War** featured large three-decker sailing ships of traditional design equipped with removable screw propellers. That war also saw the development of large fleets of steam gunboats for inshore service. Such gunboats later saw service in numerous imperial campaigns.

Rapid technical change throughout the nineteenth century led to a number of naval scares—notably in 1847, 1859, and 1884—in which it was feared that the foreign, and usually French, introduction of whole new types of ship would make the Royal Navy obsolete at a blow. The French launched the steam ironclad *La Gloire* in 1859, leading the British to respond with the much larger *H.M.S. Warrior,* equipped with both steam engines and sails and a combination of breech-loading and muzzle-loading guns. Rapid improvements in guns, armor, and steam technology led to an arms race featuring many curious hybrid ships; it was a race that, following France's defeat by **Prussia** in 1870, Britain won by default. The Victorian navy systematized the recruitment of both men and officers, introducing for ratings long service in place of the practice of engagement for a single sailing, and a system of naval colleges for officers. Technical change led to a need for engineer officers and for skilled mechanics, or artificers, as well as specialist gunnery officers. *H.M.S. Excellent,* founded in 1830, trained the latter, and was one of a number of specialized technical schools created by the nineteenth-century navy to replace the old informal system of training at sea. Originally tolerated as unpleasant necessities, engineer officers were integrated into the naval rank structure as the century went on, although the full equivalence of engineer and deck officers was only pushed through, against some resistance, in 1903. The first ship without masts at all was *H.M.S. Devastation* of 1873; henceforth battleships, as they were beginning to be called, began to take their twentieth-century form, featuring guns in turrets, steam engines, and massive belts armor, especially around key areas. Other novel types were introduced in the late nineteenth and early twentieth centuries, including the torpedo boat, the destroyer, and the submarine.

The 1905 launch of *H.M.S. **Dreadnought,*** the brainchild of Sir John **Fisher,** the first all-big gun turbine-driven battleship, made all other ships afloat obsolete. It also did much to accelerate the Anglo-German naval race. The naval race led the admiralty to withdraw from service many older and obsolete ships, especially from far-flung corners of the empire, in part to save money but also in obeisance to the blue water theories promulgated by A. T. **Mahan** and many others. The command of ships on distant imperial stations necessarily involved a great deal of initiative and autonomy on the part of relatively low ranking officers, but the battleship fleets on the Home and Mediterranean stations came be characterized by rigid command structures and, to some critics, a fetish for paint and polish. It was a syndrome highlighted by the 1893 sinking of *H.M.S. Victoria,* the flagship of the Mediterranean fleet, in a collision caused by unquestioning obedience to orders. Throughout the nineteenth century an attempt was made to preserve the Royal Navy at a strength known as the **two-power standard.** During the Edwardian era, the Anglo-German naval race replaced that standard, it then being assumed that the primary enemy would be Germany. The famous clash of Dreadnought-class battleships at Jutland in 1916, the British forces being commanded by Sir John **Jellicoe,** demonstrated that Britain had effectively won the Anglo-German naval race, albeit narrowly. *See also* British Empire; Napoleonic Wars; Navalism; Nelson, Horatio; Risk Fleet Theory; *Weltpolitik.*

FURTHER READING: Herman, Arthur. *To Rule the Waves: How the British Navy Shaped the Modern World.* New York: Harper Collins, 2004; Kennedy, Paul M. *The Rise and Fall of British Naval Mastery.* London: A. Lane, 1976; Massie, Robert K. *Castles of Steel: Britain, Germany and the Winning of the Great War at Sea.* New York; Randon House, 2003; Padfield, Peter. *Rule Britannia:*

The Victorian and Edwardian Navy. London: Routledge, 1981; Rodger, N.A.M. *The Command of the Ocean: A Naval History of Britain.* London: Allen Lane, 2004.

MARK F. PROUDMAN

Royal Titles Act (1876)

An act of Parliament making the sovereign of England the Empress (or Emperor) of **India.** British control of the subcontinent, although briefly contested during the Mutiny of 1857, had by that point long been an effective fact. But the abolition of **East India Company** rule and the imposition of formal British sovereignty by the **India Act** of 1858, along with the abolition of the Mogul Emperor, left a formal if not a real void at the top of the polyglot Indian political system. The creation of a British empress raised some liberal hackles in England, but was thought by many to appeal to an oriental taste for rank and splendor. The British had been reminded by the **Indian Mutiny** that a massive empire could not be controlled by force alone. The Imperial Durbar of January 1, 1877, formally made Queen **Victoria** Empress, or *Victoria Regina et Imperatrix,* and was in fact a successful imperial spectacle. *See also* British Empire; Disraeli, Benjamin; Rāj.

FURTHER READING: James, Lawrence. *Rāj: The Making and Unmaking of British India.* New York: St. Martin's, 1997.

MARK F. PROUDMAN

Rumania

Rumania was created in 1858 by the merging of the **Danubian principalities** of Moldavia and Wallacia, which were rebellious Christian provinces of the **Ottoman Empire** subject to Russian intervention. Austria occupied the provinces between 1854 and 1857 until the Treaty of **Paris** guaranteed their autonomy. Rumania remained Ottoman until full sovereignty resulted from the **Russo-Turkish War** of 1877–1878. Prince Charles of Hohenzollern-Sigmaringen ruled as King Carol I from 1881 until 1914. Rumania participated in the Second **Balkan War** and acquired Southern Dobrudja as a territorial prize. Carol I maintained ties with the Triple Alliance, partly in resentful reaction against Russian favoritism toward Bulgaria in the Russo-Turkish War, and came progressively within Germany's sphere of influence, permitting direct railroad communication from Berlin and Vienna through Rumania to Constantinople in 1898. Rumania declared itself neutral when war broke out in 1914 but was induced to join the war on the Allied side in August 1916 with promises from France of Russia of territorial reward. *See also* Eastern Question.

FURTHER READING: Duggan, Stephen. *The Eastern Question: A Study in Diplomacy.* New York: AMS Press, 1970; Hitchins, Keith. *Rumania, 1866–1947.* Oxford: Clarendon Press, 1994.

CARL CAVANAGH HODGE

Rush-Bagot Treaty (1817)

An exchange of notes between Richard Rush, acting U.S. secretary of state, and Charles Bagot, British minister in Washington on April 28 and 29, 1817, in which the two nations agreed to limit their naval forces on the Great Lakes. President James Monroe officially proclaimed the exchange on April 28, 1818. After the War of 1812, intense Anglo-American naval competition had developed on Lake Ontario. To reduce the dangers, the agreement limited each nation to one vessel, maximum 100-ton burden with one 18-pound cannon, appropriate for enforcing revenue laws. On the Upper Lakes, each nation was limited to two vessels of like size and armament. All other warships would be decommissioned and no others would be built or armed.

The treaty, a mark of the rising continental power of the **United States,** was an important step in the long process of Anglo-American rapprochement and Canadian-American partnership building. The transatlantic and continental relationships that the treaty presaged were to shape international affairs throughout the twentieth century. *See also* Anglo-American War; Canada; Manifest Destiny.

FURTHER READING: Miller, Hunter, ed. *Treaties and Other International Acts of the United States of America.* Vol. II. Washington, DC: U.S. Government Printing Office, 1931, pp. 645–654; Perkins, Bradford. *Castlereigh and Adams: England and the United States, 1812–1823.* Berkeley: University of California Press, 1964.

KENNETH J. BLUME

Russell, Lord John (1792–1878)

A reforming prime minister of Great Britain, John Russell entered politics as a young man, and was by both family connection and conviction a reformist Whig and an admirer of Charles James **Fox.** He opposed the repressive measures of Lord **Liverpool**'s government, and became an early advocate of parliamentary reform. Although never a democrat, and opposed to a universal manhood suffrage, he played a prominent role in pushing the 1832 Reform Act, and the abortive bills that preceded it only to be rejected in the House of Lords, through the House of Commons. Russell became home secretary in under Lord Melbourne in the 1830s, where he pursued reformist policies, particularly with respect to Ireland. As the topic of the **Corn Laws** became prominent, Russell was one of the first Whigs to see the issue as a weapon with which to divide the Tories of Sir Robert **Peel.** When the Tories did in fact split in 1846, Russell succeeded Peel as prime minster.

Always friendly on principle to self-government, he had considerable doubts about the introduction of responsible government in **Canada,** fearing that an autonomous Canadian government might embroil Britain in quarrels with the **United States.** It was nevertheless under his premiership that the principle was conceded, establishing the model for colonial governance elsewhere in the settlement empire. With the Tories split, Russell's governments survived until 1852, when a dispute with his Foreign Secretary Lord **Palmerston** brought down the Whig government. Russell served as British plenipotentiary to negotiations with the Russia during the Crimean War, but found himself embarrassed by policy changes in London over the neutralization of the Black Sea. Russell was out of office until 1859, when Russell and Palmerston, the two leading Whigs, agreed to put aside their personal differences. Russell became foreign secretary under Palmerston, in which post he gave fulsome support to Italian unification. He also, however, incurred some blame for the British government's equivocal attitude toward the **American Civil War** and its negligence in allowing the Confederate ship *Alabama* to be built in a British yard. On Palmerston's death in 1865, Russell succeeded him, becoming once more prime minister. Russell brought in a reform bill promising a substantial extension of the franchise, which was defeated in 1866 owing to opposition from the antidemocratic section of his own party. Russell was succeeded in power by the Conservative administrations of Lord **Derby** and Benjamin **Disraeli.** Russell's primary concerns were in the realm of domestic reform, although for him, this category included Ireland. He was less bellicose than Palmerston, but like him supported European nationalists and liberals. His imperial policies were ad hoc, and in that respect typical of his age. *See also* Durham, John George Lambton, First Earl of.

FURTHER READING: Prest, John. *Lord John Russell.* London: MacMillan, 1972; Walpole, Spencer. *The Life of Lord John Russell.* London: Longman, Green and Co, 1891.

MARK F. PROUDMAN

Russian-American Company (RAC)

The Russian-American Company (RAC) (*Rossiisko-Amerikanskaia kompaniia*) was Russia's first joint-stock charter company; it oversaw the **Russian Empire**'s North American colony—"Russian America," mainly present-day **Alaska**—from 1799 until its transfer to the **United States** in 1867. The RAC was involved in a number of ventures, including the importation of tea and other products from **China** into Russia, but its primary specialty was the North Pacific fur trade. The company's distinguishing characteristic was its reliance on indigenous hunters to harvest marine mammals. It should be noted that there were never more than about 600 Russian colonists in all of Russian America at any one time. These colonists lacked the specialized skills necessary for hunting sea otters. To compensate for this lack of personnel and skills, the RAC employed thousands of Aleuts, Alutiiqs and "Creoles," people of mixed Russian and indigenous parentage.

The RAC was formed in 1799 out of the remnants of several Siberian merchant companies. Some of the merchants and government officials reasoned at the time that a single united Russian company, with government support, would be better equipped than the smaller companies to compete in the North Pacific fur trade against British and American rivals. They also hoped that a large united company would be more effective in securing potential territorial expansion. The RAC's name and structure indicate that it was modeled on the charter companies of other European countries, such as the **Hudson's Bay Company** and the **East India Company** of Great Britain. The mechanism of an ostensibly commercial company managing territory, populace, and resources on behalf of an empire had been unprecedented in Russia's colonial experience. Placed under the emperor's protection, and granted for a period of 20 years the exclusive right to profit from the resources of Russian America, the RAC functioned in practice as the Russian Empire's colonial contractor. The charter was renewed and revised twice in 1821 and 1844, and the company continued to preside over Russian America until 1867. With each charter renewal, the RAC became more enmeshed in Russia's imperial bureaucracy: that said, the company maintained its commercial function to the very end.

Merchants and nobles could purchase RAC shares. Those who owned 10 or more were eligible to vote at the annual general meeting of shareholders. The shareholders elected by majority vote four, later five, directors, who headed the main office of the company, located after 1800 in St. Petersburg. The main office functioned as the company's headquarters: it made the central business decisions, kept the government apprised of the company's activities, and sent orders to the colonial administration in Russian America and various RAC offices throughout Russia.

The colonial administration of Russian America was headquartered on Kodiak Island before 1808 and at Novo-Arkhangel'sk—present-day Sitka, Alaska—from 1808. Before 1818, the chief manager (in effect, governor) of Russian America was Aleksandr Baranov, a merchant with extensive experience in the Siberian and North American fur trade. After his retirement, only officers of Russia's imperial navy served as governors of Russian America. These naval officers, who belonged to the noble estate, were selected by the RAC main office from a list of eligible officers, and served in Novo-Arkhangel'sk for terms of up to five years. For a number of reasons, ranging from the precipitous fall in the population of marine fur-bearing animals to general conditions on the fur market, the RAC's fortunes peaked in the early nineteenth century and declined after Baranov's departure. In 1867, the Alaska Commercial Company of San Francisco purchased the North American property of the RAC. *See also* Canada.

FURTHER READING: Dmytryshyn, Basil. "The Administrative Apparatus of the Russian-American Company, 1798–1867." *Canadian-American Slavic Studies* 28/1 (1994): 1–52; Taylor, Alan. *American Colonies: The Settling of North America.* New York: Viking, 2001; Vinkovetsky, Ilya. "The Russian-American Company as a Colonial Contractor for the Russian Empire." In Alexei Miller and Alfred J. Rieber, eds. *Imperial Rule.* Budapest: Central European University Press, 2004, pp. 161–176; Wheeler, Mary E. "The Origins of the Russian-American Company." *Jahrbücher für Geschichte Osteuropas* 14/4 (1966): 485–494.

ILYA VINKOVETSKY

Russian Empire

During the nineteenth century, tsarist Russia was the largest contiguous empire in the world. Stretching from Polish lands in the west to the Vladivostok on the Pacific Ocean, the Russian Empire was a Eurasian power and consequently played a major role in international relations in Europe, the Middle East, Central Asia, and East Asia.

Expansion, East and West

The Russian Empire had its origins in the rise of the principality of Moscow. Starting as one among several competing Russian principalities, Moscow took the lead in overthrowing the yoke of Mongol overlordship, and the Grand Princes of Moscow succeeded subsequently in gathering the Russian lands under their singular authority. In the process, the rulers of Moscow transformed into autocratic sovereigns who held the title tsar. Ivan IV, "the Terrible" (1533–1584), was the first Muscovite ruler to be crowned tsar. During his reign, the Tsardom of Muscovy expanded beyond its Slavic, Orthodox Christian core. In the 1550s, Ivan conquered the Muslim Tatar khanates of Kazan and Astrakhan along the Volga River. By the time of his death in 1584, the Khanate of **Siberia** had also fallen to Moscow. Thus Russia was poised for expansion to the east across the Asian land mass. During the seventeenth century, tsarist control extended across Siberia all the way to Kamchatka, and Russia gained a border with the Chinese Empire by 1648. Simultaneously, Muscovy expanded westward by exerting its sovereignty over the cossacks of Ukraine.

Under Peter the Great (1689–1725), Muscovy became officially the Russian Empire. Peter took the title of Emperor in 1721 after having defeated Sweden in the Great Northern War (1700–1721). Thanks to this victory, Russia gained access to the Baltic Sea coast and incorporated the Baltic lands of Estonia and Latvia into the empire. As part of his goal to make Russia a great power in the European states system, Peter left the city of Moscow and built a new capital city on the Baltic at St. Petersburg. Peter bequeathed a legacy of modernization along Western lines that turned Russia into a major military power in the eighteenth century. In partnership with Austria, Peter tried to roll back the **Ottoman Empire** along the Black Sea coast and in the Balkans. Although Peter himself failed to achieve this objective, his successors brought the plan to fruition. Under Catherine the Great (1762–1796), Russia waged successful campaigns against the Ottomans and finally managed to gain territories along the Black Sea coast, including the Crimean Peninsula. In cooperation with Austria and Prussia, Russia participated in three partitions of Polish lands (1772, 1793, 1795) so that the independent Kingdom of **Poland** ceased to exist by the end of the century.

The Napoleonic Wars

In the first half of the nineteenth century, Russia reached its zenith in terms of power and prestige in the European states system. In general, Russia pursued a foreign policy that opposed France and cooperated with Austria and Prussia but during the first decade of the 1800s, during the **Napoleonic Wars,** Russia repeatedly suffered reversals at the hands of the French Emperor **Napoleon.** Under Tsar **Alexander I** (1801–1825), Russia joined the coalitions against Napoleonic France. When Napoleon invaded Austria in 1805, Russia came to the aid of its ally. Napoleon decisively defeated the Austrian and Russian armies at the battle of **Austerlitz,** however, and forced Alexander to retreat. The next year Napoleon attacked Prussia. Again, Alexander sent Russian forces to help stop the French—with similarly poor results. Alexander sued for peace. The resulting Treaty of **Tilsit** (1807) brought Russia into partnership with France. Alexander professed to hate the British as much as Napoleon did and promised to join Napoleon's **Continental System** by refraining from any trade with Britain. In return, Napoleon effectively made Russia the dominant power in Eastern Europe by giving Russia a free hand to expand against the Ottoman Empire on the Black Sea coast and against Sweden on the Baltic. Alexander took the opportunity to wage a predatory war against Sweden; the **Russo-Swedish War** of 1808–1809 ended with Russia gaining control of **Finland** as a grand duchy. Meanwhile, Russia also extended its reach temporarily to the southwest by occupying the Danubian principalities of Wallachia and Moldavia at the expense of the Ottomans, although these territories were evacuated in 1812. Despite these gains from the peace with Napoleon, the potential for conflict with France remained. Much to Napoleon's irritation, Alexander never seriously enforced the ban on trade with Britain. For his part, Napoleon had created the Grand Duchy of **Warsaw** out of Prussian territory to serve as a French satellite state for the Poles; the duchy posed a constant threat to the Polish lands under Alexander's control because it held out the prospect that Napoleon might restore an independent Poland at Russian expense. These latent conflicts moved both sides to prepare for an outbreak of hostilities.

Napoleon struck first. In June 1812, he crossed the border of the Russian Empire with a total force of 600,000 soldiers. Alexander's army had been expecting the attack but had underestimated the size of Napoleon's forces. Outnumbered and with their forces divided, the Russians hastily retreated. The French gave chase and forced the Russians to make a stand outside the city of Moscow at the Battle of **Borodino** in September 1812. After heavy fighting, the Russian army withdrew from the field and Napoleon entered Moscow. There the French Emperor waited for the Russians to come to terms, but Alexander refused to negotiate until every French soldier had left Russian soil; in the meantime, the army was reformed and re-equipped. With winter approaching, Napoleon decided to retreat from Moscow. Harried by the Russian army, the French retreat turned into a rout as only roughly 30,000 troops managed to escape. The victory of 1812 meant that Russia played a key role in the campaigns that ultimately defeated Napoleon and thereby became the dominant land power with the largest standing army in Europe.

Russian Great Power Diplomacy

The struggle against Napoleon affected Tsar Alexander deeply. He concluded that any revolutionary threat in Europe had to be crushed lest it facilitate the rise of another potential Napoleon. With that goal in mind, he initiated the **Holy Alliance,** which was to be a coalition of all the Christian monarchs of Europe dedicated to preserving the social and political status quo. Austria and Prussia joined the Holy Alliance on September 26, 1815, and, by doing so, laid the groundwork for cooperation among the three conservative monarchies. As part of the peace settlement at the Congress of **Vienna** in 1815, the majority of Polish land was consolidated into the Congress Kingdom of Poland with Alexander as its constitutional king. Russia, Prussia, and Austria had a common interest in preserving their control over their Polish dominions and in buttressing the monarchical principle against revolutionary and nationalistic challenges to its legitimacy.

The conservative and anti-French orientation of Russian policy continued under Alexander's brother and successor **Nicholas I** (1825–1855). Nicholas earned the epithet "the gendarme of Europe" for his willingness to use Russian military power to suppress revolution at home and abroad. When in 1830–1831 the Poles revolted to reclaim their national independence, Nicholas dispatched the Russian army to crush the uprising and in 1832 suspended the Polish constitution, effectively placing the Polish Kingdom under direct Russian rule. When revolutionary upheavals broke out across Europe in 1848, Nicholas sent troops into the Austrian Empire to help the Habsburg emperor defeat the Hungarian national revolt.

Under Tsar Nicholas, Russia projected its power into the lands of the Ottoman Empire and expanded into the **Caucasus.** When Nicholas came to the throne, the Greek War of Independence (1821–1832) from the Turks was already underway. Torn between supporting the Ottoman sultan as legitimate sovereign against revolution or backing the Greeks as fellow Orthodox Christians against their Muslim overlords, Nicholas at first stayed out of the conflict. Eventually, however, he resolved to come to the aid of the Greeks, and Russia defeated the Turks in the **Russo-Turkish War** of 1828–1829. By the end of the 1820s, Russia won out in the struggle against the Ottomans and Iranians for hegemony in the Caucasus region. The Kingdom of Eastern Georgia had already been annexed by Russia in 1801, but, thanks to its latest victories, by 1829 Russia also established a permanent presence in Transcaucasia, including eastern Armenia and all of the historic Georgian Kingdom. As part of the peace with the Ottomans, Russia secured an administrative role in the Ottoman territories of Moldavia and Wallachia.

Nicholas sought to keep relations with the Ottomans bilateral, but British and French interests in the region were growing; neither Western power recognized a special position for Russia in Ottoman affairs. In 1831, the French supported **Mehmet Ali** of Egypt in his campaign in Syria against the Ottoman sultan. In desperation, the sultan turned to Nicholas for help. In return for Russian aid to defend the Ottomans, the Turks permitted only Russian warships through the Turkish Dardanelles and Bosporus Straits as part of the secret Treaty of **Inkiar Skelessi** in 1833. The treaty marked the height of Russian influence in the Ottoman Empire, as the straits were closed to the French and British—a gain that was not reversed until the **Straits Convention** of 1841. Russia's position in the Ottoman Empire was then challenged by the French Emperor Napoleon III in the 1850s. In response to French moves to gain control of the keys to the Holy Places in Bethlehem and Jerusalem for the Catholic Church, in 1853 Nicholas sent an ultimatum to the Ottomans demanding that control of the keys be returned to the Orthodox Church. The deployment of Russian forces across the Danube into Moldavia and Walachia resulted in the outbreak of the **Crimean War** (1853–1856) in which Russia fought alone against the Ottoman Empire, Britain, France, and Sardinia. While the war was in progress, Nicholas died in 1855.

The Redirection of Imperial Ambition

Russia's defeat in the Crimea called its prestige into question because its large army ultimately proved ineffective against the industrial power of Britain and France. The new tsar, **Alexander II** (1855–1881), concluded the Treaty of Paris to end the Crimean War in 1856. The treaty's terms placed Turkey under the protection of all the European powers, which guaranteed Ottoman territorial integrity and thereby ended the unique position for Russia as the sole protector of Ottoman Christian populations. In addition, the Black Sea was neutralized, so that neither Russia nor Turkey could maintain fortifications or a fleet there, and Russia also lost the territory of southern Bessarabia and dominance over the Danubian principalities.

After the Crimean conflict, Russian policymakers were obsessed with bringing about a revision of the treaty. Russia was no longer a supporter of the status quo and was instead becoming a reactive power willing to embrace nationalisms and revolutions to change international circumstance in its favor. Taking to heart the lesson of Crimea—not to be caught without an ally—Russia tried to mend fences with France, but Napoleon III's support of the Polish Revolt in 1863 squelched any long-term understanding between the two powers. Russia's more passive policies toward Europe played an important role in enabling Prussia to bring about German unification. In return for supporting Prussia against Austria, for example, Russian foreign minister Alexander **Gorchakov** obtained German support to renounce the Black Sea treaty clauses and reestablish a Russian navy.

Another consequence of the Crimean defeat was increasing Anglo-Russian rivalry leading to the **Great Game** in Central Asia. Russia had a strong strategic interest in the Central Asian khanates, and the importance of Central Asia in Russian strategic planning developed further in the middle of the nineteenth century. It is true that there had been Russian military advances toward **Khiva** in the early decades of the eighteenth century, but it is an indication of a lack of strategic motive that no other Khivan campaigns occurred for the rest of that century. The strategic importance of the region evolved out of Russia's concerns about Britain. During the Crimean War, Britain had attempted to apply pressure to Russia through Central Asia by concluding an agreement with **Afghanistan** in 1855, and the possible approach to the Russian frontier of a strong British force caused considerable concern in St. Petersburg. So Britain's activities during the Crimean period gave direct impetus to a tsarist Central Asian policy.

In the post-Crimean era, Russia advanced from the Kazakh steppe into the Uzbek khanates of **Bukhara, Khiva,** and Kokand for reasons of geography and military prestige. Local military commanders stressed the advantage of pressuring the British in India by advancing into Central Asia as part of a Russian strategy to gain leverage over the British in the Ottoman Empire. In a memorandum written in 1861, policymakers voiced concern that if Britain managed to create a strong Afghanistan before the Russians got to Tashkent, the **British Empire** would rule Central Asia. Russian officers also sought glory and career advancement through easy and dramatic victories over the larger but less effective native forces of the khanates; having suffered a humiliating defeat in the Crimean War, they hoped to refurbish Russia's military image as a great imperial power in a region where the risks were low. In the period 1864–1873, Russian forces defeated each of the Uzbek khanates and either annexed the territory or created protectorates over them.

The Russia Empire again became militarily involved in the Balkans in the 1870s. In 1876, **Serbia** and Montenegro declared war against the Turks, but Ottoman armies easily defeated the two small Slavic states. Russia came to the aid of the rebels and imposed an armistice on the Turks that October. In preparation for a war against the Turks, the Austrians and the Russians agreed on the spoils of war beforehand, most notably on an arrangement on separate **spheres of influence:** Austria would get Bosnia, and Russia would gain a lesser **Bulgaria** as a protectorate. After signing a convention with Romania to transit Russian troops across its territory to fight Turkey, Russia declared war on the Ottoman Empire on April 12, 1877, thus initiating the Russo-Turkish War of 1877–1878. With Russian forces victorious and camped outside the Ottoman capital of Constantinople at the village of San Stefano, the Russians proclaimed the creation of a greater Bulgaria as a Russian protectorate. Under the terms of the Treaty of **San Stefano,** Russia gained free navigation of the straits, and Serbia and Romania were to gain territory. San Stefano aggravated British fears about an expanding Russia and upset Austria, whose government had agreed to the creation of only a lesser Bulgaria. German Chancellor Otto von **Bismarck** offered to mediate through an international congress in Berlin in 1878; as a result of this Congress of **Berlin** in 1878, the size of Bulgaria was reduced, but it was to remain in Russia's orbit. Furthermore, Austria gained administrative control over Bosnia, although the province remained technically a part of the Ottoman Empire. Russian dissatisfaction over having to relinquish the more spectacular gains of San Stefano, and Austria gained Bosnia without having fired a shot, fired an anti-German sentiment and helped to bring about the Austro-German defensive alliance against Russia.

Under Tsar **Alexander III** (1881–1894), who ascended the throne after revolutionaries assassinated his father, Russian policy turned away from the Balkans and again towards Asia. The tsar exhibited personal animosity toward Prince of Bulgaria Alexander of Battenberg and sought to have that prince removed from power by sanctioning his kidnapping; then in October 1886, Alexander broke off diplomatic relations with Bulgaria and never restored them for the remainder of his life. Thus Bulgaria ceased to be under Russian influence. In the meantime, Alexander's military forces continued to advance in Central Asia by conquering the Turkmen tribes along the Trans-Caspian area of present-day Turkmenistan between 1881 and 1885. Russian expansion then turned eastward, and a series of border encroachments almost led to war between Russia and Britain over control of Afghanistan. Nevertheless, cooler heads prevailed, as each side desired to avoid armed conflict in the heart of Asia; subsequently, Russia and Britain jointly delimited the borders of a neutral Afghanistan to serve as a buffer state between the two empires in 1895.

In Europe, a Franco-Russian alliance took shape between 1891 and 1894. After exchanging some official military visits, the warming culminated in a formal defensive alliance. The Franco-Russian **Dual Alliance** brought about a fundamental alteration in the European balance of power, for autocratic Russia and republican France had been bitter ideological foes and great power rivals for decades. The turnabout was largely influenced by strategic considerations. France was looking for an ally against Germany and saw in Russia a military counterweight on Germany's eastern border. Confronted by the Austro-German military alliance and experiencing tense relations with Britain in Central Asia, Russia also needed a Great Power ally and so committed to rendering military aid to France in the event of a German attack. The alliance endured for more than 20 years and contributed to the strategic tensions leading to World War I in 1914.

As a way to increase the Russian presence in Asia, the tsarist minister of finance, Sergei **Witte,** embarked in 1891 on the construction of the 6,000-mile long **Trans-Siberian Railroad** linking Moscow with Vladivostok in the Far East. Witte proposed the railroad as the chief solution to a variety of problems facing the empire. He reasoned that the railroad could be used to develop the Russian hinterland by providing the means to move people to the east. By facilitating homesteading on the Asian steppe lands of **Kazakhstan,** the population pressure of peasants in Central Russia would be eased, and new production zones would be developed in the east. This would in turn make the empire a player in world commerce because Russia would be positioned to engage directly in trade in China faster and more cheaply than its rivals. The railway to China could also position Russia to become an imperial actor inside China; as a shortcut, Witte arranged for a line of the Russian railroad to be built and operated across the territory of the Chinese Empire in Manchuria. The railroad had far-reaching consequences. The penetration of Russian commercial and strategic interests into Manchuria aroused the suspicions of **Japan.** Witte placed commercial interests ahead of military calculation in the region and desired to have peaceful cooperation with the Japanese in East Asia. Witte was dismissed by Tsar Nicholas II (1894–1917) in 1903, however, and the Japanese apprehension at Russian aggrandizement in East Asia, especially Korea, led to the **Russo-Japanese War** of 1904–1905, a military disaster for Russia.

Crisis at Home and Abroad

Defeat at the hands of Japan had profound effects on the Russian Empire, domestically and internationally. Domestically, the Russian Empire had governed autocratically more than 100 different subject nationalities and peoples practicing the Christian, Muslim, and Buddhist faiths; the tsar ruled as the sole source of power and authority without any legal constraint. Russia's poor performance in the Russo-Japanese War, however, now called into question the whole legitimacy of tsarist autocracy and contributed directly to the outbreak of the 1905 Revolution, which combined social unrest in Russia with nationalist uprisings in Poland and the Baltic provinces. In response to the gathering revolutionary pressures, Nicholas II was forced to grant constitutional concessions and the establishment of a parliamentary body known as the Duma. The tsar could no longer rule as an absolute monarch. Internationally, Russian policy now sought to reach accommodations in Asia, quickly securing understandings with Japan and Britain on the limits of its future ambitions there, while returning primary attention to the European theater. In 1907, the Anglo-Russian Convention resolved most of the outstanding territorial conflicts in Asia and established buffer zones between the rival empires in central Persia and Afghanistan. Russia gained a sphere of influence in northern Persia, while Britain acquired southern Persia along the Persian Gulf coast. Also, both powers renounced interest in Tibet. The convention thus eased longstanding tensions and paved the way for a more cooperative relationship between St. Petersburg and London that eventually yielded the **Entente Cordiale** of Russia, France, and Britain in 1914.

Weakened by war and revolution, Russia was in no position to handle a military conflict when another crisis erupted in the Balkans. In 1908, Austria formally annexed Bosnia, causing much consternation to Serbia, Russia's ally, whose government also had territorial designs on the former Ottoman province. The Serbs appealed to the Russians to compel the Austrians to renounce the annexation, but when Russia tried to pressure Vienna, Austria turned to its ally Germany for help. Germany threatened Russia with war unless St. Petersburg recognized Austria's annexation of Bosnia. Faced with the military might of Germany, Russia had to back down. This episode, known as the Bosnian Annexation Crisis (1908–1909), spurred Russia to view Austria as an aggressive threat to the entire Balkan region. To meet that perceived threat, Russian diplomacy therefore fostered a series of cooperative military alliances among the small Balkan states to serve as a bulwark against Austrian expansion into southeastern Europe. Under Russian auspices, the **Balkan League** brought together Serbia, Bulgaria, Greece, and Montenegro by September 1912. Unfortunately for St. Petersburg, the obstreperous Balkan states proved more interested in starting a war against the Turks than in holding back the Austrians. In October 1912, the Balkan League attacked the Turks in the First **Balkan War** and then fought among themselves in the second. Not wanting to choose among its erstwhile Balkan allies, Russia remained neutral and refused to mediate the territorial disputes that had arisen, but the inability to manage the situation by preventing war and controlling its small allies further eroded Russia's prestige in Europe. When the dust settled, Bulgaria had become hostile to St. Petersburg, and Serbia alone remained an important Russian ally in the Balkans. By 1914, St. Petersburg desperately sought some kind of diplomatic victory to prove that Russia still mattered as a great power and that its interests had to be respected by the Austro-German alliance. Thus when Serbia was threatened with an ultimatum from Austria after the assassination of the Austrian Archduke Francis Ferdinand in July 1914, the Serbs again looked to St. Petersburg for help, just as they had during the Bosnian crisis. Having been forced to retreat before the German-Austrian partnership once before, Russia felt compelled to draw the line this time to assert its status as a legitimate Great Power. Accordingly, St. Petersburg declared the mobilization of its army to come to the aid of the Serbs. In response, Germany declared war on Russia, and World War I began.

Russia's poor performance in World War I brought about the downfall of the tsarist empire. In the first weeks of the war, Russia honored its commitment to its French ally and launched an offensive into Germany. As a consequence of the haste of the mobilization and poor coordination among the Russian generals, however, the two Russian armies entering East Prussia were not at full strength and easily divided. The Germans dealt the Russians such a crushing defeat at the Battle of Tannenberg in August 1914 that Russia never threatened German soil for the remainder of the war. Russia fared better against Austria, as its armies advanced to the Carpathian Mountains. But Germany came to the aid of its Austria ally. Suffering a severe equipment shortage—only one-third of its soldiers had rifles—the Russian army had no choice but to retreat before the German onslaught. By September 1915, the German offensive had driven the Russians out of tsarist Poland and had advanced into the Baltic territories. In response to the long retreat, Nicholas II left St. Petersburg and assumed personal command of Russian forces in the field. This proved disastrous, as Russia's military problems and political incompetence eroded the remaining legitimacy of tsarist authority. In March 1917, mass demonstrations in the Russian capital turned into a revolution, and Nicholas was forced to abdicate. The Provisional Government that replaced the Tsar was itself overthrown by the Bolsheviks in November 1917, thus officially ending the Russian Empire. *See also* Appendix Words and Deeds, Docs. 3, 6, 12, 13; French Empire; German Empire; Habsburg Empire; Japanese Empire.

FURTHER READING: Geyer, Dietrich. *Russian Imperialism: The Interaction of Domestic and Foreign Policy, 1860–1914.* New York: Berg, 1987; Hosking, Geoffrey. *Russia, People and Empire.* Cambridge, MA: Harvard University Press, 1997; Kennan, George. *The Fateful Alliance: France, Russia, and the Coming of the First World War.* New York: Pantheon, 1984; Lieven, Dominic. *Empire, The Russian Empire and Its Rivals.* New Haven, CT: Yale University Press, 2002; Ragsdale, Hugh. *Imperial Russian Foreign Policy.* Cambridge: Cambridge University Press, 1993; Rywkin, Michael. *Russian Colonial Expansion to 1917.* London: Mansell, 1988; Seton-Watson, Hugh. *The Russian Empire, 1801–1917.* Oxford: Clarendon, 1967.

JONATHAN GRANT

Russian Far East

A somewhat elastic term referring to Russia's Pacific littoral, stretching from Vladivostok in the south to the Anadyr Peninsula in the north, and including the Amur region, Kamchatka Peninsula, and **Sakhalin.** Before the late nineteenth century, the region was administered as part of **Siberia** but has since been administered separately. Those living in the region are keen to distinguish themselves from Siberians proper.

As early as 1700, Cossack explorers arrived on the Kamchatka Peninsula, where they established the port of Petropavlovsk. This served as a departure point for the

Great Northern Expeditions led during the 1730s by Vitus Bering, who discovered the straits that bear his name. The Russians went on to acquire Alaska, build Fort Ross in northern California, and even appear briefly on Hawai'i. Russia's hold on these latter regions proved temporary, but it retained its role as a major power in the North Pacific.

It nonetheless paid little attention to the region before the mid-nineteenth century. Problems with logistics and communications bedeviled St. Petersburg's ability to do much in the Far East, and its focus was directed west and south. Russia's humiliation in the **Crimean War** combined with the decline of Qing China, however, sparked a renewed interest in the East. In the late 1850s, eastern Siberia's Governor-general Nikolai Nikolaevich Muravev easily wrested the vast, resource-rich Amur region from China. Imperial visionaries saw the Amur River as a "Russian Mississippi" and hoped it would prove a conduit for trade throughout the Pacific. Nikolaevsk-on-the-Amur was founded at the mouth of the river, followed in 1860 by Vladivostok ("Ruler of the East") on the southernmost point of Russia's Pacific shoreline. Both ports supported the settlement and annexation of Sakhalin, especially after the **St. Petersburg Treaty** of 1875.

Imperial visionaries' dreams remained unrealized, however. Vast expanses separated the Russian Far East from Siberia's most important cities, such as Irkutsk, Eniseisk, and Tobolsk, and so communications and logistics problems remained stumbling blocks. Indeed, the first contiguous motorway linking Vladivostok to the interior was only constructed in the 1990s. Also, despite the emancipation of the serfs in 1861, strict government control over land allocation stymied free migration to the region. As a result, the Russian Far East rapidly became an extension of "the enormous prison without a roof" that was Siberia. This was especially the case with Sakhalin, which became a tsarist penal colony.

Nevertheless, a milestone 1889 migration law as well as construction of the **Trans-Siberian Railroad**—contiguously linked in 1904, but serviceable several years earlier—facilitated the Russian Far East's free settlement during the empire's final years. The region also experienced considerable immigration from **Korea** and **China.** By 1911, the Russian Far East boasted a total population of 855,000. Its population density was only .4 person per square *verst*—a *verst* equaling two-thirds of a mile—but settlement was overwhelmingly concentrated in the south. Vladivostok, for example, grew from 14,500 in 1890 to 107,900 by 1926.

The railroad and the migration law grew out of the "Far Eastern Policy" originating after Russia's defeat in the Crimean War. The rhetorical formulas used to justify this policy demonstrate a uniquely Orthodox Christian and Slavic version of the "white man's burden." Russia's construction of the Manchurian Railroad and its occupation of **Port Arthur** on Korea's Liaotung Peninsula were to a large extent physical manifestations of its notion of a "divine right" to dictate terms to East Asia's inhabitants, but also reflected more rationally conceived strategies to rebuff Japan's own imperialistic maneuvers. War with Japan was the result and led, as had the Crimean War of a half century earlier, to another defeat that undermined Russians' faith in their tsar. *See also* Japanese Empire; Manchuria; Russian Empire; Russo-Japanese War.

FURTHER READING: Bassin, Mark. *Imperial Visions: Nationalist Imagination and Geographical Expansion in the Russian Far East, 1840–1865.* Cambridge: Cambridge University Press, 1999;

Stephan, John J. *The Russian Far East: A History.* Stanford, CA: Stanford University Press, 1994; Treadgold, Donald W. *The Great Siberian Migration: Government and Peasant in Resettlement from Emancipation to the First World War.* Princeton, NJ: Princeton University Press, 1957.

ANDREW A. GENTES

Russian Revolution (1905)

The Russian Revolution of 1905 was the first act in the collapse of tsarist rule in Russia. The main reason for the outbreak of the first Russian Revolution of 1905 was the slowness of social and cultural reforms in response to the disparity of accelerated economic modernization that began much later than in Western Europe and the **United States** than in Russia.

The peasant liberation of 1861 resulted in a massive migration, from the countryside into the cities of the Russian Empire, of unskilled and uneducated workers who were not able to adapt to a modern urban life and therefore provided a breeding ground for social unrest in the cities. After the Napoleonic Wars and the Crimean War, Russian intellectuals were discontented with reforms in education and resented the rigid control and censorship imposed since Alexander III. Although willing to modernize the empire, Russia's bureaucratic and military elite were ultraconservative and sought to keep their privileges intact.

An adventurist foreign policy in Asia, the disaster of the **Crimean War,** and finally the humiliation of the **Russo-Japanese War** of 1904–1905 also revealed the incompetence and corruption of the tsarist regime. The Russian revolution of 1905 began in the Russian capital, in St Petersburg on January 22, 1905, when troops fired on a defenseless crowd of workers. This "bloody Sunday" was followed by a series of riots and strikes that encompassed all regions of the Russian Empire, all social classes, and all nationalities from St Petersburg to Vladivostok. A general strike forced Tsar **Nicholas II** to issue the **October Manifesto,** granting civil liberties and a parliament, the Duma, to be elected democratically. The limited power of the Duma, however, did not satisfy the rebelling workers, peasants, and nationalities. As the revolution of 1905 spread to non-Russian provinces of the empire, it stimulated national movements in the Baltic region, in **Poland,** Finland, the Caucasus, and Central Asia. In many regions, revolts were put down by antirevolutionary, ultra-extremist Black Hundreds who massacred socialists, Jews, and Muslims. In 1905, revolution in Russia failed, although the tsarist autocracy changed to a constitutional monarchy, and 1905 became the prelude to the revolution of 1917. Social discontent and nationalism went hand in hand and created an explosive mixture that burst forth with World War I. *See also* Bolsheviks.

FURTHER READING: Ascher, Abraham. *The Revolution of 1905: A Short History.* Stanford, CA: Stanford University Press, 2004; Weinberg, Robert. *The Revolution of 1905 in Odessa.* Bloomington: Indiana University Press, 1993.

EVA-MARIA STOLBERG

Russo-Khokandian War (1864–1865)

The inauguration of the Russian conquest of Khokand khanate. During the middle of the 1860s, Russia and the Khokand khanate competed for the same territories in Central Asia. This led to the 1864–1865 war over territories mostly in the area of present-day Uzbekistan and Kazakhstan. Before Russian entry into the oases areas of Central Eurasia, Khokand's main competitor was the emirate of Bukhara. The Khokand khanate was a vigorously productive and expanding state in the first half of the nineteenth century. Squabbles with Bukhara and internal political turmoil in the 1850s and early 1860s greatly weakened Khokand.

Russia started making its first sustained advance into Central Asia as early as about 1730. The Russians carried out a period of gradual conquest throughout the rest of the eighteenth century and early-nineteenth century across the Kazakh steppe. By mid-century, the Russian military machine was in position to use its vast and superior resources against the Central Eurasian states and peoples. After brief interludes to focus on the Crimean War and the revolt of Shamil in the Caucasus, by the 1860s Russia was ready to make an assault on the southern part of the Kazakh steppe. Under the command of General Mikhail **Cherniaev,** the Russian forces took the southern Kazakh city of Aulie-ata (in less than two hours) in June 1864. Cherniaev believed that Chimkent would fall as easily, but victory there was much more difficult to achieve. After a failed initial attack, Cherniaev retreated to Turkestan for reinforcements. The second Russian attack on Chimkent, in September 1864, was an unqualified success. This was to mark, for the Russian administration, the final victory for Russia in Central Eurasia; however, Cherniaev's decision to attack Tashkent altered that.

Russian forces advanced on Tashkent in 1865, against the expressed opinion of the Russian government and foreign minister Alexander Mikhailovich **Gorchakov.** Gorchakov believed that if Russians advanced beyond Chimkent, the empire ran the risk of involving itself in endless wars with Central Eurasian states and peoples. Despite official government opinion, General Cherniaev led the Russian military attack on Tashkent, feeling that the Russian forces would be unstoppable. He was largely correct on this score, as the Russians captured Tashkent and Cherniaev earned the nickname "The Lion of Tashkent." He was dismissed from his military duties in Central Eurasia, however, following this victory at Tashkent. The Russian conquest of Tashkent cleared the way for the creation of the 1865 Steppe Commission led by Minister of War Dimitry Miliutin and the formal establishment of the **Turkestan** colony in 1867. *See also* Afghanistan; Bukhara Emirate; Great Game; Russian Empire.

FURTHER READING: Allworth, Edward, ed. *Central Asia: 130 Years of Russian Dominance, A Historical Overview.* Durham and London: Duke University Press, 1994; MacKenzie, David. *The Lion of Tashkent: The Career of General M. G. Cherniaev.* Athens: University of Georgia Press, 1974.

SCOTT C. BAILEY

Russo-Japanese War (1904–1905)

A conflict between Russia and Japan that epitomized the violent struggles between powerful nations in the age of **imperialism.** As **China**'s strength and prestige ebbed in the face of Western aggression, the tsar's government attempted to consolidate its Maritime Provinces around Vladivostok, which it had founded in 1860. Accordingly, the Russians planned to control **Manchuria** and **Korea,** which the Chinese were unable any longer to protect. Japan had defeated the Chinese in 1895, but its own plans to take over Port Arthur and to dominate the rest of southern Manchuria were thwarted by the intervention of the Russians, Germans, and French. Bitterly humiliated by losing the fruits of its military success, and by the lease that the Russians subsequently acquired over **Port Arthur,** Tokyo determined to go to war to expel the Russians from Korea and southern Manchuria.

Japanese success in the ensuing conflict astonished most Western observers who had exaggerated Russian and deprecated Japanese power. Russia had, after all, long been considered one of the most powerful European nations with the largest army; Japan had been forced to open its ports to outside trade only in the 1850s and still tended to be bracketed with China, despite its victory over the Chinese in 1895. Negotiations between Russia and Japan for a compromise were broken off and, on February 8, 1904, the Japanese landed troops in Korea, despite half-hearted opposition from the Russian gunboat, Korietz. They also launched a preemptive, night-time torpedo boat strike on the Russian fleet moored outside Port Arthur.

The Japanese won every subsequent battle of importance on land and sea. They secured their position in Korea and, despite opposition from 30,000 Russian troops, crossed the Yalu river into Manchuria in May 1904. Here they fought numerous lesser battles and two decisive ones, involving hundreds of thousands of soldiers, at **Liaoyang** in August 1904 and at **Mukden** in February and March 2005. In both cases they forced the Russians out of their entrenchments back along the railway to the north. General Alexey Kuropatkin, the Russian commander, could not allow his rail communications to be menaced or his forces to be encircled. The Russians' withdrawal by 40 miles from Liaoyang in August was reasonably orderly, but, after the loss of Mukden, Russian troops panicked and the retreat turned into a rout. Even though the retreating forces consolidated their position further north around Harbin, morale was, not surprisingly, very low and Sir Montagu Gerard, the senior British officer with the Russian forces, commented that "all the foreign officers, whom I have met, consider the defeat at Mukden to be absolutely decisive and that nothing short of a brilliant naval success can ever change the situation."

In the south of Manchuria, Russian forces in Port Arthur had been cut off in May and besieged from June 1904 onward. The port acted as a magnet to General Maresuke Nogi's forces because it was here that the powerful Russian Pacific fleet was based. At great cost the Japanese drove the port's defenders backward until they could bring their siege train to bear on the fleet using observers on 203 Metre Hill. This was the key point in the defenses and was finally captured after bitter fighting on November 30. Previously, the Russian warships had made one serious attempt to escape to Vladivostok on August 10, 1904. They might have succeeded, according to Captain Pakenham, the British officer observing the battle from the Japanese fleet, but the flagship, *Tsarevitch*, was disabled at long range, throwing the Russian line into disorder, and their ships retreated again into harbor. The fleet was destroyed by the Japanese artillery in December 1904, and with its principal raison d'être gone, the port itself and 25,000 Russian personnel surrendered the next month.

Tsar **Nicholas II**'s government sent mass reinforcements thousands of miles along the newly built **Trans-Siberian Railway,** raising the carrying capacity of the line from 9 trains a day each way to 16 or 17 during the course of the fighting. For the tsarist regime, the line was usually under the management of someone who had been appointed for his efficiency, rather than rank. "Prince" Khilkoff had risen from poverty, gaining experience of running railways in Pennsylvania and Venezuela before returning to Russia. In contrast, Russian efforts to send reinforcements by sea to East Asia, typified the incompetence of the regime. In October 1904, the Baltic fleet began its 21,000-mile journey around the world to challenge Admiral Togo's warships. The Russians achieved notoriety by firing on British fishing boats in the North Sea in October 1904 after mistaking them for torpedo boats. In the volatile political atmosphere, this might have brought Britain into the war and thus compelled the French to help their Russian allies. Fortunately, a compromise was reached under which the Russians paid compensation for the damage. Thus Rear-Admiral Zinovy Rojestvensky's ships made their way slowly round the world, coaled with Welsh fuel by the Hamburg-Amerika Line, until the jumble of old and new warships, pressed into service because of Russia's desperate situation, was obliterated by the Japanese in the Straits of **Tsushima** on May 27, 1905.

Most of the Great Powers had no interest in seeing the war spread or even continue. The French government feared their alliance with Russia would embroil them with Britain just when they were hoping to improve relations. Britain had allied with Japan in 1902 to deter Russian expansion in East Asia without increasing its own forces there, but it had not expected its new ally to attack. It was content to see Russia weakened but not to the point where Germany would dominate the continent. President Theodore **Roosevelt** asserted Washington's international position by bringing the belligerents to the negotiating table at Portsmouth, New Hampshire, in August 1905. The Russian negotiators were led by Count Sergey Witte, the former Minister of Transport and Finance, who had been largely responsible for the rapid industrialization of the country; the Japanese were led by the Foreign Minister Jutaro Komura. The Russians quickly accepted the verdict of the war, including Japan's paramount position in Korea, the evacuation of southern Manchuria, and the handing over to Japan of the lease on Port Arthur and the Liaotung Peninsula. But the Russians refused to pay reparations or to accept formal limitations on their naval forces in the Pacific and, under pressure from Roosevelt, the Japanese gave way.

The Treaty of **Portsmouth,** signed on September 5, allowed Japan to dominate Korea for the next 40 years, despite the bitter opposition of the Korean people, which began as a guerrilla uprising by what the Koreans called the Righteous Armies. Japan was also predominant in southern Manchuria, but Russia was left in control of **Vladivostok** and of the northern part of **Sakhalin.** Given the utter failure of Russian armed forces and the widespread revolution that ensued in Russia, Witte had played a weak hand to brilliant effect, and Japanese nationalists demonstrated their disappointment by staging mass riots. After 1895, the Japanese had paid for their war against China, the expansion of their armed forces and the costs of their royal family, by squeezing indemnities out of the Chinese, but it was many years before the loans raised for the war against Russia were repaid.

Militarily, the Russo-Japanese War was important because it presaged many of the features of World War I including trenches, barbed wire, machine guns, heavy artillery, and the comparative impotence of cavalry. It demonstrated the difficulty of advancing against well-prepared troops and of controlling the hundreds of thousands of soldiers whom modern technology could move to the battlefield.

Geopolitically, it was important because it was the first time that a European power had been defeated by Asiatics using modern technology, and it encouraged anticolonial nationalists from India to Egypt. Diplomatically, it meant first that Japan had to be considered one of the Great Powers and its views taken into account. Second, Russia's weakening paved the way to the **Triple Entente** of France, Britain, and Russia, which confronted Germany and Austria-Hungary in the run-up to World War I.

The Russo-Japanese War was also important for what it did not do. While European and American commentators were shocked by the number of casualties and the suffering caused to the Koreans and Chinese, they chose not to dwell so much on the horrors of war and thus the danger of a conflict between the European nations. Rather, the numerous war correspondents and editorial writers who followed the war's progress mainly saw it as a proof of **Social Darwinism,** that international relations were a constant struggle for survival and that the weak would be destroyed. China and Korea could no longer protect themselves, so they would be crushed and colonized by the strong. Russia had proved itself too weak and must rearm and develop its industry to reassert its position among the nations. Thus the war made a significant contribution to the political atmosphere and diplomatic tensions that led up to the greater catastrophe in August 1914. *See also* Japanese Empire; Russian Empire; Sino-Japanese War.

FURTHER READING: Connaughton, Richard. *Rising Sun and Tumbling Bear: Russia's War with Japan.* London: Weidenfeld and Nicolson, 2003; Ethus, Raymond A. *Theodore Roosevelt and Japan.* Seattle: University of Washington Press, 1974; Warner, Dennis, and Warner, Peggy. *The Tide at Sunrise.* London: Frank Cass, 2002; White, John Albert. *The Diplomacy of the Russo-Japanese War.* Princeton, NJ: Princeton University Press, 1964.

PHILIP TOWLE

Russo-Swedish War (1808–1809)

A secondary theater of the **Napoleonic Wars** brought on by the provisions of the 1807 Treaty of **Tilsit,** which made allies of France and Russia. After the treaty the two countries demanded that Sweden abandon the Fourth Coalition and declare war on Britain. Sweden's quixotic King Gustavus IV refused, whereupon a Russian army invaded Finland, an integral part of the Swedish Empire since 1154. The decisive engagement was joined at the fortress of Sveaborg in Helsinki harbor, where a garrison of 7,000 Swedes and Finns held off the Russian invaders for three months before surrendering on May 3, 1808. The tsar declared Finland a grand duchy of Russia, and Gustavus was toppled in a coup d'état in March 1909. Swedish forces continued the fight until the following September, when the Treaty of Frederikshavn gave Finland and the Åland Islands to Russia. *See also* Russian Empire.

FURTHER READING: Rothenberg, Gunther E. *The Napoleonic Wars.* London: Cassell, 1999.

CARL CAVANAGH HODGE

Russo-Turkish War (1806–1812)

A secondary conflict occasioned by the **Napoleonic Wars.** Emboldened by the Russian defeat at **Austerlitz,** the **Porte** replaced the Russophile hospodars of Moldavia and Wallachia with Ottoman appointees without consulting with the Tsar's government. In the absence of consultation, Russia had the official *causus belli*, but an additional factor was the fear of an Ottoman alliance with France that might close the Straits to Russian warships. In response to a Russian ultimatum supported by Britain, the Porte relented over the hospodar appointments, but the tsar demanded further concessions and occupied Moldavia and Wallachia with 40,000 troops, both as a hedge against a French attack in the region and as prod to rebellious Christian enclaves in the Balkans to make common cause with Russia against the **Ottoman Empire.** The Porte therefore declared war on December 22, opening a war for which neither side was prepared and dragged on for six years. Ultimately, Britain mediated the conflict, and the Treaty of Bucharest acknowledged Ottoman control of Moldavia and Wallachia in exchange for an adjustment of the Russian border that gave Bessarabia to the tsar. *See also* Danubian Principalities; Russian Empire.

FURTHER READING: Rothenberg, Gunther E. *The Napoleonic Wars.* London: Cassell, 1999.

CARL CAVANAGH HODGE

Russo-Turkish War (1828–1829)

A conflict occasioned by Russia's opportunistic support for Greek independence to secure for itself new territorial leverage in the Caucasus and the Balkans at the expense of the **Ottoman Empire.** Russia issued a declaration of war to the **Porte** on April 28, 1828, and launched a two-pronged offensive, one southward into Walachia across the Danube and ultimately against the fortified port of Varna on the west coast of the Black Sea, the other southeast against Kars, Erivan, and Adrianople. When Adrianople was captured on August 20, 1829, Constantinople came under threat and the Porte sought terms. The Treaty of **Adrianople** improved Russia's position by giving it control of the mouth of the Danube and the eastern Black Sea shore and establishing a *de facto* **protectorate** over Moldavia and Wallachia. *See also* Danubian Principalities; Eastern Question; Russian Empire.

FURTHER READING: Anderson, M. S. *The Eastern Question 1774–1923.* London: Macmillan, 1966; Jelavich, Barbara. *A Century of Russian Foreign Policy 1814–1914.* Philadelphia: J. B. Lippincott, 1964.

CARL CAVANAGH HODGE

Russo-Turkish War (1877–1878)

The fourth armed conflict between the Russians and the Turks in the nineteenth century, this war was a pivotal turning point in the history of the **Eastern Question.** It resulted in independence for **Serbia, Rumania,** and Montenegro. It also led to Austrian occupation of Bosnia and Russian dominance in Bulgaria.

After Turkish troops had ruthlessly suppressed revolts by Orthodox Christian subjects in Bosnia and Bulgaria in 1875–1876, Serbia and Montenegro declared war against Turkey. Although the Russian government stood aside, Russian military volunteers, including General Chernaiev, a Russian war hero from the Central Asian campaigns, flocked to join Serbian forces to aid in the fight against the Turks. By 1876, these forces had failed miserably and the tsarist government stepped in diplomatically to preserve Serbian autonomy from Turkish repression. When the

Turks proved resistant to administrative reforms proposed by Russia, Austria, and Germany, the tsarist government prepared for war. To gain Austrian acquiescence, Russia promised to allow Austrian occupation of Bosnia in return for Austrian recognition of a small Bulgaria under Russian protection. Austria pledged its neutrality in the event of a Russo-Turkish conflict by signing the Treaty of Budapest on January 15, 1877. By February 1877, Russian forces were massing for an offensive out of the south through Rumania. The Rumanians granted Russia permission to transit through their country on April 4, 1877, and they offered Rumanian troops to join in the fight. Russia rejected the offer of Rumanian military assistance, but did cross through Rumania after officially declaring war on Turkey on April 24.

The military campaigns were fought in two theaters, Bulgaria and the Caucasus, and lasted until the armistice on January 31, 1878. The Russians advanced to the Danube River on June 22, and the Turks began to retreat. The largest body of Turkish troops regrouped at the fortress of Plevna, which guarded the western approach to Sofia. At Plevna, Ottoman armies under the command of Osman Pasha and armed with American-made repeater rifles and German steel artillery held off superior Russian numbers through two assaults and forced the Russians to look to Rumania for additional troops. In the Third Battle of Plevna in September 1877, combined Russian and Rumanian forces totaling 118,000 failed to take the fortress by storm, and the Russians abandoned the attack for siege operations. In December the Turks at Plevna finally surrendered, clearing the way for a Russian advance to the outskirts of Constantinople. *See also* Crimean War; Ottoman Empire; Russian Empire.

FURTHER READING: Breyfogle, Nicholas B. *Heretics and Colonizers: Forging Russia's Empire in the South Caucasus.* Ithaca, NY: Cornell University Press, 2005; Geyer, Dietrich. *Russian Imperialism: The Interaction of Domestic and Foreign Policy, 1860–1914.* New York: Berg, 1987; Macfie, A. L. *The Eastern Question, 1774–1923.* London: Longman, 1996; Seton-Watson, Hugh. *The Russian Empire, 1801–1917.* Oxford: Clarendon, 1967.

JONATHAN GRANT

S

Saar

Also known as Saarland or Saar Territory, a region comprising approximately 991 square miles and located in southwestern Germany. It is bordered by France in the south and west and by Luxembourg in the northwest. Control of the Saar was a source of conflict between Germany and France for centuries. Named after the major river running through the region, the Saar's population is predominately Catholic and German-speaking. Until the late eighteenth century, Saar was divided between France and other German principalities, but in 1797, the Treaty of Campo Formio ceded it to France. The 1815 Treaty of **Paris** divided the Saar territory between **Bavaria** and **Prussia.**

In the era before World War I, both nationalism and industrial competition made Saarland and Alsace-Lorraine important regions to both France and Germany. Not only did both territories have historical and cultural ties to both nations, but the iron ore deposits in Lorraine and the extensive coalfields of Saarland enabled the region to serve as a center for heavy industry. After the **Franco-Prussian War** in 1871, Germany gained Alsace-Lorraine and capitalized on its industrial potential in combination with the Saar territory. *See also* German Empire.

FURTHER READING: Cowan, L. Gray. *France and the Saar, 1680–1948.* New York: Columbia University Press, 1950; Russell, Frank Marion. *The Saar: Battleground and Pawn.* Stanford, CA: Stanford University Press, 1951.

ERIC MARTONE

Sadowa, Battle of

See Königgrätz, Battle of

Sakhalin

A large, sturgeon-shaped island north of Hokkaidō in the Pacific. Despite the island's exploration and mapping by Chinese, Japanese, and Dutch explorers centuries earlier, by the mid-nineteenth century its population, with the exception of a few Japanese seasonal fisherman, still consisted of Ainu, Giliak, and Orok natives. In the 1850s, the **Russian Empire,** seeing in Sakhalin a fortress to protect the mouth of the Amur River and having discovered its coal deposits, sought to dominate it. Although Japan declared sovereignty over the island as early as 1845, in 1855 it signed the Treaty of **Shimoda,** giving its northern half to Russian and its southern half to Japan. By 1859, both private and state mines were operating on the island. A foreign concern named Oliphant & Company briefly operated several mines, but it was soon excluded by a regulation forbidding such foreign ownership.

Russia formally annexed Sakhalin in the 1875 Treaty of **St. Petersburg,** when Japan ceded its half to Russia in exchange for the Kuril Islands to the east of Sakhalin. That same year I. N. Butkovskii, a tsarist state councilor, obtained a highly favorable mining lease that permitted him the use of convict laborers. This, combined with the collapse of the penal labor system (*katorga*) on the mainland and limitations on free migration, led to Sakhalin's transformation into a penal colony—tsarist Russia's version of New Caledonia. Convicts and their families were shipped halfway around the world from Odessa and, by 1905, accounted for the bulk of the island's population of 40,000.

Dreams of an autarkic colony failed to materialize, however, as turning convicts into farmers generally proved impossible. Sakhalin became instead a drain on the treasury and an indictment of tsarism. Conditions were dreadful in the prisons but even worse in the countryside, where a Hobbesian netherworld developed to witness parents marketing their young daughters as prostitutes. Conditions somewhat improved before the Japanese invaded in early July 1905—the only invasion of Russian territory during the **Russo-Japanese War.** But as if to pass final judgment on the penal colony, inmates razed its main prison. The Treaty of **Portsmouth** changed possession of Sakhalin again, this time awarding to Japan all territory south of 50° north latitude. *See also* Japanese Empire.

FURTHER READING: Chekhov, Anton. *The Island: A Journey to Sakhalin.* Translated by Luba and Michael Terpak. Westport, CT: Greenwood Press, 1967; Stephan, John J. *Sakhalin: A History.* Oxford: Clarendon Press, 1971.

ANDREW A. GENTES

Salisbury, Robert Arthur James Gascoyne-Cecil, Marquess of (1830–1903)

Salisbury was three times Conservative prime minister of the United Kingdom, most notably during the Second Boer War of 1899–1902. Salisbury was elected as Lord Robert Cecil to Parliament as a Tory in 1853 and also made a name for himself as a trenchant if polemical journalist and reviewer. He was briefly secretary of state for **India** in the Tory government of 1866 but resigned in opposition to Benjamin **Disraeli**'s 1867 reform bill, which he thought too democratic. He became Indian secretary again in Disraeli's 1874 government and was promoted foreign secretary in 1878. In the latter post, he played a prominent role in the **Berlin Conference** of 1878, which temporarily settled a complicated series of Balkan problems occasioned by the decline of the Turkish Empire, while avoiding a wider war between the great powers. Although Salisbury was at the Foreign Office during the Second Afghan War of 1878–1881, and the Zulu War of 1879, both of those campaigns had been instigated by local officials acting under the authority of the Colonial Office, and he deplored the tendency of ambitious or impatient local proconsuls—the "man on the spot" in the famous Victorian phrase—to push the frontiers of empire forward at the cost of repeated wars. Although no anti-imperialist, Salisbury was as skeptical of imperialist enthusiasm as he was of other kinds, and for all his profound conservatism, he was no kind of militarist.

Salisbury served as a minority prime minster from June 1885 to January 1886. After the split of the **Liberal Party** over William **Gladstone**'s Irish **Home Rule** project in 1886, he had a solid majority from 1886 to 1892. The Tories and their allies again did well in the election of 1895, and once more in the so-called Khaki election of 1900, during the Boer War. Salisbury served as his own foreign secretary for 11 of his 14 years as prime minister. Foreign policy was his chief intellectual and political interest, and he viewed the Empire as a tool of British policy rather than the reverse. Although the period saw a great deal of popular and political pressure for imperial expansion, especially in east and west Africa, Salisbury's priority was the smooth management of relations with the other great powers, chiefly France and Germany, rather than the expansion of British rule in Africa or anywhere else. In Salisbury's view, Britain's highest interest was peace, and to that interest he subordinated most others.

The years of Salisbury's last two governments, from 1895 on, saw repeated imperial crises as the major powers jockeyed for position in the remaining unclaimed areas of the world. The defeat of the **Jameson Raid** on the Transvaal in December 1895 provoked the kaiser's congratulatory telegram to Transvaal President Paul Kruger, which embittered Anglo-German relations. Although Salisbury appears to have been unaware of preparations for the raid, his Colonial Secretary Joseph **Chamberlain** did have prior knowledge that Jameson's force was preparing to intervene. The freelance invasion also embittered relations with the Boer republics, leading to war four years later, contrary to Salisbury's hopes that Boer resistance to incorporation into a British South Africa would collapse of its own accord.

The Italian defeat at **Adowa** in east Africa in 1897 prompted Salisbury's government to send an expedition under General **Kitchener** south into the Sudan, against the Islamist government of that country, headed by the son of General Charles **Gordon**'s old enemy the Mahdi. Victory at **Omdurman** in September 1898 led to a further advance up the Nile to Fashoda, provoking the famous collision with Captain Marchand's small French force, which had marched overland from French West Africa. The **Fashoda Crisis** was resolved by a French retreat in November 1898. In the meantime, crises over imperial and trade advantages in China erupted between Germany, Russia, and Britain, **China** being famously described by Salisbury in the vaguely Darwinist argot of the time as a "dying nation." Salisbury was able to avoid the threat of major war over China, and cooperated with the other western powers in putting down the **Boxer Insurrection** of 1900.

Salisbury's government made good relations with the **United States** a priority, notwithstanding Salisbury's Tory antipathy to that country. He agreed in 1897 to an arbitrated settlement of disputes with the United States concerning the border between Venezuela and British Guyana and signed the **Hay-Pauncefote** Treaty of 1901, by which Britain dropped its objections to the American project for a Panamanian canal. During the **Spanish-American War** of 1898, Salisbury worked to keep the other European powers neutral, a policy that was effectively pro-American. Salisbury's government also made significant concessions on the Canadian-Alaskan border.

But the greatest crisis of the period was in South Africa between the Boer republics of the Transvaal and the Orange Free State and the British authorities, who demanded political rights for the British miners attracted by the Transvaal's gold. The Boers resolved to preserve their political independence; the British, led by Salisbury's proconsul Sir Alfred Milner, were determined to force the two republics into a united, British-dominated South Africa. War broke out in October 1899. Although the British were eventually successful at subduing the Boers after two years of guerrilla war, characterized by scorched earth and concentration camps, the war became the most costly purely imperial war ever fought by the empire. The Peace of **Vereeniging,** by which the Boer forces laid down their arms on May 31, 1902, specified that South African self-government would precede any consideration of the native franchise, thereby laying the groundwork for South Africa's twentieth-century history of racial government.

In domestic politics, Salisbury, who began as an opponent of reform, became the emblematic leader of the middle-class Tory party of "villa Conservatism," the Primrose League, and the Liberal Unionist alliance. Salisbury solidified the reputation of the Tories, first invented by Disraeli, as the party of imperial and unionist patriotism, although he was himself no imperial enthusiast. Salisbury's skillful diplomacy guarded British interests while avoiding collision with any of the great powers; it is nevertheless the case that the blunders that led to the Boer war must remain a significant blot on the escutcheon of a prime minister whose forte—in his own mind above all—was foreign policy. Salisbury retired in July 1902 and died at his seat of Hatfield on August 22, 1903. *See also* Africa, Scramble for; Balance of Power; Boer Wars; Conservative Party; Milner, Alfred.

FURTHER READING: Cecil, Lady Gwendolyn. *The Life of Robert, Marquis of Salisbury.* 4 vols. London: Hodder and Stoughton, 1932; Kennedy, A. L. *Salisbury, 1830–1903.* London: J. Murray, 1953; Lowe, C. J. *Salisbury and the Mediterranean, 1886–1896.* London: Routledge & K. Paul, 1965; Roberts, Andrew. *Salisbury: Victorian Titan.* London: Weidenfeld and Nicolson, 1999.

MARK F. PROUDMAN

Salonica

A cosmopolitan city of the **Ottoman Empire,** Salonica was peopled by Jews from the Iberian Peninsula; Orthodox Christians, mostly Greeks, some Bulgarians; Ma'mins, Jewish converts to Islam; Vlachs, Christians speaking a Romance language similar to Rumanian; gypsies; and Western Europeans, mostly Italians.

The assumptions of racial nationalism, which shaped European thinking in the nineteenth century, did not reflect how the inhabitants saw themselves. Religion dictated their identities and it was through the efforts of a minority of educated elite imbued with the European nationalist creeds that the people were converted and mobilized. The Macedonian struggle in the late nineteenth century, which dominated life in Salonica, began as a religious conflict among its Christians, but turned into a way for nationalists to introduce national identities: Greek, Bulgarian, and even "Macedonian." This threatened the cosmopolitan identity of the city. Hellenic and Bulgarian nationalists fought over Salonica, but were also divided among themselves.

In 1871, a few Bulgarians in Salonica left the Greek-speaking Orthodox community and joined the Bulgarian Exarchate. By 1912, they numbered 6,000. Initially, this move was a religious-linguistic inspiration, but with Russian and later Bulgarian government support, it became nationalistic. Irredentist leaders in Sofia clamored for the incorporation of "the Macedonians" into Bulgaria. In 1893, a militant anarchist group was founded in Salonica and proclaimed autonomy for Macedonia. The group was called the Internal Macedonian Revolutionary Organization (IMRO) and had the slogan "Macedonia for the Macedonians." A Bulgarian governor would rule Macedonia from Salonica, all officials would be Bulgarian Slavs, and Bulgarian and Turkish would be the official languages.

The IMRO conducted terrorist activities against Muslim and Christian officials, assassinating gendarmes, tax-collectors, and other civilian officials. On April 28–29, 1903, its radicals bombed various foreign and Ottoman places in Salonica, resulting in a crackdown by Ottoman soldiers. A few months later, on St. Elias's day, the IMRO leadership organized an uprising, which only resulted in Ottoman troops killing several thousand peasants in retaliation. The European powers wanted to uphold the status quo but forced the Ottoman Sultan Abdul Hamid to accept European supervision of policing.

The Greek Patriarchate viewed the Bulgarian Exarchate as a blow to the unity of the Orthodox Christians, but Hellenic nationalists feared that Macedonia was slipping into Bulgarian hands. In the 1904 Ottoman census, there were 648,962 followers of the Patriarchate and 557,734 faithful of the Exarchates in Macedonia, and nearly 250,000 of the former had identified themselves as Bulgarian speakers. Between 1904 and 1908, Hellenized Slavs and Albanians loyal to the Patriarchate beat reluctant peasants, shot Exarchates, and burned "hostile" villages. Greek operations were based in Salonica's consulate, where a young cadet, Athanasios Souliotis-Nikolaides, organized interrogation and assassination squads. Souliotis even published a brochure in Slavic, which he circulated among the peasantry titled *Prophecies of Alexander the Great,* to convince them that only Greeks could liberate them from Ottoman rule. In 1907, Souliotis urged the boycotting of Exarchist and Bulgarian businesses, and Greeks were warned not to hire enemy workers. Those that did were shot. The Bulgarians were just as violent as the Greeks in what effectively became a reign of nationalist terror.

In 1912, Salonica changed masters. Fears that **Italy** or Albanian rebels might seize parts of it resulted in various bilateral agreements between **Montenegro, Serbia, Bulgaria,** and **Greece** to attack the **Porte.** The Greek army, with Crown Prince Constantine at its head, marched into Salonica only hours before the Bulgarians. This event ushered in efforts to make the city Greek. The 1913 census showed how cosmopolitan Salonica really was. The population numbered 157,889, of whom just under 40,000 were listed as Greeks, 45,867 as Muslims, and 61,439 as Jews.

FURTHER READING: Mazower, Mark. *Salonica, City of Ghosts: Christians, Muslims and Jews, 1430–1950.* London: Harper Collins, 2004.

ANDREKOS VARNAVA

Samoan Crisis (1889)

A three-cornered diplomatic confrontation, involving competing American, British, and German claims to the Samoan Islands in the South Pacific west of Tahiti. British missionaries had been active in Samoa since the 1830s, but the largest commercial presence was that of plantations established by the German company Godeffroy and Son. The company acquired such a dominant position in cotton, coffee, rubber, and cocoa that it interfered in the clan disputes of the local population. In 1878, the **United States** established a naval base at Pago Pago, and the next year the three powers agreed to govern jointly the town of Apia. In 1885, however, Germany sought to answer anti-German sentiment among the Samoan population by seizing control of Apia and the Mulinuu Peninsula. When the Samoans sought American protection against the German claims, the U.S. Consul Berthold Greenbaum declared Samoa to be under American protection. As he had done this without the authorization of his government, U.S. Secretary of State Thomas Bayard opted instead for a conference to resolve the issue. Held in Washington in June and July 1887, however, the conference failed to find a compromise between American support for King Malietoa and German insistence that Chief Tamasese replace him.

The dispute edged toward crisis when, in August 1887, Germany attempted to topple Malietoa, and the United States sent a warship, *U.S.S. Adams*, to Apia in October. Matters deteriorated further in September 1888 when German warships began shelling Samoan coastal villages in response to a revolt and seized an American vessel in the process. President Grover **Cleveland** denounced the action, but German Chancellor Otto von **Bismarck** proposed a three-nation conference, this time in Berlin, as American, British, and German warships converged on Apia harbor. The conference met in late April, but in the interim a hurricane struck Samoa and sunk six of the seven warships at Apia. The disaster helped to establish a climate of cooperation, so that in June 1889 the General Act of Berlin established a three-power **protectorate**. Supplementary agreements signed in 1900 gave the islands west of 171° west longitude to Germany and the islands to the east of the line to the United States. Britain, suddenly preoccupied with the Second Boer War, withdrew its claims in Samoa in return for territorial concessions elsewhere. *See also* Boer Wars; British Empire; German Empire; Navalism.

FURTHER READING: Hoyt, Edwin Palmer. *The Typhoon That Stopped a War.* New York; D. McKay Co., 1968; Kennedy, Paul M. *The Samoan Tangle: A Study in Anglo-German-American Relations, 1878–1900.* Dublin: Irish University Press, 1974.

CARL CAVANAGH HODGE

Sand River Convention (1852)

An agreement between Great Britain and the Boer population of the **Transvaal.** The agreement was brought about by the action of Sir Henry Smith, governor of the Cape Colony, in conquering the Orange River sovereignty on his own authority in 1848. The Russell and Derby governments in Britain resented Smith's expansionist adventure and repudiated his conquest in order to lighten the burden to taxpayers of Britain's obligations in South Africa. In the convention Britain recognized the independence of the Transvaal Boers in return for a promise to abolish slavery in the Transvaal along with British a commitment not to interfere in the affairs of the Orange River sovereignty. The convention also provided for the flow of trade across the borders of British and Boer territory, as well as the extradition of criminals. The Boers considered the British annexation of the Transvaal in 1877 to be a violation of the convention and the principal *casus belli* of the First Boer War. *See also* Boer Wars; British Empire; Orange Free State.

FURTHER READING: Farwell, Byron. *The Great-Anglo-Boer War.* New York: Norton, 1990; Surridge, Keith, and Denis Judd. *The Boer War.* London: John Murray, 2002.

CARL CAVANAGH HODGE

San Martín, José Francisco de (1778–1850)

The general who led armies of liberation in **Argentina, Chile,** and Peru during the concluding phases of the Wars of Independence in Spanish America. San Martín was born in Corrientes to Spanish parents who supervised his education in Spain. He entered the Spanish military and served in three campaigns between 1789 and 1793 and was active in secret societies that supported liberal reforms and the independence of the American colonies during and after his resignation from the Spanish military in 1811.

While in London, through his membership in the Great American Assembly of Francisco Miranda, he met a number of Latin American independence leaders, including Manuel Moreno—the brother of Mariano Moreno—and Carlos de Alvear. In 1812, San Martín traveled to Buenos Aires, where he offered his services to the newly formed government of the United Provinces of the Río de la Plata. He became active in politics in Buenos Aires. In 1813, after winning victories against Loyalist forces on two occasions, the ruling junta named him as the commander of the expeditionary force then engaged in fighting Spanish forces on the frontier between Argentina and Bolivia. Hoping that an indirect attack would yield better results, San Martín pushed for the recruitment and training of an army between 1814 and 1817 that crossed the Andes and invaded Chile. A series of engagements in alliance with Chilean independence forces against the Spanish defenders led to the liberation of Chile by 1818.

With support from the governments in Buenos Aires and in Santiago de Chile, he led an invasion force against the Spanish in Peru beginning in 1820. Although the Royalist forces were significantly larger than the invading forces, the ensuing campaign produced a string of victories that quickly forced Spanish and loyalist troops from Peru. On July 28, 1821, a council in Lima declared their country independent. San Martín had hoped to unite Argentina, Chile, and Peru—if not all of South America—into a single nation. Although his exact plans remain unknown, contemporaries believed that he hoped to help create a constitutional monarchy and a federation of states.

As the battle to liberate Ecuador and Bolivia continued, San Martín met with Simón de **Bolívar** on July 25, 1822, in Guayaquil. No record of their discussion appeared and what their discussion covered remains unknown. After a series of meetings, San Martín returned to Lima, where he resigned his commission and titles granted by the Peruvian government. He returned to Argentina, but he retired from politics and military affairs. After meeting briefly with government officials, he departed for England in 1824. Although he resided briefly in Montevideo, Uruguay, in 1828, and he offered to help the dictator Juan Manuel de Rosas lift an attempted French blockade of Buenos Aires in 1838, he remained for the rest of his life in Europe. *See also* Spanish Empire.

FURTHER READING: Lynch, John. *Spanish American Revolutions 1808–1826.* New York: W. W. Norton, 1986; Mitre, Bartolomé. *The Emancipation of South America. Being a condensed translation by William Pilling of the History of San Martin by Bartolomé Mitre.* New York: Cooper Square Publishers, 1969.

DANIEL K. LEWIS

San Stefano, Treaty of (1878)

Signed on March 3, 1878, the Treaty of San Stefano concluded the war between Russia and the **Ottoman Empire** that had begun the previous year. Negotiated by the Russian ambassador at Constantinople, it was very favorable to the Russians, forcing the Turks to cede significant territory along the eastern shore of the Black Sea. It also proposed the creation of several new states: a large Bulgarian state to be occupied by Russian troops for two years and an autonomous **Bosnia-Herzegovina** under Austrian and Russian supervision. The treaty was so unacceptable to Austria and other concerned nations, such as Great Britain, that it was immediately rejected and nearly resulted in a new war. In the end, Otto von **Bismarck** negotiated a new agreement at the Congress of **Berlin** in June 1878 that was far less generous to the Russians. *See also* Russo-Turkish War.

FURTHER READING: Crankshaw, Edward. *The Shadow of the Winter Palace: Russia's Drift to Revolution, 1825–1917.* New York: Viking Press, 1976; Macfie, A. L. *The Eastern Question 1774–1923.* London and New York: Longman, 1989.

LEE A. FARROW

Santiago Bay, Battle of (1898)

A naval engagement of the **Spanish-American War.** Four days after the American declaration of war on Spain, Admiral Pascual Cervera sailed for **Cuba** on April 29, 1898, in command of the armored cruisers *Almirante Oquendo, Cristóbal Colón, Infanta María Theresa,* and *Vizcaya,* and the destroyers *Furor* and *Pluton.* His squadron evaded American patrols and arrived in Santiago, Cuba, on May 19. Soon discovered by American warships, the Spanish warships remained in port through June, blockaded by American warships that regularly patrolled the port's exit.

Fearing that advancing U.S. troops overland would capture his warships and knowing that the blockading American warships hopelessly overmatched his force, Cervera led his squadron out on July 3. He hoped to evade the American warships and escape, but American Admiral William S. Sampson had carefully deployed his warships; and those on station that day, the battleships *Indiana, Iowa, Oregon,* and *Texas,* the armored cruiser *Brooklyn,* and two converted yachts, intercepted and engaged the Spanish warships, sinking them one by one in a running battle.

The Spanish suffered 323 killed and 1,720 captured of the 2,227 men in the squadron, whereas only one American died in the one-sided battle. The victory ignited a fierce controversy between Commodore Winfield Scott Schley, whom Sampson left in command of the blockade before departing with the warships that needed to refuel. Both men claimed credit for the victory and the ensuing Sampson-Schley controversy festered for a decade despite a court of inquiry meant to settle it as they and their supporters continued to press their cases. *See also* Manila Bay, Battle of; Navalism; Spanish Empire; United States.

FURTHER READING: O'Toole, G.J.A. *The Spanish War, and American Epic—1898.* New York: W. W. Norton, 1986; Trask, David. *The War with Spain.* New York: Free Press, 1981.

STEPHEN K. STEIN

Santo Domingo

The eastern two-thirds of a Caribbean island shared with Haiti and a target for European penetration dating to the arrival of Christopher Columbus under a Spanish flag in 1492. Santo Domingo became the first permanent European settlement in Western Hemisphere and the base for the Spanish conquest of the Americas, but in 1697 Spain nevertheless recognized French dominion over Haiti. After gaining independence from France in 1804, Haiti invaded Santo Domingo and ruled it until 1844. Between 1861 and 1863, Santo Domingo returned to Spanish rule but threw it off and gained full independence in 1865. That year also marked the end of the **American Civil War** and the beginning of the increasing interest of the **United States** in the Caribbean.

The Grant administration sought to annex Santo Domingo to secure a naval base at Samaná Bay, but the Senate rejected the annexation treaty. When in 1904 Santo Domingo, now the Dominican Republic, fell into bankruptcy and civil war, fear of European intervention moved President Theodore **Roosevelt** to declare the **Roosevelt Corollary** to the **Monroe Doctrine.** Annexation, however, was out of the question. "I have about the same desire to annex it," Roosevelt note, "as a gorged boa constrictor might have to swallow a porcupine wrong-end-to." Still, in 1916, President Woodrow **Wilson** sent the United States Marines to the Dominican Republic, and United States Marines occupied and administered it directly until 1924. *See also* Navalism; Spanish Empire.

FURTHER READING: Cooper, John Milton, Jr. *The Warrior and the Priest: Woodrow Wilson and Theodore Roosevelt.* Cambridge, MA: Belknap, 1983; McDougall, Walter A. *Promised Land, Crusader State: The American Encounter with the World since 1776.* Boston: Houghton Mifflin, 1997.

CARL CAVANAGH HODGE

Sarajevo

Under Ottoman rule, the administrative center of **Bosnia-Herzegovina** in the mid-nineteenth century. When Austria-Hungary occupied Bosnia and Herzegovina in the aftermath of the Congress of **Berlin** in 1878, the Austro-Hungarian administration was located in Sarajevo, too. The multiethnic city with large Croatian, Serbian, and Muslim communities was modernized and prospered, but conflicts between the major ethnic groups and between parts of the Slav population and Austro-Hungarian authorities could never be settled.

In the aftermath of the annexation of Bosnia and Herzegovina in 1908, the new provincial diet was established in Sarajevo. Several political organizations that shunned parliament and tried to get rid of Habsburg rule by propaganda campaigns and political violence were active in Sarajevo. Gavrilo Princip, a member of Young Bosnia (Mlada Bosna), a group supported by the Belgrade-based **Black Hand,** assassinated the Austro-Hungarian heir apparent, Archduke Francis Ferdinand and his wife in Sarajevo on June 28, 1914, precipitating the **July Crisis.** Austria-Hungary's leaders decided to use the assassination of Francis Ferdinand as legitimate cause for an ultimatum and finally a war against **Serbia.** *See also* Habsburg Empire.

FURTHER READING: Malcolm, Noel. *Bosnia: A Short History.* New York: New York University Press, 1994; Strachan, Hew. *The First World War.* New York: Oxford University Press, 2001.

GUENTHER KRONENBITTER

Sardinia

See Piedmont-Sardinia, Kingdom of

Satsuma Rebellion (1877)

Known in Japan as the *seinan senso,* or "Southwest War," the Satsuma Rebellion was the greatest of the series of samurai rebellions that rocked the newly established Meiji regime between 1874 and 1877. The eight-month engagement pitted 60,000 troops of the new national conscript army against the 42,000 samurai warriors from the former feudal fiefdom of Satsuma. Suppression of the rebellion in September 1877 marked the end of significant armed opposition to the new regime.

The **Meiji Restoration** of 1868 brought the end of feudal Japan and the beginning of a new, modern national polity. Although the founders of the Meiji state came from the *samurai* class, among their modernizing reforms was the elimination of privileges that had guaranteed samurai supremacy in the early modern period: the exclusive right to bear arms (two swords), to receive a stipend from the local lord, to wear the hair in a top-knot, to possess a surname and family crest, and to ride on horseback. The new central government chipped away at these rights between 1870 and 1876, provoking a series of five major uprisings.

Although the Satsuma Rebellion far exceeded the next largest disturbance, the 1874 Saga Rebellion of 2,500 samurai, it followed a general pattern of samurai protest. As with its predecessors, the origins of 1877 lie in the 1873 debate over a proposed invasion of **Korea.** Disgruntled by the decision to prioritize internal modernization over foreign invasion, several members of the ruling circle quit the national government for their native lands and assumed leadership of growing local disaffection with Tokyo.

Directing the Satsuma Rebellion was Saigo Takamori, popularized in a 2003 Hollywood film as *The Last Samurai.* Saigo had played a pivotal role in toppling the feudal regime and in promoting modernizing reforms. But after the 1873 split, he returned to his native Kagoshima and renounced public life. Moved by the sincerity of Satsuma resistance to the increasingly crass materialism of the nation, he agreed in February 1877 to lead a samurai march on Tokyo. An imposing figure of almost 6 feet, 240 pounds and piercing gaze, Saigo was already a celebrity in his time. His ritual suicide in the name of purity is legend and has ensured his place as modern Japan's greatest hero. *See also* Japanese Empire.

FURTHER READING: Ravina, Mark. *The Last Samurai: The Life and Battles of Saigo Takamori.* Hoboken, NJ: John Wiley & Sons, 2004.

FREDERICK R. DICKINSON

Scandinavia

Politically, the region is made up of **Finland, Sweden, Norway, Denmark, Iceland,** and their dependencies. Iceland retained ties to the Danish crown until 1944. The nations bear many culturally similarities, with the Lutheran confession as official religion. Scandinavian languages—Swedish, Norwegian, Icelandic, and Danish—belong to the Germanic group that, with exception of Icelandic, could be mutually understood by its practitioners. Finnish, on the other hand, belongs to the Finnish-Ugrian group and so does the language of the Samí minority, living in northern Scandinavia and the Kola Peninsula.

Between 1839 and 1850, the pan-Scandinavian movement was influential among Scandinavian intellectuals. It was partly a result of increased focus on the common history and heritage of the Scandinavian peoples, but it was also derived from the increasing pressure from outside great powers, most notably Russia and **Prussia.** It came up short, however, in confrontation with the realities of politics and the growing nationalism of each country.

For Scandinavia, the **Napoleonic Wars** were the final chapter of more than 800 years of struggle for regional hegemony. For the latter 500 years, the Danish and Swedish Kings were the main contestants; the former had sided with defeated France, the latter with the victors. Yet from 1814 to 1914, Scandinavia was little affected by the squabbles among the great powers. Instead, the region saw a period of growth of civic society, democracy, and modernization. In Finland, Sweden, and Norway, forestry had always been a major export; in the latter two, mining also contributed economically. Norway, and Denmark's dependency, Iceland, also had rich fisheries. Denmark enjoyed an export-oriented farming sector, shifting from grain to dairy and meat preserves in the 1870s. The first railroads were laid down in the 1850s, and railroad networks expanded in Scandinavia from the mid-nineteenth century. From 1870, industry was expanding, applying the latest technologies, using local raw material such as ore and wood pulp, and in Norway and Sweden, benefiting from development of hydroelectric power. Industrialization also created a new, urban working class, which grew into a significant social and political force at the turn of the century. Norway also had a significant merchant fleet, which grew from the eighth to the third largest during the nineteenth century.

By the 1814 Kiel peace treaty, Norway passed from Danish to Swedish rule. Norway had brought Iceland, the Faeroe Islands and Greenland into the union with

Denmark in 1380, but these possessions remained with the latter. The Norwegian constitution of 1814 was one of the most democratic of its time, and its adaptation was enabled by the absence of any Norwegian nobility. It was under constant attack from the ruling Swedish King, however, until the mid-nineteenth century, when the Norwegian Parliament took to the offensive leading to independence in 1905. Parliamentary government was also introduced in 1884.

Finland was lost by Sweden to Russia in 1809, and became a Grand Duchy directly under the tsar. Tsar **Alexander I** (1777–1825) gave Finland extensive autonomy. While Norway's independence developed gradually, Finland experienced repression under Russian Tsars **Alexander III** (1845–1894) and **Nicholas II** (1868–1917). Finland gained full independence as a consequence of the 1917 Russian Revolution and a bloody civil war lasting through 1918.

Both Sweden and Denmark entered the period as absolute monarchies and with a landed aristocracy that hampered development of democratic institutions. Reforms began in the mid-nineteenth century, but parliamentarism was not established before World War I. Universal suffrage was also obtained by both sexes in Finland in 1906, Norway in 1913, Denmark and Iceland in 1918, and Sweden in 1921. *See also* Russian Empire; Russo-Swedish War.

FURTHER READING: Andersson, Ingvar. *A History of Sweden.* Translated by Carolyn Hannay. London: Weidenfeld and Nicholson, 1956; Jones, Gwyn. *Denmark: A Modern History.* London: Croom Helm, 1986.

FRODE LINDGJERDET

Scharnhorst, Gerhard Johann von (1755–1813)

A distinguished officer in the Prussian Army during the Napoleonic period who is known as a remarkable reformer and administrator rather than as a battlefield commander. Hanoverian by birth, Scharnhorst transferred to Prussian service in 1801. He served as chief-of-staff first to the Duke of Brunswick at the disastrous Battle of Auerstädt on October 14, 1806, where he was slightly wounded, and towards the end of the campaign with Gerhard von **Blücher,** later to become **Prussia**'s distinguished commander-in-chief. As a major general Scharnhorst headed the reform commission appointed to rebuild and reorganize the Prussian army, and it was in this capacity that his considerable talents were revealed. He advocated the creation of a national army based on wide conscription, the opening up of officers' commissions based on merit, and the creation of a national militia—all of which led to the establishment of the new fighting force, which in 1813 helped drive the French from Germany in that year. Scharnhorst became Blücher's chief of staff in 1813 but died from an infected wound received at the Battle of Lützen. *See also* Gneisenau, August Wilhelm von; Napoleonic Wars; Moltke, Helmuth von; Roon, Albrecht von.

FURTHER READING: Craig, Gordon A. *The Politics of the Prussian Army: 1640–1945.* London: Oxford University Press, 1964; Dupuy, Trevor N. *A Genius for War: The German Army and General Staff, 1807–1945.* Fairfax: Hero Books, 1964; Goerlitz, Walter. *History of the German General Staff: 1657–1945.* New York: Frederick A. Praeger Publishers, 1953; Paret,

Peter. *Yorck and the Era of Prussian Reform: 1807–1815*. Princeton, NJ: Princeton University Press, 1966.

GREGORY FREMONT-BARNES

Schleswig-Holstein

A region comprised of two of the three duchies on the lower Jutland Peninsula between **Denmark** and the Elbe River—the third being Lauenburg—with predominantly German-speaking populations yet subject to Danish rule for centuries. Holstein was given to the **German Confederation** in 1815 as punishment for Denmark's alliance with Napoleon **Bonaparte.** During the revolutions of 1848, Denmark sought to annex the duchies, but the local population resisted and was supported by Prussian troops. A conference in London in 1852 achieved a compromise among competing claims, but after the death of Frederick VII of Denmark in 1863, his successor, Christian X, whipped up Danish national enthusiasm for annexation against Austrian and Prussian counter-claims. Schleswig-Holstein thereupon became the first of the wars of German unification under Otto von **Bismarck,** when Austria and **Prussia** combined to defeat the Danes by October 1864.

Having disposed of Denmark with Austrian help, Bismarck contrived to eliminate Austria as well. First, he set about establishing **Kiel** as a Prussian naval base, a provocation to Austria that was temporarily settled by the Gastein Convention giving Schleswig and Launenburg to Prussia and Holstein to Austria; he thereupon orchestrated a war with Austria by charging that its government was violating the convention by continuing to encourage competing claims to the duchies. Following the **Austro-Prussian War** of 1866, Prussia dissolved the German Confederation and annexed Schleswig-Holstein. *See also* Habsburg Empire.

FURTHER READING: Clark, Christopher. *Iron Kingdom: The Rise and Downfall of Prussia, 1600–1947.* Cambridge, MA: Belknap, 2006; Showalter, Dennis. *The Wars of German Unification.* London: Arnold, 2004.

CARL CAVANAGH HODGE

Schlieffen Plan

Germany's infamous military deployment plan of 1914, named after Alfred Count von Schlieffen, chief of the Prussian general staff from 1892–1905. By the time the plan was implemented in August 1914, it should more aptly be called "Moltke-Plan," as it had been changed and updated by Schlieffen's successor, Helmuth von **Moltke,** in the years 1906–1914.

Schlieffen's war planning was conducted against the background of international developments in Europe at the beginning of the twentieth century. Germany felt itself "encircled" by hostile alliances, and its military planners feared that it would most likely have to fight a war on two fronts if a European war were to break out. Schlieffen attempted to find an answer to the dilemma of how to win such a two-front war when faced with superior enemy numbers. As chief of the general staff, he had changed his predecessors' strategy of concentrating on the enemy in the East—Russia. Instead, he reversed years of planning by focusing on the enemy in the West—France. Russia, he felt, could retreat into its vast terrain and avoid a decisive battle, but Germany would be too stretched to fight on two fronts and needed to secure an early victory, at least on one of those fronts. France seemed to offer that chance; Russia would be slow to mobilize and could be dealt with later. In 1905, faced with an enforced retirement, he put some of his thoughts to paper in a now infamous memorandum, intended to point his successor, the younger Helmuth von Moltke, in the right direction.

The timing of this memorandum is important, as it was written against the background of the **Russo-Japanese War** of 1904–1905. As a result of this conflict, which Russia lost, it was eliminated as a serious threat to the European status quo for the foreseeable future. Russia would first of all have to recover from defeat and revolution. For Germany's military leaders who feared Russia as a potential future enemy, this was a perfect time to consider "preventive war," for Germany still had a chance to defeat Russia if it chose to become involved in a European war. In the not-too-distant-future, Germany's military planners predicted, Russia would become invincible. The so-called Schlieffen Plan was developed against this background and designed primarily as a war against France—and if necessary Britain—in 1905. France, allied to Russia, would not be able to count on its ally's support in 1905, so this constellation offered a real opportunity to Schlieffen that Germany could avoid a two-front war altogether and concentrate solely on fighting in the west. With one enemy removed, Russia would in future be much less of a threat to Germany.

Schlieffen therefore saw Germany's best chance of victory in a swift offensive against France; in the east, the German army was initially to be on the defensive. He counted on the fact that that German victory in the west would move quickly and that Russian mobilization would be slow, so that a small German force would suffice to hold back Russia until France was beaten. After a swift victory in the west, the full force of the German army would be redirected eastward against Russia. In effect, this strategy would turn the threatening two-front war into two sequential one-front wars. The plan further entailed that Germany would have to attack France while avoiding the heavy fortifications along the Franco-German border. Instead of a "head-on" engagement, which would lead to position warfare of inestimable length, the opponent should be enveloped and its armies attacked on the flanks and rear, using the existing railway lines, which would ensure a swift German deployment. In addition, Luxembourg, the Netherlands, and Belgium were not expected to put up much resistance and their neutrality would not be respected in a German advance. Schlieffen intended to concentrate all effort on the right wing of the German advancing armies. The plan involved violating the neutrality of Luxembourg, the **Netherlands,** and **Belgium;** however, the political ramifications of this act of aggression were considered insignificant.

This was the result of years of planning and of strategic exercises designed to find the best solution to the problem of a two-front war. Schlieffen put this version to paper in December 1905 in a memorandum written on the eve of his retirement. In the following years, his plan was adapted to changing international circumstances by his successor, the younger Helmuth von Moltke. The underlying principle—that of seeking to fight France before attempting to defeat Russia, and of attempting to envelope the opponent—remained the same until August 1914, however, when Germany's deployment plan was put into action.

In 1914, the plan imposed severe restrictions on finding a diplomatic solution to the **July Crisis,** particularly because of its narrow timeframe for the initial deployment of troops into Luxemburg, Belgium, and France. Particularly the need to capture the fortified town of Liège quickly put severe time pressure on the German advance. The escalation of the diplomatic crisis into full-scale war was in no small measure a consequence of Germany's offensive war plans.

Germany began the war with a deployment of the majority of its troops in the west. Seven armies were deployed there, and one army was deployed in the east, where the task of holding back the Russian army was to be shared with the Austro-Hungarian troops. The quick victory in the west, however, was not achieved; in the east the Russians were quicker to mobilize and deploy than had been anticipated, and the much needed support from the Austrians was less substantial than hoped for. What had seemed a sound strategy for winning a war on two fronts ultimately failed in August and September 1914, when trench warfare put an end to the idea of a quick victory on the western front. Arguably, Germany could not win a long war against numerically superior enemies, particularly once Britain entered the war and the naval blockade took effect. Once Moltke's interpretation of the Schlieffen Plan had failed, it seemed only a matter of time before Germany would lose the war.

After the war was lost and the victors blamed Germany and German militarism for its outbreak, details of the Schlieffen Plan were kept secret. Official document collections made no mention of it. In private correspondence and in their memoirs Germany's failed military leaders and former members of the general staff nonetheless frequently referred to Schlieffen's "recipe for victory," which had, in their opinion, been squandered by Moltke. Details of the memorandum did not become public until after World War II, when the German historian Gerhard Ritter published it and other documents in an effort to prove that German militarism was indeed to some extent responsible for the outbreak of war. Since then, generations of historians have come to accept that German military planning, epitomized by the Schlieffen Plan, was one of the factors for the outbreak of hostilities in August 1914.

This certainty has recently been questioned by the American historian Terence Zuber, who denies the existence of the Schlieffen Plan. Zuber's contention is that the famous 1905 memorandum did not amount to a military plan and that Schlieffen never intended to launch an attack on France via Belgium, Holland, and Luxembourg. This thesis has provoked a heated debate but has largely failed to convince critics that there was no Schlieffen Plan. Equally, Zuber's apologetic interpretation that Germany did not have an offensive war plan in 1914 has found little support. Nevertheless, the debate has reemphasized what others had already pointed out: that there never existed a perfect recipe for victory, that Schlieffen's hapless successor adulterated his plan, and that it would be prudent to think carefully about the terminology used to describe Germany's military plans of the prewar years. The notion of the Schlieffen Plan as a convenient way of summarizing German military strategy in August 1914 is inaccurate. The responsibility for the plans that were put into practice in August 1914 lay with Helmuth von Moltke, who had adapted Schlieffen's ideas to changing international and domestic conditions. Although the principle remained the same, the plans differed in important ways, such as Moltke's planned *coup de main* on Liège, which was intended to avoid a violation of Dutch neutrality. It would still be fair to say that the German war plan of 1914 contributed significantly to the outbreak of fighting, but to blame Schlieffen for what followed thereafter is misleading. *See also* German Empire; Strategy.

FURTHER READING: Bucholz, Arden. *Moltke, Schlieffen and Prussian War Planning.* New York: Berg, 1991; Ehlert, Hans, Michael Epkenhans, and Gerhard P. Gross, eds. *Der Schlieffenplan. Analyse und Dokumente.* Paderborn: Schöningh. 2006; Mombauer, Annika. *Helmuth von Moltke and the Origins of the First World War.* New York: Cambridge University Press, 2001; Ritter, Gerhard. *The Schlieffen Plan. Critique of a Myth.* London: O. Wolff, 1958; Zuber, Terence. *Inventing the Schlieffen Plan.* New York: Oxford University Press, 2003.

ANNIKA MOMBAUER

Schmoller, Gustav von (1838–1917)

Among the leading economists of Imperial Germany and founder of the "younger historical school," Schmoller attempted to square Germany's waxing industrial strength and accelerating social change with the monarchic and authoritarian traditions of Prussia by advocating paternalist social reforms to meet the material needs of the working class. He further viewed overseas expansion as a way to offset the social effects of a rapidly increasing population in Germany. To avoid resorting to domestic political repression, Schmoller advised, the Reich would have to pursue social reconciliation at home while participating fully in great power struggles overseas. *See also Weltpolitik.*

FURTHER READING: Grimmer-Solem, Erik. *The Rise of Historical Economics and Social Reform in Germany, 1864–1894.* Oxford: Clarendon, 2003.

CARL CAVANAGH HODGE

Schönbrunn, Treaty of (1809)

A peace treaty signed on October 14 between France and Austria, which ended the 1809 War of the Fifth Coalition following Napoleon **Bonaparte**'s victory at **Wagram,** also signed by Napoleon's ally, Russia. The treaty expressed Napoleon's dominant position, as Austria was required to give up territories to the French emperor, who would then reallocate them. Salzburg and Berechtesgaden, together with part of Upper Austria, would later pass to **Bavaria.** The county of Görz, Montefalcone, Trieste, the province of Carniola, together with the parts of Carinthia and civilian Croatia, six Regiments (the Karlstadt and Banal districts) of the Military Frontier, Fiume and the Hungarian Littoral (coast), plus Austrian Istria lying to the west of the Save River would pass to the Kingdom of **Italy.**

These territories would later be consolidated with French-held Dalmatia into the Kingdom of Illyria under Napoleon's rule. Austria also ceded Razuns, an enclave in eastern Switzerland. The king of Saxony had been a new French ally in the 1809 war and was rewarded with enclaves within Saxony previously attached to Habsburg Bohemia. The Saxon king was also ruler of the duchy of Warsaw and was awarded the Austrian territories in Poland taken under the 1795 Third Partition, that is West Galicia. For its half-hearted support in the war, Russia received a small part of eastern Galicia around Brody. Austria recognized the changes of monarch in

Spain, Portugal, and Naples, while also joining the **Continental System** blockade against the United Kingdom. The Austrian army was reduced to 150,000 men and the **Habsburg Empire** was to pay an indemnity of 85 million French francs. *See also* Napoleonic Wars; Russian Empire.

FURTHER READING: Petre, F. L. *Napoleon and the Archduke Charles*. London: J. Lane, 1909; Rothenberg, Gunther E. *The Napoleonic Wars*. London: Cassell, 1999; Schroeder, Paul W. *The Transformation of European Politics, 1763–1848*. Oxford: Clarendon, 1994.

DAVID HOLLINS

Schwarzenberg, Prince Felix (1800–1852)

A Habsburg statesman, Prince Schwarzenberg was born in October 1800 in Krummau, a member of the highest ranks of the Bohemian aristocracy. He joined the Austrian army and switched to the diplomatic service after a few years, where he made an impressive career. In the revolution of 1848, Schwarzenberg reentered the military service, fighting against the Italians. Field-marshal Alfred Prince von Windischgraetz, his brother-in-law and the most influential counter-revolutionary general, made sure that Schwarzenberg became prime minister and foreign minister of the Habsburg monarchy in November 1848.

As prime minister, Schwarzenberg reestablished the Habsburg regime, dissolved the constitutional assembly and paved the way to neo-absolute rule. The new emperor, Francis Joseph, relied on Schwarzenberg's advice in domestic and international affairs. Schwarzenberg managed to restore the Great Power status of the Habsburg monarchy and the **German Confederation.** Yet when he died in April 1852, he had failed to strengthen Austria's position in the Confederation beyond the status quo ante. *See also* Habsburg Empire.

FURTHER READING: Crankshaw, Edward. *The Fall of the House of Habsburg*. New York: Viking, 1963.

GUENTHER KRONENBITTER

Second Opium War

See Arrow War

Sedan, Battle of (1870)

The most decisive German victory of the **Franco-Prussian War.** With the French Army of the Rhine under Marshal Bazaine besieged in Metz, the last hope for France rested with the Army of Châlons, commanded by Marshal Patrice **MacMahon.** MacMahon's options were to either race east to Bazaine's aid or to retire to the west and use the strong fortifications around Paris to support his defense. The stronger course of action would be to retreat west, but MacMahon was under great pressure from the Empress Eugénie and her advisors. Furthermore, the Emperor Napoleon III himself was with MacMahon's army, and retreat would have dealt a grave blow to the political stability of the Empire. The Army of Châlons marched east.

To counter this threat, the German commander, General Helmuth von **Moltke,** split his forces into four armies. Leaving two to keep Bazaine contained at Metz, he ordered the other two to head west and find MacMahon. German cavalry probing ahead found indications that the Army of Châlons was heading northeast, perhaps to reach Metz via Sedan and Thionville, hugging the Belgian border. It would have been a grave risk for the Germans if they had turned north to pursue, only to find the French were not there. If the French move was a feint, Moltke would be presenting his left flank to MacMahon. On the other hand, if MacMahon was retiring to safety around Paris, the Germans would lose as much as a week reforming and chasing after the French, giving them ample time to bolster the defenses of Paris. Moltke was prepared to gamble and accordingly ordered the two armies to turn north and cut off MacMahon's line of advance. Through forced marches, the Germans caught up with the French and stopped the Army of Châlons at the town of Sedan, a few miles from the Belgian border, on August 31.

The Army of Châlons was now caught in a triangle-shaped position, surrounded by German forces on all sides. On September 1, the Germans commenced their final assault. Early in the action MacMahon was severely wounded, but there was confusion as to who would take his place. MacMahon appointed General Auguste Ducrot as acting commander; however, a more senior general and recent arrival, Emmanuel Wimpffen, refused to take orders from Ducrot and insisted he was now in charge. The two commanders disagreed over which direction the army should attempt a breakout. Ducrot advocated a breakout to the west and a return to Paris; Wimpffen ordered an attack to the east and a continuation of the drive to relieve Metz. Either option was doomed to failure. The German artillery controlled the heights above Sedan on all sides and was able to rain down artillery fire from different directions on the French troops below. There was no cover, and thousands of French soldiers and horses were cut to pieces. A few units were able to sneak to the north and into neutral **Belgium,** where they were interned, but the rest either died or were captured. By the end of the day, the French had suffered 3,000 men killed, 14,000 wounded, and 21,000 more taken prisoner, including the Napoleon III and MacMahon; over the next few days, the total French prisoner count reached nearly 100,000. The Germans' total losses—killed, wounded, and missing—were only 9,000, the vast majority of which had been incurred by a few ill-advised infantry assaults by commanders too impatient to let the artillery do their work for them. The defeat at Sedan was the last gasp of the French Second Empire and opened the road to Paris for the victorious German armies. *See also* Bismarck, Otto von; Bonaparte, Louis Napoleon; German Empire.

FURTHER READING: Howard, Michael. *The Franco-Prussian War.* New York: Collier, 1969; Wawro, Geoffrey. *The Franco-Prussian War: The German Conquest of France, 1870–1871.* New York: Cambridge University Press, 2003; Wetzel, David. *A Duel of Giants: Bismarck, Napoleon II and the Origins of the Franco-Prussian War.* Madison: University of Wisconsin Press, 2001.

DAVID H. OLIVIER

Senegal

Senegal was the largest, most important, and most democratic French colony in West Africa. Senegal was used as a jumping-off point for further colonial conquests during the scramble for **Africa.** A European presence in the area dates to the mid-fifteenth century, when the Portuguese established trading bases along the coast for commerce in gold and slaves. By the seventeenth century, the Portuguese had given way to the French and British who operated coastal forts on the Senegal and Gambia Rivers, respectively. During the next two centuries Anglo-French conflicts caused the French forts to repeatedly fall into British hands until the end of the **Napoleonic Wars** permanently restored French control over St Louis, Gorée, Dakar, and Rufisque.

Interest in the interior remained limited until the arrival of Governor Louis Faidherbe in 1854. Driven by a desire to make Senegal financially self-sustaining through the creation of plantations and convinced by his own experiences as an army officer in **Algeria** that peaceful coexistence with Muslims was impossible, Faidherbe acted on his own initiative and repeatedly provoked border conflicts with al-Hadjj Umar's neighboring Tukolor Empire as a means of expanding the French presence into the interior. France subsequently spent the period from Faidherbe's 1865 retirement until the mid 1880s, digesting its holdings in Senegal and creating an export economy centered around peanuts, ivory, and gum arabic. Once the Scramble for Africa began, however, French forces simultaneously completed the conquest of Senegal and then joined with counterparts from the French Congo and Algeria in a bid to conquer the interior and establish a band of French held territory stretching from the Atlantic Coast to the Nile River.

In addition to its financial importance, Senegal also occupied a unique place as the most democratic colony in French Africa. Although the majority of Senegalese were considered subjects and were ruled directly by French colonial administrators, the policy of assimilation meant that from the mid-nineteenth century, Africans born in the so-called Four Communes of Dakar, Gorée, Rufisque, and St Louis were French citizens with full voting rights, eventually culminating in the 1914 election of Blaise Diagne as the first African member of the French National Assembly. Senegal's unique political status was further strengthened in 1895 when Dakar was selected as the capital of the newly created federation of **French West Africa.** *See also* Fashoda Crisis; French Empire.

FURTHER READING: Clark, A. F. *From Frontier to Backwater: Economy and Society in the Upper Senegal Valley (West Africa), 1850–1920.* Lanham, MD: University Press of America, 1999; Crowder, Michael. *Senegal: A Study of French Assimilation Policy.* London: Methuen, 1967; Johnson, G. Wesley. *Double Impact: France and Africa in the Age of Imperialism.* Westport, CT: Greenwood Press, 1985; Manning, Patrick. *Francophone Sub-Saharan Africa 1880–1995.* Cambridge: Cambridge University Press, 1998.

KENNETH J. OROSZ

Sepoy

A corruption of *Sip-ah,* Persian for "army," and a general term commonly, although somewhat inaccurately, used to refer to an infantryman of the lowest rank in the British-led Indian armies. Sepoys were recruited from the native Indian population by the British East India Company as early as 1667 and later by the British government in response to the French adoption of the practice. Many British army units in **India** initially had native officers of high rank, but they were gradually replaced by officers of European origin. The term was therefore applied to any Indian soldier below officer rank who had been trained and equipped according to European tradition. Sepoys were serious, in equal parts possibly, about religion and military professionalism. Hindu and Muslim holy men typically blessed regimental colors and sent sepoys into action with a prayer, but sepoys also sought to face the same risks in battle as their British counterparts and often resented the practice of putting British troops in the positions of greatest danger. *See also* East India Companies; Indian Mutiny.

FURTHER READING: Farwell, Byron. *Queen Victoria's Little Wars.* New York: W. W. Norton, 1972; James, Lawrence. *Raj: The Making and Unmaking of British India.* New York: St. Martin's, 1997.

CARL CAVANAGH HODGE

Serbia

A rebellious Ottoman possession in the Balkans and fully independent after 1878. The defeat of the medieval kingdom of Serbia by the Ottoman Turks on Kosovo Polje in 1386 was the prelude of centuries of foreign rule. After the mid-sixteenth century, the **Ottoman Empire** fell into slow decline before emerging a modern European state in the twentieth century, and when southeast Europe was hit by waves of nationalism in the first half of the nineteenth century, both environment and inspiration lay ready for a growing Serb independence. On the eve of World War I, however, the region was Europe's most backward. Communications were poor, the majority of the population was illiterate, and the emerging nationalist sentiments fused with existing feudal structures and not the emerging national-states of the more central parts of Europe.

The Serbs had managed to maintain their culture, language, and orthodox Christianity. Many fled west to the Habsburg lands, settling in modern Croatia. In 1713, a Serb archbishopric was established there, and in this period ties with the Russian Orthodox Church were also strengthened. The population in Serbia had risen from around 1 million in the early nineteenth century, to 2.5 million by 1900. Belgrade had 100,000 inhabitants. In 1804, a tax increase triggered a Serb rebellion led by Djordje Petrovic (Karadjordhević, 1762–1817), but its underlying cause was strengthened by Serb national awareness. The revolt was quashed as the promised Russian support never materialized, but an uprising in 1813–1814 under Miloš Obrenović (1780–1860) managed to carve out some Serb autonomy. A struggle developed between Petrovic and Obrenović. The assassination of the latter, plotted by the former in 1818, began a conflict between their families that marked Serb politics until the twentieth century.

Meanwhile, the Ottoman *millet* system had divided society along religious lines, so that religion in large part constituted the Serb nation. Realizing that the Church was the sole unifying national institution, literary reformer Vuk Karadžić managed in the 1820s to establish language, too, as a defining factor of "Serbdom," enabling the inclusion of Muslim and Catholic South **Slavs** into the Serb nation-building project. This also entailed reforms and standardization of the written Serbo-Croat language. Under the weak Prince Alexander (1806-1885) from 1842-1858, Prime Minister Ilija Garašani, built up a hierarchical and centralized government apparatus after an Ottoman model, enforced by a standing army. Still formally subservient to the Turks, Garašani had no problem justifying this approach. He also formulated the program of unification of all South Slavs under Serb leadership, which heralded the later creation of Yugoslavia. He also coveted **Bosnia-Herzegovina**

The Turkish garrison in the capital Belgrade left in 1867, but full Serb independence was reached in the Treaties of **San Stefano** and Berlin only after the Ottomans were defeated by Russia in the Russo-Turkish War of 1877–1878. New territory was added in the southeast, including Niš, Serbia's second largest city from then on. Although Russian aid was welcomed, leaders like Garašani were careful not to become puppets of the tsar and let Russian designs limit Serbia's national ambitions. In 1882, Serbia was proclaimed a monarchy.

Thereafter, the increasing appeal of pan-Slavism—a call for unification of all Slav nations—troubled Serbia's relations with Austro-Hungary, itself a home of numerous Slav peoples. The situation was aggravated by the 1903 coup, bringing the throne to the Karadjordhević family and forging stronger Serb ties with Russia. The 1908 crisis over Bosnia-Herzegovina was prevented from escalating only after Germany pressured Russia to persuade Serbia to accept Austria's annexation, but new conflict soon erupted to the east.

In alliance with **Greece** and newly independent **Bulgaria,** Serbia attacked the Ottoman Empire in 1912, adding **Montenegro** to the kingdom and reducing the European possessions of the Turks to their current borders. Fighting broke out again the next year among the victors over the spoils, and Austria intervened to prevent further expansion of Serbia's territory.

On June 28, 1914, Archduke **Francis Ferdinand,** heir to the Austro-Hungarian throne, was shot and killed on a visit in Sarajevo, the provincial capital of Bosnia-Herzegovina. The assassin, Gavrilo Princip, a young student, was a member of the underground organization Mlada Bosna (Young Bosnia) with supposed ties to another organization, the **Black Hand.** The latter was known to be under the influence of Serb officers. The Austrians claimed that the Serbian government had staged the assassination and thus triggered the diplomatic crisis that led to World War I. Serbia was overrun in 1915, but in 1918 liberated Serbia could fulfill the goal of uniting South Slavs when Yugoslavia was established. *See also* Balkan Wars; Croatia-Slavonia; July Crisis; Russian Empire; Slavism.

FURTHER READING: Cox, John K. *The History of Serbia.* Westport, CT: Greenwood Press, 2002; Jelavich, Barbara. *Russia's Balkan Entanglements, 1806–1914.* New York: Cambridge University Press, 1991; Ranke, Leopold von. *A History of Servia and the Servian Revolution.* Translated by Mrs. Alexander Kerr. New York: Da Capo Press, 1973.

FRODE LINDGJERDET

Sevastopol, Siege of (1854–1855)

The culminating action of the **Crimean War.** The principal objective of the Allied army during the war was the capture of Russia's principal Black Sea port at Sevastopol, situated on the southern coast of the Crimean peninsula. After landing nearby in September 1854, the siege began on October 8 when the Russians' southern defenses were still incomplete. Indeed, the northern section was never invested, and supplies and reinforcements continued to pass in and out of the city for the entire period of operations. Bombardment of the city began on October 17, by which time the Russian engineers had rendered the place virtually impregnable to assault. The besiegers fought successfully at **Balaklava** on October 25 and **Inkerman** on November 5 to stop a Russian field army from disrupting their operations against Sevastopol, and suffered terribly from freezing conditions over the winter months. Normal operations resumed in April 1855, followed by two extremely costly Allied assaults on June 8 and September 8, the second of which, although only partly successful, convinced the defenders to evacuate the devastated city that evening. *See also* Ottoman Empire; Russian Empire.

FURTHER READING: Fletcher, Ian, and Ischchenko, Natalia. *The Crimean War: A Clash of Empires*. Staplehurst: Spellmount Publishers, 2004; Ponting, Clive. *The Crimean War*. London: Chatto & Windus, 2004; Royle, Trevor. *Crimea: The Great Crimean War, 1854–1856*. London: Little, Brown, 1999.

GREGORY FREMONT-BARNES

Seven Weeks War

See Austro-Prussian War

Shaka Zulu (1783–1828)

Founder and king of the Zulu nation of southern Africa. The Zulu and related or preceding Nguni tribes were preliterate societies, so precise details of Shaka's early career are uncertain. Shaka was probably the illegitimate son of a chief; he entered the service of another chief as a young man and rapidly became a successful warrior with a following in his own right. In 1824, he made contact with British ivory traders who had landed at what is now Durban; the diary of their medic, Henry Francis Fynn, is one of the few primary sources available. Shaka was a military innovator in both tactics and organization, and his army expanded with his conquests. Zulu conquests, largely in the area that subsequently became Natal but also extending into the eastern Cape, played a role in precipitating the massive movements of peoples in southeast Africa known collectively as the *mfecane*, movements that left large areas relatively sparsely populated at the time of the arrival of the Boer Voortrekkers.

Shaka was always suspicious of revolt and refused to acknowledge any sons, often killing or exiling women he had made pregnant. In 1828, he was killed by his followers, including his half-brother Dingane, who succeeded him as Zulu king. Shaka had made the Zulu into a powerful military nation, but also bequeathed to them a persistent succession problem. A subsequent succession dispute was referred to the British for arbitration, and played a role in embroiling them in the **Zulu War** of 1879. That war opened with the catastrophic British defeat of **Isandhlwana,** but ended with the final breaking of Zulu military power. Shaka's legacy was claimed by various future movements. He became a mythic figure for Zulu leaders and among African nationalists more widely; he also became a symbol of an exclusive ethnic identity, and was deployed to this end by the Apartheid regime in South Africa.

FURTHER READING: Fynn, Henry Francis. *The Diary of Henry Francis Fynn*. Pietermaritzburg: Shuter and Shooter, 1969; Morris, Donald. *The Washing of the Spears*. New York: Simon and

Schuster, 1965; Omer-Cooper, John D. *The Mfecane Aftermath.* London: Longmans, Green, 1966.

MARK F. PROUDMAN

Shanghai

Situated at the mouth of the Yangtze River in east central **China,** Shanghai was one of the five original **treaty ports**—along with Canton, Fuzhou, Xiamen, and Ningbo—opened to foreign commerce in 1842. Shanghai grew quickly into China's largest city, commercial and, later, industrial centre. By 1850, the surrounding swampland had been drained and the river banks shored up, thus accommodating an influx of foreign shipping. The city also became the focal point of foreign cultural influence and economic interests in China. The latter were concentrated in the International Settlement, administered by the quasi-autonomous Shanghai Municipal Council, elected by the richest among the Western firms and businessmen. *See also* Nanjing, Treaty of.

FURTHER READING: Davidson-Houston, James Vivian. *Yellow Creek: The Story of Shanghai.* Philadelphia: Dufour Editions, 1964; Johnson, Linda Cooke. *Shanghai: From Market Town to Treaty Port, 1074–1858.* Stanford, CA: Stanford University Press, 1995.

NIELS P. PETERSSON

Sherman, William Tecumseh (1820–1891)

A prominent Union military leader during the **American Civil War,** William T. Sherman was the son of an Ohio judge. At 16, Sherman obtained an appointment to the U.S. Military Academy and graduated seventh in his class in 1849. He served in the second Seminole War and the **Mexican-American War** and was promoted to captain. In 1853, he resigned his commission and held a number of positions in San Francisco, New Orleans, and St. Louis.

With the outbreak of the Civil War, Sherman enlisted as a colonel in the regular army. He rapidly moved up the ranks and, by the spring of 1863, was a major general and an Army Corps commander under his friend, Ulysses **Grant.** When, in 1864, Grant went east to take command of the Union war effort, Sherman was placed in command of the Army of Tennessee. By the fall of 1864, Sherman was convinced that the only way to end the war was to crush the South's economic ability to wage war. After the capture of Atlanta in the fall of 1864, he led his army on the famous "March to the Sea," during which the army pillaged its way from Atlanta to Savannah. In the spring of 1865, he used the same tactics in South Carolina, marching through Columbia and into North Carolina. There he accepted the surrender of the last remaining Confederate army east of the Mississippi, effectively ending resistance.

When Grant was elected president in 1868, he appointed Sherman commander-in-chief of the army. In that position, he used the same scorched earth tactics against Indian tribes who resisted being moved onto reservations. He implemented a policy of slaughtering the buffalo on the Great Plains, understanding that this would force the Indians to either stay on the reservations or starve. Once the Indians were on the reservations, he worked to make sure they were fed and spoke out forcefully, although not particularly effectively, against the civilian government mistreatment of them. Sherman's policy against the Confederacy and the Plains Indians was controversial then and now. His campaigns presaged the "total war" of the twentieth century; for better or worse, he has been called "the first modern general." *See also* Sioux Wars; United States.

FURTHER READING: Athearn, Robert G. *William Tecumseh Sherman and the Settlement of the West.* Norman: University of Oklahoma Press, 1956; Hirshson, Stanley P. *The White Tecumseh: A Biography of General William T. Sherman.* New York: J. Wiley, 1997; Sherman, William T. *Personal Memoirs of Gen. W. T. Sherman.* 2 vols. New York: D. Appleton, 1875.

JOSEPH ADAMCZYK

Shimoda, Treaty of (1855)

An agreement marking the opening of official diplomatic relations between the **Russian Empire** and Japan. The treaty was sought by Russia for two principal reasons: the Russian Empire was territorially overextended, stretching into Central Asia, Siberia, Alaska, and Northern California; and Russia was simultaneously troubled by competition from the **United States** for entry into Japan, symbolized in the visit of Commodore Matthew Perry and the Treaty of **Kanagawa** in 1854. Russia sought an Asian partner in trade for the development of its far-flung territories, as well as a wedge against American and British influence over Japan. The Shimoda treaty opened the ports of Hakodate, Nagasaki, and Shimoda to Russian commerce. It also defined the border between the two countries, rather inconclusively, through the Kuril Islands and determined joint influence over the island of **Sakhalin**, which the two divided in 1858. *See also* Japanese Empire; Manchuria; Russian Far East; Sakhalin.

FURTHER READING: Kim, Key-Hiuk. *The Last Phase of the East Asian World Order: Korea, Japan and the Chinese Empire, 1860–1882.* Berkeley: University of California Press, 1980; Stephan, John J. *The Russian Far East: A History.* Stanford, CA: Stanford University Press, 1994.

CARL CAVANAGH HODGE

Shimonoseki, Treaty of (1895)

Signed on April 17, 1895, the Treaty of Shimonoseki ended the **Sino-Japanese War** in which a modernized and westernized Japanese military had defeated handily the antiquated forces of the **Qing Dynasty.** The treaty was negotiated by Count Hirobumi Ito for the Japanese and Li Hongzhang for the Chinese, and imposed harsh terms on a defeated **China.** The Chinese were forced to pay an indemnity of 200 million taels of silver and to recognize the autonomy and independence of **Korea,** as well to cede Formosa (present-day Taiwan) and the Pescadores Islands to Japan. In addition China was to cede **Port Arthur** and the Liaodong Peninsula, and open new treaty ports in Shashi, Chongqing, Suzhou, and Hangzhou. The harsh terms of the treaty prompted the so-called Triple Intervention by Russia, France, and Germany, which pressured Japan to renounce its claims to Port Arthur and the Liaodong peninsula in return for a larger Chinese indemnity. *See also* Russo-Japanese War.

FURTHER READING: Kim, Key-Hiuk. *The Last Phase of the East Asian World Order: Korea, Japan and the Chinese Empire, 1860–1882.* Berkeley: University of California Press, 1980; Morse, H. B. *The International Relations of the Chinese Empire.* 3 vols. New York: Longmans, Green, and Co., 1918; Myers, Ramon H., and Mark R. Peattie, eds. *The Japanese Colonial Empire, 1895–1945.* Princeton: Princeton University Press, 1984.

ADRIAN U-JIN ANG

Siam

Siam, contemporary Thailand, was the only country of the Far East, besides Japan and **China,** never to experience colonial rule. In the early nineteenth century, Siam's leaders concentrated on rivalry with neighboring Burma until realizing that the main threat came from the British and French Empires. King Mongkut, an acute observer of international affairs, managed to come to terms with the British by granting them **extraterritoriality** and **free trade** in the Bowring treaty of 1855.

Mongkut and his son Chulalongkorn relied on a mixture of modernization, diplomacy, and sometimes good fortune to defend Siam's independence. Under their leadership, limited but real reforms were introduced, often with the help of experts and advisers recruited from the European colonial services. A Western-style government and a centralized provincial administration were created in the 1890s, as well as an independent judiciary, a body of codified law, and a competent administration of the country's finances. Reforms helped preserve financial independence, prevent incidents that might provide pretexts for intervention, and win back jurisdiction over British subjects in 1909. Britain was interested chiefly in stability and free trade, whereas France, pursuing territorial rather than economic interests, was harder to placate. Repeatedly, Siam had to offer territorial concessions, beginning with the "Siam Crisis" of 1893 when French gunboats forced their way to Bangkok. After France had accepted to restrain her ambitions in Siam in the **Entente Cordiale** and Siam had ceded further territory to France in 1907 and Britain in 1909, independence was finally secure.

Except through the settlement of Siam's lowlands by people escaping from the control of the nobility and producing rice for export after the introduction of free trade in 1855 and the immigration of Chinese traders and laborers into Bangkok, Siamese society changed very little and only at the top. Chulalongkorn had received a partly Western education and from the 1880s, princes were educated in Europe. Administrative reforms and the creation of a modern army were accompanied by the training of new staff and resulted in the appearance of a small modern middle class. Universal education remained a distant prospect, however, held back by cautious fiscal policies that also hampered efforts at economic diversification. Siam managed to secure independence and create the structures of a modern state, but social and economic change was limited. *See also* Burma; French Empire; Indochina.

FURTHER READING: Wyatt, David K. *Thailand: A Short History.* New Haven, CT: Yale University Press, 1984.

NIELS P. PETERSSON

Siberia

For nineteenth-century Russia, Siberia was a resource frontier like the legendary American West for the **United States.** Until the peasant liberation of 1861, migration to Siberia was mostly compulsory. Exiles were forced to work in Siberian mines. By 1858, nearly 3 million people lived in Siberian, 1.7 million in the western and 1.3 million in the eastern part. Suspicious of British engagement in China after the **Opium Wars,** the tsarist government began to develop the Siberian frontier. Fearing British expansionism and taking advantage of China's weakness, Russia annexed in the 1850s and 1860s parts of China's northern borderlands, specifically the Amur region and the nearby Pacific shore where the harbor Vladivostok was founded in 1860.

In 1861, the so-called great Siberian migration began. **Alexander II** gave peasants from European Russia who wanted to settle in Siberia free homestead on state land and exempted migrants to the borderlands from taxes. Between 1882 and 1890, nearly 200,000 peasants settled in Siberia, but the construction of the **Trans-Siberian Railroad** accelerated this process. The project of the Trans-Siberian Railroad was not only ambitious, but also a serious drain on the national budget as the construction swallowed up a sum between 770 million and 1 billion dollars. Nevertheless, the economic development of the Siberian frontier before World War I would have been unthinkable without the Trans-Siberian Railroad. Thanks to the railroad, 2.5 million peasants migrated to Siberia between 1896 and 1904. Migration contributed to the Russification of the frontier. By the outbreak of World War I, the Siberian population was overwhelmingly Russian. In the same period Siberia's agriculture was booming thanks to the import of American machinery. The most famous Siberian product on the world market was butter. The nineteenth century also saw the birth of a strong regional movement in Siberia. For many Russian exiles, Siberia became a homeland where they propagated their democratic conviction that the people in Siberia were freer and more egalitarian than in European Russia. They envisioned Siberia as a "second America" and believed that the natural resource base of Siberia would accelerate industrial revolution and democratization. In the nineteenth century, however, the majority of intellectuals and officials in European Russia rejected any westernization and democratization and stressed Russian national exceptional status independent from Europe and America alike. Ultraconservative tsars like Alexander III and Nicolas II feared Siberian separatism, so that any autonomy or federalist plans for the Russian Empire were rejected. *See also* Russian Empire; Russian Far East.

FURTHER READING: Kotkin, Stephan, and David Wolff, eds. *Rediscovering Russia in Asia: Siberia and the Russian Far East.* Armonk, NY: M. E. Sharpe, 1995; Stolberg, Eva-Maria, ed. *The Siberian Saga. A History of Russia's Wild East.* New York: Peter Lang, 2005.

EVA-MARIA STOLBERG

Sicily

See Italy

Sierra Leone

Sierra Leone was the first British colony in Africa, aside from the coastal forts of the Gold Coast region. It was founded in 1787 under the influence of evangelical abolitionists, who wanted to resettle liberated slaves and other blacks in Africa, thereby creating "legitimate" trade as an alternative to the **slave trade.** The colony did not prosper, and was refounded under the Sierra Leone Company, notwithstanding its name a philanthropic enterprise, in 1791. Approximately 1,200 loyalist blacks were transported there from **Nova Scotia,** along with maroons from **Jamaica** following the 1797 rebellion. Sierra Leone became at this time the first jurisdiction in which free blacks were granted political rights.

Zachary Macaulay, the evangelical father of T. B. **Macaulay,** governed the colony from 1794–1799, and is credited with making it a permanent concern. In response to concern about the expansion of French West Africa, a British **protectorate** for the interior region around Sierra Leone was established in 1896. As a result of Admiralty interest in using it as a naval base, Sierra Leone became a crown colony in 1808 and was used thereafter as a destination for slaves liberated from slave ships by the **Royal Navy.**

FURTHER READING: Fyfe, C. F. *A History of Sierra Leone.* London: Oxford University Press, 1962.

MARK F. PROUDMAN

Sikh Wars (1845–1846, 1848–1849)

Two short but particularly brutal wars waged by British forces against the **Khalsa,** the army of the Sikh religious sect, for control of the **Punjab** in northwest **India.** The First Sikh War followed hot on the East India Company's failed effort in **Afghanistan,** 1838–1842. The British presence in Afghanistan and annexation of Sind in 1843 provoked first apprehension and then a preemptive response from the Sikh court in Lahore, which quite rightly feared a British attack. A Khalsa force estimated between 12,000 and 20,000 men crossed the Sutlej River into British India on December 11, 1845, and seized Ferozepore two days later. When it pressed its offensive further southward, it was met and defeated by an Anglo-Indian force of 10,000 under General Sir Hugh Gough at Mudki. Gough's army then attacked and captured in bitter fighting Sikh entrenchments at **Ferozeshah,** after which the Khalsa withdrew across the Sutlej. When in January 1846 the Sikhs again crossed the frontier, the British forces were ready. They inflicted defeats on the Khalsa at Ludhiana and **Aliwal** before capturing the village of **Sobraon** near Lahore. Hostilities ended with a treaty signed at the Sikh capital on March 11, 1846, whereupon the Punjab became a British protectorate and the Sikhs were forced to pay an indemnity of £1.5 million.

The second war was the product of a conviction on the part of Khalsa that it had never been truly defeated and an ambition on the part of Lord **Dalhousie,** the new governor-general of India, to annex the Punjab outright. Both sides, in other words, were hankering for a return bout when the murder of two British officers at Lahore provided Dalhousie with appropriate outrage to invade the Punjab protectorate. After a bloody but indecisive engagement at Chilianwala in January 1849—the battle cost 2,300 British casualties and prompted a call to replace Gough as commander-in-chief in India—the British force captured Multan and then shattered a combined Sikh-Afghan force of 50,000 with his artillery at **Gujarat.** Gough, who thereby concluded the war and made himself a hero before he could be fired, described Gujarat as "a victory, not over my enemies, but over my country." The Punjab was annexed on March 30. *See also* British Empire; East India Companies; Singh, Ranjit.

FURTHER READING: Bruce, George. *Six Battles for India: The Anglo-Sikh Wars, 1845–6, 1848–9.* London: Arthur Baker, 1969; Farwell, Byron. *Queen Victoria's Little Wars.* New York: W. W. Norton, 1972.

CARL CAVANAGH HODGE

Silk Road

English translation of *Seidenstrasse,* a term coined by the German geographer and traveler Baron Ferdinand von Richthofen (1833–1905) to describe the network of land and sea trading routes connecting **China** to **India** and the Near East and whose heart was in Central Asia. For more than a thousand years, from the second century to the fourteenth century, the Silk Road was a medium of commercial and cultural exchange between East and West. The trade route fell into disuse from the fourteenth century with the eclipse of Mongol power, whose stabilizing influence had encouraged trade, and the subsequent rise of maritime trade routes based in Western Europe. For several centuries the route was largely forgotten.

The mid-nineteenth century witnessed the intensification of Anglo-Russian rivalry in Central Asia as the **Russian Empire** advanced steadily southward to threaten British India. In this context, Central Asia became a contesting ground between Russian and British adventurers and influence peddlers on whose heels arrived a host of scholars and explorers intent on studying the culture along the former Silk Road while pursuing their own host nation's interests. Most notable among such explorers were the Swede Sven Hedin (1865–1952) and the naturalized Englishman Aurel Stein (1862–1943). Sven Hedin is credited with opening up the region for exploration after his groundbreaking journeys through the Taklamakan Desert in the 1890s. Stories of the region's archaeological treasures soon attracted explorers representing Britain, France, Germany, Russia, and Japan. The effect of this intense period of activity, which lasted nearly up to the outbreak of World War I and in many ways mirrored larger imperial rivalries, was the birth of Central Asian studies. In the process, however, innumerable artifacts and ancient documents were looted from the region and taken to European museums and libraries. *See also* Great Game.

FURTHER READING: Hopkirk, Peter. *Foreign Devils on the Silk Road: The Search for the Lost Cities and Treasures of Chinese Central Asia.* London: John Murray, 1980.

DANIEL C. KANE

Singapore

An island abutting on southern tip of the Malay Peninsula in the narrow waters joining the Malacca Strait to the South China Sea, originally named *Singapura,* Sanskrit for "Lion City." A lease on it was acquired by Sir Stanford **Raffles** in the name of the East India Company from the Sultan of Jahore in 1819. Raffles established a free-trade port city in Singapore that quickly eclipsed other ports as the entrepôt servicing trade between **India** and **China,** Japan, Indonesia, and **Australia.** Singapore encouraged immigration, by virtue of which it acquired a cosmopolitan character and a population composed of Malays, Javanese, Indians, Chinese, and English.

In 1826, Singapore came under the united administration of Singapore, Malacca, Penang, and Province Wellesley in the Straits Settlements, and in 1858 the East India Company ceded the entire Straits Settlement to the British crown. With the opening of the Suez Canal in 1869, Singapore became an important link to Middle Eastern trade as well. As a naval station, it ranked as one of Admiral John Fisher's "five strategic keys" to the British Empire. *See also* British Empire; East India Companies; Free Trade; Royal Navy.

FURTHER READING: Bowle, John. *The Imperial Achievement: The Rise and Transformation of the British Empire.* Boston: Little, Brown, 1975; Tarling, Nicholas, ed. *The Cambridge History of Southeast Asia.* 2 vols. New York: Cambridge University Press, 1999.

CARL CAVANAGH HODGE

Singh, Ranjit (1780–1839)

The architect of the **Khalsa** Kingdom of **Punjab.** In 1792, at the age of 12, Ranjit succeeded to the leadership of Sukerchakia *misl* (principality), which controlled the territory between Lahore and Attock. By the first decade of the nineteenth century, he was able to establish control over the whole of Punjab. The Napoleonic Empire fascinated him, and he also kept well informed regarding the British anxiety about the advance of tsarist Russia into Central Asia. Whenever he got a chance, he discussed military affairs with foreign visitors.

In 1805, Jaswant Rao Holkar arrived in Punjab, retreating before the British General Lord Gerard Lake. Ranjit mediated peace between the two parties. He visited Jaswant and heard with astonishment about the war exploits of the British, concluding that infantry disciplined and equipped in the Western style along with field artillery would enable him to survive against the onslaught of the British East India Company. From 1807, Ranjit trained Western-style infantry equipped with Brown Bess muskets from the deserters of the company's troops and demobilized soldiers of the Maratha armies; he depended on ex-Napoleonic officers for training his army and establishing gun foundries. In total, more than 100 European officers were employed by Ranjit. Despite the opposition from his *sirdars* in particular and the Sikh community in general, who were votaries of light cavalry, Ranjit was successful in westernizing part of his army and took personal care of its westernized contingents, spending three to four hours every day watching the parade and frequently rewarded soldiers for good performance. After Ranjit's death on June 29, 1839, the court lost control over the Khalsa. This encouraged the company to invade Punjab. *See also* British Empire; East India Companies; India; Sikh Wars.

FURTHER READING: James, Lawrence. *Raj: The Making and Unmaking of British India.* New York: St. Martin's, 1997; Singh, Amandeep and Parmot Singh. *Warrior Saints: Three Centuries of Sikh Military Tradition.* New York: I. B. Tauris, 1988.

KAUSHIK ROY

Sinn Féin

Gaelic for "ourselves alone" or "we ourselves," Sinn Féin is a nationalist movement for Irish political and economic autonomy originating in Dublin during

1905–1907. Conceived as a nonviolent resistance to English imperial rule, by the eve of World War I, Sinn Féin transformed itself into an active political party dedicated to establishing an independent Irish parliament. Britain's distraction with World War I became an opportunity for Irish separatists to stage an uprising during Easter 1916.

Although militarily unsuccessful, the Easter Rebellion and subsequent English repression produced a wave of Irish nationalism that catapulted Sinn Féin to prominence. Sinn Féin coordinated and became identified with nationalist policies during the Anglo-Irish guerrilla war (1918–1921), which ended with Home Rule established in the Irish Free State. In the years after instituting dominion status and the partitioning of **Ireland,** Sinn Féin reorganized as the political voice of the Irish Republican Army. *See also* Home Rule.

FURTHER READING: Davis, Richard P. *Arthur Griffith and the Non-violent Sinn Fean.* Dublin: Anvil Books, 1974; Feeney, Brian. *Sinn Fean: A Hundred Turbulent Years.* Madison: University of Wisconsin Press, 2003.

JONATHAN GANTT

Sino-French War (1883–1885)

A conflict between **China** and France over Vietnam. The Sino-French War revealed the inadequacy of China's modernization efforts such as the Self-Strengthening Movement of the 1860s, as the imperial Qing government was unable to act effectively and decisively while facing a national crisis. Historically, Vietnam was China's major **protectorate** in the south. Since 1664, the rulers of Vietnam had sent more than 50 tribute missions to Beijing. During the mid-nineteenth century, however, France began to colonize southern Vietnam by sending its forces to protect Catholic priests and their converts. In 1874, a Franco-Vietnamese treaty of "Peace and Alliance" was reached. The French acquired the right to navigate the Red River and began to expand into northern Vietnam by stationing troops in Hanoi and Haiphong. Facing the growing French encroachment, the ruling Nguyen dynasty of Vietnam asked the Chinese for protection. Unwilling to concede its influence in the region, the Chinese government dispatched troops in 1883 from the Yunnan and Guangxi Provinces across border into Tonkin, where they engaged the French in a series of battles.

While the hostilities dragged on the frontline without decisive victories, the Chinese imperial court was divided between the appeasement wing of Viceroy Li Hongzhang (1823–1901) and the Purists' hard-line advocacy of war to defend China's honor and uphold its obligations to a tributary state. After further French advances, Prince Gong (1832–1898) and the Grand Council were dismissed, and Zhang Zhidong (1837–1909) was appointed governor general of Guangdong and Guangxi, in charge of military affairs with the French. Concurrently on the diplomatic front, in May 1884 Li Hongzhang managed to negotiate a settlement with France in which the two countries agreed to make the area a joint protectorate. Although no indemnity was required, the so-called Li–Fournier agreement specified the Chinese withdrawal and the recognition of French interests in Vietnam. This agreement, however, was rejected by the Chinese government when the conservative war party emerged with force and began to pressure the court to take a hawkish approach against the French aggression. Therefore, fighting resumed when a French ultimatum expired in August 1884, and both sides dispatched reinforcement troops to northern Vietnam.

Although on the land the French forces stayed on the offensive, taking control of the delta region and pushing toward the Chinese border in March 1885, the Chinese army recaptured the strategic Zhennan Pass, a surprising turn of events that led to the downfall of the French cabinet. Along the Chinese coast, the newly established imperial Qing navy was nonetheless no match for the French fleet. Although China had more than 50 modern warships, they were under four separate commands of the Beiyang, Nanyang, Fujian, and Guangdong fleets. Because of bureaucratic rivalry, there was no coordinated national war, as Li Hongzhang and Zeng Gongquan (1824–1890) were reluctant to mobilize the two major fleets under their commands. When facing the French assault, the Chinese naval officers were poorly trained, ill informed, disorganized, and indecisive. In August 1884, French warships attacked Jilong in northern Taiwan and destroyed 11 vessels of the Chinese Fujian Fleet established by Viceroy Zuo Zongtang (1812–1885), and demolished the Fuzhou Shipyard constructed in 1866 with the aid of French engineers. After an extra year of costly warfare, the wavering Qing government was ready for a new settlement. Finally in June 1885, Li signed a peace treaty in Paris based on the original Li–Fournier agreement. Consequently, the French protectorate of Vietnam was recognized, and the historical Sino-Vietnamese tributary relationship was terminated. *See also* Annam; French Empire; Indochina; Qing Dynasty; Tonkin.

FURTHER READING: Chere, Lewis M. *The Diplomacy of the Sino-French War 1883–1885: Global Complications of an Undeclared War.* Notre Dame, IN: Cross Cultural Publications, 1989; Eastman, Lloyd E. *Throne and Mandarins: China's Search for a Policy during the Sino-French Controversy, 1880–1885.* Cambridge, MA: Harvard University Press, 1967.

WENXIAN ZHANG

Sino-Japanese War (1894–1895)

The result of a dispute between **China** and Japan over influence in **Korea,** which was rooted in an ongoing rivalry between the two nations for dominance in the region. Through the Treaty of Kanghwa in 1876, China had de facto allowed Japan to recognize Korea as an independent state—although it was technically Chinese territory—and the subsequent attempt by the Chinese to reassert influence over the peninsula became a source of dispute between the two nations. To avoid open conflict, the Li-Ito Convention was concluded in 1885, requiring both nations to withdraw their armies from Korea and to provide notification of any new military deployments there.

In 1894, a rebellion occurred in Korea in the wake of the assassination of its pro-Japanese reformist prime minister, prompting China and Japan to intervene militarily. Having crushed the rebellion, Japan refused to withdraw its forces and instead sent further reinforcements. War was officially declared on August 1, 1894, and Japanese forces handily defeated the Chinese armies at Seoul and Pyongyang and proceeded north into China proper. By November 21, the Japanese had advanced and captured **Port Arthur** on the Liaodong peninsula. At sea, the

Chinese Beiyang fleet lost 8 of 12 warships in an engagement in the Yellow Sea and was forced to retreat behind the fortifications of the naval fortress at **Weihaiwei.** The remnants of the fleet were destroyed in harbor by Japanese forces in a flanking landward attack from the Liaodong peninsula, which then proceeded to besiege Weihaiwei.

With the easing of harsh winter conditions and the fall of Weihaiwei on February 2, 1895, Japanese armies continued their advance into **Manchuria.** This advance prompted the Chinese to sue for peace and the Treaty of **Shimonoseki,** which ended the war, was signed on April 17, 1895. In China, the humiliating defeat at the hands of an "inferior" state and the harsh terms of the peace treaty prompted calls for further reforms and accelerated modernization. For Japan, victory in the war was viewed as vindication of the modernization programs of the **Meiji Restoration** and would encourage further encroachment into China. *See also* Japanese Empire; Russo-Japanese War.

FURTHER READING: Morse, H. B. *The International Relations of the Chinese Empire.* 3 vols. New York: Longmans, Green, and Co., 1918; Nish, Ian. *Japanese Foreign Policy, 1869–1942: Kasumigaseki to Miyakezaka.* London: Routledge, 1977; Paine, S.C.M. *The Sino-Japanese War of 1894–1895: Perceptions, Power, and Primacy.* Cambridge: Cambridge University Press, 2003.

ADRIAN U-JIN ANG

Sioux Wars (1862, 1876–1877, 1890–1891)

A series of conflicts between the **United States** and one of the great confederacies of plains Indians occasioned by the westward expansion of white settlement and the seizure of indigenous lands, often in violation of treaty agreements. In the uprising of 1862, the **American Civil War** prompted the Sioux of the Minnesota Territory to exploit the division within the growing white population to rise in revolt. In attacks on farms along a 200-mile stretch of the Minnesota River Valley 800 whites were slain, many of them women and small children. A militia raised for a punitive expedition defeated the Sioux in a skirmish at Wood Lake, after which a trial sentenced 303 Sioux to death. This number was reduced to 38 by President Abraham **Lincoln,** but the subsequent hanging was nonetheless the largest mass execution in North American history.

The Great Sioux War of 1876–1877 was the largest operation of the U.S. Army since the Civil War. The conflict resulted from a campaign to force the Sioux led by Sitting Bull and Crazy Horse out of the Black Hills of Montana and on to the Great Sioux Reservation against their will. It began with a Sioux attack on Fort Pease, Montana, in early 1876 and was not concluded until the defeat of the Sioux at the Battle of Rosebud Creek in May of 1877. Its most storied engagement was the defeat of the U.S. Seventh Cavalry under Major General George Custer by a combined Sioux and Cheyenne force at Little Bighorn in June 1876. The Messiah War of 1890–1891 arose when a religious revival led to an uprising among the Sioux of the Black Hills Reservation, sometimes referred to as the Ghost Dance Disturbances. It ended with the defeat of the Teton Sioux at Wounded Knee, North Dakota. *See also* Indian Wars; Riel Rebellion.

FURTHER READING: Brown, Dee. *Bury My Heart at Wounded Knee: An Indian History of the American West.* New York: Henry Holt, 2001; Vandervort, Bruce. *The Indian Wars of Mexico, Canada and the United States.* New York: Routledge, 2006.

CARL CAVANAGH HODGE

Slave Trade

For most of the nineteenth century a commerce in human misery was in steady decline among the imperial powers. The Atlantic slave trade during the sixteenth century was initially established by Spain and Portugal for the transport of enslaved African labor to the Americas. In the seventeenth century, both Britain and the **Netherlands** also became deeply involved, in Britain's case the Royal Africa Company established in 1662 claiming an official if not actual monopoly on the sale of slaves in the English colonies. Markets such as the **United States, Brazil,** and other South American plantation economies, and the Caribbean accounted for the transport in the most appalling conditions of some 12 million Africans to the fate of forced labor and early death in the New World.

Beginning in the 1780s, humanitarian movements dedicated to the abolition of slavery and the slave trade based on Christian humanity were progressively reinforced by the industrialization of European economies and the increasing political influence of a bourgeois class to whom slave labor epitomized the economic backwardness of agrarian interests. **Denmark** banned slave trading within its empire in 1792, followed by Britain and the United States in 1807, and France in 1815. Largely as the result of British insistence, the Congress of **Vienna** adopted a resolution banning the slave trade, yet left it to each of the powers present to decide when to act on the sentiment. The trade in slaves continued illegally well into the 1860s, and the use of slave labor was not banned in the **British Empire** until 1833 and in the United States not until the defeat of the Confederacy and its slave-based economy in 1865. The Netherlands waited until 1863 to ban slavery. Although France banned the trade in 1815, the trafficking of slaves and use of slave labor lasted for decades in many French colonial possessions. Because after the Battle of Trafalgar the **Royal Navy** was omnipotent on the high seas, it was in a position to repress the slave trade and made an honest attempt to do so. It had the greatest impact on the Atlantic passage. Elsewhere, such as the Arab slaving network stretching across the Indian Ocean and deep into the African interior, the sheer volume of the commerce often exceeded the navy's capacity. Moreover, variations on slave labor and its legacy persisted in corners of the British Empire. British missionaries inveighed against the cruel treatment of native Africans by the Boers, and British circuit courts in the Cape Colony took legal action. The Slachter's Nek Rebellion of 1815 erupted when a farmer charged with mistreating a Khoikhoi laborer refused to appear in court. When a force of colonial police consisting partly of Khoikhoi regulars was sent to arrest him, a skirmish ensued in which the farmer was killed. Several of his supporters were subsequently tried and hanged. The episode provoked outrage among Boers who thought it absurd that a farmer be punished for abusing a Koikhoi, and it presaged the tension between South African Boers and British authority that eventually led to the Anglo-Boer Wars. *See also* American Civil War; Pax Britannica; Portuguese Empire; Spanish Empire.

FURTHER READING: Johnson, Paul. *The Birth of the Modern: World Society, 1815–1830.* New York: Harper Collins, 1991; Klein, Herbert. *The Trans-Atlantic Slave Trade.* Cambridge: Cambridge University Press, 1999; St. Clair, William. *The Door of No Return: Cape Coast Castle and the Slave Trade.* New York: Bluebridge, 2007; Toledano, Ehud R. *The Ottoman Slave Trade and Its Suppression, 1840–1890.* Princeton, NJ: Princeton University Press, 1982.

CARL CAVANAGH HODGE

Slavism

A movement with roots in Slavic Romanticism stirred up by the French Revolution and human ideals of liberty, equality, and fraternity but also influenced by idealistic German philosophers such as Johann Gottfried von Herder. Slavism was a literary and intellectual movement. The most prominent writers and philosophers were Pavel J. Savarik (1795–1861) and Frantisek Palacky (1798–1876) among the Czechs and Slovaks, Bronislaw Tretowski (1808–1869) and Adam Mickiewicz (1789–1866) among the Poles, Valentin Vodnik (1758–1819) and Ljudant Gaj (1809–1872) from the Balkans, Mikhail P. Pogodin (1800–1875) and Fyodor I. Tyuchev (1803–1875) among the Russians. **Pan-Slavism** was by contrast political and envisioned the unification of all Slavic peoples. It was supported by Slavic nationalities in the **Habsburg Empire** and **Ottoman Empire** and was also a foreign policy tool of the **Russian Empire.**

Like Pan-Germanism, Pan-Slavism was awakened by the **Napoleonic Wars.** Slavs rediscovered their history, philology, and folklore to create a sense of national unity. Pan-Slavism had many facets, like the call for the independence of the Poles, Czechs, Slovaks, and southern Slavic peoples, but also for the inseparable union of the Russian Empire. On the one hand, it stood for self-determination and independence, on the other for the cultural superiority of the Slavic people over non-Slavic nationalities within the Russian Empire. During the revolution of 1848, the movement held its first congress in Prague. There was the idea of a Pan-Slavic University in Warsaw and three Slavic empires: the Russian Empire, including all territories east of the Vistula; a Western Slavic empire with Prague as its capital; and a southern Slav empire with Belgrade as its capital. But these ideas remained utopian. The problem was that western Slavs were overwhelmingly loyal to the Habsburg Empire, whereas the Balkan Slavs, in particular the Serbs, were loyal to the Russian Empire.

From the very beginning, in fact, the Pan-Slavist movement was divided. The Poles showed strong anti-Russian tendencies, whereas minor Slavic nationalities feared that the Russians would dominate the movement and exploit the vision of Slavic unity to make the nationalities of Central Europe and the Balkans into Russia's vassals. Russian Pan-Slavists believed that, because they had not experienced Habsburg or Ottomans rule, Russians were the "true" Slavs and the natural leaders of the movement. Some proponents even thought that the other Slavic nationalities should adopt Russian as the *lingua franca* of all Slavs, the Orthodox religion, and even Cyrillic writing. Russian Pan-Slavists sought less the emancipation than the Russification of Slavic peoples.

Before World War I, Czechs and Slovaks aimed more autonomy within the Habsburg Empire—the so-called Austro-Slavism—but southern Slavs openly advocated complete independence from Habsburg and Ottoman rule. The Serbs sought to unite all of the Balkan Slavs under their rule and turned to Russia for support.

The Serbs were at the fore of the Slavic independence movement and were less compromising than the Czechs or Slovaks who favored the solution of the Slavic question through modernization and democratization. Whereas western Slavs were oriented toward the ideals of Western Europe, the orthodox Serbs shared a more Slavic-centered ideology with Russian Slavophiles. Russian Slavism had been influenced by philosophers like A. S. Khomiakov (1804–1860), I. V. Kireevskii (1806–1856), and K. S. Aksakov (1817–1860), who rejected Western ideas based on rationalism and materialism that would destroy Slavic spiritualism. They propagated a return to old Slavic tradition through a renaissance of conservative social and political structures and considered the peasant communalism as the ideal social structure, because most regions of Eastern Europe were agrarian. Aksakov rejected any modernization as degenerate.

From the mid-nineteenth century, Russian pan-Slavism became more aggressive. The defeat of Russia in the **Crimean War** of 1853 and the inner reforms of the 1860s were considered symptoms of decay. Humiliation in foreign policy and domestic modernizations based on Western models drove Russian Pan-Slavists to foster an idea of national salvation for all Slavic nationalities through the rejection of industrialization and urbanization and the embrace of agrarian society and the simple life of Slavic peasants as a human ideal. Russian Pan-Slavists also believed in the mission of the Orthodox religion as a universal idea that attracted their orthodox brethren in Serbia. Between 1806 and 1815, the Serbs became autonomous of the Ottoman **Porte** and were very soon seeking expansion in the Balkans in order to bring all southern Slavs under Serbian rule. This aim endangered the unity of the Habsburg Empire, so Vienna pursued an extremely repressive course in domestic politics that fueled the fire of southern Slavic nationalism and would eventually lead to the **July Crisis** of 1914.

In Poland, Pan-Slavism had a difficult quality, because the Poles had known oppressive occupation under by the Russian Empire and viewed the movement as a tool of Russification. As the Russian movement became more aggressive after Russia's defeat in the Crimean War and the Polish January Revolt of 1863, Russo-Polish animosity revealed deep strains within Pan-Slavism. Polish delegates did not take part in the Pan-Slavist Congress in Moscow in 1867. The Czech delegation under the leadership of the Czech historian Frantisek Palacky spoke up for a Russo-Polish rapprochement, but the Russians clung to their leadership of a movement that under Russian predominance defended Russia's imperial policy. During the Balkan crisis of 1875–1878, the Pan-Slavist movement propagated an aggressive policy toward the Ottoman Empire, including the conquest of Constantinople as the future capital of a Slavic Union. Western Slavs had no interest in southern Slav irredentism and Russian expansionism. Although they preferred a compromise with Vienna, Czechs and Slovaks were nonetheless not free of radicalism, especially where cultural autonomy was concerned. An extensive pamphlet literature and a series of journals revealed a tone not of reconciliation but of confrontation. Pan-Slavism in the Habsburg Empire, furthermore, provoked anti-Slavism. Hungarians defended their exclusive rights within an empire in which Hungarian had to be the second public language. The Slovaks and Serbs of Hungary criticized the privileged status of Hungarians.

Nevertheless, Pan-Slavism was no more aggressive than other nationalist movements such as German and Hungarian nationalism, and it had a profound impact on Slavic identity. From the mid-nineteenth century until World War I, Slavic nationalities within Austria-Hungary and the Ottoman Empire experienced a cultural renaissance, as Slavs rediscovered a history dating to the Middle Ages before Habsburg and Ottoman domination—a period that appeared to have been a golden age. The *fin-de-siècle* Slavic language experienced a rebirth in journals and schoolbooks. Merchants, the clergy, and teachers supported Slavic cultural renaissance. As each Slavic nationality—Polish, Czech, Slovak, southern Slav, Russian—was grounded in a different historical tradition, Pan-Slavism had never been a homogeneous movement. The two main and opposing factions—a conciliatory policy favored by western Slavs of Catholic belief faith that followed the Western European model of national development, and a violent variant propagated by Serbs and Russians of Orthodox belief who rejected the Western model of the nation-state—represented the divergent paths of gradual transformation and eruptive confrontation. In contrast to Orthodox Pan-Slavism, Austro-Slavism had the character of a democratic national federalism. Czechs recognized that true national and cultural emancipation required a break with imperialism. The main reason for this difference was religion. Western Slavs were influenced by a liberal Catholicism that was an important bond with Austria-Hungary. Russia, as an Orthodox Great Power, was suspicious of conciliatory Austro-Slavism that gained influence in the Balkans among the Croats and Slovenians and in Galicia among the Polish and Ukrainian national movements. From the mid-nineteenth century onward, the comments on Czech Austro-Slavism in Russian periodicals were highly negative, and Austro-Slavism was rejected as a betrayal of the Pan-Slavist ideal. Croatian and Slovenian loyalty to the Habsburg Empire endangered Serb and Russian influence in the Balkans, and conflict among Slavists contributed to a confrontation between the Habsburg and the Russian Empire that led to World War I. *See also* Balkan Wars; Bosnia-Herzegovina; Croatia-Slavonia; Serbia.

FURTHER READING: Kohn, Hans. *Pan-Slavism: Its History and Ideology.* Notre Dame, IN: University of Notre Dame Press, 1953; MacKenzie, David. *The Serbs and Russian Pan-Slavism, 1875–1878.* Ithaca, NY: Cornell University Press, 1967; Milojkovic-Djuric, Jelena. *Panslavism and National Identity in Russia and the Balkans, 1830–1880.* Boulder, CO: East European Monographs, 1994; Rabow-Edling, Susanna. *Slavophile Thought and the Politics of Cultural Nationalism.* Albany: State University of New York Press, 2006.

EVA-MARIA STOLBERG

Smith, Adam (1723–1790)

The founding theorist of classical political economy, Adam Smith was educated at Glasgow, where he came to know many of the key figures of the Scottish enlightenment, and at Balliol, Oxford. He became friends with David Hume and, in 1751, was offered a post as professor of logic at Glasgow, where he also taught moral philosophy. Smith's first book, *The Theory of Moral Sentiments* was as much about the psychology as the ethics of moral feelings: in it he first used his famous phrase "an invisible hand," conveying a notion that the world was a rational system characterized by natural balances. It was an idea that carried forward into Smith's major work, the *Wealth of Nations* of 1776. Smith was influenced both by his meetings with contemporary French political economists and by his acquaintance with Charles Townshend, chancellor of the exchequer under William Pitt the Elder, and the prominent

Scottish politician Sir Henry Dundas (later Lord **Melville**). *Wealth of Nations* was a work of two volumes, treating numerous topics of political and economic—two categories not then separate—relevance, but focusing, as its title implied, on the historical, geographical, and political factors that made a nation wealthy or poor. Smith's most famous argument related to the division of labor, which, enabled by its necessary concomitant, trade, made "the progress of opulence" possible.

Smith began by describing wealth as the sum of material assets in a society, from which "the necessaries and conveniences of life" were supplied, and that wealth was originally the creation of labor. These ideas were directly opposed to the mercantilist doctrine then current that bullion was equivalent to wealth. International trade, he taught, should be freed of protectionist impediments designed to accumulate specie. For Smith, society progressed through various stages of history, although there is little trace of determinism in his account. No opponent of class privilege—class differences being for him a simple fact of life—Smith nevertheless argued that a prosperous nation was one in which the poor had a basic standard of living above mere subsistence. *The Wealth of Nations* had no great immediate impact—the British political world being somewhat preoccupied with the wars of 1775–1783—but in subsequent decades it came to be regarded as a canonical work. It influenced William **Pitt** the Younger's 1786 trade agreement with France and became the standard point of reference for subsequent political economists. Although to some degree Smith was overtaken as a theoretical economist by David **Ricardo** and John Stuart **Mill,** and was superseded by the marginal economics of W. S. Jevons later in the century, his arguments for **free trade** became a standard text for politicians in the nineteenth century, and his name has remained a touchstone for free market advocates to this day. Smith was a strong supporter of the Scottish Union, which had opened imperial markets to Scottish merchants, as well as an advocate of an Irish Union.

In directly imperial matters, Smith's distaste for the bullion-centered theories of wealth led him to emphasize the corrupt character of the **Spanish Empire,** and by contrast the wholesome character of the **British Empire** of settlement. His opposition to protectionism on grounds of the theory of comparative advantage led him to oppose closed mercantilist colonial schemes as counterproductive and at any rate unenforceable. He thought the British colonies in America the most productive in the world and attributed this to "plenty of good land, and liberty to manage their own affairs," although he thought they were of no direct value to England. Smith was a determined opponent of chartered companies of the East India type, holding that theirs was the worst of all governments. He was not, however, a dogmatic free trader, recognizing that some public purposes, such as defense, were more important than trade. The wider impact of *Wealth of Nations,* beyond its specific policy arguments, was to function as the canonical text of the idea that free markets, and more generally capitalist economies in the round, were a progressive force making not merely for the "progress of opulence" but for the improvement of all concerned. Such ideas permeated Victorian thought and formed the environment in which both the imperialist and the anti-imperialist arguments of the nineteenth century were constructed. *See also* Anti-Corn Law League; Free Trade; Liberalism.

FURTHER READING: Muller, Jerry. *Adam Smith in His Time and Ours.* New York: Maxwell Macmillan International, 1993; Ross, Ian Simpson. *The Life of Adam Smith.* Oxford: Clarendon,

1995; Smith, Adam. *An Inquiry into the Nature and Causes of the Wealth of Nations.* 2 vols. London: W. Strahan and T. Cadell, 1776.

MARK F. PROUDMAN

Smolensk, Battle of (1812)

An indecisive battle on Napoleon **Bonaparte**'s march to Moscow. French delays earlier in the campaign allowed the Russians to combine two armies, commanded by Generals Barclay de Tolly and Peter Bagration, at Smolensk, about 280 miles east of Moscow, and the Russian force now numbered about 50,000 men. Napoleon did little on August 15, allowing the Russians to prepare for battle. Battle came the next day as the two sides clashed in the suburbs, each sustaining heavy casualties. On August 17, Napoleon sent three corps against the city walls, but this was ineffective and both sides again sustained heavy losses. A lull on August 18 allowed Bagration to withdraw his army eastward, with Barclay soon following suit. Prompt French action could have been decisive, but General Junot failed to properly pursue and the Russians successfully retired, leaving a burning city to the French. Napoleon considered staying there for the winter, but ultimately marched east toward **Borodino** and Moscow. *See also* Napoleonic Wars; Russian Empire.

FURTHER READING: Austin, Paul Britten. *1812: The March on Moscow.* London: Greenhill Books, 1993; Markham, J. David. *Imperial Glory: The Bulletins of Napoleon's Grande Armée 1805– 1814.* London: Greenhill, 2003.

J. DAVID MARKHAM

Smuts, Jan Christiaan (1870–1950)

Prime minister of **South Africa,** a British imperial statesman, and a Boer general during the Boer War of 1899–1902, Jan Smuts went on to become a British field marshal and an advocate of Commonwealth unity. Smuts was the son of a prosperous South African farmer, and was educated at the University of the Cape of Good Hope and at Cambridge. He was an outstanding student and was trained as a lawyer in England. He entered cape politics as a supporter of the Afrikaner Bond in 1895, and, in a theme that persisted throughout his career, called for the two white races of South Africa to unite against black "barbarians." Following the **Jameson Raid,** however, he became an ardent opponent of British imperialism, and joined Paul **Kruger**'s Transvaal government. He led ultimately unsuccessful efforts to negotiate a solution to the issue that led to the South African War, the franchise for British immigrants to the Transvaal.

In that war, he placed his hopes for victory on international intervention. Originally a civilian, he became a a guerilla commander, remaining in the field after the British occupation of Pretoria. In the discussions that led to the peace of **Vereeniging,** he insisted that the question of the native franchise be left to a self-governing South Africa, a decision with fateful consequences. After the war, he became a leading Afrikaner politician, consistently opposed to political rights for Africans. In 1914, he supported the Union of South Africa's entry into the war on the British side, suppressing a rebellion by some of his former Afrikaner nationalist comrades. He commanded South African forces in their invasion of southwest Africa, and then took command of British forces in east Africa, with the rank of lieutenant general in the British army. Representing South Africa in London in 1917, he was made a member of the war cabinet and became influential with David **Lloyd George.**

In contrast to his rigid opposition to black rights at home, and his vision of a settler-dominated Africa, he was in extra-African affairs a keen liberal internationalist. He produced a pamphlet urging a League of Nations, resisted the vindictive aspects of the Treaty of Versailles, and, in the aftermath of the World War II, he drafted the preamble of the United Nations Charter. The latter was quoted back at him, and at subsequent South African leaders, by human rights advocates. In commonwealth affairs, he was an advocate of **dominion** autonomy. Nevertheless, in domestic South African politics, he lost Afrikaner support and found himself in alliance with the English population and mining interests; the latter identification was reinforced by violent action against strikers both black and white. He led a sorely divided South Africa into World War II, becoming again a key figure in imperial politics, and a trusted confidant of **Churchill.** But he was defeated by the pro-apartheid and anti-imperial National Party in 1948. An intellectually ambitious man, Smuts attempted to reconcile religion and evolution and ecology through his philosophy of "holism." Smuts died in 1950, lauded with honors internationally but increasingly irrelevant in South African affairs. *See also* Boer Wars; Vereeniging, Treaty of.

FURTHER READING: Danziger, Christopher. *Jan Smuts.* Cape Town: Macdonald South Africa, 1978; Geyser, O. *Jan Smuts and His International Contemporaries.* Johannesburg: Covos Day, 2001; Hancock, W. K. *Smuts.* 2 vols. Cambridge: Cambridge University Press, 1968.

MARK F. PROUDMAN

Sobraon, Battle of (1846)

The final showdown of the First **Sikh War** fought on February 10, 1846, near the village of Sobraon. The Sikhs had constructed 3,000 yards of entrenchments in a semicircle, with each end touching the Sutlej River. Construction was shoddy, especially on the right side, as the Sikh generals practically wanted defeat. General Sire Hugh Gough, with his 15,000 troops, rightly wanted to launch the main assault against the Sikh right flank and then attack the center and left. The battle began at dawn with artillery fire for two to three hours, but the British quickly ran low of ammunition. Gough ordered an infantry charge, which was initially repulsed, but finally succeeded in pushing back the Sikh army. Because Tej Singh had removed much of the pontoon bridge that went across the Sutlej, many Sikh soldiers were forced to retreat into the river, which quickly became clogged with dead and dying men. British casualties amounted to nearly 2,300, of whom 300 were killed. The Sikhs had upwards of 8,000 casualties. The British victory at Sobraon broke the **Khalsa,** and fighting in the First Sikh War came to an end. *See also* India; Punjab.

FURTHER READING: Bruce, George. *Six Battles for India: The Anglo-Sikh Wars, 1845–6, 1848–9.* London: Arthur Barker, 1969; Cook, Hugh. *The Sikh Wars: The British Army in the Punjab, 1845–1849.* London: Leo Cooper, 1975; Crawford, E. R. "The Sikh Wars, 1845–9." In Brian

Bond, ed. *Victorian Military Campaigns.* New York: Frederick A. Praeger Publishers, 1967; Farwell, Byron. *Queen Victoria's Little Wars.* New York: W. W. Norton & Co., 1972.

DAVID TURPIE

Social Darwinism

An ideological trend widespread at the end of the nineteenth and the beginning of the twentieth centuries advocating laws of human social and political development based on crude association with the laws of biological evolution theorized by Charles **Darwin.** Competition, natural selection, struggle for existence, and survival of the most adaptive individuals are recognized as basic determinants of social life and in a wider context applied to social theory, arguing the necessity of competition for social progress. It originated in the specific historical, cultural, political, and economic context of the end of nineteenth century, characterized by wars over resources, competition in the world market, rising militarism and territorial expansionism, class struggle, social tensions, and antagonistic nationalisms. In such situations it became convenient to believe that the world of nations was organized according to the same basic principle as the animal world and that predatory behavior afforded the best chances of survival.

Aspects of social Darwinism are found in the ideas of English economist and priest Thomas R. **Malthus** (1766–1834), according to whom contradictions and difficulties of social progress were explained by eternal and absolute laws of nature. Malthus was well known for his "natural law" of human population growth and regulation. A theoretical expression of social-Darwinist views is found in works of the English philosopher and sociologist Herbert Spencer (1820–1903). It was Spencer who coined and put into circulation in social science the concept of "struggle for existence." In nature the best chance for survival belongs to the best-adapted organisms, the organisms with the highest degree of functional differentiation. According to Spencer, in a social context, the higher the internal differentiation of the society, the higher its capacity to adapt. Spencer neglected the role of the state and of any political institutions in society regulation. At his later period he underlined primacy of the individual in the industrial society; the role of the state he considered as secondary and non-necessary in the process of social development. As a result of Spencer's significant impact and influence on the development of social Darwinism's theoretical base, this direction in social thought sometimes is also called spencerism.

In Great Britain Darwinist ideas applied to social behavior were sometimes used as an argument to attack privileges, but they were also used to explain failure. The most politically liberal form of social Darwinism was developed in the **United States** and is associated with a new generation of industrialists such as John D. Rockefeller and Andrew Carnegie who considered their success in business as the best proof of the social Darwinist principle that competition inevitably leads to progress. The least liberal form of social Darwinism saw an inherent virtue in competitive nationalism and militarism, at its worst justifying, in an age of rampant colonial competition, the subjugation of inferior peoples by their "natural" superiors. *See also* Race.

FURTHER READING: Bannister, Robert C. *Social Darwinism: Science and Myth in Anglo-American Thought.* Philadelphia: Temple University Press, 1979; Crook, David Paul. *Darwinism,*

War and History: The Debate over the Biology of War from the "Origin of Species" to the First World War.
Cambridge: Cambridge University Press, 1994; Hawkins, Mike. *Social Darwinism in European and American Thought, 1880–1946: Nature as Model and Nature as Threat.* Cambridge: Cambridge University Press, 1997; Hofstadter, Richard. *Social Darwinism in American Thought.* New York: G. Braziller, 1959.

OLENA V. SMYNTYNA

Solferino, Battle of (1859)

The last engagement of the second War of Italian Independence. It was fought in Lombardy between an Austrian army and a Franco-Piedmontese army and resulted in the annexation of most of Lombardy by **Piedmont-Sardinia,** thus contributing to the unification of **Italy.**

After its defeat at the Battle of **Magenta** on June 4, the Austrian army of about 120,000 men had retreated eastward, and Emperor **Francis Joseph** had arrived to dismiss General Count Franz von Gyulai and take personal command. The Franco-Piedmontese army, of approximately equal size, under the command of Napoleon III of France and Victor Emmanuel II of Piedmont-Sardinia, pursued the Austrians. Neither side had accurate information about the other's troop movements, and on June 24, they unexpectedly clashed, in and around Solferino, four miles southeast of Castiglione della Stiviere in Lombardy at a time when the French expected to engage only the Austrian rear guard, and the Austrians expected to engage only the French advance units. The battle developed in a confused and piecemeal fashion until midday. After extremely costly fighting, the French broke the Austrian center in mid-afternoon. Smaller actions, including a vigorous delaying action by the Austrian general Ludwig von Benedek, continued until dark, leaving the French and Piedmontese too exhausted to pursue the defeated Austrians.

The Austrians lost 14,000 men killed and wounded and more than 8,000 missing or prisoners; the Franco-Piedmontese lost 15,000 killed and wounded and more than 2,000 missing or prisoners. These heavy casualties contributed to Napoleon III's decision to seek the truce with Austria that effectively ended the Second War of Italian Independence. The bloodshed also inspired Henri Dunant to lead the movement to establish the International Red Cross. *See also* Bonaparte, Louis Napoleon; Habsburg Empire.

FURTHER READING: Di Scala, Spencer M. *Italy: From Revolution to Republic, 1700 to the Present.* Boulder, CO: Westview Press, 1998; Hearder, Harry. *Italy in the Age of the Risorgimento, 1790–1870.* New York: Longman, 1983.

GUENTHER KRONENBITTER

Somaliland

Located along the Horn of Africa, a territory carved into three **protectorates,** French Somaliland and British Somaliland along the Red Sea, and Italian Somaliland along the Indian Ocean. Until the early 1870s, the **Ottoman Empire** exercised a nominal sovereignty over the Red Sea Coast until the Egyptians expanded into the area all the way to Cape Guardafui. When they evacuated, European powers followed, expanding their influence through the establishment of protectorates over native rulers. The British established a protectorate over the Red Sea port of Zeila, while the French, seeking to contain further British expansionism and to establish trade with Ethiopia, occupied the port of Djibouti. Finally, the Sultan of Zanzibar, nominal sovereign over the Benadir cities, the Obbia, and Mijjertein sultanates negotiated protectorates with the Italians in 1887–1893.

All three colonial powers faced the same problems: native uprisings, investment costs to develop their colonies, and an increasingly expansionist Ethiopian Empire. The most serious native uprising occurred in British Somaliland between 1899 and 1905 when Mohammed ben Abdullah and his Dervishes rebelled and raided British and Italian Somaliland. And, though bribed with land in southeastern British Somaliland, his presence required a British garrison and hindered development. With an ill-defined border, Ethiopian warriors constantly raided the British and Italian protectorates. The French were investing in a massive railroad project to build a line from Djibouti to Addis Ababa, the Empire's capital, while the Ethiopians continued to press more and more demands. The Italian government was the last to start investing in its colony, having only assumed governmental control in 1905. *See also* Africa, Scramble for; British Empire; Egypt; Ethiopia; French Empire; Italy.

FURTHER READING: Hess, Robert. *Italian Colonialism in Somalia.* Chicago: University of Chicago Press, 1966; James, Lawrence. *The Rise and Fall of the British Empire.* New York: St. Martin's Press, 1994.

FREDERICK H. DOTOLO

Soor, Battle of

See Burkersdorf, Battle of

South Africa Act (1910)

An act of Parliament creating the Union of **South Africa,** a federal **dominion** within the British Empire, consisting of four provinces, the **Cape Colony,** Natal, the **Transvaal,** and the **Orange Free State.** The latter two were Afrikaner-dominated formerly independent states conquered during the South African or Boer war of 1899–1902. The Cape Colony and Natal were in general dominated by their Anglophone or British populations. All had a large majority of Africans who, with few exceptions, were disenfranchised. The South Africa Act was passed by the Liberal government of H. H. **Asquith,** many of whose supporters had opposed the conquest of the Boer republics and believed strongly in the principle of self-government. By the terms of the Peace of **Vereeniging,** which had concluded the South African War, however, the question of the African franchise was left to the white voters of the new Union of South Africa. Despite a brief Afrikaner rebellion in 1914, the Union of South Africa, under the premiership of the former Boer general Louis **Botha,** remained loyal to Britain in World War I, providing one of the most prominent imperial statesmen, Jan Christiaan **Smuts.** *See also* Boer Wars; Transvaal.

FURTHER READING: Wilson, Monica, and Leonard Thompson, eds. *Oxford History of South Africa.* 2 vols. Oxford: Clarendon, 1971.

MARK F. PROUDMAN

Southwest War

See Satsuma Rebellion

Spanish Empire (1516–1714)

An empire in final decline and disintegration in the nineteenth century, starting with the loss of the Louisiana Territory in 1800 in the context of the Napoleonic Wars and ending with the loss of **Cuba, Puerto Rico,** the **Philippines,** and Guam after the **Spanish-American War** of 1898.

The Age of Expansion of the Spanish Empire had started early in the sixteenth century, under the Habsburg dynasty, of Austrian origin, brought about by the succession to the throne of Carlos I (1516–1556). Carlos was also known as Holy Roman Emperor Charles V, the grandson of Isabella and Ferdinand, who sponsored the "discovery" of America. The map of Spanish holdings in the Americas up to the dawn of the nineteenth century would start in the north with the Louisiana Territory, founded in 1699 by the French who lost it to Spain after the Seven Years' War. France briefly regained control of Louisiana in 1800, under Napoleon **Bonaparte,** who sold it to the **United States** in 1803. Spain disputed the borders of Louisiana, however, because the United States considered it to include territory corresponding to Texas, part of New Mexico, and West Florida, which Spain still regarded as colonies. Part of the squabble was settled in 1819, with the Adams-Onís Treaty, whereby Spain also ceded all of Florida to the United States.

The **Napoleonic Wars** generally undermined Spain's control of its American colonies. The Battle of **Trafalgar** in 1805, a resounding victory for the **Royal Navy,** resulted in the destruction of the Spanish fleet, leaving Spain without the means to enforce its administrative control in the Americas. The tables were turned in 1808, with the **Peninsular War,** when Napoleon's troops invaded Spain and Portugal, which were supported this time by Great Britain. The war ended with the British army crossing the border into France and Napoleon's abdication in 1814. The Spanish economy nevertheless went in freefall for most of the nineteenth century. By 1825, Spain had lost all its mainland American colonies.

The Spanish holdings in the Americas were organized and administered as viceroyalties. The first ones to be created, in the sixteenth century, were the Viceroyalty of New Spain, containing the North and Central American territories, and the Viceroyalty of Peru, covering most of South America. In the eighteenth century the Viceroyalty of Peru, created in 1542, was modified through the addition of the Viceroyalties of New Granada and of Río de la Plata, and left with the territory of what today is Chile and Peru. These two countries obtained their independence in 1818 and 1821, respectively, thus marking the end of the Viceroyalty of Peru.

The Viceroyalty of New Granada was created in 1717 for administrative reasons, because Lima, the capital of the Viceroyalty of Peru, was not easily accessible. It included present-day Colombia, Ecuador, Panama, and Venezuela. Revolutionary movements of independence emerged in this area in 1810, under the leadership of Simón **Bolívar** (1783–1830) and Francisco de Paula Santander (1792–1840). In 1819, these territories declared their independence as the confederation of the Republic of Gran Colombia. It lasted until 1830, when Ecuador and Venezuela proclaimed their independence. Panama remained a Columbian department until

1903, when it seceded from Colombia and declared its independence, emboldened by the United States, whose government immediately was granted exclusive rights to build and administer the **Panama Canal.**

The Viceroyalty of Río de la Plata was created in 1776 and covered the territory of what today is **Argentina,** Bolivia, Paraguay, and Uruguay. In 1778, Portugal annexed the Uruguay territory, which would become part of Brazil when it declared its independence in 1822. A revolt started in 1825 and in 1828 Uruguay declared its independence. With the Spanish fleet devastated in the Battle of Trafalgar in 1805, military enforcement of Spanish dominion in the area became impossible. British troops repeatedly attacked Buenos Aires and Montevideo in 1806 and 1807 but were successfully overcome by local forces, raising hopes for self-rule. Paraguay declared its independence in 1811 and Argentina in 1816. Bolivia had proclaimed itself independent in 1809, but strife continued until 1825, when a republic was finally established.

The Viceroyalty of New Spain was the first to be created, in 1525, and the last to fall apart. It covered the Spanish territories in North and Central America. The territorial disputes with the newly established United States, stirred by Napoleon's sale of the Louisiana Territory in 1803, were settled through the **Adams-Onís Treaty** of 1819, and New Spain ceased to exist in 1821 when Mexico gained its independence along with all the Central American territories, except for the Caribbean islands of Cuba and Puerto Rico.

The Philippines had also been annexed to New Spain in 1565 and continued to remain under Spanish domination after 1821. Late in the nineteenth century, Spain colonized the Palau Islands, located in the Pacific Ocean, east of the Philippines, and in 1899 sold them to Germany. Also in the Pacific Ocean there were the Marshall Islands, first explored by Alonso de Salazar in 1529. Spain claimed them in 1874, but in 1885 they became a German protectorate. The struggle for independence intensified toward the end of the century, particularly in Cuba and the Philippines, duly supported by the United States. This led to the Spanish-American War of 1898 and the Treaty of **Paris,** whereby the United States took over Cuba, Puerto Rico, Guam, and the Philippines. Cuba was granted conditional independence in 1902, through the **Platt Amendment,** but the United States continued to exercise strict control over its affairs and even occupied it between 1906 and 1909.

The colonies that Spain managed to hold on to the longest were several small north African territories. In 1778 Spain had received territorial and commercial rights in the Gulf of Guinea from Portugal in exchange for South American land rights. The respective area would become Spanish Guinea in 1885, a Spanish claim reinforced by the 1898 Treaty of Paris. Only in 1968, under international pressure, was the Guinea protectorate declared an independent state and renamed Equatorial Guinea. The **Berlin Conference** of 1884–1885 parleyed the colonization of Africa by European powers, and one of the consequences was that Spain and France went on to collaborate in controlling northwestern Africa, mainly the Algerian, Moroccan, and Western Saharan territories, until well after World War II. *See also* Portuguese Empire.

FURTHER READING: Balfour, Sebastian. *The End of the Spanish Empire, 1898–1923.* Oxford: Oxford University Press, 1997; Cortada, James W., ed. *Spain in the Nineteenth-Century World: Essays on Spanish Diplomacy, 1789–1898.* Westport, CT: Greenwood, 1994; Esdaile, Charles

J. *Spain in the Liberal Age: From Constitution to Civil War, 1808–1939.* Oxford: Blackwell, 2000; Tortella, Gabriel. *The Development of Modern Spain: An Economic History of the Nineteenth and Twentieth Centuries.* Translated by Valerie Herr. Cambridge, MA: Harvard University Press, 2000.

GEORGIA TRES

Spanish-American War (1898)

A conflict marking the beginning of American **imperialism.** As Secretary of State John Hay put it, the conflict was indeed, in many respects, a "splendid little war," in that it was popular, short, and relatively cheap; it brought easy victories at a low human cost; it was fought for the sake of a noble cause; and it eventually made the **United States** a world power.

American economic policy was indirectly responsible for the Cuban war. The tariff of 1894, which put high duties on Cuban sugar, worsened economic conditions on the island and triggered a new revolt against Madrid's autocratic rule in February 1895. The Spaniards vainly tied to put down the rebellion, and the conflict was a constant source of irritation to the United States. There were frequent naval incidents and destruction of American property. Approximately 50 million dollars were invested in Cuban plantations, sugar refineries, and factories. Moreover, there existed the risk of a European intervention in support of Spain, as Great Powers on the whole sympathized with Madrid, although none committed itself openly.

The part then played by the anti-Spanish "yellow press" and the response of public opinion were crucial elements in the outbreak of hostilities. The Cuban Junta in New York City had other powerful allies in organized labor, notably the American Federation of Labor, Protestant clergymen who disliked "Pope-ridden" Spain, Republican expansionists, and even Democrats who thought that "a little 'Jingo'" could do no harm in the coming presidential election of 1896.

By contrast, the attitudes of the last two presidents of the nineteenth century, Grover Cleveland and William McKinley, were strikingly similar: neither wanted to precipitate American involvement in the conflict. By March 1898, the country was nonetheless in a frenzied state owing to a number of occurrences, notably the explosion of the battleship *U.S.S. Maine* in Havana harbor—accidental, as it later turned out—on February 15, which brought public indignation and anti-Spanish sentiment to the highest pitch. The role of Congress was essential in that it somewhat prodded a cautious chief executive into declaring war. Recent scholarship tends to describe the president's diplomacy as patient, firm, and courageous. In his war message of April 11, 1898, McKinley asked Congress for authority to use the military and naval forces to terminate hostilities in **Cuba** and ensure peace. The Congress responded with a joint resolution that amounted to a declaration of war, inasmuch as it proclaimed Cuba to be free, demanded the withdrawal of Spain, and empowered the president to use the armed forces for these purposes. The Teller Amendment specified that the United States did not intend to annex the island of Cuba. President McKinley signed the resolution and, by an act of Congress, war was retroactively declared on April 21, 1898.

According to most accounts the U.S. expeditionary corps was ill-equipped and ill-trained, and the Cuban campaign a bungle. But the Spaniards fared no better, and the United States easily got the better of declining Spain. The most famous victory was probably Commodore George Dewey's destruction of the Spanish fleet on May 1, 1898, at **Manila Bay** in the Philippines, a long way from Cuba. The most popular feat of the Santiago campaign was undoubtedly Rough Rider Colonel Theodore **Roosevelt**'s charge up San Juan Hill. Hostilities ended on August 12, 1898. The peace negotiations opened in Paris on October 1, and a treaty was signed on December 10, 1898.

The outcome of the Spanish-American War was the creation of a new colonial power at the expense of Spain, which lost Puerto Rico, occupied by American troops toward the end of the war, Guam in the Marianas, and the **Philippines,** whose main seaport, Manila, came under American control. The benefits of the Cuban venture for the United States were threefold. First, the Caribbean—and more generally the Americas—had been freed from European influence in accordance with the principles enunciated in the **Monroe Doctrine,** and the United States could keep closer watch over the future isthmian canal in Central America. Second, the United States had made her strength known to the world and acceded to the status of a Great Power, which would imply increasing and unavoidable world commitments in the near future. Third, the United States had acquired colonial possessions that were deemed by some to be vital strategically and economically.

The future as a world power now had to be faced. Before the government made momentous choices and decisions, a debate went on throughout the country, in the press and in Congress—perhaps the most important since the founding of the Republic. The arguments of the imperialists were based on **Manifest Destiny** and the civilizing mission of the United States. Furthermore, the strategic importance of both Cuba and the Philippines impressed itself on the advocates of American naval power. In addition, economic motives were far from negligible as the **Open Door** was threatened in China. Unlike Cuba or **Puerto Rico,** where U.S. trade and investments were a reality, however, the Philippines interested part of the business community for their commercial potential, and not everyone in that community was convinced that its promise would be realized. Puerto Rico's case was different. Annexation was simply inevitable from an imperial point of view because of the island's vital strategic situation in the Caribbean near the Isthmus of Panama, as well as the growth of American trade and investments there.

The anti-imperialist opposition was a motley crowd: Democrats from the East and the Plains states, old-generation Republicans, intellectuals, scholars and writers, union leaders who anticipated a steady flow of cheap imported Filipino labor, top business people who were indifferent or hostile to the siren song of overseas expansion and feared competition from Philippine products. The anti-imperialists on the whole reasoned primarily in terms of moral principles and tradition. They referred to Washington and Jefferson's warning against foreign entanglements; they invoked the principles of the Declaration of Independence and the Constitution, as well as Abraham **Lincoln**'s teachings, and insisted that governments derived their powers from the consent of the governed; they doubted the wisdom of transplanting American institutions into alien lands whose peoples differed so from the Americans in culture, race, and speech—and of doing so against their will. Could there be such a thing as an imperial republic with democracy at home—possibly threatened by the attendant militarism—and despotism in the colonies? The issue of unconstitutionality was raised. For the first time the United States was to acquire territories that it had no intention of Americanizing and developing into states. Still, the Supreme Court in the so-called Insular Cases of 1901 agreed with the imperialists that the Constitution did not follow the flag. Many anti-imperialists also rejected expansion on economic grounds and warned the country against the predictable increase in defense expenditures for the sake of a business minority whose profitable investments overseas were to be safeguarded with public money.

McKinley, who groped for the most satisfactory solution, eventually instructed the American Peace Commissioners in Paris to negotiate the cession and ultimately the purchase of the whole Philippine archipelago for $20 million. In addition an executive order on December 21, 1898, extended American military rule over all of the islands. The peace treaty, signed on December 10, 1898, was ratified by a narrow margin of two votes on February 6, 1899, after a heated debate. Rejection of the treaty, many senators felt, would have been tantamount to a repudiation of the president and to national humiliation.

Just as the debate over ratification had confused the issues by reducing approval of the treaty to a choice between support or disavowal of the president's policies, the election of 1900 confused them by mixing imperialism with free silver and prosperity. Whereas the Democrats at first did their best to make imperialism "the paramount issue" of the campaign in their muddled Philippine plank, the Republicans tried to defuse that issue by focusing on William Jennings Bryan's advocacy of free silver, by stressing the prosperity enjoyed during McKinley's first term, by posturing as the only true patriots. Many Republicans later interpreted McKinley's sweeping victory as a mandate for imperialism. Obviously, things had not been as simple and straightforward as that. Many anti-imperialists were probably reluctant to vote for Bryan because of his financial theories, which they feared might endanger the economic recovery. All in all, domestic problems certainly influenced the electorate more decisively than foreign policy, which possibly won a consensus by inertia.

FURTHER READING: Gould, Lewis L. *The Presidency of William McKinley*. Lawrence: University Press of Kansas, 1983; Linderman, Gerald F. *The Mirror of War: American Society and the Spanish-American War*. Ann Arbor: University of Michigan Press, 1974; May, Ernest R. *Imperial Democracy: The Emergence of America as a Great Power*. Chicago: Imprint Publications, 1991; O'Toole, George J. A. *The Spanish War: An American Epic—1898*. New York: Norton, 1986; Smith, Joseph. *The Spanish-American War: Conflict in the Caribbean and the Pacific*. New York, 1994; Tompkins, E. Berkeley. *Anti-Imperialism in the United States: The Great Debate, 1890–1920*. Philadelphia: University of Pennsylvania Press Paperbacks, 1972; Trask, David F. *The War with Spain in 1898*. New York: Macmillan, 1981.

SERGE RICARD

St. Petersburg, Treaty of (1875)

A temporary compromise over Russo-Japanese rivalry in the Western Pacific. Signed on May 7, 1875, between foreign minister Aleksandr Mikhailovich **Gorchakov** of Russia and Admiral Enomoto Buyo of Japan, it gave Russia sovereignty over **Sakhalin** in return for Japanese sovereignty over the central and northern Kurile Islands. Supplementary articles signed in Tokyo on August 22 allowed for the Japanese still living on Sakhalin to retain their nationality, continue in their business and industrial enterprises, chiefly fishing, and exemption for life from all taxes and duties. Sakhalin's Ainu population, however, were forced to declare themselves subjects of either the Russian or Japanese emperor; in the latter case they were to be transferred to Hokkaido. Approximately 800 were transported after the island's formal transfer in September.

Japan's decision to renounce its claims to land it had discovered and sparsely settled long before the Russians arrived was based on recognition of the Russian Empire's preponderant strength at the time. Since the 1850s, Russia had been populating the island with a mix of soldiers and convicts, and had established several major settlements and a coal-mining industry. By 1875, plans were in place for a full-scale penal colony, and Sakhalin's Slavic population already outnumbered the small cohort of Japanese fishermen living there. Thus Tokyo faced something of a *fait accompli.* Japanese officials had nevertheless turned attention to colonizing Korea and Formosa instead of the climatically less hospitable island. By signing the treaty, Japan avoided a diplomatic and possible military standoff with Russia and gained several decades of peace with which to increase its military and economic strength. The fledgling empire was therefore well placed to defeat Russia during the 1904–1905 war, invading Sakhalin in June 1905. Japan subsequently annexed the southern half of the island, which it retained until the end of World War II. *See also* Japanese Empire; Russian Empire; Russo-Japanese War.

FURTHER READING: Stephan, John J. *Sakhalin: A History.* Oxford: Clarendon Press, 1971; Stephan, John J. *The Russian Far East: A History.* Stanford, CA: Stanford University Press, 1994.

ANDREW A. GENTES

Stanley, Sir Henry Morton (1841–1904)

British-American journalist, politician, and explorer whose expeditions to find David **Livingstone** and explore the **Congo** river basin opened the African interior to European expansion and touched off the Scramble for **Africa.** Born John Rowlands, he left Britain in 1859 as a deck hand on a ship bound for New Orleans and on arrival took the name of a local businessman who befriended him. After serving in the **American Civil War,** the newly renamed Stanley began his career as a journalist working for the *Missouri Democrat* and then the *New York Herald.*

Stanley's coverage of the 1868 Abyssinia War led the *New York Herald* to send him to Africa in search of David Livingstone, the British missionary who had disappeared while exploring the lakes region of central Africa. Stanley traveled overland from **Zanzibar,** finally finding Livingstone in November 1871. After returning to Europe to publish an account of his exploits, he resumed his African explorations in 1874 with a new expedition that circled Lakes Victoria and Tanganyika and then followed the Congo from its source to the Atlantic. Shortly thereafter he was hired by **Leopold II** of Belgium and worked from 1879–1884 overseeing the construction of trading stations and signing treaties with local chieftains who gave Leopold control over the Congo. Stanley returned to Africa in 1887 to lead an expedition to rescue Emin Pasha, the Egyptian governor of **Sudan** who had been cut off by the **Mahdi**'s revolt. Although the mission was a success, the expedition's heavy losses and his reputation for violence and brutality earned on earlier expeditions significantly damaged Stanley's reputation.

Shortly after his return to England in 1889, he married, became a re-naturalized British subject, and ran for Parliament as a member of the Liberal Unionist party. He was knighted in 1899 and retired to his country estate in Surrey the following year. *See also* Abyssinia; Berlin, Conference of; Egypt.

FURTHER READING: Bierman, John. *Dark Safari: The Life behind the Legend of Henry Morton Stanley.* New York: Alfred A. Knopf, 1990; Dugard, Martin. *Into Africa: The Epic Adventures of Stanley and Livingstone.* New York: Doubleday, 2003; McLynn, Frank. *Stanley: The Making of an African Explorer.* London: Constable, 1989; Newman, James L. *Imperial Footprints: Henry Morton Stanley's African Journeys.* Washington, DC: Brassey's, 2004.

KENNETH J. OROSZ

Steamboats/Steamships

As revolutionary a development for transportation over water as the advent of the **railroad** for transportation over land. In combination with railroad transportation, in fact, shallow-draft steam-driven riverboats that could negotiate narrow waterways with or against the current were as vital in opening up the interior of the United States on rivers such the Mississippi and the Ohio as in penetrating the African continent by way of the Congo and Nile. The first successful steamship, the *Charlotte Dundas*, towed barges on the Forth and Clyde Canals starting in 1801. Without either the vast interior or an interconnecting river network of the **United States,** however, Britain took the lead in building ocean-going steamships. The first passenger steamer crossed the English Channel from Brighton to Le Havre in 1816, and, in 1825, the 120-horse power *Enterprize* made Calcutta in 113 days.

The **Royal Navy** was initially unimpressed with the implications of steam power, so that the commercial development of it initially outstripped its military use. At the time of its ill-fated maiden voyage in 1912, the White Star Line's *Titanic* displaced 50,000 tons and could make 25 knots; when the Vickers shipyard completed *Kongo*—36,000 tons and 27 knots—for sale to Japan, the gap had long since been closed. In the interim armed shallow-draft, steam-driven vessels called "gunboats" carried imperial firepower upriver into **Burma** in the name of the East India Company in the 1820s and were critical to Britain's victory in the **Opium Wars** of the 1840s. The era of "gunboat diplomacy" for all the imperial powers lingered in various manifestations until World War I. The opening of the **Suez Canal** in 1869 put an end to the age of sail clippers for commercial use, both because steam engines had become more efficient in the use of coal while steamships could now reach any far eastern port faster than sail. In 1860, the Royal Navy launched *H.M.S. Warrior,* the first iron-hulled battleship, twice the length of Nelson's *Victory* and propelled 5,200 horsepower engines to a speed of 14 knots. The *U.S.S. Monitor,* a turreted warship launched the same year, introduced another revolutionary development. The combination of steel hulls, gun turrets, and ever-improving steam power propelled warship development through the predreadnought era of the Russo-Japanese and Spanish-American Wars toward the next revolutionary change with the launch of *H.M.S. Dreadnought* in 1906. *See also* East India Companies; Great White Fleet; Navalism; Tirpitz Plan.

FURTHER READING: Headrick, Daniel. *The Tools of Empire: Technology and European Imperialism in the Nineteenth Century.* New York: Oxford University Press, 1981; Herman, Arthur. *To Rule the Waves: How the British Navy Shaped the Modern World.* New York: Harper Collins, 2004; Spector, Ronald H. *At War at Sea.* Harmondworth: Penguin, 2001.

CARL CAVANAGH HODGE

Stein, Friedrich Karl Reichsfreiherr vom und zum (1757–1831)

The leading member of the group of the so-called Prussian reformers who, as a state minister, set the stage for **Prussia**'s modernization at the beginning of the nineteenth century. After Prussia's crushing defeat by Napoleon **Bonaparte,** Stein and his followers launched a revolution from above by introducing important liberal reforms in all areas of public life. In his efforts Stein was helped by a widespread demand for change, which, however, faltered increasingly once Napoleon's fortunes declined.

Stein studied law at the university of Göttingen where he was influenced by modern constitutional ideas, especially of British and French origin. After completion of his studies, he entered the Prussian civil service, starting in the mining administration. Nominated Prussian secretary for finance and the economy in 1804, he tried in vain to prepare the kingdom for the impending military confrontation with Napoleonic France. In the wake of the defeat at **Jena** and Auerstädt, King Frederick William III dismissed him on January 3, 1807.

In the ensuing leisure time Stein argued in the instantly-famous "Nassau memorandum" for the need for profound change in the political, economical, societal, and military fields. Reinstated after the humiliating peace of **Tilsit** on September 30, 1807, which reduced Prussian territory and population by nearly half, Stein became first minister of the Prussian state. Napoleon's victory demonstrated that Prussia was moribund if it did not embrace reform, particularly in the military field, a fact that at least temporarily outflanked ultraconservative and reform-resistant circles such as the *Junkers*. Fighting for Prussia's immediate survival and long-term future, in the next 14 months Stein tackled a myriad of scene-setting reforms.

The most important of these were the emancipation of the peasants and the initiation of municipal self-government. After Stein's dismissal, the introduction of the freedom of trade in 1811, the emancipation of the Jews in 1812, and major reforms in the educational sector, as well as in the armed forces, among others, followed suit. Collectively they marked a watershed in the slow transformation of Prussia from an absolutist agrarian to a modern constitutional and industrial state. At the time Prussia still had a long way to go to, but Stein, together with Karl August von Hardenberg, paved the way for its ultimate ascendancy and the resounding military successes of the years 1864–1870. Although most of these reforms had been devised before Stein rose to the highest public office, his determination and tenacity in realizing the blueprints proved decisive.

Stein's efforts did not meet with general approbation. Confronted with only slightly diminished resistance from conservative circles, Stein's reform effort slackened all too quickly. Voices calling for his resignation multiplied, and Napoleon, too, interfered. On November 24, 1808, Frederick William gave in to these demands, and Stein was dismissed for the second time within two years. The French outlawed him soon after, and he had to flee to Austria from where he fanned the flames of opposition to Napoleon. After becoming political adviser to Tsar **Alexander I** in 1812, Stein returned to Germany with the Russian military offensive against France. He remained in Russian service until 1815 and took part in the Congress of **Vienna.** Failing in his efforts to secure the formation of a unified Germany, Stein withdrew into private life. Although he remained politically active until his death, he exercised no further influence on affairs of state. *See also* Gneisenau, August Wilhelm von; Roon, Albrecht von; Scharnhorst, Gerhard Johann David von.

FURTHER READING: Clark, Christopher. *Iron Kingdom.* Cambridge: Belknap, 2006; Craig, Gordon. *The End of Prussia.* Madison: University of Wisconsin Press, 1984; Haas, Stefan. *Die Kultur der Verwaltung: Die Umsetzung der preußischen Reformen 1800–1848.* Frankfurt/Main: Campus-Verlag, 2005; Herre, Franz. *Freiherr vom Stein. Sein Leben, seine Zeit.* Cologne: Kiepenheuer & Witsch, 1973; Huch, Ricarda. *Stein, der Erwecker des Reichsgedankens.* Berlin: Atlantis Verlag, 1932; Ritter, Gerhard. *Freiherr vom Stein. Eine politische Biographie.* Frankfurt/Main: Fischer-Verlag, 1983.

ULRICH SCHNAKENBERG

Straits Question

See Bosporus; Dardanelles; London Straits Convention

Strategy

The use made of military force or the threat of force to achieve political goals. Carl von **Clausewitz** initially defined strategy narrowly as "the employment of the battle to gain the end of the War" but immediately conceded that strategy is inherently theoretical, because the application of force is always based on conjectures "some of which turn out incorrect." Because Clausewitz defined war itself as "a mere continuation of policy by other means," policy dictated the goals of strategy and required that strategy incorporate instruments other than the purely military into the pursuit of such goals. He was, moreover, explicit in distinguishing strategy from tactics, the latter involving the thought behind the deployment of armed forces in an engagement, the latter representing the overarching logic behind not only the use of military forces but all the capabilities of a nation—economic, technological, diplomatic—to achieve the foreign policy objectives of the nation in war *and* peace.

During and after the **Napoleonic Wars,** the major European powers either established or reconstituted academies for the education of staff officers. Meanwhile, the most ambitious military literature of the time was, like Clausewitz, concerned with analyzing the fundamental strategic principles revealed by the Napoleonic Wars, as well as with their application to future conflict. Because Napoleon **Bonaparte** had demonstrated the effectiveness of waging war with the full force of national energy, strategy in the nineteenth century concentrated evermore attention to the matter of how best to bring national energy to bear against the most probable adversary or coalition of adversaries. The **American Civil War,** for example, demonstrated the advantages of superior **railway** transport to the Union cause. The Prussian general staff of the 1860s, contemplating future conflict with traditional foes, France in the

West and Russia in the East, came to view the construction of a dense domestic railway network as indispensable in bringing its military forces to bear quickly and in large numbers on whatever front they might be needed.

By 1900, European staff colleges were accustomed to abstract war planning, and general staffs were developing elaborate war plans, Germany's **Schlieffen Plan** and France's Plan 17 being the most noteworthy. Each was notable for its inflexibility, high secrecy, and remarkable *lack* of attention to the political, economic, diplomatic, and moral dimensions Clausewitz deemed crucial to the comprehensive and coherent vision of war that in the twentieth century was referred to as grand strategy. *See also* Mackinder, Halford; Mahan, Alfred Thayer; Navalism.

FURTHER READING: Gray, Colin. *Modern Strategy.* Oxford: Oxford University Press, 1999; Howard, Michael. *War in European History.* Oxford: Oxford University Press, 1976; Keegan, John. *The First World War.* New York: Alfred A. Knopf, 1998; Kennedy, Paul, ed. *Grand Strategies in War and Peace.* New Haven, CT: Yale University Press, 1991; Luttwak, Edward. *Strategy.* Cambridge, MA: Belknap Press, 1990.

CARL CAVANAGH HODGE

Sudan

A largely desert country to the south of **Egypt,** extending along the Nile from the second cataract in the north to Uganda in the south, and encompassing large tracts of desert on either side. It is inhabited by Islamic and ethnically Arab peoples in the north, but by black Africans in the south. Originally animist, many of the latter were converted to Christianity by Western missionaries in the nineteenth century. Slavery, largely practiced by the Islamic population at the expense of the equatorial Africans, was a consistent feature of Sudanese life and also provided both a motivation and a pretext for imperial intervention.

Although the Nile—its source uncertain for much of the nineteenth century— does not begin in the Sudan, it ensured that those with interests in Egypt thought of the Sudan as a strategic territory, providing a further motive for imperial interest. Long claimed by the rulers of Egypt, the nineteenth century saw a succession of largely unsuccessful Egyptian expeditions into the Sudan, and these drew in European opportunists and evangelists, many in the Egyptian service. General Charles **Gordon** was made governor-general of the Sudan, under claimed Egyptian suzerainty, in 1873, where he conscientiously tried to abolish slavery. The British occupation of Egypt in 1882 caused Britain to inherit Egypt's troubles to the south. An uprising by a self-proclaimed **Mahdi** led to bloody defeats for the British-officered Egyptian army, and to a call in London to do something. In response, Gordon was sent back to arrange a withdrawal. Gordon decided on his own initiative to stay instead, and his 1885 death at the hands of the Mahdi's forces made him a martyr in the eyes of much British opinion.

The subject remained dormant until the Italian defeat at Adowa in 1896 raised the specter of an Islamic empire in east Africa. The government of Lord **Salisbury** resolved to send an expedition to avenge Gordon. It proceeded deliberately up the Nile under the leadership of General Herbert **Kitchener,** capturing Khartoum after the battle of **Omdurman** in 1898. Notwithstanding plans to develop a cotton industry, the Sudan remained henceforth a backwater of empire. Formally under the joint rule of Egypt and Britain, a fiction that was increasingly a source of anger to Egyptian nationalists, the Anglo-Egyptian Sudan became independent in 1956. *See also* Adowa, Battle of; British Empire; Slave Trade.

FURTHER READING: Holt, P. M. *The Mahdist State in Sudan, 1881–1898.* Oxford: Clarendon, 1958; Pakenham, Thomas. *The Scramble for Africa.* New York: Random House, 1991.

MARK F. PROUDMAN

Suez Canal

A 100-mile long sea-level canal in **Egypt,** across the isthmus of Suez between Port Said on the Mediterranean and the Gulf of Suez at the north end of the Red Sea, opened in 1869. It was built by a French consortium led by Ferdinand de **Lesseps,** the then-viceroy of Egypt taking a percentage of its shares. The canal was built in the face of British opposition, both because it competed with a British-owned railway from the Nile to Suez, and because in the opinion of Lord **Palmerston,** it would cause numerous diplomatic complications. Transit through Egypt to India and the Far East had grown rapidly after the introduction of **steamship** services in the Red Sea in the 1840s; the canal led to even more traffic, avoiding the long Cape route by traveling through Egypt. Most of this traffic, given the predominance of the British merchant marine and British control of **India,** was British.

In 1875, Benjamin **Disraeli** engineered the British purchase of the financially pressed Khedive's shares, largely to keep complete control of the canal out of French hands. In 1882, in part in response to fears of instability on the canal's doorstep, the British occupied Egypt, nominally a Turkish vassal state, and landed an army in the Canal Zone. The British army stayed there until 1954, notwithstanding much talk about the temporary or limited nature of the occupation. In 1914, Britain declared a **protectorate** over Egypt, and the Canal Zone became a large strategic base area, not merely because of the canal but also as a base from which to attack Turkish territories in the Middle East. The Suez Canal, "the swing door of empire," came to have a key place in the British imperial imagination, a place that lasted until the divisive intervention against Nasser's nationalization of the canal in 1956. *See also* Panama Canal; Steamboats/Steamships.

FURTHER READING: Farnie, D. A. *East and West of Suez.* Oxford: Clarendon, 1969; Karabell, Zachary. *Parting the Waters: The Creation of the Suez Canal.* New York: Random House, 2003; Marlowe, John. *World Ditch: The Making of the Suez Canal.* New York: Macmillan, 1963.

MARK F. PROUDMAN

Sun Yatsen (1866–1925)

Chinese revolutionary leader educated in Honolulu, Canton, and Hong Kong, where he was baptized and trained as a doctor. Living in exile in Japan, Indochina, and Europe since 1894, Sun led various revolutionary groups and organized numerous abortive uprisings in **China.** Surprised by the outbreak of the revolution of October 1911 while touring the **United States,** Sun returned and was elected president by an assembly representing the provinces that supported the revolution.

He agreed to step down in favor of Yuan Shikai in a deal arranging for the abdication of the **Qing Dynasty** in January 1912. Sun and the Kuomintang party he led turned against Yuan's increasingly authoritarian regime in the "second revolution" of 1913. Defeated, Sun went to Japan but returned in 1916 to participate in the chaotic politics of the warlord era before reorganizing the Kuomintang with Soviet help and seizing power in Peking. *See also* Boxer Insurrection.

FURTHER READING: Yu, George T. *Party Politics in Republican China, The Kuomintang, 1912–1924.* Berkeley: University of California Press, 1966.

NIELS P. PETERSSON

Suttee

Suttee, or *sati,* is a Hindu custom in which widows immolated themselves on the funeral pyre of their husbands. Suttee was supposed to be voluntary, but it was in fact often coerced. The practice was banned in Indian territory held by some of the European powers and as early as 1515 by the Portuguese in Goa. The British, far and away the most powerful imperial force on the subcontinent, tolerated it into the nineteenth century, although individual officers made attempts to suppress it. In 1812, the Bengali reformer, Ram Mohan Roy, started a campaign to ban suttee, and it was formally suppressed in 1829 by Governor-General William **Bentinck.** *See also* India.

FURTHER READING: James, Lawrence. *Raj: The Making and Unmaking of British India.* New York: St. Martin's, 1997.

CARL CAVANAGH HODGE

Sweden

A declining Great Power and industrial power of **Scandinavia.** King Gustavus IV Adolphus (1779–1837) pushed his luck in the **Napoleonic Wars,** lost Finland to Russia in 1808, and was forced to resign. A leading power in the military revolution of the seventeenth century, Sweden emerged from the Napoleonic Wars as a second-rate power despite being on the winning side. Superior organizational skills and a technological edge could no longer compensate for a small population as the ideas of modern warfare spread throughout Europe. All of Sweden's possessions along the eastern and southern shores of the Baltic were lost, and by the Treaty of **Kiel** in 1814, Sweden confirmed the loss of Finland to Imperial Russia, but it acquired control over Norway in exchange. The Norwegians maintained their constitution and legislature, and the Swedish king gradually lost control over Norway until full independence was achieved in 1905.

Sweden also largely withdrew as a player in European diplomacy. Its strategy of nonalignment in peace and neutrality in war lasted until World War I and well beyond; even the 500-year long struggle for Scandinavian hegemony was suspended despite the fact that Sweden was now the most powerful Nordic nation. A brief exemption from neutrality was made in 1848, when Sweden sent troops to **Denmark** to preempt a German assault. In 1809, Sweden adopted a new constitution. The king maintained control over the executive, but the legislature was transferred to a parliament based on the division into estates. Through an 1840 administrative reform, departments headed by ministers were introduced, and in 1866 a bicameral system replaced the estates. An 1842 reform also introduced local government to which farmers and workers with a certain level of income were enfranchised. From 1858, some freedom of religion was granted. A proportional vote was adopted in 1911, parliamentary government in 1917, and adult universal suffrage in 1921. Introduction of full democracy followed the development of associations and organizations through all aspects of Swedish public life, from trade unions to social and religious societies.

The wealth accumulated through one-and-half century of expansion was reinvested into mining and emerging industries, making Sweden one of the wealthiest European nations, despite its nonparticipation in the general race for overseas possessions. Sweden participated in the exploration of the Arctic, and the territories offered rich fisheries and whaling. It was cut of from this arena, however, when Norway gained independence in 1905. A technology-intensive industrialization gained momentum toward the end of the nineteenth century, concentrating on products like ball bearings, dynamite, electromotors, and telephones. Swedish iron ore was also of a unique quality, providing industry with prime raw material as well as export income. The building of the Göta Canal, 1810–1832, across southern Sweden greatly improved internal communications, and, in 1856, the first railroad between Örebro and Ervala was opened. After 1870, Sweden became more pro-German, which affected the orientation of the economy and cultural life. Sweden introduced compulsory military service for men in 1901 and increased defense budgets, but stayed neutral in World War I. *See also* Norway; Russian Empire; Russo-Swedish War.

FURTHER READING: Aberg, Alf. *A Concise History of Sweden.* Translated by Gordon Elliott. Stockholm: LTs Förlag, 1985; Andersson, Ingvar. *A History of Sweden.* Translated by Carolyn Hannay and Alan Blair. New York: Praeger, 1970.

FRODE LINDGJERDET

Syria

During the nineteenth and early twentieth centuries, Syria comprised the area that today contains the modern states of Syria, Lebanon, Israel, and Jordan. For the **Ottoman Empire** the area was divided into four provinces: Aleppo, Damascus, Tripoli, and Sidon. Religion was the oldest source of European interest in the region and derived from the existence of the Holy Places in Palestine, which had never ceased to attract a flow of pilgrims, and from the presence of various communities of Eastern Christians to which different European powers gave protection. The Russians claimed to speak for the Greek Orthodox and the French for the Catholics.

The Damascus uprising in July 1860, in which between 5,000 and 10,000 Christians were massacred, turned the scale in favor of European intervention in the form of a French army. Napoleon III was obliged to appease outraged French Catholic opinion. France insisted on major governmental reforms in Lebanon. Under the new system, introduced in 1861, and revised in 1864, Mount Lebanon—not including Beirut, the Biqa', Tripoli, or Sidon—was to be autonomous under international guarantee with a Christian governor assisted by an elected council on which all communities were represented. The strategic position of Syria was another source of European interest in the region. From the late eighteenth century the European powers manifested a greater interest in the Levant, and, with the enlargement of her Indian empire, Britain became concerned about the safety of communications through the Levant. To sever these communication lines, Napoleon landed at Alexandria on July 1, 1798, defeated the Mamluks on July 21, and occupied Cairo. Then **Bonaparte** set off into Syria, but was checked at Acre in May 1799 and returned to **Egypt** where he abandoned his army and sailed back to France.

Thereafter, the European powers did as they could to retain the integrity of the Ottoman Empire. Muhammad Ali of Egypt was determined to conquer Syria, which he had been promised for his assistance in suppressing the Greek uprising. In November 1831, **Ibrahim Pasha** invaded the region. The Ottomans resisted and on December 27, 1832, were beaten at Konya. There appeared to be nothing to prevent the Egyptian forces from advancing to Istanbul. The Ottomans appealed to other states for assistance, and received it from Russia, which sent troops to the Bosporus and signed a defensive alliance with the Ottomans on July 8, 1833, called **Inkiar Skelessi.** Russian policy was in line with her 1829 decision to preserve the Ottoman Empire, but to the other European powers, it seemed as though Russia had acquired a protectorate over the Ottoman Empire.

The object of British policy was to undo the effects of Inkiar Skelessi and to support the independence and integrity of the Ottoman Empire against all threats. The opportunity to undo the 1833 arrangement arose in 1839. In April 1839, the Ottomans attacked Muhammad Ali, hoping to expel him from **Syria** by force. Instead, the Egyptians defeated the Ottoman army at Nazib on June 24, and shortly afterwards the Ottoman fleet deserted to Egypt. The new sultan, Abd al-Majid, appeared helpless and his empire likely to collapse. To prevent this, the European powers decided on joint mediation between the sultan and Muhammad Ali. They took action to force Muhammad Ali out of Syria and leave him with only the hereditary possession of Egypt still within the bonds of the Ottoman Empire. During World War I France and Britain divided **Syria** between themselves: Syria and Lebanon under French mandate and Transjordan and Palestine under British mandate. *See also* British Empire; Crimean War; French Empire.

FURTHER READING: Karsh, Efraim, and Inari Karsh. *Empires of the Sand: The Struggle for Mastery in the Middle East 1789–1923.* Cambridge, MA: Harvard University Press, 2001; McCarthy, Justin. *The Ottoman Peoples and the End of Empire.* London: Arnold, 2001; Yapp, M. E. *The Making of the Modern Near East: 1792–1923.* London: Longman, 1987.

MOSHE TERDMAN

T

Taft, William Howard (1857–1930)

An American politician who served as chief civil administrator in the **Philippines** (1901–1904), secretary of war (1904–1908), twenty-seventh President of the **United States** (1909–1913), and Chief Justice of the U.S. Supreme Court (1921–1930). William Howard Taft was born in 1857 in Cincinnati, Ohio. His education was geared toward law and political life, following in his father's footsteps and graduating from Yale University. He later obtained his law degree from the University of Cincinnati and subsequently entered private practice.

Taft's main ambition was to one day be appointed to the U.S. Supreme Court, and it was in pursuit of this that he began his political career. In 1900, President McKinley asked Taft to serve as president of the commission to oversee the newly won Philippines. Between 1900 and 1903, Taft was devoted to his work as governor in the Philippines, so much so that he turned down two offers to serve on the Supreme Court from McKinley's successor, Theodore **Roosevelt,** so that he could finish what he had started.

After returning to the United States, Taft became Roosevelt's secretary of war and quickly gained the president's full confidence. Roosevelt had sworn not to serve another term and backed Taft's ascension to the presidency in the belief that Taft would continue his reform programs. Taft shied away from domestic progressivism yet sought to follow through on Roosevelt's foreign policy. The centerpiece of his approach became known as "Dollar Diplomacy" and involved enhancing American international influence through the use of economic power with the cultivation of trade and the promotion of loans from private banks in support of overseas projects involving American interests. Taft used his dollar diplomacy to protect American interests in the **Panama Canal** region, buying off Latin American debts to European powers and refinancing Haiti's debt, setting the stage for future plans there. This policy also extended to Asia, where Taft convinced banks to help finance railroad construction in China in both cooperation and competition with Britain, France, and Germany.

Although Taft was successful in extending American influence internationally, he caused suspicion and resentment among the European powers involved in China, and his dollar diplomacy did not survive the revolution that erupted in China in 1912. His aversion to progressivism lost him support not only from his own party, but also from the American public. He handily lost his second election, an outcome he was not particularly saddened by. His lifetime dream nonetheless was realized in 1921 when President Warren G. Harding appointed him to the U.S. Supreme Court. *See also* Mexico; Open Door.

FURTHER READING: Coletta, Paolo E. *The Presidency of William Howard Taft.* Lawrence: University Press of Kansas, 1973; Minger, Ralph Eldin. *William Taft and United States Foreign Policy: The Apprenticeship Years, 1900–1908.* Urbana: University of Illinois Press, 1975; Rosenberg, Emily S. *Financial Missionaries to the World: The Politics and Culture of Dollar Diplomacy, 1900–1930.* Durham, NC: Duke University Press, 2004.

ARTHUR HOLST

Taiping Rebellion (1850–1864)

A rebellion against the **Qing Dynasty** of China. It began in China's southern Guangxi province under the leadership of Hong Xiuquan (1813–1864), a teacher and failed civil service exam candidate from nearby Guangzhou (Canton). Hong had been the victim of a hallucinatory episode in 1837 following his fourth failure to pass the state civil service examination. Reading some early Protestant teachings circulating in Guangzhou, Hong came to believe he was the son of God and brother of Jesus Christ come to save China. In collaboration with Feng Yünshan, a Christian convert, Hong founded the "God Worshipper's Society," composed mostly of disaffected peasants of Guanxi province. In 1850, Hong led the society in rebellion and the next year declared the establishment of a new dynasty, the Taiping Tianguo—Heavenly Kingdom of Great Peace—proclaiming himself its heavenly king.

With growing membership and efficient organization, the Taiping rebels scored a series of stunning early victories and, by spring 1853, had captured the major Chinese city of Nanjing, which they made their new capital. The Taipings set off on a broad program of social and land reform that promulgated social equality and a peculiar version of Christianity while repudiating Confucianism. Initially curious as to the nature of the rebellion and its Christian and reformist aspects, several Western powers dispatched envoys to the Taiping capital to learn more and initially opted to take a neutral stance toward the rebels.

While the Taiping was wracked by infighting in 1856, the Qing government began to see some successes in the form of an army led by the talented official and scholar, Zeng Guofan (1811–1872). Zeng's well-trained forces, all from his native Hunan province, were able to put the Taiping on the defensive. Following its defeat in the **Arrow War** of 1856–1860, the Qing Dynasty opted for a more cooperative attitude with the West. This, combined with a second Taiping attack on Shanghai, a treaty port open to Western trade, instigated Western support of the Qing against the Taiping. It came in the form of the "Ever-Victorious Army," a foreign mercenary force headed first by the American Frederick Townsend Wade and then the Englishman Charles George **Gordon.** From 1862, with the combined assault of Qing and

Western troops, the Taiping was in retreat. Hong died of illness during the siege of Nanjing in June 1864, and the city's fall the following month brought an effective end to the rebellion.

The Taiping Rebellion cost more than 20 million lives and bequeathed a legacy of tremendous destruction. Although the Qing Dynasty was able to defeat it, the rebellion was severely weakened by the effort and never able to restore full central authority before its eventual fall in 1912. Although defeated, the egalitarian and revolutionary ideas the Taiping rebels espoused have had a lasting impact on Chinese society. *See also* Boxer Insurrection.

FURTHER READING: Gregory, J. S. *Great Britain and the Taipings.* London: Routledge and Kegan Paul, 1969; Reilly, Thomas H. *The Taiping Heavenly Kingdom: Rebellion and the Blasphemy of Empire.* Seattle: University of Washington Press, 2004; Spence, Jonathan. *God's Chinese Son: The Taiping Heavenly Kingdom of Hong Xiuquan.* New York: Norton, 1996.

DANIEL C. KANE

Taisho Democracy

A term associated with the reign of the Taisho Emperor Yoshihito and used to symbolize the wave of liberal reform that swept Japan in the early twentieth century. Although Yoshihito occupied the throne only between 1912 and 1925, "Taisho Democracy" more generally refers to the critical transition period between the **Russo-Japanese War** of 1904–1905 and the Manchurian Incident of 1931.

The Meiji Emperor **Mutsuhito** died in 1912. But military victory over the great continental empire of Russia, signaled the triumph by 1905 of the principal goals of his reign: national unity, industrialization, military might, empire, and imperial sovereignty. By contrast, postwar developments hinted at a new and unsettling era: the rise of individualism, public opposition to war and excessive armaments, mounting labor agitation, a plot to assassinate the emperor, and the emergence of modern China, not on the model of Japanese constitutional monarchy but of American republicanism. The death of the Meiji emperor in July 1912 confirmed the end of an exalted age. Only seven months later, a coalition of political parties toppled an oligarchic cabinet for the first time in Japanese history.

World War I spurred the most dramatic reforms associated with Taisho. Propelled by an enormous boost in overseas trade, Japan experienced a new wave of industrialization, urbanization, and commercialization that spawned a new middle class. The principal consequence was the rise of political party government in place of oligarchic rule. By 1918, Japan welcomed its first party cabinet. From 1924 to 1932, two bourgeois political parties commanded policy-making in Japan. At the same time, new advocacy groups championed the rights of urban labor, rural tenants, women, and outcastes.

The 1920s also brought dramatic change in Japanese external affairs. After the steady advance of empire and arms under Meiji, the interwar years invited a retraction of empire, disarmament, and a new commitment to internationalism. Japan became a charter member of the League of Nations in 1920; withdrew troops from Shandong, China, and **Siberia;** slashed naval arms in compliance with the Washington 1922 and the London 1930 naval treaties; and cut four divisions from the Imperial Army. When members of the Japanese "Guandong Army" sparked an "incident" along the Manchuria Railway in 1931, they signaled their strong displeasure of these dramatic symbols of "Taisho democracy." *See also* Japanese Empire; Manchuria; Meiji Restoration; Russian Empire.

FURTHER READING: Silberman, Bernard S., and H. D. Harootunian, eds. *Japan in Crisis: Essays in Taisho Democracy.* Princeton, NJ: Princeton University Press, 1974.

FREDERICK R. DICKINSON

Talleyrand-Périgord, Charles Maurice de (1754–1838)

A remarkable French foreign minister, with many political lives, serving in turn governments during the French Revolution, the First Empire, and the Bourbon restoration. Born in Paris into an aristocratic family, he was sent to the seminary at Saint-Sulpice where he took holy orders in 1779. He was consecrated bishop of Autun a decade later and became politically involved in the French Revolution. In July 1792, the government sent him on a diplomatic mission to London, but while away he was condemned as a traitor and took refuge in the **United States** until 1795. Through connections with Paul Barras, he was appointed foreign minister in July 1797 and the next year proposed the sending of an expedition to Egypt to threaten British interests in India. He resigned from office in July 1798 when he failed to prevent the formation of a Second Coalition of powers against France. Offering strong support to Napoleon **Bonaparte** during the young general's coup d'état of November 1799, Talleyrand was reinstated as foreign minister shortly thereafter. He was instrumental in arranging the **Concordat of 1801** with the pope, negotiated the Treaty of Amiens with Britain in 1802, and helped establish the **Confederation of the Rhine** in 1806. In the wake of the Treaty of **Tilsit,** in which Napoleon made peace with Russia and **Prussia,** Talleyrand began to distant himself from his emperor's policies, and he left his post in August 1807.

Napoleon nevertheless continued to consult with Talleyrand, who strongly opposed French intervention in Spanish internal affairs, especially the emperor's decision to remove King Charles IV and Crown Prince Ferdinand from power. After a heated exchange with Napoleon in January 1809, in which the emperor accused him of treachery, Talleyrand lost his post of grand chamberlain of the court, although he continued to exercise some influence over imperial affairs through his role as vice grand elector. By the time invading forces neared Paris in 1814, Talleyrand had already established secret communication with the sovereigns accompanying Allied headquarters. Having assembled some of Napoleon's disaffected marshals to discuss their emperor's abdication, Talleyrand then entertained Tsar **Alexander** of Russia, whose influence led to Talleyrand's taking charge of the provisional government, which reached an agreement with the restored Bourbon king, **Louis XVIII.** Talleyrand was created a prince and appointed foreign minister, once again, in May 1814.

In short order, he represented the new regime at the Congress of **Vienna,** where he virtually single handedly restored his defeated country to the status of a Great Power by playing one victor off against the other to secure concessions for France. After Napoleon's second abdication in 1815, Talleyrand served as prime minister for a few months before retiring to his estate to write his much-biased memoirs, which only appeared in print long after his death. During the revolution of 1830,

Talleyrand returned to Paris to aid Louis Philippe's accession to power. He served as ambassador to Britain from September 1830 to August 1834. *See also* French Empire; Napoleonic Wars.

FURTHER READING: Copper, Duff. *Talleyrand.* London: Weidenfeld & Nicolson, 2001; Dwyer, Philip. *Talleyrand.* London: Longman, 2002; Lawday, David. *Napoleon's Master: A Life of Prince Talleyrand.* London: Jonathan Cape, 2006.

GREGORY FREMONT-BARNES

Tampico and Vera Cruz Incidents (1914)

Incidents between the **United States** and **Mexico,** arising indirectly from the overthrow of the elected government of Francisco Madero by José Victoriano **Huerta.** Unlike the European powers, the administration of Woodrow **Wilson** in Washington refused to recognize the Huerta dictatorship and sought to isolate it from foreign sympathy and aid. In April 1914, American sailors from the *U.S.S. Dolphin* were arrested by Mexican authorities in Tampico on a charge of having entered a restricted area. Although the sailors were released with an apology, the local American commander peremptorily demanded the hoisting of the American flag and a 21-gun salute from the Mexican port commander and was refused.

Wilson asked for and received congressional permission to use force to secure U.S. rights, and American forces had already landed on Mexican soil when a German warship arrived with munitions and supplies for the Mexicans. The Americans blocked delivery of the supplies and, on April 21, American forces bombarded Vera Cruz and occupied the city. Huerta promptly broke diplomatic relations. The two countries were on the brink of war when they accepted the mediation of the **ABC Powers**. *See also* Monroe Doctrine.

FURTHER READING: Link, Arthur S. *Wilson: Confusions and Crises, 1915–1916.* Princeton, NJ: Princeton University Press, 1964; McDougall, Walter A. *Promised Land, Crusader State: The American Encounter with the World since 1776.* Boston: Hougton Mifflin, 1997.

CARL CAVANAGH HODGE

Tariff Reform League

A lobby formed in London July 21, 1903, to advocate the adoption of tariff protection for British or imperial industry and the abandonment of unilateral **free trade.** It was formed in reaction to Colonial Secretary Joseph **Chamberlain**'s call for the rejection of Britain's post-**Corn Law** adhesion to free trade, in favor of a system of **imperial preference.** Free trade had been increasingly challenged in the previous two decades, beginning with the founding of the Fair Trade League in 1881.

The increased popularity of protectionist ideas derived from increasing foreign competition, from the obvious successes of protectionist countries such as Germany and the **United States,** and from a desire to establish more formal bonds within the empire. The cause attracted much support from former members of the Imperial Federation League. Chamberlain's call for protection nevertheless aroused strong resistance, especially, but not only, from the **Liberal Party,** the inheritor of the tradition of free trading radicalism. Britain abandoned free trade, largely for revenue reasons, during World War I. Imperial preference gained a victory at the 1931 Ottawa conference, but the interests of the different parts of the empire were so varied that the movement never produced the kind of unified imperial market that its supporters wanted.

FURTHER READING: Marsh, Peter. *Joseph Chamberlain.* New Haven, CT: Yale University Press, 1992; Semmel, Bernard. *Imperialism and Social Reform: English Social-Imperial Thought, 1895–1905.* London: George Allen and Unwin, 1960.

MARK F. PROUDMAN

Tatars

A Turkic-speaking people originally from the Crimea. In the nineteenth century the Tatars, settling along the river Volga and on the Crimea, developed a sophisticated discourse about their nationality and its relationship to the Russians while the tsarist government tried to incorporate non-Russians, especially the Asian nationalities, into a politically, socioeconomically, and culturally homogenous Russian state. The main question for Russian intellectuals and the tsarist administration was how the Tatars and other Asian nationalities could be assimilated into the Russo-European nation. Tatars sought to keep their nationality vital within the empire. Although at the beginning of the nineteenth century there were some Tatar voices who demanded a secularization of Tatar-Muslim culture, they were isolated.

The great discussion on the future of the Tatar identity began after the **Crimean War** of 1853. The confrontation with the Western powers was not only for Russians but also for Russian Muslims a trauma, because Tatars understood that the Muslim world had become a colonial object of European powers. One of the most influential Tatar leaders of the nineteenth century was Ismail Bey **Gaspirali** (1851–1914). In a century where industrialization and modernization meant a Russian political, economic superiority, Gaspirali demanded an educational and spiritual renewal of Tatar identity to overcome Tatar backwardness. In 1881, Gaspirali wrote a book entitled *Russian Islam: Thoughts, Notes and Observations of a Muslim* in which he propagated a Tatar-Muslim renaissance that could be done—in his opinion—only in concert with the tsarist government. Gaspirali was convinced that a coexistence of different cultures was possible, and through Tatar-Russian cooperation, the tsarist government would give up its hostility toward Muslims. Gaspirali was also a spokesman of women's rights and emancipation. He emphasized that the Qur'an demanded a fair treatment of women and that the veil was nothing more than an Asian relict. Gaspirali understood that without women's emancipation, it would be difficult for the Tatar-Muslim society to follow Russia's modernization. As a reformer (jadidist), however, Gaspirali faced opposition from the traditional Tatar-Muslim elite, as well as the Russian conservative Pan-Slavists. *See also* Russian Empire.

FURTHER READING: Fisher, Alan. *Between Russians, Ottomans, and Turks: Crimea and Crimean Tatars.* Istanbul: Isis Press, 1998; Frank, Allen J. *Islamic Historiography and "Bulghar" Identity among the Tatars and Bashkirs of Russia.* Leiden: Brill, 1998.

EVA-MARIA STOLBERG

Telegraph

From the Greek word meaning distant writing—*tele* distant, *graphein* to write—the invention of telegraphy revolutionized communications as it was adopted by government offices, press, business, military, and the travel industry. Count Alessandro Volta (1745–1827) invented in 1800 the voltaic pile (battery) for producing continuous electric current. Hans Christian Oersted (1777–1851) discovered the relationship between electric current and magnetism. An electromagnetic telegraph was developed by Paul Schilling (1768–1837) in 1832, and Joseph Henry (1797–1878) operated the electromagnetic telegraph. Charles Wheatstone and William F. Cook made significant advances in the 1830s. Much of the credit is given to Samuel Finley **Morse** (1791–1872) as "father of the telegraph." Morse applied existing technology commercially, particularly that of Joseph Henry, and worked out a viable communication system using combinations of short clicks (dots) and long clicks (dashes) for the letters of the alphabet. These were transmitted by electrical pulses from a sender along a wire. By means of an electromagnetically controlled pencil, the receiver prepared dots and dashes equivalent to the extent of the current. On May 24, 1844, Morse sent the message, *What hath God wrought,* the first one over long distance between Washington and Baltimore. In spite of strong opposition in some quarters, like the office of postmaster-general of the **United States,** Congress approved the Morse Bill. Skilled operators sent and received messages with great speed with Morse code. As it was difficult to convert Morse code into plain language, David E. Hughes (1831–1900) solved the problem by inventing a printing telegraph having a rotating wheel with alphabets. The use of punched paper tape began in 1858, and a new era in telecommunications was ushered in by the Atlantic cable of 1866 joining Europe and the United States.

The **Crimean War** witnessed the first military use of the telegraph, when a submarine cable running from the Crimea to Varna, **Bulgaria,** and standard cable from Varna to London and Paris gave the allies direct communication with the theater of war. Telegraph was also used during the **Indian Mutiny, American Civil War,** and the **Franco-Prussian War.** The telegraph also changed diplomatic communication, but its most famous use before 1914 was in the most undiplomatic use of the **Ems Telegram** by Otto von **Bismarck** to provoke the Franco-Prussian conflict. *See also* Railways.

FURTHER READING: Brooks, John. *Telephone: The First Hundred Years.* New York: Harper & Row, 1976; Gordon, John Steele. *A Thread across the Ocean: The Heroic Story of the Transatlantic Cable.* New York: Perennial, 2003; Standage, Tom. *The Victorian Internet: The Remarkable Story of the Telegraph and the Nineteenth Century's On-Line Pioneers.* New York: Berkley, 1999.

PATIT PABAN MISHRA

Teller Amendment (1898)

Part of a Joint Resolution of the **United States** Congress authorizing President William McKinley to use force to secure the independence of **Cuba** from Spain. The Teller Amendment disclaimed "any disposition or intention to exercise sovereignty, jurisdiction, or control over said Island [Cuba] except for the pacification thereof, and asserts its determination, when that is accomplished, to leave the government and control of the Island to its people." The resolution came in response to McKinley's message to Congress on April 11, 1898, in which he requested permission to forcibly intervene in Cuba to stop the fighting between Spain and its rebellious colony. Congressional opponents of the McKinley administration feared that intervention would lead to annexation and wanted to restrict the president's actions by recognizing the Cuban Republic. McKinley opposed the action but submitted to the Teller Amendment as a compromise measure. *See also* Foraker Amendment; Spanish Empire.

FURTHER READING: Healy, David. *The United States in Cuba, 1898–1902: Generals, Politicians, and the Search for Policy*. Madison: University of Wisconsin Press, 1963.

JAMES PRUITT

Terrorism

A distinct organized practice considered to have emerged in the second half of the nineteenth century in which the systematic use of fear or terror is used as a means of coercion against a people or government. The term was introduced through the French language, in the context of the French Revolution, as *terrorisme*, derived from the Latin verb *terrere*, meaning "to frighten." It appeared in 1795 and it was used to characterize Jacobin rule known as the "Reign of Terror" (1793–1794), involving arrest and execution, usually by guillotine, of opponents to the revolutionary government. The term therefore was initially applied to the acts of a regime, not those of its opponents.

In mid-nineteenth century anarchists like the Russian Mikhail **Bakunin** (1814–1876) and later the Italian Errico Malatesta (1853–1932) regarded the use of violence as necessary, and even moral, in the pursuit of social reform. Some Russian anarchists and nihilists, organized in secret societies, engaged constantly in acts of violence, which culminated with the assassination of Tsar **Alexander II** in 1881. In **Italy,** too, there were several attempts to assassinate members of the royal family. In Great Britain there appeared what was to become known as "republican terrorism"—attacks organized and carried out by the Irish Republican Brotherhood, a nationalist group founded in Dublin in 1858 that called themselves **Fenian Brotherhood** and organized the failed Fenian Rising of 1867. The group reemerged in 1910 and then organized another revolt, also doomed, the Easter Rising of 1916. They were the precursors of the Irish Republican Army. The American counterpart of the Irish Republican Brotherhood was the Clan na Gael, founded in New York by Irish immigrants who also pursued the goal of an independent Irish republic. By 1868, they even raised an army for this purpose, made up mostly of veterans of the **American Civil War.** In support of the cause of Irish independence, they planned attacks on British military bases in **Canada** between 1866 and 1871. Other terrorist occurrences in the **United States** included the Haymarket Riot in Chicago in 1886; the assassination in 1901 of President William McKinley by anarchist Leon Czolgosz; and the bombing of the *Los Angeles Times* building in 1910, which killed 20 workers.

Other heroes of *fin-de-siècle* "nationalist terrorism," besides the Irish, were the members of the Bulgarian Macedonian-Adrianople Revolutionary Committee, which pursued Bulgarian and Macedonian independence. It was founded by Bulgarians in 1893 in Thessaloniki, now part of Greece but then under Ottoman occupation, like **Macedonia** and parts of **Bulgaria.** The group changed its name in 1902 and again in 1906, and, since 1920, it has been known as the Internal Macedonian Revolutionary Organization. It was revived in the 1990s as a nationalist political party in both Macedonia and Bulgaria. It was also an act classified as terrorism that marked the end of the Age of **Imperialism**—the assassination of the Habsburg Archduke **Francis Ferdinand** of Austria and his wife Sophie on June 28, 1914, in Sarajevo, by Bosnian Serb nationalist Gavrilo Princip, a member of both the Bosnian nationalist youth organization Young Bosnia and the Serbian nationalist secret society **Black Hand**. *See also* July Crisis; Nationalism.

FURTHER READING: Laqueur, Walter. *A History of Terrorism.* Somerset, NJ: Transaction, 2001; Sinclair, Andrew. *An Anatomy of Terror: A History of Terrorism.* London: Pan Macmillan, 2004.

GEORGIA TRES

Texas

A Spanish possession for three centuries when **Mexico** became independent in 1821. By opening the territory to immigrants from the **United States,** the Mexican government eventually defeated its own settlement scheme. By the mid-1820s, Americans were pouring in, lured by an attractive colonization plan, of which Moses and Stephen Austin made the most. These immigrants would outnumber, by four to one, and displace the natives. There was little the distant Mexican government could do to forbid slavery within its borders or force Protestants to become Roman Catholics as stipulated in their contracts.

Worried by the growing American influence in Texas, the Mexican Congress in 1830 vainly tried to cut off further immigration from the United States. When in 1835 Mexican President Antonio López de Santa Anna attempted to impose a new constitution establishing a centralized government and curtailing state rights, the North American settlers, led by Sam Houston, revolted, expelled the Mexican garrison, and set up a provisional government. The March 5, 1836, disaster of the **Alamo**—the fortress of San Antonio where 200 Texans were wiped out at great cost by a force 3,000-strong—was followed by an American victory, and revenge, under the slogan "Remember the Alamo," at San Jacinto on April 21. The new Texan constitution was ratified and slavery legalized. The Texans elected Sam Houston president and sought annexation to, or recognition by, the United States. President Andrew **Jackson** recognized the Lone Star Republic on March 3, 1837, on his last full day in office. Britain and France also recognized Texas.

Yet annexation did not come about, owing to northern opposition, the danger of upsetting the fragile balance between free states and slave states, the risk of war with Mexico, and the Panic of 1837. Another treaty was denied ratification by the Senate in 1843. North and South were naturally at cross-purposes over what was likely to imperil the Union most, the success or failure of annexation. Outgoing President John Tyler obtained a joint resolution of both houses on February 28, 1845, and the new chief executive, James K. Polk, concluded the negotiations. On March 6, 1845, the Mexican minister to Washington solemnly protested and left the American capital. The Lone Star Republic formally accepted in July 1845 and thus became the 28th state of the Union, an event that was to trigger off hostilities between Mexico and the United States. *See also* Manifest Destiny; Mexican-American War.

FURTHER READING: Brands, H. W. *Lone Star Nation: How a Ragged Army of Volunteers Won the Battle for Texas Independence—and Changed America.* New York: Doubleday, 2004; Fehrenbach, T. R. *Lone Star: A History of Texas and the Texans.* New York: Da Capo Press, 2000; Haynes, Sam W., and Morris, Christopher, eds. *Manifest Destiny and Empire: American Antebellum Expansionism.* College Station: Texas A&M University Press, 1997.

SERGE RICARD

Thailand

See Siam

Thiers, Adolphe (1797–1877)

In succession, a lawyer, journalist, historian of the French Revolution and the Napoleonic era, minister of the interior under Louis Philippe, prime minister in 1836 and 1840, suppressor of the **Paris Commune** in 1871, and the first president of the French Third Republic. Thiers negotiated with Otto von **Bismarck** the terms for the peace to follow the **Franco-Prussian War** and was subsequently responsible for securing the German evacuation of French territory by promptly paying off the financial indemnity arising from the treaty. Thiers enjoyed the support of the Versailles Assembly as well most of provincial France in the campaign to defeat the Paris Commune, the military prosecution of which lasted from April 1 to May 28, 1871 and witnessed piles of dead ultimately numbering in the tens of thousands. The fighting killed so many anarchists and socialists that it guaranteed the moderate and bourgeois character of the Third Republic yet simultaneously became a potent symbol to the insurrectionalist left in France. *See also* Haussmann, Georges Eugène.

FURTHER READING: Bury, J.P.T. *Thiers, 1797–1877: A Political Life.* London: Allan & Unwin, 1986; Zeldin, Theodore. *France 1848–1945.* New York: Oxford University Press, 1979.

CARL CAVANAGH HODGE

Thugs

A corruption of *thagi*, from the Sanskrit *sthaga* for "scoundrel," applied in **India** to a cult of Hindu, Muslim, and occasionally Sikh assassin-priests who preyed above all on travelers with large-scale robbery and murder, usually by strangulation. The practice was common all over India until its suppression by Lord William **Bentinck** in the 1830s. By 1837, some 3,000 thugs and been arrested and incarcerated on the power of an 1836 act that provided for a life sentence for the convicted. By 1840, the practice had been all but eradicated. The popular novel by Philip Meadows Taylor, *Confessions of a Thug,* introduced the word to the English language in 1839. *See also* Suttee.

FURTHER READING: Rosselli, John. *Lord Willian Bentinck: The Making of a Liberal Imperialist, 1814–1839.* London: Sussex University Press, 1974.

CARL CAVANAGH HODGE

Tientsin, Treaties of (1858)

A set of agreements that opened China to further foreign penetration. It was one of the unequal treaties signed between China and the Imperial powers. The First **Opium War** had started the process of active foreign aggression against China. The treaty of **Nanjin,** concluded between Britain and China in August 1842, had forced China to open its doors for foreign commerce. The Second Opium War, or **Arrow War,** was the result of tension between China and foreign powers after 1842. The immediate causes were the murder of a Catholic missionary and the seizure of a British registered ship, the *Lorcha Arrow.* Anglo-French troops took Guangzhou and Tientsin, forcing the Chinese to accept a treaty. It was signed at Tientsin, the largest commercial city in Chih-li, the metropolitan province of China and hence the name of the treaty. The first phase of the Arrow War was over. France, Britain, Russia, and the **United States** were party to the treaties, and the preamble of each treaty affirmed the "lasting and sincere friendship" between sovereign of the Chinese Empire and the respective governments.

China provided 10 new ports, including Niuzhuang, Danshui, Hankou, and Nanjing for foreign trade and commerce. Britain, France, Russia, and the United States were also permitted legations in the closed city of Beijing. The Yangtze River became free for foreign ships, and even the warships could anchor at 15 Chinese ports. Where the treaty of Nanjin had opened up 5 ports, 10 more were now added. Toleration for Christianity and missionary activity was guaranteed. Foreigners with passports could travel to interior regions of China for trade. The humiliation was complete when China agreed to pay a huge war indemnity to Britain and France. The opium trade was legalized and millions of Chinese became addicted. It took two years to ratify the treaty. Meanwhile, hostilities broke again in 1859. The imperial summer palace was burned and Beijing besieged. By the Beijing Convention in October 1860, the terms of the treaties of Tientsin were confirmed and the weakness of China fully exposed. *See also* Boxer Insurrection.

FURTHER READING: Beeching, Jack. *The Chinese Opium Wars.* London: Hutchinson, 1975; Epstein, Israel. *From Opium War to Liberation.* Hong Kong: Joint Publishing Co, 1980; Polachek, James M. *The Inner Opium War.* Cambridge, MA: Harvard University Press, 1992; Waley, Arthur. *The Opium War through Chinese Eyes.* Stanford, CA: Stanford University Press, 1968.

PATIT PABAN MISHRA

Tilsit, Treaties of (1807)

The peace ending the War of the Fourth Coalition. The French Emperor Napoleon I (see **Bonaparte, Napoleon**) was at the zenith of his power following the French occupation of **Prussia** in October 1806 and the defeat of the Russians at **Friedland** on June 14, 1807. Napoleon and **Alexander I** met at Tilsit on a raft in the River Niemen to discuss the terms of peace. Sharing common hatred of the

British, a persuasive Napoleon brought Alexander I to agree to observe the **Continental System** and recognize the Confederation of the Rhine. A secret clause bound Alexander to declare war against **Denmark, Sweden,** and Portugal if they permitted British shipping in their ports. Russia was also given a claim on Finland, which the tsar then tested against Sweden in 1809. The tsar recognized Napoleon as the emperor in Western Europe in return for his own claim to rule the East. Prussia lost all territory west of the Elbe River; the Kingdom of Westphalia established with Jérôme Bonaparte as its monarch; and Danzig was restored as a free city. Two of Napoleon's other brothers were given the thrones of Holland and Naples, and France agreed to share certain European territories of the **Ottoman Empire** with Russia. The Franco-Russian alliance lasted until 1810, when the tsar allowed neutral ships to land in ports of Russia and Napoleon invaded Russia in 1812. *See also* Napoleonic Wars; Portuguese Empire; Russian Empire; Russo-Swedish War.

FURTHER READING: Alexander, R. S. *Napoleon.* London: Arnold, 2001; Englund, S. *Napoleon: A Political Life.* New York: Scribner, 2004; Markham, J. D. *Napoleon's Road to Glory: Triumphs, Defeats and Immortality.* London: Brassey's, 2003.

PATIT PABAN MISHRA

Timbuctu

In the late eighteenth and early nineteenth centuries, Timbuctu was a prized destination for competing European adventurers. Located in the contemporary West African country of Mali, Timbuctu had for centuries been an established scholarly center and locus for trans-Saharan trade in salt and gold. During the medieval period, the great empire of Mali and its successor, Songhay, incorporated the city within their dominion. Timbuctu gained international prestige in the fourteenth century after the Malian ruler, Mansa Musa, made an extravagant pilgrimage to Mecca. During the journey, his entourage dispersed gold so freely in Cairo that the value of the precious metal was depressed in the city for several months after his departure. After this event, tales of Timbuctu's wealth reached foreign lands and shaped European perceptions of the city for centuries to come. By the nineteenth century, however, this longstanding perception was in stark contrast to Timbuctu's reality of steady decline following a devastating Moroccan conquest in 1591.

As European explorers and adventurers descended on every corner of Africa during the nineteenth century, Timbuctu remained an elusive prize. Several Europeans perished in their quest to reach the city, including British military officer Alexander Gordon Laing, who reached Timbuctu in 1826, but was murdered before returning home. Frenchman René Caillié entered the city two years later and was able to return to Europe to relate his findings. Several decades later, German Heinrich Barth reached Timbuctu in 1853. Their accounts of the city's appearance and meager resources shattered the centuries-old view of Timbuctu's wealth. By the late nineteenth century, a European colonial infrastructure was being established in West Africa, and Timbuctu was captured and controlled by French forces in 1894. *See also* French Empire; French West Africa.

FURTHER READING: Bovill, Edward W. *The Golden Trade of the Moors: West African Kingdoms in the Fourteenth Century*. Princeton, NJ: Markus Wiener Publishers, 1995; Caillié, René. *Travels through Central Africa to Timbuctu, and across the Great Desert, to Morocco, Performed in the Years 1824–1828*. London: Cass, 1968.

BRENT D. SINGLETON

Tirpitz, Alfred von (1849–1930)

A key figure in German domestic and foreign policymaking as the naval minister of Kaiser **Wilhelm II** from the late 1890s until his dismissal in 1916. Tirpitz was born in Kuestrin on the River Oder on March 19, 1849 into an upper middle class family. His father was a judge. Tirpitz himself had an undistinguished school career and left at age 16 to join the Prussian navy. In those years, this navy was in poor shape and offered opportunities for a young officer who had now found his vocation. Tirpitz proved to be a skilled organizer who was keen to modernize the navy, even more so after the unification of Germany in 1871 as an officer of the new Imperial navy. When from 1877 onward the torpedo boat became a weapon of the future, Tirpitz helped to develop it in a systematic fashion that was also the hallmark of his later organizational efforts.

By the early 1890s, Tirpitz had risen to a staff position at the Naval High Command, which, after a recent larger reorganization of the entire naval administrative structure, had been charged with training and war planning. It is in these years that Tirpitz pushed for a shift in strategic thinking away from cruiser warfare and the preparation for conflicts with other colonial powers in distant waters toward a fleet prepared to do battle in the home waters, and here not just against France or Russia, but also against Britain, then the dominant naval power in the world. This new strategy required the building of battleships rather than cruisers.

In 1897, Wilhelm II put Tirpitz in charge of the Reich Navy Office where he had to deal with the naval budget and with obtaining the financial resources for a planned expansion of the navy from a reluctant national assembly, the Reichstag. With the help of a well-oiled naval propaganda department and pressure groups such as the recently founded Navy League, Tirpitz convinced the deputies to ratify the First Navy Law in 1898, followed by another one in 1900, thereby securing the next stage of his grand plan, thereafter named the **Tirpitz Plan,** to build a navy of no fewer than 60 battleships by 1918.

For several years until 1911–1912, Tirpitz was a towering figure in the Reich government, supported by a monarch who had signed on to his naval secretary's design—a building program that, once completed, would enable Wilhelm II, as supreme commander and man in charge of German foreign policymaking, to conduct "a great overseas policy," as Tirpitz once told him. By 1907–1908, however, this policy had run into serious trouble. It promoted the diplomatic isolation of the country when, in 1904, Britain and France formed the **Entente Cordiale** followed in 1907 by the addition of Russia to create the **Triple Entente.** This left Germany in the middle with its only reliable ally, the ramshackle Austro-Hungarian Empire. Moreover, by then the **Royal Navy** had engaged Tirpitz in a quantitative and qualitative arms race in big ships, with the launch of the *Dreadnought,* which he lost a few years later.

By 1914, with his position in the government and public opinion badly battered, Tirpitz realized that the Imperial navy was too weak to confront Britain at sea. Accordingly, his battleships remained bottled up at Kiel and Wilhelmshaven throughout the war, except for a brief sortie that resulted in a strategic defeat by the British in the Battle of Jutland in 1916. In the meantime, the Imperial navy had begun a frantic buildup of a submarine fleet, which, physically and symbolically, was the opposite of Tirpitz's dream of a proud and very presentable fleet of 16 battleships. The kaiser dismissed him rather ignominiously in 1916.

Tirpitz, however, had always been too political an officer to begin a quiet retirement at age 57. He was among the founders of the extreme right-wing Fatherland Party, a movement that agitated for a continuation of the war until a final German victory and large territorial annexations were achieved. As this victory became ever more elusive, the Fatherland Party stepped up its chauvinistic, antisocialist, and anti-Semitic propaganda. After Germany's defeat in 1918, Tirpitz fell silent for a number of years until the conservative-nationalist *Deutschnationale Volkspartei* that had absorbed some of the elements of the Fatherland Party in 1918 persuaded him to stand as a candidate for the 1924 **Reichstag** elections. He gained a seat and used the aura of his name in right-wing circles to advance a radical revisionism in German foreign policy aiming at the destruction of the hated Versailles peace treaty. In 1929, he tried to persuade Paul von **Hindenburg,** then president of the Weimar Republic, to withhold his signature from the Young Plan, the renegotiated reparations settlement that replaced the Dawes Plan of 1924.

Tirpitz died on March 6, 1930. Apart from the conservative-nationalist Stahlhelm veterans association, Adolf Hitler's Stormtroopers also attended his funeral. The "Tirpitz Myth" of a powerful German navy was carried forward by his admirers in the naval officer corps under Hitler who, via the so-called Z-Plan, were happy to begin the building of world-class fleet of super battleships and aircraft carriers to be completed by the mid-1940s. *See also* British Empire; Fisher, John Arbuthnot, Lord Fisher; *Weltpolitik*.

FURTHER READING: Hubatsch, W. *Die Ära Tirpitz*. Göttingen: Musterschmidt, 1955; Scheck, Raffael. *Alfred von Tirpitz and German Right-Wing Politics*. Atlantic Highlands, NJ: Humanities Press, 1998; Steinberg, Jonathan. *Yesterday's Deterrent: Tirpitz and the Birth of the German Battle Fleet*. London: Macdonald, 1968; Weir, Gary E. *Building the Kaiser's Navy: The Imperial Naval Office and German Industry in the von Tirpitz Era*. Annapolis, MD: Naval Institute Press, 1992.

VOLKER R. BERGHAHN

Tirpitz Plan

Named after its creator, Alfred von **Tirpitz,** and related to the contemporaneous notion of *Weltpolitik* of Kaiser **Wilhelm II,** the Tirpitz plan called for an ambitious expansion of the German Imperial Navy. The term *Tirpitz Plan* was not in use at the time it was conceived in the late 1890s. Rather, its full dimensions emerged 60 years later when the files of the Reich Navy Office became available to researchers for the first time. These files had been held under lock and key by the German navy after World War I until they were captured by the Allies in 1945 and housed uncatalogued in Cambridge, England. After their return to West Germany in the 1960s, scrutiny of the massive holdings revealed a program for the expansion of the Imperial Navy that was much more ambitious than earlier scholarship had assumed.

There was, to begin with, a highly technical side to the Tirpitz Plan. In a narrow sense it was concerned with the replacement of older ships and the building of additional new ones. Toward this end, Tirpitz and his team of naval officers arranged, as a first step, the older battleships and cruisers in such a way that they came up for replacement in a sequence of two per annum. If, because of an earlier building tempo, more than two came up, the replacement would be stretched so as to secure a regular tempo of two ships.

However, Tirpitz's ambition was to launch three ships per annum. Accordingly, one new ship was added to the two replacements, resulting in what came to be called an annual "3-tempo." These three ships were then to be replaced again after 20 years, producing in the meantime a fleet of 60 big ships. There were two considerations behind this systematic design not revealed in Tirpitz's First Navy Law of 1898. First, this law stipulated that those 60 ships were to be automatically replaced after 20 years, so that the start of the renewal cycle in 1918 would not require any further budgetary approval by the **Reichstag.** Second, it provided funding for only three years, 1898–1900, and the Reich Navy Office kept silent about the intention to introduce a second bill in 1900 that would extend the 3-tempo for a further four or five years. After that period more bills were to be submitted until 1918 when the gap would be filled with the building of three battleships per annum.

Because the deputies were not told in 1898 and 1900 that there were more bills to come to extend the 3-tempo all the way until 1918, they also did not appreciate that the 20-year replacement rule in the 1898 law was intended to deprive them of their budgetary powers over the navy. This means that in 1918, Tirpitz would have been independent of the vagaries of the Reichstag approval process. The navy of 60 big ships would be replaced automatically and hence be at the disposal, without interference from the democratically elected assembly, of the monarch who was in exclusive charge of German foreign policy.

Apart from this antiparliamentary calculation, the Tirpitz Plan to expand the Imperial navy in several stages to a total of 60 battleships in 20 years was also adopted with Britain in mind. If London had realized from the start that the kaiser aimed to have all those ships, the British would have been so alarmed that they would have tried to "outbuild" the Germans. Because of the initially veiled German buildup in stages, they recognized rather belatedly what Tirpitz was planning, but when they did, they engaged Germany in a naval arms race that began in 1905–1906.

This plan to establish a 3-tempo over 20 years with its cool antiparliamentary and anti-British considerations emerge clearly from the memoranda and tables that the Reich Navy Office drew up at the turn of the century. Not familiar with this material, historians in the early post-1945 period believed that the strengthening of the navy had a purely defensive purpose to protect the country's overseas interests and colonies at a time when other great powers were also building ships. Others have seen the systematic planning in the Reich Navy Office as part of a bureaucratic power struggle in which Tirpitz, as navy minister, tried to assert himself against the high command, in charge of war planning, and the admiralty staff, responsible for personnel policy. Here Tirpitz is seen as a skillful administrative infighter in a struggle that also revolved around the question of whether the German fleet should consist of cruisers or battleships.

The third position argues that Tirpitz was a very political officer who, with his program, pursued two major long-term objectives. The first one was, as already indicated, to liberate the Imperial navy from the shackles of budgetary approval by the

Reichstag and to achieve an "iron budget" that could not be reduced. Here the army was the model. After 1918, only further additions to the fleet of 60 ships could be voted on, and calculations have in fact survived in the files that show an increase in the 3-tempo to four ships per annum. The German army had a similarly untouchable budget.

Apart from its domestic role, however, the Tirpitz Plan also had a veiled foreign policy angle. Once completed, the 60-battleship fleet was deemed by Tirpitz and his advisers to be powerful enough to defeat the Royal Navy in a do-or-die battle in the North Sea; for they had also reckoned that over the next 20 years, London would not be able to build more than 90 ships. Naval doctrine of the time assumed that a fleet with a one-third inferiority had a genuine chance of defeating an opponent, provided the latter was the attacker. If this attack ever came, Tirpitz hoped to defeat the Royal Navy in their home waters. Britain would then have lost its dominant position in the world in one bold stroke. If, on the other hand, London sat tight, Tirpitz expected the 60-battleship fleet to provide the kaiser with the diplomatic leverage to extract concessions at the conference table when it came to the much-vaunted "redistribution of the world" in the twentieth century. This is where the ambitions of the Tirpitz Plan became connected with those of Wilhelmine *Weltpolitik*.

The plan failed just as *Weltpolitik* did. Suspecting that the Germans were up to something sinister—that they wanted "to steal our clothes"—the British engaged the kaiser in a quantitative naval arms race, more and more ships, as well as a qualitative arms race, and bigger and bigger ships. The launching of the ***Dreadnought*** class from 1906 suddenly made Tirpitz's existing ships obsolete. He tried to keep up by also building both more and bigger ships, but he was defeated by the escalating costs. It proved more and more difficult to persuade the deputies who, after all, still had to approve the naval budget to allocate the additional resources needed to keep up with the **Royal Navy.** By 1912, the original design was in disarray. The army came along and demanded the priority in defense that the navy had enjoyed in previous years. Germany returned to a continental strategy and the war that broke out in July 1914 was fought on land. Tirpitz's navy remained idle for most of the war, and submarines became the instrument of German naval warfare.

FURTHER READING: Berghahn, V. R. *Der Tirpitz-Plan: Genesis und Verfall einer innenpolitischen Krisenstrategie unter Wilhelm II.* Düsseldorf: Droste, 1971; Brézet, F. E. *Le plan Tirpitz, 1897–1914: une flotte de combat allemande contre l'Angleterre.* Paris: Librairie d'l'Inde, 1998; Herwig, H. H. *Luxury Fleet.* London: Allen & Unwin, 1980; Steinberg J. *Yesterday's Deterrent.* London: Macdonald, 1968.

VOLKER R. BERGHAHN

Tisza, István (1861–1918)

Hungarian prime minister and statesaman. István Tisza was born April 22, 1861, in Budapest. His father, Kálmán Tisza, was the leader of Hungary's Liberal Party. In 1886, István Tisza became a member of the Hungarian parliament. He was prime minister of Hungary from 1903 to 1905, when his Liberal Party was defeated at the polls. In a time of deep controversy about Hungary's status within the Habsburg monarchy and of political instability, Tisza managed to take control of the Liberal

Party and to rein in the opposition in parliament. Leader of the lower house from 1912 and prime minister again from June 1913, Tisza dominated Hungarian politics until he resigned in June 1917. In the **July Crisis** of 1914, he insisted on the importance of preliminary diplomatic steps to be taken against Serbia before any military action to avoid a great power war. During the war, however, he supported the war effort wholeheartedly. After his resignation, he was assassinated by a Hungarian leftist in October 1918.

FURTHER READING: Albertini, Luigi. *The Origins of the War of 1914.* 3 vols. Translated by Isabella Mellis Massey. New York: Oxford University Press, 1952; Wilson, Keith, ed. *Decisions for War.* New York: St. Martin's, 1995.

GUENTHER KRONENBITTER

Tisza, Kálmán (1830–1902)

Founder of the Hungarian Liberal Party, Tisza was born in December 1830 in Geszt, into a Calvinist family belonging to the Magyar gentry. In the revolution of 1848–1849, Tisza joined the revolutionary regime and was exiled by the Habsburg authorities after the Hungarian defeat. After his return to **Hungary,** he held an important position in the efforts to restore Hungarian autonomy within the Habsburg monarchy. Since 1875, Tisza supported the status quo of 1867, the Ausgleich between Hungary and Austria. He became the leader of the new Liberal Party, which represented the interests of the nobility, business elites, and landowners. Tisza was prime minister of Hungary from 1875 to 1890 during which the country was modernized. He died in March 1902. *See also* Habsburg Empire; Hungary.

FURTHER READING: Evans, R.J.W. *Austria, Hungary and the Habsburgs: Essays on Central Europe, 1683–1867.* New York: Oxford University Press, 2006.

GUENTHER KRONENBITTER

Togo

A West African territory colonized by Germany in the late nineteenth century as part of an effort to flex diplomatic muscle, preserve international trading rights, and placate interest groups at home. German interest in Togo began in the late 1840s with the arrival of missionaries and a series of small German merchant firms along the coast trading in palm products, cocoa, cotton, and rubber. In the 1880s, Britain's decision to raise import duties along the **Gold Coast** triggered fears that German merchants would be shut out of local markets completely. Otto von **Bismarck,** the German chancellor, responded in July 1884 by sending an armed expedition under the command of Gustav Nachtigal to encourage west African chiefs along the coast of **Cameroon** to sign treaties of protection that would place them under German control. Along the way Nacthigal made an unsanctioned stop in Togo where he obtained similar treaties and announced the creation of a German **protectorate.** Other colonial powers soon recognized Germany's new colony and during the next 15 years the Germans expanded into the interior in the hopes of gaining access to the Niger River. Those hopes were ultimately dashed by a combination of resistance from the indigenous Ewe peoples and simultaneous expansionist efforts of Britain and France. Togo's final borders were set in 1900 via a series of treaty negotiations between Britain, France, and Germany.

Despite early hopes for Togo's financial future, before the turn of the century its small size and limited trade opportunities discouraged investment, leaving most financial enterprises in the hands of small German merchant firms. By 1900, however, **railway** construction and other infrastructure projects facilitated commercial access to the interior and attracted a variety of larger trading companies. Mirroring earlier coastal operations, both the colonial administration and these new trading companies focused their energies on running plantations and encouraging the indigenous peoples to harvest cash crops, thereby turning Togo into the most lucrative of all Germany's African possessions.

Despite Togo's reputation as a model colony, its financial success barely masked growing racial tensions between colonizer and colonized. Starting in 1900, the Ewe increasingly protested their lack of rights, the extensive use of corporal punishment, and the ongoing economic discrimination that they faced. These protests in turn helped give rise to a nascent nationalist movement that partially explains the rapid collapse of German forces in the face of a joint Anglo-French invasion in August 1914. The decision of the victorious allies to split Togo between them was ratified in 1922 when the newly created League of Nations granted Britain and France mandates over the former German colony. *See also* Africa, Scramble for; Berlin, Conference of; German Empire.

FURTHER READING: von Albertini, Rudolf, ed. *European Colonial Rule, 1880–1940. The Impact of the West on India, Southeast Asia, and Africa.* Westport, CT: Greenwood Press, 1982; Henderson, W. O. *The German Colonial Empire 1884–1919.* London: Frank Cass, 1993; Knoll, Arthur J. *Togo under Imperial Germany 1884–1914: A Case Study of Colonial Rule.* Stanford, CA: Hoover Institution, 1978; Stoecker, Helmuth, ed. *German Imperialism in Africa.* London: C. Hurst & Company, 1986.

KENNETH J. OROSZ

Tokugawa Shōgunate (1600–1868)

The hereditary feudal military dictatorship of Japan, passed down the male line of the Tokugawa clan, which was toppled in 1868 and resulted in the **Meiji Restoration.** In 1603, following the warring-states period, political power was centralized by Ieyasu Tokugawa, who took the title of shōgun or military dictator. The shōgun ruled Japan from Edo (present-day Tokyo); the figurehead emperor and the imperial court were kept isolated in Kyoto. The Tokugawa shōgunate maintained a rigid feudal class structure, with the warrior-caste of samurai at the top of the hierarchy and farmers, artisans, and traders at the bottom. The *daimyo,* or feudal lords, attempted to challenge the rule of the Tokugawa clan but the shōguns were able to dominate them politically and militarily by virtue of their monopoly on the importation of gunpowder. Ieyasu Tokugawa had been in favor of foreign trade but his successors, fearful of foreign influence, placed heavy restrictions on contact with the outside world.

The isolationist policies of the Tokugawa shōgunate have been credited for two centuries of relative political stability, but they also resulted in economic stagnation. The appearance of Commodore Matthew Perry's squadron in Tokyo Bay in

July 1853 threw the Tokugawa shōgunate into a state of political turmoil. Hoping to avoid the fate of Qing China, the shōguns signed a series of "unequal treaties" with the **United States,** Britain, France, and Russia, which opened up Japanese ports to foreign trade, granted extraterritorial rights to Western citizens, and ceded control of Japan's foreign trade tariffs to the Western Powers. The *daimyo* of Chosu and Satsuma used the opening of Japan to foreign trade to acquire gunpowder superior to the old saltpeter of the shōgunate, and a Tokugawa army dispatched to quell the rebellion in Chosu and **Satsuma** was defeated. Sensing the weakness of the shōgun, the *daimyo* allied themselves with the new Meiji emperor, who, in January 1868, declared his own restoration to full sovereignty and the abolition of the shōgunate. The shōgun, Yoshinobu, declared the emperor's act illegal and attacked Kyoto but was defeated by imperial forces and surrendered unconditionally in May 1868.

FURTHER READING: Duus, Peter. *Feudalism in Japan.* New York: McGraw-Hill, 1993; Jansen, Marius, ed. *Warrior Rule in Japan.* Cambridge: Cambridge University Press, 1995; Mass, Jeffrey P., and William B. Hauser, eds. *The Bakufu in Japanese History.* Stanford, CA: Stanford University Press, 1985.

ADRIAN U-JIN ANG

Tonkin

The northernmost territory of French **Indochina,** part of **Annam,** which became the target of strong military action against China by the government of Jules **Ferry** in the Third French Indochina War of 1881–1885. When in May 1883, a French expedition was ambushed and wiped out by Chinese "Black Flags," a stronger expeditionary force composed of Foreign Legion and Algerian colonial forces was sent in retaliation and, through 1884, campaigned from Haiphong into the interior to clash with the Black Flags at Tuyen Quang and then to capture Lang Son near the Chinese border. Although the heavy losses and cost of the expedition toppled Ferry's government, French forces had prevailed by April of 1885, when China signed a treaty. The Chinese momentarily renounced the peace, but the bombardment of Hanoi and Haiphong produced a second and final peace in August 1885, whereupon Tonkin became a French **protectorate**. *See also* French Empire.

FURTHER READING: Quinn, Frederick. *The French Overseas Empire.* Westport, CA: Praeger, 2002; Wesseling, H. L. *The European Colonial Empires 1815–1919.* New York: Longman, 2004.

CARL CAVANAGH HODGE

Toussaint l'Ouverture (c. 1743–1803)

Known originally as François-Dominique Toussaint, Toussaint l'Ouverture was a self-educated former slave who became one of the leaders of the revolt in St. Domingue that overthrew French rule and created the independent nation of **Haiti.** As the French Revolution unfolded in Europe, slaves in the north of St. Domingue staged their own rebellion in 1791 in a bid to gain their freedom. Although initially uncommitted, Toussaint l'Ouverture joined the rebels when the white planters refused to honor earlier promises to grant voting rights and citizenship to all free men regardless of color. After rising quickly through the ranks of the rebel army and briefly allying himself with invading Spanish forces from the neighboring colony of Santo Domingo, in 1794 l'Ouverture declared himself a French patriot following the decision in Paris to grant freedom to all slaves who fought on behalf of the Revolution.

From 1794 to 1801, Toussaint l'Ouverture used his forces to end foreign military intervention and capture Santo Domingo on behalf of the French Republic. Shortly thereafter he drafted a new constitution for the colony, which formally abolished slavery and named him governor-general for life. Because these actions threatened Napoleon **Bonaparte**'s plans to restore St. Domingue to its former status as a profitable plantation colony, the newly crowned French emperor ignored Toussaint l'Ouverture's claims of continued allegiance and launched an invasion in 1802 to restore French authority on the island. After several months of fighting, Toussaint l'Ouverture signed a truce in May 1802 and retired to his farm. Three weeks later he was arrested and deported to France where he died in prison. Less than a year later, his followers defeated the French and declared independence. *See also* French Empire; Slavery.

FURTHER READING: Alexis, Stephen. *Black Liberator: The Life of Toussaint L'Ouverture.* New York: Macmillan, 1949; James, C.L.R. *The Black Jacobins: Toussaint L'Ouverture and the San Domingo Revolution.* London: Allison & Busby, 1980; Moran, Charles. *Black Triumvirate: A Study of L'Ouverture, Dessalines, Christophe.* New York: Exposition Books, 1957; Ros, Martin. *Night of Fire: The Black Napoleon and the Battle for Haiti.* New York: Sarpedon, 1994.

KENNETH J. OROSZ

Trafalgar, Battle of (1805)

The most decisive naval engagement of the **Napoleonic Wars,** in which a **Royal Navy** fleet of 27 ships under Admiral Horatio **Nelson** routed a combined French and Spanish fleet of 33 ships commanded by Rear-Admiral Pierre Charles Villeneuve. It took place off Cape Trafalgar on the southwestern coast of Spain on October 21, 1805.

Weather conditions on the morning of that day were such that Nelson was able to approach the Franco-Spanish line from the northwest to catch Villeneuve's ships downwind and sailing a northerly course. To attack Nelson formed his ships in two parallel lines and ordered them to close on Villeneuve's fleet, forming a line-ahead formation north-to-south, at right angles. This tactic had in fact been anticipated by Villeneuve, yet he had no counter to it and indeed had difficulty keeping his line orderly owing to its awkward position to the wind. One column of ships, headed by Nelson's flagship *Victory,* steered into and split off the top third of Villeneuve's line; the other, headed by Vice-Admiral Wilfrid Collingwood's *Royal Sovereign,* split off the bottom third. Nelson's tactics ran the danger of exposing his ships to punishing fire as they closed on Villeneuve's line. Yet they also temporarily separated a third of the French admiral's ship from action as the two British columns tore into the Combined Fleet's line and engaged it at close range. Once this had been accomplished, the gunlock firing mechanism of the Royal Navy's cannon and the superior discipline of its gun crews was able to deliver a volume and rate of fire that inflicted casualties and damage disproportionate to what was received. Villeneuve's line broke apart as Nelson's ships fell among them, *Royal Sovereign* alone engaging no fewer than eight enemy ships. *Victory,* and in succession the ships that followed her into the French line, fired broadsides into Villeneuve's flagship, *Bucentaure,* toppling its masts, shattering it timbers with solid shot, and tearing up its crew with grapeshot. Nelson lost no ships yet managed to sink or capture 19 of the Combined Fleet; 449 British died against 4,000 French and Spanish. In Britain, national jubilation at so spectacular a victory was submerged in grief at the news of Nelson's death from the ball of a sniper.

Trafalgar did not, technically, save Britain from invasion. Napoleon's plans in this direction had already been all but abandoned. It nonetheless guaranteed Britain's survival and economic prosperity, which in turn permitted her to continue the struggle for the next decade and to support her continental allies in the effort. Napoleon had, in 1805, not yet reached the zenith of his success, but, as he eventually stretched his ambition and resources to Spain and Russia simultaneously, having an implacable foe such as Britain meant that Trafalgar was a defeat of strategic dimensions. This was even more so for Spain whose loss of a fleet at Trafalgar emboldened its colonies to rebellion had hastened the demise of a vast overseas empire. Lastly, it gave Britain almost the century of naval predominance that enabled it to preserve and extend it own imperial interests, a fact that, by the 1890s, moved Mahan to cite Trafalgar in making the case for the influence of sea power on history. *See also* Mahan, Alfred Thayer; Navalism; Pax Brittanica; Tirpitz Plan.

FURTHER READING: Davies, David. *Fighting Ships.* London: Constable and Co., 1996; Keegan, John. *The Price of Admiralty.* London: Hutchinson, 1988; Kennedy, Paul M. *The Rise and Fall of British Naval Mastery.* London: A. Lane, 1976; Rodger, N.A.M. *The Command of the Ocean: A Naval History of Britain, 1649–1815.* New York: W. W. Norton, 2004.

CARL CAVANAGH HODGE

Transcontinental Treaty

See Adams-Onís Treaty

Trans-Siberian Railway

A railroad across Russia, between Moscow and Vladivostok, part of Russia's industrialization plan at the end of the nineteenth century. Officially begun on May 31, 1891, the project received financial and administrative support from Minister of Finance Sergei **Witte.** Moreover, a special committee was created to oversee the project that included the heir to the throne, **Nicholas II.** Nevertheless, the project was plagued by labor and material shortages, as well as the constant threat of disease and attacks by mosquitoes and tigers. Moreover, the harsh weather and difficult terrain regularly slowed construction. The work force on this enormous project included Turks, Italians, Chinese, and Russians, some of whom were convicts. This railroad promoted Russia's penetration of northern China, thus heightening tensions with Japan. Although there are technically three routes, the most common, from Moscow to Vladivostok, runs 5,810 miles and takes about a week to travel. *See also* Manchuria; Russian Empire; Russian Far East; Russo-Japanese War.

FURTHER READING: Marks, Steven G. *Road to Power: The Trans-Siberian Railroad and the Colonization of Asian Russia, 1850–1917.* London: I. B. Tauris, 1991; Von Laue, Theodore. *Sergei Witte and the Industrialization of Russia.* New York: Columbia University Press, 1963.

LEE A. FARROW

Transvaal

A Boer state established north of the Vaal River in South Africa during the Great Trek in 1852. It was annexed by Britain in 1877 in an agreement with the Boers who sought protection against the predations of the **Zulu** at a time of insolvency for the Transvaal's finances. Outright annexation was never popular among the Boers. They considered it a violation of the principles of the **Sand River Convention,** were annoyed by the taxes and parsimony of British administrations, and outraged at the abuses to themselves and their property by misbehaving British troops. They were also led to hope for the recovery of their independence by William **Gladstone**'s attack on the Conservative government of Benjamin **Disraeli** as "drunk with imperialism" and the annexation of a free and tenacious protestant community as a gross offense to liberal principle. When Gladstone returned to office and decided instead that the Boers should accept the liberty afforded them by confederation, they revolted. The First Boer War is therefore occasionally referred to as the Transvaal War. Transvaal was again annexed by Britain after the Second Boer War. *See also* Boer Wars; Orange Free State.

FURTHER READING: Wilson, Monica and Leonard Thompson, eds. *The Oxford History of South Africa.* 2 vols. Oxford: Clarendon, 1971.

CARL CAVANAGH HODGE

Treaty of 1818

See Anglo-American Treaty (1818)

Treaty Ports

Ports in China, Japan, and Korea that were opened to the trade and residence of foreigners under pressure from Western powers. The Treaty of **Nanjing** ending the **Opium War** in 1842 forced China to open five treaty ports; a second list of ports was opened after the **Arrow War,** so that by 1917 there were 92, some of them opened on China's own initiative. Western activity in the Far East concentrated in the treaty ports, where consulates exercised **extraterritorial** jurisdiction and, in the larger ports—**Shanghai,** Tientsin, Hankow—settlements administered exclusively by the European inhabitants, "concessions" as they were commonly called, were created. Japan opened Shimoda and Hakodate in 1854 and added five more ports in 1858.

FURTHER READING: Greenberg, Michael. *British Trade and the Opening of China.* Cambridge: Cambridge University Press, 1951.

NIELS P. PETERSSON

Treitschke, Heinrich von (1834–1896)

Born in Dresden, Heinrich von Treitsche was one of the most well-known German historians of the later nineteenth century. Appointed as Leopold von **Ranke**'s successor at the Humboldt University in 1874, Treitschke's name is closely associated with his unswerving support for German nationalism. After German unification in 1871, he also held a seat as a National Liberal in the **Reichstag.** He edited the monthly *Preussische Jahrbücher* and became in 1886 Prussian state historian. In his *German History in the Nineteenth Century,* published in a series of volumes between 1879 and 1894, Treitschke sought to provide a historical justification for German unification and expansion. His aim was to arouse in the hearts of his readers "the pleasure of living in the Fatherland." Full of vitriol for the British, whom he described as "dreadful hypocrites" with an Empire based on an "abundance of sins and outrages," his works were extremely well received and inspired leading figures such as Bernhard von **Bülow.** *See also* German Empire; Prussia.

FURTHER READING: Davis, H. W. Careless. *The Political Thought of Heinrich von Treitschke.* Westport, CT: Greenwood, 1973; McCabe, Joseph. *Treitschke and the Great War.* London: T. F. Unwin, 1914.

PAUL LAWRENCE

Trent Affair (1861)

A diplomatic incident that threatened to bring about a war between Britain and the **United States** in the midst of the **American Civil War.** On November 8, 1861, a Union warship commanded by Charles Wilkes intercepted a British mail packet, the *Trent,* in the Bahaman channel. Wilkes removed two Confederate diplomats bound for Europe, James M. Mason and John Slidell, and took them to Boston where they were confined as prisoners. Wilkes clearly had violated international law: the two Confederates had sailed under the protection of a neutral flag. According to law, the most that Wilkes should have done was to seize the ship and take it to port for an admiralty court to judge whether the *Trent* had done anything wrong. Instead he had seized only the two men. Worst of all, the removal of the Confederate diplomats had insulted Britain whose **Royal Navy** was accustomed to dominate the high seas.

Public opinion in the Northern states applauded Captain Wilkes' bold action, but public opinion in Britain was outraged. Prime Minister Lord **Palmerston** began preparations for war. For him this was a matter of national honor and not part of any pro-Confederate policy. Foreign Secretary Lord John **Russell** and Prince Consort Albert, then struggling with a terminal illness, persuaded Palmerston to moderate his demands in the diplomatic note that he sent to Washington. The British diplomat there, Lord Lyons, delayed until December 23 his formal presentation of the note to give passions a chance to cool. After Secretary of State William H. **Seward** received the note, he reluctantly conceded the British demand for the release of Mason and Slidell, as did President Abraham **Lincoln.** It was not realistic for the United States to risk a naval war with Britain while fighting a civil war with the seceding states of the Confederacy. As Lincoln said, "one war at a time." Historians are divided about how serious the danger of war had been but agree that if Britain had declared war on the United States, the Confederacy might well have secured its independence. In January 1863, the Confederate diplomats were released, Mason going to London and Slidell to Paris, where neither of them accomplished anything.

FURTHER READING: Warren, Gordon H. *Fountain of Discontent: The Trent Affair and the Freedom of the Seas.* Boston: Northeastern University Press, 1981.

DAVID M. FAHEY

Trieste

An ancient port city at the northeastern corner of the Adriatic Sea, which in the eighteenth and nineteenth centuries became the most important sea harbor of the Habsburg monarchy because it offered direct access to the Mediterranean. The city was occupied three times by French troops during the Revolutionary and **Napoleonic Wars.** From 1857 to 1918, Trieste was among the most prosperous harbors on the Mediterranean, but it was also home to a strong irredentist movement seeking annexation to Italy. On the eve of World War I, approximately two-thirds of the population of Trieste were Italians, most of the rest Croats or Slovenes. James Joyce spent almost a decade in Trieste and for a time taught English to officers of at the Habsburg naval base in nearby Pola. After World War I, Italian troops occupied the city in accordance with the treaty of London of 1915. *See also* Habsburg Empire.

FURTHER READING: Cornwall, Mark, ed. *The Last Years of Austria-Hungary: A Multi-National Experiment in Early Twentieth Century Europe.* Exeter: University of Exeter Press, 2002.

GUENTHER KRONENBITTER

Triple Alliance (1882)

A secret alliance of Austria-Hungary, Germany, and **Italy** pledging mutual assistance in the event of an attack by France. Franco-Italian relations had been strained since the Italian occupation of Rome in 1870. When France formalized its protectorate over Tunis in 1881, Italy decided to pursue an alliance with Austria-Hungary, already allied with Germany.

Germany and Austria-Hungary were initially cool to Italian advances, as there appeared to be no benefits to them. Berlin was in fact happy to see France diverted by North African adventures, while Vienna had made it clear that Austria-Hungary was unwilling to go to war against France on Germany's behalf and even less willing to enter a war for the sake of Italy. A crisis in the Habsburg province of Bosnia over the autumn and winter of 1881–1882, however, led to a reevaluation of the situation by both. Though Russia had remained officially neutral during the crisis, prominent ministers and generals had spoken in favor of Franco-Russian alliance in support of the Bosnians. Fear of such sentiments drove Germany and Austria-Hungary into the arms of Italy.

The alliance was signed on May 20 as an agreement renewable every five years. Like the Dual Alliance, which it replaced, it was a defensive pact designed to work against France or against "two or more Great Powers not members of the alliance." In the event of an Austro-Russian war, Italy was pledged to benevolent neutrality.

Finally, to allay Italian fears, the pact stated that it "cannot . . . in any case be regarded as directed against England." The Triple Alliance provided the greatest benefit to Italy by making her part of the Great Power system and providing her with stronger partners in the event of conflict with France. For Germany and Austria-Hungary, the gains were minimal, as the alliance removed the threat of an additional partner for Russia and posed for France a complication in any war with Germany. The pact was renewed until 1912. The Italians chose not to enter World War I in 1914, because, they argued, the terms of the alliance had not been met. *See also* Bosnia-Herzegovina; German Empire; Habsburg Empire; July Crisis; Triple Entente.

FURTHER READING: Langer, William L. *European Alliance and Alignments 1871–1890.* New York: Alfred A. Knopf, 1962; Strachan, Hew. *The First World War.* New York: Oxford University Press, 2001; Tranter, Nigel. *Triple Alliance.* London: Coronet, 2002.

DAVID H. OLIVIER

Triple Entente (1907)

A term commonly used to refer to cooperation among Britain, France, and Russia after 1907. It was not an alliance and was composed of three diplomatic agreements: the Franco-Russian alliance on 1894, the 1904 **Entente Cordiale** between Great Britain and France, and the 1907 Anglo-Russian agreement. These separate arrangements were initially settlements of disputes rather than positive diplomatic commitments, and the three powers involved did not craft a military alliance until after the outbreak of World War I, at which point they agreed, on September 3, 1914, that none of them would sign a separate peace treaty with Germany or Austria-Hungary. That alliance did not survive the war. With the revolution of 1917, the Bolshevik government in Russia renounced the alliance and in 1918 signed the Treaty of Brest-Litovsk with Germany. *See also* British Empire; French Empire; Russian Empire.

FURTHER READING: Howard, Michael Eliot. *The Continental Commitment.* London: Ashfield, 1989; Langer, William L. *European Alliance and Alignments 1871–1890.* New York: Alfred A. Knopf, 1962; Williamson, Samuel R. *The Politics of Grand Strategy: Britain and France Prepare for War, 1904–1914.* Cambridge, MA: Harvard University Press, 1969.

CARL CAVANAGH HODGE

Tripoli

A city located in northwest Libya on the Mediterranean coast. Tripoli was the capital of the former Ottoman province of Tripolitania in western Libya. The city's climate was mitigated by the Mediterranean, but the desert winds that swept the region during the summer rendered widescale agriculture expensive and impractical. The Turks, therefore, used Tripoli mainly as a port along the Sudan-Sahara trade route. In 1714, the Karamanli dynasty seized control of Tripoli and, with the city-states of Tunis, Morocco, and Algiers, formed the Barbary States. Their pirate fleets seized European and American trade in the Mediterranean in return for tribute and ransoms. In the Barbary Wars of 1801–1805 and 1815, the **United States** defeated the pirates, forcing them to either lower or abandon their blackmail. The wars also allowed the Turks to return.

The Ottomans reestablished authority over Tripoli in 1835 but were unable to impose strong centralized rule, and instead relied on Arabs and Europeans to help administer the province. One Arab tribe was the Islamic fundamentalist brotherhood, the Senussi, founded in 1837 by Muhammad bin Ali al-Sanusi (1791–1859). Italian emigrants in Tripoli opened up branches of the Bank of Rome throughout Tripolitania and Cyrenaica to handle the provinces' trade. Each group mistrusted the other and were jealous of their prerogatives.

In 1911, Italian imperialists pressured the government into launching a colonial war against Turkey for Libya on the pretext that the Turks were restricting Italian economic rights. During the Italo-Turkish War (1911–1912), the Italians bombarded and occupied Tripoli, installed a government, and formally annexed Tripolitania and Cyrenaica by royal decree. Tripoli became capital of the Italian colony of Tripolitania. *See also* Italo-Turkish War; Italy; Ottoman Empire.

FURTHER READING: Beehler, W. H. *The History of the Italian-Turkish War.* Annapolis, MD: Advertiser-Republican, 1913; McCarthy, Justin. *The Ottoman Peoples and the End of Empire.* London: Arnold, 2001.

FREDERICK H. DOTOLO

Troppau, Congress of (1820)

The third meeting of the **Congress System,** at the village of Troppau—Opava in the contemporary Czech Republic—involving Austrian, Prussian, and Russian delegations with British and French observers. The meeting dealt with the outbreak of liberal revolutionary upheavals in **Italy** and Spain. Dominated by Prince von **Metternich**—with the enthusiastic cooperation of Tsar **Alexander I,** who had recently been shaken by upheaval and conspiracy in Russia—the meeting produced the Protocol of Troppau, according to which "States which have undergone a change of government due to revolution, the results of which threaten other States, *ipso facto* cease to be members of the European Alliance and remain excluded from it until their situation gives guarantees for legal order and stability." It went on to pledge that "the Powers bind themselves, by peaceful means, or if need be by arms, to bring back the guilty State into the bosom of the Great Alliance." Britain endorsed Austrian intervention in Italy but rejected the thrust of the protocol that intervention was justified to defeat any liberal revolt in Europe. *See also* Aix-la-Chapelle; Laibach; Prussia; Russian Empire; Vienna, Congress of.

FURTHER READING: Kissinger, Henry. *A World Restored: Metternich, Castlereagh and the Problems of Peace.* London: Weidenfeld & Nicolson, 1957.

CARL CAVANAGH HODGE

Trotha, Adrian Dietrich Lothar von (1848–1920)

A commander of German colonial troops who is most noted for his defeat of the **Herero Revolt** in **German Southwest Africa.** Von Trotha had joined the Prussian army at 17, served previously in the **Austro-Prussian War** and the **Franco-Prussian War,** and also led the First East Asian Brigade against the **Boxer Insurrection.** In the latter case he had used mass reprisals against the defeated Chinese that he developed into a *Vernichtungspolitik* or "policy of annihilation" that he applied to the Herero. The policy stated that the Herero people would no longer be considered German subjects and further that any Herero who remained within German territory, armed or unarmed, was to be shot. Woman and children were to be driven into the desert. Public outcry against von Trotha's actions prompted Chancellor von **Bülow** to have him relieved of his command, by which time the Herero had been reduced through shooting, starvation, and overwork from an estimated population of 80,000 to some 15,000 survivors. *See also* Maji-Maji Revolt.

FURTHER READING: Drechsler, Horst. *Let Us Die Fighting: The Struggle of the Herero and Nama against German Imperialism.* London: Zed, 1980; Hull, Isabel V. *Absolute Destruction: Military Culture and Practices of War in Imperial Germany.* Ithaca, NY: Cornell University Press, 2005.

CARL CAVANAGH HODGE

Trotsky, Lev Davidovich (1879–1940)

One of the primary leaders of the **Bolshevik** Revolution in Russia. Trotsky was born Lev Davidovich Bronstein—he assumed the name Trotsky in 1902—the son of a Jewish farmer in a small village in the Ukraine. His early revolutionary activities resulted in his arrest, exile, and eventual movement abroad, where he met V. I. **Lenin** in London in 1902. In the 1903 meeting of the Russian Social Democrats, Trotsky rejected Lenin's idea of a small, restrictive party, preferring that of Julius Martov, who favored a broader party membership, open to all who embraced Marx's theories. Over the next years, Trotsky remained more or less isolated, not linked to any one revolutionary group, criticizing Lenin and warning that his vision for a centralized party would inevitably result in the dictatorship of one man. Despite his isolation, Trotsky became well known, largely on the strength of his exceptional writing and oratory skills.

In early 1905, Trotsky emerged as a leader of the Petersburg Soviet, although he was later arrested and again went abroad. During the spring of 1917, he returned to Russia and joined the Bolsheviks and by the early fall, he was leading the party while Lenin was in hiding. When the actual insurrection began in late October, Trotsky directed the revolutionaries' activities, ordering the seizure of major city installations, such as phone and transportation offices. In the immediate aftermath of the coup, when some socialists refused to participate in the new government, Trotsky gave his famous speech in which he told these opponents to go "into the dustbin of history." In the new Soviet government, Trotsky took the position of Commissar of Foreign Affairs. In 1918, as commissar of war, he was the Soviet representative during the negotiations for the Treaty of Brest Litovsk with Germany. After Lenin's death in 1924, Trotsky was isolated and expelled from the party by Joseph Stalin's aggressive maneuvering to become the country's new leader. Trotsky's ideas about permanent revolution and world revolution were cast aside in favor of Stalin's argument for socialism in one country. In 1928, he was forced to leave Russia and moved from country to country until he finally settled in a suburb of Mexico City, where he worked with other Marxists such as Frida Kahlo and Diego Rivera. Even here he was not outside of Stalin's reach and ultimately was murdered by one of Stalin's agents in 1940. *See also* Russian Empire.

FURTHER READING: Figes, Orlando. *A People's Tragedy: The Russian Revolution, 1891–1924*. New York: Penguin, 1996; Trotsky, Leon. *My Life: An Attempt at an Autobiography*. New York: Pathfinder Press, 1970; Volkhogonov, Dmitrii. *Trotsky: The Eternal Revolutionary*. Translated by Harold Shukman. New York: The Free Press, 1996; Wolfe, Bertram D. *Three Who Made a Revolution*. New York: Dial Press, 1964.

LEE A. FARROW

Ts'u Hsi (1835–1908)

Known as the "Empress Dowager," Ts'u Hsi was a leading figure of the **Qing Dynasty**'s last decades in power in China. Ts'u Hsi took over the regency for her son T'ung-chih in 1861. She relinquished power in 1889, but reestablished the regency when her adoptive son, Emperor Kuang-hsü, embraced radical reformist ideas in 1898. In 1900, she allied herself with supporters of the **Boxer Insurrection,** apparently believing that they might well succeed in expelling foreigners from China, but had to flee from the international intervention forces. Back in power, she supported conservative reformers, specifically by issuing an edict in 1906 promising a new constitution and reforms of China's administrative structure, including the establishment of a national assembly. Suspiciously, Kuang-hsü died one day before Ts'u Hsi.

FURTHER READING: Preston Diana. *The Boxer Rebellion: China's War on Foreigners, 1900*. London: Robinson, 2002.

NIELS P. PETERSSON

Tsushima, Battle of (1905)

Fought May 27, Tsushima was the decisive naval battle of the **Russo-Japanese War,** a Japanese victory as spectacular as Horatio **Nelson**'s at **Trafalgar** 100 years earlier. With the destruction of the Russian Pacific Fleet in the Battle of Shantung, the Baltic fleet was dispatched to help break the blockade of **Port Arthur.** In a feat of seamanship, Admiral Zinovi Petrovitch Rozhdestvenski led his fleet 18,000 nautical miles to the Pacific only to find that Port Arthur had fallen. Rozhdestvenski decided to sail for Vladivostok instead but was intercepted by the Japanese fleet under Admiral Heihachiro Togo in the Tsushima Straits.

The two fleets joined battle on the afternoon of May 27, and the Japanese managed to "cross the T" of the Russian fleet twice and proceeded to destroy it systematically. Nearly the entire Russian fleet was sunk or captured; three cruisers made it to Manila where they were interned and two damaged destroyers and supply vessels made it to Vladivostok. Tsushima had two immediate and profound consequences: it hastened the day when **Tsar Nicholas II** would seek terms with the **Japanese Empire** and marked the emergence of Japanese naval power as a force to reckoned with. *See also* Navalism.

FURTHER READING: Busch, Noel Fairchild. *The Emperor's Sword: Japan vs. Russia in the Battle of Tsushima*. New York: Funk & Wagnalls, 1969; Corbett, J. S. *Maritime Operation in the Russo-Japanese War*. Annapolis, MD: Naval Institute Press, 1995.

ADRIAN U-JIN ANG

Tunis/Tunisia

The North African city of Tunis was ruled by a succession of foreign rulers, beginning with the ancient city of Carthage situated across from it. Carthage, including Tunis, fell in the hands of the Romans in 146 B.C. The Vandals conquered Tunis in 439 A.D. In the sixth century, Flavius Belisarius conquered Tunis and it became part of the Byzantine Empire. The seventh century saw the Arabs invading Tunis. Under the Almohade dynasty in the twelfth century and the Hafsid dynasty from 1206 till 1534, Tunis flourished and became a thriving Islamic city, with strong commercial links with Europe and the rest of the Mediterranean world. From the years 1534 to 1881, the city was in the Ottoman orbit, with temporary Spanish rule from 1553 to 1569 and from 1573 to 1574. For much of the nineteenth century, Tunis was autonomous and, in 1837, secured an alliance with Britain to balance Ottoman dominance and French ambition.

From the 1870s, however, Tunis came increasingly under the influence of France in neighboring **Algeria,** a fact formally acknowledged at the Congress of **Berlin** in 1878. Tunisia was then annexed outright by France in May 1881. Although its administration resembled that of a colony, it was officially a French **protectorate.** As a French dependency, the *Bey* had a title of *Possesseur de Royaume* and his administration was considered to be a sufficiently strong basis for government. A rebellion against the *Bey* for capitulating to the French was suppressed by French military forces. From then on, Tunis was run by French civil and military administration, and every person within Tunisia was bound by a French code. It was granted independence in 1956. *See also* Africa, Scramble for; French Empire; Ottoman Empire.

FURTHER READING: Ganiage, Jean. *Les origins du protectorate français en Tunisie, 1861–1881.* Paris: Presses universitaires de France, 1959; Pakenham, Thomas. *The Scramble for Africa.* New York: Random House, 1991.

NURFADZILAH YAHAYA

Turkestan

A Russian colony in Central Asia during the nineteenth and early twentieth centuries. Russian colonial administration in Turkestan became necessary following the conquest of Tashkent in 1865. The colony lasted until the collapse of the Russian imperial regime in 1917. Turkestan's colonial apparatus was set up through the 1865 Steppe Commission, led by Minister of War Dimitry Miliutin. The commission decided to govern Turkestan with an eye toward allowing the peoples of the region to maintain many of their traditional governmental practices. It advocated a gradual integration into the **Russian Empire.** It was also decided, however, that Turkestan would be governed by military rule under a governor-general. The commission's findings were formalized in 1867 by **Alexander II.**

Turkestan's territory consisted of most of the oasis lands of the present-day countries of southern Kazakhstan, Kyrgyzstan, Uzbekistan, Tajikistan, and Turkmenistan, minus the protectorates of **Khiva** and **Bukhara.** Much of this territory was gained through military operations from the 1860s until the 1880s. Throughout most of its history, Turkestan was a unique colony of the Russian Empire that maintained many traditional religious and cultural practices, as well as a degree of political and juridical autonomy at the local level. Despite some opinions to the contrary, it was decided that Islam should be both allowed and even encouraged within the territory. The administration even decided that individuals wishing to make the hajj, the Islamic pilgrimage, be granted the right to do so.

Konstantin von **Kaufman** ruled the colony as governor-general from 1867 until his retirement in 1881. He encouraged ethnographic research on the peoples of the region. Kaufman saw Turkestan as a uniquely multiethnic and multireligious colony, which he hoped could be gradually integrated into a uniform whole. In 1886, a reform statute for the colony was approved, based on the findings of Fedor Girs. He found that the colony needed to strengthen the "civic spirit" of the people by furthering the integration of Russia's civilian administrative and legal system in Turkestan.

The Transcaspian Railway completed a line to Tashkent from Orenburg and was opened for business in 1906. This allowed for the increased migration of Slavic peoples into Turkestan, which caused growing discontent among the local populations. Scarce water and land resources were a major source of dispute between the Turkic peoples and the new Slavic settlers. A major revolt in Turkestan called the Basmachi revolt began in 1916 and lasted well into the 1920s. *See also* Great Game; Slavism.

FURTHER READING: Brower, Daniel. *Turkestan and the Fate of the Russian Empire.* London: Routledge Courzon, 2003; Khalid, Adeeb. *The Politics of Muslim Cultural Reform: Jadidism in Central Asia.* Berkeley: University of California Press, 1998; Schuyler, Eugene. *Turkistan.* New York: F. A. Praeger, 1966.

SCOTT C. BAILEY

Two-Power Standard

The idea, current throughout the nineteenth century but first articulated officially in the Naval Defence Act of 1899, that the **Royal Navy** should be able to defeat the combined fleets of the next two most powerful nations. The two powers whose combined navies the British feared were usually France and Russia. The rise of other navies, including the American, the Italian, the Japanese, and of course the German, led to talk of a three-power standard at the end of the century.

The polarization of Europe between the entente and the central powers in the Edwardian era, and the threat of what Churchill called the German luxury fleet, led, however, to the effective adoption during the Anglo-German naval race of a one-power standard, that power being Germany. These evolving standards often had something of a *post-hoc* quality to them: they were as much descriptions of the current state of naval power as policies laid down at the admiralty, although they did serve as motivational slogans on occasions, such as the 1884 naval scare, when the British feared that technical change was about to cost them their superiority. The standard began to lose its relevance when the launch of *H.M.S. **Dreadnought*** so altered the naval arms with Germany that the comparative balance of capital ships became less important. The standard was dropped by First Sea Lord Winston

Churchill in 1912 in favor of a 60 percent British lead in dreadnoughts over any other one fleet. *See also* Mahan, Alfred Thayer; Navalism; Tirpitz Plan.

FURTHER READING: Kennedy, Paul M. *The Rise and Fall of British Naval Mastery.* London: A. Lane, 1976; Mackinder, Halford J. *Britain and the British Seas.* Oxford: Clarendon, 1922.

MARK F. PROUDMAN

U

Uganda

A territory in East Africa, which became a British colony during the Scramble for **Africa.** During the late nineteenth century, Britain obtained control of many territories in Africa simply because British policymakers feared that their acquisition by other European powers—especially France and Germany—could represent a strategic threat to the British Empire. By the late 1880s, Prime Minister Lord **Salisbury** was convinced that control of Uganda was necessary to defend the Upper Nile. To minimize the cost to the British taxpayer Salisbury turned to the British East Africa Company to establish a presence in the area and, in December 1890, the company's representative, Frederick **Lugard,** marched into the kingdom of Buganda, southern Uganda, and made a treaty with Kabaka Mwanga, who accepted the company as his overlord.

The region offered little by way of trade, and the costs of Lugard's expedition quickly undermined the financial position of the company. In 1891, the company proposed that the British Government build a **railway** from the East African coast to Uganda to maintain the company's presence and strengthen British strategic control of the region. There was a great deal of political prevarication, but the issue was resolved by a combination of pressure from missionary societies eager to see extension of British control over an area in which slavery was still evident and Colonial Secretary Joseph **Chamberlain,** who favored schemes for the economic development. In 1895, a decision was taken to go ahead with the 580-mile railway, built at a cost of £5.5 million.

The financial weakness of the British East Africa Company prompted the British government to establish a **protectorate** over Uganda in 1894. Before 1914, just 40 British officials administered a population of more than 3 million in Uganda through a system of **indirect rule,** in which local tribal chiefs maintained their authority subject to British overrule. One clear indication of the extent of British control was the redrawing of the frontiers between Uganda and Kenya in 1902. A large area of the Ugandan highlands east of Lake Victoria was assigned to Kenya, which was becoming attractive to small numbers of British settlers eager to grow cash crops such as coffee. In Uganda the major cash crop was cotton, which by 1918 accounted for 80 percent of its exports. *See also* British Empire; Fashoda Crisis; German East Africa.

FURTHER READING: Apter, David. *The Political Kingdom in Uganda.* London: Routledge, 1997; Low, D. A. *Buganda in Modern History.* Berkeley: University of California Press, 1971; Twaddle, Michael. *Kakungulu and the Creation of Uganda, 1868–1928.* London: James Currey, 1993.

CARL PETER WATTS

Ulm, Capitulation at (1805)

A mass surrender of Austrian forces during the War of the Third Coalition. Having established a military alliance in August 1805, Russia and Austria sent armies toward the Danube, en route to France, while Napoleon **Bonaparte** shifted the army he intended to use for the invasion of England to meet this threat from the east. The French crossed the Rhine on September 26, while General Karl Mack, the Austrian commander, about 100 miles west of Munich and unaware of Napoleon's rapid advance, found his army gradually enveloped by large enemy columns forming a wide concentric arc to the north and east of his position. By the time Mack realized that his lines of communication were severed and his retreat cut off, Napoleon had completed the encirclement, and after an unsuccessful attempt to break out at Elchingen on October 14, Mack capitulated his army of nearly 30,000 men three days later. Napoleon's turning movement proved a strategic tour de force which, when combined with his decisive victory at **Austerlitz** on December 2, broke further Austrian resistance. *See also* Napoleonic Wars.

FURTHER READING: Bowden, Scott. *Napoleon and Austerlitz.* Chicago: The Emperor's Press, 1997; Chandler, David. *The Campaigns of Napoleon.* London: Weidenfeld & Nicolson, 1995.

GREGORY FREMONT-BARNES

Ulster

See Ireland; Union

Union

In British imperial history, "union" signifies the idea of combining smaller legislative units into a larger one. Specifically, it referred to the Scottish Union of 1707, by which the Scottish Parliament voted itself out of existence and Scotland acquired seats in the Union Parliament at Westminster. By the Act of Union of 1800, the Irish Parliament did the same. The Scottish Union, despite periodic Jacobite risings, at length successfully integrated Scotland into the United Kingdom. The Irish Union was notably less successful and eventually disintegrated following the Easter rising of 1916 and the Anglo-Irish treaty of 1921. The idea of Union was in many ways a liberal idea, as it sought to downplay national differences, and to eliminate corrupt and aristocratically dominated local legislatures, by including Scots and Irish alongside the Welsh and the English as ostensible equals represented in the "mother of Parliaments" at Westminster. *See also* British Empire; Ireland.

FURTHER READING: Morgan, Kenneth O., ed. *Oxford History of Britain*. Oxford: Oxford University Press, 2001.

MARK F. PROUDMAN

Unionist Party

See Liberal Party, Liberal Unionist Party

United States of America

Between 1800 and 1914, the United States nearly quadrupled its national territory, became a world power, and created three overlapping and intimately connected forms of empire: a transcontinental empire, an informal empire, and an overseas colonial empire. American expansion was accelerated by the spectacular economic and population growth of the nation, the successful integration of vast territories through a unifying communication and transportation network, a powerful expansionist ideology that at times encountered substantial anti-expansionist opposition, and a cultural setting conducive to the practice of empire-building.

Transcontinental Empire

Throughout the nineteenth century, the United States steadily expanded its national territory by diplomacy and war. The most important steps included the 1803 **Louisiana Purchase,** through which the United States acquired almost 530 million acres from France for $15 million, and the 1819 Transcontinental Treaty, through which the United States acquired Florida from Spain and extended its boundaries to the Oregon coast in exchange for $5 million and a temporary recognition of Spanish claims to Texas. The United States then annexed **Texas** in 1845, the **Oregon** Territory in 1846, and large territories in the West and Southwest in 1848 as part of the Treaty of **Guadalupe-Hidalgo,** which ended the **Mexican-American War.** The cessions from Mexico alone, including Texas, equaled the Louisiana Purchase and made the United States 10 times the size of Britain and France combined and equal in size to the Roman Empire. The Gadsden Purchase of southern Arizona from Mexico in 1853 and the acquisition of **Alaska** from Russia for $7.2 million in 1867 completed the transcontinental empire.

The United States exploited imperial rivalries among the European powers and thereby replaced their dominion over enormous stretches of territory by way of a dual strategy of negotiated land transfers and financial compensation. But to ensure full control over these territories inhabited by indigenous American peoples the U.S. government relied not only on diplomacy but also on war and internal colonization. In this process, the Indian nations, pressured by ever accelerating Euro-American settler colonialism, experienced a rapid demographic decline, and were forced to accept negotiated land transfers to the central government. Their legal status was successively downgraded from sovereign nations to dependent wards, as resistance was punished with forced removals and continuous warfare. By the late nineteenth century, Native Americans had been militarily defeated, confined to a reservation system, and exposed to intrusive assimilation programs designed to eradicate indigenous cultural identities.

Warfare was used not only to secure control over land transferred by European colonial powers and indigenous peoples but also to contain potential imperial contenders for North American territory. Accompanied by a surge of nationalist sentiment, the United States fought a victorious war against Mexico in 1846–1847 and, in the 1848 Treaty of Guadalupe-Hidalgo, acquired 500,000 square miles of territory—today the states of California, New Mexico, Utah, and Nevada, as well as parts of Arizona, Colorado, and Wyoming—for $15 million. The annexation of all Mexico would have been militarily possible but was rejected on racial grounds; opponents interpreted the inclusion of a large Hispanic population as detrimental to the American body politic. Nonetheless, rapid territorial expansion—combined with the retention of slavery in the southern states, the expansion of freehold agriculture in the western territories, and the accelerated industrialization of the northeast—led in 1861 to the **American Civil War,** the greatest crisis of American nationhood.

The expansive dynamism of the transcontinental empire was fueled by, and in turn contributed to, rapid economic growth and population increase. The American continental economy profited from great expanses of rich agricultural land, bountiful raw materials, and new technological innovations, such as **railways,** the steam engine, and mining equipment, for the development of those resources. It also encountered comparatively few social and geographical constraints, a relative absence of significant foreign threats, and a steady flow of foreign and domestic investment capital. The development of this economic powerhouse was accompanied by an increase of the population from 3.9 million in 1790 to almost 76 million by 1900.

In accordance with the Northwest Ordinance of 1787, new territories were required to pass through stages of political development before they could be admitted to the Union. During that time, they were ruled in a quasi-colonial manner with no political representation and limited rights for the inhabitants and were policed by the U.S. Army, which ensured control over trading routes and strategic positions. At the same time, these territories were integrated into an emerging national transportation and communication network, in which the evolution of the American railway system was particularly vital. In the 1830s, local railroads covered only short distances, but during the period between the Civil War—in which superior railways gave the Union a critical strategic advantage—and the 1880s, the available track increased 10-fold from 9,000 to 93,000 miles. In the early years of the twentieth century, the figure reached more than 200,000 miles. The completion of the first transcontinental railroad in 1869, by the combined Union Pacific and Central Pacific Railroads, symbolized the western integration through transportation networks.

Accelerating transportation opportunities were accompanied by equally revolutionary developments in communications technology. At the beginning of the nineteenth century, it took 25 days for news to travel from the eastern seaboard of the new republic to its western frontier. By 1900, news could be transmitted almost instantaneously through new media such as telephone, **telegraph,** and wireless communication; more than 1.4 million telephones were in service, 1 for every 60 inhabitants. At the same time the experimental use of wireless, or radio, was beginning to usher in a new era of communications technology. George Washington had lamented that it took six to nine months to deliver a letter to Paris in 1779, but

Marconi's instantaneous transmission of radio messages across the Atlantic in 1901 heralded a new era that would successfully challenge Britain's monopoly on the global information infrastructure after World War I.

The creation of a transcontinental empire with hemispheric ambitions and a global outlook was legitimated and popularized through a coherent ideology of expansion. This consisted of a quasi-religious missionary zeal concerning the exceptional nature of American national development and the idea of the United States as a nation embodying universal values. Despite marginal changes over time, those core convictions were a persistent feature of American expansion and provided a rationale for reconciling it with a republican form of government. Since the early days of the Republic, in fact, the missionary myth drew on biblical ideas such as the millenarian concept of a coming kingdom and interpreted American history as a project in salvation, the United States as redeemer nation. Concrete manifestations of this national ideology often varied radically: Whereas one mode of popular transmission advocated the exemplary role of the Republic as a "city upon the hill," another demanded an active role for the United States in reshaping the world. Even before national independence, Thomas Paine offered one of the most powerful and enduring expositions on America's world role. In *Common Sense,* Paine's "idealistic internationalism" emphasized the fundamental differences between old and new worlds, suggested a congruence of American and international democratic aspirations, and emphasized the beneficial impact of mutual trade interdependence on the international system.

In contrast to Montesquieu and others who had warned that republics could not expand by conquest and expect to successfully reproduce their constitutional system, founding fathers of the United States, such as Alexander Hamilton, James Madison, Benjamin Franklin, Thomas Jefferson, James Monroe, and John Quincy Adams, argued in one way or another that extensive territory and republican government were compatible, indeed necessary. Adams was the author of the precocious **Monroe Doctrine** of 1823, according to which the United States had a natural and abiding interest in the entire Western Hemisphere. Inconsistencies were ironed out with the argument that extensive territory was a blessing for a republic founded on popular sovereignty, as it served as insurance against the corruption of virtue and thus ultimate decline. A continuously expanding nation would prevent powerful interests from dominating the republic's affairs. At the same time, expansion was also interpreted as a prudent defense against potential of European imperial incursions in North America. Thus, the anticolonial spirit of the Revolutionary period was directed against Great Power Europe while territorial expansion was made an integral aspect of the national security of the United States.

Informal Empire

The completion of a transcontinental polity was accompanied by a growing strategic and commercial interest beyond the confines of North America. Some considered the Asian mainland, the North Pacific, and the Caribbean Basin to be natural spheres of interest, and others regarded Hawaii and Cuba appendages to the United States. The interest in outlying territory did not translate immediately into a quest for colonial dependencies, but it did accelerate the elaboration of informal empire with instruments ranging from commercial penetration and punitive military expeditions to missionary reform and educational modernization.

By the late nineteenth century, this informal empire then provided justification for the acquisition of colonies, which in turn provided an even stronger rationale for the extension of informal control over adjacent areas.

In Asia, the United States played a prominent role in the "opening" of Japan and **Korea** to Western influence and simultaneously sough access to the commercial potential of **China.** To secure new customers for surplus production and simultaneously contain social instability at home, successive administrations developed the strategy of economic penetration within a conceptual framework that praised the simultaneous benefits of trade for commercial profit, social stability at home, development overseas, and international stability through mutual interdependence. And although the imagined riches of a Chinese market with 400 million people eager to purchase American products did not materialize, the United States nonetheless greatly enhanced its role in Asian affairs. The **Open Door** Notes of 1899 and 1900 and American participation in the western military intervention during the **Boxer Insurrection** of 1900 jointly underlined Washington's insistence on access to the Asian mainland. The Hawaiian Islands were considered an important stepping-stone to commercial opportunities in Asia. Located more than 2,500 miles off the California coast, Hawaii had been of major importance for whaling and trade in the North Pacific since the late eighteenth century. During the nineteenth century, American **missionaries** and planters assumed important government positions in the independent kingdom, maneuvered Hawaii into increasing political and economic dependency with the United States, and repeatedly lobbied Washington for formal annexation of the islands.

The U.S. government supported many private initiatives, extended the Monroe Doctrine to Hawaii to prevent annexation of the islands by a European contender, granted Hawaiian sugar duty free entry into the United States in the Reciprocity Treaty of 1875, and received naval rights at Pearl Harbor. In 1893, Washington even supported a coup d'état against Hawaiian ruler Queen Lilioukalani's efforts to contain American influence in the islands. At the same time, however, concern over inclusion of a racially diverse body of Chinese, Japanese, and native Hawaiian inhabitants postponed incorporation until 1898, when the Pacific colonies won in the Spanish-American War increased American concern over Japanese influence in the North Pacific provided the rationale for annexation. In the Caribbean basin, too, American power oscillated between informal and formal empire, as the United States contained European influence in the region and used commercial hegemony, cultural penetration, and military intervention to secure virtual sovereignty over a number of countries such as **Cuba, Haiti,** Dominican Republic, **Panama,** Nicaragua, Honduras, and El Salvador.

Cuba was a prized asset of this informal empire. Strategically located at the entrance to the Gulf of Mexico and the Caribbean Sea, the island was part of Spain's colonial empire between 1511 and 1899. During the nineteenth century, the Cuban struggle for independence was accompanied by a growing American commercial and cultural presence on the island while the government in Washington assumed a position of political noninvolvement for much of the century. Many contemporary observers preferred Spanish rule to possible instability and its anticipated negative effects on U.S. commercial interests. But in 1898, the William **McKinley** administration intervened in the Cuban War for Independence, and the **Spanish-American War** effectively ended Spanish colonial rule in the western hemisphere. The reasons for American military intervention and the "splendid little war" of 1898 included public outrage over the brutal oppression of the Cuban population by Spanish troops, in particular the strategy of forced removals (*reconcentrado*), fear of instability in the Caribbean, the explosion of the *U.S.S. Maine* in Havana harbor blamed on Spanish sabotage, and the desire to protect American commercial investments.

The U.S. Congress, however, prohibited annexation with the **Teller Amendment** and limited the military occupation to Cuban pacification. From 1898 to 1902, U.S. troops disbanded the Cuban revolutionary army, worked on infrastructure improvements, and laid the foundations for health and educational reforms. To secure control over Cuban affairs beyond the immediate period of military occupation, the McKinley administration developed a legal framework for Cuban-American "ties of singular intimacy." Through the **Platt Amendment** of 1901, which became part of the Cuban constitution, and the U.S.-Cuban Treaty of 1903, the United States was not only granted naval rights at Guantánamo Bay but reserved the right to intervene in Cuban affairs and established virtual sovereignty over Havana's foreign and economic affairs. Between 1906 and 1909, Cuba, which had effectively become a U.S. protectorate, was again placed under American military occupation with additional military interventions in 1912 and 1917.

An even stronger quasi-colonial relationship was the result of America's unorthodox approach to nation-building in Panama. After France's failure to build an interoceanic canal and British permission to assume sole responsibility, the United States selected Panama, Colombia's northernmost province, as the site for the monumental construction. After the government in Bogotá rejected the terms, a U.S.-backed rebellion secured Panamanian independence. The new country gratefully acknowledged American intervention rights and provided Washington with a 10-mile wide canal zone, which constituted a quasi-colony, sometimes referred to as a "government owned reservation." The **Panama Canal,** completed in August 1914, became the strategic center of America's informal empire in the Caribbean. It provided commercial stimulation by completing a net of interoceanic shipping links, and represented a strategic asset of utmost importance for American security. It also completed the integration of the transcontinental empire by linking the Atlantic and Pacific coasts and simultaneously confirming the central position of the United States within a new set of global transportation and communication routes between East and West.

Colonial Empire

After victory in the Spanish-American War of 1898, the United States acquired a colonial empire in the **Philippines,** Guam, parts of **Samoa, Puerto Rico,** and **Hawaii.** The proponents of overseas expansion celebrated these new possessions as logical extensions of transcontinental empire, strategic adjuncts to the informal empire, and the nation's entrance ticket into the exclusive club of colonial powers. Their arguments invoked the **Manifest Destiny** that had accompanied the quest for transcontinental empire and added progressive reform enthusiasm along with a strong dose of Anglo-Saxonism.

Anglo-Saxonism advanced the argument that the civilization of the English-speaking nations was superior to that of any other nation, by virtue of inherited racial characteristics, in particular industry, intelligence, adventurousness, and talent for self-government. Those abilities were contrasted with the accomplishments of other races in a hierarchy of racial success. Advocates emphasized that Anglo-Saxonism had provided the basis for the perfection of democratic government and that Britain and America were thus ideally suited for the civilizational mission of the imperial mandate; it also fused with a **social Darwinist** conception of international relations and turned colonialism into a mission and obligation for the betterment of global conditions. This set of ideas also provided the intellectual glue and ideological rationale for the "great rapprochement" between the **British Empire** and the United States This transformation from confrontation to cooperation was characterized by peaceful crisis management in the **Venezuelan** Boundary **Crisis** (1895–1896), the extension of mutual support in the Spanish-American and Anglo-Boer Wars, and intensified diplomatic relations embedded in a general sense of kinship between the two nations.

Closely connected to a transatlantic racial legitimation of imperialism was the notion that the rigors of colonial vocation would enable American men to escape the emasculating influences of civilization. Discursive constructions of manliness accompanied the national debate on the merits of empire, as expansionists framed the colonial project as a test of character, manhood, and the martial spirit. Many imperialists tapped into widespread cultural concern in turn-of-the-century America about effeminacy, racial decadence, and the worry that modern civilization produced soft, self-absorbed, and materialistic middle class men who would weaken both the national fiber and the political system.

The opponents of empire, mostly organized in the Anti-Imperialist League, meanwhile shared many of the racial assumptions of Anglo-Saxonism but emphasized the fundamentally contradictory nature of an imperial republic and argued that the quest for colonial possessions violated the nation's core political values. They rejected the notion of national reinvigoration through imperialism, stressed the detrimental impact of tropical life on the human condition, and suggested that the negative record of the United States in dealing with its indigenous population, as well as the enduring legacies of slavery, hardly qualified the nation to provide for the educational uplift of colonized races. Although the critics of empire and the Anti-Imperialist League's many prominent members—William Jennings Bryan, Edward Atkinson, Andrew Carnegie, Carl Schurz, and Mark Twain among them—attracted much public attention, they ultimately failed to translate their agenda into political power. The proponents of imperial expansion carried the debate with William McKinley's reelection in 1900.

Despite the electoral victory for imperialism, the optimistic assumptions of its enthusiasts were severely tested in America's largest colony, the Philippines, where the American project of colonial state-building was accompanied by one of the bloodiest and most costly colonial wars ever. Between 1899 and 1913, American forces fought against the Filipino independence movement under Emilio Aguinaldo and militarily pacified the southern Muslim part of the archipelago. After the independence forces then embarked on a campaign of guerrilla warfare, American forces increasingly confronted unexpected challenges and ultimately embarked on a campaign characterized by massive retaliatory measures against the archipelago's civilian population. By 1902, more than 130,000 American soldiers had fought in a war that killed more than 4,200 of them and wounded another 3,500. During those first four years only, approximately 20,000 Filipino soldiers were killed, one-quarter of the armed forces of the independence movement. Conservative estimates assess the number of civilian casualties at least as high as 250,000, and some studies suggest that losses may have been as high as 750,000, or approximately 10 percent of the prewar population.

The fighting was accompanied by an extensive pacification program designed to co-opt the local population into the American colonial regime. In the Philippines, as in Puerto Rico, the United States perceived its rule as mandate for benevolent tutelage and introduction to eventual self-government. Although political independence remained a mirage for Puerto Ricans and was granted to Filipinos only after World War II, initial military governments, as well as subsequent civilian colonial commissions, reaffirmed this outlook and logic of the colonial project. They placed great emphasis on local political participation and strongly supported public education. Those measures were complemented in both cases by social engineering and economic development, as the United States embarked on public health programs, infrastructure improvements, land reform, and commercial investments designed to transform fundamentally the colonial possessions consistent with notions of civilizational development common to the Progressive Reform era in the United States.

Other possessions such as American Samoa and Guam were excluded from the project of political tutelage. Their functions as naval and coaling stations, ruled by the U.S. Navy, limited their colonial status to that of strategic outposts and confined the concerns of Americans posted there to the maintenance of stability and order. As political transformation was assumed to be counterproductive, Washington accepted **indirect rule** and governed through local hereditary chiefs in Samoa and traditional functional elites in Guam. The colonized were exposed neither to political education nor civil government, and the possessions were largely excluded from capital investment or integration into the American economic system.

Americans approached the task of colonial state-building with a dual strategy: they looked to the British Empire for guidance and transferred know-how on a wide range of issues from colonial administration to colonial military policies to urban planning and social engineering. They also used the experience of the transcontinental empire to develop a durable basis for a colonial policy in accordance with established precedents and traditions.

This dual positioning of the American colonialism was embedded in the cultural context of a comparatively insular empire built on accepted traditions, myths, and practices that had celebrated westward expansion as a formative factor in the rise of an exceptional nation. The cultural production of the West entailed a measure of racism and social Darwinism as part of a frontier myth that permeated nineteenth-century American society. This myth found its cultural outlet in a wide range of cultural artifacts ranging from dime novels to ethnographic displays and Wild West reenactments. The overseas empire prompted an equally impressive outpouring of travelogues, poems, and novels that not only introduced Americans to the conditions in the new possessions but also integrated the colonial adventure into the national tradition of expansion. In addition, international expositions and world fairs, such as the Louisiana Purchase Exposition in 1904, served as a popular platform for imperial propaganda in the years leading up to World War I. These fairs illustrated and interpreted America's overlapping expansionist projects for a mass audience in a meaningful way and provided a synthesis of the driving forces, aspirations, and manifestations of American history from the founding to the early twentieth-century. Through the uses of ethnographic displays, American international expositions provided national self-assurance and suggested multiple linkages and continuities between the westward continental expansion and the late nineteenth century colonial acquisitions. As the United States consolidated its international position, Americans became more assertive and reinvigorated their claim to exceptional national development. Despite continued close association between Britain and the United States, Americans increasingly rejected the British Empire as a trusted reference point, underlined the violent and exploitative attitude of European colonial powers, and boasted the transformational accomplishments of U.S. colonial rule. By World War I, this claim to a unique and temporary imperial role coincided with an increasing disillusionment of the American public with the colonial project, a growing belief in the benefits of decolonization, and a renewed interest in the advantages of informal rule from strategic positions of strength that soon became the hallmark of the "American Century." *See also* Appendix Words and Deeds, Docs. 4, 7; Anglo-American War; Hay-Pauncefote Treaty; Mahan, Alfred Thayer; Navalism; Roosevelt, Theodore; Root, Elihu; Webster-Ashburton Treaty.

FURTHER READING: Darby, Philip. *Three Faces of Imperialism: British and American Approaches to Asia and Africa, 1870–1970.* New Haven, CT: Yale University Press, 1987; Go, Julian, and Anne L. Foster, eds. *The American Colonial State in the Philippines: Global Perspectives.* Durham, NC: Duke University Press, 2003; Hunt, Michael. *Ideology and U.S. Foreign Policy.* New Haven, CT: Yale University Press, 1987; Kaplan, Amy. *The Anarchy of Empire in the Making of U.S. Culture.* Cambridge, MA: Harvard University Press, 2002; LaFeber, Walter. *The American Search for Opportunity, 1865–1913. The Cambridge History of American Foreign Relations Vol. II.* Cambridge: Cambridge University Press, 1993; Langley, Lester, and Thomas Schoonover. *The Banana Men: American Mercenaries and Entrepreneurs in Central America, 1880–1930.* Lexington: University Press of Kentucky, 1995; Miller, Stuart C. *"Benevolent Assimilation": The American Conquest of the Philippines, 1899–1902.* New Haven, CT: Yale University Press, 1982; Ninkovich, Frank. *The United States and Imperialism.* Malden, MA: Blackwell Publishers, 2001; Onuf, Peter S. *Jefferson's Empire: The Language of American Nationhood.* Charlottesville, VA: University of Virginia Press, 2000; Osborne, Thomas J. *Empire Can't Wait: American Opposition to Hawaiian Annexation, 1893–1898.* Kent, OH: Kent State University Press, 1981; Paolino, Ernest N. *The Foundations of the American Empire: William Henry Seward and U.S. Foreign Policy.* Ithaca, NY: Cornell University Press, 1973; Prucha, Francis Paul. *The Great Father: The United States Government and the American Indians.* Lincoln: University of Nebraska Press, 1984; Rydell, Robert W. *All the World's a Fair: Visions of Empire at American International Expositions, 1876–1916.* Chicago: University of Chicago Press, 1984; Schoonover, Thomas. *Uncle Sam's War of 1898 and the Origins of Globalization.* Lexington: University Press of Kentucky, 2003; Stephanson, Anders. *Manifest Destiny. American Expansion and the Empire of Right.* New York: Hill and Wang, 1995.

FRANK SCHUMACHER

Uruguay

Uruguay, known as the *Banda Oriental* or Eastern Bank during South America's colonial era, had developed in tandem with **Argentina** as a center of extensive ranching and mercantile trade. Its ports were rivals to Buenos Aires, the regional capital that dominated the region's trade and its politics. When Spanish authority in Buenos Aires weakened after 1806, Montevideo became a center of Loyalist sentiment despite the port city's dependence on illegal trade with Portuguese and British merchants.

The collapse of the Spanish monarchy in the wake of Napoleon **Bonaparte**'s invasion of the Iberian Peninsula in 1807 transformed the military and political conditions in Uruguay. Beginning in 1811, popular forces in the rural areas surrounding Montevideo rebelled. Under the leadership of José Gervasio **Artigas,** the rebels joined with an invading army from Argentina and surrounded the port. Concerns about the ambitions of the independence movement in Buenos Aires led Artigas and his army to abandon the siege. When Montevideo surrendered in 1814, Uruguay in turn rebelled against the government of the United Provinces of the Río de la Plata.

Artigas declared a social revolution that promised broader political participation and the distribution of land to Native Americans, people of mixed race heritage, and the landless poor. He also promoted federalism, which helped him gain allies in the interior provinces of Argentina. The radical nature of his proposals and his military achievements, however, also produced powerful enemies. Paraguay, under the dictatorial leadership of Jose Rodríguez Gaspar de Francia, moved to separate Uruguay from its allies in northern Argentina. The Imperial government of Portugal, displaced to Rio de Janeiro in **Brazil** by Napoleon's invasion of Iberia, moved to quell rebellions in its southern territories.

Although Artigas did retake Montevideo in 1815, a major invasion by Portuguese forces reduced his army and forced him into exile after 1818. Uruguay fell under Portuguese authority until 1825, when a nationalist rebellion set in motion a war that would pit Argentina against Portuguese Brazil. Negotiations led to the creation of an independent Uruguay in 1828. The country's final borders would not be secured until the defeat of Paraguay in the War of the Triple Alliance, 1864–1870. *See also* Portuguese Empire; Spanish Empire.

FURTHER READING: Bushnell, David, and Neill MacAuley. *The Emergence of Latin America in the Nineteenth Century.* 2nd ed. New York: Oxford University Press, 1994; Street, John. *Artigas and the Emancipation of Uruguay.* Cambridge: Cambridge University Press, 1959.

DANIEL K. LEWIS

V

Valikhanov, Chokan Chinggisovich (1835–1865)

Widely considered the first Western-trained Kazakh intellectual, Valikhanov was important for furthering imperial connections between the Russians and Kazakh peoples. He worked closely with, and received the financial support of, the Russian Geographical Society and traveled widely across Semirech'e, Eastern Turkestan, and Lake Issyk-kul regions, documenting both the natural environment and describing the peoples whom he encountered in his journeys. Valikhanov also collected and produced the first written translation in Russian of the Kyrgyz epic poem "Manas."

Valikhanov's ancestors included his grandfather, who was a Kazakh khan, and his father, who served the Russian imperial administration in **Siberia.** He was educated at the imperial Russian city of Omsk at the Siberian Cadets Corps Institute, which was considered the best educational institution in the region in those years. While there Valikhanov studied Western languages and developed a particular interest in ethnography. In 1856, he met Petr Semenov Tian-shanskii, who recommended to the Russian administration that Valikhanov be used in spying and diplomatic missions to Eastern Turkestan, particularly to Kashgar. This was considered an extremely dangerous mission, but one that he was well suited for because of his knowledge of the cultures and languages of this region. Chokan disguised himself on this mission to blend in with the Kashgar environs.

During the latter 1850s and early 1860s, Valikhanov traveled around the Kazakh steppe and collected information on the history and culture of the Kazakhs and during this time cultivated a close personal relationship with exiled Russian writer Fyodor Dostoevsky. Both men spent time in and around the city of Semipalatinsk, discussing history, literature, and other subjects. In 1861, Valikhanov chose to return to his home in the Semipalatinsk region after the onset of illness. During his final years, he continued to write and to collect information, which was published posthumously as his *Collected Works* by the Kazakh Academy of Sciences. He advised the Russian government against dealing with nomadic peoples the same way as other subjects of the empire. He argued that if they were dealt with on their own unique terms, the imperial relationship would be more fruitful. Valikhanov died in 1865 of lung complications. *See also* Russian Empire; Turkestan.

FURTHER READING: Valikhanov, Chokan and Mikhail Ivanovich Venyukov. *The Russians in Central Asia*. London: E. Stanford, 1865.

SCOTT C. BAILEY

Venezuelan Crisis (1895)

A border dispute that occasioned a confrontation between Britain and the **United States.** For the most part the jungle-covered boundary between British Guiana and Venezuela had never been properly surveyed, so the discovery of gold would suddenly make it a hotly disputed area. Venezuela broke diplomatic relations with London, and Britain's aggressive attitude in the controversy, as well as her refusal to arbitrate, represented from the American perspective a challenge to the time-honored Monroe Doctrine. In the hope of increasing U.S. influence in Latin America, Secretary of State Richard Olney decided to take a firm stance and forcefully warned London on July 20, 1895, that "to-day the United States is practically sovereign on this continent, and its fiat is law upon the subjects to which it confines its interposition. [. . .] because in addition to all other grounds, its infinite resources combined with its isolated position render it master of the situation and practically invulnerable against any or all other powers."

The haughty language reflected a new self-confidence, and the American public applauded as expected this vigorous twisting of the lion's tail. Republican expansionists and nationalists heartily supported the Democratic administration of Grover Cleveland. Britain's condescending response to Olney's note raised a jingoistic flurry across the Atlantic and even prompted short-lived rumors of war. President Cleveland further dramatized the issue in his Annual Message to Congress of December 1895, when he asked for funding for a survey crew and hinted at the possible use of armed force.

If in the end Britain agreed to arbitration, it was not out of fear of American might but because the Boer crisis in South Africa demanded her attention. British restraint also evidenced the incipient Anglo-American rapprochement and London's shift in world priorities, notably its admission of Washington's paramount interest in the Americas, recognized as its natural sphere of influence. *See also* Monroe Doctrine.

FURTHER READING: Cleveland, Grover. *The Venezuelan Boundary Controversy*. Princeton, NJ: Princeton University Press, 1913; Perkins, Dexter. *A History of the Monroe Doctrine*. New rev. ed. Boston: Little, Brown, 1963; Perkins, Dexter. *The Monroe Doctrine, 1867–1907*. Baltimore: The Johns Hopkins Press, 1937.

SERGE RICARD

Venizelos, Eleutherios (1864–1936)

A dynamic Greek statesman who presided over transformation of **Greece** from a tiny and poor kingdom to a modern and enlarged state in a matter of years. Divisions between himself and the monarch, King Constantine, over the participation of Greece in World War I undid much of his major achievements.

After studying law in Athens, Venizelos founded the Liberal Party in Crete and in 1896 led the movement against Ottoman rule. In 1909, Venizelos decided to enter the Greek parliament, but in August a group of disgruntled Greek military officers presented an ultimatum to the Athens government demanding military and political reorganization that precipitated the government's collapse. The Military League was inexperienced and called on Venizelos. He established a National Assembly that revised the constitution and led the league to dissolve. Elected to parliament in August 1910, within two months he became the prime minister. When the old leaders obstructed him, Venizelos coolly called an election in which his Liberal Party won 300 of the 364 seats. He then instituted reforms. In 1911, the British were contracted to reorganize the navy, the French the army, and the Italians the gendarmerie.

Venizelos's ambition to see a modern, liberal Greece take its place alongside other Mediterranean powers gathered pace. Because of his prudence in shaking-up the army and fleet, the country was prepared for the **Balkan Wars** of 1912 and 1913 and was able to seize parts of Epirus, **Macedonia,** and some of the Aegean Islands. Prince Constantine became king after the assassination of his father, King George I, in 1913. Although in 1914 Venizelos supported an alliance with the Entente, believing that Britain and France would win the war, Constantine wanted to remain neutral. Venizelos resigned in February 1915.

Venizelos's party again won the elections and formed a government, although he promised to remain neutral. Bulgaria's attack on Serbia, with which Greece had an alliance treaty, obliged him to abandon that policy. Again the king disagreed, and again Venizelos resigned. He did not take part in the next election, as he considered parliament's dissolution unconstitutional.

In 1916, Venizelos's supporters organized a military movement in Thessaloniki, called the Temporary Government of National Defense. There they founded a new state including northern Greece and Aegean Islands. On May 1917, after the exile of Constantine, Venizelos returned to Athens and allied with the Entente. After the war he took part in Paris Peace Conference in 1919 and signed, as Greece's representative, the Treaty of Neuilly in November 1919 and the Treaty of Sèvres in August 1920.

FURTHER READING: Dakin, D. *The Unification of Greece, 1770–1923.* London: Benn, 1972; Forster, Edward Seymour. *A Short History of Modern Greece.* Westport, CT: Greenwood, 1977.

ANDREKOS VARNAVA

Vera Cruz Incident

See Tampico and Vera Cruz Incidents

Vereeniging, Treaty of (1902)

The treaty bringing the Boer War to an end in May 1902, following a number of abortive efforts to find a compromise between the Afrikaner Republics and the British government. Many Boer commandos wished to continue fighting to preserve their independence but, when they convened at Vereeniging on May 15, the 60 Boer representatives reluctantly agreed to accept the British terms. The Afrikaner governments met Lords **Kitchener** and **Milner** at Pretoria on May 31 and signed the treaty concluding the war.

The Afrikaner Republics of the **Orange Free State** and **Transvaal** lost their independence, but their white citizens had full rights in South Africa and came to dominate its politics. The guerrillas were to receive an amnesty unless they had committed offenses "contrary to the usages of war." The Boer farmers were compensated for their losses and given livestock for their burned-out farms. Originally, the British said they would provide the Afrikaners with £3 million for reconstruction by giving, at least, £25 to every Boer who had suffered. In practice, the distribution was often unfair because it was hurried so that the 200,000 Boer farmers could be sent homewards to plant harvests as quickly as possible. On the other hand, the daughter of the Boer leader, General Smuts, estimated that, in the end, compensation amounted to £9.5 million.

This was, no doubt, poor recompense for the destruction and for the sufferings of the Boer families who had been removed from their farms and concentrated in camps to prevent them from helping the commandos. But the compensation was unique in this period; it had, for example, been the vanquished Chinese who had to compensate the victorious Japanese in 1895. Britain's relative generosity stemmed from the desire of the Conservatives to build up the new country and from the guilt felt by many about the destruction of the small Boer Republics.

What the treaty did not do was protect the rights of the Africans. Indeed Article 8 promised that "the question of granting the Franchise to Natives will not be decided until after the introduction of self-government." The war had increased the bitterness between the Africans and the Afrikaners, not least because the Boers complained of African attacks, while the Africans protested Boer brutality. To that extent it was a flawed treaty, but its generosity to the defeated was rightly held up 17 years later by one of the Boer leaders, General Botha as an example to be followed at the negotiations that followed World War I. *See also* Boer Wars; British Empire; Cape Colony.

FURTHER READING: Beak, G. B. *Aftermath of War.* London: Edward Arnold, 1906; Kestell, J. D. *Through Shot and Flame.* London: Methuen 1903; Meintjes, Johannes. *General Louis Botha: A Biography.* London: Cassell, 1970; Nasson, Bill. *The South African War, 1899–1902.* London: Arnold, 1999; de Wet, Christiaan Rudolf. *Three Years War.* London: Constable, 1902.

PHILIP TOWLE

Verona, Congress of (1822)

The last full meeting of the **Congress System,** its main item of business a proposal by France to send an expeditionary force into Spain to crush a liberal rebellion. Castlereagh was not present to represent Britain—having taken his own life shortly before he was due to depart Britain—so that the Duke of **Wellington** became the British delegate. Prince **Metternich** of Austria supported the French intervention, in large part to keep the support of Tsar **Alexander I** of Russia, but Wellington opposed intervention on behalf of a restoration in Spain both to maintain Britain's alliance with it and to keep Spanish ports open to commerce. In this, Wellington was representing the policy of Britain's new foreign secretary, George **Canning,** but he was also personally annoyed at a conference resolution that he deemed misleading regarding the intention of the continental powers in Spain. He therefore withdrew from the conference.

When French troops then marched into Spain the next year, Canning's government declared that its sympathies were with the rebels, thereby signaling the rupture of the Congress System. Equally, Canning sought to avoid both a royalist restoration anywhere in the Spanish Americas and any Russian intervention in that hemisphere, so it was partly at the prodding of Canning that John Quincy **Adams,** the American secretary of state, drafted the **Monroe Doctrine** against any and all European intervention in the Americas. *See also* Wellington, Arthur Wellesley, Duke of.

FURTHER READING: Kissinger, Henry. *A World Restored.* London: Weidenfeld & Nicolson, 1957; Schroeder, Paul M. *The Transformation of European Politucs, 1763–1848.* Oxford: Clarendon Press, 1994.

CARL CAVANAGH HODGE

Vicksburg, Siege of (1862–1863)

A pivotal action of the **American Civil War.** Vicksburg, Mississippi lies on high bluffs above the eastern bank of the Mississippi River. In May 1862, Confederate forces began fortifying the bluffs at Vicksburg with artillery to block Union passage on the Mississippi River. Union naval forces attacked the city and its fortifications but were unable to capture the city. Confederate operations against Union supply and artillery forces on the Louisiana side of the Mississippi River were without lasting success.

Above Vicksburg, the mouth of the Yazoo River was guarded by Fort Pemberton. The Yazoo River was the entryway to a delta land rich in cotton production. During the fall and winter of 1862 and into the spring of 1863, Union forces commanded by General Ulysses S. **Grant** fought a number of engagements against Confederate Major General John C. Pemberton. The latter was inhibited in his operations because he had been issued conflicting orders by General Joseph E. Johnston and by President Jefferson Davis.

Grant drove the Confederates out of the Mississippi capital of Jackson on May 14 and then defeated Pemberton at Champion Hill on May 16 and Big Black River the following day, forcing Pemberton into Vicksburg. In June 1863, the attempt by Johnston to relieve Vicksburg was blocked by superior Union forces. In Vicksburg nine miles of Confederate earthen fortifications protected 30,000 troops. Outside were 12 miles of Union earth works with 50,000 soldiers. Continual bombardments by heavy Union guns took a heavy toll of civilians, soldiers, and the dwindling livestock. Vicksburg surrendered on July 4, 1863. The news of the fall of Vicksburg was paired with the Union victory at **Gettysburg.** In Europe it spelled the end of Confederate hopes for European support.

FURTHER READING: Bearss, Edwin C. *The Vicksburg Campaign.* 3 vols. Dayton: Morningside, 1995.

ANDREW JACKSON WASKEY

Victor Emmanuel II (1820–1878)

The King of **Piedmont-Sardinia** (1849–1861) and **Italy** (1861–1878), Victor Emmanuel II of Savoy assumed the throne of Piedmont after the Austrians defeated his father Charles Albert at the Battle of Novara in March 1849 and forced him to abdicate. The former king had been a leader in the effort to unify the peninsula, but his delay in intervening on behalf of Milan cost him and the House of Savoy much good will and aroused suspicion of his real intentions. When Turin rose in the revolutionary fervor that gripped Italy in February and March 1848, Charles Albert granted his kingdom a constitution and prepared to help the Milanese defend themselves against the Austrians. With aid arriving from the other Italian states, Charles Albert preferred to delay for the right moment to strike. Some Liberals saw in this move a monarch's attempt to undermine a popular revolution. The resulting in-fighting weakened the revolutionary governments and allowed the Austrians to take Venice and Milan, and defeat the Piedmontese.

Victor Emmanuel II had to be extremely careful in dealing with the Austrians, who demanded the negation of the constitution, and the radicals, who wanted him to keep it. The king did not enjoy the goodwill of republicans who believed his father had betrayed the cause, and so had to worry about an insurrection. But he had no intention of revoking the constitution or of losing control of the monarchy. Instead, the king cracked down on the radicals in parliament by issuing the famous Moncalieri Proclamation of 1849, stating that if parliament was not to his liking, he would not be held responsible for its future. The ploy worked, because the subsequent election brought a group of moderate reformers, led by Count Camillo Benso di **Cavour,** to power. Cavour quickly came to the king's attention as a hardheaded politician who would do whatever it took to achieve unification, and so the king asked Cavour to form a government in 1852. Cavour did exactly what Victor Emmanuel wanted and unified Italy under the Kingdom of Piedmont. *See also* Victor Emmanuel III.

FURTHER READING: Di Scala, Spencer. *Italy from Revolution to Republic: 1700 to the Present.* Boulder, CO: Westview, 1998.

FREDERICK H. DOTOLO

Victor Emmanuel III (1869–1947)

King of **Italy** from 1900–1947, Victor Emmanuel III of Savoy came to the throne in July 1900 at the age of 29 after his father, Umberto I, was assassinated by the anarchist Gaetano Bresci. The ascension of this young prince occurred at a critical junction in Italy's political life, near the end of constitutional government and a possible military dictatorship. The collapse of the Crispi government in 1896 had demonstrated the weakness of Italy's political consensus. The political right was opposed by a growing socialist movement, which had made gains in parliament amid political violence unleashed by extremists. General Luigi Pelloux, head of the current government, circumvented parliament to deal with the problems by having King Umberto issue royal decrees. In June, this practice was declared unconstitutional so the government demanded new parliamentary elections hoping to bypass the opposition. When he lost the vote, Italy was on the verge of a coup.

Victor Emmanuel III abandoned the reactionary politics of his father and embraced a policy of political reconciliation and governmental reform. He appointed a well-known reformer, one of the leaders of the parliamentarian alliance that opposed Pelloux, Zanardelli to form the new government. When Zanardelli retired for health reasons, the king appointed his deputy, Giovanni **Giolitti.** While politics of the son and father were different, it was their character that was even more remarkably different. Umberto was larger than life, romantic, decisive, and unafraid to enter politics. Not so Victor Emmanuel who could be very indecisive and timid.

FURTHER READING: Di Scala, Spencer. *Italy from Revolution to Republic: 1700 to the Present.* Boulder, CO: Westview, 1998.

FREDERICK H. DOTOLO

Victoria, Queen of Great Britain (1819–1901)

Queen of the United Kingdom of Great Britain and Ireland from 1837 until her death, Victoria was the central icon of the nineteenth-century **British Empire.** A granddaughter through one of the younger sons of **George III,** she inherited the throne at the age of 18 on the death of her uncle William IV. Raised in deliberate isolation from her scandal-ridden Hanoverian relatives, she was initially popular, and her tutors made a deliberate point of emphasizing her Englishness, in contra-distinction to the German heritage of her ancestors. Although later in her reign Victoria acquired a reputation for being pro-Tory, she was initially influenced by her first prime minister, the Whig Lord Melbourne. Victoria married Prince Albert of Saxe-Coburg, to whom she was devoted, in 1840. Victoria had nine children, many of whom married into other royal families, with the result that by the end of her reign, she had some familial connection to most of the royal houses in Europe. Victoria's eldest son became **Edward VII.** Albert's death in 1861 plunged Victoria into a deep depression, from which she emerged only slowly and grudgingly. Her reluctance to perform her royal duties led to a brief republican movement in the early 1870s, led by among others Sir Charles **Dilke.**

Victoria took a particular liking to the Tory prime minister of that decade, Benjamin **Disraeli,** a liking accentuated by the **Royal Titles Act,** making her Empress of India. She also developed, and failed entirely to dissemble, a dislike for William **Gladstone;** she was more comfortable with his successor, the Tory peer Lord **Salisbury.** Victoria fostered a close relationship between the crown and military, taking a close interest in the campaigns and in the welfare of the soldiery during the **Crimean War** and again during the Boer War of 1899–1902, and taking a personal part in the creation of the Victoria Cross during the former. Victoria did much to create the image of the royal family as an exemplar of bourgeois domesticity, notwithstanding the racier life led by her son, Edward VII. Victoria's silver and diamond jubilees of 1887 and 1897 were celebrations not merely of her reign but of the empire. An imperial theme, complete with colorful displays and troops from around the empire, was deliberately chosen for the diamond jubilee of 1897. For a woman who lived through years of massive change, her name remains somewhat unfairly associated with old-fashioned prudery; her name is more accurately associated with imperial Britain at its height. *See also* Boer Wars.

FURTHER READING: Charlot, Monica. *Victoria: The Young Queen.* Oxford: Blackwell, 1991; Weintraub, Stanley. *Victoria: An Intimate Biography.* New York: Dutton, 1987.

MARK F. PROUDMAN

Vienna, Congress of (1815)

A major international conference held in the Austrian capital from September 1814 to June 1815, the Congress of Vienna convened to consider the multifarious political problems to be tackled at the end of the **Napoleonic Wars,** particularly the reconstruction of Europe. The principal delegates included Count **Metternich** representing Austria, Tsar **Alexander I** and several advisors from Russia, Lord **Castlereagh** and the Duke of Wellington present for Britain, King Frederick William III and Count Hardenberg representing **Prussia,** and Prince **Talleyrand** from France. Most of the important decisions were reached by the four major victorious powers, although Talleyrand managed to have France included in much of the process, not least by playing off one side against the other and sowing the seeds of suspicion between states with rival claims. Each seeking to satisfy a different agenda, practically every European state, large and small, sent a representative to plead its case respecting a range of issues including borders, political claims, financial compensation, and commercial rights.

In the settlement reached on June 9, 1815, the congress declared the creation of two new countries: the Kingdom of the **Netherlands,** to include Holland, **Belgium,** and Luxembourg; and the **German Confederation,** to comprise 39 states with no central governing body and only tenuous links to one another. It also created the kingdom of Lombardy-Venetia, over which Austria was to exercise strong influence, with Francis I as king. **Poland** was restored, albeit in a reduced form of its eighteenth-century self and under direct Russian administration. The old dynasties of a number of states were restored: Spain, Naples, Piedmont, Tuscany, and Modena. The Swiss Confederation was reestablished and its permanent neutrality guaranteed. Austrian domains increased as a result of the annexation of Dalmatia, Carniola, Salzburg, and Galicia. Prussia annexed Posen, Danzig, much of the former Kingdom of Saxony, large parts of former Westphalia, and **Sweden**'s possessions in Pomerania on the Baltic coast of Germany. In return, Sweden received **Norway.** Britain retained a number of conquests including **Malta, Heligoland, Cape Colony** in southern Africa, Ceylon, Tobago, St. Lucia, and **Mauritius.** The Ionian Islands, including Corfu, were granted to Britain as a protectorate, with effect for nearly 50 years.

The congress also guaranteed the free navigation of the Rhine and the Meuse, condemned the **slave trade,** extended the civil rights of Jews, particularly in Germany, and established the precedent of international conferences as a diplomatic device in seeking redress and settling disputes between nations.

FURTHER READING: Chapman, Tim. *The Congress of Vienna: Origins, Process and Results.* London: Routledge, 1998; Dallas, Gregor. *The Final Act: The Roads to Waterloo.* New York: Henry Holt, 1997; Ferrero, Guglielmo. *The Reconstruction of Europe: Talleyrand and the Congress of Vienna, 1814–1815.* New York: Norton, 1963; Kissinger, Henry A. *A World Restored: Metternich, Castlereagh and the Problems of Peace, 1812–22.* London: Weidenfeld & Nicolson, 1957; Nicolson, Harold. *The Congress of Vienna: A Study in Allied Unity: 1812–1822.* Gloucester: Peter Smith, 1973; Webster, Charles. *The Congress of Vienna, 1814–1815.* New York: Barnes & Noble, 1969.

GREGORY FREMONT-BARNES

Vladivostok

An important Russian city and port in the Far East. Vladivostok occupies a natural basin dominating the tip of the Muravyov-Amursky Peninsula on the Sea of

Japan. Vladivostok means "ruler of the east" in Russian, a name chosen upon the establishment of a Russian military post there in 1860, shortly after the territory was acquired from Qing China with the Treaty of **Aigun** in 1858 and Conventions of **Beijing** in 1860. Vladivostok became a port in 1862 and a city in 1880. From 1871, it was also the headquarters of the Russian Far Eastern Fleet. With the completion of the Trans-Siberian Railway in 1905, the city was linked with St. Petersburg. This, combined with the Russian loss of **Port Arthur** to Japan in 1905, soon made Vladivostok the major Russian port in the Far East. From 1905 to 1907, the city was the site of serious uprisings by workers and soldiers that contributed to Russia's prerevolutionary crisis. *See also* Japanese Empire; Russian Empire; Russo-Japanese War.

FURTHER READING: Stephan, John J. *The Russian Far East: A History.* Stanford, CA: Stanford University Press, 1994.

DANIEL C. KANE

Wagner, Richard (1813–1883)

Richard Wagner was a German composer who was controversial in his own time and beyond. Wagner wrote 13 operas, mostly with themes from Germanic mythology, among them *Lohengrin, Tannhäuser, Parsifal, The Flying Dutchman, Tristan and Isolde,* and *The Ring of the Nibelung.* Wagner is not only famous because of his compositions and an astonishing number of books and articles, but also because of his influence on German culture. According to his contemporary, Nietzsche, this influence was, in the end, malignant, incorporating *reichsdeutsch* nationalism and anti-Semitism. His name has appeared in connection to almost all major trends in German history of the nineteenth and twentieth centuries. *See also* German Empire.

FURTHER READING: Chancellor, John. *Wagner.* London: Weidenfeld & Nicolson, 1978.

MARTIN MOLL

Wagram, Battle of (1809)

The decisive battle of Napoleon **Bonaparte**'s campaign of 1809 against Austria. Wagram was a costly, slogging match fought only days after the French emperor's first defeat at **Aspern-Essling**. The French had already captured Vienna on May 13, but the main Austrian army under Archduke **Charles** remained concentrated on the north bank of the Danube. After Napoleon crossed the river, on July 5 Charles attempted to turn the French left in an effort to prevent him from withdrawing back across the Danube. After the first day's indecisive fighting, on the second day Napoleon tried to envelop the Austrian left, while Charles attempted to do the same to his opponent. Charles made little progress, but the French gained ground against staunch resistance and determined counterattacks. After massing artillery against the Austrian center, Napoleon unleashed a massive infantry attack and drove in Charles's center. The Austrians withdrew in good order, with losses of more than 60,000 casualties; the French lost about 40,000. *See also* Habsburg Empire; Napoleonic Wars.

FURTHER READING: Castle, Ian. *Aspern and Wagram 1809: Mighty Clash of Empires.* Oxford: Osprey Publishing, 1994; Chandler, David. *The Campaigns of Napoleon.* London: Weidenfeld & Nicolson, 1995; Hourtoulle, F. G. *Wagram: At the Heyday of the Empire.* Paris: Histoire and Collections, 2002; Lapouge, Gilles. *The Battle of Wagram.* London: Hutchinson, 1988; Rothenberg, Gunther. *The Emperor's Last Victory: Napoleon and the Battle of Wagram.* London: Weidenfeld & Nicolson, 2004.

GREGORY FREMONT-BARNES

Wahhabi/Wahhabism

An Islamic sect named for Muhammad Abd al Wahhab, who was born at 'Uyaynah in central Arabia in 1703. His father was a local Islamic judge (*qadi*) and a follower of the Hanbali school of Islamic law. Wahhab became an Islamic judge. While studying at Medina he read the works of Taqiyyudin Ahmad ibn Taymiyyah (1263–1328). Wahhab was concerned about what he believed was a decline in Muslim strength. In Taymiyyah, he found inspiration for dealing with Islamic spiritual decay and methods of religious reform.

According to Wahhab's analysis of the times, the weakness of Islam was caused by a weakening of the monotheistic purity of the faith. The solution was to put great emphasis upon *tawid,* or the unity of Allah. With *tawid* as his chief guide, Wahhab initiated a global Islamic reform movement. Wahhab's teachings might have come to naught had he not met the military champion of his movement, Muhammad Ibn Sa'ud. In 1744, Wahhab moved to Dar'iyyah, a small village in east central Arabia area of Najd. He encouraged enforcement of *tawid,* and **jihad** against those with a different Islamic theology.

Muhammad Ibn Saud died in 1766. He was succeeded by his son Abd al-Aziz ibn Saud and the by his grandson Sa'ud Ibn 'Abd al-Aziz, who carried on the Wahhabi movement. Wahhab died at Dar'iyyah in 1792, but in the early 1800s the Wahhabi army captured the Hejaz cities of Mecca and Medina. They "purified" them of the buildings, books, and other things that were offensive to *tawid.* The activities of the Wahhabi were viewed by the Sultan in Turkey as a challenge to his spiritual leadership. He sent **Mehmet Ali** to Arabia to fight the Wahhabi. In 1818, Ali defeated the Wahhabi and destroyed Dar'iyyah. He sent Abd al-Aziz to Istanbul where he was beheaded. In the following decades of the nineteenth century, the Al-Saud family continued to follow the teachings of Wahhab. In 1902, Abdul Aziz ibn Saud, a direct descendant of both al-Wahhab and the first Ibn Saud, captured the city of Riyadh.

In the decades that followed Ibn Saud organized a band of Wahhabi warriors, the *Ikhwan,* or brotherhood. With them he unified much of the Arabian Peninsula. During World War I, he made an alliance with the British to fight against the Turks. *See also* Ottoman Empire.

FURTHER READING: Algar, Hamid. *Wahabbism: A Critical Essay.* Oneota: Islamic Publications, 2002; DeLong-Bas, Natana J. *Wahhabi Islam: From Revival and Reform to Global Jihad.* Oxford: Oxford University Press, 2004.

ANDREW JACKSON WASKEY

Waitangi, Treaty of

See New Zealand

Wales

Comprising the western peninsula of the island of Britain, Wales was officially part of England since 1536. The last independent Welsh prince, Llywelyn ap Gruffydd, died in 1283, after which Wales was administered directly by England and in 1536 was joined to England by the Act of **Union.** Even though the majority of Welsh people spoke Welsh as a first language, there was no longer any official difference between the two countries. The government was the same, the established church was the same, and only English could be used as an official language in the law courts. As a comparatively remote and rural part of the British Isles, Wales was not much affected by the early stages of British **imperialism.** Some Welsh people called Dissenters, however, did move to the American colonies for religious reasons, especially to Pennsylvania.

The Industrial Revolution transformed the British Isles and was the engine of growth behind British imperialism. This transformation was not just economic but also political and social. Its end result was the creation of a global economic system with the imperialist countries at its center. Wales was intimately connected to this growth of imperialism and was itself transformed as part of the process. The rich coalfields of south and northeast Wales provided a large percentage of the energy, which fueled the industrial revolution. They also made these areas centers for steel and other industrial production, as well as major shipping and trading centers. These in turn created a large demand for industrial labor. Initially this demand was met from within Wales, but increasingly workers moved to Wales from other parts of Britain. At the beginning, Welsh remained the language of work and of religious and social occasions. These industrial regions were Welsh in language and strongly involved in both religious and labor union organization. Welsh remained dominant in religious life, but over time English became the more important language. English was the language of influence in this industrial and imperialist world, and it opened new horizons for many Welsh people in Britain and the empire. The Welsh were active in industrial organization. They also took their skills with them to other parts of the **British Empire** and to the **United States.** The education of this workforce was addressed by the Education Act of 1870, which required school attendance. Education was compulsory and it was in English. Wales was still distinctive, but it was at the center of the industrial British Empire and was proud of its place in this empire.

FURTHER READING: Davies, John. *A History of Wales.* London: Penguin, 1995; Morgan, Kenneth O. *Modern Wales: Politics, Places and People.* Cardiff: University of Wales, 1995; Williams, Gwyn. *When Was Wales?* London: Penguin, 1985.

MICHAEL THOMPSON

War of 1812

See Anglo-American War (1812–1815)

War of Liberation

See Liberation, War of

War of the Pacific (1879–1882)

A conflict waged by Chile against Bolivia and Peru over control of the Atacama Desert, a region rich in deposits of nitrates newly being used by the explosives industry. In 1873, Bolivia and Peru made a secret alliance to protect their access to the Atacama; in 1875 Peru seized control of Chilean nitrate companies on what it deemed to be its territory. When Bolivia followed suit three years later, the Chilean president, Anibal Pinto, declared war on both countries in April 1879.

The war's first engagements were at sea—hence its name—but after the Chilean navy had taken the Peruvian port of Callao and blockaded Bolivia's Pacific coast, Chilean land forces marched inland and defeated a combined Peruvian-Bolivian force near Iquique. Bolivia was out the war quickly thereafter, but the Chileans were required to campaign against the Peruvian capital, Lima, to prevail. They took Lima in January 1881. The **United States** mediated treaties in 1883 and 1884, officially ending hostilities. Chile gained territory from both states, but Bolivia was the main loser insofar as the Treaty of Valparaiso blocked its access to the Pacific.

FURTHER READING: Farcau, Bruce W. *The Ten Cents War.* Westport, CT: Praeger, 2000.

CARL CAVANAGH HODGE

Wars of the Coalitions (1792–1815)

See Napoleonic Wars

Washington, Treaty of (1871)

An agreement settling several outstanding issues involving Britain, **Canada,** and the **United States.** British and American delegates met in Washington in 1871 to address financial compensation for American ship owners' losses caused by the British-built and equipped Confederate commerce-raider *C.S.S. Alabama;* the Pacific coast boundary in the Straits of Georgia; and American inshore fishing rights in Newfoundland. The final treaty was signed on May 8, 1871. Most of the issues were put to arbitration, with the United States receiving possession of the San Juan Islands, $15.5 million as settlement of the *Alabama* claims, and limited inshore fishing rights. In return, Canada received free access for its fish to American markets. The Washington Treaty is notable for three features. It was the first time a Canadian delegate—Prime Minister Sir John A. Macdonald—represented Canadian interests in foreign affairs. It recognized the principle of putting contentious international issues to arbitration by third parties. Finally, it codified the responsibilities of neutrals during a war at sea. *See also* British Empire.

FURTHER READING: Campbell, Charles S. *The Transformation of American Foreign Relations, 1865–1900.* New York: Harper and Row, 1976.

DAVID H. OLIVIER

Waterloo, Battle of (1815)

The most decisive battle of the **Napoleonic Wars.** Waterloo brought a final end to Napoleon **Bonaparte**'s reign and the military threat posed by France since 1792.

Fought in **Belgium** between Napoleon's army and an Anglo-Allied force under Field Marshal the Duke of **Wellington,** aided by elements of the Prussian army under Field Marshal Gerhard von **Blücher,** Waterloo demonstrated nothing of the finesse of earlier Napoleonic battles: it was a slogging match, pure and simple. On June 17, Wellington deployed his army on a low rise called Mont St. Jean, south of Brussels, with many of his troops concealed behind the reverse slope. On the following morning the French had approximately 72,000 men arrayed against 68,000 British, Hanoverians, and Dutch-Belgians under Wellington, who counted on the support of tens of thousands of Prussians engaged at the same time against Marshal Grouchy at Wavre, nine miles to the east.

Fruitlessly waiting for the ground to dry out after the previous night's rain, Napoleon opened the engagement around 11:30 A.M. by launching General Reille's corps against the farm of Hougoumont, a heavily fortified position in Wellington's center right. This was intended to serve as a mere diversion to draw in the Duke's reserves while the main French thrust was to be made by d'Erlon's corps. In fact, the French attack on Hougoumont unwittingly intensified, attracting more and more French infantry to the fighting with no decisive result. D'Erlon advanced at 2:00 P.M., only to be driven off in disorder by counterattacking cavalry, which, after cutting through the infantry, advanced far behind French lines where they were largely destroyed. To the east, the Prussians began to reach the fringes of the battlefield—albeit in piece-meal fashion—thus obliging Napoleon to detach a corps under Count Lobau in the center to delay them at Plancenoit.

Then, inexplicably, Marshal Michel **Ney,** the de facto commander in the field, proceeded to launch most of the reserve cavalry, unsupported by infantry and artillery, against the Allied center. Numerous attempts to break the British infantry, all safely deployed in squares, failed, with massive losses to Napoleon's mounted arm. By 5:30 P.M. the charges had ceased, with nothing to show for their effort but gallantry on a grand scale. At the same time, although elements of Napoleon's Imperial Guard had thus far managed to hold off the Prussians at the village of Plancenoit on the French right flank, steadily increasing numbers of Blücher's men were beginning to bear against weakening resistance. Allied victory was by no means assured, however, for the fortified farm of La Haye Sainte, in Wellington's center, fell to the French in the late afternoon, leaving a large gap in the Allied line. Wellington managed to shift troops to avert catastrophe, and by the time Napoleon had ordered forward the Imperial Guard around 7:30 P.M., the opportunity to exploit his temporary success had been lost. In the event, when these elite troops were repulsed by point-blank musket and artillery fire—a catastrophe rendered still more calamitous by the knowledge that the Prussians were now on the field in strength—French morale broke all along the line, with whole formations dissolving in the ensuing rout. Napoleon fled the field, leaving behind 25,000 killed and wounded and 8,000 prisoners; Wellington lost 15,000 killed and wounded, and the Prussians suffered approximately 7,000 casualties. *See also* Ligny, Battle of; Prussia; Quatre Bras, Battle of.

FURTHER READING: Adkin, Mark. *The Waterloo Companion: The Complete Guide to History's Most Famous Land Battle.* London: Aurum Press, 2001; Barbero, Alessandro. *The Definitive History of the Battle of Waterloo.* London: Atlantic Books, 2005; Chalfont, Lord, ed. *Waterloo: Battle of Three Armies.* London: Sedgwick and Jackson, 1979; Hibbert, Christopher. *Waterloo: Napoleon's Last Campaign.* Blue Ridge Summit: Cooper Square Books, 2004; Howarth, David. *Waterloo: A Near Run Thing.* London: Weidenfeld & Nicolson, 2003; Roberts, Andrew. *Waterloo: Napoleon's*

Last Gamble. London: HarperCollins 2005; Wooten, Geoffrey. *Waterloo 1815.* Oxford: Osprey, 1992.

GREGORY FREMONT-BARNES

Webster-Ashburton Treaty (1842)

A pact between the **United States** and Great Britain regarding the Canadian-American border, the illegal slave trade, and nonpolitical extraditions. Negotiated by U.S. Secretary of State Daniel Webster and British Minister Alexander Baring, First Baron Ashburton, the agreement was signed August 9, ratified by the U.S. Senate on August 20, and proclaimed on November 10, 1842.

Anglo-American relations had badly frayed by 1840. The boundary between Maine and New Brunswick, and from Lake Superior to Lake of the Woods, remained unresolved. Enforcement of the ban on slave trading brought the two nations into conflict. Furthermore, the United States refused to extradite a Canadian involved in sinking a gun-running vessel on the Niagara River. By 1842, however, the two nations realized the mutual benefits of compromise. The treaty set the boundary between New Brunswick and Maine, New York and Quebec at Lake Champlain, and Lake Superior and Lake of the Woods; provided for British-American naval cooperation in pursuing slavers; and established the principle of extradition in nonpolitical criminal cases. The treaty was a boon to Anglo-American relations. In addition the United States improved the security of its northern border and gained thousands of square miles, including Minnesota's rich Mesabi iron fields. *See also* Canada; Oregon Question; Rush-Bagot Treaty.

FURTHER READING: Jones, Howard. *To the Webster-Ashburton Treaty: A Study in Anglo-American Relation, 1783–1843.* Chapel Hill: University of North Carolina Press, 1977.

KENNETH J. BLUME

Weihaiwei

A port city and Chinese naval base in Shantung province. It was briefly seized by the Japanese in the **Sino-Japanese War** from 1894 to 1895 and leased by Britain in 1898. Regarded as a purely "cartographic consolation" by Lord **Salisbury** for the acquisition of **Kiaochow** and **Port Arthur** by Germany and Russia, Weihaiwei was ruled by only a handful of British officials, preserving traditional Chinese institutions long after modernizing reforms had swept them away in China herself. The port was nonetheless useful for monitoring the activity of both Germany and Russia in the region. In 1902, Britain then looked to Japan for help in shielding Manchuria and Korea from Russian encroachment. Weihaiwei was handed back to China in 1930. *See also* Anglo-Japanese Alliance; Japanese Empire; Russian Empire.

FURTHER READING: Langer, William L. *The Diplomacy of Imperialism, 1890–1902.* New York: Alfred A. Knopf, 1968.

NIELS P. PETERSSON

Wellesley, Richard Colley (1760–1842)

The eldest brother of Arthur Wellesley, Duke of **Wellington.** Richard Wellesley became the second earl of Mornington on the death of his father. He served as governor-general of **India** from 1797 to 1805, during which time he defeated the Mahrathas and conquered Mysore, largely with his brother Arthur in command of the forces of the Crown and the East India Company. During Wellesley's tenure, British India expanded to include the Carnatic and part of Oudh, although Wellesley's frequent disagreements with the directors of the East India Company obliged him to return to Britain in 1805. He was appointed ambassador to Spain in 1809 and served simultaneously until 1812 as foreign secretary. From 1821–1828 and again from 1833–1834 he was Lord Lieutenant of **Ireland.** *See also* East India Companies.

FURTHER READING: Butler, Iris. *The Eldest Brother: The Marquess Wellesley, the Duke of Wellington's Eldest Brother.* London: Hodder & Stoughton, 1973; Severn, John K. *A Wellesley Affair: Richard, Marquess Wellesley and the Conduct of Anglo-Spanish Diplomacy, 1809–1812.* Tallahassee: University Presses of Florida, 1981.

GREGORY FREMONT-BARNES

Wellington, Arthur Wellesley, Duke of (1769–1852)

With the possible exception of John Churchill, Duke of Marlborough, the Duke of Wellington was Britain's greatest general, with an almost uninterrupted string of battlefield successes, most notably at **Waterloo** in 1815, in the Iberian Peninsula and southern France (1808–1814) during the **Napoleonic Wars.** Wellington made his name first in **India** in 1797–1805 where he won two notable victories against the Mahrathas before serving briefly as chief secretary of **Ireland** in 1807–1809.

In 1808, he was sent to Portugal and the next year became commander-in-chief of Allied forces in the peninsula. He successively drove back the French, most notably at Salamanca on July 22, 1812, and Vitoria on June 21, 1813, demonstrating a masterful use of tactics and topography while almost always commanding a numerically inferior force. After Waterloo he became ambassador to France and later served briefly as prime minister from 1828–1830, during which time he brought in the bill for Catholic emancipation. *See also* Maratha Wars; Peninsular War; Verona, Congress of; Wellesley, Richard Colley.

FURTHER READING: Guedalla, Philip. *The Duke.* London: Wordsworth Editions, 1997; Holmes, Richard. *Wellington: The Iron Duke.* London: HarperCollins, 2003; James, Lawrence. *The Iron Duke: A Military Biography of Wellington.* London: Pimlico, 2002; Longford, Elizabeth. *Wellington: Pillar of State.* London: Weidenfeld & Nicolson, 1972; Longford, Elizabeth. *Wellington: The Years of the Sword.* London: HarperCollins, 1971; Shaw, Matthew. *The Duke of Wellington.* London: British Library Publishing Division, 2005.

GREGORY FREMONT-BARNES

Weltpolitik

A concept of foreign policy emerging in the late nineteenth century in Imperial Germany against the background of the country's rise as a major industrial and trading nation. Coming out of the period of retarded economic growth known as the Great Depression of 1873–1895, German entrepreneurs were pushing for the acquisition of colonies in search of raw materials and markets for their goods. Already in the 1880s, Reich chancellor Otto von **Bismarck** had responded to these pressures and, in the larger context of the European "scramble for colonies," had acquired territories in Africa and Asia. His successors, and Bernhard von **Bülow** in particular, promoted this overseas expansion even more vigorously after becoming the trusted adviser of Kaiser **Wilhelm II,** first as foreign secretary and from 1900 as chancellor. He was the person who coined such popular slogans of imperialist power politics as that of Germany seeking "a place in the sun" next to the other Great Powers. In the twentieth century, he added, Germany would either be "the hammer or the anvil" of world politics when it came to a redistribution of colonies and the allocation of territories that had not yet been annexed by the Europeans. Nor did he leave any doubt that he wanted Germany to be a hammer.

Given these claims, there has been a good deal of debate among historians as to the meaning of *Weltpolitik.* In the early years after World War II, most scholars tended to interpret it as some rather aimless yearning for prestige and for recognition of Germany as a latecomer to the international system, especially by Britain, then the dominant power in the world. No doubt *Weltpolitik* lacked precision in the public discourse of the time. But later work, based on newly discovered archival sources, has shown that this indeterminacy was more deliberate and that behind the slogans of the day there was a precise and well-thought-out strategy to make certain that Germany would succeed at the bargaining table when, as was widely expected, there would be a redistribution of colonies in the new century. Thus the ailing **Portuguese Empire** was thought to be an object of future power-political negotiation.

The kaiser and his advisers in the late 1890s were convinced that the German voice would not be heard unless it was backed up by military might. Although Germany had the strongest army in Europe, it was also clear that it would be useless against British naval power. Only a large German navy would be able to buttress future German claims. This is why it has been argued more recently that *Weltpolitik,* the vagueness of its definition for popular consumption notwithstanding, did have a hardcore plan to expand the Imperial navy into a powerful instrument that was capable of challenging even the Royal Navy. The fate of *Weltpolitik* was therefore inseparably linked to the success or failure of the kaiser's naval program. By 1910–1911, both had run into serious trouble. In 1909 Bülow lost his job, not least because his *Weltpolitik* diplomacy had led to the isolation of Germany. He could not prevent the conclusion of the Anglo-French **Entente Cordiale** in 1904, nor the formation of the **Triple Entente** of 1907, which brought in Russia. By 1911, it was also evident that the **Tirpitz Plan** was at its end, because the British, suspicious of German naval expansion, had "outbuilt" the kaiser in the arms competition that also began around 1904–1905.

Weltpolitik was now replaced by a retreat by Germany to the European continent. Stepped-up expenditure for the army began to replace the earlier massive funding of the navy. Berlin began to support its only reliable ally, the Austro-Hungarian Empire, and developed a siege mentality that contributed to the attempt to break out of the perceived encirclement of this Dual Alliance by Britain, France, and Russia in July 1914. The unleashing of World War I was therefore a preventive strike against France and Russia before the position of the two Central European powers had deteriorated to the point where the armies of the former could no longer be defeated, that is, before it was too late and the latter would become the "anvils" of the great power system. *See also* German Empire; Habsburg Empire; Morocco Crisis; Triple Alliance.

FURTHER READING: Dehio, L. *Deutschland und die Weltpolitik im 20. Jahrhundert.* Vienna: Verlag für Geschichte und Politik, 1955; Hillgruber, Andreas. *Deutsche Grossmacht und Weltpolitik im 19. und 20. Jahrhundert.* Düsseldorf: Droste, 1977; Mommsen, Wolfgang J. *Grossmachtstellung und Weltpolitik.* Frankfurt am Main: Propyläen, 1993.

VOLKER R. BERGHAHN

White Man's Burden

The term *white man's burden* came from Rudyard **Kipling**'s 1899 poem of that name, signifying the idea that empire was a philanthropic duty of the advanced or civilized nations. Kipling directed the injunction at the **United States,** which, in the **Spanish-American War,** had for the first time acquired overseas colonies. To many current minds, the idea is repulsively racist, and of course it does use a racial category. It is nevertheless significant that Kipling felt imperialism justified not because it served the metropolitan power but because it served humankind. Earlier generations of imperialists had been more forthrightly self-interested. *See also* Imperialism.

FURTHER READING: Mason, Philip. *Kipling: The Glass, the Shadow, and the Fire.* London: J. Cape, 1975.

MARK F. PROUDMAN

Wilhelm I, Kaiser of Germany (1797–1888)

Wilhelm I was king of **Prussia** (1861–1888) and German emperor (1871–1888). Born Wilhelm Friedrich Ludwig of Prussia in Berlin, the son of Friedrich Wilhelm III and Queen Louise of Mecklenburg-Strelitz, he served in the **Napoleonic Wars** and in 1848 used his military experience to help put down the liberal revolts stirring the country. When he ascended the throne of Prussia as Wilhelm I in 1861, he appointed Otto von **Bismarck** to the office of first Prussian minister and thereby did more for his country in one stroke than the rest of his reign could account for. Bismarck thereafter guided domestic affairs and foreign policy through the wars of German unification and the proclamation of the **German Empire** in the Hall of Mirrors in January 1871. *See also* German Empire; Hohenzollern Dynasty.

FURTHER READING: Clark, Christopher. *Iron Kingdom: The Rise and Downfall of Prussia, 1600–1947.* Harvard: Belknap, 2006.

CARL CAVANAGH HODGE

Wilhelm II, Kaiser of Germany (1859–1941)

King of **Prussia** and German emperor from 1888–1918, Wilhelm was born in Berlin on January 27, 1859. He was the first son of Crown Prince Friedrich of Prussia and his English wife Princess Victoria, a daughter of Queen **Victoria.** After a troubled birth that left him with a paralyzed left arm, and following a difficult childhood, in which his parents attempted to make up for his physical deficiencies with a harsh upbringing, he came to the throne at the age of 29 on June 15, 1888, following his father's premature death from cancer.

As a young prince, he had begun to reject his parents' liberalism. His reign began with a conflict with Chancellor Otto von **Bismarck,** as the young kaiser was determined to establish his own "personal rule." Wilhelm soon dismissed the aged chancellor who had been reluctant to yield his powers. Following Under Wilhelm's rule, Germany's relations with its European neighbors, previously stabilized by Bismarck's alliance policy, steadily declined, and Europe divided into rival alliances. Despite the monarch's attempts to come to alliance agreements with some of his neighbors, Germany found itself increasingly isolated and unable to win over either Russia or Britain. During several international crises, European relations steadily worsened, and the kaiser's foreign policy made it appear as if Germany were spoiling for a fight. Under his auspices, for example, Germany began to build a powerful navy designed to challenge British naval supremacy, the so-called **Tirpitz Plan.** With the pursuit of *Weltpolitik* and European hegemony, moreover, Wilhelm II and his entourage helped cultivate suspicion of Germany among her neighbors. On several occasions, most notably during the infamous "war council" of December 1912, he demanded war, although in July 1914, when war was almost unavoidable, he advocated mediation between **Serbia** and Austria-Hungary.

Wilhelm II appears to have suffered from a number of personality defects that may well have been caused by the difficult circumstances of his birth and upbringing. He was prone to bellicose outbursts and frequently cruel to friends and subordinates. Although many contemporaries attributed him with great intelligence and a quick wit, he was often bored by the business of ruling Germany, preferring to spend his time traveling and indulging in his favorite past-time of hunting. His companions were frequently subjected to his monologues and practical jokes, and his friendship with a number of homosexuals also led to speculation about his own sexuality, although frequent and ill-disguised affairs with women have cast doubt on the theory. He was also prone to anti-Semitic outbursts, and he saw himself in a leading role when it came to defending Europe against the "yellow peril," such as during the **Boxer Insurrection** of 1900.

During the war that he had so often wished for and then shied away from, Wilhelm II's powers were restricted. It has been argued that he was only a "shadow Emperor" from 1914–1818. In particular, he had to compete for public recognition with **Hindenburg** and Ludendorff whose military successes had come to overshadow the **Hohenzollern** kaiser's majesty. In November 1918, when the war was lost for Germany, Wilhelm resisted both the call to resign, a move that might have saved the Prussian monarchy, and calls to seek a heroic death on the battlefield. Instead, he sought exile in the neutral **Netherlands,** taking with him a large part of his possessions. After his inglorious flight from Germany, Wilhelm II lived in Doorn in the Netherlands for 23 years, hoping for a restoration of the German monarchy, but he never returned to Germany.

Historians have long debated the importance of Wilhelm II's personal rule—whether he was really in a position to determine his own policies, particularly foreign policy, or manipulated by cunning statesmen around him. His role in the events that led to the outbreak of war has also been the subject of historiographical controversy, not least because the victorious Allies of 1918 demanded the Emperor's extradition as a war criminal, considering him "the criminal mainly responsible for the war." In recent years, German historians have begun to accept some of the views of those such as John C. G. Röhl who argue for Wilhelm II's pivotal role in German decision making and in the events that led to the outbreak of the World War I, although a consensus has not yet been reached. *See also* Bülow, Berhard von; German Empire; Habsburg Empire; July Crisis; Morocco Crisis.

FURTHER READING: Cecil, Lamar. *Wilhelm II.* 2 vols. Chapel Hill: University of North Carolina Press, 1996; Clark, Chris. *Kaiser Wilhelm II.* New York: Longman, 2000; Mombauer, Annika, and Wilhelm Deist, eds. *The Kaiser. New Research on Wilhelm II's Role in Imperial Germany.* New York: Cambridge University Press, 2004; Röhl, John. *Young Wilhelm. The Kaiser's Early Life, 1859–1888.* New York: Cambridge University Press 1998; Röhl, John. *Wilhelm II. The Kaiser's Personal Monarchy, 1888–1900.* New York: Cambridge University Press, 2004; Röhl, John. *The Kaiser and His Court. Wilhelm II and the Government of Germany.* New York: Cambridge University Press, 1994.

ANNIKA MOMBAUER

Wilson, Woodrow (1856–1924)

The 28th President of the **United States** (1913–1921), Woodrow Thomas Wilson, the son of Joseph Ruggles Wilson and Janet Woodrow, attended Davidson College, a small Presbyterian school in North Carolina, of which his father was a trustee. Although Wilson was interested in English literature, he nonetheless had a gift for politics and during his last year at college he published an essay, "Cabinet Government in the United States," in the *International Review.*

In 1885, a book-length expansion of his earlier essay on Congress sold well. Wilson published *The State*, a lengthy textbook analyzing the political nature of society in 1889. He became a professor at Princeton University in 1890 and its president in 1902. Wilson's presidency at Princeton coincided with the advent of the Progressive Era in American politics. His educational reforms were radical, but his social and political outlook remained largely conservative.

Colonel George B. Harvey, editor of *Harper's Weekly*, who was instrumental in shifting Wilson's interests to politics, suggested that Wilson would make a good Democratic presidential candidate. Wilson sought and won the governorship of New Jersey and won the Democratic presidential nomination of 1912, thereafter coasting to an election victory as a result of a split of the Republican vote between President William Howard **Taft** and the "Bull Moose" candidate, former President Theodore **Roosevelt.** At the top of Wilson's list of ideas was that of lower tariff rates to free American consumers from artificially protected monopolies. He established the Federal Trade Commission in 1914 to ensure that one company or group of companies did not gain control of an entire industry and force up prices artificially.

Although elected to reform domestic politics, Wilson spent the better part of his tenure dealing with foreign policy. Wilson's predecessors—McKinley, Roosevelt, and Taft—viewed the United States as an emerging power and had significantly expanded American influence abroad with the establishment of colonies and protectorates in the Caribbean and Pacific. Wilson did not share their imperial outlook, yet in 1913 he refused to recognize the revolutionary government in **Mexico,** and he intervened with force repeatedly there and in Central America. With the outbreak of World War I in Europe, Wilson sought to abide by a policy of neutrality, a policy evermore difficult to uphold as American public sentiment sided increasingly with the Entente powers. After Germany resumed unrestricted submarine warfare in 1917, Wilson took the United States to war on the Allied side, yet with the goal above all to "make the world safe for democracy." What Wilson sought at the Paris Conference after the war, however, was to make the postwar world unsafe for European imperialism. His Fourteen Points became the foundation of the conference and amounted, taken as whole, to a proposal for the reconstitution of international relations on principles wholly different from those animating European diplomacy between 1800 and 1914. In this he only partly succeeded, even though the application of his doctrine of the self-determination of peoples in effect dismembered the **Habsburg** and **Ottoman Empires.**

Wilson offered not only the most compelling critique of imperialism but also the most thoughtful alternative—a liberal internationalism that served the United States well in the second half of the twentieth century. His belief in international cooperation through an association of nations led to the creation of the League of Nations, an institution hobbled from the outset by the refusal of the Senate to have the United States join it. For his efforts in this direction, he was awarded the 1919 Nobel Peace Prize. Wilson died on February 3, 1924, and was buried in the National Cathedral in Washington, D.C.

FURTHER READING: Ambrosius, Lloyd. *Woodrow Wilson and the American Diplomatic Tradition: The Treaty Fight in Perspective.* New York: Cambridge University Press, 1990; Auchincloss, Louis. *Woodrow Wilson: A Penguin Life.* New York: Viking Press, 2000; Cooper, John, *Breaking the Heart of the World: Woodrow Wilson and the Fight for the League of Nations.* Cambridge: Cambridge University Press, 2001; Daniels, Josephus. *The Life of Woodrow Wilson.* Westport, CT: Greenwood, 1971; Gilderhus, Mark. *Pan American Visions: Woodrow Wilson and the Western Hemisphere, 1913–1921.* Tucson: University of Arizona Press, 1986.

JITENDRA UTTAM

Witte, Sergei (1849–1915)

An outstanding statesman who played a decisive role in the industrialization of the **Russian Empire** before World War I. Witte was born and had spent his childhood in the Caucasus, studied mathematics at the Novorossiysk University in Odessa, and in the 1870s and 1880s started a career in different private enterprises. Because of his administrative skills he was appointed as director of railroad affairs within the ministry of finance between 1889 and 1891 and one year later became minister for transportation.

Witte recognized that an industrialization of the vast empire was not thinkable without railroad construction, and in 1891 he started the greatest project during his career, the construction of Russia's transcontinental railroad, the **Trans-Siberian Railroad,** and the **Chinese Eastern Railway** through northern **Manchuria.** In 1892, Witte also took over the ministry of finance in which portfolio he attracted loans from France and foreign investment, and he also introduced the gold standard in the Russian Empire in 1897. Under his supervision Russia experienced an economic boom, especially in the sectors of transportation and resource extraction. Because of his strong engagement for an accelerated modernization and gradual penetration of Manchuria, Witte opposed an aggressive policy toward Japan and was ousted from his position in 1903. After Russia's defeat in the **Russo-Japanese War** of 1904–1905, he was instructed by Tsar **Nicholas II** to negotiate the Treaty of **Portsmouth** in which Russia lost her Great Power status in East Asia. During the

Russian Revolution of 1905, Witte advised Nicholas to issue the **October Manifesto** and was appointed prime minister to test his own counsel. Witte put a new constitution and the convocation of Russia's first parliament, the Duma, into action yet simultaneously managed to secure an Anglo-French loan of £80 million, which made the government less dependent on the Duma for finance, and was vigorous in the repression of all open rebellion. Yet all this came too late; as radical left-wing parties got the upper hand in the Duma, Witte lost the support of Nicholas and political reactionaries, and was forced to resign. Shortly before the outbreak of World War I, Witte, remembering the disaster of 1905, warned that the Russian Empire should avoid another conflict or face unavoidable decline.

FURTHER READING: Sidney, Harcave. *Count Sergei Witte and the Twilight of Imperial Russia: A Biography.* Armonk: M. E. Sharpe, 2004.

EVA-MARIA STOLBERG

Wolseley, Garnet Wolseley, Field Marshal Viscount (1833–1913)

Among the most successful British soldiers of the nineteenth century, Garnet Wolseley was the son of an impecunious Anglo-Irish army officer. Unable to afford a commission, he was granted one by the Duke of **Wellington** on the strength of his father's service. True to his own dictum that it was the duty of an ambitious young officer to try to get himself killed, Wolseley transferred to a regiment going out to Burma, where he both distinguished himself and acquired a leg wound that bothered him for the rest of his life. He served in the **Crimean War,** again with distinction, and then in **India** during and after the **Indian Mutiny** of 1857, and in China during the **Opium War** of 1859–1860. In **Canada** during **American Civil War,** he took the opportunity to visit the headquarters of the Confederate army. Remaining in Canada after the war, he commanded the 1870 Red River expedition against Metis rebels in what became the Canadian province of Manitoba.

In 1869, Wolseley published the *Soldier's Pocket Book,* a manual of military skills that went through many editions and did much to establish Wolseley's reputation as a scientific and reforming officer. Wolseley commanded the British expedition of 1873–1874 against the **Ashanti,** a quick and victorious operation in which British losses—from either enemy action or disease—were few, in stark contrast to many contemporary African expeditions. Following the **Ashanti War** the expression "all Sir Garnet" indicated something well done; Wolseley also became Gilbert and Sullivan's "very model of a modern major-general." Wolseley was the first governor-general of **Cyprus** after the British annexation of 1878, and then commanded the forces that defeated Colonel Arabi's nationalist rebellion in **Egypt** in 1882. The September 13, 1882, victory at Tel el-Kebir gave an enormous fillip to his reputation. He commanded the unsuccessful relief expedition to the **Sudan** in 1884–1885. Although Wolseley was closely associated with the Liberals, having served at the War Office under the reforming Secretary Edward Cardwell, he was privately scathing about both liberalism and democracy, and never ceased to blame William **Gladstone** for the death of his friend General Charles **Gordon** in Khartoum. Wolseley became commander-in-chief of the British army in 1895, but he was sidelined by illness and old age in 1897. A skillful self-promoter, Wolseley gathered about himself a group of officers known as the "Wolseley ring," who simultaneously promoted both army reform and each others' careers. Wolseley's significance to the theme of imperialism lies in his service as a normally successful local commander in colonial wars from the 1850s to the 1880s. *See also* Riel Rebellions.

FURTHER READING: Kochanski, Halik. *Sir Garnet Wolseley: Victorian Hero.* London: Hambledon, 1999; Lehmann, Joseph H. *The Model Major General: A Biography of Field-Marshal Lord Wolseley.* Boston: Hougton Mifflin, 1964.

MARK F. PROUDMAN

Wood, Leonard (1860–1927)

A proconsul in the American Empire created by the **Spanish American War,** Leonard Wood directed civil and military governments in both **Cuba** and the **Philippines.** Wood joined the U.S. Army in 1885 and won the Congressional Medal of Honor for his participation in the final campaign against the Apache Chief Geronimo. At the start of the Spanish-American War, Wood and Theodore **Roosevelt** formed the First United States Volunteer Cavalry, popularly known as the Rough Riders. After the war, General Wood remained as governor of Santiago Province and eventually became military governor of Cuba.

Tasked with setting Cuba on the road to independence, Wood rebuilt the infrastructure; battled sanitation problems, disease, and hunger; and reorganized the Latin government along Anglo-Saxon lines. In close association with Secretary of War Elihu **Root,** Wood held local and national elections and supervised the organization and subsequent work of the Cuban Constitutional Convention. He played a leading role in securing Cuban acceptance of the **Platt Amendment** and in getting the **United States** to negotiate the **Cuban Reciprocity Treaty.** After the inauguration of the new Cuban government, President Roosevelt sent Wood to extend direct American control over the Muslim inhabitants of the Philippines. Wood, determined to make the American presence felt, worked to abrogate the existing **Bates Agreement** and coerce the Moros into respecting American laws, including an end to slavery and piracy. To punish noncompliant Moros, Wood launched the **Moro Punitive Expeditions.** After his service in the Moro Province, Wood became head of the Philippine Division and eventually chief-of-staff of the U.S. Army. In 1920, Wood unsuccessfully ran as a candidate for the Republican nomination for president. He returned to the Philippines as governor-general in 1921 and served in that capacity until his death in 1927.

FURTHER READING: Hagedorn, Hermann. *Leonard Wood: A Biography.* New York: Harper & Brothers, 1931; Hitchman, James H. *Leonard Wood and Cuban Independence, 1898–1902.* The Hague: Nijhoff, 1971; Lane, Jack C. *Armed Progressive: General Leonard Wood.* San Rafael, CA: Presidio Press, 1978.

JAMES PRUITT

Wounded Knee, Battle of (1890)

In 1890, the U.S. Army went to the Sioux reservation in South Dakota to arrest Chief Sitting Bull. The federal government feared that Sitting Bull was encouraging the Sioux to attack white settlements. As the army attempted to arrest the chief, a soldier shot and killed Sitting Bull. The Indians who were living on Sitting Bull's campground fled. The next day, December 29, 1890, a small band of Sioux were captured by the army and forced into the Wounded Knee Creek at South Dakota. The Indians were told to surrender their weapons. As they were giving up their guns, a rifle discharged. In response, the army opened fire. More than 300 men, women, and children were killed. The wounded attempted to crawl away, but a heavy snow fell that evening and many were found dead the next day. The Battle of Wounded Knee was the last act of Indian resistance in the western part of the **United States.** *See also* Indian Wars; Sioux Wars.

FURTHER READING: Brown, Dee. *Bury My Heart at Wounded Knee: An Indian History of the American West.* New York: Henry Holt, 2001.

GENE C. GERARD

X-Y

Xhosa Wars

See Kaffir Wars

Yalu River, Battle of (1904)

An early action of the **Russo-Japanese War.** At the end of April 1904, Russian forces under General Zasulich met Japanese forces under the command of General Kuroki at the point where the Yalu River meets the Ai River. The Japanese forces consisted of the three divisions of the First Army: 2,000 cavalrymen, 28,000 infantry, and 128 field guns, including some brand new Krupp 4.7-inch howitzers. The Russian forces were the Eastern Detachment and had 5,000 cavalry, 15,000 infantry, and only 60 guns.

Strategically, the Battle of Yalu River showed the use of subterfuge, a relatively new concept in this context. Between April 25 and 27, Japanese engineers built a bridge intended as a diversion. The Russians fired on it, showing the Japanese where the Russian guns were. Tactically, the battle was dominated by new technologies. The Japanese Krupp howitzers could fire from further away than the Russian artillery. Thus the safe distance for the Russians guns was greater than their effective range. Both sides in this conflict were equipped with breech loading rifles, but only the Japanese grasped what this meant on a tactical level. The Japanese attacked in a long line, allowing them to cover a large field of fire. The Russians mocked this strategy and attacked using tactics best suited for single-shot muzzle loading weapons.

The battle itself was surprisingly one-sided. The Japanese attacked in the morning on May 1, and by 5:30 P.M., the Russian forces were retreating in disarray. The majority of the Russians escaped, and casualties were relatively minor: 1,300 Russians dead and 600 captured; 160 Japanese dead and 820 wounded. Symbolically, however, the Japanese had shown that an Asian army could win against a European power. As with much of the Russo-Japanese War, this symbolic victory was more significant than the military victory. *See also* Japanese Empire; Russian Empire.

FURTHER READING: Jukes, Geoffrey. *The Russo-Japanese War, 1904–1905*. Oxford: Osprey, 2002.

MICHAEL TIMONIN

Yellow Sea, Battle of (1904)

A major naval battle of the **Russo-Japanese War.** As Japanese forces closed on **Port Arthur,** Czar **Nicholas II** ordered the Russian fleet to break out and sail to **Vladivostok** to join the Russian warships there. Commanded by Admiral Wilgelm Vitgeft, the Russian fleet of 6 battleships, 3 cruisers, and 14 smaller ships sortied on August 10, 1904. Admiral Heihachiro Togo's larger Japanese fleet intercepted the Russians, and Japan's 4 modern battleships and 11 cruisers dominated the battle. Japanese shells shattered the bridge of the *Tsesarevich,* killing Vitgeft. The Russian fleet fell into confusion and fled in disorder. The pursuing Japanese sank only one Russian cruiser. Five battleships and most of the smaller ships evaded the Japanese and returned to Port Arthur. Two cruisers and the heavily damaged *Tsesarevich* escaped to neutral ports. Japan's strategic victory trapped the Russian fleet in Port Arthur and ensured Japanese control of the seas for the duration of the war. *See also* Japanese Empire; Russian Empire; Tsushima, Battle of.

FURTHER READING: Corbett, J. S. *Maritime Operation in the Russo-Japanese War.* Annapolis, MD: Naval Institute Press, 1995; Jukes, Geoffrey. *The Russo-Japanese War, 1904–5.* Oxford: Osprey, 2002; Warner, Denis, and Peggy Warner. *The Tide at Sunrise: A History of the Russo-Japanese War, 1904–1905.* London: Frank Cass, 2002.

STEPHEN K. STEIN

Young Ireland

Young Ireland was a group of Protestant and Catholic nationalists associated with the *Nation* newspaper in the 1840s. Thomas Osborne Davis, a Protestant, and Charles Gavin Duffy and John Blake Dillon, both Catholics, founded the weekly *Nation* in 1842. It quickly acquired a readership of 250,000. Contemporaries gave the men associated with the *Nation* an impressive name, Young Ireland. Liberal and romantic nationalists, notably Giuseppe **Mazzini**'s **Young Italy,** challenged traditionalists in many European countries. Unlike them, Young Ireland did not base its nationalism on a distinctive language.

The *Nation*'s contributors were youthful compared with the elderly Daniel O'Connell, the hero of Catholic Emancipation (letting Roman Catholics serve in the British Parliament). Young Ireland can be viewed as a generational and ideological revolt against O'Connell's leadership. It regarded O'Connell as too closely allied with the Whigs in London and the Roman Catholic bishops in **Ireland.** Like O'Connell, it wanted the repeal of the 1801 **Act of Union** to restore a separate Irish Parliament, but unlike him it refused to be distracted by lesser reforms. O'Connell rejected and Young Ireland accepted a British proposal for nondenominational colleges. Although it refused to condemn violence, Young Ireland's Irish Confederation, organized in 1847, was cautiously constitutional in its tactics. Nearly all the middle class intellectuals and paternalistic landlords who made up Young Ireland lacked sympathy with radical antilandlord peasants. As an exception, John Mitchel, a Protestant, called for a rent strike and a refusal to pay the local taxes, called rates.

It was the example of revolutions in France and elsewhere on the continent that induced the essentially moderate Young Irelanders to adopt the rhetoric of revolutions in 1848. Without any realistic planning, William Smith O'Brien led a pathetic uprising in County Tipperary. Several Young Irelanders were exiled to **Australia.**

Young Ireland had little impact on Irish history, certainly less than the **Irish famine** of the 1840s. The main significance of Young Ireland was that it was nonsectarian in a country in which religion increasingly colored national identity. Of the individuals, Davis was the most influential. Before he died in 1844, still in his early thirties, he helped inspire a secular Irish nationalism rooted in history and hostility to English culture. His ballad, "A Nation Once Again," enjoyed widespread popularity. *See also* Home Rule.

FURTHER READING: Davis, Richard P. *The Young Ireland Movement.* Dublin: Gill and Macmillan, 1987.

DAVID M. FAHEY

Young Italy (1831)

A secretive revolutionary, religious-nationalist movement founded and led by Giuseppe **Mazzini** (1805–1872). While exiled in Marseilles in 1831, Mazzini formed Young Italy, an energetic, national revolutionary organization as an alternative to the Carbonari secret society that had failed to either drive the Austrians from **Italy** or end monarchial rule. Mazzini recruited men under the age of 40 to his movement, believing that only the youth were passionate enough and willing to risk martyrdom for the cause of national liberation. Young Italy believed that the Italian nation had a divine mission to lead all of humanity into a new democratic age, which was reflected in its motto, "God and the People." Foreign occupation, authoritarianism, and social inequality prevented Italy from achieving this destiny, and so were all to be opposed. Young Italy pursued goals of national liberation and revolution through propaganda, insurrection, assassination, and other acts of political violence in the name of a republican Italy.

Headed by a central office, which convened outside of the country, the leadership of Mazzini and his advisers handled propaganda and coordinated insurrections. A provincial office handled similar functions in every Italian province. Initiators recruited and trained new members, who were armed with a knife, a gun, and 30 rounds of ammunition, and were expected to take part in any insurrection or act directed from the central or provincial offices. Young Italy launched several failed plots against King Charles Albert of **Piedmont-Sardinia** and insurrections in 1831 and 1833, but lost much of its prestige through its use of violence and unwillingness to compromise. Moderate nationalists displaced Young Italy until the outbreak of revolutions of 1848 when the group made another appearance in the short-lived Roman Republic (1848–1849).

FURTHER READING: Berkeley, G.F.H. *Italy in the Making 1815 to 1846.* Cambridge: Cambridge University Press, 1932.

FREDERICK H. DOTOLO

Young Turks

Originally a coalition of young dissidents based in Salonika who ended the Ottoman sultanate, the Young Turk movement consisted of college students and dissident soldiers. Formally known as The Committee on Union and Progress, founded in 1889, the Young Turks succeeded in 1908 in forcing Abdülhamid II to reinstitute the 1876 constitution and recall the legislature. They deposed him the next year, reorganized the government, and started modernizing and industrializing Ottoman society. During the **Balkan Wars,** in which the **Ottoman Empire** suffered significant territorial losses, the influence of the nationalists eclipsed that of the liberals. The Young Turks government aligned the Ottoman Empire with the Central Powers during World War I. In 1915, in response to the formation of anti-Turkish Armenian battalions, they deported 1.75 million Armenians to Syria and Mesopotamia, in the course of which 600,000 to 800,000 Armenians were killed or died of starvation. Facing defeat in 1918, the Young Turks resigned a month before the war ended. A number of leading Young Turks, including Enver Pasha, unsuccessfully sought Soviet help to overthrow Mustafa Kemal Atatürk in the postwar period.

FURTHER READING: Hanioglu, M. Sükrü. *Preparation for a Revolution: The Young Turks, 1902–1908.* New York: Oxford University Press, 2001.

ANDREKOS VARNAVA

Z

Zaibatsu

A Japanese term for the large financial combines, literally, "financial cliques," that were the pillar of the Japanese economy from the 1880s through 1945. Organized around individual families and their holding companies, the *zaibatsu* comprised intricate networks of financial, industrial, and commercial concerns tied through interlocking directorships and mutual shareholding. They served the critical function of concentrating capital, skilled labor, and technological know-how at a time of scarcity during the rapid transition from feudal to industrial Japan.

Although two—Mitsui and Sumitomo—of the four—Mitsui, Mitsubishi, Sumitomo, Yasuda—largest *zaibatsu* had their origins as commodities dealers in the Tokugawa period, the *zaibatsu* coalesced, in particular after the early 1880s, when the national government, in an effort to control spiraling inflation, sold off most state-owned enterprises. The men who purchased these enterprises enjoyed close personal ties with the ruling elite, with whom they shared a background as lower-level samurai. They benefited immensely from bargain-basement prices for state industries and from special contracts and loans obtained from the government.

They also profited greatly from modern Japan's series of wars. Mitsui financed the imperial forces in their bid to topple the supreme warlord, the shōgun, in the 1868 **Restoration War.** Mitsubishi got its start when the new national government leased, then donated, 13 ships to founder Iwasaki Yataro to ferry troops on a punitive expedition to Taiwan in 1874. The provision of ships, docks, warehouses, fuel, metals, chemicals, and funding during the **Sino-Japanese War** earned the head of the Mitsui conglomerate the title of baron.

Although their enormous resources would also become critical in the prosecution of World War II, the *zaibatsu* were never a causal factor in Japanese continental expansion. The Japanese economy remained primarily agricultural when imperial forces engaged China in war in 1894. And the military instigators of the Manchurian Incident of 1931 initially hoped to exclude the *zaibatsu* from their newly developed territory in northeast Asia. Despite this, the allied occupation of Japan made dissolution of the *zaibatsu* a central component of the democratizing agenda after 1945. *See also* Japanese Empire; Meiji Restoration.

FURTHER READING: Roberts, John G. *Mitsui: Three Centuries of Japanese Business.* New York: Weatherhill, 1973; Wray, William D. *Mitsubishi and the N.Y.K., 1870–1914: Business Strategy in the Japanese Shipping Industry.* Cambridge, MA: Harvard University Press, 1984.

FREDERICK R. DICKINSON

Zanzibar

A small island off the coast of Africa. The first European to visit Zanzibar was the Portuguese navigator Vasco de Gama in 1499; by 1503, the Portuguese had gained control of Zanzibar, and soon they held most of the East African coast. In 1698, Arabs from Oman ousted the Portuguese from Zanzibar. The Omanis gained nominal control of the islands, but until the reign of Sayyid Said (1804–1856), they took little interest in them. Said recognized the commercial value of East Africa and increasingly turned his attention to Zanzibar and Pemba, and in 1841 he permanently moved his court to Zanzibar.

Said brought many Arabs with him, and they gained control of Zanzibar's fertile soil, forcing most of the Hadimu to migrate to the eastern part of the island. The Hadimu were also obligated to work on the clove plantations. Said controlled much of the East African coast, and Zanzibar became the main center of the East Africa ivory and slave trade. Some of the slaves were used on the clove plantations, and others were exported to other parts of Africa and overseas. Zanzibar's trade was run by Omanis, who organized caravans into the interior of East Africa; the trade was largely financed by Indians resident on Zanzibar, many of whom were agents of Bombay firms.

From the 1820s, British, German, and American traders were active on Zanzibar. As early as 1841, the representative of the British government on Zanzibar was an influential adviser of the sultan. This was especially the case under Sir John Kirk, the British consul from 1866 to 1887. In a treaty with Great Britain in 1873, sultan Barghash agreed to halt the **slave trade** in his realm. During the Scramble for **Africa** territory among European powers, Great Britain gained a protectorate over Zanzibar and Pemba by a treaty with Germany in 1890. The sultan's mainland holdings were incorporated in German East Africa (later Tanganyika), British East Africa (later Kenya), and Italian Somaliland. The British considered Zanzibar an essentially Arab country and maintained the prevailing power structure. The office of sultan was retained, although stripped of most of its power; and Arabs, almost to the exclusion of other groups, were given opportunities for higher education and were recruited for bureaucratic posts. The chief government official from 1890 to 1913 was the British consul general, and from 1913 to 1963 it was the British resident. *See also* Heligoland-Zanzibar Treaty.

FURTHER READING: Bennett, Norman Robert. *A History of the Arab State of Zanzibar.* London: Methuen, 1978; Ingrams, William Harold. *Zanzibar: Its History and Its People.* London: Frank Cass, 1967.

MOSHE TERDMAN

Z-Flag

The flag hoisted by Admiral Heihachiro Togo on the flagship *Mikasa* immediately before engaging the Russian Baltic Fleet at **Tsushima** Straits on May 27, 1905.

The flag was the code of the day, meaning "The fate of the Empire depends on this battle. Let every man do his utmost." It was modeled on Admiral Horatio **Nelson**'s famous exhortation to his fleet before the 1805 Battle of **Trafalgar:** "England expects that every man will do his duty." The decimation of the Russian Baltic Fleet ensured that the Battle of Tsushima Straits lived on in memory as Imperial Japan's greatest naval victory. Likewise, the Z-flag continued to have special significance. On December 6, 1941, Vice Admiral Nagumo Chuichi read Admiral Yamamoto Isoroku's battle order—a verbatim rendition of Togo's Z-flag code—and hoisted the very flag from the Battle of Tsushima Straits on the departure of the air fleet for Pearl Harbor.

FURTHER READING: Watts, Anthony J., and Brian G. Gordon. *The Imperial Japanese Navy.* London: Macdonald, 1971.

FREDERICK R. DICKINSON

Zionism

A movement for the establishment of a national homeland for the Jews, arising in the 1880s from a reaction to anti-Semitism in Europe, not only in the form of pogroms in the **Russian Empire**—popular outbreaks of violence directed against Jews including the destruction of property and massacre, encouraged by the legal persecution of Jews led by Alexander III—but also evidenced in the **Dreyfus Affair** in a far more liberal society such as France. The movement was founded by Theodor Herzl (1860–1904), a Hungarian-Jewish journalist whose leadership led in 1897 to the First Zionist Conference in Basle, Switzerland.

While Herzl lived the Zionist movement was run from Vienna, but after his death its offices moved first to Cologne and then to Berlin. Although many Jews fled persecution in Europe for the **United States,** in 1891 alone 300,000 from Russia, Herzl's book *The Jewish State* posed the issue of the founding of a Jewish state in the historic homeland Palestine, a goal not realized until after the Holocaust and the establishment of Israel in 1948. Zionism was thus in large part a product of the coarsening of European politics by way of popular nationalism and heightened international tension between 1880s and 1914, a phenomenon which many Jews rightly calculated was only going to get worse.

FURTHER READING: Bein, Alex. *Theodore Herzl: A Biography.* Translated by Maurice Samuel. Philadelphia: Jewish Publication Society of America, 1941.

CARL CAVANAGH HODGE

Zollverein

A customs union formed by **Prussia** and neighboring German states in 1834 to stimulate trade. In retrospect, the German *Zollverein* can be considered as a predecessor of the **German Empire,** as it encompassed, already in the 1850s, most of the states that were to found the **Reich** in 1871. At its inception, however, the *Zollverein* was not intentionally designed to accelerate German political unity but rather to improve commerce and economic development. In this aspect the customs union proved an unqualified success, while it cannot be denied that the exclusion of Austria from the *Zollverein* paved the way for the *kleindeutsch*—a "lesser" Germany, excluding Austria—solution of the question of Austro-Prussian dualism.

At the beginning of the nineteenth century, trade in Germany was severely hampered by the existence of a kaleidoscope of 39 different states and free cities, many of them imposing their own tariffs and issuing their own currencies. This posed a problem especially in northern Germany where Prussia's western provinces were separated from the main body of the kingdom. To overcome these difficulties, the Prussian government passed a law in May 1818 that created a unified internal market by abolishing all custom dues within the scattered territories of the kingdom. In addition, the government announced its intention to conclude free trade agreements with her neighbors. Prussia imposed comparably low tariffs on imports and abolished all export tariffs.

It is wrong to say that with the formation of the *Zollverein* on January 1, 1834, German unification under Prussian leadership was a foregone conclusion. Before Bismarck finally achieved unity in 1871, another generation elapsed and several wars had been fought. On the contrary, several of the *Zollverein*'s members had been outright opposed to unification, especially to a *kleindeutsch* solution under Prussian leadership. As nearly all participating governments were jealously guarding their sovereignty, the customs union was forged primarily out of economic considerations and was an unmitigated success right from its inception. With the *Zollverein* a huge common market came into existence; both the agricultural and the industrial sectors were protected by tariffs; and a uniform system of measures and weights was adopted. Although payment transactions were eased by the mounting dominance of the Prussian *Taler*, every new member gave the *Zollverein* more power and thus it became easier to conclude more advantageous trade agreements with foreign states. Also, the *Zollverein* made it less difficult to coordinate the building of roads and railways, which soon expanded with breathtaking speed. On the other hand, between 1834 and 1844, administrative costs of tariff collection decreased by 50 percent and net income through custom dues grew by 90 percent. All these factors combined to stimulate growth and tied the participating states closer together. In turn, because of the success of the *Zollverein*, its economies became increasingly competitive internationally. Public opinion, which used to view the project rather skeptically, now emphatically embraced it.

Driving forces behind the propagation of the *Zollverein* were visionaries like the Prussian minister of finance, Friedrich von Motz, and the economist Friedrich **List.** List, initially a supporter of free trade, turned increasingly into an advocate of protectionism because of the growing import of cheap British commodities. British export industry was in fact less of a threat to the *Zollverein* than List thought. While Great Britain exported mostly manufactured goods to, and imported mainly agrarian products from, Germany, the *Zollverein* nonetheless enjoyed a favorable trade balance. Indeed, Prussia had been exporting more than it was importing since the early 1820s.

The apparent triumph made the customs union more and more attractive to other German states. Before long, Baden, Nassau, and the free city of Frankfurt joined, although Hanover, Oldenburg, and most of the smaller northern states enclaved by Prussia stood aloof until the 1850s. Austria remained voluntarily outside the *Zollverein*. Although Prince **Metternich** saw the success of the customs union with growing unease, he stubbornly refused to take part in it because of the consequences this would have for the **Habsburg Empire**'s economy. Until 1848, Austria pursued a policy of mercantilist protectionism, and her industry was hardly in a position to compete with the *Zollverein*'s. Yet when Austria changed its mind after the aborted German Revolution, Prussia would no longer accept it as a member. After the humiliation of the Punctuation of Olmütz on November 29, 1850, when Prussia was forced to renounce its plans of German political unity, its was not prepared to give way to Austria in the economic sphere, too. By now Prussia fully realized the potential of the *Zollverein* as a weapon in the struggle for German supremacy. As a result initial hopes of the smaller German states to establish a counterweight to dominant Prussia by inviting Austria into the *Zollverein* soon disintegrated. Prussia's economic potential was superior to Austria's as early as 1834, and the *Zollverein* enhanced this advantage.

In spite of several serious crises, the *Zollverein* also proved resilient. Neither the question of admittance of Austria nor the secular conflict between advocates of free trade and proponents of protectionism were able to destroy it. The customs union even survived the military confrontations between several of its members in the Austro-Prussian War. By 1867, most of the states of the future Empire adhered. The *Zollverein* lasted until 1918. *See also* Austro-Prussian War; German Empire; North German Confederation.

FURTHER READING: Burg, Peter. *Die deutsche Trias in Idee und Wirklichkeit. Vom alten Reich zum Deutschen Zollverein.* Stuttgart: Steiner Verlag, 1989; Doeberl, Michael. *Bayern und die wirtschaftliche Einigung Deutschlands.* Munich: Verlag der Bayerischen Akademie der Wissenschaften, 1915; Hahn, Hans-Werner. *Wirtschaftliche Integration im 19. Jahrhundert. Die hessischen Staaten und der Deutsche Zollverein.* Göttingen: Vandenhoeck und Ruprecht, 1982; Henderson, William Otto. *The Zollverein.* London: Cass, 1959.

ULRICH SCHNAKENBURG

Zoological Gardens

Initially private menageries of the royal and wealthy, later public parks devoted to the amusement and education of the metropolitan populace on the one hand and the scientific study of animal species on the other. This was in part the product of political change—the Jardin des Plantes Zoological Gardens incorporated the surviving animals of the Versailles menagerie in 1793 in the wake of France's revolutionary upheaval—but it was equally influenced by the expansion of European colonial empires in the second half of the nineteenth century.

In some instances colonial administrators had a direct hand in the process. Sir Thomas Stamford **Raffles** indulged a personal love of natural history by developing a vast collection of anthropological, botanical, and zoological specimens and was a cofounder of the Zoological Society of London at the comparatively early date of 1826. Zoos were also about prestige, a showcase for the exotica of empire. King William IV identified the Zoological Society in 1831 as symbolic of Britain's international position. Mid-century Europe also experienced a new interest in "acclimatization," the transplanting of organisms to different locations for the purpose of developing the abilities of species to perpetuate themselves in radically different conditions, which, for France and Britain in particular, flourished in overseas settler colonies pursuing protectionist programs of economic development. At the darkest end of the scientific and moral spectrum was the phenomenon of the **human zoo** popularized between the 1870s and World War I, in which the indigenous peoples of overseas colonies were displayed much like caged animals.

FURTHER READING: Hoage, R. J., and William A. Deiss, eds. *New Worlds, New Animals: From Menagerie to Zoological Park in the Nineteenth Century.* Baltimore: Johns Hopkins University Press, 1996; Osborne, Michael A. *Nature, the Exotic, and the Science of French Colonialism.* Bloomington: Indiana University Press, 1994; Ritvo, Harriet. *The Animal Estate: The English and Other Creatures in the Victorian Age.* Cambridge, MA: Harvard University Press, 1987.

CARL CAVANAGH HODGE

Zulu War (1879)

A brief conflict between the Zulu Kingdom of southern Africa and the **British Empire.** When British colonial possessions in southern Africa expanded through the annexation of the **Transvaal** in 1877, the Zulu people, under their chief Cetewayo, found themselves threatened by a far greater adversary than the neighboring Boers. The British, with designs on Zululand as part of their efforts to create a British federation encompassing the whole of southern Africa and anxious at the Zulus' martial power, issued an ultimatum on December 11, 1878, deliberately designed to be rejected and therefore to serve as a *casus belli.* After receiving no reply from Cetewayo, a force under Lord Chelmsford, consisting of 5,000 British and 8,000 native troops, invaded Zululand in three columns. Cetewayo had at his disposal 40,000 highly disciplined and well-trained warriors, largely armed with spears. On January 22, 1879, a Zulu army caught the British center column, consisting of 900 British and more than 500 native levies, completely by surprise in their unfortified camp at **Isandhlwana,** annihilating the force.

The Zulus followed up their victory by attacking on the same evening and through the following morning the nearby British base at **Rorke's Drift,** where fewer than a hundred British soldiers tenaciously held their position against successive Zulu assaults. A second British force, meanwhile, became besieged at Eshowe, although this was relieved after another column, having driven off a Zulu attack at Gingindhlovu on April 3, reached the defenders the next day. Two further battles, at Hlobane and Kambula on March 28 and 29, respectively, and fought by separate British columns, favored the British, but in both cases the Zulus exhibited their usual fanatical bravery in the assault.

A hiatus in fighting followed during April and May as Chelmsford awaited reinforcements from home. In June he opened a new offensive, marching on the Zulu capital, Ulundi, in the vicinity of which he confronted a force of 10,000 warriors with his own 4,200 British and Cape colonial troops and 1,000 native levies. His men deployed in a large hollow square, with cavalry sheltered inside, Chelmsford was assailed several times by the Zulus, who in each wave lost heavily to the concentrated rifle and machine gun fire of their technologically superior opponents. With the Zulus checked, the cavalry then emerged from the square and put the Zulus to rout. The war was effectively over, the fugitive Cetewayo was eventually captured, and his kingdom annexed to Natal. *See also* Boer Wars.

FURTHER READING: Barthorp, Michael. *The Zulu War: Isandhlwana to Ulundi.* London: Weidenfeld & Nicolson, 2002; Castle, Ian. *Zulu War, 1879.* Westport, CT: Greenwood

Publishing, 2005; David, Saul. *Zulu: The Heroism and Tragedy of the Zulu War of 1879*. New York: Viking Press, 2004; Knight, Ian. *Brave Men's Blood: The Epic of the Zulu War, 1879*. London: Greenhill Books, 1990; Morris, Donald R. *The Washing of the Spears: The Rise and Fall of the Great Zulu Nation*. New York: Simon and Schuster, 1965.

GREGORY FREMONT-BARNES

PRIMARY DOCUMENTS

1. Prime Minister William Pitt Replies to Critics of His War Policy (February 17, 1806)

Challenged in Parliament by the Whig MP George Tierney to explain the policy of his government in joining the war against France, British Prime Minister William Pitt the Younger (1759–1806) replied with an eloquent sarcasm. Pitt explained that British national security alone dictated policy, but he also revealed his utter contempt for both the French Revolution and "its child and champion," Napoleon Bonaparte.

The hon. Gentleman defies me to state, in one sentence, what is the object of the war. In one word, I tell him that it is security—security against a danger, the greatest that ever threatened the world—security against a danger which never existed in any past period of society. This country alone, of all the nations of Europe, presented barriers the best fitted to resist its progress. We alone recognized the necessity of open war, as well with the principles, as the practice of the French revolution. We saw that it was to be resisted no less by arms abroad, than by caution at home; that we were to look for protection no less to the courage of our forces than to the wisdom of our councils; no less to military effort than to legislative enactment. At the moment when those, who now admit the dangers of Jacobinism while they contend that it is extinct, used to palliate this atrocity, this House wisely saw that it was necessary to erect a double safeguard against a danger that wrought no less by undisguised hostility than by secret machination. But how long is it that the hon. Gentlemen and his friends have discovered that the dangers of Jacobinism have ceased to exist? How long is it that they found that the cause of the French revolution is not the cause of liberty? How or where did the hon. gentleman discover that the Jacobinism of Robespierre, of Barrère, of the triumvirate, of the five directors, has all disappeared, because it has all been centered in one man who was reared and nursed in its bosom, whose celebrity was gained under its auspices, who was at once *the child and the champion* of all its atrocities? Our security in negotiation is to be this Buonoparté, who is now the sole organ of all that was formerly dangerous and pestiferous in the revolution. . . .

I trust this country is ready to exert its efforts to avail ourselves of the assistance of our allies to obtain real security, and to attain solid peace. It is true, that in this contest different opinions may exist as to the means by which the danger is to be resisted. The emperor of Russia may approve of one course, the emperor of Germany another. But is it not strange that the hon. gentlemen should be so displeased that we are desirous of the cooperation of the emperor of Germany, who has no gone so far in his declarations on the subject of the war as the emperor of Russia? Is it a ground of objection with the hon. Gentleman, that we should avail ourselves of the assistance of those who do not declare themselves in favor of that object which he professes himself particularly to disapprove? Without changing our objects, may we not avail ourselves of the aid of other powers, though the motives of the cooperation may not be those which dictate our own exertions? Admitting that the emperor of Germany has no other view but to regain possession of the Netherlands, to drive the enemy back to the Rhine, to recover the fortresses he was forced to abandon, are these objects which have no connection with British safety? . . .

The hon. Gentleman said that the war could not be just, because it was carried on for the restoration of the house of Bourbon; and that it could not be necessary, because we had refused to negotiate for peace when an opportunity was offered us. As to the first proposition, he has assumed the foundation of the argument, and has left no ground for controverting it, or for explanation, because he says that any attempt at explanation upon this subject is the mere ambiguous language of *ifs* and *buts* and of special pleading. Now, Sir, I never had much liking to special pleading; and if ever I had any, it is by this time almost entirely gone. He has, besides, so abridged me of the use of particles, that though I am not particularly attached to the sound of an *if* or a *but*, I would be much obliged to him of he would give me some others to supply in their places.

Is this, however, a light matter, that it should be treated in so light a matter? The restoration of the French monarchy, I consider as a most desirable object, because I think that it would afford the best security to this country and to Europe. *But* this object may not be attainable; and if not attainable we must be satisfied with the best security we can find independent of it. Peace is most desirable to this country, *but* negotiation may be attended with greater evils than could be counterbalanced by any benefits which would result from it. And *if* this be found to be the case; *if* it afford no prospect of security; *if* it threaten all the evils which we have been struggling to avert; *if* the prosecution of the war afford the prospect of attaining complete security; and *if* it may be prosecuted with increasing commerce, with increasing means, and with increasing prosperity, except what may result from the visitations of the seasons; then, I say, that it is prudent in us not to negotiate at the present moment. These are my *buts* and my *ifs*. It is my plea, and on no other do I wish to be tried, by God and country.

Source: See Hans J. Morgenthau and Kenneth W, Thompson, eds. *Principles and Problems of International Politics* (New York: Alfred A. Knopf, 1950), pp. 349–351.

2. French Foreign Minister Talleyrand Criticizes Napoleon's War Policy (1807)

In his memoirs, Charles Maurice de Talleyrand (1754–1838), foreign minister to Napoleon Bonaparte from 1799 to 1807, noted how Napoleon's invasion of Spain and the ensuing Peninsular War marked the beginning of his ultimate defeat eight years later.

If ever the success of an enterprise should have appeared infallible, it was assuredly an enterprise in which reason had combined everything in such a manner as to leave nothing to be done by force of arms. It must have seemed impossible that Spain, invaded before she could possibly expect it, deprived of her government and of a portion of her strongholds, with a regular army mediocre in number, and more mediocre in quality, without harmony between her provinces, and almost without the means of establishing any, could think a moment of offering resistance, or of attempting to do so except for her ruin. However, those who knew Spain and the Spaniards judged otherwise, and were not deceived. They predicted that Spanish pride would calculate neither ultimate result nor present dangers, but would find in indignation and despair, a vigor and resource continually renewed.

Napoleon, in menacing England with an invasion, had forced her to create an army of considerable strength, and thus, without foreseeing it, had prepared help for the Peninsula. Seventeen thousand English, and some thousand Portuguese, made the French evacuate Portugal; the latter re-entered momentarily, but were unable to establish a firm footing there. The Portuguese soon had a numerous army, brave and well-disciplined, and, with the English, developed into the auxiliaries and the support of the resistance which had burst forth simultaneously over all parts of Spain, and which could be entirely suppressed only by immense armies, which it was impossible to maintain in that country, because it was impossible to nourish them. The title "invincible" that the continual victories over regular armies had attached to the name of Napoleon became contestable, and it was from Spain that Europe learned that he could be conquered, and how it could be done. The resistance of the Spaniards, in setting a precedent prepared that made later by the Russians, and led to the fall of the man who had promised himself the domination of the world. Thus was verified what Montesquieu had said of the projects of a universal monarchy: *that they could not fail in a single point without failing everywhere.*

At the first indications they had in France of the projects of Napoleon in Spain, a few persons said: "This man is undertaking a thing which, if it fail, will ruin him; and if it succeed will ruin Europe." It has failed enough to ruin him, and perhaps it has succeeded sufficiently to ruin Europe.

Source: The Duc de Broglie, Ed. *Memoirs of the Prince de Talleyrand.* 5 Vols. Trans. Raphaël Ledos de Beaufort (New York: G. P. Putnam's, 1891), I, pp. 291–292.

3. Johann Gottlieb Fichte Calls Upon Germans to Redeem Their Nation (1808)

The German philosopher Johann Gottlieb Fichte (1762–1814) delivered 14 Addresses to the German Nation, which denounced Napoleonic dominion over Europe. In the final address, Fichte called on his countrymen to redeem the honor of their ancestors by self-sacrifice in the cause of the survival of the German nation.

To all you, whatever position you may occupy in society, these addresses solemnly appeal; let every one of you who can think, think first of all about the subject here suggested, and let each do for what lies nearest to him individually in the position he occupies.

Your forefathers unite themselves with these addresses, and make a solemn appeal to you. Think that in my voice there are mingled the voices of your ancestors of the hoary past, who with their own bodies stemmed the onrush of Roman world dominion, who with their blood won the independence of those mountains, plains, and rivers which under you have fallen prey to the foreigner. They call to you: "Act for us; let the memory of us which you hand on to posterity be just as honorable and without reproach as it was when it came before you, when you took pride in it and in your descent from us. Until now, the resistance we made has been regarded as great and wise and noble; we seemed the consecrated and the inspired in the divine world purpose. If our race dies out with you, our honor will be turned to shame and our wisdom to foolishness. For if, indeed, the German stock is to be swallowed up in Roman civilization, it were better that it had fallen before the Rome of old than before a Rome of today. The former we resisted and conquered; by the latter you have been ground to dust. Seeing that it is so, you shall now not conquer them with temporal weapons; your spirit alone shall rise up against them and stand erect. To you has fallen the greater destiny, to found the empire of the spirit and of reason, and completely to annihilate the rule of brute physical force in the world. If you do this, then you are worthy of descent from us."

Then, too, there mingle with these the voices the spirits of your more recent forefathers, those who fell in the holy war for the freedom of belief and of religion. "Save our honor too," they cry to you. "To us it was not entirely clear what we fought for; besides the lawful resolve not to let ourselves be dictated to by external force in matters of conscience, there was another and a higher spirit driving us. To you it is revealed, this spirit, if you have the power of vision in the spiritual world; it beholds you with eyes clear and sublime. The varied and confused mixture of sensuous and spiritual motives that has hitherto ruled the world shall be displaced, and spirit alone, pure and freed from all sensuous motives, shall take the helm of human affairs. It was in order that this spirit might have freedom to develop and grow to independent existence—it was for this that we poured forth our blood. It is for you to justify and give meaning to our sacrifice, by setting this spirit to fulfill its purpose and rule the world. If this does not come about as the final goal to which the whole previous development of our nation has been tending, then the battles we fought will turn out to be a vain and fleeting farce, and the freedom of conscience and of spirit that we won is a vain word, if from now on spirit and conscience are to be no more."

Source: See Johann Gottlieb Fichte, *Adresses to the German Nation.* Trans. R. F. Jones and G. H. Turnbull. Ed. George Armstron Kelly (New York: Harper Torchbooks, 1968), pp. 225–226.

4. Osip P. Kozodavlev Seeks Advice on Russia's North American Colonies (1812)

In an 1812 letter to the minister of commerce on foreign affairs, Russian Minister of Internal Affairs Osip P. Kozodavlev (1754–1819) advised caution in dealing with the commercial precociousness of the young republic of the United States of America.

Gracious Sir, Count Nikolai Petrovich,

Your Excellency is undoubtedly aware of the present situation regarding the affairs of the Russian American Company and its colonies. The settlements which the North Americans are planning to establish at the mouth of the Columbia River threaten to put an end to the Company's enterprises, and the [Russian] colonies are at hazard because these same Americans have supplied the Indians with firearms and have instructed them in their use.

Although Your Excellency has informed the Main Administration of the Russian American Company of the proposal of the New York-based company of [Adrian] Bentzon, [to halt the sale of firearms to natives and to export furs to Russia], the Company finds this proposal inimical to its business affairs and feels it should not be adopted. It hopes it will have support from the gracious patronage of His Imperial Majesty.

Before any decisive action is taken concerning this, I feel obliged to submit my thoughts, Gracious Sir, based only on general observations. I believe that any means which uses force or firearms to deflect the attempts of the North Americans, even though such attempts would undoubtedly be successful, would not be appropriate in this case. I firmly believe that any action which would breach government relations for the benefit of a private company would be ill-conceived. Thus I believe it would be better to utilize the efforts of our Chargé d'Affaires in the United States to end the ventures of the Americans [detrimental to the Interests of the Russian American Company]. If all arguments and importunities on our part are ineffectual in persuading the Americans to do this, then Bentzon's proposal, especially with some restrictions, would be a most plausible means, because it would establish a balance in the fur trade and raise a barrier to monopoly, in case the Russian American Company had it in mind to establish a monopoly there. By conducting a large part of its fur trade with Kiakhta, the Company would lose much less profit than by permitting settlement on the Columbia River. In submitting this opinion for Your Excellency's attention, I find that I must turn your thoughts away from important Imperial concerns, and I most humbly request, my Gracious Sir, that you briefly review these circumstances. Because of your long administrative experience and skill in handling foreign affairs, you are much more familiar with the procedures. Kindly honor me with your gracious advice, which will guide me in this matter.

Source: See *The Russian American Colonies: A Documentary Record, 1798–1867.* Eds. and Trans. Basil Dmytryshyn, E.A.P. Crownhart-Vaughan, Thomas Vaughan (Portland: Oregon Historical Press, 1989), pp. 202–203.

5. President James Monroe Proclaims His Doctrine (December 2, 1823)

In his seventh annual message to the U.S. Congress, President James Monroe (1758–1831) delivered a warning drafted by Secretary of State John Quincy Adams against any and all European interference in the Western Hemisphere.

At the proposal of the Russian Imperial Government, made through the minister of the Emperor residing here, a full power and instructions have been transmitted to the minister of the United States at St. Petersburg to arrange by amicable negotiation the respective rights and interests of the two nations on the northwest coast of this continent. A similar proposal has been made by His Imperial Majesty to the Government of Great Britain, which has likewise been acceded to. The Government of the United States has been desirous by this friendly proceeding of manifesting the great value which they have invariably attached to the friendship of the Emperor and their solicitude to cultivate the best understanding with his Government. In the discussions to which this interest has given rise and in the arrangements by which they may terminate the occasion has been judged proper for asserting, as a principle in which the rights and interests of the United States are involved, that the American continents, by the free and independent condition which they have assumed and maintain, are henceforth not to be considered as subjects for future colonization by any European powers . . .

It was stated at the commencement of the last session that a great effort was then making in Spain and Portugal to improve the condition of the people of those countries, and that it appeared to be conducted with extraordinary moderation. It need scarcely be remarked that the results have been so far very different from what was then anticipated. Of events in that quarter of the globe, with which we have so much intercourse and from which we derive our origin, we have always been anxious and interested spectators. The citizens of the United States cherish sentiments the most friendly in favor of the liberty and happiness of their fellow-men on that side of the Atlantic. In the wars of the European powers in matters relating to themselves we have never taken any part, nor does it comport with our policy to do so. It is only when our rights are invaded or seriously menaced that we resent injuries or make preparation for our defense. With the movements in this hemisphere we are of necessity more immediately connected, and by causes which must be obvious to all enlightened and impartial observers. The political system of the allied powers is essentially different in this respect from that of America. This difference proceeds from that which exists in their respective Governments; and to the defense of our own, which has been achieved by the loss of so much blood and treasure, and matured by the wisdom of their most enlightened citizens, and under which we have enjoyed unexampled felicity, this whole nation is devoted. We owe it, therefore, to candor and to the amicable relations existing between the United States and those powers to declare that we should consider any attempt on their part to extend their system to any portion of this hemisphere as dangerous to our peace and safety. With the existing colonies or dependencies of any European power we have not interfered and shall not interfere. But with the Governments who have declared their independence and maintain it, and whose independence we have, on great consideration and on just principles, acknowledged, we could not view any interposition for the purpose of oppressing them, or controlling in any other manner their destiny, by any European power in any other light than as the manifestation of an unfriendly disposition toward the United States. In the war between those new Governments and Spain we declared our neutrality at the time of their recognition, and to this we have adhered, and shall continue to adhere, provided no change shall occur which, in the judgment of the competent authorities of this Government, shall make a corresponding change on the part of the United States indispensable to their security.

The late events in Spain and Portugal show that Europe is still unsettled. Of this important fact no stronger proof can be adduced than that the allied powers should have thought it proper, on any principle satisfactory to themselves, to have interposed by force in the internal concerns of Spain. To what extent such interposition may be carried, on the same principle, is a question in which all independent powers whose governments differ from theirs are interested, even those most remote, and surely none of them more so than the United States. Our policy in regard to Europe, which was adopted at an early stage of the wars which have so long agitated that quarter of the globe, nevertheless remains the same, which is, not to interfere in the internal concerns of any of its powers; to consider the government de facto as the legitimate government for us; to cultivate friendly relations with it, and to preserve those relations by a frank, firm, and manly policy, meeting in all instances the just claims of every power, submitting to injuries from none. But in regard to those continents circumstances are eminently and conspicuously different.

It is impossible that the allied powers should extend their political system to any portion of either continent without endangering our peace and happiness; nor can anyone believe that our southern brethren, if left to themselves, would adopt it of their own accord. It is equally impossible, therefore, that we should behold such interposition in any form with indifference. If we look to the comparative strength and resources of Spain and those new Governments, and their distance from each other, it must be obvious that she can never subdue them. It is still the true policy of the United States to leave the parties to themselves, in hope that other powers will pursue the same course.

Source: See *Documents of American History.* Ed. Henry Steele Commager (New York: Appleton-Century-Crofts, Inc., 1949), pp. 235–237.

6. Carl von Clausewitz Assesses the Military Legacy of Napoleon (1832)

In his classic military treatise *On War*, published after his death, Carl von Clausewitz (1780–1831)—soldier, military reformer, and writer—summed up the consequences of Europe's response to Napoleon Bonaparte's challenge.

Thus matters stood when the French Revolution broke out; Austria and Prussia tried their diplomatic Art of War; this very soon proved insufficient. Whilst, according to the usual way of seeing things, all hopes were placed on a very limited military force in 1793, such a force as no one had any conception of made its appearance. War had again suddenly become an affair of the people, and that of a people numbering in the thirty millions, every one of whom regarded himself as a citizen of the State. Without entering here into the details of the circumstances with which this great phenomenon was attended, we shall confine ourselves to the results which interest us at present. By this participation of the people in the War instead of a Cabinet and an Army, a whole nation with its natural weight came into the scale. Henceforward, the means available—the efforts which might be called forth—had no longer any definite limits; the energy with which the War itself might be conducted had no longer any counterpoise, and consequently the danger for the adversary had risen to the extreme.

If the whole of the Revolution passed over without all this making itself felt in its full force and becoming quite evident, if the Generals of the Revolution did not persistently press on to the final extreme, and did not overthrow the monarchies in Europe; if the German Armies now and again had the opportunity of resisting with success, and checking for a time the torrent of victory—the cause lay in reality in that technical incompleteness with which the French had to contend, which showed itself first amongst the common soldiers, then in the Generals, lastly, at the time of the Directory, in the Government itself.

After all this was perfected by the hand of Buonaparte, this military power, based on the strength of the whole nation, marched over Europe, smashing everything in pieces so surely and certainly, that where it only encountered the old-fashioned Armies the result was not doubtful for a moment. A reaction, however, awoke in due time. In Spain, the War became of itself an affair of the people. In Austria, in the year 1809, the Government commenced extraordinary efforts, by means of Reserves and *Landwehr,* which were nearer to the true object, and far surpassed in degree what this State had hitherto conceived possible. In Russia, in 1812, the example of Spain and Austria was taken as a pattern, the enormous dimensions of that Empire on the one hand allowed the preparations, although too long deferred, still to produce effect; and, on the other hand, intensified the effect produced. The result was brilliant. In Germany, Prussia rose up first, made the War a National Cause, and without either money or credit and with a population reduced one-half, took the field with an Army twice as strong as that of 1806. The rest of Germany followed the example of Prussia sooner or later, and Austria, although less energetic than in 1809, still came forth with more than its usual strength. Thus it was that Germany and Russia, in the years 1813 and 1814, including all who took an active part in, or were absorbed in these campaigns, appeared against France with about a million of men. [. . .]

Thus, therefore, the element of War, freed from all conventional restrictions, broke loose, with all its natural force. The cause was the participation of the people in this great *affair of State,* and this participation arose partly from the effects of the French Revolution on the internal affairs of countries, partly from the threatening attitude of the French towards all Nations.

Now, whether this will be the case always in the future, whether all Wars hereafter in Europe will be carried on with the whole power of the States, and, consequently, will only take place on account of great interests closely affecting the people, or whether a separation of the interests of the Government from those of the people will again gradually arise, would be a difficult point to settle; least of all shall we take it upon ourselves to settle it. But every one will agree with us, that bounds, which to a certain extent existed only in unconsciousness of what is possible, when once thrown down, are not easily built up again; and that, at least, whenever great interests are in dispute, mutual hostility will discharge itself in the same manner as it has done in our times.

Source: See Carl von Clausewitz, *On War.* Trans. J. J. Graham (Harmondsworth: Penguin, 1982), pp. 384–387.

7. Viscount Palmerston Counsels Diplomatic Pragmatism in British Foreign Policy (1835)

As foreign secretary in a Whig government, Henry John Temple, Lord Palmerston (1784–1865), applied liberal principles to British diplomacy. Done for British Prime Minister, Lord Melbourne, the following assessment of a report from Undersecretary of State William Fox-Strangways on a conversation with Count Metternich demonstrates Palmerston's pragmatic sense of Britain's strategic interests.

I dare say this is a pretty correct summary of Metternich's conversations with Strangways; but after all what does it amount to? And what foundation does it afford for any system of European policy to be built upon the basis of an Austrian alliance?

There are indeed abundant declarations of a desire to be the most intimate ally of England: and of a conviction that an alliance with England is the best and most useful for Austria. But when Metternich comes to explain the nature of the alliance which he contemplates, it turns out to be one, which is impracticable for us; and when we inquire what advantages we should derive from it, we are at a loss to discover any whatever.

He begins by describing France as the natural enemy both of Austria and England; and it is manifest that his notion of an alliance with England presupposed an estrangement of both Austria and England from France. Now its is needless to point that to come to such a new system we must abandon all the objects we have been striving for during the last five years, undo all that we have been doing, and, as we should at once become Tories abroad, we ought to begin by becoming Tories at home; for such a change of system would infallibly lose much support of that party, by whom we are at present upheld. Metternich, in short, sighs for a return of the state of things which existed during the war against Buonaparte, when all of Europe was united against France; and when, by the by; if the fate of Europe had depended upon the vigor of Austrian councils, and the enterprise of Austrian armies, we never should have had a Treaty of Paris. But he would wish all Europe to be leagued now against France in diplomatic and moral hostility, as it was at that period in active warfare. But here again he takes for granted, that, which to say no more of it, is in the highest degree doubtful, namely that if England was to abandon France in order to take to Austria, France would find no other ally to take the place of England; and what I should like to know, should we gain, if while we exchanged active, powerful, and neighboring France for sluggish and temporizing and distant Austria, Russia were to make the converse of our exchange and instead of being united with Austria, who, though subservient, acts as a clog, she were to strike up an intimacy with France, and gain a more active, ambitious and a *naval* ally? It does not appear to me that such a change of partners would increase our chance of winning the rubber.

For what are the advantages he holds out to us as likely to result from this entire change in our system of policy? First of all, that we are to shape our course by his, and to make temporizing not even a means but an end, and with respect to whom? Why, with respect to Russia, whom he admits to be a constantly increasing Power? Now nothing can be clearer than that if you pursue a system of temporizing, which in other words means perpetually giving way, while your adversary pursues a system of perpetual encroachment, the only problem to be solved, *how soon* you will be received. Metternich's principle is to submit to everything that is done, thinking that he has got out of all embarrassment by saying "c'est un fait accompli." This is an excellent doctrine for one's adversary to hold, but a very inconvenient maxim to serve as a rule of conduct for a friend and ally in difficult times.

Then again what flimsy and fallacious assumptions he puts forward, as grounds on which to build a system of measures upon great national interests! The personal character of Nicholas, for instance, is represented by him, as a sufficient guarantee of the *conservative* policy of Russia. Now we happen also to know something of the personal character of Nicholas: and I confess that I am disposed to draw from that personal character conclusions exactly the reverse of those which Metternich seems to have formed. I take Nicholas to be ambitious, bent upon great schemes, determined to make extensive additions to his dominions; and laboring to push his political ascendancy far beyond the range of his Ukases, animated by the same hate to England which was felt by Napoleon, and for the same reasons, namely that we are the friends of national independence, and the enemies of conquerors. We are an obstacle in his path; he would cajole us if he could; he would crush us if he were able; not being equal to either; he only hates us.

The conclusion which seems to follow from all this, that we should not quit or loosen our connection with France, but should encourage the friendly disposition of Austria towards us, as far as we can; without departing from our own course in order to please her; and to express on every favorable occasion a strong wish to see her friendly dispositions evinced by acts as expressed in conversations and dispatches.

Source: See Sir Charles Webster, *The Foreign Policy of Palmerston, 1830–1841.* 2 Vols. (London: G. Bell & Sons, 1951), II, pp. 841–843.

8. Marquis de Custine Indicts Russian Absolutism (1839)

Astolphe Louis Lénor, Marquis de Custine (1790–1857), published his Letters from Russia in 1839; in the following excerpt, he is unsparing in his attack on the tsar and Russian society.

You can believe what I say about the effects of absolute government, for when I came to study this country, it was in the hope of finding here a cure for the ills that threaten our own. If you find that I judge Russia too harshly, you must blame the involuntary impressions that I receive here daily from peoples and things, impressions that any friend of mankind would receive in my place were he to make the same effort as I do to look beyond what he is shown.

Immense as it is, this Empire is simply a prison to which the Tsar holds the key, and in this state, which lives only on its conquests, nothing in peacetime equals the misfortune of his subjects, except the misfortune of their ruler. A jailer's life has always seemed to me so nearly similar to that of the prisoner that I am filled with astonishment at the imaginary prestige that makes one of these two men think himself infinitely less to be pitied than the other.

Mankind here experiences neither the true social pleasures of a cultivated mind, nor the absolute and brutal freedom of the savage or the barbarian. I can see no compensation for the misfortune of being born under this regime, other than the illusions of pride and hope of domination: I come back to this passion every time that I try to analyze the spiritual life of the inhabitants of Russia. The Russian thinks and lives as a soldier—a conquering soldier.

A true soldier, whatever his country, can barely be called a citizen, and less so here than anywhere else. He is a prisoner sentenced to life to guard prisoners.

Note that in Russia the world 'prison' signifies something more than it does elsewhere. One trembles to think of all the subterranean cruelties concealed from our pity by the discipline of silence, in a country where every man learns at birth to be discreet. Coming here, you learn to hate reserve: all this caution reveals a secret tyranny, the ever-present image of which raised before me. Every facial movement, every sign of reticence, every inflection of voice teaches me the dangers of trust and spontaneity.

Even the mere appearance of the houses calls my thoughts back to the miserable conditions of human life in this country [. . .] As I endure the dampness of my room, I think of the poor devils exposed to the dampness of the submarine dungeons at Kronstadt, or the Petersburg fortress and many other political tombs, the very names of which are unknown to me. The haggard look of the soldiers whom I see passing in the street suggests the plunder and corruption of their army quartermasters. [. . .] With every step I take here, I see rising before me the specter of Siberia, and I think of all that is implied in the name of that political desert, that abyss of miseries, that graveyard of the living, a world of mythical sorrow, a land populated by infamous criminals and sublime heroes, a colony without which this Empire would be as incomplete as a mansion without cellars.

Source: See Marquis de Custine, *Letters from Russia.* Translated and edited by Robin Buss (London: Penguin, 1991), pp. 106–107.

9. John L. O'Sullivan Proclaims America's Destiny (1839)

As the founding editor of the *United States Magazine & Democratic Review*, a magazine espousing the territorial expansion of the United States in the 1840s, John

O'Sullivan (1813–1895) coined the term "manifest destiny" as an article of faith of the American national mission. O'Sullivan initially broached the issue in the1839 article "The Great Nation of Futurity," wherein he connected the American role in the world to the very origin and nature of the republic.

The American people having derived their origin from many other nations, and the Declaration of National Independence being entirely based on the great principle of human equality, these facts demonstrate at once our disconnected position as regards any other nation; that we have, in reality, but little connection with the past history of any of them, and still less with all antiquity, its glories, or its crimes. On the contrary, our national birth was the beginning of a new history, the formation and progress of an untried political system, which separates us from the past and connects us with the future only; and so far as regards the entire development of the natural rights of man, in moral, political, and national life, we may confidently assume that our country is destined to be the great nation of futurity.

It is so destined, because the principle upon which a nation is organized fixes its destiny, and that of equality is perfect, is universal. It presides in all the operations of the physical world, and it is also the conscious law of the soul—the self-evident dictates of morality, which accurately defines the duty of man to man, and consequently man's rights as man. Besides, the truthful annals of any nation furnish abundant evidence, that its happiness, its greatness, its duration, were always proportionate to the democratic equality in its system of government . . .

What friend of human liberty, civilization, and refinement, can cast his view over the past history of the monarchies and aristocracies of antiquity, and not deplore that they ever existed? What philanthropist can contemplate the oppressions, the cruelties, and injustice inflicted by them on the masses of mankind, and not turn with moral horror from the retrospect? America is destined for better deeds. It is our unparalleled glory that we have no reminiscences of battle fields, but in defense of humanity, of the oppressed of all nations, of the rights of conscience, the rights of personal enfranchisement. Our annals describe no scenes of horrid carnage, where men were led on by hundreds of thousands to slay one another, dupes and victims to emperors, kings, nobles, demons in the human form called heroes. We have had patriots to defend our homes, our liberties, but no aspirants to crowns or thrones; nor have the American people ever suffered themselves to be led on by wicked ambition to depopulate the land, to spread desolation far and wide, that a human being might be placed on a seat of supremacy.

We have no interest in the scenes of antiquity, only as lessons of avoidance of nearly all their examples. The expansive future is our arena, and for our history. We are entering on its untrodden space, with the truths of God in our minds, beneficent objects in our hearts, and with a clear conscience unsullied by the past. We are the nation of human progress, and who will, what can, set limits to our onward march? Providence is with us, and no earthly power can. We point to the everlasting truth on the first page of our national declaration, and we proclaim to the millions of other lands, that "the gates of hell"—the powers of aristocracy and monarchy—"shall not prevail against it." The far-reaching, the boundless future will be the era of American greatness. In its magnificent domain of space and time, the nation of many nations is destined to manifest to mankind the excellence of divine principles; to establish on earth the noblest temple ever dedicated to the worship of the Most High—the Sacred and the True. Its floor shall be a hemisphere—its roof the firmament of the star-studded heavens, and its congregation a Union of many Republics, comprising hundreds of happy millions, calling, owning no man master, but governed by God's natural and moral law of equality, the law of brotherhood—of "peace and good will amongst men." . . .

Yes, we are the nation of progress, of individual freedom, of universal enfranchisement. Equality of rights is the cynosure of our union of States, the grand exemplar of the correlative equality of individuals; and while truth sheds its effulgence, we cannot retrograde, without dissolving the one and subverting the other. We must onward to the fulfillment of our mission—to the entire development of the principle of our organization—freedom of conscience, freedom of person, freedom of trade and business pursuits, universality of freedom and equality. This is our high destiny, and in nature's eternal, inevitable decree of cause and effect we must accomplish it. All this will be our future history, to establish on earth the moral dignity and salvation of man—the immutable truth and beneficence of God. For this blessed mission to the nations of the world, which are shut out from the life-giving light of truth, has America been chosen; and her high example shall smite unto death the tyranny of kings, hierarchs, and oligarchs, and carry the glad tidings of peace and good will where myriads now endure an existence scarcely more enviable than that of beasts of the field. Who, then, can doubt that our country is destined to be *the great nation* of futurity?

Source: See Dennis Merrill and Thomas G. Paterson, eds., *Major Problems in American Foreign Relations.* 2 Vols. (Boston: Houghton Mifflin, 2000), I, p. 231.

10. Lady Florentia Sale Describes the Retreat from Kabul (1842)

Lady Florentia Sale (1790–1853) was in Kabul during the First Afghan War. She took part in the British retreat from the city during which soldiers and civilians alike came under attack. In this excerpt from her journal, she describes the final stage of the disaster.

January 13: From Soorkhab the remnant of the column moved towards Gundamuk: but as the day dawned the enemy's numbers increased; and unfortunately daylight soon exposed to them how very few fighting men the columns contained. The force now consisted of twenty officers, of whom Major Griffiths was the senior, fifty men of the 44th, six of the horse artillery, and four or five Sipahees. Amongst the whole there were but twenty muskets; 300 camp followers still continued with them.

Being now assailed by an increased force, they were compelled to quit the road, and take up a position on the road adjoining. Some of the Afghan horsemen being observed at short distance were beckoned to. On their approach there was cessation of firing; terms were proposed by Capt. Hay to allow the force to proceed without further hostilities to Jellalabad. These persons not being sufficiently influential to negotiate, Major Griffiths proceeded with them to a neighboring chief for that purpose: taking with him Mr. Blewitt, formerly a writer in Capt. Johnson's office, who understood Persian, that he might act as an interpreter.

Many Afghans ascended the hill where our troops awaited the issue of the conference; and exchanges of friendly words passed between both parties. This lasted upward of an hour; but hostilities were renewed by the Afghans who snatched the firearms of the men and officers. This they of course resisted; and drove them off the hill: but the majority of the enemy, who occupied the adjoining hills commanding our position, commenced a galling fire upon us. Several times they attempted to dislodge our men from the hill, and were repulsed; until, our ammunition being expended, and our fighting men reduced to about thirty, the enemy made a rush, which in our weak state we were unable to cope with. They bore our men down knife in hand; and slaughtered all the party except Capt. Souter and seven or eight men of the 44th and artillery. This officer thinks that this unusual act of forbearance towards him originated in the strange dress he wore: his poshteen having opened during the last struggle exposed to view the color he had wrapped around his body; and they probably thought they had secured a valuable prize in some great bahdur, for whom a large ransom might be obtained.

Eighteen officers and about fifty men were killed at the final struggle at Gundamuk. Capt. Souter and the few remaining man (seven or eight) that were taken alive from the field, after a detention of a month in the adjoining villages, made over to Akbar Khan and sent to the fort of Buddeeabad in the Lughman valley, where they arrived on the 15th of February.

Source: See *A Journal of the First Afghan War.* Edited by Patrick Malloy (New York: Oxford University Press, 1969), pp. 125–126.

11. Richard Cobden Laments the Cost of British Rule in India (June 27, 1853)

In an 1853 House of Commons speech, free trade champion Richard Cobden (1804–1865) used the outbreak of the Second Anglo-Burmese War (1852) as an occasion to criticize the costs of imperial rule in India generally and the activities of the East India Company in particular.

I will now call the attention of the House to a point of considerable importance, which was strikingly illustrated by the facts attending the commencement of the Burmese war in which we are now engaged. It is another fact, which is a proof of the precipitancy with which the measure has been brought forward, and I believe it has not been noticed before in the course of the debate. I wish to refer to the state of the relations between the vessels of war in the Indian waters and the Government of India; and, in illustration of what I mean, I beg leave to state what has taken place on the breaking out of this war. In the month of July, 1851, a small British vessel arrived at Rangoon, the captain of which was charged with throwing a pilot overboard, and robbing him of 500 rupees. The case was brought before the Governor of Rangoon; and, after undergoing a great many hardships, the captain was mulcted in the amount of rupees.

A month after this, another English vessel arrived, having on board two coolies from the Mauritius, who secreted themselves in the vessel when she left. On their arrival, they said that the captain had murdered one of the crew during the voyage. The captain was tried for this, and he was mulcted also. An application was made to the Governor-General for redress, and a demand was made on the Burmese authorities to the amount of 1,900£ for money extorted, for demurrage of the vessels, and other injuries inflicted. The Governor-General ordered an investigation of the case, and he awarded 920l£ as sufficient. At this time there was lying in the Hooghly a vessel of war commanded by Commodore Lambert, and the Governor-General thought that the presence of this vessel afforded a good opportunity for obtaining redress.

The House should understand that there was no other case to be redressed than these two; that the parties in them were British subjects, and that the Governor of Rangoon did not adjudicate between Burmese subjects and British subjects. Commodore Lambert was furnished with very precise instructions indeed. He was first to make inquiry as to the validity of the original claim, and, if he found that it was well founded, he was to apply to the Governor of Rangoon for redress; and, in case of a refusal on his part, he was furnished with a letter from the Governor-General to the King of Ava, to be sent up by him to the capital; and he was then to proceed to the Persian Gulf, for which place he was under orders. He was told not to commit any act of hostility, if redress was refused, till he had heard again from the Governor-General. These were very proper and precise instructions. On the arrival of the Commodore at Rangoon, he was met by boats filled with British subjects, who complained of the conduct of the Governor of Rangoon. If the House wishes for an amusing description of the British subjects of Rangoon, I would recommend them to read Lord Ellenborough's sketch of them in a speech which he delivered in the House of Lords. Rangoon is, it appears, the Alsatia of Asia, and is filled by all the abandoned characters whom the other parts of India are too hot to hold. Commodore Lambert received the complaints of all these people; and he sent off the letter to the King of Ava at once, which he was instructed to send only in case redress was refused; and he made no inquiry with respect to the original cause of the dispute, and the validity of the claims put forward. He also sent a letter from himself to the Prime Minister of the King of Ava, and demanded an answer in thirty-five days. The post took from ten to twelve days to go to Ava, and at the end of twenty-six days an answer came back from the King to the Governor-General, and to Commodore Lambert from the Prime Minister.

It was announced that the Governor of Rangoon was dismissed, and that a new Governor was appointed, who would be prepared to look into the matter in dispute, and adjust it. Commodore Lambert sent off the King of Ava's letter to the Governor-General, with one from himself, stating that he had no doubt the King of Ava and his Government meant to deal fairly by them. Meantime, the new Governor of Rangoon came down in great state, and Commodore Lambert sent three officers on shore with a letter to him. The letter was sent at twelve o'clock in the day, and when they arrived at the house they were refused admittance, on the plea that the Governor was asleep. It was specifically stated that the officers were kept waiting a quarter of an hour in the sun. At the end of that quarter of an hour they returned to the ship, and, without waiting a minute longer, Commodore Lambert, notwithstanding that he had himself declared that he had no doubt justice would be done, ordered the port to be blockaded, having first directed the British residents to come on board. During the night, he seized the only vessel belonging to the King of Ava, which he towed out to sea.

This brings me to the point to which I am desirous of calling the attention of the House. Lord Dalhousie had no power to give orders to Commodore Lambert in that station; he could merely request and solicit the co-operation of the commanders of the Queen's forces, just as we might solicit the co-operation of a friendly foreign Power. See what the effect of this system is. If Commodore Lambert had been sent out with orders from the First Lord of the Admiralty, he would not have dared to deviate from them in the slightest respect, much less to commence a war. Owing, however, to the anomalous system existing in India, Commodore Lambert felt at liberty to act on his own responsibility; and hence the Burmese war. Why has not this blot been hit upon by the framers of the present Bill? Can there be a stronger proof of the undue precipitancy with which the Government measure has been introduced than this—that it leaves the great defect which I have pointed out—a defect leading to results of immense gravity—uncured? The Government cannot plead ignorance; they cannot allege that their attention had not been directed to the matter. On the 25th of March, Lord Ellenborough referred to the subject in the House of Lords; and on that occasion Lord Broughton, who had just left office, stated that he had received an official communication from Lord Dalhousie relative to the anomalous character of the relations subsisting between the Governor-General and the Queen's commanders, and expressing a hope that the evil would be corrected in the forthcoming Charter Act. But there is nothing on this important subject in the present Bill; and is not this another ground for delay till we have obtained further information?

I have now to say a few words on the subject of the finances of India; and, in speaking on this subject, I cannot separate the finances of India from those of England. If the finances of the Indian Government receive any severe and irreparable check, will not the resources of England be called upon to meet the emergency, and to supply the deficiency? Three times during the present century the Court of Directors has called on the House of Commons to enable them to get rid of the difficulties which pressed upon them. And do you suppose, that if such a case were to occur again, that England would refuse her aid? Why, the point of honour, if there were no other reason, would compel us to do so. Do you not hear it said, that your Indian Empire is concerned in keeping the Russians out of Constantinople, which is, by the way, 6,000 miles distant from Calcutta; and if we are raising outworks at a distance of 6,000 miles, let no man say that the finances of England are not concerned in the financial condition of India. The hon. Member for Guildford (Mr. Mangles), referring to this subject on Friday night, spoke in a tone that rather surprised me; he taxed those who opposed the measure with a readiness to swallow anything, and twitted my hon. Friend (Mr. Bright) with saying that the debt of India, contracted since the last Charter Act, was 20,000,000£. The hon. Gentleman (Mr. Mangles) said it was only 9,000,000£. There has, he said, been 13,000,000£ increase of debt, but that there was 4,000,000£ of reserve in the Exchequer. I will quote the evidence of Mr. Melvill, who signed all the papers that have come before the Committee on this point. Mr. Melvill, being asked what the amount of the debt was, says:—'The amount of the debt is over 20,000,000£.' After this answer of Mr. Melvill, what becomes of the statement of the hon. Member for Guildford? But I must say that there is a very great difference in the opinions and statements of Indian authorities. The evidence of Mr. Prinsep was different from that of the hon. Gentleman (Mr. Mangles); that of the hon. Gentleman was different from the opinion of the hon. Member for Honiton (Sir J. Hogg); that of Mr. Melvill was different from all of them, and Mr. Melvill was sometimes of a different opinion from his own papers. I want to give you an opportunity of making up your minds on this subject, and of correcting the statements that come before you, for you are to judge of the financial results of your management of India. Now, if I could treat this question as many persons do; if I could believe that the East India Company is a reality; if I believed that they could transfer India to the management of some other body, and that England would be no more responsible; that we could have the trade of India, and be under no obligations in reference either to its good government or its future financial state, I should not be the person to come forward and seek a disturbance of that arrangement.

Other people may not share in my opinion; but I am under the impression that, so far as the future is concerned, we cannot leave a more perilous possession to our children than that which we shall leave them in the constantly-increasing territory of India. The English race can never become indigenous in India; we must govern it, if we govern it at all, by means of a succession of transient visits; and I do not think it is for the interest of the English people, any more than of the people of India, that we should govern permanently 100,000,000 people, 12,000 miles off. I see no benefit which can arise to the mass of the English people from their connection with India, except that which may arise from honest trade; I do not see how the millions of this country are to share in the patronage of India, or to derive any advantage from it, except through the medium of trade; and therefore, I say emphatically, that if you can show me that the East India Company is the reality which many persons suppose it to be, I shall not be the party to wish to withdraw their responsible trust and to place it again in the hands of a Minister of the British Crown. But when I see that this vast territory is now being governed under a fiction, that the Government is not a real one, but one which one of the most able and faithful servants of the Company has declared to be a sham, I say, "Do not let the people of this country delude themselves with the idea that they can escape the responsibility by putting the Government behind a screen."

I wish therefore to look this question fairly in the face; I wish to bring the people of this country face to face with the difficulties and dangers with which I think it is beset. Let it no longer be thought that a few gentlemen meeting in Leadenhall Street can screen the people of England from the responsibility with which they have invested themselves with regard to India. Since the granting of the last Charter, more territory has been gained by conquest than within any similar period before, and the acquisition of territory has been constantly accompanied with a proportionate increase of debt. We have annexed Sattara, and our own blue-books prove that it is governed at a loss; we have annexed Scinde, and our own books prove that it, too, is governed at a loss; we have annexed Pegu, and our own authorities said that this annexation also will involve a loss. All these losses must press on the more fertile provinces of Bengal, which are constantly being drained of their resources to make good the deficit. Let me not be told, by-and-by, that the annexation of Pegu and Burmah will be beneficial. What said Lord Dalhousie? He said in his despatch—and the declaration should not be forgotten—that he looked upon the annexation of Pegu as an evil second only to that of war itself; and if we should be obliged to annex

Burmah, then farewell to all prospect of amelioration in Indian affairs. Well, then, believing that if this fiction be destroyed—if this mystery be exterminated—the germ of a better state of things in reference to this question will begin to grow; and believing that as yet we are profoundly ignorant of what was wanted for India, I shall vote for the Amendment, that we should wait for two years; and I hope sincerely that the House will agree to it.

Source: Richard Cobden, *Speeches by Richard Cobden.* Eds. John and James E. Thorold Rogers Bright (London: T. Fisher Unwin, 1908) [Online] http://www.econlib.org/library/YPD Books/Cobden/cbdSSP1html

12. Yokoi Shōnan Advocates Japanese Naval Power (1860)

Yokoi Shōnan (1809–1869), a mid-ranking scholar-samurai of the late Tokugawa period in Japan, responded to the challenge of Western encroachment in Asia by making a series of policy recommendations to Matsudaira Shugaku, lord of Echizen, which include—in the following excerpt—a stressing of the importance of naval power to Japan's ability to compete among the Great Powers and "forestall indignities."

In discussing arms for the present day, we can continue using the traditional hand-to-hand fighting, or we can stress the fierce Western rifle columns. What are their respective advantages and disadvantages?

In the old days, either way would do for Japan at home, but today we cannot refuse contacts with the overseas countries that have greatly developed their navigation. In the defense of an island country like ours, a navy is of prime importance in strengthening out military. In Japan up to the present, nothing had been heard concerning regulations for a navy, so how could we know how to apply them? Navigation has progressed so much in the world today that we must start our discussion with the importance of the navy. Let us put aside for the time being the problem of Japan.

In Asia there is China, a great country facing the sea in the east. Early on, it developed a high material culture, and everything, including rice, wheat, millet and sorghum, has been plentiful for the livelihood of the people. In addition, there has been nothing lacking within its [China's) borders in regard to knowledge, skills, arts, goods of daily use, and entertainment. [But] from the imperial court on down to the masses of the common people, extravagant habits have come to prevail. Although China permits foreigners to come and carry on trade, it has no intention of going out to seek goods. Moreover, it does not know how to obtain knowledge from others. For this reason, its arms are weak, and it must suffer indignities from various countries.

Europe is different from China. Its territory touches Asia on the east and is surrounded by seas on three sides. It is located in the northwest part of the earth, and compared with Asia it is small and is lacking in many things. Hence it was inevitable it [Europe] should go out in quest of things. It was natural that its nations should develop navigation to carry on trade, to fight one another with warships, and to attempt establishing possessions with monopoly controls.

This year [1860] English and French forces attacked the Manchu empire, taking Tientsin and threatening the capital at Beijing. Russia is watching from the sidelines to take advantage of the stalemate and is like a tiger waiting to pounce on its prey. If Russia has designs of dominating China, then a great force must be mustered to prevent this. England must also be feared.

With the situation beyond the seas like this and growing worse all the time, how can Japan arouse its martial vigor when it alone basks in peace and comfort and drills its indolent troops as though it were child's play? Because there is no navy, a defense policy simply does not exist. . .

For several decades Russia had been requesting permission for trade in vain. England's requests also had been rejected. Therefore America laid out its plan long and carefully, and in 1853 its warships entered Uraga Bay, and bluffing with its armed might, it eventually unlocked our closed doors. Thereafter in succession, the Russians, English, and French came and instituted procedures for peaceful trade.

Japan has consequently learned some information about conditions beyond the seas. But we still cling to our antiquated views and depend on our skill in hand-to-hand fighting. Some believe that we can quickly learn to fire in rifle formations and thus avoid indignities. Indeed, our outmoded practices are pitiable.

Consider England: it prevents indignities being committed by foreigners, and it rules possessions. In 1848 there were 673 well-known English navy ships, of which 420 were operating. Steamboats are included in these figures. There were about 15,000 cannons, 29,500 sailors, 13,500 marines, and 900 officers. In wartime, France had 1,000 navy ships and 184,000 sailors. Today it has more than 700 steam naval vessels, 88,000 fighting men, and 240 armored warships. Compared with earlier times, it has twice as many fighting men. In 1856 it had more than 200,000 troops.

In our Bonroku era [1592–1595] during the Toyotomi campaign in Korea, Japan had 350,00 troops, not an inconsiderable figure when compared with England's. Moreover the circumstances of Japan and England are very much alike, and therefore our militarization should be patterned after that of England, with 420 naval vessels, 15,000 cannon, 29,500 sailors, 13,500 fighting men, and 900 officers in the navy. Military camps must be set up in the vicinity of our open port, and warships must be stationed there in preparation for emergencies. They can go to one another's assistance when circumstances require, and they should be adequate to forestall any indignities. England is situated in the northwest, and its land is not good. But with all the advantages of a maritime power, it has seized distant territories and today has become a great power.

Better yet, Japan lies in the central part of the earth, and we excel in the advantages of a sea environment. If the shogunate issued a new decree, aroused the characteristic vigor and bravery of the Japanese, and united the hearts of the entire nation with a firmly established military system based on clarified laws, not only would there be no need to fear foreign countries, but we could sail to various lands within a few years. And even if these lands should make armed attacks, we could, with our moral principles and courage, be looked up to for our benevolent ways.

Even though we need a navy, it cannot be built without an order from the shogunate. Nevertheless, if each province were to take action . . . we could first of all, take those from the samurai class who have the desire to become apprentices in navigation and, in accordance with their ability, give them a moderate salary so that they could take care of their daily needs. They should live near the sea. At first they could sail fishing vessels and catch fish or sail to foreign lands in merchant vessels Thus they would learn about the wind and waves while on the sea.

In addition, the shogunate should build two or three vessels of the cutter-schooner type . . . According to this plan, each vessel would engage in trade, whaling, or the like. If it makes a profit from the trade, it should be divided among the members of each ship. The original fund would again be put to use. With this experience in seeking profits according to man's normal impulses, impoverished samurai and others would greatly benefit. They could be trained in techniques while enjoying their work.

Furthermore, those with an interest could be taught the skills of sailing or astronomical observation. These can be learned in actual work in the field. The samurai who constantly go back and forth to foreign countries could broaden their knowledge through observation . . . Hence when the shogunate finally issues a new decree, they will most certainly be able to offer their services in the navy.

We have now discussed how navigation must be learned first and how this knowledge can eventually be put to naval use. But how can this [alone] be called strengthening the military (kyohei)? It is said that no military reform surpassed the Way of the warrior (bushido), which is to cultivate that spirit in actual practice.

Source: See William Theodore de Bary, Carol Gluck, and Arthur E. Tiedemann, eds., *Sources of Japanese Tradition.* 2 Vols. (New York: Columbia University Press, 2005), II, p. 645–647.

13. Prussian Chancellor Otto von Bismarck Issues His "iron and blood" Statement on the German Future (September 30, 1862)

In response to a resolution tabled by the liberal member Max von Forkenbeck, the newly appointed Chancellor of Prussia Otto von Bismarck (1815–1898) urged the lower house to vote for increases in military spending and warned its members ominously not to overestimate their constitutional powers.

He would like to go into the budget for 1862, though without making a prejudicial statement. An abuse of constitutional rights could be undertaken by any side; this would then lead to a reaction from the other side. The Crown, e.g., could dissolve [parliament] twelve times in a row, that would certainly be permitted according to the letter of the constitution, but it would be an abuse. It could just as easily reject cuts in the budget, immoderately; it would be hard to tell where to draw the line there; would it be at 6 million? at 16? or at 60?—There are members of the National Association [Nationalverein]—of this association that has achieved a reputation owing to the justness of its demands—highly esteemed members who have stated that all standing armies are superfluous. Yes, if only a public assembly had this view! Would not a government have to reject this?!—There was talk about the "sobriety" of the Prussian people. Yes, the great independence of the individual makes it difficult in Prussia to govern with the constitution (or to consolidate the constitution?); in France things are different, there this individual independence is lacking. A constitutional crisis would not be disgraceful, but honorable instead.

Furthermore, we are perhaps too "well-educated" to support a constitution; we are too critical; the ability to assess government measures and records of the public assembly is too common; in the country there are a lot of catiline characters who have a great interest in upheavals. This may sound paradoxical, but everything proves how hard constitutional life is in Prussia.

Furthermore, one is too sensitive about the government's mistakes; as if it were enough to say "this and that [cabinet] minister made mistakes,["] as if one wasn't adversely affected oneself. Public opinion changes, the press is not [the same as] public opinion; one knows how the press is written; members of parliament have a higher duty, to lead opinion, to stand above it. We are too hot-blooded, we have a preference for putting on armor that is too big for our small body; and now we're actually supposed to utilize it. Germany is not looking to Prussia's liberalism, but to its power; Bavaria, Württemberg, Baden may indulge liberalism, and for that reason no one will assign them Prussia's role; Prussia has to coalesce and concentrate its power for the opportune moment, which has already been missed several times; Prussia's borders according to the Vienna Treaties are not favorable for a healthy, vital state; it is not by speeches and majority resolutions that the great questions of the time are decided—that was the big mistake of 1848 and 1849—but by iron and blood. Last year's appropriation has been carried out; for whatever reasons, it is a matter of indifference; he (Bismarck is here referring to himself) is sincerely seeking the path of agreement: whether he finds it does not depend on him alone. It would have been better if one had not made a fait accompli on the part of the Chamber of Deputies.—If no budget comes about, then there is a *tabula rasa;* the constitution offers no way out, for then it is one interpretation against another interpretation; *summum ius, summa iniuria;* the letter killeth. He is pleased that the speaker's remark about the possibility of another resolution of the House on account of a possible bill allows for the prospect of agreement; he, too, is looking for this bridge; when it might be found is uncertain.—Bringing about a budget this year is hardly possible given the time; we are in exceptional circumstances; the principle of promptly presenting the budget is also recognized by the government; but it is said that this was already promised and not kept; [and] now [it's] "You can certainly trust us as honest people." He does not agree with the interpellation that it is unconstitutional to make expenditures [whose authorization had been] refused; for every interpretation, it is necessary to agree on the three factors.

Source: See Otto von Bismarck, *Reden, 1847–1869,* ed., Wilhelm Schüßler, vol. 10, Bismarck: *Die gesammelten Werke,* ed. Hermann von Petersdorff. (Berlin: Otto Stolberg, 1924–1935), pp. 139–140. Translation: Jeremiah Riemer.

14. British Prime Minister Benjamin Disraeli Champions the Defense of the British Empire (August 11, 1876)

In answer to charges from the opposition that his Conservative government was insensitive to atrocities committed by Ottoman troops against rebellious Christian subjects in Bulgaria, Disraeli answered, in the following excerpt, that Britain's policy was, and always ought to be, based on the maintenance of the Empire.

We are, it is true, allies of the Sultan of Turkey—so is Russia, so is Austria, so is France, and so are others. We are also their partners in a tripartite treaty, in which we not only generally, but singly guarantee with France and Austria the territorial integrity of Turkey. These are our engagements, and they are engagements that we endeavor to fulfill. And if these engagements, renovated and repeated only four years ago by the wisdom of Europe, are to be treated by the honorable and learned gentleman as idle wind chaff, and if we are told that our political duty is by force to expel the Turks to the other side of the Bosphorus, then politics cease to be an art, statesmanship becomes mere mockery, and instead of a House of Commons faithful to its traditions and which is always influenced, I have ever thought, by sounds principles of policy, whoever may be its leaders, we had better at once resolve ourselves into one of those revolutionary clubs which settle all political and social questions with the same ease as the honorable and learned gentleman.

Sir, we refused to join in the Berlin note because we were convinced that if we made that step we should very soon see a material interference with Turkey; and we were not of the opinion that by a system of material guarantees the great question which the honorable and learned gentlemen has averted to, would be solved either for the general welfare of the world or for the interests of England, which after all must be our sovereign care. The Government of the Porte was never for a moment misled by the arrival of the British fleet in Besika Bay. They were perfectly aware when that fleet came there that it was not to prop up any decaying or obsolete Government, nor did its presence there sanction any of those enormities which are the subjects of our painful discussion tonight. What may be the fate of the eastern part of Europe it would be arrogant for me to speculate upon, and if I had any thought on the subject I trust I should not be so imprudent or indiscreet to as to take this opportunity to express them. But I am sure that as long as England is ruled by English Parties who understand the principles on which our Empire is founded, and who are resolved to maintain that Empire, our influence in that part of the world can never be looked upon with indifference. If it should happen that the Government which controls the greater portion of these fair lands is found to be incompetent for its purpose, neither England nor any of the Great Powers will shrink from fulfilling the high political and moral duty which will then devolve upon them.

But, Sir, we must not jump at conclusion so quickly as is now the fashion. There is nothing to justify us talking in such a vein of Turkey as has, and is being this moment entertained. The present is a state of affairs which required the most vigilant examination and the most careful management. But those who suppose that England ever uphold, or at this moment particularly is upholding, Turkey from blind superstition and from want of sympathy with the highest aspirations of humanity, are deceived. What our duty is at this critical moment is to maintain the Empire of England. Nor will we agree to any step, though it may obtain for a moment comparative quiet and a false prosperity, that hazards the existence of that Empire.

Source: T. E. Kebbel, ed. *Selected Speeches of the Late Right Honourable Earl of Beaconsfield.* 2 Vols. (London: Longmans, Green, and Co., 1882), II, pp. 159–160.

15. Lord Augustus Loftus Defends British Support for Turkey (1877)

In the wake of the capture of Plevna by Russian forces in the Russo-Turkish War of 1877–1878, the British ambassador to St. Petersburg, Lord Augustus Loftus (1817–1904), found himself in conversation with the Russian foreign minister and forced to defend his government's obvious sympathy for Turkey as a barrier against Russian encroachment. In this excerpt from his memoirs, he recounts the exchange.

After the fall of Plevna the Emperor returned on the 22nd December to St. Petersburg, attended by Prince Gortschakoff. A congratulatory address was presented to His Majesty by the nobles of St. Petersburg on his return from the seat of war. An Imperial Rescript was issued by the Emperor, conferring the Grand Cross of St. George on the Grand Duke Nicholas, Commander-in-Chief; the Second Class of same Order on the Cesarewich; also the Second Class on General Todleben, General Nepokoichitzi, and General Miliutine, Minister of War, and a gold sword in diamonds Grand Duke Vladimir. The title of Count was conferred on General Ignatieff, Senior, President of the Council of Ministers; and his son, General Ignatieff, Junior, previously Ambassador at Constantinople, was created a member of the Council of the Empire.

I had an interview with Prince Gortschakoff on the 25th, and after congratulating His Highness on his return, which was the object of my visit. I said that I had no communication to make, as I had received no official information bearing on the war or peace.

Prince Gortschakoff said that the moment was one of considerable importance. He said that he could not understand the cause of the feverish alarm and agitation in England. "We have," said His Highness, "been frank and straightforward with England. At the commencement of the war we were told of British interests—well, when they were submitted in form, we gave the most explicit assurances that these interests should be duly respected, and they were considered as satisfactory to your Government. There was the Isthmus of Suez; the road to India; the possession of Constantinople. What could we do more? We could not beforehand state that we shall not cross the Balkans—that we may not be under the necessity of advancing to Constantinople (although we have no wish to do so)—in order to force our enemy to sue for peace. But we have given solemn assurances that we have no intention of keeping possession of Constantinople, and we have pledged ourselves to respect any British interests which may be supposed to be endangered." "Now," continued His Highness, "what are those British interests which all of a sudden are springing up and producing this alarm? Name them to us, and we shall than know what is their nature, their value, and how they can best be safeguarded."

I replied to His Highness that every country must be the judge of its own interests, and that their safeguard and protection could not be confided to other hands. It could not be denied that the passage of the Balkans by a colossal Russian army constituted a danger which threatened the existence of the Turkish Empire in Europe, and it was therefore incontestably the duty of England, in view of such a contingency to be prepared for the protection of her interests, but that I could not see that the performance of this duty intimated any intention of hostility, or even bore the character of an inimical act towards Russia.

Prince Gortschakoff refuted the idea that the existence of the Turkish Empire in Europe would be threatened by the advance of a Russian army across the Balkans, and added that, should it so happen, it was England, and England alone, that would be the cause of it.

"If", said His Highness, "you should determine to occupy Gallipoli, or any other point, and to send your fleet into the Bosphorus, you will be encouraging Turkey to prolong her resistance, and you will be thereby participating in her hostility to Russia."

To this I could not agree, and I again I repeated that in my opinion the measures which might be necessary for the protections of our interests did not in any imply hostility to Russia, but could only be considered of a precautionary and defensive nature.

I observed to His Highness that I could not understand why such vehement invectives were launched against England by the Russian Press, whilst during the whole course of the war our attitude had differed in no respect from that of Austria and Germany.

Prince Gortschakoff replied that he could not admit that we had maintained the same attitude as Austria and Germany. The two Imperial Governments had acted, and were acting, in perfect accord and in harmony with that of Russia. He stated that the policy of the Austrian Cabinet had been consistent throughout, and that he placed entire confidence in Austria and in Germany. As regarded France, His Highness observed that her attention had been absorbed by internal affairs, and could not therefore be directed to external questions, but he had received very satisfactory assurances from the new Minister of Foreign Affairs. England, therefore, he said, was quite isolated.

I replied to His Highness that it was not the first time that England had taken her own line of policy, and that she was sufficiently great and powerful to defend her own interests alone.

Prince Gortschakoff said that he had always supported a pacific solution of the Eastern question. "I have always," said His Highness, "admired and respected England, and I have always wished to maintain amicable relations with her; but I can never 'prostrate' myself before her (*mais me prosterner devant elle—jamais!*).

This conversation was conducted in a very friendly and conciliatory tone.

Notwithstanding the signature of the armistice and the preliminaries of the peace, signed at Adrianople on January 31st, 1878, the Russian armies continued their march on Constantinople.

Source: Lord Augustus Loftus, *The Diplomatic Reminiscences of Lord Augustus Loftus, 1862–1879.* 2 Vols. (London: Cassell and Company, 1894), II, pp. 239–243.

16. Peter Alexandrovitch Saburov Explains the European Situation to Tsar Alexander II (1880)

Saburov, appointed ambassador to Berlin in January 1880, outlined for Tsar Alexander II his impressions of the European situation and stressed the importance of Germany to the defense of Russia's interests.

Our interests in the east are of a double character: some clash with England, the other with Austria. The security of our military and political position in the Black Sea comes under the first category. The emancipation and political organization of the kindred races in the Balkan Peninsula comes under the second. The latter was the object of our efforts in the last campaign. Immense progress has been made in this direction. We can now settle down with pride and wait a while. The task would be too heavy indeed if Russia, pursuing two aims at one and the same time, came into collision with a reunited England and Austria.

The moment seems favorable to separate these two adversaries. The present situation in Europe even makes it a duty for us. We know that hostility to Austria will involve us in a probable conflict with Germany. Accordingly, the most elementary prudence counsels us to halt on the road which had the last war as its consequence, and devote our attention to another aspect of the Eastern question—the one which touches the interests of security of the Empire more directly. In other words, let us be less Slav and more Russian.

The present inclinations of the German Cabinet favor this in a remarkable manner. Prince Bismarck anticipates these ideas. It suits him infinitely better to see Russia orientate her policy in a direction which leaves the interests of Austria alone. He voluntarily agrees to make things easy for us, in consenting to protect, with his new ally, the vulnerable point where England can strike us. Agreements concluded on these bases would complete our plan of defense, and make an attack from this side very difficult, if not impossible, for England.

So it would be desirable, in my humble judgment, to agree to the counter-project of Prince Bismarck, and in place of an arrangement between these two parties, to give the preference to the conclusion of a treaty between three, whilst assigning to the German Chancellor the responsibility of making Austria participate in it.

We must choose one of two alternatives; either Austria will accept, and then our interests in the Straits, as Prince Bismarck has rightly explained, will have secured a more efficacious safeguard than that from an Entente between us and Germany.

Or Austria will refuse. There will likely result from that a coolness in her relations with Germany; the seed of mistrust will have been sown, and Germany, by a natural reaction of things, will once more remove the principal centre of her political affinities from Vienna to St. Petersburg.

In either case, we shall have gained. May I be allowed to finish these lines with a general consideration?

All the impressions that I have received at Berlin only confirm my conviction on the matter of the necessity of persevering in the way of an understanding with Germany, in conformity with the decision taken by the Emperor. This conviction is based on the following reflection:

The real source of the distrust which has made its appearance in Germany with respect to us lies in the fact of her geographical position between two great military States, of which one is animated by a desire for revenge, whilst the intentions of the other remain unknown.

Observing anxiously the march of our affairs, the Germans think they see, in the manifestations of the daily press and even in our Government circles, currents of opinion surging round the throne in a struggle for supremacy. It is of the highest importance for them to know which of these currents will finally prevail in a lasting manner in the guidance of our foreign policy.

Therefore—and I do not hesitate to say it—the most conclusive argument which I have employed when talking with Prince Bismarck has been drawn from the uneasiness inspired in him by the possibility of a rapprochement between France and ourselves, and from the prospect of bringing to an end this nightmare which haunts him, at the price of the loyal co-operation of Germany would afford us the safeguarding of our national interests.

I have reason to believe that the Prince has grasped the whole import of this idea, and that he sincerely sticks to it, for he sees in it a serious pledge for the security of Germany herself!

The situation would entirely change in aspect today if we were to go back upon our steps. The mistrust, of which we already had a foretaste last summer, would arise again on both sides with redoubled intensity. It will become embittered by questions of military susceptibilities which, in their turn, will not be slow to translate themselves into defensive measures and concentrations of troops on both sides of the frontier.

Politically, Germany is at this moment in such a situation that she could become, should it so happen, the centre of a formidable coalition against us. The elements of this coalition are already indicated. It will be formed before France, torn by factions, has had time to clear up her ideas and shake off the English alliance, to which she is fettered.

In this respect it would be impossible to deceive one's self. The first act of that coalition will be the creation of an intermediary State formed out of the fragments of the ancient Poland which they would succeed in snatching from us. For, whatever be the past political declarations of Prince Bismarck on the subject of the Poles, they were only real when they formed part of a system of alliance with us. They would change entirely in the event of conflict. The re-establishment of a Poland, armed with age-long hatred, would then become for Germany a barrier necessary for her future security.

Such is the general effect of my impressions. I dare to submit them to the Imperial Government with the frankness which the Emperor had deigned to allow me.

Source: See J. Y. Simpson, *The Saburov Memoirs or Bismarck and Russia* (London: Cambridge University Press, 1929), pp. 123–126.

17. Jules Ferry Defines French Colonial Expansion as a Struggle of Survival (1884)

In a speech before the French parliament in 1884, Prime Minister Jules-François-Camille Ferry (1832–1893) defended the cause of colonial expansion in terms of an imperative thrust on the nation by an ever-increasing international economic competition in which the loss of Great Power status would be the inevitable price of abstention or neglect—and provokes both outrage and support with his remarks.

The policy of colonial expansion is a political and economic system that I would say could be connected to three sets of ideas: economic ideas; civilizational ideas of the greatest consequence; and ideas of a political and patriotic order. In the area of economics, I am placing before you, with the support of some figures, the considerations that justify the policy of colonial expansion, as seen from the perspective of a need, felt more and more urgently by the industrialized population of Europe and especially the people of our rich and hard-working country of France: the need for outlets.

Is this some sort of fantasy? Is it something for the future or is this not a pressing need, one may say a crying need, of our industrial population? I merely express in a general way what each one of you, from the various parts of France, can see for himself. Yes, what our major industries, steered irrevocably by the treaties of 1860 toward exports, lack more and more are outlets. Why? Because next door Germany is setting up trade barriers; because across the ocean the United States of America have become protectionists, and extreme protectionists at that; because not only are these major markets perhaps too closing but shrinking, becoming more and more difficult for our industrial goods to access, but these great states are beginning to pour into our own markets products not seen there before. [. . .]

That is a great complication, a huge economic challenge; we have spoken many times of it from this rostrum when the government was questioned by M. Langlois about the economic situation; it's an extremely serious problem. It is so serious, gentlemen, so troubling, that the least informed persons are already forced to acknowledge, foresee, and take precautions against the time when the great South American market that has, in a manner of speaking, belonged to us forever will be contested and perhaps taken away from us by North American products. Nothing is more serious; there is no graver social problem; and these matters are linked intimately to colonial policy. [. . .] Gentlemen, we must speak more openly and honestly! We must declare openly that the higher races indeed have a right over the lower races.

- M. Jules Maigne: Oh! You dare to say in the country that has proclaimed the universal rights if man!

- M. de Guilloutet: It's a justification for the enslavement and trading of negroes! [. . .]

I repeat that the superior races have a right because they have a duty. They have the duty to civilize the inferior races [. . .] These duties, gentlemen, have often been misunderstood in the history of past centuries; and certainly when the Spanish soldiers and explorers introduced slavery into Central America, they did not fulfill their duty as men of a higher race. But in our time I maintain that European nations meet this superior civilizing duty with generosity, with grandeur, and in good faith.

- M. Paul Bert: France always has! [. . .]

I say that French colonial policy, the policy of colonial expansion, the policy that has taken us under the Empire to Saigon, to Cochinchina, led us to Tunisia, brought us to Madagascar—I say that this policy of colonial expansion was inspired by a reality, to which it is nevertheless to direct your attention an instant: the fact that a navy such as ours cannot do without safe harbors, defenses, supply centers on the high seas. Are you unaware of this? Look at a map of the world. [. . .]

Gentlemen, these are considerations that merit the full attention of patriots. The conditions of naval warfare have greatly changed. At present, as you know, a warship, however perfect its design, cannot carry more than fourteen days' supply of coal; and a vessel without coal is a wreck on the high seas abandoned to the first occupier. Hence the need to have places of supply, shelters, ports for defense and provisioning. And that is why we needed Tunisia; that is why we needed Saigon and Cochinchina; that is why we need Madagascar, why we are at Diego-Suarès and Vohemar and why we shall never leave them! Gentlemen, in Europe as it is today, in this competition of the many rivals we see rising up around us, some by military or naval improvements, others by the prodigious development of incessant population growth; in a Europe, or rather in a universe such as this, a policy of withdrawal or abstention is simply the high road to decadence! Nations in our time are great only through activity; it is not by "peaceful radiance light of their institutions" that they are great in these times. [. . .] Spreading light without acting, without taking part in the affairs of the world, staying clear of all European alliances and viewing all expansion into Africa or the Orient as a trap, a misadventure—for a great nation to live this way is, believe me, to abdicate and, in less time than you may think, to sink from the first rank to the third and fourth.

Source: Discours et Opinions de Jules Ferry. 7 Vols. Ed. Paul Robiquet (Paris: Armand Colin, 1897), V, p. 199–200, 210–211, 215–216, 217–218.

18. Former President Ulysses S. Grant Blames the American Civil War on Expansionism (1885)

Commander of the Union forces during the American Civil War and 18th President of the United States (1869–1877), Ulysses S. Grant (1822–1885) completed his personal memoirs in June 1885. In the following excerpt, he cites territorial greed in the acquisition of Texas leading to the Mexican War of 1845–1846 as the source for the bloodshed of 1861–1865.

Texas was originally a state belonging to the republic of Mexico. It extended from the Sabine River on the east to the Rio Grande on the west and from the Gulf of Mexico on the south and east to the territory of the United States and New Mexico—another Mexican state at the time—on the north and west. An empire in territory, it had a very sparse population, until settled by Americans who had received authority from Mexico to colonize. These colonists paid very little attention to the supreme government, and introduced slavery to the state almost from the start, though the constitution of Mexico did not, nor does it now, sanction that institution. Soon they set up an independent government of their own, and war existed, between Texas and Mexico, in name from that time until 1836, when active hostilities very nearly ceased upon the capture of Santa Anna, the Mexican President. Before long, however, the same people—who with the permission of Mexico had colonized Texas, and afterwards set up slavery there, and then seceded as soon as they felt strong enough to do so—offered themselves and the State to the United States, and in 1845 their offer was accepted. The occupation, separation and annexation were, from the inception of the movement to its final consummation, a conspiracy to acquire territory out of which slave states might to be formed for the American Union.

Even if the annexation itself could be justified, the manner in which the subsequent war was forced upon Mexico cannot. The fact is, annexationists wanted more territory than they could possibly lay any claim to, as part of the new acquisition. Texas, as an independent State, never had exercised jurisdiction over the territory between the Nueces River and the Rio Grande. Mexico had never recognized the independence of Texas, and maintained that, even if independent, the State had no claim south of the Nueces. I am aware that a treaty, made by the Texans with Santa Anna while he was under duress, ceded all territory between the Nueces and the Rio Grande; but he was a prisoner of war when the treaty was made, and his life was in jeopardy. He knew, too, that he deserved execution at the hands of the Texans, if they should ever capture him. The Texans, if they had taken his life, would have only followed the example set by Santa Anna himself a few weeks before, when he executed the entire garrison of the Alamo and the villagers of Goliad.

In taking military possession of Texas after annexation, the army of occupation, under General Taylor, was directed to occupy the disputed territory. The army did not stop at the Nueces and offer to negotiate for a settlement of the boundary question, but went beyond, apparently in order to force Mexico to initiate war. It is to the credit of the American nation, however, that after conquering Mexico, and while practically holding the country in our possession, so that we could have retained the whole of it, or made any terns we chose, we paid a round sum for the additional territory taken; more than it was worth, or was likely to be, to Mexico. To us it was an empire of incalculable value; but it might have been obtained by other means. The Southern rebellion was largely the outgrowth of the Mexican war. Nations, like individuals, are punished for their transgressions. We got our punishment in the most sanguinary and expensive war of modern times.

Source: See U. S. Grant. *The Personal Memoirs of U. S. Grant* (Lincoln: University of Nebraska Press, 1996), pp. 37–38.

19. Francesco Cucchi Reports on Otto von Bismarck's Thinking (July 24, 1889)

Francesco Crispi (1819–1901), the prime minister of Italy, received a letter from Francesco Cucchi (1834–1913), who had been sent to Germany to confer with Chancellor Bismarck, in which Cucchi transmitted Bismarck's thoughts on the likelihood of French belligerence toward Italy. In this excerpt, the chancellor reveals not only his interpretation of European circumstance but also some of his cherished wishes for future developments.

I will give you a résumé of my conversations with the Prince.

He has absolutely no faith in the possibility of an attack on Italy such as implied by the information you have received, and which I communicated to him. He says that such an act would arouse the indignation of the civilized world. The responsibility of having brought about war in Europe by an act of brigandage (his very words) would cost France immensely dear. It might even signify the *finis Galliæ* (again his own words), and there would be no avoiding the consequences with five billions of money as in 1870. He added from a purely military and practical point of view this insane attack might be desirable. In high military circles in Germany they would prefer to have war at once or in the spring, rather than two years hence, when France will have completed her armament and fortifications, and filled her ranks. In any case, the Prince says Germany has her eyes open and is keeping her powder dry. She has long been prepared to meet any form of danger, threat, or unexpected attack. In ten days' time 1,200,000 men could invade France. All requisites of war and the provisions for victualling this huge army for one month, are ready in the cities and fortresses on the banks of the Rhine, Lorraine and Alsace. Besides all this, matters have been so arranged that attack need be feared on the part of Russia, with which country the Prince still hopes it would be possible to avoid a rupture, or at least to keep her out of it, until France has received one serious set-back. In this case, as everything is prepared with a view to making the first great battle absolutely decisive, the weight that Russia would throw into the battle would be greatly diminished.

As regards the quality of the French army, they are of the opinion here that it is wanting in cohesion and discipline. Without these attributes great numbers would be of no avail, and might, indeed, prove fatal under certain conditions. They do not doubt, however, that the French army will be better led, at least in the beginning, than it was in 1870–71. The Chief of the General-Staff, General Miribel, is greatly respected. The Germans believe their artillery is stronger, especially that for purposes of siege. They know that the Lebel rifle is excellent, but by next spring the entire German army of the first line will be supplied with new rifles, which are more perfect than any heretofore known. These are being quietly but swiftly manufactures in the arsenals, and 4000 are being turned out every day.

The Prince has great faith, not only in England's good will, but also that she would help, should France be the first to declare war. He is pleased with the clever way in which you cultivate English friendship, without minding whether Salisbury or Gladstone be in office. Should England really take an active part, as would seem probable, the combined action of the three fleets would completely paralyze that of the French, and oblige it either to take refuge in its arsenals or risk battle against overwhelming odds. This, the Prince says, would greatly facilitate the operations of the land forces against France. By the three fleets he means the English, German, and Italian. I asked the Prince why he did not count on the Austrian fleet as well. He replied that although he has a good opinion of the Austrian marines, he did not believe the ship themselves were worth much. On the whole I noticed a certain coolness toward Austria in his conversation. [. . .] It would take me too long to set down all the views the Prince expressed concerning the policies of England, Russia, Austria, and Turkey, and the attitudes these Powers would be likely to assume should France attack Germany and Italy, or Russia attack Austria and Turkey. I will report them verbally.

Source: The Memoirs of Francesco Crispi. Trans. Mary Prichard-Agnetti. 3 Vols. (London: Hooder and Stoughton, 1912), II, pp. 411–414.

20. Alfred Thayer Mahan Makes the Case for American Naval Power (1890)

In his book, *The Influence of Sea Power upon History, 1660–1783*, Alfred Thayer Mahan (1840–1914) explains in the following excerpt the importance of a first-class navy to the vital interests of the United States at the beginning of a decade in which the American republic emerged as an international force to be reckoned with.

The influence of the government will be felt in its most legitimate manner in maintaining an armed navy, of a size commensurate with the growth of its shipping and importance of the interests connected with it. More important even than the size of the navy is the question of its institutions, favoring a healthful spirit and activity, and providing for rapid development in time of war by an adequate reserve of men and ships and by measures for drawing out that general reserve power which has before been pointed to, when considering the character and pursuits of the people. Undoubtedly under this second head of warlike preparation must come the maintenance of suitable naval stations, in those distant parts of the world to which the armed shipping must follow the peaceful vessels of commerce. The protection of such stations must depend either upon direct military force, as do Gibralter and Malta, or upon a surrounding friendly population, such as the American colonists once were to England, and it may be presumed, the Australian colonists now are. Such friendly surroundings and backing, joined to a reasonable military provision, are the best of defenses, and when combined with decided preponderance at sea, make a scattered and extensive empire, like that of England, secure: for while it is true that an unexpected attack may cause disaster in some one quarter, the actual superiority of naval power prevents such a disaster from being general or irremediable. History has sufficiently proved this. England's naval bases have been in all parts of the world; and her fleets have at once protected them, kept open communications between them, and relied upon them for shelter.

Colonies attached to the mother-country afford, therefore, the surest means of supporting abroad the sea power of the country. In peace, the influence of the government should be felt in promoting by all means a warmth of attachment and a unity of interest which will make the welfare of one the welfare of all, and the quarrel of one the quarrel of all; and in war, or rather for war, by including such measures of organization and defense as shall be felt by all to be a fair distribution of a burden of which each reaps the benefit.

Such colonies the United States has not and is not likely to have. As regards purely military naval stations, the feeling of her people was probably accurately expressed by an historian of the English navy a hundred years ago, speaking then of Gibralter and Port Mahon. "Military governments," he said, "agree so little with the industry of a trading people, and are in themselves so repugnant to the genius of the British people that I do not wonder that men of good sense and of all parties have inclined to give up these, as Tangiers was given up." Having therefore no foreign establishments, either colonial or military, the ships of war of the United States, in war, will be like land birds, unable to fly far from their own shores. To provide resting-places for them, where they can coal and repair, would be one of the first duties of a government proposing to itself the development of the power of the nation at sea . . .

The question is eminently one in which the influence of the government should make itself felt, to build up a navy which, if not capable of reaching distant countries, shall at least be able to keep clear the approaches to its own. The eyes of the country have for a quarter of a century been turned from the sea; the results of such a policy and of its opposite will be shown in the instance of France and of England.

Without asserting a narrow parallelism between the case of the United States and either of these, it may safely be said that it is essential to the welfare of the whole country that the conditions of trade and commerce should remain, as far as possible, unaffected by an external war. In order to do this, the enemy must be kept not only out of our ports, but far away from our coasts.

Source: Alfred Thayer Mahan, *The Influence of Seapower upon History, 1660–1783* (Boston: Little, Brown and Company, 1890), pp. 82–83, 87.

21. Frederick Lugard Espouses a Philosophy for Colonial Missionaries (1893)

The epitome of the British colonial administrator in Africa and the principal inventor of the practice of indirect rule, Frederick John Dealtry Lugard (1858–1945) published extensively on his experiences. In *The Rise of Our East African Empire*, he gives his views on the nature of missionary work and the proper attitude of the missionary to his colonial flock.

A word as to missions in Africa. Beyond doubt I think the most useful missions are the Medical and the Industrial, in the initial stages of savage development. A combination of the two is, in my opinion, an ideal mission. Such is the work of the Scotch Free Church on Lake Nyasa. The medical missionary begins work with every advantage. Throughout Africa the ideas of the cure of the body and of the soul are closely allied. The "medicine man" is credited, not only with a knowledge of the simples and drugs which may avert or cure disease, but owing to the superstitions of the people, he is also supposed to have a knowledge of the charms and *dawa* which will invoke the aid of the Deity or appease His wrath, and of the witchcraft and magic (*ulu*) by which success in war, immunity from danger, or a supply of rain may be obtained. As the skill of the European in medicine asserts its superiority over the crude methods of the medicine man, so does he in proportion gain an influence in his teaching of the great truths of Christianity. He teaches the savage where knowledge and art cease, how far natural remedies produce their effects, independent of charms or supernatural agencies, and where divine power overrules all human efforts. Such demonstration from a medicine man, whose skill they cannot fail to recognize as superior to their own, has naturally more weight than any mere preaching. A mere preacher is discounted and his zeal is not understood. The medical missionary, moreover, gains an admission to the houses and homes of the natives by virtue of his art, which would not be so readily accorded to another. He becomes their adviser and referee, and his counsels are substituted for the magic and witchcraft which retard development.

The value of the Industrial mission, on the other hand, depends, of course, largely on the nature of the tribes among whom it is located. Its value can hardly be overestimated among such people as the Waganda, both on account of their natural aptitude and their eager desire to learn. But even the less advanced and more primitive tribes may be equally benefited, if not only mechanical and artisan work, such as the carpenter's and blacksmith's craft, but also the simpler expedients of agriculture are taught. The sinking of wells, the system of irrigation, the introduction and planting of useful trees, the use of manure, and of domestic animals for agricultural purposes, the improvement of his implements by the introduction of the primitive Indian plough, etc.—all of these, while improving the status of the native, will render his land more productive, and hence, by increasing his surplus products, will enable him to purchase from the trader the cloth which shall add to his decency, and the implements and household utensils which shall produce greater results for his labor and greater comforts in his social life.

In my view, moreover, instruction (religious or secular) is largely wasted upon adults, who are wedded to custom and prejudice. It is the rising generation who should be educated to a higher plane, by the establishment of schools for children. They, in turn, will send their children for instruction; and so a progressive advancement is instituted, which may produce really great results. I see, in a recent letter, that Dr. Laws supports this view, and appositely quotes the parallel of the Israelites after their exodus from Egypt, who were detained for forty years in the desert, until the generation who had been slaves in Egypt had passed away. The extensive schools at his mission at Bandawi were evidence of the practical application of his views. These schools were literally thronged with thousands of children, and chiefs of neighboring tribes were eagerly offering to erect schools in their own villages at their own cost. [. . .]

One word as regards missionaries themselves. The essential point in dealing with Africans is to establish a respect for the European. Upon this—the prestige of the white man—depends his influence, often his very existence, in Africa. If he shows by his surroundings, by his assumption of superiority, that he is far above the native, he will be respected, and his influence will be proportionate to the superiority he assumes and bears out by his higher accomplishments and mode of life. In my opinion—at any rate with reference to Africa—it is the greatest possible mistake to suppose that a European can acquire a greater influence by adopting the mode of life of the natives. In effect, it is to lower himself to their plane, instead of elevating them to his. The sacrifice involved is wholly unappreciated, and the motive would be held by the savage to be poverty and lack of social status in his own country. The whole influence of the European in Africa is gained by this assertion of a superiority which commands the respect and excites the emulation of the savage. To forego this vantage ground is to lose influence for good. I may add, that the loss of prestige consequent on what I should term the humiliation of the European affects not merely the missionary himself, but is subversive of all efforts for secular administration, and may even invite insult, which may lead to disaster and bloodshed. To maintain it a missionary must, above all things, be a gentleman; for no one is more quick to recognize a real gentleman than the African savage. He must at all times assert himself, and repel an insolent familiarity, which is a thing entirely apart from friendship born of respect and affection. His dwelling house should be as superior to those of the natives as he is himself superior to them. And this, while adding to his prestige and influence, will simultaneously promote his own health and energy, and so save money spent on invalidings to England, and replacements due to sickness or death. In these respects the Scotch missions in Nyasaland have shown a most useful example.

I am convinced that the indiscriminate application of such precepts as those contained in the words to "turn the other cheek also to the smiter," and to be the servant of all men, is to wholly misunderstand and misapply the teaching of Christ. The African holds the position of a late-born child in the family of nations, and must as yet be schooled in the discipline of the nursery. He is neither the intelligent ideal crying out for instruction, and capable of appreciating the subtle beauties of Christian forbearance and self-sacrifice, which some well-meaning missionary literature would lead us to suppose, nor yet, on the other hand, is he universally a rampant cannibal, predestined by Providence to the yoke of the slave, and fitted for nothing better, as I have elsewhere seen him depicted. I hold rather with Longfellow's beautiful lines—

> In all ages
> Every human heart is human;
> There are longings, yearnings, strivings
> For the good they comprehend not.
> That the feeble hands and helpless,
> Groping blindly in the darkness,
> Touch God's right hand in that darkness.

That is to say, that there is in him, like the rest of us, both good and bad, and that the innate good is capable of being developed by culture.

Source: F. D. Lugard. *The Rise of our East African Empire.* 2 Vols. (Edinburgh: William Blackwood and Sons, 1893), I, pp. 69–75.

22. Joseph Chamberlain Explains the True Conception of Empire (March 1897)

The colonial secretary in the Conservative cabinet of Lord Salisbury, Joseph Chamberlain (1836–1914) addressed the annual dinner of the Royal Colonial Institute in March 1897. In his speech, he presented a defense of the British Empire as an evolving mission of civilization that had become an obligation of the British nation to humanity rather than a project of selfish plunder.

What is that conception? As regards the self-governing colonies we no longer talk of them as dependences. The sense of possession has given way to the sentiment of kinship. We think and speak of them as part of ourselves, as part of the British Empire, united to us, although they may be dispersed throughput the world, by ties of kindred, of religion, of history, and of language, and joined to us by the seas that seemed to divided us.

But the British Empire is not confined to the self-governing colonies and the United Kingdom. It includes a much greater area, a much more numerous population in tropical climes, where no considerable European settlement is possible, and where the native population must always vastly outnumber the white inhabitants; and in these cases also the same change has come over the Imperial idea. Here also the sense of possession has given place to a different sentiment—the sense of obligation. We feel now that our rule over these territories can only be justified if we can show that it adds to the happiness and prosperity of the people, and I maintain that our rule does, and has, brought security and peace and comparative prosperity to countries that never knew these blessings before.

In carrying out this work of civilization, we are fulfilling what I believe to be our national mission, and we are finding scope for the exercise of those faculties and qualities which have made of us a great governing race. I do not say that our success has been perfect in every case, I do not say that all of our methods have been beyond reproach; but I do say that in almost every instance in which the rule of the Queen has been established and the great Pax Britannica has been enforced, there has come with it greater security to life and property, and a material improvement in the condition of the bulk of the population. No doubt, in the first instance when these conquests have been made, there as been bloodshed, there has been loss of life among the native populations, loss of still more precious lives among those who have been sent out to bring these countries in to some kind of disciplined order, but it must be remembered that that is the condition of the mission we have to fulfill. There are, of course, among us—there are always among us, I think—a very small minority of men who are ready to be the advocates of the most detestable tyrants, provided their skin is black—men who sympathize with the sorrows of Prempeh and Lobengula, and who denounce as murderers those of their countrymen who have gone forth at the command of the Queen, and who have redeemed districts as large as Europe from barbarism and the superstition in which they had been steeped for centuries. I remember a picture by Mr. Selous of a philanthropist—an imaginary philanthropist, I will hope—sitting cosily by his fireside and denouncing the methods by which British civilization was promoted. This philanthropist complained of the use of Maxim guns and other instruments of warfare, and asked why we could not proceed by more conciliatory methods, and why the *impis* of Lobengula could not be brought before a magistrate, and fined five shillings and bound over to keep the peace.

No doubt there is a humorous exaggeration in this picture, but there is gross exaggeration in the frame of mind against which it was directed. You cannot have omelettes without breaking eggs; you cannot destroy the practices of barbarism, of slavery, of superstition, which for centuries have desolated the interior of Africa, without the use of force; but if you will fairly contrast the gain to humanity with the price which we are bound to pay for it, I think you may well rejoice in the result of such expeditions as those which have been recently conducted with such signal success in Nyassaland, Ashanti, Benin, and Nupé—expeditions which may have, and indeed have, cost valuable lives, but as to which we may rest assured that for one life lost a hundred will be gained, and the cause of civilization and the prosperity of the people will in the long run be eminently advanced. But no doubt such a state of things, such as mission as I have described, involves heavy responsibility. In the wide dominions of the Queen the doors of the temple of Janus are never closed, and it is a gigantic task we have undertaken when we have determined to wield the scepter of empire. Great is the task, great is the responsibility, but great is the honor; and I am convinced that the conscience and the spirit of the country will rise to the height of its obligations, and that we shall have the strength to fulfill the mission which our history and our national character have imposed upon us.

Source: Charles W. Boyd, ed. *Mr. Chamberlain's Speeches.* 2 Vols. (Boston: Houghton Mifflin, 1914), II, pp. 2–4.

23. Winston Churchill Assesses the Afghan Tribesmen (1897)

Commissioned as an officer in the Fourth Hussars and posted to his regiment in Bangalore, India, Winston S. Churchill (1874–1965) offered his services to the *Daily Telegraph* as an expedient to get him to the Northwest frontier. On September 6, 1897, he posted a letter, in typically strong language, describing the qualities of the Afghan tribesmen then at war with the British Empire.

Let us begin, then, as we hope to end, with the enemy. In the examination of a people it is always best to take their virtues first. This clears the ground and leaves sufficient time for the investigation of the predominant characteristics. The Swatis, Bonerwals, Mohmands and other frontier tribes with whom the Malakand Field Force is at present engaged are brave and warlike. Their courage has been abundantly displayed in the present campaign. They charge home, and nothing but a bullet stops their career. Their swordsmanship—neglecting guards—concerns itself only with cuts and, careless of what injury they may receive, they devote themselves to the destruction of their opponents. In the selection of positions they exhibit considerable military skill, and as skirmishers their use of cover and preservation of order entitle them to much praise. It is mournful to be compelled to close the catalogue of their virtues thus early, but the closest scrutiny of the facts which have been placed before me has resulted in no further discovery in this direction. From year to year their life is one of feud and strife. They plough with a sword at their sides. Every field has its protecting tower, to which the agriculturalist can hurry at the approach of a stranger. Successful murder—whether by open force or treachery—is the surest road to distinction among them. A recent writer had ascribed to these people those high family virtues which simple races so often possess. The consideration of one pregnant fact compels me reluctantly to abandon even this hope. Their principal article of commerce is their women—wives and daughters—who are exchanged for rifles. This degradation of mind is unrelieved by a single elevated sentiment. Their religion is the most miserable fanaticism, in which cruelty, credulity and immorality are equally represented. Their holy men—the Mullahs—prize as chief privilege a sort of *droit de seigneur.* It is impossible to imagine a lower type of beings or a more dreadful state of barbarism.

I am aware of the powerful influence of climate upon character. But the hill man cannot even plead the excuse of a cold and barren land for their barbarism. The valleys they inhabit are fertile and often beautiful. Once the spots where their squalid huts now stand were occupied by thriving cities, and the stone 'sangars' from which they defy their foes are built on the terraces which nourished the crops of a long forgotten civilization. Everywhere are the relics of the old Buddhists on whom these fierce tribes, thrown out of that birthplace of nations, Central Asia, descended. Their roads, their temples, their ruins have alone survived. All else has been destroyed in that darkness which surrounds those races whose type is hardly on the fringe of humanity. But it may be argued, "However degraded and barbarous these people may be, they have a right to live unmolested on the soil that their fathers conquered." "They have attacked your posts,' says the Little Englander, carefully disassociating himself from anything British, "but why did you ever put your posts there?" To answer this question it is necessary to consider the whole matter from a wider point of view than the Swat Valley affords.

Starting with the assumption that our Empire in India is worth holding, and admitting the possibility that others besides ourselves might wish to possess it, it obviously becomes our duty to adopt measures for its safety. It is a question of a line of defense. The Indus is now recognized by all strategists as being useless for this purpose. The most natural way of preventing an enemy from entering a house is to hold the door and windows; and the general consensus of opinion is that to secure India it is necessary to hold the passes of the mountains. With this view small military posts have been built along the frontier. The tribes whose territories adjoin have not been interfered with. Their independence has been respected and, their degradation undisturbed. More than this, the influence of the flag that flies from the fort on the hill has stimulated the trade of the valley, and increased the wealth of its inhabitants. Were the latter amenable to logical reasoning, the improvement of their condition and strength of their adversaries would have convinced them of the folly of an outbreak. But in a land of fanatics common sense does not exist.

The defeat of the Greeks sent an electric thrill through Islam. The Ameer—a negative conductor—is said to have communicated it to the 'Mullahs', and they have generated the disturbance through the frontier tribes. The ensuing flash has kindled a widespread conflagration. This must now be dealt with courageously and intelligently. It is useless, and often dangerous, to argue with an Afghan. Not because he is degraded, not because we covet his valleys, but because his actions interfere with the safety of our Empire, he must be crushed. There are many in Europe, though they live amid the prosaic surroundings of a highly developed country, where economics and finance reign supreme, who yet regard, with pleasure and with pride, the wide dominions of which they are trustees.

These, when they read that savages have been killed for attacking British posts and menacing the security of our possessions, will not hesitate to say, with firmness and without reserve, 'So perish all who do the like again.'

Source: See Frederick Woods, ed. *Young Winston's Wars: The Original Despatches of Winston S. Churchill, War Correspondent, 1897–1900* (New York: Viking, 1972), pp. 8–10

24. Bernhard von Bülow Calls Upon Germany to Be a Hammer (December 11, 1899)

As secretary of foreign affairs for Kaiser Wilhelm II, Berhard von Bülow (1849–1929) defended German *Weltpolitik* generally and the country's colonial policy specifically increasingly in terms of a fight for survival among the Great Powers. His most storied contribution to the sense of intensified imperial competition, the Hammer and Anvil Speech to the Reichstag of December 11, 1899, is excerpted here.

In our nineteenth century, England has increased its colonial empire—the largest the world has seen since the days of the Romans—further and further; the French have put down roots in North Africa and East Africa and created for themselves a new empire in the Far East; Russia has begun its mighty course of victory in Asia, leading it to the high plateau of the Pamir and to the coasts of the Pacific Ocean. Four years ago the Sino-Japanese war, scarcely one and a half years ago the Spanish-American War have put things further in motion; they've led to great, momentous, far-reaching decisions, shaken old empires, and added new and serious ferment. [. . .] The English prime minister said a long time ago that the strong states were getting stronger and stronger and the weak ones weaker and weaker. [. . .] We don't want to step on the toes of any foreign power, but at the same time we don't want our own feet tramped by any foreign power (Bravo!) and we don't intend to be shoved aside by any foreign power, not in political nor in economic terms.(Lively applause.) It is time, high time, that we [. . .] make it clear in our own minds what stance we have to take and how we need to prepare ourselves in the face of the processes taking place around us which carry the seeds within them for the restructuring of power relationships for the unforeseeable future. To stand inactively to one side, as we have done so often in the past, either from native modesty (*Laughter*) or because we were completely absorbed in our own internal arguments or for doctrinaire reasons—to stand dreamily to one side while other people split up the pie, we cannot and we will not do that. (*Applause.*) We cannot for the simple reason that we now have interests in all parts of the world. [. . .] The rapid growth of our population, the unprecedented blossoming of our industries, the hard work of our merchants, in short the mighty vitality of the German people have woven us into the world economy and pulled us into international politics. If the English speak of a 'Greater Britain;' if the French speak of a 'Nouvelle France;' if the Russians open up Asia; then we, too, have the right to a greater Germany (Bravo! from the right, laughter from the left), not in the sense of conquest, but indeed in the sense of peaceful extension of our trade and its infrastructures. [. . .] We cannot and will not permit that the order of the day passes over the German people [. . .] There is a lot of envy present in the world against us (calls from the left), political envy and economic envy. There are individuals and there are interest groups, and there are movements, and there are perhaps even peoples that believe that the German was easier to have around and that the German was more pleasant for his neighbors in those earlier days, when, in spite of our education and in spite of our culture, foreigners looked down on us in political and economic matters like cavaliers with their noses in the air looking down on the humble tutor. (Very true!—*Laughter.*) These times of political faintness and economic and political humility should never return (*Lively Bravo.*) We don't ever again want to become, as Friedrich List put it, the 'slaves of humanity.' But we'll only be able to keep ourselves at the fore if we realize that there is no welfare for us without power, without a strong army and a strong fleet. (Very true! from the right; objections from the left) The means, gentlemen, for a people of almost 60 million—dwelling in the middle of Europe and, at the same time, stretching its economic antennae out to all sides—to battle its way through in the struggle for existence without strong armaments on land and at sea, have not yet been found. (Very true! from the right.) In the coming century the German people will be a hammer or an anvil.

Source: See Buchners Kolleg Geschichte, *Das Kaiserreich, 1871 bis 1918* (Bamberg: C. C. Buchners Verlag, 1987), p. 137.

25. Rudyard Kipling Calls upon Americans to Take Up the White Man's Burden (1899)

Rudyard Kipling (1865–1936) wrote a poem, "The White Man's Burden," which became both famous and infamous for its treatment of colonialism as a noble self-sacrifice. The poem was occasioned by the U.S. colonization of the Philippines and originally published in *McClure's* magazine as a challenge to the American people to join the other imperial powers in civilizing the non-European world.

The White Man's Burden
Take up the White Man's burden—
Send forth the best ye breed—
Go bind your sons to exile
To serve your captives' need;
To wait in heavy harness,
On fluttered folk and wild—
Your new-caught, sullen peoples,
Half-devil and half-child.
Take up the White Man's burden—
In patience to abide,
To veil the threat of terror
And check the show of pride;
By open speech and simple,
An hundred times made plain
To seek another's profit,
And work another's gain.
Take up the White Man's burden—
The savage wars of peace—
Fill full the mouth of Famine
And bid the sickness cease;
And when your goal is nearest
The end for others sought,
Watch sloth and heathen Folly
Bring all your hopes to nought.
Take up the White Man's burden—
No tawdry rule of kings,
But toil of serf and sweeper—
The tale of common things.
The ports ye shall not enter,
The roads ye shall not tread,
Go mark them with your living,
And mark them with your dead.
Take up the White Man's burden—
And reap his old reward:
The blame of those ye better,

The hate of those ye guard—
The cry of hosts ye humor
(Ah, slowly!) toward the light:—
"Why brought he us from bondage,
Our loved Egyptian night?"
Take up the White Man's burden—
Ye dare not stoop to less—
Nor call too loud on Freedom
To cloke your weariness;
By all ye cry or whisper,
By all ye leave or do,
The silent, sullen peoples
Shall weigh your gods and you.
Take up the White Man's burden—
Have done with childish days—
The lightly proferred laurel,
The easy, ungrudged praise.
Comes now, to search your manhood
Through all the thankless years
Cold, edged with dear-bought wisdom,
The judgment of your peers!

Source: See Irving Howe, ed., *The Portable Kipling* (New York: Penguin, 1982), p. 602.

26. Colonel C. E. Calwell Counsels Ruthlessness in Fighting Guerrillas (1906)

In 1906, Colonel C. E. Calwell (1859–1928) published *Small Wars*, a handbook on colonial warfare in which he dealt forthrightly with the methods to be employed against guerrilla fighters.

The adoption of guerilla methods by the enemy almost necessarily forces the regular troops to resort to punitive measures directed against the possessions of the antagonists. It must be remembered that one way to get the enemy to fight is to make raids on his property—only the most cowardly of savages and irregulars will allow their cattle to be carried off or their homes to be destroyed without making some show of resistance. Antagonists who will not even under such circumstances strike a blow, can only be dealt with by depriving them of their belongings or burning their dwellings. When operations are being carried out against guerrillas scattered over great tracts of country, it has generally been found very useful to send raiding parties consisting of mounted men great distances, to carry off the enemies' flocks and herds or to destroy encampments and villages. As already mentioned the Russians have put this method of warfare in force in Central Asia, and the French made large use of it in some of their Algerian campaign. [. . .] In the Indian Mutiny, a campaign for the suppression of a rebellion where the most drastic measures were justified by the events at its outset, guerrilla warfare was not a feature, except in the Central Provinces and in some few localities after the rebel armies had been overthrown. The nature of the campaign was indeed such that the insurgents were so roughly handled in action that the country was practically pacified on the battle-field. But in South Africa in 1851–52, in 1877, and again in 1896, rigorous treatment was meted out to the enemy in crushing out disaffection, and with good results; the Kaffir villages and Matabili kraals were burnt, their crops destroyed, their cattle carried off. The French in Algeria, regardless of the maxim, "les représailles sont toujours inutiles," dealt very severely with the smoldering disaffection of the conquered territory for years after Abd el Kader's power was gone, and their procedure succeeded. Uncivilized races attribute leniency to timidity. A system adapted to La Vendée is out of place among fanatics and savages, who must be brought thoroughly to book and cowed or they will rise again.

Source: Colonel C. E. Calwell, *Small Wars: Their Principles and Practice,* (London: H.M.S.O, 1906), Ch. XII.

27. Sir John Fisher Thanks God and Machiavelli for His Own Genius (1907)

In correspondence with King Edward VII, First Sea Lord John Fisher (1841–1920) explained how the development of the *Dreadnought* had given Great Britain a victory in the Anglo-German naval race.

Our only probable enemy is Germany. Germany keeps her *whole* fleet always concentrated within a few hours of England. We must therefore keep a Fleet twice as powerful concentrated within a few hours of Germany.

If we kept the Channel and Atlantic Fleets *always* in the English Channel (say in the vicinity of the Nore), this would meet the case, but this is neither feasible nor expedient, and if, when relations with foreign powers are strained, the Admiralty attempt to take the proper fighting precautions and move our Channel and Atlantic Fleets to their proper fighting position, then *at once* the Foreign Office and the Government veto it, and say such a step will precipitate war! This actually happened on the recent occasion of the German Government presenting an ultimatum to acquire a coaling station at Madeira, and the German Minister was ordered to leave Lisbon at 10 p.m. on a certain Sunday night, and war was imminent, as Lord Landsdowne had told Portugal England would back her. The Board of Admiralty don't intend ever again to subject themselves to this risk, and they have decided to form a new Home Fleet always at home, with its Headquarters at the Nore and its cruising ground the North Sea.

("Your battle ground should be your drill ground,"said Nelson!) The politicians and the diplomatists will not be the people the Public will hang if the British Navy fails to annihilate the whole German Fleet and gobble up every single one of those 842 German merchant steamers now daily on the ocean! *No*—it will be the Sea Lords! [. . .]

In March this year *it is an absolute fact* that Germany had not laid down a single Dreadnought, nor had she commenced building a single ship for 18 months (*Germany has been paralysed by the Dreadnought!*). The more the German Admiralty looked into her qualities, the more convinced they became that they must follow suit, and the more convinced they were that the whole of the existing battle fleet was useless *because utterly wanting in gun power!* (Half of their whole fleet are only equal to our armored cruisers!) The German Admiralty wrestled with the Dreadnought problem for 18 months and did nothing. *Why?* Because it meant spending 12 1/2 millions sterling on widening and deepening the Kiel Canal and dredging all their harbors and all the approaches to their harbors, because if they did not do so it would be no use building German Dreadnoughts, because they couldn't float anywhere in the harbors of Germany! *But there is another reason never yet made public.* Our *existing* battleship of the latest type draw too much water to get close into the German waters, but the German Admiralty is going (is *obliged*) to spend 12 1/2 millions sterling [in dredging] to allow our existing ships to go and fight them! It was a Machiavellian interference of Providence on our behalf that brought about the evolution of the *Dreadnought!*

Source: See Fear God and Dread Nought: The Correspondence of the Admiral of the Fleet Lord Fisher of Kilverstone. 2 Vols. Ed. Arthur J. Marder. (London: Jonathan Cape, 1956), II, pp. 103, 139–140.

28. Sir Eyre Crowe Drafts a Historic Memorandum (1907)

Only seven years before the outbreak of World War I, one of the leading officials of the British Foreign Office, Sir Eyre Crowe (1864–1925), drafted an extraordinarily perceptive and coherent memorandum, excerpted here, in which he attempted to clarify policy options in dealing with Germany as a naval power.

If it be considered necessary to formulate and accept a theory that will fit all ascertained facts of German foreign policy, the choice must lie between the two hypotheses:

Either Germany is definitely aiming at a general political hegemony and maritime ascendancy, threatening the independence of her neighbors and ultimately the existence of England;

Or Germany, free from any such clear-cut ambition, and thinking for the present merely of using her legitimate position and influence as one of the leading Powers in the council of nations, is seeking to promote her foreign commerce, spread the benefits of German culture, extend the scope of her national energies, and create fresh German interests all over the world wherever and whenever a peaceful opportunity offers, leaving it to an uncertain future to decide whether the occurrence of great changes in the world may not assign to Germany a larger share of direct political action over regions not now part of her dominions, without that violation of the established rights of other countries which would be involved in any such action under existing political conditions.

In either case Germany would clearly be wise to build as powerful a navy as she could afford. [. . .]

It maybe recalled that the German Empire owes such expansion as has already taken place in no small measure to England's cooperation or spirit of accommodation, and to the British principle of equal opportunity and no favor. It cannot be good policy for England to thwart such a process of development where it does not direct conflict either with British interests or with those of other nations to which England is bound by solemn treaty obligations. If Germany, within the limits imposed by thee two conditions, finds the means peacefully and honorably to increase her trade and shipping, to gain coaling stations or other harbors, to acquire landing rights for cables, or to secure concessions for the employment of German capital or industries, she should never find England in her way.

Nor is it for British Governments to oppose Germany's building as large a fleet as she may consider necessary or desirable for the defense of her national interests. It is the mark of an independent state that it decides such matters for itself, free from any outside interference, and it would ill become England with her large fleets to dictate to another State what is good for it in matters of supreme national concern. Apart from the question of right and wrong, it may also be urged that nothing would be more likely than any attempt at such dictation, to impel Germany to persevere with her shipbuilding programs. And also, it may be said in parenthesis, nothing is more likely to produce in Germany the impression of the practical hopelessness of a never-ending succession of costly naval programs than the conviction, based on ocular demonstration, that for every German ship England will inevitably lay down two, so maintaining the present British preponderance.

It would be of real advantage if the determination not to bar Germany's legitimate and peaceful expansion, nor her schemes of naval development, were made as patent and pronounced as authoritatively as possible, provided care were taken at the same time to make it quite clear that this benevolent attitude will give way to determined opposition at the first sign of British or allied interests being adversely affected. This alone would probably do more to bring about lastingly satisfactory relations with Germany than any other course. [. . .]

Here, again, however, it would be wrong to suppose that any discrimination is intended to Germany's disadvantage. On the contrary, the same rule will naturally impose itself in the case of all other Powers. It may, indeed, be useful to cast back a glance on British relations with France before and after 1898. A reference to the official records will show that ever since 1882 England had met a growing number of French demands and infringements of British rights in the same spirit of ready accommodation which inspired her dealing with Germany. The not unnatural result was that every successive French Government embarked on a policy of "squeezing" England, until the crisis came in the year of Fashoda, when the stake at issue was the maintenance of the British position on the Upper Nile. The French Minister for Foreign Affairs of that day argued, like his predecessors, that England's apparent opposition was only half-hearted, and would collapse before the persistent threat of French displeasure. Nothing would persuade him England could in a question of this kind assume an attitude of unbending resistance. It was this erroneous impression, justified in the eyes of the French Cabinet by their deductions from British political practice, that brought the two countries to the verge of war. When the Fashoda chapter had ended with the discomfiture of France, she remained for a time very sullen, and the enemies of England rejoiced, because they believed that an impassable gulf has now been fixed between the two nations. As a matter of fact, the events at Fashoda proved to be the opening of a new chapter of Anglo-French relations. These, after remaining for some years rather formal, have not since been disturbed by any disagreeable incidents. France behaved more correctly and seemed less suspicious and inconsiderate than had been her wont, and no fresh obstacle arose in the way which ultimately led to the Agreement of 1904.

Although Germany has not been exposed to such a rebuff as France encountered in 1898, the events connected with the Algeciras Conference appear to have had on the German Government the effect of an unexpected revelation, clearly showing indication of a new spirit in which England proposes to regulate her own conduct towards France on the one hand and to Germany on the other. That the result was a very serious disappointment to Germany has been made abundantly manifest by the turmoil which the signature of the Algerciras Act has created in that country, the official, semi-official, and unofficial classes vying with each other in giving expression to their astonished discontent. The time which has since elapsed has, no doubt, been short. But during that time it may be observed that our relations with Germany, if not exactly cordial, have at least been practically free from all symptoms of direct friction, and there is an impression that Germany will think twice before she now gives rise to any fresh disagreement. In this attitude she will be encouraged if she meets on England's part with unvarying courtesy and consideration in all matters of common concern, but also with a prompt and firm refusal to enter into any one-sided bargains or arrangements, and the most unbending determination to uphold British rights and interests in every part of the globe. There will be no surer or quicker way to win the respect of the German Government and of the German nation.

Source: See Hans J. Morgenthau and Kenneth W. Thompson, eds. *Principles and Problems of International Politics* (New York: Alfred A. Knopf, 1950), pp. 258–261.

29. Austria-Hungary Threatens Serbia with War (July 23, 1914)

Three weeks after the assassination of Archduke Franz Ferdinand in Sarajevo, the Austro-Hungarian government submitted the ultimatum below to Serbia to seize the opportunity presented by the crisis to settle longstanding grievances with Serbia. Sir Edward Grey, the British Foreign Secretary, commented that he had "never before seen one state address to another independent state a document of so formidable a character."

On the 31st of March 1909 the Serbian Minister at Vienna on the instructions of his Government, made the following declaration to the Imperial and Royal Government:

"Serbia recognizes that her rights have not been affected by the *fait accompli* created in Bosnia-Herzegovina and that consequently she will conform to such decisions as the Powers may take in conformity with Article XXV of the Treaty of Berlin. In deference to the advice of the Great Powers, Serbia undertakes henceforward to renounce the attitude of protest and opposition which she has adopted with regard to the annexation since last autumn and she further engages to modify the direction of her present policy with regard to Austria-Hungary and to live henceforward on a footing of good neighborliness."

The history of recent years and in particular the painful events of the 28 June have demonstrated the existence in Serbia of a subversive movement the aim of which is to detach from the Austro-Hungarian Monarchy certain parts of its territories. This movement which had its birth under the eye of the Serbian Government has gone so far as to manifest itself beyond the territory of the Kingdom by of acts of terrorism, by a series of outrages and murders.

The Royal Serbian Government, far from fulfilling the formal pledges contained in the declaration of the 31 March, 1909, has done nothing to repress these movements; it has tolerated the criminal machinations of various societies and associations directed against the Monarchy, unrestrained language on the part of the press, glorification of the perpetrators of outrages, participation of officers and officials in subversive agitation, unwholesome propaganda in public education, in short tolerated all the manifestations of a nature to inculcate in the Serbian population hatred of the Monarchy and contempt of its institutions.

This culpable tolerance of the Royal Government of Serbia had not ceased at the moment when the events of the 28 June last revealed its disastrous consequences to the whole world.

It is shown results by the depositions and confessions of the criminal authors of the outrage of the 28 June that the Sarajevo assassinations were planned in Belgrade, that the arms and explosives with which the murderers were found to be provided had been given them by Serbian officers and officials belonging to the *Narodna Odbrana* and finally that the passage into Bosnia of the criminals and their arms was organized and effectuated by the chiefs of the Serbian frontier service.

The results here mentioned of the preliminary investigation do not permit the Imperial and Royal Government to pursue any longer the attitude of expectant forbearance which they have for years observed towards the machinations concentrated in Belgrade and thence propagated in the territories of the Monarchy; the results on the contrary impose on them the duty of putting an end to the intrigues which form a permanent threat to the tranquility of the Monarchy.

It is to achieve this end that the Imperial and Royal Government sees itself obliged to demand from the Serbian Government a formal assurance that it condemns the propaganda directed against the Austro-Hungarian Monarchy; that is to say the aggregate of tendencies, the ultimate aim of which is to detach from the Monarchy territories belonging thereto, and that it undertakes to suppress by every means this criminal and terrorist propaganda.

In order to give a formal character to this undertaking the Royal Government of Serbia shall cause to be published on the front page of the *Official Journal* of the 26/13 July the following declaration:

"The Royal Government of Serbia condemns the propaganda directed against Austria-Hungary, i.e., the aggregate of tendencies, the ultimate aim of which is to detach from the Austro-Hungarian Monarchy territories which form part thereof, and it sincerely deplores the fatal consequences of these criminal proceedings."

"The Royal Government regrets that Serbian officers and officials have participated in the above-mentioned propaganda and thereby compromised the good neighborly relations to which the Royal Government had solemnly pledged itself by its declaration of the 31 of March 1909."

"The Royal Government, which disapproves and repudiates all idea or attempt at interference with the destinies of the inhabitants of any part whatsoever of Austria-Hungary, considers it its duty formally to warn officers, officials and all population of the Kingdom that henceforward they will proceed with the utmost rigor against all persons who may render themselves guilty of such machinations which it will use all its efforts to forestall and repress."

This declaration shall simultaneously be communicated to the Royal Army as an order of the day by His Majesty the King and shall be published in the *Official Bulletin of the Army*.

The Royal Serbian Government shall further undertake:

1. To suppress any publication which incites to hatred and contempt of the Monarchy and the general tendency of which is directed against its territorial integrity;
2. To dissolve immediately the society styled *Narodna Odbrana*, to confiscate all its means of propaganda, and to proceed in the same manner against other societies and their branches in Serbia which engage in propaganda against the Austro-Hungarian Monarchy; the Royal Government will take the necessary measures to prevent the dissolved societies from continuing their activities under another name and form;
3. To eliminate without delay from public instruction in Serbia, both as regards the teaching body and the methods of instruction, all that serves or might serve to foment the propaganda against Austria-Hungary;
4. To remove from the military service and the administration in general all officers and officials guilty of propaganda against the Austro-Hungarian Monarchy and of whom the Imperial and Royal Government reserves to itself the right to the names and deeds to the Royal Government;
5. To accept the collaboration in Serbia of organs of the Imperial and Royal Government in the suppression of the subversive movement directed against the territorial integrity of the Monarchy;
6. To take judicial proceedings against accessories to the plot of the 28 June who are on Serbian territory; organs delegated by the Imperial and Royal Government will take part in the investigation relating thereto;
7. To proceed without delay to the arrest of Major Voija Tankosic and of a certain Milan Ciganovic, a Serbian State employee implicated by the findings of the preliminary investigation at Sarajevo;
8. To prevent by effective measures the cooperation of the Serbian Authorities in the illicit traffic in arms and explosives across the frontier; to dismiss and severely punish the officials of the Šabac and Ložnica frontier service guilty of having assisted the authors of the Sarajevo crime by facilitating their passage across the frontier;
9. To furnish the Imperial and Royal Government with explanations regarding the unjustifiable utterances of high Serbian officials both in Serbia and abroad, who, notwithstanding their official position, have not hesitated since the crime of the 28 June to express themselves in interviews in terms of hostility towards the Austro-Hungarian Monarchy, finally;
10. To notify the Imperial and Royal Government without delay of the execution of the measures comprised under the preceding heads.

The Imperial and Royal Government expects the reply of the Royal Government at the latest by 5 o'clock on Saturday 25 of this month at 5 p.m.

Source: See Luigi Albertini, *The Origins of the War of 1914.* 3 Vols. Trans. Isabella M. Massey (New York: Oxford University Press, 1952), II, pp. 286–288.

30. Viscount Ishii Remembers Russian and German Arrogance (1936)

In his memoirs, published in 1936, Viscount Kikujiro Ishii (1866–1945) explained the Japanese perspective on the emergence of hostilities with Russia, the alliance with Britain, and the impact of both on the calculations of Germany.

The Negotiations between Japan and Russia in 1903 opened under foreboding conditions. Up to that time Japan had been exercising such self-restraint in the face of the impending national danger that even foreign nations wondered at it. Since the Tripartite Intervention, however, Japan's diplomacy had developed some perspicacity, and when Britain now extended a hand to her, Japan gladly grasped it and the Anglo-Japanese Alliance was formed. Germany was now delighted with her handiwork. France was much distressed by this troublesome development, as it left no course open to her but to continue her unwholesome association with Russia. Probably to offset the Anglo-Japanese Alliance, France and Russia quickly formed and announced a fresh pact between them.

By this time Russia's fever for East Asiatic conquest had become incurable. Japan she considered too insignificant to bother about, while Britain she thought ruined by the South African War. As for the Anglo-Japanese Alliance, Russia did not think it worth the paper it was written on. Indeed, there seemed to be no cure for Russian militarism except a major surgical operation. Thus when the curtain arose on the Russo-Japanese negotiations, the Russian attitude was menacing and overbearing. Russia would tolerate no interference from any power except China in the liquidation of Manchuria, inasmuch as this was territory "which had been conquered by the might of Russian arms." Mr. Komura, the Japanese foreign minister, reminded the Russian representatives of the facts of the Manchurian affairs, but his soft-spoken words fell on deaf ears. In the opinion of the Russian militarists, if Russo-Japanese negotiations were to be held at all, it would have to be at some point south of the Yalu River. They implied that Japan's sphere of influence was not recognized north of the Daido River. At the same time the Russian advanced such impossible proposals as the lease of Masanpo and generally made it clear that, instead of looking for a fair settlement of the issues, they were prolonging the discussions merely to gain time to strengthen their army and navy and place Japan in a helpless position.

The details of the negotiations with Russia will not be recited here, as they were published when the war broke out and are now generally known. The war between greedy militarism and righteous civilization did not last long. The loss of Port Arthur, the defeat at Mukden and the annihilation of the Baltic fleet in the Straits of Tsushima were the three stages of Russia's collapse that brought her to the peace table at Portsmouth. The Portsmouth Conference, lasting only one month, changed the political geography of the Far East. The Russia so dreaded by Bismarck, which had startled the world by directing its limitless population and energy toward the Far East, was now a thing of yesterday, withdrawing from Korea and abandoning its fortresses and railways in North China and South Manchuria. It seemed that Russia was at last awakened from her dream of an ice-free port and cured of her fever for eastward conquest. But for this cure she paid dearly.

We can understand now why Germany exulted when she learned of the formation of the Anglo-Japanese Alliance. Her scheme matured almost as she had planned it. Russia's lust for eastward expansion had to be aroused; Japan had to be emboldened against Russian might; Japan would not quail but fight Russia if allied with Britain; and the ensuing war would be a long drawn out affair in which neither side would be overwhelmingly victorious. Outside of the short duration of the war and Japan's smashing victory, the situation developed as contemplated, and Germany's mighty neighbor, who used to cause Bismarck sleepless nights, had now fallen, in fighting strength, to the position of a third-rate European power. As for France, she stood completely isolated. The Kaiser had every reason to be pleased with his statecraft. If he had been wise and prudent, the Hohenzollern house today might be ruling securely, with Germany the mistress of the world. Flushed with success, however, the Kaiser flourished his mailed fist, rattled his saber, invaded the Mediterranean and disturbed its smooth waters at Morocco, and by stirring up trouble everywhere incurred the ill-will of the powers. Not only did he make enemies in Europe, but he needlessly irritated Japan with his Yellow Peril propaganda. He is said to have exhibited at different European courts an oil painting depicting Japan as a second Ghenghis Khan trampling down white civilization. The seeds of resentment sown by him all over Europe and the Orient grew and bore fruit, and when the World War broke out enemies of Germany arose all over the world to ruin his empire and destroy his family.

Source: See Viscount Kikujiro Ishii, *Diplomatic Commentaries.* Trans. and Ed. William R. Langdon (Baltimore: The Johns Hopkins Press, 1936), pp. 63–65.

SELECTED BIBLIOGRAPHY

Abernethy, David B. *The Dynamics of Global Dominance: European Overseas Empires, 1415–1980*. New Haven, CT: Yale University Press, 2000.

Adams, Frederick Upham. *Conquest of the Tropics: The Story of the Creative Enterprises Conducted by the United Fruit Company*. Garden City, NY: Doubleday, 1914.

Adas, Michael. *Machines as the Measures of Men: Science, Technology, and Ideologies of Western Dominance*. Ithaca, NY: Cornell University Press, 1989.

Ageron, Charles Robert. *Modern Algeria: A History from 1830 to the Present*. Trenton: Africa World Press, 1991.

Ahmad, Feroz. *The Making of Modern Turkey*. London: Routledge, 1993.

Alatas, Syed Hussein. *Thomas Stamford Raffles, 1781–1826: Schemer or Reformer?* Singapore: Angus and Robinson, 1971.

Albertini, Luigi. *The Origins of the War of 1914*. 3 vols. Translated by Isabella Mellis Massey. New York: Oxford University Press, 1952.

Albertini, Rudolf von. *European Colonial Rule, 1880–1940: The Impact of the West on India, Southeast Asia, and Africa*. Westport, CT: Greenwood Press, 1982.

Aldrich, Robert. *Greater France: A History of French Overseas Expansion*. New York: St Martin's, 1996.

Alexander, R. S. *Napoleon*. London: Arnold, 2001.

Alfonso, Oscar M. *Theodore Roosevelt and the Philippines, 1897–1909*. Quezon City: University of the Philippines Press, 1970.

Algar, Hamid. *Wahabbism: A Critical Essay*. Oneota, NY: Islamic Publications, 2002.

Al-Rasheed, Madawi. *A History of Saudi Arabia*. New York: Cambridge University Press, 2002.

Ambrosius, Lloyd. *Woodrow Wilson and the American Diplomatic Tradition: The Treaty Fight in Perspective*. Cambridge: Cambridge University Press, 1990.

Ammon, Harry. *James Monroe: The Quest for National Identity*. Charlottesville: University Press of Virginia, 1990.

Anderson, Eugene N. *The First Moroccan Crisis, 1904–1906*. Hamden, CT: Archon Books, 1966.

Anderson, M. S. *The Eastern Question 1774–1923*. London: Macmillan, 1966.

Anderson, Margaret Lavinia. *Practicing Democracy: Elections and Political Culture in Imperial Germany*. Princeton, NJ: Princeton University Press, 2000.

Andersson, Ingvar. *A History of Sweden*. Translated by Carolyn Hannay and Alan Blair. New York: Praeger, 1970.

Andrew, Christopher M. *Théophile Delcassé and the Making of the Entente Cordiale: A Reappraisal of French Foreign Policy, 1898–1905*. London: Macmillan, 1968.

Ansari, Ali. *Iran*. New York: Routledge, 2004.

Anscombe, Frederick F. *The Ottoman Gulf: The Creation of Kuwait, Saudi Arabia, and Qatar*. New York: Columbia University Press, 1997.

Arberry, A. J. *The Legacy of Persia*, Oxford, Clarendon Press, 1953.

Arnold, J. *Marengo and Hohenlinden*. Lexington, VA: Napoleon Books, 1999.

_____. *Napoleon Conquers Austria*. Westport, CT: Praeger, 1995.

Auchincloss, Louis. *Woodrow Wilson: A Penguin Life*. New York: Viking Press, 2000.

Baer, George W. *One Hundred Years of Sea Power: The U.S. Navy, 1890–1990*. Stanford, CA: Stanford University Press, 1993.

Balfour, Sebastian. *The End of the Spanish Empire, 1898–1923*. New York: Oxford University Press, 1997.

Bannister, Robert C. *Social Darwinism: Science and Myth in Anglo-American Thought*. Philadelphia: Temple University Press, 1979.

Banton, Michael. *Racial Theories*. Cambridge: Cambridge University Press, 1987.

Barraclough, Geoffrey. *From Agadir to Armageddon: Anatomy of a Crisis*. London: Weidenfeld & Nicolson, 1982.

Barthorp, Michael. *Heroes of the Crimea: Balaclava and Inkerman*. London: Blandford, 1991.

———. *The Zulu War: Isandhlwana to Ulundi*. London: Weidenfeld & Nicolson, 2002.

Barton, H. Arnold. *Sweden and Visions of Norway: Politics and Culture, 1814–1905*. Carbondale: Southern Illinois University Press, 2003.

Basham, A. L., ed. *A Cultural History of India*. Oxford: Clarendon, 1975.

Bassin, Mark. *Imperial Visions: Nationalist Imagination and Geographical Expansion in the Russian Far East, 1840–1865*. Cambridge: Cambridge University Press, 1999.

Bauer, K. Jack. *The Mexican War, 1846–1848*. Lincoln: University of Nebraska Press, 1992.

Bausani, Alessandro. *The Persians: From the Earliest Days to the Twentieth Century*. New York: St. Martin's Press, 1971.

Bayly, C. A. *The Birth of the Modern World, 1780–1914: Global Connections and Comparisons*. Oxford: Blackwell, 2004.

Beale, Howard K. *Theodore Roosevelt and the Rise of America to World Power*. Baltimore: The Johns Hopkins University Press Paperbacks, 1984.

Beasley, William G. *The Rise of Modern Japan: Political, Economic and Social Change since 1850.* London: Weidenfeld & Nicholson, 2000.

_____. *The Meiji Restoration.* Stanford, CA: Stanford University Press, 1972.

Beeching, Jack. *The Chinese Opium Wars.* London: Hutchinson, 1975.

Beehler, W. H. *The History of the Italian-Turkish War.* Annapolis, MD: Advertiser-Republican, 1913.

Beller, Steven. *Francis Joseph.* London, New York: Longman, 1996.

Bemis, Samuel Flagg. *John Quincy Adams and the Foundations of American Foreign Policy.* New York: Alfred E. Knopf, 1949.

Benedict, Ruth. *Race and Racism.* London: Routledge & Kegan Paul, 1983.

Bennett, Norman Robert. *A History of the Arab State of Zanzibar.* London: Methuen, 1978.

Bérenger, Jean. *A History of the Habsburg Empire.* London, New York: Longman, 1994.

Bergeron, Louis. *France under Napoleon.* Princeton: Princeton University Press, 1981.

Berghahn, Volker R. *Imperial Germany, 1871–1914.* Providence: Berghahn Books, 1994.

_____. *Germany and the Approach of War in 1914.* London: Macmillan, 1993.

_____. *Der Tirpitz-Plan: Genesis und Verfall einer innenpolitischen Krisenstrategie unter Wilhelm II.* Düsseldorf: Droste, 1971.

Berkeley, G.F.H. *Italy in the Making 1815 to 1846.* Cambridge: Cambridge University Press, 1932.

_____. *The Campaign of Adowa and the Rise of Menelik.* London: Archibald Constable, 1902.

Berkhofer, Robert F., Jr. *The White Man's Indian. Images of the American Indian from Columbus to the Present.* New York: Vintage Books, 1979.

Bernstein, R. B. *Thomas Jefferson.* Oxford: Oxford University Press, 2003.

Bierman, John. *Dark Safari: The Life behind the Legend of Henry Morton Stanley.* New York: Alfred A. Knopf, 1990.

Bilgrami, Asghar H. *Afghanistan and British India, 1793–1907: A Study in Foreign Relations.* New Delhi: Sterling, 1972.

Birmingham, David. *Trade and Empire in the Atlantic, 1400–1600.* New York: Routledge, 2000.

Black, Jeremy. *The British Seaborne Empire.* New Haven, CT: Yale University Press, 2004.

Blake, Robert. *Disraeli.* London: Eyre and Spottiswoode, 1966.

Blom, J.C.H., and Emiel Lamberts, eds. *History of the Low Countries.* Translated by C. Kennedy. New York: Berghahn, 2005.

Bordo, Michael D., Alan M. Taylor, and Jeffrey G. Williamson, eds. *Globalization in Historical Perspective.* Chicago: University of Chicago Press, 2003.

Bowden, Scott. *Napoleon and Austerlitz.* Chicago: The Emperor's Press, 1997.

Brands, H. W. *Lone Star Nation: How a Ragged Army of Volunteers Won the Battle for Texas Independence—and Changed America.* New York: Doubleday, 2004.

_____. *T. R.: The Last Romantic*. New York: BasicBooks, 1997.

Bridge, F. R. *From Sadowa to Sarajeva: the Foreign Policy of Austria-Hungary 1860–1914*. London: Routledge & Kegan Paul, 1972.

Broers, Michael. *Europe under Napoleon, 1799–1815*. London: Arnold, 1996.

Brookner, Anita. *Romanticism and Its Discontents*. New York: Viking, 2000.

Brooks, John. *Telephone: The First Hundred Years*. New York: Harper & Row, 1976.

Broome, Richard. *Aboriginal Australians: Black Responses to White Dominance, 1788–1994*. St. Leonards: Allen and Unwin, 2002.

Brower, Daniel. *Turkestan and the Fate of the Russian Empire*. London: Routledge Courzon, 2003.

Bruce, George. *Six Battles for India: The Anglo-Sikh Wars, 1845–6, 1848–9*. London: Arthur Barker, 1969.

Bucholz, Arden. *Moltke, Schlieffen, and Prussian War Planning*. New York: St. Martin's, 1991.

Buckner, Phillip A. *The Transition to Responsible Government: British Policy in British North America, 1815–1850*. Westport, CT: Greenwood Press, 1985.

Bunau-Varilla, Philippe. *Panama: The Creation, Destruction, and Resurrection*. New York: McBride, Nast and Co., 1914.

Bushnell, David. *Simón Bolívar: Liberation and Disappointment*. New York: Longman, 2003.

Cain, Peter J., and A. G. Hopkins, *British Imperialism, 1688–2000*. Harlow: Longman, 2001.

Campbell, Charles S., Jr. *Anglo-American Understanding, 1898–1903*. Baltimore: The Johns Hopkins Press, 1957.

Canale, Jean-Suret. *French Colonialism in Tropical Africa 1900–1945*. New York: Pica Press 1971.

Carbonnier, Jeanne. *Congo Explorer, Pierre Savorgnan de Brazza, 1852–1905*. New York: Scribner, 1960.

Castle, I. *Aspern & Wagram 1809*. Oxford: Osprey, 1996.

Castle, Ian. *Zulu War, 1879*. Westport, CT: Greenwood, 2005.

Cecil, Lamar. *Wilhelm II*. Chapel Hill: University of North Carolina Press, 1996.

Chandler, David G. *The Campaigns of Napoleon*. London: Weidenfeld & Nicolson, 1995.

_____. *Jena 1806: Napoleon Destroys Prussia*. London: Osprey, 1993.

Chandra, Bipan, *Essays on Contemporary India*. New Delhi: Har-Anand, 1993.

Chapman, Tim. *The Congress of Vienna: Origins, Process and Results*. London: Routledge, 1998.

Chernow, Rob. *Alexander Hamilton*. New York: Penguin Books, 2004.

Chickering, Roger. *Imperial Germany and the Great War, 1914–1918*. Cambridge: Cambridge University Press, 2004.

Churchill, Rogers Platt. *The Anglo-Russian Convention of 1907*. Cedar Rapids, IA: Torch Press, 1939.

Clark, Chris, *Kaiser Wilhelm II*. New York: Longman, 2000.

Clark, Christopher. *Iron Kingdom: The Rise and Downfall of Prussia, 1600–1947*. Cambridge: Belknap Press, 2006.

Clausewitz, Carl von. *On War*. Princeton, NJ: Princeton University Press, 1984.

Cleveland, William L. *A History of the Modern Middle East*. Boulder, CO: Westview, 1994.

Cohen, Warran I., ed. *The Cambridge History of American Foreign Relations*. 4 vols. New York: Cambridge University Press, 1993.

Cohen, William B. *The French Encounter with Africans: White Response to Blacks, 1530–1880*. Bloomington: Indiana University Press, 2003.

Collin, Richard H. *Theodore Roosevelt's Caribbean: The Panama Canal, the Monroe Doctrine, and the Latin American Context*. Baton Rouge: Louisiana State University Press, 1990.

Collins, Robert O. *The Southern Sudan, 1883–1898: A Struggle for Control*. New Haven, CT: Yale University Press, 1964.

Connaughton, Richard M. *Rising Sun and Tumbling Bear: Russia's War with Japan*. New York: Cassell, 2003.

Cook, Hugh. *The Sikh Wars: The British Army in the Punjab, 1845–1849*. London: Leo Cooper, 1975.

Cooke, James J. *New French Imperialism 1880–1910: The Third Republic and Colonial Expansion*. Hamden, CT: Archon Books, 1973.

Copper, Duff. *Talleyrand*. London: Weidenfeld & Nicolson, 2001.

Craig, Gordon A. *The Politics of the Prussian Army: 1640–1945*. London: Oxford University Press, 1964.

Crankshaw, Edward. *Bismarck*. New York: Viking Press, 1981.

Crone, Patricia, and Martin Hinds. *God's Caliph: Religious Authority in the First Centuries of Islam*. Cambridge: Cambridge University Press, 1986.

Cunninghan, Noble E. *The Presidency of James Monroe*. Lawrence: University of Kansas Press, 1996.

Dallas, Gregor. *The Final Act: The Roads to Waterloo*. New York: Henry Holt, 1997.

_____. *At the Heart of a Tiger. Clemenceau and His World 1841–1929*. New York: Carroll & Graf, 1993.

Daniel, Elton L. *The History of Iran*. New York: Greenwood, 2000.

Darby, Philip. *Three Faces of Imperialism: British and American Approaches to Asia and Africa, 1870–1970*. New Haven, CT: Yale University Press, 1987.

Davenport, R., and C. Saunders. *South Africa: A Modern History*. London: Macmillan, 2000.

Davenport, T.R.H. *South Africa: A Modern History*. Basingstoke: MacMillan, 1987.

David, Saul. *Zulu: The Heroism and Tragedy of the Zulu War of 1879*. New York: Viking Press, 2004.

_____. *The Indian Mutiny, 1857*. London, Viking, 2002.

DeConde, Alexander. *The Quasi-War: The Politics and Diplomacy of the Undeclared War with France, 1797–1801.* New York: Charles Scribner's Sons, 1966.

DeLong-Bas, Natana J. *Wahhabi Islam: From Revival and Reform to Global Jihad.* Oxford: Oxford University Press, 2004.

Di Scala, Spencer. *Italy from Revolution to Republic: 1700 to the Present.* Boulder, CO: Westview, 1998.

Dixon, Peter. *Canning: Politician and Statesman.* London: Weidenfeld & Nicolson, 1976.

Dobson, John. *Reticent Expansionism: The Foreign Policy of William McKinley.* Pittsburgh: Duquesne University Press, 1988.

Dodwell, Henry. *The Founder of Modern Egypt: A Study of Muhammed Ali.* Cambridge: Cambridge University Press, 1931.

Duffy, Michael. *The Younger Pitt.* New York: Longman, 2000.

Dugard, Martin. *Into Africa: The Epic Adventures of Stanley and Livingstone.* New York: Doubleday, 2003.

Dunlop, Ian. *Edward VII and the Entente Cordiale.* London: Constable, 2004.

Dupuy, Trevor N. *A Genius for War: The German Army and General Staff, 1807–1945.* Fairfax: Hero Books, 1964.

Duus, Peter. *The Abacus and the Sword: The Japanese Penetration of Korea, 1895–1910.* Berkeley: University of California Press, 1995.

_____. *Feudalism in Japan.* New York: McGraw-Hill, 1993.

Dwyer, Philip. *Talleyrand.* London: Longman, 2002.

Dwyer, T. Ryle. *Eamon de Valera.* Dublin: Gill & Macmillan, 1980.

Dziewanowski, M. K. *Alexander I: Russia's Mysterious Tsar.* New York: Hippocrene Books, 1990.

Ehrman, John. *The Younger Pitt: The Consuming Struggle.* London: Constable, 1996.

Eldridge, C. C. *Disraeli and the Rise of a New Imperialism.* Cardiff: University of Wales Press, 1996.

Elliott, Jane. *Some Did It for Civilization, Some Did It for Their Country: A Revised View of the Boxer War.* Hong Kong: The Chinese University Press, 2002.

Ellis, Geoffrey J. *Continental Blockade: The Case of Alsace.* Oxford: Oxford University Press, 1989.

———. *Napoleon's Continental Blockade.* Oxford: Clarendon Press, 1981.

Ellis, Joseph J. *Passionate Sage: The Character and Legacy of John Adams.* New York: W. W. Norton, 2001.

_____. *American Sphinx: The Character of Thomas Jefferson.* New York: Knopf, 1997.

Embree, Ainslie T., ed. *Encyclopedia of Asian History.* 4 vols. New York: Scribner's, 1988.

Englund, S. *Napoleon. A Political Life.* New York: Scribner, 2004.

Epstein, Israel. *From Opium War to Liberation.* Hong Kong: Joint Publishing Co., 1980.

Erickson, Edward J. *Defeat in Detail: The Ottoman Army in the Balkans, 1912–1913.* Westport: Praeger, 2003.

Esdaile, Charles. *The French Wars, 1792–1815*. London: Routledge, 2001.

_____. *The Wars of Napoleon*. London: Longman, 1995.

Ewans, Martin. *Afghanistan: A Short History of Its People and Politics*. New York: Harper Perennial, 2002.

Farwell, Byron. *The Encyclopedia of Nineteenth Century Land Warfare*. New York: W. W. Norton, 2001.

_____. *The Great Anglo-Boer War*. New York: Harper & Row, 1976.

_____. *Queen Victoria's Little Wars*. New York: W. W. Norton, 1972.

Featherstone, Donald. *Omdurman 1898: Kitchener's Victory in the Sudan*. Oxford: Osprey Publishing, 1994.

_____. *India from the Conquest of Sind to the Indian Mutiny*. London: Blandell, 1992.

Fehrenbach, T. R. *Lone Star: A History of Texas and the Texans*. New York: Da Capo Press, 2000.

Ferrer, Ada. *Insurgent Cuba: Race, Nation, and Revolution, 1868–1898*. Chapel Hill: University of North Carolina Press, 1999.

Ferrero, Guglielmo. *The Reconstruction of Europe: Talleyrand and the Congress of Vienna, 1814–1815*. New York: Norton, 1963.

Feuchtwanger, E. J. *Bismarck*. New York: Routledge, 2002.

Fichtner, Paula Sutter. *The Habsburg Empire. From Dynasticism to Multinationalism*. Malabar: Krieger, 1997.

Finer, S. E. *The History of Government from the Earliest Times*. 3 vols. Oxford: Oxford University Press, 1997.

Fisher, Alan. *Between Russians, Ottomans, and Turks: Crimea and Crimean Tatars*. Istanbul: Isis Press, 1998.

Fisher, Godfrey. *Barbary Legend: War, Trade, and Piracy in North Africa*. Westport, CT: Greenwood Press, 1974.

Fisher, H.A.L. *Bonapartism*. Oxford: Clarendon, 1908.

Fisher, Sydney Nettleton, and William Ochsenwald. *The Middle East: A History*. New York: MacGraw-Hill, 1990.

Fletcher, Ian, and Natalia Ischchenko. *The Crimean War: A Clash of Empires*. Staplehurst: Spellmount Publishers, 2004.

Flower-Smith, Malcolm, and Edmund Yorke, eds. *Mafeking: The Story of a Siege*. New York: Covos-Day Books, 2000.

Förster, Stig, Wolfgang J. Mommsen and Ronald Edward Robinson, eds. *Bismarck, Europe and Africa: The Berlin Africa Conference 1884–1885 and the Onset of Partition*. Oxford: Oxford University Press, 1988.

Foster, R. F. *Modern Ireland,* London: Allen Lane, 1988.

Frank, Allen J. *Islamic Historiography and "Bulghar" Identity among the Tatars and Bashkirs of Russia*. Leiden: Brill, 1998.

Frei, Henry P. *Japan's Southward Advance and Australia: From the Sixteenth Century to World War II*. Melbourne: Melbourne University Press, 1991.

Freidel, Frank. *The Splendid Little War.* New York: Dell, 1958.

Fremont-Barnes, Gregory, and Todd Fisher. *The Napoleonic Wars: The Rise and Fall of an Empire.* Oxford: Osprey Publishing, 2004.

_____. *The French Revolutionary Wars.* Oxford: Osprey Publishing, 2001.

_____. *The Napoleonic Wars, Vol. 4: The Fall of the French Empire, 1813–1815.* Oxford: Osprey, 2001.

Gaillard, Jean-Michel. *Jules Ferry.* Paris: Fayard, 1989.

Gann, L. H., and Peter Duignan. *The Rulers of German Africa 1884–1914.* Stanford, CA: Stanford University Press, 1977.

Gardner, Brian. *Mafeking: A Victorian Legend.* London: Cassell, 1966.

Gat, Azar. *A History of Military Thought: From the Enlightenment to the Cold War.* New York: Oxford University Press, 2001.

Gates, David. *The Napoleonic Wars, 1803–1815.* London: Arnold, 1997.

Gernet, Jacques. *A History of Chinese Civilization.* Translated by J. R. Foster. New York: Cambridge University Press, 1982.

Gerolymatos, André. *The Balkan Wars: Conquest, Revolution, and Retribution from the Ottoman Era to the Twentieth Century and Beyond.* New York: Basic Books, 2002.

Giddens, Paul Henry. *The Early Petroleum Industry.* Philadelphia: Porcupine Press, 1974.

Glatz, Ferenc., ed. *Hungarians and Their Neighbors in Modern Times, 1867–1950.* New York: Columbia University Press, 1995.

Glenny, Misha. *The Balkans: Nationalism, War, and the Great Powers, 1804–1999.* New York: Viking, 2000.

Goetz, Robert. *1805—Austerlitz: Napoleon and the Destruction of the Third Coalition.* London: Greenhill Books, 2005.

Goldschmidt, Arthur, Jr. *Modern Egypt: The Formation of a Nation-State.* Boulder, CO: Westview, 1988.

_____. *A Concise History of the Middle East.* Boulder, CO: Westview, 1983.

Gordon, John Steele. *A Thread across the Ocean: The Heroic Story of the Transatlantic Cable.* New York: Perennial, 2003.

Gould, Lewis L. *The Presidency of William McKinley.* Lawrence: University Press of Kansas, 1983.

Graebner, Norman A. *Empire on the Pacific: A Study in American Continental Expansion.* Santa Barbara: ABC-Clio, 1983.

Grainger, John D. *The Amiens Truce: Britain and Bonaparte, 1801–1803.* Rochester, NY: Boydell Press, 2004.

Gregory, J. S. *Great Britain and the Taipings.* London: Routledge and Kegan Paul, 1969.

Guedalla, Philip. *The Duke.* London: Wordsworth Editions, 1997.

Gullick, Edward Vose. *Europe's Classical Balance of Power.* Ithaca, NY: Cornell University Press, 1955.

Hale, William. *Turkish Foreign Policy 1774–2000.* London: Frank Cass, 2000.

Hall, Richard C. *The Balkan Wars, 1912–1913: Prelude to the First World War*. London: Routledge, 2000.

Harbaugh, William H. *Power and Responsibility: The Life and Times of Theodore Roosevelt*. 1961. Newtown: American Political Biography Press, 1997.

Harrington, Peter. *Peking 1900: The Boxer Rebellion*. London: Greenwood, 2005.

Harris, John. *The Indian Mutiny*. London: Wordsworth Editions, 2000.

Hart, Robert A. *The Great White Fleet: Its Voyage around the World, 1907–1909*. Boston: Little, Brown, 1965.

Hayes, Carlton J. H. *A Political and Social History of Modern Europe, 1815–1924*. New York: Macmillan, 1926.

Hazareesingh, Sudhir. *The Legend of Napoleon*. London: Granta, 2004.

Healy, David. *The United States in Cuba, 1898–1902: Generals, Politicians, and the Search for Policy*. Madison: University of Wisconsin Press, 1963.

Hearder, Harry. *Italy in the Age of the Risorgimento 1790–1870*. New York: Longman, 1983.

Heckscher, Eli F. *The Continental System: An Economic Interpretation*. Oxford: Clarendon Press, 1922.

Henderson, C. E. *Culture and Customs of India*. Westport, CT: Greenwood Press, 2002.

Henderson, W. O. *The German Colonial Empire 1884–1919*. London: Frank Cass, 1993.

_____. *Friedrich List. Economist and Visionary, 1789–1846*. London: Frank Cass, 1983.

_____. *Studies in German Colonial History*. Chicago: Quadrangle, 1962.

_____. *The Zollverein*. London: Cass, 1959.

Hernández, José M. *Cuba and the United States: Intervention and Militarism, 1868–1933*. Austin: University of Texas Press, 1993.

Herrmann, David G. *The Arming of Europe and the Making of the First World War*. Princeton, NJ: Princeton University Press, 1997.

Herwig, H. H. *Luxury Fleet: The Imperial German Navy, 1888–1918*. London: Allen and Unwin, 1980.

Hess, Robert. *Italian Colonialism in Somalia*. Chicago: University of Chicago Press, 1966.

Hiery, Herman J. *The Neglected War: The German South Pacific and the Influence of World War I*. Honolulu: University of Hawaii Press, 1995.

Hietala, Thomas R. *Manifest Design: Anxious Aggrandizement in Late Jacksonian America*. Ithaca, NY: Cornell University Press, 1985.

Hinde, Wendy. *Castlereagh*. London: Collins, 1981.

_____. *George Canning*. London: Collins, 1973.

Hiro, Dilip. *Inside India Today*. London: Routledge and Kegan Paul, 1976.

Hobhouse, Hermione. *The Crystal Palace and the Great Exhibition*. London: 2002.

Hochschild, Adam. *King Leopold's Ghost*. New York: Houghton Mifflin, 1998.

Hofschröer, Peter. *Waterloo 1815: Quatre Bras and Ligny*. London: Leo Cooper, 2005.

Hollins, D. *Marengo*. Oxford: Osprey Military Publishing, 2000.

Holt, P. M. *The Mahdist State in the Sudan, 1888–1898: A Study of Its Origins, Developments and Overthrow*. Oxford: Clarendon Press, 1970.

Hopkirk, Peter. *The Great Game: The Struggle for Empire in Central Asia*. New York: Kodansha International, 1994.

_____. *Foreign Devils on the Silk Road: The Search for the Lost Cities and Treasures of Chinese Central Asia*. London: John Murray, 1980.

Horsman, Reginald. *Race and Manifest Destiny: The Origins of American Racial Anglo-Saxonism*. Cambridge, MA: Harvard University Press, 1981.

Howard, Michael. *The Franco-Prussian War: The German Invasion of France, 1870–71*. New York: Macmillan, 1961.

Hsieh, P. C. *The Government of China, 1644–1911*. Baltimore: The Johns Hopkins University Press, 1925.

Hsü, Immanuel C. *The Rise of Modern China*. New York: Oxford University Press, 2000.

Hull, Isabel V. *Absolute Destruction: Military Culture and the Practices of War in Imperial Germany*. Ithaca, NY: Cornell University, 2005.

Hurd, Douglas. *The Arrow War: An Anglo-Chinese Confusion, 1856–1860*. New York: Macmillan 1968.

Huttenback, Robert A. *Kashmir and the British Raj, 1847–1947*. Oxford: Oxford University Press, 2004.

Iliffe, John. *Tanganyika under German Rule, 1905–1912*. Cambridge: Cambridge University Press, 1969.

Jackson, J. Hampden. *Clemençeau and the Third Republic*. New York: Collier, 1962.

James, Lawrence. *Raj: The Making and Unmaking of British India*. London: Little, Brown and Company, 1997.

Jansen, Marius, and Kenneth B. Pyle, eds. *Warrior Rule in Japan*. Cambridge: Cambridge University Press, 1995.

_____. *The Emergence of Meiji Japan*. Cambridge: Cambridge University Press, 1995.

_____. *The Making of Modern Japan*. Lexington, MA: Heath, 1978.

Jarausch, Konrad H. *The Enigmatic Chancellor*. New Haven, CT: Yale University Press, 1973.

Jelavich, Barbara. *The Habsburg Empire in European Affairs, 1814–1918*. Hamden, CT: Archon, 1975.

_____. *A Century of Russian Foreign Policy 1814–1914*. Philadelphia: J. B. Lippincott, 1964.

Jenkins, Roy. *Gladstone*. London: MacMillan, 1995.

_____. *Asquith*. London: Collins, 1964.

Jespersen, Knud J. V. *A History of Denmark*. Basingstoke: Palgrave 2004.

Jessup, Philip C. *Elihu Root*. New York: Dodd, Mead, 1938.

Johnson, G. Wesley. *Double Impact: France and Africa in the Age of Imperialism*. Westport, CT: Greenwood Press, 1985.

Joll, James. *The Origins of the First World War*. London: Longman, 1984.

Jones, Greta. *Social Darwinism and English Thought: The Interaction between Biological and Social Theory*. Brighton: Harvester Press, 1980.

Judd, Denis. *The Lion and the Tiger: The Rise and Fall of the British Raj, 1600–1947*. New York: Oxford University Press, 2004.

Judd, Denis, and Keith Surridge. *The Boer War*. London: John Murray, 2003.

Jukes, Geoffrey. *The Russo-Japanese War, 1904–5*. Oxford: Osprey, 2002.

Karabell, Zachary. *Parting the Desert: The Creation of the Suez Canal*. New York: Random House, 2003.

Karsh, Efraim, and Inari Karsh. *Empires of the Sand: The Struggle for Mastery in the Middle East 1789–1923*. Cambridge, MA: Harvard University Press, 2001.

Kazemzedeh, Firuz. *Russia and Britain in Persia, 1864–1914*. New Haven, CT: Yale University Press, 1968.

Keegan, John. *The First World War*. New York: A. Knopf, 1999.

Keene, Donald. *Emperor of Japan: Meiji and His World, 1852–1912*. New York: Columbia University Press, 2002.

Kendle, John Edward. *The Colonial and Imperial Conferences, 1887–1911: A Study in Imperial Organization*. London: Longman, 1967.

Kennedy, Paul, ed. *Grand Strategies in War and Peace*. New Haven, CT: Yale University Press, 1991.

_____. *The Rise of the Anglo-German Antagonism 1860–1914*. London: George Allen & Unwin, 1982.

_____. *The Rise and Fall of British Naval Mastery*. London: A. Lane, 1976.

Kerr, Ian J. *Building the Railways of the Raj, 1850–1900*. Delhi: Oxford University Press, 1995.

Khalid, Adeeb. *The Politics of Muslim Cultural Reform: Jadidism in Central Asia*. Berkeley: University of California Press, 1998.

Kissinger, Henry. *A World Restored: Metternich, Castlereagh and the Problems of Peace*. London: Weidenfeld & Nicolson, 1957.

Knoll, Arthur J. *Togo under Imperial Germany 1884–1914: A Case Study of Colonial Rule*. Stanford, CA: Hoover Institution, 1978.

Kohn, Hans. *American Nationalism: An Interpretative Essay*. New York: Macmillan, 1957.

Kutolowski, John F. *The West and Poland: Essays on Governmental and Public Responses to the Polish National Movement, 1861–1881*. New York: Columbia University Press, 2000.

Kuykendall, Ralph Simpson. *The Hawaiian Kingdom*. 3 vols. Honolulu: University of Hawaii Press, 1965.

LaFeber, Walter. *The American Search for Opportunity, 1865–1913*. Cambridge: Cambridge University Press, 1993.

_____. *The Panama Canal: The Crisis in Historical Perspective*. New York: Oxford University Press, 1989.

Lambert, Andrew D. *Nelson: Britannia's God of War*. London: Faber, 2004.

————. *The Crimean War,* Manchester: University Press, 1990.

Lambert, Nicholas A. *Sir John Fisher's Naval Revolution.* Columbia: University of South Carolina Press, 1999.

Langer, William L. *The Diplomacy of Imperialism, 1890–1902.* New York: Alfred A. Knopf, 1968.

————. *European Alliances and Alignments 1871–1890.* New York: Alfred A. Knopf, 1962.

Langley, Lester, and Thomas Schoonover. *The Banana Men: American Mercenaries and Entrepreneurs in Central America, 1880–1930.* Lexington: University Press of Kentucky, 1995.

Laqueur, Walter. *A History of Terrorism.* Somerset: Transaction, 2001.

Laue, Theodore von. *Sergei Witte and the Industrialization of Russia.* New York: Columbia University Press, 1963.

Lawday, David. *Napoleon's Master: A Life of Prince Talleyrand.* London: Jonathan Cape, 2006.

Lawrence, James. *The Rise and Fall of the British Empire.* London: Little, Brown & Company, 1994.

Leopold, Richard W. *Elihu Root and the Conservative Tradition.* Boston: Little, Brown, 1954.

Lewis, David Levering. *The Race to Fashoda: European Colonialism and African Resistance in the Scramble for Africa.* New York: Weidenfeld & Nicholson, 1987.

Libæk, Ivar, and Øivind Stenersen. *A History of Norway: From the Ice Age to the Age of Petroleum.* Trans. Jean Aase. Oslo: Grøndahl Dreyer, 1999.

Lieven, D.C.B. *Russia and the Origins of the First World War.* New York: St. Martin's Press, 1983.

Lincoln, W. Bruce. *The Great Reforms: Autocracy, Bureaucracy, and the Politics of Change in Imperial Russia.* DeKalb: Northern Illinois University Press, 1990.

Linn, Brian M. *The U.S. Army and Counterinsurgency in the Philippine War, 1899–1902.* Chapel Hill: University of North Carolina Press, 1989.

Louis, William Roger, ed. *Oxford History of the British Empire.* 6 vols. Oxford: University Press, 1998.

Lowe, C. J. *The Reluctant Imperialists: British Foreign Policy 1878–1902.* New York: Macmillan, 1969.

Lowe, John. *The Concert of Europe: International Relations, 1814–70.* London: Hodder & Stoughton, 1991.

Luttwak, Edward. *Strategy.* Cambridge: Belknap, 2001.

Macartney, Carlile A. *The Habsburg Empire, 1790–1918.* London: Weidenfeld & Nicolson, 1971.

Macfie A. L. *The End of the Ottoman Empire.* London: Longman, 1998.

————. *The Eastern Question 1774–1923.* London and New York: Longman, 1989.

Mack, Gerstle. *The Land Divided: A History of the Panama Canal and Other Isthmian Canal Projects.* New York: Octagon Books, 1974.

MacKenzie, David. *Imperial Dreams, Harsh Realities: Tsarist Russian Foreign Policy, 1815–1917.* Fort Worth, TX: Harcourt Brace College Publishers, 1994.

_____. *The Lion of Tashkent, the Career of General M. G. Cherniaev.* Athens: University of Georgia Press, 1974.

_____. *The Serbs and Russian Pan-Slavism, 1875–1878.* Ithaca, NY: Cornell University Press, 1967.

Mackinnon, Aran S. *The Making of South Africa.* Upper Saddle River, NJ: Prentice Hall, 2000.

Mahan, A. T. *The Influence of Sea Power upon History, 1660–1783.* London: Sampson, Low, Marston, 1890.

Maier, Charles S. *Among Empires: American Ascendancy and Its Predecessors.* Cambridge, MA: Harvard University Press. 2006.

Manning, Patrick. *Francophone Sub-Saharan Africa 1880–1995.* Cambridge: Cambridge University Press, 1998.

Marcus, Harold G. *A History of Ethiopia.* Berkeley: University of California Press, 1994.

Marder, A. J. *From the Dreadnought to Scapa Flow: The Royal Navy in the Fisher Era.* 5 vols. London: Oxford University Press, 1970.

Markham, J. D. *Napoleon's Road to Glory: Triumphs, Defeats and Immortality.* London: Brassey's, 2000.

Marks, Frederick W., III. *Velvet on Iron: The Diplomacy of Theodore Roosevelt.* Lincoln: University of Nebraska Press, 1979.

Marks, Steven G. *Road to Power: The Trans-Siberian Railroad and the Colonization of Asian Russia, 1850–1917.* London: I. B. Tauris, 1991.

Martel, Gordon, *The Origins of the First World War.* Longman: London 2003.

Mass, Jeffrey P., and William B. Hauser, eds. *The Bakufu in Japanese History.* Stanford, CA: Stanford University Press, 1985.

Massie, Robert K. *Dreadnought: Britain, Germany and the Coming of the Great War.* London: Pimlico, 2004.

Matsusaka, Yoshihisa Tak. *The Making of Japanese Manchuria, 1904–1932.* Cambridge, MA: Harvard University Asia Center, 2001.

Matthew, H.C.G. *The Liberal Imperialists.* Oxford: University Press, 1973.

May, Stacy, and Galo Plaza Lasso. *The United Fruit Company in Latin America.* Washington, DC: National Planning Association, 1958.

McCarthy, Justin. *The Ottoman Peoples and the End of Empire.* London: Arnold, 2001.

McConnell, Allen. *Tsar Alexander I.* New York: Crowell, 1970.

McCord, Norman. *The Anti-Corn Law League: 1838–1846.* London: George Allen and Unwin, 1958.

McCullough, David. *John Adams.* New York: Touchstone, 2001.

McDougall, Walter. *Promised Land, Crusader State: The American Encounter with the World since 1776.* Boston: Houghton Mifflin, 1997.

McGrath, Ann, ed. *Contested Ground: Australian Aborigines under the British Crown.* St. Leonards: Allen and Unwin, 1995.

McLynn, Frank. *Stanley: The Making of an African Explorer.* London: Constable, 1989.

McMurray, Jonathan S. *Distant Ties: Germany, the Ottoman Empire, and the Construction of the Baghdad Railway.* Westport, CT: Praeger, 2001.

Meaney, Neville. *The Search for Security in the Pacific, 1901–14.* Sydney: Sydney University Press, 1976.

Mercer, Patrick. *Give Them a Volley and Charge!: The Battle of Inkerman, 1854.* Staplehurst: Spellmount, 1998.

———. *Inkerman 1854: The Soldier's Battle.* Oxford: Osprey Publishing, 1998.

Merk, Frederick. *The Oregon Question: Essays in Anglo-American Diplomacy and Politics.* Cambridge, MA: Harvard University Press, 1967.

———. *Manifest Destiny and Mission in American History: A Reinterpretation.* New York: Knopf, 1963.

Merry, Sally E. *Colonizing Hawai'i: The Cultural Power of Law.* Princeton, NJ: Princeton University Press, 1999.

Miller, Stuart C. *"Benevolent Assimilation": The American Conquest of the Philippines, 1899–1902.* New Haven, CT: Yale University Press, 1982.

Mishra, Patit Paban. *A Contemporary History of Laos.* New Delhi: National Book Organization, 1999.

Mombauer, Annika and Wilhelm Deist, eds. *The Kaiser. New Research on Wilhelm II's Role in Imperial Germany.* Cambridge: Cambridge University Press, 2003.

———. *Helmuth von Moltke and the Origins of the First World War.* New York: Cambridge University Press, 2001.

Morgan, Gerald. *Anglo-Russian Rivalry in Central Asia: 1810–1895.* London: Frank Cass, 1981.

Morris, Donald R. *The Washing of the Spears: The Rise and Fall of the Great Zulu Nation.* London: Cape, 1966.

Morris, Edmund. *Theodore Rex.* New York: Random House, 2001.

Moses, Jonathon Wayne. *Norwegian Catch-Up: Development and Globalization before World War I.* Aldershot: Ashgate Publishing, 2005.

Myer, Ramon H., and Mark R. Peattie, eds. *The Japanese Colonial Empire, 1895–1945.* Princeton, NJ: Princeton University Press, 1984.

Myint-U, Thant. *The Making of Modern Burma.* New York: Cambridge University Press, 2001.

Nahm, Andrew C. *Korea: Tradition and Transformation: A History of the Korean People.* Seoul: Hollym International Corporation, 1996.

Nasson, Bill. *The South African War, 1899–1902.* London: Arnold, 1999.

Negash, Tekeste. *Italian Colonialism in Eritrea, 1882–1941: Policies, Praxis, and Impact.* Stockholm: Uppsala University, 1987.

Neillands, Robin. *The Dervish Wars: Gordon and Kitchener in the Sudan 1880–1898.* London: John Murray, 1996.

Neu, Charles E. *An Uncertain Friendship: Theodore Roosevelt and Japan, 1906–1909.* Cambridge, MA: Harvard University Press, 1967.

Newbury, Colin. *The Diamond Ring: Business, Politics and Precious Stones in South Africa, 1867–1947.* Oxford: Clarendon, 1989.

Nicholson, Harold. *The Congress of Vienna: A Study in Allied Unity, 1812–1822.* New York: Viking Press, 1946.

Ninkovich, Frank. *The United States and Imperialism.* Malden: Blackwell Publishers, 2001.

Nipperdey, Thomas. *Deutsche Geschichte, 1800–1866: Bürgerwelt und starker Staat.* Munich: C. H. Beck, 1984.

Nish, Ian H. *Japanese Foreign Policy, 1869–1942: Kasumigaseki to Miyakezaka.* London: Routledge, 1977.

_____. *The Anglo-Japanese Alliance: The Diplomacy of Two Island Empires, 1894–1907.* London: Athlone Press, 1966.

Nolan, Cathal J. *The Greenwood Encyclopedia of International Relations.* 4 vols. Westport, CT: Greenwood, 2002.

O'Brien, Philips, ed. *The Anglo-Japanese Alliance.* New York: Routledge, 2004.

O'Toole, G.J.A. *The Spanish War, and American Epic—1898.* New York: W. W. Norton, 1986.

Okey, Robin. *The Habsburg Monarchy. C. 1765–1918 from Enlightenment to Eclipse.* Basingstoke: MacMillan Press, 2001.

Olcott, Martha Brill. *The Kazakhs.* Stanford, CA: Stanford University Press, 1987, 1995.

Olson, James S., and Robert Shadle, eds. *Historical Dictionary of the British Empire.* 2 vols. Wesport, CT: Greenwood, 1996.

Omer-Cooper, J. D. *A History of Southern Africa.* Oxford: James Currey Publishers, 1997.

Onuf, Peter S. *Jefferson's Empire: The Language of American Nationhood.* Charlottesville: University of Virginia Press, 2000.

Osborne, Thomas J. *Empire Can't Wait: American Opposition to Hawaiian Annexation, 1893–1898.* Kent, OH: Kent State University Press, 1981.

Osgood, Robert E. *Ideals and Self-Interest in America's Foreign Relations.* Chicago: University of Chicago Press, 1953.

Osterhammel Jürgen, and Niels P. Petersson. *Globalization: A Short History.* Princeton, NJ: Princeton University Press, 2005.

_____. *Colonialism: A Theoretical Overview.* Princeton, NJ: Markus Wiener, 2002.

Paine, S.C.M. *The Sino-Japanese War of 1894–1895: Perceptions, Power, and Primacy.* Cambridge: Cambridge University Press, 2003.

Pakenham, Thomas. *The Scramble for Africa: The White Man's Conquest of the Dark Continent from 1876 to 1912.* New York: Random House, 1991.

_____. *The Boer War.* New York: Random House, 1979.

Palmer, Alan. *Napoleon in Russia.* London: Andre Deutsch, 1967.

Palmer, A. W. *A Dictionary of Modern History, 1789–1945.* Harmondsworth: Penguin, 1962.

Paolino, Ernest N. *The Foundations of the American Empire: William Henry Seward and U.S. Foreign Policy.* Ithaca, NY: Cornell University Press, 1973.

Paret, Peter, and Craig, Gordon, eds. *Makers of Modern Strategy from Machiavelli to the Nuclear Age.* Princeton, NJ: Princeton University Press, 1986.

_____. *Clausewitz and the State*. Oxford: Oxford University Press, 1976.

_____. *Yorck and the Era of Prussian Reform: 1807–1815*. Princeton, NJ: Princeton University Press, 1966.

Parkinson, Roger. *Clausewitz*. London: Wayland, 1970.

Patterson, A. T. *Jellicoe: A Biography*. London: MacMillan, 1969.

Pérez, Louis A. *The War of 1898: The United States and Cuba in History and Historiography*. Chapel Hill: University of North Carolina Press, 1998.

_____. *Cuba under the Platt Amendment, 1902–1934*. Pittsburgh: University of Pittsburgh Press, 1986.

Perkins, Dexter. *The Monroe Doctrine, 1867–1907*. Baltimore: The Johns Hopkins Press, 1937.

Perras, Arne. *Carl Peters and German Imperialism 1856–1918: A Political Biography*. Oxford: Clarendon Press, 2004.

Perry, Glenn E. *The Middle East: Fourteen Islamic Centuries*. Upper Saddle River, NJ: Prentice-Hall, 1997.

Petre, F. Loraine. *Napoleon's Conquest of Prussia, 1806*. London: Greenhill Books, 1993.

Pletcher, David M. *The Diplomacy of Annexation: Texas, Oregon, and the Mexican War*. Columbia: University of Missouri Press, 1973.

Polachek, James M. *The Inner Opium War*. Cambridge, MA: Harvard University Press, 1992.

Pollock, John. *Kitchener*. London: Constable, 2001.

Porch, Douglas. *Wars of Empire*. London: Cassell, 2000.

_____. *The French Foreign Legion*. New York: Harper Collins, 1991.

Porter, Bernard. *The Lion's Share: A Short History of British Imperialism 1850–2004*. New York: Longman, 2004.

Porter, Brian A. *When Nationalism Began to Hate. Imagining Modern Politics in Nineteenth Century Poland*. New York: Oxford University Press, 2000.

Power, Thomas F. *Jules Ferry and the Renaissance of French Imperialism*. New York: King's Crown Press, 1944.

Preston, Diana. *Besieged in Peking: The Story of the 1900 Boxer Rising*. London: Constable 1999.

Quataert, Donald. *The Ottoman Empire, 1700–1922*. New York: Cambridge University Press, 2000.

Quinn, Frederick. *The French Overseas Empire*. Westport, CT: Praeger, 2002.

Rabow-Edling, Susanna. *Slavophile Thought and the Politics of Cultural Nationalism*. Albany: State University of New York Press, 2006.

Radan, Peter and Aleksandar Pavkovic, eds. *The Serbs and Their Leaders in the Twentieth Century*. Aldershot: Ashgate, 1997

Ravina, Mark. *The Last Samurai: The Life and Battles of Saigo Takamori*. Hoboken, NJ: John Wiley & Sons, 2004.

Reilly, Thomas H. *The Taiping Heavenly Kingdom: Rebellion and the Blasphemy of Empire*. Seattle: University of Washington Press, 2004.

Rich, Norman. *Friedrich von Holstein. Policy and Diplomacy in the Era of Bismarck and Wilhelm II.* 2 vols. Cambridge: Cambridge University Press, 1964.

Ridley, Jasper. *Garibaldi.* London: Constable, 1974.

Riste, Olav. *Norway's Foreign Relations—A History.* Oslo: Universitetsforlaget, 2001.

Roberts, John. *The Battleship Dreadnought.* London: Conway Maritime, 1992.

Rodger, N.A.M. *The Command of the Ocean: A Naval History of Britain, 1649–1815.* London: Allan Lane, 2004.

Rolo, P.J.V. *Entente Cordiale: The Origins of the Anglo-French Agreements of April 8, 1904.* New York: St. Martin's, 1969.

Rose, John Holland, A. P. Newton, and E. A Benians. *The Cambridge History of the British Empire.* 8 vols. Cambridge: Cambridge University Press, 1959.

_____. *The Revolutionary and Napoleonic Era, 1789–1815.* London: Cambridge University Press, 1935.

Rosenberg, Emily S. *Financial Missionaries to the World: The Politics and Culture of Dollar Diplomacy, 1900–1930.* Cambridge, MA: Harvard University Press, 1999.

Ross, Steven T. *European Diplomatic History, 1789–1815: France against Europe.* Garden City: Anchor Books, 1969.

Rotberg, Robert I. *The Founder: Cecil Rhodes and the Pursuit of Power.* New York: Oxford University Press, 1988.

Rothenberg, Gunther. *The Napoleonic Wars.* London: Cassell, 1999.

Royle, Trevor. *Crimea: The Great Crimean War, 1854–1856.* New York: Palgrave, 2000.

_____. *The Kitchener Enigma.* London: M. Joseph, 1985.

Said, Edward W. *Culture and Imperialism.* London: Vintage, 1994.

Schneid, F. C. *Napoleon's Italian Campaigns: 1805–1815.* Westport, CT: Praeger, 2002.

Schroeder, Paul W. *The Transformation of European Politics, 1763–1848.* Oxford: Clarendon, 1994.

Schurman, Jacob Gould. *The Balkan Wars, 1912–1913.* New York: Cosimo Classics, 2005.

Schuyler, Eugene. *Turkistan.* New York: F. A. Praeger, 1966.

Seager, Robert. *Alfred Thayer Mahan: The Man and His Letters.* Annapolis, MD: Naval Institute Press, 1977.

Shaha, Rishikesh. *Modern Nepal: A Political History 1769–1955.* 2 vols. New Delhi: Manohar, 1990.

Showalter, Dennis. *The Wars of German Unification.* London: Hodder Arnold, 2004.

_____. *Railroads and Rifles: Soldiers, Technology, and the Unification of Germany.* Hamden, CT: Archon Books, 1975.

Sidney, Harcave. *Count Sergei Witte and the Twilight of Imperial Russia: A Biography.* Armonk: M. E. Sharpe, 2004.

Siegel, Jennifer. *Endgame: Britain, Russia, and the Final Struggle for Central Asia.* New York: I. B. Tauris, 2002.

Silberman, Bernard S., and H. D. Harootunian, eds. *Japan in Crisis: Essays in Taisho Democracy.* Princeton, NJ: Princeton University Press, 1974.

Simkins, Peter. *Kitchener's Army: The Raising of the New Armies, 1914–16.* Manchester: Manchester University Press, 1988.

Sinclair, Andrew. *An Anatomy of Terror: A History of Terrorism.* London: Pan Macmillan, 2004.

Singh, Amandeep, and Parmot Singh. *Warrior Saints: Three Centuries of Sikh Military Tradition.* New York: I. B. Tauris, 1988.

Smith, Iain R. *The Origins of the South African War, 1899–1902.* New York: Longman, 1996.

Smith, Page. *John Adams.* 2 vols. Garden City, NY: Doubleday, 1962.

Smith, Woodruff D. *The German Colonial Empire.* Chapel Hill: University of North Carolina Press, 1978.

Soucek, Svat. *A History of Inner Asia.* Cambridge: Cambridge University Press, 2000.

Spence, Jonathan. *God's Chinese Son: The Taiping Heavenly Kingdom of Hong Xiuquan.* New York: Norton, 1996.

_____. *The Search for Modern China.* London: Hutchinson, 1990.

Sprigge, Cecil. *The Development of Modern Italy.* New York: Fertig, 1969.

Steinberg, Jonathan. *Yesterday's Deterrent: Tirpitz and the Birth of the German Battle Fleet.* London: MacDonald, 1965.

Stephan, John J. *The Russian Far East: A History.* Stanford, CA: Stanford University Press, 1994.

Sternhell, Zeev. *Neither Right Nor Left: Fascist Ideology in France.* Translated by David Maisel. Princeton, NJ: Princeton University Press, 1996.

Strachan, Hew. *The First World War.* New York: Oxford University Press, 2001.

Stuart-Fox, Martin. *A History of Laos.* Cambridge: Cambridge University Press, 1997.

Sugden, John. *Nelson, A Dream of Glory.* London: Pimlico, 2005.

Tanner, Stephen. *Afghanistan: A Military History from Alexander to the Fall of the Taliban.* Karachi: Oxford University Press, 2003.

Taylor, A.J.P. *The Struggle for Mastery in Europe, 1848–1918.* Oxford: Clarendon, 1954.

Temperley, Harold. *The Foreign Policy of Canning, 1822–1827.* Hamden, CT: Archon, 1966.

Tilchin, William N. *Theodore Roosevelt and the British Empire: A Study in Presidential Statecraft.* New York: St. Martin's Press, 1997.

Trani, Eugene P. *The Treaty of Portsmouth: An Adventure in American Diplomacy.* Lexington: University of Kentucky Press, 1969.

Vincent, Edgar. *Nelson: Love and Fame.* New Haven, CT: Yale University Press, 2003.

Waley, Arthur. *The Opium War through Chinese Eyes.* Stanford, CA: Stanford University Press, 1968.

Waller, Bruce. *Bismarck.* Oxford: Blackwell, 1997.

Ward, Colin. *Anarchism: A Very Short Introduction.* Oxford: Oxford University Press, 2004.

Warner, Denis, and Peggy Warner. *The Tide at Sunrise: A History of the Russo-Japanese War, 1904–1905*. London: Frank Cass, 2002.

Warren, Gordon H. *Fountain of Discontent: The Trent Affair and the Freedom of the Seas*. Boston: Northeastern University Press, 1981.

Wawro, Geoffrey. *The Austro-Prussian War: Austria's War with Prussia and Italy in 1866*. New York: Cambridge University Press, 1996.

Weber, Eugen Joseph. *Action Française*. Stanford, CA: Stanford University Press, 1962.

Webster, Sir Charles. *The Foreign Policy of Castlereagh, 1812–1815: Britain and the Reconstruction of Europe*. London: G. Bell and Sons, 1963.

Weeks, William Earl. *John Quincy Adams and the American Global Empire*. Louisville: University Press of Kentucky, 1992.

Wehler, Hans Ulrich. *The German Empire, 1871–1918*. New York: Berg Publishers, 1997.

Weir, Gary E. *Building the Kaiser's Navy: The Imperial Naval Office and German Industry in the von Tirpitz Era*. Annapolis, MD: Naval Institute Press, 1992.

Wesseling, H. L. *The European Colonial Empires, 1815–1919*. Harlow: Longman, 2004.

Wetzel, David. *A Duel of Giants: Bismarck, Napoleon III, and the Origins of the Franco-Prussian War*. Madison: University of Wisconsin Press, 2001.

Williamson, D. G. *Bismarck and Germany, 1862–1890*. New York: Longman, 1998.

Wiltshire, David. *The Social and Political Thought of Herbert Spencer*. Oxford: Oxford University Press, 1978.

Wolff, Robert Paul. *In Defense of Anarchism*. Berkeley: University of California Press, 1998.

Wolpert, Stanley. *A New History of India*. New York: Oxford University Press, 2005.

Wong, J. Y. *Deadly Dreams: Opium, Imperialism, and the Arrow War in China*. New York: Cambridge University Press, 1998.

Woodham-Smith, Cecil. *The Reason Why*. London: Readers' Union, 1957.

Wyatt, David K. *Thailand: A Short History*. New Haven, CT: Yale University Press, 1984.

Yapp, M. E. *The Making of the Modern Near East 1792–1923*. London: Longman, 1987.

Zeldin, Theodore. *France 1848–1945*. New York: Oxford University Press, 1979.

Zewde, Bahru. *A History of Modern Ethiopia, 1855–1974*. London: J. Currey, 1991.

Zimmermann, Warren. *First Great Triumph. How Five Americans Made Their Country a World Power*. New York: Farrar, Straus and Giroux, 2002.

Zuckerman, Larry. *The Rape of Belgium*. New York: New York University Press, 2004.

ABOUT THE EDITOR
AND CONTRIBUTORS

Editor

Carl Cavanagh Hodge is an associate professor of political science at the University of British Columbia-Okanagan. His is a former Senior Volkswagen Research Fellow with the American Institute of Contemporary German Studies at the Johns Hopkins University and a former NATO-EAPC fellow. His books include *Atlanticism for a New Century: The Rise, Triumph and Decline of NATO* (Prentice-Hall, 2004); *Politics in North America: Canada, Mexico and the United States,* with Robert J. Jackson, Gregory Mahler, and Holly Reynolds (Prentice-Hall, 2003); *NATO for a New Century: Expansion and Intervention in the Atlantic Alliance* (Praeger, 2002); *Redefining European Security* (Garland, 1999); *All of the People, All of the Time: American Government at the End of the Century* (Peter Lang, 1998); *The Trammels of Tradition: Social Democracy in Britain, France, and Germany* (Greenwood,1994); *Shepherd of Democracy? America and Germany in the Twentieth Century,* co-edited with Cathal J. Nolan (Greenwood, 1992).

Contributors

Joseph Adamczyk is an independent scholar.

Scott Anderson is a doctoral candidate in history at the School of Oriental and African Studies at the University of London.

Adrian U-jin Ang is a doctoral candidate in the Department of Political Science at the University of Missouri-Columbia.

Scott C. Bailey is a doctoral candidate in history at the University of Hawaii at Manoa. His doctoral dissertation is tentatively titled, "Russian Scientific, Ethnographic, and Geographic Travel to Central Eurasia for the Benefit of Empire, 1856–1905." He is currently preparing doctoral fields in world history, Central Eurasian history, Russian/Soviet history, and Islamic history. He received a bachelor's degree in history from East Tennessee State University and his master's degree in history from Murray State University.

Gábor Berczeli is assistant professor of British and American history at Kodolányi János University College, Hungary. His research interests include the history of the British Empire in Africa and U.S. naval history from the Spanish-American War to World War I on which he has published several journal articles.

Volker R. Berghahn is Seth Low Professor of History at Columbia University. He specializes in modern German history and European-American relations. He received his MAfrom the University of North Carolina, Chapel Hill, in 1961 and his PhD from the University of London in 1964. He taught in England and Germany before coming to Brown University in 1988 and to Columbia 10 years later. His publications include *Der Untergang des alten Europas, 1900–1929* (1999), *Quest for Economic Empire*, ed. (1996), *Imperial Germany* (1995), *The Americanization of West German Industry, 1945–1973* (1986), *Modern Germany* (1982), and *Der Tirpitz-Plan* (1971). His *America and the Intellectual Cold Wars in Europe* appeared in 2001.

Kenneth J. Blume is a professor of history in the Department of Arts and Sciences of Albany College of Pharmacy. He holds a PhD from SUNY-Binghamton, and his research explores various aspects of nineteenth-century American diplomatic, maritime, and naval history. He is the author of the *Historical Dictionary of U.S. Diplomacy from the Civil War to World War I* (2005), the *Historical Dictionary of U.S. Maritime Industry* (2007), and *Advancing American Seapower: The Story of Richard W. Meade III (1837–1897)* (2007). He is currently working on studies of the Naval Efficiency Boards of 1855–1857 and African-American diplomats between the Civil War and World War I.

David M. Carletta is a doctoral candidate in Latin American history at Michigan State University.

John Connor is a senior historian at the Australian War Memorial, Canberra, where he is writing a volume of the *Official History of Australian Peacekeeping and Post-Cold War Operations*. He has taught Australian history at the Menzies Centre for Australian Studies, King's College, London. His book, *The Australian Frontier Wars, 1788–1838,* received a Special Mention in the 2002 Centre for Australian Cultural Studies National Awards, was short-listed for the Royal United Services Institute for Defence Studies' 2003 Westminster Medal for Military Literature, and was highly commended in the Australian Historical Association's 2004 W. K. Hancock Prize.

Robert Davis is a doctoral candidate in modern British Empire and European diplomatic history at Ohio University. He completed a BA in history at the University of Kansas in 1998 and accepted a Masters fellowship at Ohio University's Contemporary History Institute. He spent 2005–2006 in Oslo on a Fulbright Fellowship, where he was hosted by the Contemporary History Forum at the University of Oslo and the Norwegian Institute for Defense Studies. He is currently researching NATO during the period 1956–1975 and plans to write a book on railway imperialism and the ethos of the engineers who helped build the infrastructure of the British Empire.

Frederick R. Dickinson is an associate professor of Japanese history at the University of Pennsylvania. He received master's and doctoral degrees in history from Yale University and also holds a master's degree in international politics from Kyoto

University. He is author of *War and National Reinvention: Japan and the Great War, 1914–1919*, published by Harvard University Press in 1999.

Frederick H. Dotolo finished a doctorate in modern European history at the State University of New York at Buffalo in 2001, and promptly left the country. He was spotted on various U.S. Navy vessels in the Pacific and Atlantic teaching for the NCPACE (Navy College Program Afloat for College Education) Program. It was even rumored that Dr. Dotolo got caught in a combat zone while happily teaching a course on American diplomatic history. Dr. Dotolo's dissertation was on Italian foreign policy in the Balkans in the 1920s. His research interests include the relationship between totalitarian ideology and its origins within the French Revolution, the impact of Italian fascism on the conduct of diplomacy, and the conduct of non-German Axis forces during World War II.

David M. Fahey is a professor of history at Miami University. He received his PhD from the University of Notre Dame in 1964. He specializes in modern Britain, temperance in Britain and America, theories in world and comparative history, and Anglo-American social movements. He has published on nineteenth-century temperance and fraternal societies in Britain and the Americas. His most recent monograph is *Temperance & Racism: John Bull, Johnny Reb, and the Good Templars*. He is co-editor of the international encyclopedia, *Alcohol and Temperance in Modern History*. Formerly president of the Alcohol and Temperance History Group (ATHG), he currently is a member of the executive council of its successor organization, the Alcohol and Drugs History Society (ADHS). For more than 10 years, he moderated the ADHS and ATHG listserv groups on the Internet. He served as editor-in-chief of the first two volumes of the *Social History of Alcohol and Drugs: An Interdisciplinary Journal*. He also is one of the creators of Miami's graduate field in world and comparative history. He was a list editor for H-World and H-Teach. He also has published about African American fraternal lodges.

Lee A. Farrow is an associate professor at Auburn University Montgomery in Alabama and is the author of *Between Clan and Crown: The Struggle to Define Noble Property Rights in Imperial Russia* (University of Delaware Press, 2004). Her current book project is on the U.S./Canadian visit of Russian Grand Duke Alexis in 1871–1872, about which she has published two articles: "Grand Duke Alexis in Memphis and the Reconstruction of Southern Identity During Reconstruction" in the West Tennessee Historical Society *Papers,* vol. 59 (2005), and "Grand Duke Alexei and the Origins of Rex, 1872: Myth, Public Memory and the Distortion of History" in the *Gulf South Historical Review,* vol. 18, no. 1 (Fall 2002).

Gregory Fremont-Barnes holds a doctorate in modern history from the University of Oxford. An independent historian, he has written numerous books on eighteenth- and nineteenth-century military and naval history, particularly of the Napoleonic era. He is also editor of the three-volume *Encyclopedia of the French Revolutionary and Napoleonic Wars* and co-editor of the five-volume *Encyclopedia of the American Revolutionary War.*

Jonathan Gantt is a visiting assistant professor of history at Columbia College in Columbia, South Carolina. His research interests include United States foreign relations, American-European transnational exchanges, modern imperialism, and international terrorism. His article "Irish-American Terrorism and Anglo-American Relations, 1881–1885" was published in the October 2006 issue of the *Journal of the Gilded Age and Progressive Era.*

Andrew A. Gentes earned his PhD in history from Brown University and is currently lecturer in Russian and European history at the University of Queensland, Australia. He researches pre-Soviet Siberian exile and his articles have appeared in *Sibirica, Ab Imperio, Journal of Asian History, Jahrbücher für Geschichte Osteuropas,* and elsewhere. His forthcoming book is entitled *Exile to Siberia, 1590–1822: Corporeal Commodification and Administrative Systematization in Russia* (Palgrave).

Gene C. Gerard earned a master's degree in European religious history from the University of Oklahoma in 1992. Since then he has held 14 teaching positions at various colleges and universities in the Southwest. He is currently an adjunct instructor in history at Tarrant County College in Arlington, Texas. He has contributed to eight books and published numerous articles in both American and international publications.

Mohammad Gharipour is a visiting lecturer with the Southern Polytechnic State University, a doctoral candidate at the Georgia Institute of Technology, and an expert on Islamic and Japanese architecture and history of garden design. He has written more than 40 encyclopedia entries and book articles.

Daniel Gorman is a post-doctoral fellow in the Department of History at York University, and has taught at Trent University. His PhD is from McMaster University. He has published on imperial and global history in *The Historian, The Journal of Colonialism and Colonial History, Personal Perspectives: World War I* (ABC-CLIO), and *Personal Perspectives: World War II* (ABC-CLIO). He is currently working on a book on ideas of internationalism in the 1920s.

Jonathan Grant is associate professor of Russian history at Florida State University. His monographs include *Rulers, Guns, and Money, The Global Arms Trade in the Age of Imperialism* (Harvard University Press, 2007) and *Big Business in Russia, The Putilov Company in Late Imperial Russia* (University of Pittsburgh Press, 1999). In addition, he has published articles on the Ottoman Empire in *The Journal of Military History* and the *Journal of World History.*

John Faithful Hamer teaches philosophy at John Abbott College of Ste-Anne-de-Bellevue in Montreal.

David Hollins is an independent historian. He has published seven books on the Austrian Army of the Napoleonic Wars, including a book on the Marengo campaign.

Arthur Holst received his PhD in political science from Temple University. He is Government Affairs Manager for the City of Philadelphia and teaches in the MPA Program at Widener University. He has written extensively on politics, public administration, and history and the environment.

Daniel C. Kane is a doctoral candidate in Korean history at the University of Hawaii–Manoa. Along with working on his dissertation, he is currently collaborating on a translation of a twelfth-century Korean history for the Academy of Korean Studies in Seoul, Korea.

Guenther Kronenbitter is DAAD Professor of History at Emory University, Atlanta. His fields of research include political ideas and the Vienna System, Austria-Hungary, and the origins of World War I. His major publications are *Wort und Macht: Friedrich Gentz als politischer Schriftsteller* (Berlin: Duncker & Humblot, 1994); ed., *Friedrich Gentz: Gesammelte Schriften,* 12 vols. (Hildesheim: Olms-Weidmann, 1997–2004); and *"Krieg im Frieden": Die Führung der k.u.k. Armee und die Großmachtpolitik Österreich-Ungarns, 1906–1914* (Munich: Oldenbourg, 2003).

Paul Lawrence is senior lecturer in history at The Open University and has conducted research in the fields of nationalism and historiography and crime and policing. His major publications include *Nationalism: History and Theory* (Longman, 2005) and (with Barry Godfrey) *Crime and Justice, 1750–1950* (Willan, 2006).

Daniel K. Lewis is chair of the History Department at California State Polytechnic University in Pomona, California. He is author of *The History of Argentina* (Palgrave, 2003) and *A South American Frontier: The Tri-Border Region* (Chelsea House Press, 2006).

Frode Lindgjerdet is an intern at the Royal Norwegian Air War College and a freelance abstractor for ABC-Clio's *Historical Abstracts* and *America History and Life.* He is a contributor to encyclopedias on NATO and the Cold War and has also published several articles on military history and security policy.

Roger D. Long is a professor of history in the Department of History and Philosophy at Eastern Michigan University. He teaches the history of England, Canada, British Empire, and Southeast Asia. His research specialization is India. He has edited *"The Man on the Spot": Essays on British Empire History* (1995); *The Founding of Pakistan: An Annotated Bibliography* (1998); *Charisma and Commitment in South Asian History: Essays Presented to Stanley Wolpert* (2003); and *"Dear Mr Jinnah": Selected Correspondence and Speeches of Liaquat Ali Khan, 1937–1947* (2004). He is the author of a forthcoming biography of Liaquat Ali Khan.

J. David Markham is an internationally acclaimed historian and Napoleonic scholar. His major books include *Napoleon's Road to Glory: Triumphs, Defeats and Immortality* (winner of the 2004 Napoleonic Society of America Literary Award), *Imperial Glory: The Bulletins of Napoleon's Grande Armée* (winner of the International Napoleonic Society's 2003 Presidents Choice Award), and *Napoleon for Dummies* and *Napoleon and Dr Verling on St Helena.* He has been featured on the History Channel International's *Global View* program on Napoleon, the History Channel's *Conquerors* program (Napoleon's Greatest Victory; Caesar in Gaul), and *Napoleon: The Man Who Would Conquer Europe,* as well as in programs on the Learning and Discovery channels. He has served as historical consultant to History Channel and National Geographic Society programs. Markham has contributed to four important reference encyclopedias, *Leadership; World History; American Revolution; French Revolutionary and Napoleonic Wars.* He serves as the president of the Napoleonic Alliance and executive vice-president and editor-in-chief of the International Napoleonic Society. He has also organized International Napoleonic Congresses in Italy, Israel, the Republic of Georgia, and France. He was the first American scholar to present a paper at the Borodino Conference in Russia. His awards include the Legion of Merit from the International Napoleonic Society, the President's Medal from the Napoleonic Alliance, and the Marengo Medal from the province of Alessandria, Italy.

Eric Martone is a teacher at John F. Kennedy High School in Waterbury, Connecticut. He holds an MA in global history from Iona College and an MA in European history from Western Connecticut State University. He has written numerous articles on European and global history and has served as associate editor for Facts on File's forthcoming *Encyclopedia of Protest and Revolution in World History.*

Barbara J. Messamore is an instructor in Canadian history at University College of the Fraser Valley. She has a special interest in constitutional history. Her most recent publication is *Canada's Governors General, 1847–1878: Biography and Constitutional Evolution* (Toronto: University of Toronto Press, 2006).

Patit Paban Mishra is professor of history at Sambalpur University, India, where he specializes in world history, with particular reference to South Asian and South-East Asian history. He obtained his MA in history at Delhi University, and his M.Phil. (1974) and PhD (1979) at JNU New Delhi in the Centre for South, Southeast and Central Asian Studies. In 1998, Professor Mishra was awarded the D.Litt degree from Rabindra Bharati University, Kolkata. He has taught history for almost 30 years and supervised M.Phil., PhD, and D.Litt. scholars. He is the author of more than 30 research articles and has written about 300 articles in more than 30 encyclopedias.

Martin Moll is professor of modern and contemporary history in the Department for History at Graz University, where he has taught since 2003. His areas of expertise are the two World Wars and the last decades of Austria-Hungary. His noteworthy publications include *Kein Burgfrieden. Der deutsch-slowenische Nationalitätenkonflikt in der Steiermark 1900–1918* (Innsbruck 2007); *"Führer-Erlasse" 1939–1945* (Stuttgart 1997); and, together with Filip Èuèek, *Duhovniki za rešetkami/Priester hinter Gittern. Die Berichte der im Sommer 1914 in der Untersteiermark verhafteten Geistlichen an ihren Bischof* (Ljubljana 2006).

Annika Mombauer is a senior lecturer in modern European history at The Open University, in Milton Keynes, United Kingdom. She studied history at the Westfälische-Wilhelms-Universität in Münster, Germany, and at the University of Sussex, where she was awarded a doctorate in history in 1998. Her research interests are in twentieth-century German history, in particular the origins of World War I and the history of post-1945 Germany. Her publications include *Helmuth von Moltke and the Origins of the First World War* (Cambridge University Press, 2001); *The Origins of the First World War. Controversies and Consensus* (Longman, 2002); and, as editor with Wilhelm Deist, *The Kaiser. New Research on Wilhelm.*

David H. Olivier is assistant professor of history and contemporary studies at Wilfrid Laurier University. His area of expertise is the German navy in the nineteenth century. He is the author if *German Naval Strategy, 1856–1888: Forerunners of Tirpitz* (Frank Cass, 2004).

Kenneth J. Orosz is associate professor of history at the University of Maine at Farmington. In 1995, he received a Fulbright grant for dissertation research in Germany. His research interests include language policy, missionary work, and education in colonial Africa.

Niels P. Petersson is a lecturer in history at the University of Konstanz. He has worked on the history of imperialism, the world economy, European integration, and globalization. His publications include *Modernisierung und Imperialismus: Siam, China und die europäischen Mächte, 1895–1914* (Munich: Oldenbourg 2000); *Globalization: A Short History* (with Jürgen Osterhammel; Princeton: Princeton University Press, 2005); *Von der Volkssouveränität zur Völkersouveränität: Legitimationsgrundlagen einer europäischen Verfassung* (with Georg Jochum, Wolfgang M. Schröder, and Katrin Ullrich; Berlin: Duncker & Humblot 2007).

Mark F. Proudman is a historical writer who is currently preparing for publication a thesis on Victorian anti-imperialism. He is a member of the editorial board of the *Journal of the Historical Society* and holds a doctorate from the University of Oxford.

James Pruitt is a doctoral candidate in American military and diplomatic history at Texas A&M University.

Serge Ricard is professor of American Studies and U.S. History at the Sorbonne Nouvelle, Paris. He was educated at Davidson College in North Carolina and at the Sorbonne in Paris, and was twice a Fulbright research scholar and many times a visiting scholar at Harvard University. He has taught at the universities of Aix-Marseille and Montpellier, France, and was twice an exchange professor at the University of Texas at Austin. He has published extensively on Theodore Roosevelt, American expansionism and foreign policy in the late nineteenth and early twentieth centuries, and Mexican-American culture. He is the editor or co-editor of numerous books and the author, notably, of *Theodore Roosevelt: principes et pratique d'une politique étrangère* (1991), *The Mass Media in America: An Overview* (1998), and *The "Manifest Destiny" of the United States in the 19th Century* (1999).

J. Simon Rofe is lecturer in defence studies in the Defence Studies Department of the War Studies Group of King's College, London. He teaches international military officers at the Joint Services Command and Staff College within the Defence Academy of the United Kingdom. His research lies in the field of American foreign policy in the twentieth century, with a specific focus on the diplomacy of Franklin Roosevelt, the nature of the Anglo-American relationship, and competing visions of peacemaking and postwar planning. A volume entitled *'Once Chance in a Thousand': The Sumner Welles Mission to Europe, Rooseveltian Diplomacy and Anglo-American Relations during the Phoney War,* is currently under review with Palgrave. He has published a number of works on the Roosevelt era and more contemporary issues while contributing to a number of refereed journals such as *The Round Table—The Commonwealth Journal of International Affairs, International History Review,* and *The Journal of Strategic Studies.*

Kaushik Roy teaches at the History Department, Presidency College, at Kolkata. He is also affiliated with the International Peace Research Institute in Oslo and the United Nations University. Previously, he was a Nehru Memorial Museum and Library Fellow. Roy specializes in Indian military history. He has 27 articles in peer-reviewed journals and has edited contributed volumes and four books. His latest publication is *War and Society in Colonial India* from Oxford University Press, New Delhi.

Ulrich Schnakenberg is a doctoral candidate in the Department of History of the University of Kassel. He is presently working on British occupation and constitutional policy in postwar Germany.

Frank Schumacher is assistant professor of North American history at the University of Erfurt, Germany. He is the author of *Kalter Krieg und Propaganda. Die USA, der Kampf um die Weltmeinung und die ideelle Westbindung der Bundesrepublik Deutschland, 1945–1955.* He has published articles on nineteenth- and twentieth-century North America and diplomatic, military, cultural and environmental history, and is currently at work on his second book entitled *The American Way of Empire: The United States and the Quest for Imperial Identity, 1880–1920.*

Brent D. Singleton is senior assistant librarian at California State University, San Bernardino, with expertise in Islam in West Africa and Islam in the United States. His publications include *Yankee Muslim: The Asian Travels of Mohammed Alexander Russell Webb* (2007); "Minarets in Dixie: Proposals to Introduce Islam in the American Sout," (*Journal of Muslim Minority Affairs,* vol. 26, issue 3, 2006); "African Bibliophiles: Books and Libraries in Medieval Timbuktu" (*Libraries & Culture,* vol. 39, issue 1, 2004); and "The Ummah Slowly Bled: A Select Bibliography of African Muslims Enslaved in the Americas and the Caribbean" (*Journal of Muslim Minority Affairs,* vol. 22, issue 2, 2002).

Olena V. Smyntyna is a doctor of science, full professor, and head of the Department of Archaeology and Ethnology of the Ukraine, Faculty of History, Odessa I.I. Mechnikov National University in Odessa. She is a specialist in the fields of environmental history, prehistoric archaeology, and the history of ideas and theories in history, archaeology, and anthropology, and author of 140 publications, including two monographs.

David R. Snyder is an assistant professor of history at Austin Peay State University. He specializes in military history, Nazi Germany, and the Holocaust. He is author of *Sex Crimes under the Wehrmacht,* forthcoming from University of Nebraska Press.

Manu P. Sobti is an assistant professor at the University of Milwaukee and lectures on architecture and urban design in Central Asia

Stephen K. Stein is a lecturer at the U.S. Naval War College in Rhode Island. He holds bachelor's and master's degrees from the University of Colorado at Denver and a doctoral degree from The Ohio State University. He specializes in military and diplomatic history, twentieth-century U.S. history, and ancient history.

Eva-Maria Stolberg is a lecturer at the Institute of East European & Russian History at the University of Bonn. Her current research is on the "Landscape of the Vistula in Polish Historical Memory."

Moshe Terdman has a PhD from the Department of Maritime Civilizations of the University of Haifa. The title of his dissertation is "Mamluk Maritime Policy in the Eastern Mediterranean and in the Red Sea." He also holds master's and bachelor's degrees from the Department for Middle Eastern and Islamic Studies at the Hebrew University. He is a research fellow in PRISM (Project for the Research of Islamic Movements) and the director there of the Islam in Africa Project.

Michael Thompson teaches history at Miyazaki International College in Japan. He received his doctoral degree from Carnegie Mellon University. His research interests include the history of the Catholic Church, environmental history, and ethnicity and nationalism.

Mike Timonin holds a master's degree in history from James Madison University, where he currently works as an adjunct faculty member.

Philip Towle is reader in international relations at Cambridge University's Centre of International Studies, where he has taught for the last 26 years. His recent publications include *Forced Disarmament from the Napoleonic Campaigns to the Gulf War* (1997); *Democracy and Peacemaking: Negotiations and Debates 1815–1973* (2000); *From Ally to Enemy: Anglo-Japanese Military Relations, 1904–45* (2006); and, with Robert J. Jackson, *Temptations of Power: The United States in Global Politics after 9/11* (2006). He has also edited *Estimating Foreign Military Power* (1982); *Japanese Prisoners of War* (2000), with Margaret Kosuge and Yoichi Kibata; and *Anglo-Japanese Relations in the 20th Century: One Hundred Years of Trade and Prejudice* (2007), with Margaret Kosuge.

Georgia Tres is a visiting assistant professor at Oakland University. Her areas of expertise are in comparative literature, cinema, and cultural studies. She is editor of *The Greenwood Encyclopedia of Sex, Love, and Courtship* and *Women and War: A Historical Encyclopedia from Antiquity to the Present*.

David Turpie is a doctoral candidate at the University of Maine. He specializes in nineteenth- and twentieth-century U.S. foreign relations and in the nineteenth-century British Empire.

Jitendra Uttam is an assistant professor at the School of International Studies, Jawaharlal Nehru University, New Delhi, India. His area of expertise includes international political economy, with particular interest in the Asian development modes. He has recently published "Korea's New Techno-Scientific State: Mapping a Strategic Change in the 'Development State'" in the *China Report* vol. 42, no. 3 (2006).

Andrekos Varnava completed his doctoral degree in history at the University of Melbourne. He specializes in the modern history of Cyprus and the British Empire, and more generally the history of the modern Near East. His focus ranges from military, strategic, and political issues to social and cultural questions. His last three publications have appeared in *Byzantine and Modern Greek Studies*, vol. 29, no. 2, 2005; *The Cyprus Review*, vol. 17, no. 2, 2005; and in the book *Britain in Cyprus: Colonialism and Post-Colonialism 1878–2004* (2006). In October 2006, he took up the post of assistant professor of history at Cyprus College, Nicosia, and he currently holds the post of honorary fellow in the Department of History at the University of Melbourne.

Thomas D. Veve is an associate professor of history at Dalton State College. He received his bachelor's degree from Hofstra University in 1974, his master's degree in 1983 from Marquette University in 1983, and his doctoral degree from Marquette in 1990. Dr. Veve, commissioned as an infantry officer after completing ROTC at Hofstra, retired from the United States Army Reserve as a Lieutenant Colonel in 2002, after 28 years of service. He has published one book, *The Duke of Wellington and the British Army of Occupation in France, 1815–1818* (Greenwood Press, 1992) and has recently published numerous entries in several encyclopedias, including *Naval Warfare, Encyclopedia of the Second World War, French Revolutionary and Napoleonic Wars*, and *The Encyclopedia of American Military History*.

Ilya Vinkovetsky is an assistant professor of history at Simon Fraser University in British Columbia, Canada. His areas of expertise include Russian history and the history of colonialism in North America. His recent publications are "The Russian-American Company as a Colonial Contractor for the Russian Empire," in Alexei Miller and Alfred J. Rieber, eds. *Imperial Rule.* Budapest: Central European University Press, 2004; "Circumnavigation, Empire, Modernity, Race: The Impact of Round-the-World Voyages on Russia's Imperial Consciousness." *Ab Imperio,* 2001, nos. 1–2; "Why Did Russia Sell Alaska?" *Acta Slavica Iaponica,* vol. 23, 2006; "Classical Eurasianism and Its Legacy." *Canadian-American Slavic Studies,* vol. 34, no. 2, 2000; Editor and Translator: Petr Savitskii, Petr Suvchinskii, Nikolai Trubetskoi, Georgii Florovskii, *Exodus to the East: Forebodings and Events: An Affirmation of the Eurasians.* Idyllwild, CA: Charles Schlacks, Jr. Publisher, 1996.

Andrew Jackson Waskey is associate professor of social science at Dalton State College in Dalton, Georgia. He has presented lectures and papers in Europe and Asia, as well as the United States; has published scholarly papers, numerous encyclopedia articles, book chapters, and a co-authored book on American government; and has served as the editor of an encyclopedia of world history. His areas of expertise are law, politics and government, world religions, philosophy, and general history. He is a specialist on John Calvin's political thought.

Carl Peter Watts completed his doctoral thesis on the Rhodesian problem at the University of Birmingham (UK) where he was Honorary Lecturer in Modern History and Visiting Lecturer in War Studies. He has taught at Grand Valley State University, Michigan; the University of Wisconsin–Whitewater; and Indiana University–Purdue University, Fort Wayne. He has published a number of articles on Rhodesia in journals, such as the *Michigan Academician* (2004), *Twentieth Century British History*

(2005), *Diplomatic History* (2006), *Journal of Colonialism and Colonial History* (2007), and *Commonwealth and Comparative Politics* (2007). He is currently writing a book, *Rhodesia's Unilateral Declaration of Independence: A Study in International Crisis,* which will be published by Palgrave Macmillan in 2008.

Nurfadzilah Yahaya is a graduate student at the National University of Singapore. Her thesis is "Good Friends and Dangerous Enemies—British Images of the Arab Elite in Colonial Singapore (1819–1942)." The thesis investigates British colonial perceptions of the Arab elite in Singapore and traces how the Arabs maintained a distinct Arab identity, despite being of mixed Arab and Malay descent.

Jeffrey T. Zalar is an assistant professor of history at Pepperdine University in Malibu, California. His published work concerns the cultural and intellectual history of the German Empire.

Wenxian Zhang has been an associate professor at Rollins College since 1995; he serves as the head of archives and special collections in the Olin Library. He has published numerous articles in the areas of library historical research, information studies, and Chinese librarianship.

INDEX

ARCHBISHOP ALEMANY LIBRARY
DOMINICAN UNIVERSITY
SAN RAFAEL, CALIFORNIA 94901